Knowledge Management Strategies for Business Development

Meir Russ
University of Wisconsin–Green Bay, USA

BUSINESS SCIENCE REFERENCE

Hershey · New York

Director of Editorial Content:	Kristin Klinger
Senior Managing Editor:	Jamie Snavely
Assistant Managing Editor:	Michael Brehm
Publishing Assistant:	Sean Woznicki
Typesetter:	Michael Brehm
Cover Design:	Lisa Tosheff
Printed at:	Yurchak Printing Inc.

Published in the United States of America by
Business Science Reference (an imprint of IGI Global)
701 E. Chocolate Avenue
Hershey PA 17033
Tel: 717-533-8845
Fax: 717-533-8661
E-mail: cust@igi-global.com
Web site: http://www.igi-global.com/reference

Library of Congress Cataloging-in-Publication Data

Knowledge management strategies for business development / Meir Russ, editor.
    p. cm.
  Includes bibliographical references and index.
  Summary: "This book addresses the relevance of knowledge management strategies for the advancement of organizations worldwide"--Provided by publisher.
  ISBN 978-1-60566-348-7 (hardcover) -- ISBN 978-1-60566-349-4 (ebook) 1. Knowledge management. 2. Industrial management. 3. Strategic planning. I. Russ, Meir, 1968- II. Title.

  HD30.2.K6378 2010
  658.4'038--dc22

2009032732

British Cataloguing in Publication Data
A Cataloguing in Publication record for this book is available from the British Library.

All work contributed to this book is new, previously-unpublished material. The views expressed in this book are those of the authors, but not necessarily of the publisher.

In memory of my grandparents—Mayer Pillersdorf Levental and Gitla Mayer Pillersdorf; and Isaak Russ and Rozia Lewitt Bernardiener Russ—my wife's grandparents—Josef and Fani Pfeffer—my numerous uncles and aunts (Genia, Israel, Reuven, Chaim, Salka, and Rivka Russ; and Moishe-Leib and Tuaba Pillersdorf) and two cousins—Alusia Russ and Chava Pillersdorf—who perished in the holocaust and have no physical burial place.

May this book be their living virtual memory and a source of wisdom and knowledge for future generations.

Table of Contents

Section 1
Knowledge and Knowledge Management Conceptual Aspects

Section 2
Knowledge Management Audit

Section 3
Organizational Knowledge Management Strategic Dilemmas

Section 4
Knowledge Management Strategy

Section 5
Knowledge Management Functional Strategies

Detailed Table of Contents

Section 1
Knowledge and Knowledge Management Conceptual Aspects

Meir Russ, University of Wisconsin-Green Bay, USA
Robert Fineman, Independent Consultant, USA
Jeannette K. Jones, American Intercontinental University, USA

This chapter will provide the reader with two definitions of knowledge, one at the individual level, the other at the organizational level. This will be followed by connecting the knowledge base of the organization to its sustainable competitive advantage by using a multiple-layer framework of organizational knowledge. Then, the chapter will discuss the frameworks of knowledge management vision, mission and goals for the organization. Temporary and functional gap analysis frameworks will follow. The chapter will end with a brief description of three tools developed by the authors.

Kalotina Chalkiti, Charles Darwin University, Australia

This chapter investigates how the hospitality industry of the Northern Territory of Australia achieves organizational flexibility in dynamic labor environments. A case study in the Northern Territory of Australia reveals a new type of organizational flexibility, "relational flexibility." Relational flexibility is the result of behaviors, which go beyond the scope of job descriptions, used to repair the relational disruptions of labor changes and to adapt to the inevitability of labor dynamism. With relational flexibility, hospitality businesses can become flexible, responsive, and adaptable to dynamic labor environments while ensuring knowledge management activities are not inhibited. This research highlights the central role of peer relationships in dynamic labor environments and contributes to the organizational flexibility, staff turnover, and hospitality knowledge management literature.

Chapter 3

Daniel Worden, RuleSmith Corporation, Canada

Emergent strategy provides for both planned and reactive aspects of strategic planning. It also identifies that strategy as implemented will often have different characteristics than originally anticipated. Today, even traditional, non-knowledge based organizations have adopted comparatively high levels of computerization compared to a decade ago. Enterprises now rely extensively on digital systems for data handling across operational and administrative processes. This chapter maintains that detection and reporting capabilities inherent in information technology (IT) can themselves be exploited as a strategy for managing knowledge. Using feedback loops to describe the dynamics of systems lets an organization capture and communicate intended strategy and emergent characteristics of the actual strategy along with changes in the execution environment. The role of IT as an execution capability required for both business strategy and knowledge management is examined, along with the need to more quickly align the business processes that use IT services to changes in business strategies or priorities. Advances in IT assisting in requirements discovery, system design and development- including use cases, patterns, decision modeling, and aspect-oriented software-are discussed. Techniques to capture and communicate knowledge vital for aligning organizational capabilities with emerging strategies and competing priorities are evaluated. A predicted emergent business pattern as a tool for managing the capture and communication of organizational knowledge is proposed. This includes techniques for defining strategy and decision elements as data about processes that can be used during execution to trigger notification and appropriate handling of exceptional events.

Section 2
Knowledge Management Audit

Chapter 4

Meir Russ, University of Wisconsin-Green Bay, USA
Robert Fineman, Independent Consultant, USA
Jeannette K. Jones, American Intercontinental University, USA

Companies tend to start their knowledge management initiatives with a knowledge management audit. A framework used for developing this specific audit, as well as some issues encountered while utilizing the audit, are illustrated. A number of benefits and weaknesses are also identified. Finally, a detailed, open-ended audit tool is introduced, knowledge assessment review and management audit-KARMA.

Chapter 5

Philip Mattek, University of Wisconsin-Green Bay, USA

Knowledge management is many things to different people. Within complex organizations, this reality needs to be acknowledged. For an organization to utilize and enhance knowledge for competitive advantages, systems and culture need to be analyzed within the context of an organization's strategy.

Once analyzed, an honest appraisal of the knowledge systems in place and those needed to fulfill the strategic goals of the organization will have to be performed. For everyone within an organization to be able to "pull in the same direction" and achieve maximum value from a knowledge management system, that system will have to mean the same thing to all. If a knowledge management system is to be central in maintaining a competitive advantage for organizations, it will engulf the organization. To understand financial systems, audits are undertaken to ensure that systems provide the information as expected. It is well understood that for financial information to be meaningful, it must be understood. To be understood, it must be logically prepared and presented in a manner useful and timely to the end user. Through an audit process of this nature performed on knowledge management systems within the context of business strategy and culture, an organization learns what is needed to get their divergent individuals on the same page, as it were, to fulfill the promise of enhancing its most valuable resource in a competitive world. This chapter examines how to systematically conduct a knowledge management audit. By design, the audit was simplified and designed around a single specific issue. By breaking apart where the organization needs to go and combining it with a study of what it will take to get there from a knowledge management systems standpoint, individuals can come together to build the framework literally from the ground up. Companies can use this framework to assess how they plan with knowledge management as the central, differentiating factor in their business strategy.

Chapter 6

Carolina López-Nicolás, University of Murcia, Spain
Ángel L. Meroño-Cerdán, University of Murcia, Spain

Due to contradictory results obtained in knowledge management (KM) initiatives, a model of audit is presented. The main action in the international project "Strategi" is the development and application of a model to diagnose and propose suitable recommendations concerning the management of knowledge and intellectual capital of a firm. A brief description of the model is presented after the exposition of its key scientific assumptions.

Section 3
Organizational Knowledge Management Strategic Dilemmas

Chapter 7

Meir Russ, University of Wisconsin-Green Bay, USA
Robert Fineman, Independent Consultant, USA
Jeannette K. Jones, American Intercontinental University, USA

This chapter proposes the C3EEP typology as a framework of knowledge management strategies by using six knowledge based strategic dilemmas. A number of graphic presentations of the complete typology are reported. Based on the typology, nine taxonomies of knowledge management (KM) are proposed and are followed by a framework that uses the six dilemmas and the knowledge levers as leading dimensions for the development of organization's knowledge management strategy. The proposed typology and taxonomies are closing a gap in academic knowledge management and strategic management literatures.

Knowledge management is a fundamental capability in today's evolving markets. Management needs
to understand which organizational processes are necessary to trigger each of the stages in knowledge
development. The objective of this study is to outline the main concepts and stages in the process of
knowledge development in organizations and the organizational activities that have a positive influence
on those stages. A conceptual framework is proposed which combines the model of knowledge development proposed by Nonaka (1994) with the concepts of exploration and exploitation initially described
by March (1991). Information systems are seen to play a fundamental role in supporting this process,
especially in activities related to exploitation capability.

Section 4
Knowledge Management Strategy

The chapter will describe a comprehensive planning framework for developing a company's knowledge
management strategy. The framework includes the goals and game plans of the strategy and the use
of three enablers supporting such a strategy: levers, processes, and systems. This is complemented by
the development of an action plan while considering the resources needed and the constraints present.
The framework also includes the discussion of aligning the knowledge management strategy with the
company's business strategy as well as with the organization's knowledge base and core competencies.
The chapter uses two cases to illustrate some of the aspects discussed.

Aurora Health Care, Wisconsin's largest employer and healthcare provider faces intense competition,
consolidation, and reform. Its choice is to view these challenges as opportunities instead of problems. A
key component to realizing Aurora's opportunities is an aggressive knowledge management system. They
understand that to maximize their potential, they must get the most out of their knowledge management.
The purpose of this chapter is to present to you a case study of knowledge management applications

in the healthcare industry through the many lenses of Aurora Health Care. First we will describe the background of this accomplished healthcare provider. We will then look at their business and knowledge management strategies. Next will be a review of the major components: core competencies, knowledge base, culture, implementation, and key success indicators.

Managing organizational knowledge in alliances implies establishing the best possible strategic design to create, acquire, maintain, transfer, and apply organizational knowledge developed between the partners (or acquired from partners) in order to achieve competitive goals. In this chapter, the role of knowledge management strategy (KMS) in strategic alliances is analyzed in a technology-intensive company. Focusing on this, the importance of alliances for technological companies and the necessity of designing suitable KMSs in alliances–in terms of establishing objectives, knowledge management tools, and support systems–are explained first of all. This is followed by the analysis of a case study of KMS in the strategic alliances of a company currently developing different businesses in technological settings. Finally, a number of conclusions are discussed, based on how the implementation aspects concerning KMS in strategic alliances have been managed and the way they have contributed to the attainment of the company's objectives and goals.

Over the past decade, the rapid proliferation of knowledge management (KM) has been one of the most striking developments in business. Viewing KM as a key driver of competitive advantage, we attempt to provide managers with important guidance on how to create and deliver a successful KM strategy. Specifically, we develop a framework of three factors that are vital to KM success: top management support, a culture of organizational learning, and effective measures of KM performance. To offer a better understanding of the factors, their multiple facets are further investigated and discussed.

The alignment of business and knowledge strategies necessarily includes the individual and the organizational perspectives. A major problem in this context is to reconcile these perspectives into a common framework for alignment. To this end, an intermediate level is introduced–the activity domain. The activity domain is a canonical structure comprising all kinds of organizational units, irrespective of size and organizational level. The organization is regarded as a constellation of activity domains, each having a capability to produce an outcome that the organization needs in order to fulfill its goals. Alignment is defined as the management of dependencies between capabilities such that these capabilities fit the business's strategic intents. As a consequence, business and knowledge strategies can be linked to the same target–the activity domain. Practical guidelines and alignment targets for these strategies are suggested.

Section 5
Knowledge Management Functional Strategies

Chapter 14

The global economy is transforming the sources of the competitive advantages of firms, especially for firms embedded in local manufacturing systems. Based on the theoretical contributions to knowledge management and industrial districts, this chapter describes alternative firm's strategies and upgrading options by exploring the relationships among innovation, marketing, and network technologies. Starting from the analysis of the Global Competitiveness Report and the European Innovation Scoreboard, this chapter focuses on the case of firms specializing in the "Made in Italy" industries (fashion, furniture, home products) to outline a framework explaining the new competitive opportunities for SMEs. Through a qualitative analysis the chapter presents four case studies of Italian firms that promote successful strategies based on a coherent mix of R&D-based innovation, experienced marketing, and design by leveraging on ICT.

Chapter 15

In the last decade, knowledge management has been receiving managerial attention particularly in the post-Internet era. With advancements in information and communications technologies, the incentives to manage knowledge have far surpassed the costs associated with it. The sales and marketing (S&M) function is one of the important functions in an organization with a unique blend of internal and external stakeholders to cater to. Another unique feature of knowledge management in the S&M function is that it lies on the interface of the organization with its customers. Therefore, information that comes into the organization through sales and marketing employees is often collected, filtered, and assimilated in different forms and with time lags. This chapter is aimed at familiarizing the readers with the importance of managing a continuously churning ocean of knowledge in the S&M function. We address various knowledge management issues and opportunities in the context of S&M and recommend a set of guidelines to enable managers increase the effectiveness of the S&M function by using appropriate knowledge management tools and strategies.

Throughout the past decade, CRM has become such a buzzword that in contemporary terms the concept is used to reflect a number of differing perspectives. In brief, CRM has been defined as essentially relating to sales, marketing, and even services automation. CRM has also been increasingly associated with cost savings and streamline processes. Accordingly, the topic has been widely covered in terms of its alignment with business strategy. However, there appears to be a paucity of coverage with regards to the concept's alignment with knowledge management. This chapter demonstrates how CRM in fact pivots upon the dynamics of knowledge management. Furthermore, this chapter emphasises how by lieu of its conceptual underpinnings and operational dimensions, CRM is aligned with business development in the context of knowledge management. References have been made to specific strategies and tactics within the hotel industry in order to illustrate the relevance of this contended association.

Knowledge management requires people to synthesize and interpret information, and technologies to organize, make sense of, and draw conclusions from the collection of knowledge. Together, these people and technologies shape part of a sociotechnical system. The relationships between them make the sociotechnical system behave as a network, where communication and knowledge transfer can occur, and the network becomes a community once elements of the system interact in meaningful ways. The quality of a knowledge management system depends on how well these meaningful exchanges are promoted and cultivated. This chapter examines how to construct a high-quality knowledge management system, taking into consideration the challenging sociotechnical nature of such an effort. By relating the four stages of a continuous improvement process, the five measures of quality within a knowledge management system, and EASE (Expectations, Actionability, Sustainability, and Evaluation), we present an approach to examine the business processes associated with knowledge management. Managers can use this framework to assess the quality of knowledge management systems and formulate strategies for continually improving them.

Chapter 18

This chapter aims to evaluate the application of knowledge management (KM) literature in supply chains. The underlying understanding derived from this evaluation can be used to devise a valid business strategy to encourage knowledge management practices in supply chains. The concept of a supply chain encompasses businesses organised around a common goal of delivering a product or service from the initial supplier to the end customers. In this respect, the importance of knowledge management within the boundaries of supply chain management has been iterated by many authors; some underline the strategic and tactical importance of knowledge management, whereas others focus on the advantages and tools used to create knowledge in supply chains. The difficulty of assessing knowledge management is twofold when considering supply chains—first, the underlying difficulty of locating the trail of knowledge creation in supply chains and secondly how this can be utilised to devise a business strategy. On close examination of the literature in this field, we can identify a salient need for the theoretical categorisation of existing theoretical frameworks of supply chain management (SCM) on KM-related practices. This chapter explicitly looks into three supply chains, namely learning chains, virtual chains and build-to-order supply chains, and the specific challenges that these create for knowledge management and devising a valid business strategy.

Preface

INTRODUCTION

The emergence of the global and volatile service and experience based economy, global and mobile communication networks, and the Internet present new types of strategic threats and opportunities that companies of all sizes and in every industry are facing on a daily basis. Organizations' downsizing and jobs reengineering are also daily endeavors. New skills acquisition by knowledge workers and an ongoing, increased pace of changes are the new norms in the workplace. Companies are required to introduce new products or services, cut costs, reduce risks, and to reinvent themselves, or face major challenges in this unique economic environment[1].

As the new economy continues to evolve, knowledge is being recognized as a business asset and considered a crucial component of business strategy. Therefore, the ability to manage knowledge is rapidly becoming a crucial skill for securing and maintaining organizational success and surviving in the new knowledge economy. The question is: how do companies succeed in this endeavor? The basic idea is that different companies manage their knowledge in different ways, the same way they differently manage their employees, financial capital, and other assets. Companies use different strategies to manage those assets: they diversify, they penetrate, and/or they develop new products. Knowledge management (KM) requires obtaining skills that will allow management to develop knowledge-based strategies.

I see companies as distributed knowledge systems, or as knowledge repositories[2]. Instinctively, this should make sense to you, and herein lies the problem; companies use knowledge instinctively, not systematically, and as such they have limited ability to manage and control their knowledge strategies. The evidence for this claim is easy to see. When conditions change (and today they change more frequently then ever) companies have problems adjusting. How many survive? Not too many over longer periods of time. For example, the average life expectancy of a Fortune 500 company is about 40 to 50 years[3]. Some writers would claim that leading the pack is more important that adjusting to change[4]. But how many companies can do that systematically, over a long period of time? Also, in search of the competitive advantage within the new knowledge-based economy, companies invest heavily in information and communication systems. The effectiveness of such investments is questionable, however. Some researchers found a positive impact on company performances, while other researchers found at best no positive evidence and in the worst cases horror stories. Some of the horror stories described massive losses, failures, and even company closures[5].

A knowledge-based strategy is important to an organization's success because it is the base for the organization's core competencies. Our experience tells us that even companies that understand what core competencies are, are clueless about how to create and manage them. More than that, even companies that know how to manage the core competencies they currently have are clueless about how to create new ones when the need arises. In today's business environment, managing knowledge-based strategy is critical to develop the core competencies needed in a timely manner. Knowledge-based strategy is a winning strategy that will allow an organization to create and to maintain a sustainable competitive advantage in a systematic way. The key word here is **systematic**. More and more, companies are using the tools of strategic management systematically. Their management is meeting continually, at least once a year, and discussing strategic issues. The companies utilize inputs from customers, suppliers, and internally from employees to gather business intelligence, new product ideas, and so forth, and all this is then incorporated into a strategic plan. The plans are communicated and implemented, data about the outcomes is collected, and the plan is then revised. Some companies are starting to use more sophisticated tools, like strategic maps or balanced scorecards to manage their strategies, as well as capabilities. Some are even venturing into revolutionizing their business models and creating whole new industries, but to our knowledge, few companies are using any of these tools systematically to manage their knowledge base.

MISSION AND OBJECTIVE OF THE BOOK

This book is the culmination of more than 10 years of research, teaching and consulting in the area of KM strategies. More than 100 companies were involved directly through research, teaching, or consulting while I, with my colleagues, developed the tools described in this book in chapters 1, 4, 7, and 9. The mission of this book is to educate the business audience of the relevance of KM strategies for the development of business strategies. From my consulting and business experience, I know that there is a gap between the sustainable competitive advantage companies have and their use and ability to manage their core competencies. Companies also lack the ability to develop the appropriate knowledge base when they are in need of a new competency, and lastly, many companies are clueless about systematically managing the knowledge they already possess.

The objective of this book is to provide the business practitioners with a comprehensive set of tools that are designed to systematically guide them through a process that will focus on data gathering, analysis, and decision making that culminates in a strategic plan of action. I want the reader to understand that knowledge assets are a critical component in any strategic planning process. From the academic perspective, I want to introduce students studying knowledge management and business strategy to the value of utilizing the tools presented in this book as a means to quantify the strategic decision making process.

As academics, we have methods and information available to us that practitioners in the field do not. Our mission is to share the academic research and practical applications with those that can benefit the most---those that need to make the decisions. Our vision for this book, therefore, is to provide tools that can span the gap between the academic proofs and the real world practitioner. In other words, we do the ground work so you don't have to do it yourself. You can take the exclusive and non-biased information that we provide and apply it to the success of your organization. The authors of this book have developed a series of tools that allow management to manage its new or existing knowledge assets, identify knowledge gaps, create strategic action plans, implement the solutions, and track and measure the progress and results of the implementation.

THE AUDIENCE FOR THE BOOK

The authors see a huge need for a practically-oriented book that will provide a specific set of tools to business practitioners who are struggling with the dilemmas described above.

Specifically, I identified the following readers for this book:

- Executives and managers with special interest in business strategy
- Knowledge management and organizational learning executives
- Knowledge management and organizational learning specialists and practitioners
- HR and IT officers
- MBA students taking classes in business strategy and knowledge management

THE SCHOLARLY VALUE AND THE CONTRIBUTION TO THE MANAGEMENT LITERATURE

The academic and popular literature discussing KM is relatively young. About 15 years ago, the first articles and books started to be published. When I started my research in this area, I was able to read every published article and to acquire every published book for the first three years. Today, there is a proliferation of writings in this area; still, the number of books focusing on the strategic aspects of KM is relatively small. Specifically, the process of developing the KM strategies is weakly covered. I believe that at this stage, the process should be left more open so it can be tailored to the specific context of the organization, while at the same time the reader should have access to a tool kit that s/he can use when needed.

THE CHAPTERS

This book has five sections. We start section one by discussing some basic and some specific new concepts that are used in the context of KM strategy development. The second section of the book discusses and describes knowledge audits. We then continue by discussing the strategic KM dilemmas in section three. The fourth section of the book discusses KM strategy at the organizational and inter-organizational level. Lastly, we discuss some intra-organizational KM strategic issues and functional KM strategies in section five.

Section one begins with a chapter written by Meir Russ, Robert Fineman, and Jeannette Jones that provides the basic building blocks the KM novice should understand. Chapter 1 also builds a few more in-depth concepts that should enrich the KM expert. The chapter starts with the discussion of three alternative and complementary epistemologies of knowledge. The chapter details two definitions of knowledge within the business context at the individual and organizational level and defines KM and KM strategy. The authors then discuss the vision, mission, and goals that should be driving the development of an organization's KM strategy. This is followed by the gap analysis in terms of gaps in time and gaps among functions.

Chapter 2 is written by Kalotina Chalkiti and defines a new organizational capability, what the author calls, the relational flexibility, which is investigated as a case study in the context of the hospitality industry in the Northern Territory of Australia. Relational flexibility allows organizations the flexibility, responsiveness, and adaptability to dynamic labor environments while guaranteeing that KM activities are not inhibited. According to the author, relational flexibility is the result of behaviors, which go beyond the scope of job descriptions, used to repair the relational disruptions of labor changes and to adapt to the inevitability of labor dynamism.

The last chapter in the first section of this book, Chapter 3, is written by Daniel Worden and discusses the emergent aspects of the implemented KM strategy according to the author, the role of information technology (IT) as an execution capability requires that both business strategy and KM be continuously examined, along with the need to more quickly align the business processes that use IT services so that they will be aligned with the changes in business strategies or priorities. The author suggests that the use of the *predicted emergent business pattern* as a tool to capture the feedback loops, which describe the dynamics of systems, allows the organization to capture and communicate intended strategy and emergent characteristics of the actual strategy, along with changes in the execution environment.

The second section of this book starts with Chapter 4, written by Meir Russ, Robert Fineman, and Jeannette Jones, and describes an open-ended audit tool, the knowledge assessment review and management audit-KARMA. The chapter describes the framework used for developing this audit. This is followed by a discussion of some illustrative issues encountered while utilizing the audit. A number of benefits and weaknesses are also discussed. The audit tool is then detailed.

Chapter 5 is written by Phillip Mattek and is a case study of the Green Bay's Chamber of Commerce Foundation. The author is using KARMA, plus a few additional tools, to analyze the current state of affairs of KM within the organization concluding with a specific set of recommendations.

The last chapter in section two, Chapter 6, is written by Carolina López-Nicolás and Ángel L. Meroño-Cerdán. The authors begin the chapter with a brief literature review and then provide a brief description of a number of KM audit tools. This is followed by an introduction of the strategic methodology to the KM and intellectual capital audits proposed by the authors. The authors end the chapter with conclusions from early implementation of the methodology and next steps.

Section three of the book discuses KM strategic dilemmas. In Chapter 8, Mier Russ, Robert Fineman, and Jeannette Jones describe the six dimensions of the C³EEP typology of knowledge-based strategy and detail the managerial dilemmas that each dimension encompasses. Then, based on this typology, an extensive taxonomy of knowledge-based strategies is presented. The chapter ends by suggesting a framework for KM strategy that uses the dilemmas and the levers of the strategy to create a context for the KM strategy.

The second and final chapter in section three, Chapter 8, is written by César Camisón-Zornoza and Montserrat Boronat-Navarro. The authors use two of the strategic dilemmas illustrated in the previous chapter, namely the exploration-exploitation and the codification-tacitness, to propose a process of knowledge development. This chapter outlines the main concepts and stages in the process of knowledge development in organizations and the organizational activities that have a positive influence on those stages. Information systems are seen by the authors as playing a fundamental role in supporting this process, especially in activities related to exploitation capability. The chapter concludes with summary and future directions.

Section four is the principal section of this book. Here we finally get to the actual development of KM strategy at the organizational (and inter-organizational) level. The first chapter in section four, Chapter 9, is written by Meir Russ, Robert Fineman, Riccardo Paterni, and Jeannette Jones and provides a comprehensive framework for the development of KM strategy. The initial building blocks for the two pieces of the framework are the specific goals expected to be achieved by the strategy. The first piece of the framework then identifies the levers, processes, capabilities, and systems framing the context for the "game plan" facet of the strategy. This is followed by conversation about the constraints and the resources needed for the "action plan" part of the strategy resulting in outcomes. The second piece of the framework broadens the scope of the discussion by linking the knowledge base of the organization and its KM strategy with the business strategy and its core competencies framed by the internal and the external environment scanning needed for such a planning effort.

Chapter 10 is a case study written by Thomas Ginter and Jane Root, which uses some of the frameworks and tools described in the previous chapter, as well as in chapters 1, 4, and 7. The chapter describes their analysis and proposal for a KM strategy for a healthcare organization in Green Bay, WI. The authors provide a detailed background and business analysis for Aurora Health Care, as well as their specific set of goals and a game plan for using KM as a driver for the business initiatives and strategies facing their organization.

Chapter 11 is written by Mario J. Donate-Manzanares, Fátima Guadamillas-Gómez, and Jesús D. Sánchez de Pablo. The chapter broadens the scope of KM strategy to the inter-organization level by discussing a case study of a technological company's KM strategy in the context of strategic alliances. The chapter discusses the unique aspects of establishing objectives and the use of KM tools and support systems in such a context. This is illustrated by a case study. Lastly, conclusions are discussed based on how the implementation had been managed.

Chapter 12 is written by Jiming Wu, Hongwei Du, Xun Li, and Pengtao Li. The authors develop a framework of how to create and deliver a successful KM strategy that includes three factors that are vital to KM success: top management support, a culture of organizational learning, and effective measures of KM performance. Then, each one of the three is elaborated upon and their multiple facets are further investigated and discussed. The chapter concludes with a summary.

The last chapter in section four, Chapter 13, is written by Lars Taxén. The author provides for an intermediate level framework, the *activity domain,* of alignment between the business and the KM strategies, one that bridges the individual and the organizational units of analysis. Alignment is defined by the author as the management of dependencies between capabilities in a way which allows these capabilities to fit the business' strategic intents. The activity domain is defined as a canonical structure encompassing different types of organizational units, irrespective of size and organizational level. The organization is viewed as an assembly of activity domains, each having a capability to produce an outcome that the organization needs in order to fulfill its goals. Finally, practical guidelines and alignment targets for these strategies are suggested by the author.

Section five, the final section of this book, covers intra-organizational aspects of KM strategy. The first chapter in section five, Chapter 14, is written by Eleonora Di Maria and Stefano Micelli. The chapter discusses the alternative small firm's strategies that are embedded in local manufacturing systems, and upgrading options by exploring the relationships among innovation, marketing, and network technologies, based on the author's theoretical contributions to KM and industrial districts literature. This chapter focuses on the case of firms specializing in the "Made in Italy" industries (fashion, furniture, home products) to outline a framework explaining the new competitive opportunities to create competitive advantage for small firms. The authors present four case studies of Italian firms that promote successful strategies based on a coherent mix of R&D-based innovation, experienced marketing and design, and leveraging on ICT.

Chapter 15 is written by Amit Karna, Ramendra Singh, and Sanjay Verma. The authors discuss KM strategic issues for an effective sales and marketing (S&M) function within an organization. This function has a unique attribute in regard to KM, since the S&M function lies on the boundary between the organization and its customers, and as such, the function has to cater to both external and internal stakeholders. One implication of this is that the information that comes into the organization through

S&M employees is often collected, filtered, and assimilated in different forms and with different time delays. The authors address a number of KM issues and opportunities in the context of S&M and recommend a set of guidelines to enable managers to increase the effectiveness of the S&M function by using appropriate KM tools and strategies.

Chapter 16 is written by Diana Luck. The author discusses the implications of the development and implementation of CRM for KM. The author starts the chapter by reviewing the use of the CRM and database management in marketing. Then, the author extends this use into how CRM could align marketing with business development by using the KM aspects of the technology, specifically in the context of the hotel industry.

Chapter 17 is written by Nicole M. Radziwill and Ronald F. DuPlain. The authors discuss quality and continuous improvement aspects in KM. The authors define community (or organization) as a network of socio-technical systems that communicate and share knowledge in meaningful ways. This chapter investigates how to create a high-quality KM system in this context. The authors suggest using the four stages of a continuous improvement process, the five measures of quality within a KM system, and EASE (expectations, actionability, sustainability, and evaluation) heuristics they developed to assess the quality of KM systems and formulate strategies for continually improving them.

Chapter 18 is written by Ozlem Bak. The author discusses KM practice issues as relevant to supply chain management, specifically to the boundaries of organizations involved in the supply chain. The author defines the concept of supply chain as organizations organized around a common goal of delivering a product or service from the initial supplier to the end users. In this context, the complexity of assessing KM has two aspects. First, the difficulty of establishing the trail of knowledge creation in a supply chains; and second, how such situated knowledge can be utilized intentionally to develop a business strategy. For this purpose, the author suggests examining three types of chains: learning chains, virtual chains, and build-to-order supply chains. Finally, the author describes the unique challenges these create for devising a valid business strategy and for KM.

As the reader can see, this book has a wonderful mix of tools, illustrative case studies, and illuminating new theories. It is heavily focused on providing practical, process-oriented frameworks. The book is written by authors from all over the world with a concentrated attention on the KM practitioner at any level within for-profit and not-for-profit organizations. I hope you will enjoy it, and more importantly, put it to good use.

REFERENCES

Kim, W. C., & Mauborgne, R. (2004). *Blue Ocean strategy: How to create uncontested market space and make competition irrelevant.* Boston, MA: Harvard Business School Press.

Kogut, B., & Zander, U. (1996). What firms do? Coordination, identity, and learning. *Organization Science, 7*, 502-518.

Russ, M. (2009, April 15-17). Knowledge management strategy in the age of paradox and transition. In R. Hackney (Ed.), *Emergent challenges in IS/IT. Proceedings of the Annual ISOneWorld Conference.* Washington, D.C.: Information Institute Publishing.

Russ, M., & Jones, J. K. (2006). Knowledge-based strategies and information system technologies: Preliminary findings. *International Journal of Knowledge and Learning, 2*(1&2), 154-179.

Tsoukas, H. (1996). The firm as a distributed knowledge system: A constructionist approach. *Strategic Management Journal, 17*, 11-25.

ENDNOTES

[1]   For example, Russ, 2009 (ISOneWorld2009).

[2]   Tsoukas, 1996; Kogut and Zander, 1996.

[3]   See for example http://www.businessweek.com/chapter/degeus.htm downloaded June 4, 2009.

[4]   For example, Kim and Mauborgne, 2004.

[5]   See more in depth discussion in Russ and Jones, 2006.

Acknowledgment

This book is ten years in the making and long overdue. I realized in 1996 that what I had been studying under the subject matter of technology transfer (with Michael Camp) since 1994 should actually be referred to as managing knowledge. Realizing that, in 1997 I developed one of the first classes that taught knowledge management in a graduate business program. Since then, I have been researching, consulting, and teaching that subject in numerous countries and academic institutions, never having found a text that would completely satisfy my needs. I have been talking to Robert for years about the need to write a book and later with Jeannette. The IGI Global editor suggested editing a book on the subject. This book is the fruition of our dream. Four chapters in the book are ours. The reader will also find two chapters that were written by students who have taken some of my classes and I thought would be great additions to this book. The rest of the chapters are from collaborators who I came to know at different venues over the last few years, and who have graciously agreed to share their knowledge and experience as a chapter in this book.

Now, I have to thank all the people who have had a direct or indirect impact on me during the last thirteen years. This is a very long list, and I am in no position to list all of them. I apologize in advance for not mentioning all of them individually, as many of them deserve.

Still, here are those that I thank deeply and personally. First and foremost, I have to thank the love of my life, my wife Fay for her endless patience with my *meshugas* and for being an endless source of love and support in more ways than I can acknowledge. I also want to thank my children Ira, Yaara, Maytal, and Yifat, their spouses, boyfriends, and kids for being an endless source of joy and inspiration. My deceased parents (Henryk and Anna Russ), my deceased father in law (Leo Pepper) and my mother in law (Sue Pepper) were and still are an endless source of motivation and encouragement.

I cannot mention by name the many hundreds of students that I have had in my knowledge management classes over the past twelve years (at Franklin University, Columbus, OH; Roosevelt University, Chicago; University of Wisconsin—Green Bay, Silver Lake College, Northeast Wisconsin, BEM, Bordeaux, France and the GSA Master program at the University of Pisa, Italy) who asked difficult questions, forced me to think, and made comments on early ideas and drafts. I will be remiss not to mention the few who had a significant impact and helped me along the way above and beyond the usual student help. They are (in alphabetical order): Nancy Amaral, Warren Boerger, John Francis, Abe Joseph, Erik Jul, John Klaus, Phil Mattek, and Roger Pfister.

I also cannot thank personally the hundreds of business executives and managers who provided me with their time and wisdom, advice and questions, to make this book what it is. The few[1] that made a significant impact on my understanding of the strategic importance of managing knowledge are: Susan Mott at Nationwide Insurance; at Worthington Industries, John P. McConnell, John Christie; Roger Campbell, John Lamprinakos, Virgil Winland, Ralph Roberts, and John Slane; at Syngenta, John Scheuring, Khoon Min Chin, and Steve Holt; John Corbett at Awhere; Mike Sayre at Pinnacle Data Systems; Martin Dillon at

OCLC; David Ward at NorthStar Economics, Inc.; Bob DeKoch at The Boldt Company; Jim Golembeski at Bay Area Workforce Development Board; Paul Jadin and Nan Nelson at Green Bay Area Chamber of Commerce; Barb Fleisner at Advance, Green Bay Area Economic Development; Paul Linzmeyer at ISO, Inc.; Greg Gauthier at Foxwood Associates; Jerry Murphy at New North, Inc.; Tim Weyenberg and Howard Bornstein at Foth & Van Dyke, LLC; and Eitan Yudilevich at Bird Foundation.

Throughout my academic career, I have had many outstanding professors, colleagues, and personal friends that have had a major impact on my academic development in this and in related areas. This might be the right time to thank them personally. Deep thanks go to Eitan Muller, Shlomo Kalish, Elie Segev, and Shlomo Globerson at Tel Aviv University; to Morris Teubal and Tamar Yinnon at the Jerusalem Institute for Israel Studies; to Dan Carmon, Yehuda Harel, and Elie Abrahami at Yad Tabenkin; to Don Sexton, Paul Nutt, David Greenberger, Bob Backoff, Riad Ajami, and Michael Camp at The Ohio State University; to Bart Schiavo, Ray Forbes, Bill Rives, Dick Curtis, Jay Young, and Shah Hasan at Franklin University; to Karl Zehms, Fritz Erickson, and Marilyn Sagrillo at UW-Green Bay; to Miltiadis Lytras at the University of Patras; to Ray Hackney at Brunel University; to Knut Ingar Westeren at North Trondelag University College; to David A. McEntire at University of North Texas; to Ernest Sternberg at State University of New York Buffalo; to Mike Santoro at Lehigh University; to Anja Schulz at Technische Universitat Dortmund; to Jeffrey Rafn at Northeast Wisconsin Technical College; to Manuel Rodenes-Adam at Universidad Politecnica de Valencia; to Emmanuel Carre at BEM, Bordeaux Management School; to Leopold Kahn at BEM, Bordeaux Management School; to Pedro Soto Acosta at Universidad De Murcia; to Bill Hynes at Saint Norbert College in De Pere, Wisconsin; to Silvio Bianchi Martini and Marco Allegrini at the University of Pisa; to Murray Jennex at San Diego State University, and to Riccardo Paterni at Professione Lavoro.

Also, I have to thank the two Assistant Development Editors whom I worked with at IGI Global, Rebecca Beistline and Christine Bufton, as well as to Kelly Anklam (at UW-Green Bay) for her ongoing editing of my writing, without whom this book would never have been published.

Another thank you goes to the members of my editorial advisory board: Leif Edvinsson at Lund University and Kuan Yew Wong at Universiti Teknologi, Malaysia, as well as to my two reviewers: Jack Aschkenazi at American Intercontinental University and Michael Knight at UW-Green Bay.

Lastly, I have to thank my two long time academic collaborators: Robert Fineman and Jeannette Jones at American Intercontinental University for their ongoing support and help over the last twelve years. I don't think I have words to express my gratitude for the many hours they spent with me on this book.

As always, the mistakes that remain are my personal responsibility.

ENDNOTE

[1] The affiliations in this preface are listed based on where I interacted with the person at the time. Since in some cases more than twenty years have passed, they might not be affiliated with that institution today.

Section 1
Knowledge and Knowledge Management Conceptual Aspects

Chapter 1
Conceptual Theory:
What Do You Know?

Meir Russ
University of Wisconsin-Green Bay, USA

Robert Fineman
Independent Consultant, USA

Jeannette K. Jones
American Intercontinental University, USA

ABSTRACT

This chapter will provide the reader with two definitions of knowledge, one at the individual level, the other at the organizational level. This will be followed by connecting the knowledge base of the organization to its sustainable competitive advantage by using a multiple-layer framework of organizational knowledge. Then, the chapter will discuss the frameworks of knowledge management vision, mission and goals for the organization. Temporary and functional gap analysis frameworks will follow. The chapter will end with a brief description of three tools developed by the authors.

INTRODUCTION

This chapter will provide the reader with a number of theoretical aspects that we consider important as a background for understanding and effectively utilizing the later developed subjects related to knowledge management strategy discussed by us later in this book. We will begin this chapter by introducing you to three epistemologies that can and do frame the discussion about knowledge and knowledge management. We will continue by discussing two conceptual aspects of knowledge. We will define knowledge at the individual (personal) level and then at the organizational level. Once these definitions have been solidified, we will place these concepts into a practical application by describing knowledge within an organization's strategic discussion. In a practical application, it is critical for an organization to understand where their knowledge should be located. Some of this discussion might seem tedious at first, but we hope you will commit to reading through the entire discussion to see for yourself that, while it might sound theoretical or philosophical, it is actually very practical. We hope the examples will illustrate why it is crucial for you to understand the foundation of our tools.

DOI: 10.4018/978-1-60566-348-7.ch001

Following that, we will introduce you to vision, mission, and goals for KM as well as gaps. We will close the chapter by briefly introducing three tools that we have developed to make it easier for you and your organization to systematically manage knowledge as a strategic asset to create value. A more in-depth discussion of those tools can be found in this book in chapters 4, 7 and 9.

Knowledge as a Complex and Living System: Three Epistemologies

Knowledge can be viewed from different perspectives (what academics call epistemology[1]). The three epistemologies are: the cognitivist view, the connectionist view and the autopoietic view. They are detailed and illustrated in Table 1. We want the reader to realize that there is more than one way to look at knowledge, and that by using the three perspectives you can have more and richer opportunities to use knowledge effectively. You will see the use of these three perspectives again in chapters 4, 7 and 9, within this book.

First Definition of Knowledge

Any discussion of Knowledge Management must begin by defining the terms to be used. We all assume that the reader knows what knowledge is but, in fact, everyone has his or her own conceptual idea of knowledge. That unique conception creates a problem because there is no universally agreed upon accepted definition. As an old story suggests, it's like trying to understand what an elephant looks like by asking several blind men to describe an elephant based on touching a different part of the animal. Knowledge is many things to many people. Knowledge is not easily understood, managed, or quantified. Indeed, since there is no universally accepted definition of knowledge, understanding, managing, and quantifying are nearly impossible tasks. Through this book, our goal is to show you that there are empirically based measures of knowledge that can be quantified, utilized, and

exploited! If we are to be successful, however, we must be assured that the definition of the key terms we are using aligns with the definition you have of the term.

Any definition of knowledge is biased, individualized, and carries with it social, political, and cultural baggage. As we look at common usage today, we find that *knowledge, information,* and *data* are as easily interchangeable as cola and "Coke." One simple way to explore the issue is to look into their definitions in any dictionary. If you do, you will see that the definitions are circular. Each one of the three is defined by the use of the other two terms. The loop feature of the terms can make the distinction between them quite difficult to find. We have developed definitions that clearly demonstrate that these terms are distinct (related, but distinct) entities. We believe that data and information are the building blocks of knowledge. In order to clarify what we mean, we will begin by sharing our definition of knowledge and then will break down the knowledge definition into its actionable components.

Knowledge: an action, or a potential of an action, that creates, or has the potential to create, value based on data or previous knowledge, and/or information.

Data: basic building blocks

Metadata: context of the building blocks, "the baskets"

Information: meaning

In order to understand Knowledge, we have to understand its parts. Assume that data elements are the most basic building blocks of knowledge. Data are entities that are meaningless (like bytes or letters) until there is context or metadata wrapped

Table 1. Perspectives of knowledge and their implications on knowledge management and strategy Modified from Russ, 2008

PERSPECTIVE/ EPISTEMOLOGY DIMENSION[2]	COGNITIVIST	CONNECTIONIST	AUTOPOIETIC
Cardinal Idea (Brain…)	Representation. Transparency of information.	There are rules for how components operate and there are rules for connections between components. Global properties emerge spontaneously without a central control.	Is an autonomous, simultaneously open and closed, self-referencing (knowledge about itself is effecting the structure and operations).
Humans are seen as	Information processing (sequential, localized). Logic Machines. Truth seekers.	Thought and activities that result from self-organizing properties, some similar to learned states, some novel. Relationship seekers (social-psychological).	A living system, an autonomous unit, responsible for their own maintenance and growth, consider the environment only as a potential source of input for their inner functioning.
Lemma	I am, therefore I act in the world.	I know, therefore I co-act in the world.	I know, therefore I act in my world.
Organization is seen as	Input-Output entity. Problem seeker and solver. An instrument of strategic planning and forecasting.	Network of individuals connected by Information Systems (communication), rules of access, shared consensus, resources, incentives. Network of activities.	A self-similar, autopoietic system of knowledge and distinction, a living system, shared awareness. A domain of structural coupling.
Knowledge is	Time invariant. Abstract, independent of human act. Transferable.	History dependent. A state in a system of interconnected components interacting with the environment. Transferable.	Embodied, self-referencial. Allows for distinction making in observations of categories and in values. It is bringing the world forth (coupling with). It is NOT transferable.
Learning	Is a process by which an increasingly accurate definition of representations corresponding to the external world arrives.	Is an emerging behavior, history and rules dependent.	Create the potential for and change in scope of potential and actual behavior resulting in improved effectiveness.[3]
Organizational Learning	Organizations as rational entities are capable of observing (their own and others') actions, and experiences to discover effects of actions and modify actions to improve performance.[4]	"an organizational process, both intentional and unintentional enabling the acquisition of, access to, and revision of organizational memory, thereby providing direction to an organizational action[5]."	Results in change of organizational behaviors which may enhance (or not) effectiveness, which will include change in the scope of organizational potential behaviors.[6]
Environment	Given. To be represented, predefined, highly structured, bounded, limiting.	Negotiable.	Structurally coupled with knowledge.
Relationships	Adaptation.	Shaping.	Structurally coupled.
Locus of Control	Central.	Network.	Internal.
Organizational networks	Input-output device.	Network of individuals/activities.	Autopoietic system.
Boundaries	Real, limiting.	Can be modified by using new actors.	An issue of knowledge.

continued on following page

Table 1. continued

PERSPECTIVE/ EPISTEMOLOGY DIMENSION[2]	COGNITIVIST	CONNECTIONIST	AUTOPOIETIC
Strategy	The choice of product/market and the competitive thrust (focus and set of priorities) to create value for shareholders, using coordination, reinforcement, allocation and control mechanisms.[7]	Choices in regard to: 1. Value creation - a choice of which value (profit maximization versus social responsibility) and for which stakeholder (shareholders versus customers). 2. Managing imitation - sustaining competitive advantage. 3. Shaping the perimeter of the organization - defining profitable business scope using, for example, outsourcing and vertical integration.[8]	Creating value (e.g. capturing synergies) and managing uncertainties (e.g., " differentiate roles based on the strategic uncertainty decision-makers face and integrate them by way of the strategic commitment to be made.)"[9]
Business Model	Describes how the organization creates and captures value by specifying the profit generating mechanism.	Define the value created for users, within a product market (for whom and what). Define the structure of the complete value chain (from suppliers to final customers). Describe the position of the organization within the value network. Specifies the profit generating mechanism.[10]	Define the value created for users, within a product market (for whom and what) as understood by the organization. Define the structure of the complete value chain (from suppliers to final customers) as understood by the organization. Describe the position of the organization within the living eco-system. Specifies the profit generating mechanism.[11]
Internationalization	"A process of increasing involvement in international operations"[12] "is the process of mobilizing, accumulating and developing resource stocks for international activities."[13]	A "process of developing networks of business relationships in other countries through extension, penetration, and integration."[14] "the emphasis is on gradual learning and the development of market knowledge through interaction within networks."[15]	A process of changing the existing geographic business scope, and the editing mechanism of structuralizing various kinds of innovative market knowledge for the creation of new business opportunities to connect the establishment of the new organization with future of unknown international opportunities.[16]
Entrepreneurs	Opportunity identifiers, resource marshaling, knowledge acquirers, star players.	Connectors, recombining resources and opportunities, by filling up structural holes in networks. Head of a team, builders of partnerships. Knowledge holders and creators in knowledge communities within a social network.	New reality creators, creators of new eco-systems. Builders of shared domain consensus.
Entrepreneurship	"Activities to promote socio-economic stabilization and effective utilization of resources by stimulating socio-economic progress, creating new values, and providing employment opportunities."[17]	Is "a diachronic process based on multiple decisions and action..... provides opportunities to newly combine heterogeneous ideas, promote their realization, and create new activities and potentials through interactions."[18]	"activities of changing the existing business paradigms, and to the editing mechanism of structuralizing various kinds of knowledge for the creation of a new business....to connect the establishment of the new organization with future of unknown opportunities"[19]

around them; something to give the data meaning, which is what you would call information.

For example, the data that comprises written romance languages would be the 26 letters of the alphabet. The data that comprises a spoken language would be the different sounds used to identify each letter. Add to that all the different sounds available in all the romance languages and you are beginning to build quite a large database. But at this point, you still don't have anything that is instantaneously useful and that has meaning or value. Another point that adds complexity to this issue is how these elements are represented. The database is now comprised of the physical representation of letters A – Z, but the sounds require a different media, a .wav file for instance. Add to that the various pronunciations between the languages as well as the multiple dialects and regionalisms within a language. We use this example to demonstrate the variety of data and their potential inter-relationships. It's not until we get to the next step in the process that we can take a variety of data elements and begin to determine what they mean.

The next step is to understand metadata. Metadata is a frame (the context creator) wrapped around a single piece or multiple pieces of data. You can easily see the power of metadata as it transforms data into something potentially useful. If we go back to our letters example, the concept of say, names, would provide a context that would give the letters and sounds the ability to become useful. Remember, at this point there is only data with context. We now have a construct where we have the ability to take the data and metadata to the next level.

When we agree on the definition of data and metadata, we can then move on in the knowledge definition to look at the term information. We will define information as simply data plus metadata. Information lacks the actionable punch of knowledge, but it allows the transformation of six pieces of data such as J-O-S-H-U-A into a name. By wrapping the context of name around

the letters, we have something that can represent the first name of Joshua Jones. We could look at numbers in the same way. Data of 0-1-0-1-0-0 is meaningless in a vacuum. If we add the context of date, then 010100 turns into the first day of the 21st century and can be represented as 01/01/00. If we changed the context to student identification, it could just as easily represent Joshua Jones's student ID number simply by attaching that label. The name Joshua, the date 01/01/00, and the student ID number 010100, now reflect information that we can use. Therefore, information is interchangeable and totally dependent on the context or metadata.

Our favorite real world example deals with the loss of the Mars Climate Orbiter (MRO) in November of 1999[20]. Prior to the success of the two Mars rovers, there was an attempt to place the MRO in orbit over Mars that ended as a failure. A course correction had to be sent to the spaceship to align it correctly for entry into an orbit over Mars. The course correction instructions (the data) were sent but it is assumed that the craft entered the Martian atmosphere at too low an altitude and the ship crashed into the surface of the planet. We liken this to the classic metadata problem. Why? Because the data was correct. However, the context or metadata was incorrect. An investigation board concluded that NASA engineers failed to convert English measures of thrust into a metric system or newtons (the metadata context). Although the actual difference between the acceleration when using the two different units was small, it was enough to terminate a potentially successful and scientifically significant mission. Therefore, the "information," the combination of the data and metadata, that the ship was given was faulty. If we align this example to our definition, the knowledge (action step) was present, the information (meaning) was present, the metadata (context) was present but inaccurate, and the data was present. Because the metadata was incorrect, the information and overall knowledge sent to the orbiter was wrong and the result of the mission reflects this fact. We believe this example reflects our definition, but also demonstrates how fragile information that we use everyday to make strategic decisions can be. This complex circular relationship between data, metadata and information is the reason it is important to discuss and align meaning within an organization. We want to make sure that the building blocks of knowledge are housed on a solid foundation. You cannot assume the metadata is correct and understood by all concerned parties; you must confirm your assumptions at every step in the process. As you can see from this example, a simple misunderstanding or wrong assumption/context can have significant consequences on the information shared, action and outcomes.

As a general guiding principle, when determining data for a specific application, it is best to use the smallest manageable unit (lowest common denominator) as data. The most important point in this discussion is not to break down say, atoms into protons, neutrons, electrons, and then into the myriad sub-atomic particles. It is to have everyone involved understand what the data means (which makes it information). Metadata can be simple or complex, so spend the time building a consensus around the metadata. Get rid of all the assumptions! Belabor the point! Make sure everyone is talking apples and apples! If a house has a faulty foundation, it will never stand straight. If knowledge has a faulty foundation, it won't have any real value.

We've been talking about information as data and metadata and now it's time to go to the next step, knowledge. Our definition of knowledge states: *Knowledge is an action, or a potential of an action, that creates or has the potential to create, value based on data or previous knowledge, and/or information.* Consider knowledge as the outcome of a catalytic event or kinetic energy and information as potential energy. In this context, there is a vast difference between the two terms. In order for knowledge to be created, there must be an actionable event that occurs or has the po-

tential to occur. Therefore, if one starts with data and then adds metadata, information is created and the potential for knowledge or an action is in place. New knowledge is created when such potential for an actionable event occurs.

The equation would look like this: $K = ke + pe$. Where K=Knowledge, ke = kinetic energy, and pe = potential energy.

Knowledge gets more complex and gives us better insight into what is required for knowledge creation. As we look into additional equations, the process gets more complex. For example, another way to express the value proposition inherent in knowledge creation is the following equation: $K = (D+MD) \times A \ V$. Where Knowledge (K) is equal to Data plus Metadata (D+MD) times Action (A) that creates or has the potential to create Value (V).

For purposes of this illustration, assume the knowledge has been created by an individual. Only two events can occur once the knowledge has been created and stored by the individual as tacit knowledge. It can either be exploited by the individual to produce value (for example a new product or new service), or it can be transferred to other individuals. In the latter instance, the knowledge must be codified as explicit knowledge by the original knowledge creator and transferred as data to other individuals. Once they receive the data, they must add metadata and create the knowledge for themselves. Although this sounds counterintuitive, we contend that only data, metadata, and information can be transferred, but knowledge has to be re-created individually. Lots of information such as the speed of light, the number of feet in a mile, the number of days in a year, is available. Lots of knowledge is also available. For example, we know how to calculate the speed of light, we can measure the number of feet in a mile, and we have standards that allow us to determine the number of days in any given year. The difference between information and knowledge is an actionable event or the potential to create an actionable event. That event is the catalyst that transforms potential energy into kinetic energy and produces value. Therefore, using our definition, the information that reduces uncertainty to allow an action is knowledge and that action creates value. The same information, if it does not allow for an action as it has meaning to the user is NOT knowledge. It is just useless information. Knowledge is dynamic. Data and Information are static. Just because data and metadata are present does not mean that knowledge will be created; it only supplies the necessary framework for knowledge to be created. Remember an individual or organization does not have to re-invent the mousetrap; they only have to make a better one.

Let us give you another example. In a recent book "*Decoding the Universe,*" Seife[21] describes a number of examples of how information (knowledge by our definition) creates value by reducing uncertainty. He describes Paul Revere's scheme for sharing information (knowledge) about the British intentions (pp. 60-61) and the story of breaking the Japanese JN-25 code named AF (the attack on Midway, pp. 5-7). What he misses completely is the metadata and the intentions that framed this information (knowledge) and allowed this knowledge to create value. Just look into the misreading of the weak signals preceding the 9-11 events, missing the early indications of the Challenger and Discovery disasters in this country, or the Israelis missing the signals of the coming Yom Kippur war and you will see the difference.

Our reasoning of presenting this variety of examples is to support the point that information does NOT always translate to knowledge. Interestingly, we are NOT the first ones to come up with this idea. von Baeyer[22] in his recent book: "*Information: The New Language of Science*" describes three levels of complexity of information (pp. 32-33) developed originally by Shannon and Weaver[23] in their classic book about information theory. Shannon and Weaver suggest that knowledge is present only if it can answer the following questions: 1. "How accurately can information be transmitted" (p. 32)? This is what we refer to as data. 2. "How precisely do the symbols convey the desired meaning" (p. 32)? This is what we refer to as information. 3. "How effectively does the received meaning affect behavior in the desired way" (p. 32)? This is what we refer to as knowledge. Unfortunately, most experts dealing with this subject (for example, Seife and von Baeyer) refer to those three levels as nothing more than different aspects of information, missing the importance of metadata (the context) and intentions (the knowledge). For example, adding the metadata to the data will allow the sender to convey the desired meaning, (see question 2 above) or, to answer question 3, adding context and intention to the information will ensure the appropriate behavior by the receiving entity.

The real issue here is the creation of value and you can clearly see that knowledge builds on itself. In fact, as we move up the knowledge ladder, we build more and more complex structures. Since our definition allows knowledge to be based on data and previous knowledge, we have the ability to utilize existing knowledge to increase our knowledge base.

A more detailed discussion regarding the actionable event that transforms data elements into knowledge will be presented later in this chapter. Our intent for this chapter is to lay a working definition foundation. The difference between Information and Knowledge as we have just outlined is critically important. It is NOT simply an issue of semantics. Thousands of business executives and hundreds of Information Systems (IS) companies do NOT understand this issue. Organizations that purchase software and hardware intending to create a Knowledge Based System can not use these tools to capture knowledge as an asset by itself unless the system is embedded in the appropriate context. While it might have the potential to utilize knowledge, unless the system is embedded in the appropriate context, it is strictly information. This, at least to us, explains the failure of the first generation of many of the KM initiatives. Companies that bought Knowledge Based Systems assumed that the systems will work as indeed KNOWLEDGE based systems, without comprehending that knowledge has human-systems interactive aspects and is a social-technical phenomenon.

Knowledge is an asset. Good managers exploit their assets to position their companies well within their particular environment. As you will see, the ability to determine where your knowledge assets are and how to utilize those assets can start you on the road to identifying and sustaining a competitive advantage. Our intention is to provide a roadmap that will allow you and your organization to navigate the very tricky waters of knowledge management. We don't claim to have all the answers, but we hope to give the reader what he or she needs to make the trip as smooth as possible.

Second Definition of Knowledge

Until now, we have been talking about knowledge as a stand-alone entity at the individual level of analysis. If this is true, how can there be "smart" organizations and "not-so-smart" organizations? Even within your own company there are "smart" teams and "not-so-smart" teams. Although it would be easy to say that the best people are in the "smart" teams and the worst are in the "not-so-smart" teams, we know that just isn't the case. You are smart and bring a lot of knowledge to any team. You have also been on "good" teams and "not-so-good" teams. Shouldn't your knowledge have brought the "not-so-good" team to the level of a "good" team? Let's examine this last piece of the puzzle.

To help you visualize the process, draw a triangle on a piece of paper or a white board. Now label the points of the triangle People, Process, and System. These are the building blocks of knowledge creation and the drivers for the actionable event that actually creates knowledge. Now, convert the triangle into a pyramid and make it three dimensional by giving it height and label

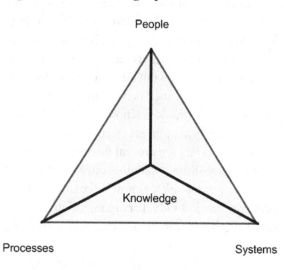

Figure 1. The knowledge space

the top Knowledge. You have just constructed a three-dimensional actionable event model of knowledge creation based on the organizational drivers People, Processes, and Systems, (see Figure 1).

Although we didn't discuss these three items in our definition of knowledge, each of the entities we labeled at the base of the triangle is a knowledge component or driver that is either active, passive, or both. The diagram you drew describes the support structure for Knowledge at the organizational level that can be represented in an equation as $K = P*(P+S+P*S)$ or *Knowledge* equals *(People)* times *(Processes* plus *Systems* plus *Processes *Systems)*; where $P*S$ is the synergy between the processes and the systems. The equation stipulates that a Person must be present in order to create knowledge. However, either Processes or Systems (or both) can be present and these variables times Person will generate knowledge. This is the genesis of the actionable event we referred to earlier.

Consider an example where a company "owns" a process that manufactures a specific product and has systems that do much of the work. This process incorporates two of the three essential ingredients, Processes and Systems, however, if there are no people who possess the knowledge to put the process and system to work (into action), the product cannot be produced. There is an exception to this and it deals with embedding knowledge into processes and systems. We'll deal with embedded knowledge later in the chapter, but a simplistic example would be driving a car. The mechanical knowledge to actually get the car moving is embedded within the vehicle, all the driver has to know is how to start the engine, how to put the car in gear and how to drive.

Organizational Knowledge-Base and Strategy

The definition of knowledge is complex at the individual level and organizational levels. Incorporating knowledge management into the strategic discussion of an organization adds yet another layer of complexity. We see the knowledge-base of the organization feeding into the core competencies and capabilities of the organization. Those are the core competencies and capabilities that allow the organization to develop a strategy and its sustainable competitive advantage. This, in turn, results in performance in the marketplace. So, the other aspect of knowledge that reinforces the complexity of knowledge management's processes is the multi-layering aspect of the interrelationships between the four layers[24] mentioned above (see also Figure 2). This complexity increases due to the potential time lag between managing the knowledge at the bottom layer and the final outcome at the top layer. There can be a time lag between the bottom layer, (managing the knowledge base), to the top layer, (final market performance) of up to 15 years. The time lag is caused by the slow movement through all four layers as they build upon each other. An analogy that illustrates this aspect is the public education system. Society is paying for education today with an expectation of a return for the next generation of the workforce. However, there is no tool that allows us to quantify that X dollars spent today

Figure 2. Organizational knowledge base and business strategy as a multilayer construct

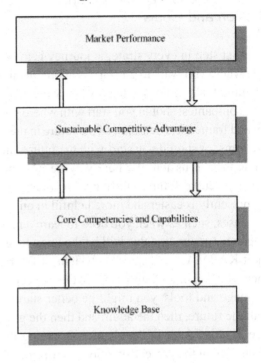

will return Y dollars in the future. Additionally, there are no tools available to allow us to see what type of education will be required for the workforce of the future. Who could have predicted the explosion of programming skills that were needed to fuel the Internet revolution?

We have provided a conceptual explanation of what knowledge is and have discussed how to make it operational. An organization can create knowledge and derive value from that knowledge. That happens in some organizations. The problem stems from the fact that, by and large, management doesn't recognize knowledge as an asset. We are not saying that knowledge is dismissed by companies; on the contrary, knowledge is prized. However, most organizations don't know where their knowledge resides, what pieces of knowledge are missing, how to value knowledge, or how it should be managed. This book will provide several tools to enable you to understand the complexities and misunderstandings of this management gap.

Where Do You Want to Go: The Knowledge-Based Vision, Mission and Goals

The first step in every strategic journey is to decide where you want to go. This is an interesting dilemma that we always have when we consult with companies: should you start with where you are and frame the discussion of the future in present terms; or should you start with the future and frame the discussion of where you are in terms of the potential future. Starting with where you are presently is easier and more helpful in only a few cases, such as when you need to learn a new language (in our case this will be the knowledge audit-KARMA, see chapter 4). BUT, in the future, once you become familiar with the concepts, language and tools, you might be better starting with the future, then the audit, and then the gaps (see Figure 5 later in the chapter). Framing the discussion of the present situation in terms of the future simply makes it easier to get there.

One way to start this discussion is to define broad and specific goals for your organization in business and KM terms. A second way is to have a discussion about your KM vision and mission statements and how they relate to your business vision and mission. Some people are better at developing the long term vision and mission before they (or usually others) go into the detailed goals. Some are better the other way around--they have the goals and they let the vision and mission bubble up. Regardless, before you are done developing the picture of the future, you will need to clearly define the vision, mission and goals. At this first stage you should develop the KM vision-mission and relate it to the business. We rarely find companies that have an explicit vision-mission statement for their KM, even when they have an explicit KM strategy, which again, few have.

We have identified a number of approaches companies have used to develop explicit or implicit vision and mission statements (see Figure 3 and Figure 4). In the technology management

Figure 3. Vision statement framework

	Product		Process	
	Explicit	Implicit	Explicit	Implicit
Internal, technology driven				
External, market/ customer driven				

literature this is called technology push or market pull.[25] High-tech companies will develop a unique knowledge, patent it, and then look for markets. Service companies will have the customers/markets and then will look for products and knowledge to satisfy their changing needs. Companies that have an explicit strategy will patent knowledge or trademark brands, realizing that they have intellectual assets to protect, while those that have an implicit strategy will not, or will do so reactively.

What is unique about knowledge that impacts how you develop your vision-mission? Since the product life cycle and the half life of knowledge are continuously shrinking (can be as short as 18-30 month today[26]), competitors are changing the "rules of the game" more frequently, and the capital investments needed for new knowledge creation are increasing. The uncertainties and the risks involved in committing long term (in some cases 10-15 years) to a knowledge path are growing continuously since by the time your knowledge embedded in a product or a service gets to the market it may be obsolete. Here, large companies e.g. large pharmaceutical companies, banks, etc., use their size muscle and transfer their business model from knowledge driven to customer driven, assuming (mostly correctly) that instead of gambling on technology, they will secure the channels of distribution to the customers and that their size and power will allow them to buy needed knowledge when risks are lower at a reasonable cost, and as such, they will leave new knowledge development to small companies that are willing to take higher risks. One problem for the large companies is that they are shifting their business models, so pharmaceutical companies have to hire more marketing and sales people and less PhDs in chemistry. In addition, if the large companies are completely losing their R&D they are putting themselves at risk of losing knowledge. Their marketing people will now have to talk to external PhDs of chemistry which sooner or later will give the knowledge provider power. So here, we can predict a shift of power to Indian and Chinese R&D companies in the long run. Also, the large companies now have to learn how to evaluate, to negotiate with external partners and to develop partnerships and relationships within the industry. This causes a shift from content/area knowledge to process knowledge-which is also one of our six strategic dilemmas. As you can see, process knowledge is tricky. American companies that tried to copy the Japanese process knowledge of TQM and Six Sigma learned this the hard way. Process knowledge can be easily embedded in some cultures but might be very difficult in others. Such knowledge is also more tacit and embedded in people, even when you put it into policies and procedures.

Once you know what kind of vision-mission you want to develop, you have to decide on the time frames and specifics. Traditionally, vision is long term and less specific, while mission is shorter term and includes specifics regarding the scope of KM in question. For example, technological scope, market scope, product/service scope. We found the following framework especially helpful in developing KM mission statements (see Figure 4).

Of course you do not have to use all of the KM scopes to define who you want to be. Just use those that are appropriate. In chapter 9 of this book we describe the case of Fiat and how the company's new CEO was able to change the path of its future by utilizing its core competency of product development and driving a new mission of their product scope to get them out of a financial crisis.

Figure 4. Mission statement framework

KM Scope	Time Horizon		
	Short	Medium	Long
Business you are in			
Business Model			
Technological Scope			
Market Scope			
Product Scope			
Geographic Scope			
Innovation Scope			
Intellectual Assets			

Once you have your vision-mission it is a good time to translate that into outcomes, or what some people call, broad goals, specific goals, and measurable key success indicators.

There is an interesting academic debate surrounding the idea of whether or not companies need specific indicators, and especially if those indicators inhibit or support innovation and creativity. Some academics[27] claim that specific indicators prevent creativity, if they are the wrong indicators, or if they are followed by a wrong reward system. We tend to fall on the other side. We think you should have specific indicators and the appropriate reward system. It is wrong to assume that more innovation is always better, but if you want that, CHANGE the indicators and the reward system but be sure to have some indicators. Why? In our minds, the answer is simple: transparency (which happens to be another strategic dilemma, see our discussion in chapter 7). We are confident that only companies that are transparent (of course by and large-not absolutely) will be successful in the future. As we will tell you later, this is probably the only way the markets (capital and human) will be able to evaluate the value and decide if they want to invest money (capital) or be employed (human), since the power is shifting from the demand side to the supply side (both capital and talent). The other reason why measurable indicators are crucial is that they force you to deal with gaps first (if you don't measure, you don't know) and second, they force you to deal with real gaps, not perceived or imaginary gaps. Our experience is telling us that many executives and managers will go a long way to avoid measurable indicators because they want to avoid the accountability trap. If you measure and you fail, someone is accountable. In the old economy this was a bad thing. You could pay with your career. We suggest using failure as a trigger for learning, not for execution. This does not mean that stupidity should be rewarded, nor does it mean that failure should be punished. This is a tricky balance. If a nurse is being sued for criminal negligence when mistakes happen, what do you think is the probability that the hospital will be able to implement a six sigma initiative? In our humble opinion balance and common sense are the answer, not a heavy-hand, regulated environment driven only by judicial concerns. Why do we believe purely judicial is not the answer? Check the cost and quality of the British healthcare system and compare it to the American and tell us what you think.[28]

What are some of the dimensions of the outcomes that are affected by KB strategies and/or are KM specific? In our consulting experience and academic research we identified two frameworks that are of interest and relevance; the intellectual capital (e.g., Edvinsson and Malone, 1997) and the balanced scorecard (Kaplan and Norton, 1992). We added a few additional potential outcomes to their recommendations, e.g., social responsibilities and talent, and arrived at ten possible goals organizations might have. Each of these possible goals is discussed in the following paragraphs.

Intellectual Property (IP)

Some of the most valuable assets companies in the knowledge economy have are intellectual assets or intellectual properties like brands names, patents etc. The intellectual asset/property values are relatively easy to quantify, since they are regulated and have markets. They incur costs, and in some cases take a long time to build, but when managed appropriately will have an enormous value. Cases of building value worth billions of dollars by IBM (patents) and Coca Cola (brand equity) are well known but are by no means unique. Companies can also choose other IPs like: trade secrets, copyrights, trademarks, and internet domain names, among others.

Sales, Earnings, etc.

Some of the most import and simple to achieve results for KM are in the area of sales. As such it should not be surprising that one of the first successful Knowledge Based Systems successfully implemented by companies is Customer Relationship Management (CRM). Recently companies moved into the next generation of CRM, one that allows them to use analytics to improve sales force and customer service effectiveness as well as to acquire the ability to identify new products or services, including after sale service. More and more companies are realizing the potential of identifying the "big fat tail" of customer markets and the potential for true one-to-one marketing and, as a result, increasing revenues and profits (see also discussions in chapters 15 and 16).

Liability, Risk Reduction

The value of the reduction of liabilities and risks is very hard to quantify, unless you have to pay for a mistake someone made. Then the costs are clear, and unfortunately, in many cases prohibitive. For example, 40% of Small and Medium Enterprises (SMEs) companies hit by a disaster (fire, flood, etc.) do not survive the 5th year after being hit by disaster[29]. The current (Nov. 2008) financial crisis is another example of financial and other risks accrued by companies. The same can be said about liabilities encountered by companies, in many cases without realizing the consequences. Foreign suppliers, outsources, etc. that can provide the company with an enormous cost advantage, can also create huge liabilities (see for example China[30]). Engineering knowledge is currently required to manage risks and liabilities reduction when designers of new products are using knowledge base tools and the risks can be quantified and the costs known. Taking that kind of thinking to the business realm requires a change in scope and tools and, as the current financial crisis illustrates, is not easy to accomplish.

Delivery Performance

At times, when Supply Chain Management (SCM) should be intertwined concurrently with innovation while creating the business model at the inception of the new business, it is seen as the next new "game breaker". Having the right goals and indicators to manage SCM could make or break a company. On time delivery and inventory management on the go are legendary for making Wal-Mart and Dell what they are. Other delivery performance indicators might be error elimination, rush orders, damaged goods, etc., (see also the discussion in chapter 18).

Cost Savings

The simplest goal to document, the easiest to implement, and the most important at the early stages of the KM journey for the organization's set of goals and indicators is the cost savings one. Early studies suggest that successful KM initiatives in this area have an extremely high rate of ROI.

Quality

Quality initiatives, TQM and/or Six Sigma (you name the buzz word of the month) are everywhere. Underlying quality is the knowledge and talent needed to support such initiatives (see also the discussion in chapter 17) as the experience and tremendous success of Toyota illustrates.[31] The goals here can be quality improvement in processes resulting in cost savings, or improving sales due to increased customer satisfaction. There is one goal that we are strongly NOT recommending (which will not make us the favorites of quality gurus) and that is the quality awards. If you want to know more, look into how many quality awards Motorola[32] received and the correlation this had with market share of profitability. Or look into companies that tried to reengineer their processes and on their journey to successful reengineering eliminated a whole slew of middle managers and resulted in losing critical knowledge.[33]

Flexibility, Agility, Responsiveness

Knowledge embedded in process management can support flexible strategic (and operational) moves, agility under attack and responsiveness to market, and customers' opportunities (see also the discussion in chapter 3). Specific goals here might be, for example, having a flexible manufacturing strategy that allows every facility in the world to manufacture every car within a specific time frame (Honda[34]) or receiving compliments from customers, translated into better location in stores or new orders from customers (Blue Rhino[35]).

Innovation, Creativity

Probably the most difficult area in which to use KM, since the systems are not so helpful, is at the fuzzy front end of the creativity and innovation process. Due to the time lag, complexities, etc. it is easy to measure lagging indicators in this area like new product sales but defining and validating leading indicators for innovation and creativity is much more difficult.

Learning, Talent Improvement

In the knowledge economy the most import assets and the most difficult to measure are related to human capital (HC), succession planning, and talent mentoring, just to mention a few. Also, relationship or social capital, learning and forgetting, and investing in and depreciation of HC are difficult to define and validate.

SOCIAL RESPONSIBILITY, SUSTAINABILITY

Social responsibility and sustainability have been recently accepted as an important set of goals and indicators, are highly debatable and are not strongly and positively reinforced by the markets and shareholders. For example, some companies are using the Leadership in Energy and Environmental Design (LEED) building rating, or some investment companies will only invest in companies that are socially responsible. So a company can make a decision that x% of it s new buildings will be LEED platinum certified, or that by a specific date it will have a chief ethics officer.

By no means is this a comprehensive list. You may want to add, eliminate, or modify it to your specific needs. As always, too few or too many is a bad thing. You also have to think about progression. It is really very hard to run unless you can walk (as any parent with toddlers can tell you). This is what absorptive capacity[36] talks about. In other words, if you are a young start-up company you can run, BUT you must have legs, and since yours have not had the time to grow and mature you have to get them from the outside: buy, hire, etc.

To find the right set of outcomes for you, you will have to go through the whole cycle a couple of times and each time refine, modify, etc. until you

find what works for you. One word of warning, though---You are NEVER done, since an accelerated pace of change is the only constant.

The Knowledge-Based Gap Analysis

The next step is to identify the gaps between where you are and where you want to be.

Starting with the vision-mission takes us back to the discussion about assumptions, or how you frame the discussion (e.g. present or future terms). Consider Amazon.com's strategic dilemma in the late 90's: if you frame the discussion of vision-mission as Amazon.com being a company selling books (present) the gaps are of one kind, BUT if you frame the discussion in terms of the future (multilayer market, retailer) then you have very different gaps. Of course, at the time only the top executives of the company were aware of this dilemma, because the rest of us saw the actions. But, this is exactly the point. What are the assumptions you have? In our opinion you are always better documenting (codifying) your assumptions if you can[37]. This documentation process will make your life easier in the future.

Regardless of where you started earlier and how you framed the discussion (see Figure 5), you now have to begin to face the music and start the hard work of identifying the gaps.

The gaps identified might be between now and the future, and/or between the KM part and the business part. Here you face an interesting and critical dilemma. We know that there is a very long time-lag between developing the knowledge base and turning it into strategy. It can take anywhere from 5 to 15 years, depending on the industry and product life cycle you are in currently. In order to arrive at a knowledge base that will drive your sustainable competitive advantage you may have to invest in a long term commitment that might turn out to useless by the time you need it for your strategy, and you may find that a much more flexible and faster changing approach is needed. Years ago companies assumed that the only way

Figure 5. Gaps and assumptions

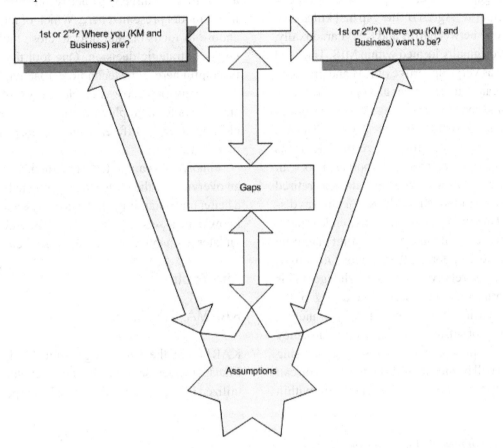

to control an entity (and its knowledge) was to own it, so they bought it. But since many mergers and acquisitions failed, companies had to learn how to partner and collaborate. They had to create joint ventures or alliances which afforded them less control, but also exposed them to less risk. The same is happening in the KM area. Fewer companies are doing the research part of the R&D part and more are doing the development. Also, not all companies that invest heavily in R&D are doing well (did we mention Ford[38]?). What is this suggesting? Companies must rapidly learn what their REAL gaps are and how they can close them quickly and at a reasonable price. If they do not, bad things will likely happen.

Next, we will discuss the different types of gaps that you might identify. For example, you might identify that you do not have an explicit

KM strategy, but you do have an explicit business strategy (most companies have) and you have a quality strategy (more and more companies have). You also might be aware of innovation issues that you have, and you begin to hear more and more about environmental issues, but you do not have those strategies explicitly stated. First you have to identify the gaps you currently have between your KM strategy, your business strategy and your quality strategy. For example, is your reward system consistent with all of your explicit strategies? We rarely find companies that have their reward system aligned with their strategies, so this is one simple test. Then you have to develop strategies in the other areas (see Figure 6) while making sure that there are no gaps. Next you have to think in terms of time horizons (see Figure 6), present (audit) and the three future time horizons (near, medium, long).

Some gaps are more important than others. For example at "Agresco" the gap that killed KM was the one between MIS and KM. Paradoxally, KM was originally located within MIS. The head of MIS was very supportive of KM and provided the KM team with resources and operated as their mentor and sponsor. But along the way, information security and hardware strategy were obstacles and issues that were difficult to resolve. KM was never truly (in our opinion) incorporated into/with MIS strategy. And so, when the team head retired and the sponsor moved on, the KM team was dissolved. This might be an extreme, endearment/survival case, but it illustrates the point that some gaps are more important than others. Obviously, over time, the relative importance changes. This change brings us to the second kind of gap, the one between time frames (see Figure 7). In another words, it is not sufficient to identify the gaps, they also must be rank ordered so the strategy (closing the gaps) will be meaningful and fruitful. You can identify up to twenty four gaps (eight gaps within

a time frame * three gaps between time frames) in our model presented here. Which of them you choose to focus on and how to close them will be your strategic decision. One tool that could be helpful here is the technology roadmap[39]. The Technology roadmap was developed by Motorola[40] and allows for a graphic description of the gaps, closing the gaps, different time frames, and complex relationships.

Finally, we want to take a moment to provide an overview of the tools we have created to give a better understanding of how to utilize and value knowledge assets. Those tools will be elaborated on later in chapters 4, 7 and 9 in this book.

The Tools

KARMA: The Audit

KARMA or the Knowledge Audit Review and Management Assessment has been developed and utilized in over 70 organizations. Its purpose is to

Figure 6. Framework A for gaps analysis

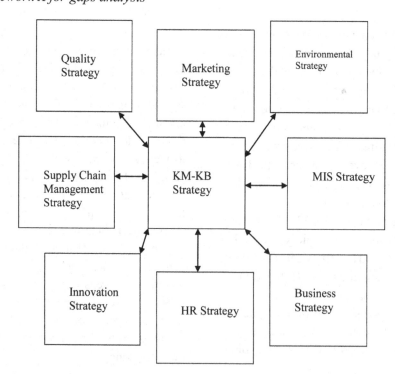

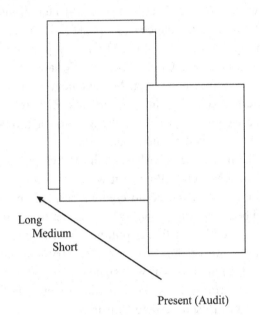

Figure 7. Framework B for gaps (between time frames) analysis

Long
Medium
Short

Present (Audit)

allow an organization to systematically assess the current status of its knowledge base. For example, KARMA allows organizations to understand what knowledge they possess as well as where their knowledge assets reside. Most organizations don't really know what knowledge they have, and those that do, usually don't know how to utilize that knowledge effectively. It should be noted that most organizations that value and use their knowledge assets, do so intuitively (not systematically). Our research affirms that there is no evidence that points to a systematic evaluation and exploitation of knowledge to support strategic management in companies.

We will take a more in depth look at KARMA in the next chapter but you should keep the following issues in mind:

- KARMA identifies where you have pockets of knowledge building blocks as well as potential "Knowledge Gaps."
- KARMA is not the driver of your knowledge management systems or your strategic plan.

- KARMA can show you where you need additional knowledge; it can't tell you how to get that knowledge.
- KARMA can show you where to put the "X."

C³EEP: The Strategic Dilemma Matrix

C³EEP (Codification, Complementary, Concealment, Exploration, External Acquisition, and Product dilemmas, see chart below) frames the data collected from KARMA and presents management with specific questions based on the organization's knowledge base. Up to this point, we have mentioned strategic thinking but here is where it begins to come into play. We have developed a matrix (Table 2) that requires management to focus on the types of knowledge it possesses or would like to posses and begins to guide management to make the most appropriate decisions based on "Where do you want to go"?

At this point we know where our knowledge assets reside. Now we have to decide what to do with those assets. We will explore the details of each decision and the ramifications of those decisions as they relate to the strategic planning process later in chapter 7.

To quickly review, we have defined earlier in this chapter what knowledge is. We also know that data is the basic building block of knowledge. Once we have the data context, or metadata, all we need is an actionable item that creates or has the potential to create value. Now that we have defined knowledge, we have a framework to identify where it resides (KARMA), and the six strategic dilemmas (C³EEP) that will put you on the road to utilizing the knowledge base to it fullest advantage. Now we can look at the final piece of the puzzle, the Action Engine. This is a tool that allows you to complete the work started earlier.

Table 2. The strategic dilemma matrix

Codification	Vs	Tacitness
Complementary	Vs	Destroying
Concealment	Vs	Transparency
Exploration	Vs	Exploitation
External Acquisition	Vs	Internal Development
Product	Vs	Process

Action Engine: The Strategic Framework

The Action Engine is a strategic tool that incorporates an organization's knowledge base. Its decisions are based on the six strategic dilemmas, systems and processes within the organization, culture, time, money, and many other inter-dependent variables that tell the organization not only where it wants to go, but the best way to get there. The output of the Action Engine tool is a Knowledge Management Action Plan. By using the tool to create an action plan, the resulting strategic framework will provide Knowledge Management Outcomes (KMOs) from a variety of sources. The outcomes might include some of the performances below (as mentioned earlier):

- Intellectual Property
- Sales, Earnings, etc.
- Liability
- Delivery, Performance
- Cost, Savings
- Quality
- Flexibility, Agility, Responsiveness
- Innovation
- Learning
- Social Responsibility

These performances are created by: KM Processes, KM/IS Systems, and KM Levers. The KM processes might include Communities of Practice, Product Councils, Functional Units, Project Teams, Informal Networks, etc. There is no predefined list and each organization will dictate the processes that it deems appropriate. The systems might include KM/IS Architecture, Security Policies, Access to Systems (internal and external), Maintenance and Update Policies, etc. The levers might include HR hiring practices, Reward Systems, Cross Functional Collaboration, Core Competencies, Top Management Support, External Relationships, Culture, and Risk Tolerance. Again, the specifics of the systems and levers will be dictated by the organization.

Think of these KMOs as the forces pulling up the KM Action Plan. If it were that simple, a management team could create a strategic plan and be on its way to success. However, there are also a number of forces pulling down from the bottom. An organization must be very familiar with the pull downs as well since we all deal with them on a daily basis. We're talking about the pull downs of Resources and Constraints.

On the Resource side, you have things like Time, Money, Physical Plant Capacity, and Real Estate for Human Resources (Offices and Cubes), Authorized Head Count, etc. On the Constraint side, you have Time (again), Money (again), Reward Systems, HR Policies, Top Management Support (or lack of), Culture, and (lack of) Risk Tolerance.

This is the most complex area to work in because there are interdependencies that actually build the plan of action. This is where strategic action is actually put in place and you can quickly see the implications and rewards of this kind of thinking. This is not an easy road to travel. Organizations will find many bumps and potholes in the road. The obstacles the organization may have to maneuver around may challenge some closely held beliefs. When we discuss the concept of KARMA later in the book, we will dig deeper into the specifics and mechanics.

CONCLUSION

To recap the highlights of this chapter, we would like to provide you with what we believe are the most important concepts to assist in your understanding of the process:

- Don't assume metadata exists – verify and make the metadata explicit.
- Managing knowledge is a complex process – use systems thinking as a framework of reference.
- Sharing data and information is not sharing knowledge – don't confuse the three definitions.
- If there is no action (or potential for action) that creates (or has the potential to create) value, there is no new knowledge created.
- For a team or an organization to create knowledge, people, and systems (and/or) processes working in tandem are required.
- Watch for assumption when you are working on the audit (KARMA).
- Frame your strategic discussions as a set of trade-offs/dilemmas.
- Your Knowledge Management strategy should be driven by outcomes, supported by People, Systems, Processes, and other KM levers, and mitigated by available resources and other restraints.

The use of these tools, KARMA, the C^{3}EEP Matrix, and the Action Engine, will give an organization the means to create and sustain a competitive advantage. The results obtained from the use of these tools may confirm management's suspicions. The tool results may point the organization in a direction that was different from its original expectations. At the very least, the results should provide insights into an organization that management never knew existed. The use of the tools may even surprise you by exposing opportunities where none were thought to exist. The use of the tools may also lead an organization to the realization that a process or technology it possesses isn't as valuable as once thought.

ACKNOWLEDGMENT

The first author wishes to acknowledge the Frederick E. Baer Professorship in Business for partial financial support. The authors wish to thank Kelly Anklam for her assistance in editing this chapter.

REFERENCES

Adamson, I. (2005). Knowledge management–the next generation of TQM? *Total Quality Management & Business Excellence*, *16*(8/9), 987–1000. doi:10.1080/14783360500163177

Ahokangas, P. (1998). *Internationalization and resources: An analysis of processes in Nordic SMSs*. Unpublished doctoral dissertation, Universitas Wasaensis, Vaasa.

Bowman, E. H. (1974). Epistemology, corporate strategy, and academe. *Sloan Management Review*, *15*, 35–50.

Brush, C. G., Greene, P. G., & Hart, M. M. (2001). From initial idea to unique advantage: The entrepreneurial challenge of constructing a resource base. *The Academy of Management Executive*, *15*(1), 64–78.

Chesbrough, H. W. (2007). Why companies should have open business models. *MIT Sloan Management Review*, *48*(2), 22–28.

Cohen, W. M., & Levinthal, D. A. (1990). Absorptive capacity: A new perspective on learning and innovation. *Administrative Science Quarterly*, *35*, 128–152. doi:10.2307/2393553

Cooper, A. C., Woo, C. Y., & Dunkelberg, W. C. (1989). Entrepreneurship and the initial size of firms. *Journal of Business Venturing, 4*(5), 317–332. doi:10.1016/0883-9026(89)90004-9

Edvinsson, L., & Malone, M. S. (1997). *Intellectual capital: Realizing your company's true value by finding its hidden brainpower.* New York: Harper Business.

Elenurm, T. (2003). Knowledge management development challenges of transition economy organisations representing different value creation models. *Electronic Journal of Knowledge Management, 1*(2), 47-56. Retrieved on November 12, 2008, from http://www.ejkm.com/volume-1/volume1-issue-2/issue2-art5-elenurm.pdf

Fiol, C. M., & Lyles, M. A. (1985). Organizational learning. *Academy of Management Review, 10*(4), 803–813. doi:10.2307/258048

Frery, F. (2006). The fundamental dimensions of strategy. *Sloan Management Review, 48*(1), 71–75.

Garcia, M. L., & Bray, O. H. (1997). *Fundamentals of technology roadmapping.* Strategic Business Development Department Sandia National Laboratories.

Hafeez, K., Zhang, Y., & Malak, N. (2002). Core competence for sustainable competitive advantage: A structured methodology for identifying core competence. *IEEE Transactions on Engineering Management, 49,* 28–35. doi:10.1109/17.985745

Holmes, J. S., & Glass, J. T. (2004). Internal R&D-vital but only one piece of the innovation puzzle. *Research Technology Management, 47*(5), 7–10.

Iaquinto, A. L. (1999). Can winners be losers? The case of the Deming prize for quality and performance among large Japanese manufacturing firms. *Managerial Auditing Journal, 14*(1/2), 28–35. doi:10.1108/02686909910245531

Ichijo, K., & Kohlbacher, F. (2007). The Toyota way of global knowledge creation the 'learn local, act global' strategy. *International Journal of Automotive Technology and Management, 7*(2/3), 116–134. doi:10.1504/IJATM.2007.014970

Ichijo, K., & Kohlbacher, F. (2008). Tapping tacit local knowledge in emerging markets–the Toyota way. *Knowledge Management Research & Practice, 6,* 173–186. doi:10.1057/kmrp.2008.8

Johanson, J., & Mattsson, L.-G. (1993). Internationalization in industrial systems–a network approach, strategies in global competition. In P. J. Buckley & P. N. Ghauri (Eds.), *The internationalization of the firm: A reader* (pp.303-22). London: Academic Press.

Johanson, J., & Vahlne, J. E. (1990). The mechanism of internationalization. *International Marketing Review, 7*(4), 11–24. doi:10.1108/02651339010137414

Kagono, T. (1988). *The cognitive theory of organization.* Tokyo: Chikura Shobou (in Japanese).

Kaplan, R. S., & Norton, D. P. (1992). The balanced scorecard-measures that drive performance. *Harvard Business Review,* (January/February): 71–79.

Lin, L.-H. (2009). Mergers and acquisitions, alliances and technology development: An empirical study of the global auto industry. *International Journal of Technology Management, 48*(3), 295–307. doi:10.1504/IJTM.2009.024950

Mikkola, J. H. (2001). Portfolio management of R&D projects: Implications for innovation management. *Technovation, 21,* 423–435. doi:10.1016/S0166-4972(00)00062-6

Mooney, L. (2007). BPM–a whole new world of opportunity. *KM World, January,* 54-55.

Mowery, D. C., & Rosenberg, N. (1979). The influence of market demand upon innovation: A critical review of some empirical studies. *Research Policy, 8*, 102–153. doi:10.1016/0048-7333(79)90019-2

Pfeffer, J. (2001). Fighting the war for talent is hazardous to your organization's health. *Organizational Dynamics, 29*, 248–259. doi:10.1016/S0090-2616(01)00031-6

Pfeffer, J. (2002). To build a culture of innovation, avoid conventional management wisdom. In F. Hesselbein, M. Goldsmith & I. Somerville (Eds.), *Leading for innovation: And organizing for results* (pp. 95-104). San Francisco: Jossey-Bass.

Phaal, R., Farrukh, C., & Probert, D. (2001). *Technology roadmapping: Linking technology resources to business objectives.* Centre for Technology Management, University of Cambridge.

Raynor, M. E. (2007). What is corporate strategy, really? *Ivey Business Journal Online, 71*(8), 1-6. Retrieved on June 28, 2009, from ABI/INFORM Global (Document ID: 1451062821)

Robey, D., Boudrea, M.-C., & Rose, G. M. (2000). Information technology and organizational learning: A review and assessment of research. *Accounting. Management & Information Technology, 10*, 125–155. doi:10.1016/S0959-8022(99)00017-X

Russ, M. (2008, January 28-30). *Do we need a new theory, or a conceptual model to explain SME internationalization or do we need to apply existing theories and conceptual models by using a different epistemology?* Paper presented in the International Business Symposium at the International Academy of Management and Business Conference in San Diego, CA.

Ruzzier, M., Hisrich, R. D., & Antoncic, B. (2006). SME internationalization research: Past, present, and future. *Journal of Small Business and Enterprise Development, 13*(4), 476–497. doi:10.1108/14626000610705705

Shahabuddin, S. (2008). Six sigma: Issues and problems. *International Journal of Productivity and Quality Management, 3*(2), 145–160. doi:10.1504/IJPQM.2008.016562

Shannon, C. E., & Weaver, W. (1949). *The mathematical theory of information.* Urbana, IL: University of Illinois Press.

Siefe, C. (2006). *Decoding the universe: How the new science of information is explaining everything in the cosmos, from our brains to black holes.* New York: Viking.

Takahashi, T., & Vandenbrink, D. (2004). Formative knowledge: From knowledge dichotomy to knowledge geography–knowledge management transformed by the ubiquitous information society. *Journal of Knowledge Management, 8*(1), 64–76. doi:10.1108/13673270410523916

Ulrich, D., & Smallwood, N. (2004). Capitalizing on capabilities. *Harvard Business Review, 82*(6), 119–127.

von Baeyer, H. C. (2003). *Information: The new language of science.* London: Weidenfeld and Nicolson.

von Krogh, G., & Roos, J. (1995). *Organizational epistemology.* London: MacMillan.

Welch, L., & Luostarinen, R. (1993). Internationalization: Evolution of a concept. In P. J. Buckley & P. N. Ghauri (Eds.), *The internationalization of the firm: A reader* (pp. 155-171). London: Academic Press.

Willyard, C. H., & McClees, C. W. (1987). Motorola's technology roadmap process. *Research Management, Sept./Oct.*, 13-19.

Yamada, J. (2004). A multidimensional view of entrepreneurship: Towards a research agenda on organisation emergence. *Journal of Management Development, 23*(4), 289–320. doi:10.1108/02621710410529776

Zaun, T. (2003, April 28). In Asia, Honda employs new tactic in building cars. *Wall Street Journal (Eastern Edition)*, A11. Retrieved on June 28, 2009, from ABI/INFORM Global (Document ID: 329642741)

ENDNOTES

[1] See Bowman, 1974, p. 49 for discussion of epistemology in the context of strategy.

[2] Based on von Krogh and Roos, 1995.

[3] Based on Robey et al., 2000.

[4] Fiol and Lyles, 1985.

[5] Robey, Boudreau, and Rose, 2000, p. 130.

[6] Based on Robey et al., 2000.

[7] Bowman, 1974, p. 46.

[8] Frery, 2006.

[9] Raynor, 2007, quoted, p. 3.

[10] Chesbrough, 2007, p. 13, exhibit 1.

[11] Modified from Chesbrough, 2007.

[12] Welch and Luostarinen, 1993, p. 156.

[13] Ahokangas, 1998; cited from Ruzzier et al. 2006, p. 479.

[14] Johanson and Vahlne, 1990, p. 20.

[15] Johanson and Mattson, 1990, cited from Ruzzier et al. 2006, p. 484.

[16] Based on Kagono, 1988; cited from Yamada, 2004.

[17] Yamada, 2004, p. 293.

[18] Cooper et al., 1995; cited from Yamada, 2004, p. 295.

[19] Kagono, 1988; cited from Yamada, 2004, p. 298.

[20] See for example the discussion about NASA's Mars Climate Orbiter in http://mars.jpl.nasa.gov/msp98/news/mco990930.html

[21] Seife, 2006, Decoding the universe.

[22] Von Baeyer, 2003, Information: The new language of science.

[23] Shannon and Weaver, 1949.

[24] See discussion in Brush et al. (2001) and by Hafeez et al. (2002).

[25] See for example Mowery and Rosenberg, 1979, or Phaal, Farrukh and Probert, 2001.

[26] see for example Ulrich and Smallwood 2004, http://kwork.org/Stars/Ulrich/Capabilities.pdf

[27] See for example Pfeffer, 2002.

[28] You can see the answer in the article in Time Magazine, June 8, 2009, vol. 173, No. 22, pp. 44-45, New Lessons From the Old World, by Eben Harrell.

[29] http://jobfunctions.bnet.com/abstract.aspx?docid=66602

[30] For example http://wistechnology.com/articles/4150/

[31] See discussion of Toyota KM and talent in for example: Pfeffer, 2001, Ichijo and Kohlbacher, 2007 and Ichijo and Kohlbacher, 2008.

[32] See examples in http://www.answers.com/topic/motorola-inc or Iaquinto, 1999 and Shahabuddin, 2008.

[33] See Adamson, 2005.

[34] See discussion of Honda's manufacturing strategy in Takahashi and Vandenbrink, 2004, or Zaun, 2003.

[35] See Mooney, 2007.

[36] Cohen and Levinthal, 1990.

[37] See example of KM assumptions in Elenurm, 2003, available at http://www.ejkm.com/volume-1/volume1-issue-2/issue2-art5-elenurm.pdf

[38] See discussions about Ford R&D in: Mikkola, 2001, Lin, 2009, Holmes and Glass, 2004.

[39] See example at Garcia & Bray, 1997 and in Phaal et al., 2001.

[40] CH Willyard, CW McClees - Research Management, 1987.

Chapter 2

Relational Flexibility:
How to Work with Labor Dynamism and Promote Knowledge Sharing in Hospitality

Kalotina Chalkiti
Charles Darwin University, Australia

ABSTRACT

This chapter investigates how the hospitality industry of the Northern Territory of Australia achieves organizational flexibility in dynamic labor environments. A case study in the Northern Territory of Australia reveals a new type of organizational flexibility, "relational flexibility." Relational flexibility is the result of behaviors, which go beyond the scope of job descriptions, used to repair the relational disruptions of labor changes and to adapt to the inevitability of labor dynamism. With relational flexibility, hospitality businesses can become flexible, responsive, and adaptable to dynamic labor environments while ensuring knowledge management activities are not inhibited. This research highlights the central role of peer relationships in dynamic labor environments and contributes to the organizational flexibility, staff turnover, and hospitality knowledge management literature.

INTRODUCTION

Creating and sustaining a competitive advantage through knowledge practices that recognize the industry's specific context and allow it to compete for customers and staff in the global marketplace is imperative (Butler, 1998; Poon, 1993). Even in the face of relatively poor staff retention and constant labor movements, hotels ought to ensure knowledge management practices are not impeded (Lundvall & Nielsen, 2007). Such issues become critical to hospitality businesses operating in remote, transient and seasonal regions like the Northern Territory of Australia where labor movement patterns and consequences manifest in forms more extreme than in other destinations. Considering the infinite nature of labor movements in hospitality, Northern Territory businesses are challenged by the need to become organizationally flexible while supporting knowledge management practices.

This chapter builds from previous research (Chalkiti & Carson, in press) and investigates how

DOI: 10.4018/978-1-60566-348-7.ch002

Northern Territory businesses can become organizationally flexible while supporting knowledge management practices despite inevitable labor changes.

This chapter begins with a literature review on the nature, consequences and management of labor dynamism in hospitality. Primary data from the Northern Territory hospitality industry will be analyzed to show how employees, teams and management deal with labor dynamism. The concept of relational flexibility will be introduced and discussed as a way to achieve organizational flexibility within dynamic labor environments. The chapter will conclude with managerial implications and limitations of the study and introduce scope for future research (Figure 1).

LABOR DYNAMISM IN HOSPITALITY: AN INTERNATIONAL PERSPECTIVE

This section describes the nature of labor dynamism in hospitality, its consequences and the ways to manage it.

Nature

Hospitality businesses are dynamic labor environments as a "critical source of change" (Timo, 2001, p. 126) stems from their human resources. A number of reasons contribute to this including the way businesses are structured to deal with ir-

regular and unpredictable demand, staff turnover and tourist destination popularity (Knox, 2002; Kvist & Klefsjo, 2006; Zhang & Wu, 2004; Zopiatis & Constanti, 2007). In Australia, the 2006 Labour Mobility Survey reported that nearly 40 per cent of all people employed in the accommodation sector stayed in their jobs for less than one year (ABS, 2006). Indeed, in remote and peripheral destinations like the Northern Territory, "obtaining and long term retaining of trained and experienced staff may be very difficult" (Hohl & Tisdell, 1995, p. 519). Finally, Australia is challenged by uncertain labor supply because of the high influx of employees seeking work, travel and living experience; and transfers due to better career opportunities (high wages, shorter working hours), emotional labor, training pressures and social life (Mohsin, 2003).

Consequences

Hospitality businesses customize their human resource processes to deal with irregular and unpredictable demand and seasonality (Knox, 2002). They engage in flexible labor strategies such as shiftwork, casual employment, multiple hiring and multi-tasking (Burgess, 1997). In this vein, it is important "to understand the effects of these resulting socially thin employment relationships" (Koene & Riemsdijk, 2005, p. 91). Employees form and participate in networks for reasons such as their shared participation in pro-

Figure 1. Chapter organization

Introduction	Labor dynamism in hospitality: An international perspective and a Northern Territory study	Relational flexibility: concept generation, literature alluding to the concept and the components of relational flexibility	Conclusion: research and managerial implications, limitations, and future research

duction processes or due to shared interests (Lee & Moreo, 2007). Networks foster knowledge management processes which make them "transactive knowledge systems" (Wegner, as cited in Cross, Parker, Prusak & Borgatti, 2001, p.216). Formal organizational structures present only the professional relationships of peers, but peers relate in a multitude of ways in a work environment (e.g. professional, social). This gives employee networks both a social and a professional facet that cannot be ignored. The existence and interdependency of social networks can positively or negatively influence business performance (Farh, Christopher & Lin, 1997; Robins & Pattison, 2006). Disrupting networks changes a business's knowledge content causing a loss of corporate memory (Adams, 1995; Carbery & Garavan, 2003; Cotton & Turtle, 1986). On a positive note, literature suggests that the knowledge base of an organization can be enhanced by a certain level of labor dynamism (Johannessen, Olaisen & Olsen, 2001). New employees bring with them experiential knowledge, relationships, networks and other that can add to the businesses knowledge base and help build competitive advantage (Burt, 2001; Mu, Peng & Love, 2008). In hospitality, where teams and peers are constantly reorganized the type and composition of social networks is affected. This rearrangement of employees suggests changes in the composition of networks as well as in their interconnection and interdependence (Cho & Johanson, 2006; Koene & Riemsdjik, 2005; Krackhardt & Porter, 1985, 1986). This threefold change of networks suggests changes in the learnt characteristics of relationships often referred to as relational disruptions (Borgatti & Cross, 2003; Singh, Hu & Roehl, 2007).

Management

Achieving organizational flexibility through human resource management can be central for managing labor dynamism in hospitality businesses (Beltran-Martin, 2008; Dalton & Krackhardt,

1983; Knox & Walsh, 2005). However, the literature tends to "mirror what is seen in mainstream human relations research and theory" (Lucas & Deery, 2004, p. 459); which is the uniform adoption of flexible labor strategies, namely: temporal, numerical and functional (Atkinson, 1984; Jolliffe & Farnsworth, 2003; Lai & Baum, 2005). Indeed, literature covering human resource management practices or organizational flexibility of the Australian hotel industry, while limited, validates the extensive use and ambiguous effectiveness of flexible labor strategies (Knox, 2002; Rodwell & Shadur, 2000; Timo, 2001). The common limitation of this line of thought is that in hospitality, where labor dynamism is inevitable and tourism labor is boundaryless and ultramobile (Hjalager & Anderson, 2001), there is little incentive to look for ways to reduce labor dynamism. Chalkiti and Carson (in press) argued that the dynamic labor nature of hospitality disrupts employee networks and affects both individual and group behavior. Therefore, the discussion of organizational flexibility should rethink whether the purpose is only to align labor supply to unstable demand. Finding a way to recover from relational disruptions in a timely fashion will not only help hospitality businesses become more adaptable and flexible to labor changes but will also ensure knowledge management activities are not inhibited (Chalkiti & Carson, in press).

Summary

Labor dynamism in hospitality creates relational disruptions which may inhibit knowledge management processes between employees. Businesses have tried to become organizationally flexible by adopting flexible labor strategies (Moorman & Harland, 2002) with questionable evidence of their effectiveness (Uzzi, 1997). Considering the relational disruptions of labor movement, it is argued that the current information about organizational flexibility in the hospitality industry is limited to suggesting ways or strategies to work with and manage labor dynamism so that it does not inhibit knowledge management. Therefore, "what are the mechanisms to provide flexibility" (Whitehouse, 1997, p. 37), "which strategy gives the best state of preparedness for high variance environments" (Riley & Lockwood, 1997, p. 419), and how do labor dynamic hospitality businesses achieve organizational flexibility without impeding the sharing of knowledge between peers?

LABOUR DYNAMISM IN HOSPITALITY: A NORTHERN TERRITORY STUDY

This section introduces the case study, the methods used and primary data on the nature, consequences and management of labor dynamism in the hospitality industry of the Northern Territory.

Methods

This section presents findings from the front office departments of a five star hotel-chain in the hospitality industry of the Northern Territory. Data was collected from six different hierarchical levels of front office departments, through semi-structured interviews (210 interviews), observation (20 meetings) and a focus group to verify the findings. Respondents discussed their perceptions of organizational flexibility, labor movements and employee relationships. They held either undergraduate or postgraduate qualifications; had been employed in hospitality for periods ranging from six months to five years; and were employed with the hotel chain for less than twelve months through which they sought career progression or working holiday opportunities.

Nature

Staff turnover, the Northern Territory as a location, and the industry's work structure amplify labor dynamism in the hospitality industry of the

Northern Territory. Staff turnover was triggered by the availability or lack of career progression opportunities and the seeking of travel-work-lifestyle experiences. Considering the intense competition in hospitality businesses in bigger Australian cities and the less frequent promotional opportunities offered, many employees moved to the Northern Territory for short periods of time to gain work experience and move up the hierarchical ladder before moving to larger population centres. Other reasons for staff turnover included the inherent limitations of the hospitality industry such as low financial rewards, emotional burnout, and unsociable hours. The Northern Territory's remoteness and isolation caused accessibility difficulties and contributed to the blurring of work and play in highly remote tourist destinations such as Jabiru and Kakadu National Park. The sheer remoteness amplified the emotional burnout of peers who interact continuously with guests and colleagues. The majority of the employees came from southern Australian states with no pre-existing local social support networks. They would usually interact with each other professionally and socially suggesting the blurring of work and play. Finally, the hotel-chain made extensive use of flexible labor strategies such as casual employment to manage unpredictable demand. This meant that although the hotels for some of the time had a stable core workforce, the use of such strategies meant that teams of peers were never the same on a daily basis.

Consequences

When asked to comment on the consequences of labor dynamism, apart from the cost and time implications, respondents also suggested it affected peer relationships and overall group dynamics. Considering that peers relate to others in a multitude of ways (e.g. trust, friends), the infinite shuffle of teams enabled them to constantly develop new relationships with peers which in some cases compromised existing relationships.

Additionally, the nature of peer relationships affected group dynamics. For example, should an employee leave, a similar intention to leave was created among the employees the individual related to socially. Thus, labor dynamism affected the ways peers related to one another giving them both the opportunity to learn how to work with one another but also influenced, sometimes negatively, the way the team worked or behaved.

Management

The opinion of frontline employees was sought to understand how they dealt with the industry's inevitable labor changes. Employees deal with and adapt to labor changes by finding ways to relationally align to their peers. To achieve this, a personal or social approach was considered to be the key to establish some sort of relational alignment between peers who were constantly shuffled. They found it possible to collaborate with peers through relationships. These different types of relationships helped peers build a "people/collaboration knowledge" base that was unique to them at that point in time. However, in an environment where nothing stands still, the constant shuffle of teams changed this people/collaboration knowledge which helped respondents learn how to interact with different people and develop people/collaboration knowledge for each peer they worked with. This collection of customized people/collaboration knowledge was what enabled them to know how to work with one another and become adaptable to sudden, predictable and inevitable labor changes while knowledge management activities never ceased.

It was also important to find out what motivates them to engage in peer relationships. Employee motivations played a role in their willingness to engage in peer relationships. Those attracted to the destination and industry to fulfil their travel-lifestyle-work experiential aspirations viewed their engagement in peer relationships as part of the overall experience. For these individuals,

striking up peer relationships was important to them as individuals and not necessarily as a way to work in a labor dynamic environment. In juxtaposition, the career driven individuals considered peer relationships as a means to an end. They acknowledged the lack of career focus in some of their peers and engaged in social relationships as a way to cooperate with them at work.

However, the employment motivations were not the only things dictating the engagement in peer relationships. Group dynamics played a role too. When first entering a team, the willingness of peers to engage in relationships was influenced by their motivations. While in the team, the decision to continue to engage in peer relationships was then affected by the quality of the relationships and the dynamics of the team. For example, friendship relationships proved to be an obstacle in both the individual's and consequently the team's performance. In such cases, this would instigate corrective action from management and would then lead to transformation and disappearance of that relationship. Therefore, although the decision to engage in peer relationships is associated to one's employment motivations, its existence and ongoing management depend on both the individuals participating in it and the group context it belongs to.

From a managerial perspective, organizational flexibility was achieved through numerical, temporal and functional flexible labor strategies such as casual and part time employment to align labor supply to unpredictable demand. Although their effectiveness was measured against labor costs, it was interesting to note that some managers recognized the relational misalignment or alignment between peers throughout the implementation of these strategies. This urged some managers to base rostering decisions on their awareness of peer relationships. Considering that the organizational values of the hotel-chain promoted cooperation by indirectly pinpointing the importance of peer relationships, apart from some exceptions as noted above, the awareness of the existence and importance of peer relationships was to a large extent ignored by management. When the organizational values inferred to the importance of peer relationships, why were they ignored by management? Reasons include management's unawareness of the practical implications of peer relationships in the workplace, and their personal belief that peer relationships should not dictate the way the hotels were managed. This suggests that although an organization may try to instil the importance of peer relationships, management's unawareness and personal beliefs can be an obstacle towards fostering an atmosphere encouraging them.

Overall, the managerial findings suggest that the formal way of achieving organizational flexibility in labor dynamic environments is through flexible labor strategies. However, the employees exposed to and required to deal with labor dynamism did so through peer relationships. The way peers related in the work environment promoted the creation of people/collaboration knowledge which is context and people specific. However, labor dynamism led to an infinite change in peer relationships resulting in the creation of a collection of people/collaboration knowledge. This collection of people/collaboration knowledge is referred to as relational knowledge and is considered to be a way to support the seamless and timely collaboration of employees and teams subject to labor dynamism (Borgatti & Cross, 2003). Peer relationships and the social benefits they create could be the key towards achieving flexibility that will continue to support knowledge management processes. Social benefits can help build dynamic and flexible work environments while promoting relational characteristics that seem to facilitate knowledge management processes such as knowledge sharing. This peer relationship approach was not required or promoted in employees' job descriptions and was not formally assessed by the hotels, which suggests it is an extra role approach (Smith, Organ & Near, 1983). These extra role approaches made it possible for peers to cope with labor dynamism and ensure critical activi-

ties such as cooperation and knowledge sharing were not inhibited. Despite the hotel-chain value system indirectly supporting peer relationships, in practice the representatives of these values (managers) blocked it. Therefore, having a value system explicitly stressing the importance of peer relationships does not necessarily mean that it will happen.

Summary

The hospitality industry of the Northern Territory suggests that peers and teams deal with labor dynamism through peer relationships. Labor changes create a collection of peer relationships and people/collaboration knowledge that make up the relational knowledge between peers in a certain context. It is this relational knowledge that enables them to repair the relational disruptions of labor dynamism while ensuring knowledge management activities are not inhibited. This leads to the question: How can hospitality businesses address the relational disruptions of labor dynamism to become organizationally flexible and ensure critical knowledge management activities are not inhibited?

RELATIONAL FLEXIBILITY

This section introduces the idea and components of Relational Flexibility; a new strategy to become organizationally flexible and promote knowledge sharing in labor dynamic environments.

Concept Generation

Accepting the inevitability of labor changes and acknowledging their beneficial impact (Peters, 1987; Pringle & Kroll, 1997; Singh et al.,, 2007) is central to progress into ways of managing their occurrence. New people bring experiential knowledge, relationships, networks and other social capital that can add to the businesses knowledge base and help build competitive advantage (Mu et al., 2008). Indeed, finding ways to work with labor changes will enable businesses to reap the knowledge management benefits deriving from people movement. Indeed, this can be achieved by "understanding how to effectively manage this competitive source [human resources] for better organizational performance... [in] hospitality establishments" (Singh et al., 2007, p. 132).

Keenoy (1999) promotes the need for fluidity and dynamism of human resource management itself. Kramar (2002) argued that Australian human resource management resembles a hologram; "as with a hologram, human resource management changes its appearance as we move around its image. Each shift of stance reveals another facet, a darker depth, a different contour" (Kramar, p. 91). Human resource management approaches should be malleable to help businesses and employees deal with labor dynamism. Therefore, we need to evolve to deal with the relational disruptions between peers in a dynamic labor environment enabling an employee to be organizationally flexible to foster knowledge sharing. In this vein, relational flexibility is proposed as a way to help employees, teams and businesses repair the relational disruptions of labor dynamism in a seamless and timely manner. This allows them to adapt and ensure knowledge management activities are not inhibited.

Depending on the level of focus, the factors triggering relational flexibility vary. For example, at the level of an employee, employment motivations drive his/her engagement to socialization activities. Similarly, at an intra-group (employee to employee), team, inter-group (team to team) and organizational level, different factors support socialization activities and consequently relational flexibility. Employees engage in peer relationships which, because of labor dynamism, evolve into a collection of customised peer relationships. This helps them build their peer's relational identity or relational knowledge or "learned characteristic" that is time, people and context specific (Borgatti

Figure 2. The evolution of relational flexibility

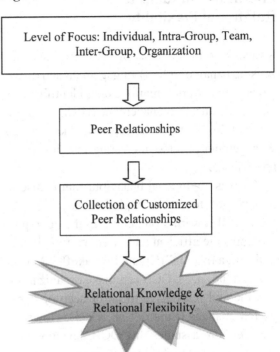

& Cross, 2003, p. 432). The creation and ongoing renewal of relational knowledge gives peers the opportunity to be relationally flexible and adaptable to labor dynamism while providing a conducive environment to ensure knowledge management activities are not inhibited (Figure 2).

By minimizing the inhibition of knowledge management, relational flexibility can help hospitality businesses become more competitive (Cross et al., 2001; Knox & Walsh, 2005; Robins & Pattison, 2006; Von Krogh, Nonaka & Aben, 2001). Indeed, it plays a catalytic role in hospitality businesses and complements product knowledge attained through work instructions and manuals. Although product knowledge may create the hospitality experience, peer relationships enable employees to put that product knowledge into use and deliver experiences. Therefore, relational flexibility can be regarded as an inimitable "core capability" (Kalleberg, 2001, p. 45).

Literature Alluding to Relational Flexibility

Research from the areas of organizational citizenship behavior (OCB), engagement and disengagement at work, organizational identification, human resources management (HRM), organizational flexibility, social capital and knowledge management provide interesting insights to our proposition.

OCB is "individual behaviour that is discretionary, not directly or explicitly recognized by the formal reward system, and in the aggregate promotes the efficient and effective functioning of the organization" (Organ, Podsakoff & MacKenzie, 2006, p. 3). OCB can make organizations flexible and responsive to unforeseen or unexpected changes (Smith et al., 1983). However, the literature assumes that OCB develops over time as opposed to short timeframes as suggested in hospitality contexts. Indeed, OCB in dynamic labor environments has been poorly researched. For example, Khalid (2006) and Chen, Hui & Sego (1998) investigated the relationship between OCB and the manifestation of withdrawal behaviors in the Malaysian hotel sector and Chinese manufacturing sector. Their findings suggest that OCB "significantly influenced employee turnover intentions" (Khalid, p. 1). Relational flexibility aims to make the relationship between OCB and turnover more explicit. Indeed, OCB is considered "as an important component in research on turnover" (Chen et al., p. 925) to investigate the organizational flexibility of dynamic labor environments. This supports the well established research gap between the influence of OCB on organizational performance (Khalid) and labor changes (Podsakoff, MacKenzie, Pain & Bachrach, 2000).

It is useful to know the factors "in which people bring themselves into or remove themselves from particular task behaviors" (Kahn, 1990, p. 692). Kahn found that psychological reasons relating to a sense of meaningfulness, safety and availability at "multiple levels of influences-individual, interpersonal, group, intergroup and organizational" engaged or disengaged employees from their work roles and behaviors (Kahn, p. 719). It is at the confluence of all these influences that employees choose to engage or disengage. The research from the Northern Territory argues that behaviors intending to relationally align one peer to another are influenced by factors that, depending on the level of focus, vary. For example, at the individual, intra-group, team, inter-group or organizational level, different factors trigger extra role behaviors to relationally align peers in dynamic labor environments.

Organizational identification suggests that the "degree to which a member defines him or her by the same attributes that he or she believes define the organization" leading to "a heightened sense of in-group trust" (Dutton, Dukerich & Harquail, 1994, p. 255) which promotes OCB. The data suggests that peers, through OCB, socially identify with one another while overcoming the difficult initial stage of being introduced and oriented in the team. This approach seems to help employees and teams cope and manage labor dynamism. On the contrary, organizational identification seems to disregard labor dynamism by denoting the availability of time to build trust. How can the creation of such an emotional attachment to the organization through such shared values like trust be possible in dynamic labor environments? (Konovsky & Pugh, 1994). Additionally, individuals through identification "form a pattern of in group and out group dynamics" that favours cooperation (Dutton et al., 1994, p. 254). This work highlights how the identification of individuals with an organization or team spin off dynamism throughout the group. What happens in labor dynamic environments where peers are constantly shuffled between teams and group dynamics continue to change? Indeed, peer identification is understudied in the area of organizational identification. Nonetheless there is some work channelling research towards the idea of relational flexibility. Koene and

Riemsdijk (2005), argued that the "identification with the organization can influence an employees perceptual attachment to the organization" and therefore their performance (Koene & Riemsdijk, p. 80). For example they can demonstrate "better in group cooperation, organizational citizenship behavior and better individual association to the organization" (Dutton et al., p. 76). Although their work is similar to Moorman and Harland (2002), they make some propositions on how to manage a flexible workforce to ensure labor and organizational alignment. One of the ways which they call "special attention" aims to "reduce the behavioral problems often encountered" (Moorman & Harland, p. 91). These behavioral problems only refer to the behavior temporary employees have towards the organization and not necessarily towards fellow peers.

There has not been much work in the HRM literature looking into the qualities or attributes of employees working in dynamic labor environments. Chapman and Lovell (2006) suggest the idea of an attitudinally and behaviorally flexible hospitality workforce as a way to remain competitive. They treat flexibility differently; the attitudinal and behavioral qualities for hospitality employees are the key towards the "social awareness and flexibility of trainees in preparing for careers in this complex industry" (Chapman & Lovell, p.80). Similarly, Beltran-Martin, Roca-Puig, Escrig-Tena & Bou-Llusar (2008) examined the role of high performance work systems (HPWS) on an organizations performance. The authors are in favour of the role of human resource flexibility to contribute towards organizational performance. This is important as they stress the need for flexibility even from those committed and involved individuals to be able to react and adapt to changing conditions (Bhattacharya et al., cited in Beltran-Martin et al). Human resource flexibility is "the extent to which employees possess skills and behavioral repertoires that can provide a firm with options to pursue strategic alternatives" (Wright & Snell, as cited in Beltran-Martin et al., p. 1014).

"Behavioral repertoires" consist of functional flexibility, skills malleability and behavior flexibility (Wright & Snell, as cited in Beltran-Martin et al., p. 1014). However, the references to behavioral flexibility refer to encouraging employees "to improvise and think of new ideas, questions and reflect on their actions" (Wright & Snell, as cited in Beltran-Martin et al., p. 1016). This relates only to work related tasks and not relational activities such as peer interaction. Indeed, it cannot help businesses operating in labor dynamic environments. This is because in such environments, the idea of commitment is disposable and the relational disruptions impeding organizational performance are not addressed within the context of behavioral flexibility. Relational flexibility extends the thinking of Beltran-Martin by arguing that behavioral flexibility should acknowledge changes in peers and the need to find ways to relate and align to them in order to work together and cooperate as opposed to being cultivated only in committed peers. Therefore, for peers and organizations operating in labor dynamic environments, behavioral flexibility should also include relational flexibility to manage the relational disruptions that labor changes cause.

In the organizational flexibility literature, it has been suggested that multiple flexible labor strategies can be managed through organizational inter-relations (Kalleberg, 2001). The network perspective here suggests a relational connection between different organizations to achieve organizationally flexibility. The drawback is that this refers to inter-organizational relationships and not necessarily peer to peer. The concern regarding the implementation of flexible labor strategies is how to "substitute one person for another" (Riley & Lockwood, 1997, p. 414). They suggest it increases "when the more personal attributes count in the job" (Riley & Lockwood, p. 414). In hospitality, experiences are central to both customers and employees. Employee experiences are formed from the interplay of personal attributes during peer interaction. Personal attributes are important but the way that an employee behaves and functions in the work environment is greatly influenced by their colleagues too. It has been shown that "staff attitudes to flexibility were generally favorable as long as the additional tasks were not widely different in terms of skills and status" (Riley & Lockwood, p. 418). However, Riley and Lockwood disregard the implications of substitutability. Substitution involves the mix and match of individuals. This substitution may create relational disruptions or create the need for relational connection. These aspects remain unaddressed throughout their paper and most importantly they fail to link the importance of personal attributes to the implications of substitution. Tourism and hospitality literature on flexibility and adaptability suggests that flexibility derives from the social interaction of peers (Woods, Heck & Sciarini, 1998; Rowley & Purcell, 2001). Timo (2001) referred to "a failure to fit" (p. 298). It is assumed that a failure to fit refers to the misalignment of peers. His work indirectly suggests that it is important to find a way for peers to be socially accepted into constantly changing teams. Indeed, the social benefit of training and development is that social ties between peers are strengthened which in turn facilitates a better understanding of the businesses goals (Rowley & Purcell).

The social capital literature is relevant and useful to this research. The rationale of social capital is that both employees and employers can benefit from workplace relationships (Taylor et al., 2004). For example, through peer relationships or membership in a social entity like a team, peers can access competitive resources such as knowledge (Lin, 2001; Portes, 1998). The same applies in this research from the Northern Territory but knowledge in this case differs from the competitive or innovative nature of knowledge described in the literature (Granovetter, 1973, 1985). This research showed that inevitable labor changes force employees to engage in new or to rejuvenate past peer relationships. This ongoing process exposes employees to a variety of rela-

tional knowledge that is people, time and context specific (Borgatti & Cross, 2003). Through time and therefore through labor changes, employees build a collection of relational knowledge, in other words knowing the way a colleague likes to be spoken to or knowing which tasks a colleague prefers, allows hotel employees to cope with and adapt to this ongoing labor dynamism while functioning as a team during a short timeframe. This collection of relational knowledge deriving from labor changes relates to relational social capital (Nahapiet & Ghosal, 1998). The notion of relational social capital suggests the presence of norms such as trust and reciprocity which in turn suggest the availability of sufficient time (Adler & Kwon, 2002; Uzzi, 1996). Indeed, Tsai and Ghosal (1998) argued that time helps the creation of trust and reciprocity norms to support critical aspects such as knowledge management activities. The findings presented here describe a context where labor stability is non-existent and therefore sufficient time to develop these norms is not present. Employees do not have the opportunity to work with a certain peer for a period lengthy enough to allow trust and reciprocity to build between them. Also, teams do not have a stable employee composition to collectively work towards creating trusting and reciprocal relationships. Labor changes occur so frequently in teams dictating the need for employees to find ways to cope with and adapt to labor changes in the absence of sufficient time, and hence, a lack of trust and reciprocity. Therefore, it could be argued that relational flexibility could be a form of relational social capital with the difference that it develops in unstable labor environments in short time frames without trust and reciprocity necessarily being present (Cohen & Prusak, 2001).

Finally, the field of knowledge management offers a good basis on which to ground relational flexibility. Recent work from Russ, Jones & Fineman (2006) and Russ and Jones (2006) offers a preliminary taxonomy of knowledge based strategies that recognise the common challenges, which they term as the codification, complementary, concealment, exploration, external acquisition and product (C³EEP) framework, that businesses face when managing their knowledge base. The combination of strategies proposed in the above work caters for a variety of business approaches to managing knowledge such as exploring existing knowledge to improve processes or re-design existing products while codifying it in an explicit form. The concept of relational flexibility can potentially play a facilitating role to such knowledge based strategies. It can be regarded as a facilitator for the codification of tacit knowledge at a variety of levels (individual, intra-group, team, inter-group or organizational). Still, the evolvement and purpose of relational flexibility differs to the purpose of the aforementioned knowledge based strategies. Russ et al and Russ and Jones rightfully argue that knowledge based strategies should be considered in relation to cultural factors (e.g. trust).

In this book chapter, the purpose of relational flexibility is to relationally align employees or teams that are subject to infinite labour changes. Relational flexibility facilitates the relational alignment of employees through people/collaboration knowledge that is time, people and context specific. Therefore, in this instance the purpose of relational flexibility is not necessarily to facilitate the codification of process or product specific tacit knowledge. On the contrary, it facilitates the codification of people, collaboration or relation-

ship knowledge to enable employees who have not worked with each other to function collectively in a seamless and timely manner. Moreover, in relation to cultural factors, trust infers the provision of sufficient time. Time is critical in this case because the inevitable and frequent occurrence of labor changes does not allow employees or teams sufficient time to nurture and create factors like trust. Therefore, relational flexibility can be viewed as a facilitator of knowledge based strategies for businesses operating in labor dynamic environments.

The Components of Relational Flexibility

The data collected from this study of the Northern Territory hospitality industry suggests that relational flexibility is facilitated by extra role behaviors. For example, at the intra-group or team level, employees engaged in general conversation with their peers on the same shift with questions such as: how was your day? where are you from?. They explained that they adopted this approach to satisfy their working holiday motivations, get through the shift, or relate to a person who they have only just met or have not worked with previously. The initial interaction between peers irrespective of their employment motivations or other factors is triggered through behaviors that are not required by the organization and employees are not formally rewarded and are not trained

Table 1. Components of relational flexibility

Level of Focus	Socialization Triggers					
	Meaningfulness	**Task characteristics**	**Disposable attitude**	**Safety**	**Availability**	**Mutuality**
Individual						
Intra-group						
Team						
Inter-group						
Organization						

to socially engage with peers. This suggests that this approach or behaviour resembles extra role behaviors which create an environment conducive to socialization which in turn promotes the creation of relational flexibility (Smith et al., 1983). This leads to the question: Depending on the level of focus, which factors facilitate behaviors that trigger the socialization process and create relational flexibility? Table 1 depicts the components of relational flexibility in five levels: individual, intra-group, team, inter-group and organization. Shaded areas show the socialization triggers that affect each level.

Meaningfulness

Participants in the study, found it meaningful to socialize because of their employment motivations and demographic characteristics. For them, social interactions helped them establish a relational bridge between themselves and their peers to help them collaborate while satisfy their socialization needs. For example, some participants chose the industry and the Northern Territory as a working holiday or a travel and work experience. This seems to be the norm in regions like the Northern Territory. The Northern Territory is known to attract a labor force that has embarked on a travel, lifestyle and work experience journey (Chalkiti & Carson, in press; Mohsin, 2003). For some employees, this is not temporary. Moving from one place to another for the sake of experiencing the way of life, interacting with new people and engaging in new or alternative employment is a way of life. This sector of seasonal found great satisfaction from their interactions with peers and guests. Indeed, "such connections are an invaluable source of meaning in peoples lives...they allow people to feel known and appreciated and that they are sharing their existential journeys with others" (Kahn, 1990, p. 707). Indeed, literature highlights that certain types of hospitality labour are motivated by the socialization opportunities of the hospitality industry., Feldman and Doerping-

haus (1992) argued that differences in non standard work arrangements might not only attract groups of workers with different demographic profiles but might also lead to differences in the attitudes in behavior of non standard employees such as more sociable people (Walsh & Deery, 1999). Lee and Moreo (2007) suggested that seasonal hospitality workers perceive different social and moral values. They are in search of pleasure experiences while having many diverse characteristics (e.g. work experience, place of origin). Similarly, research by Wildes (2007) in US hospitality found that younger age groups found the presence of fun an important aspect in their work life.

In contrast, others were attracted to the Northern Territory by career development opportunities. Socialization behaviors are not central and serve a different purpose for this segment. For these participants, socialization is a means to an end. They will do anything and everything through teamwork to get the job done but that does not necessarily mean that they have to or will enjoy it or need to have behavioral or attitudinal skills to make it happen. They pay less attention to the power of personality and interpersonal skills in their work. However, in an industry where front office departments act as the main points of guest contact and deliver experiences that are formed by peer to peer interactions, the importance of personality and interpersonal skills can not be ignored? For career driven employees, peer to peer interactions are a means to an end and often become a survival strategy to get through the shift. Indeed, career driven people pay less attention to the power of personality and interpersonal skills in their work (Hai-Yan & Baum, 2006). The challenge in such environments is how to promote collaboration between the two differing groups of career driven employees and those on a working holiday. Hai-Yan and Baum aimed to develop a picture of the skills profile, work background, educational attainment, attitudes and plans of the employees in front office departments of Chinese hotels. It was interesting to read that the career driven sample put little value on the statement that "front office work is all about personality" (Hai-Yan & Baum, p. 514), but nonetheless, because of their national culture, considers teamwork as critical.

The majority of the respondents to the Northern Territory study were between 19-25 years of age with a few exceptions of considerably older employees. The socialization of both age groups differs considerably, with the younger segment being more likely to socialize with each other. Lun and Huang (2007) found that if older employees feel attached to the organization, they are more willing to apply themselves to behaviors that are beyond the scope of their work (e.g. socialization). This is interesting because feeling attached to an organization requires time and in hospitality where labor changes are the norm it is difficult to foster and build organizational attachment. Indeed, young employees who are on working holidays do not need to feel attached to the organization to demonstrate extra role behaviors. This suggests that older employees might not cope with ever changing teams because of the need to feel attached to the organization to demonstrate extra role behaviors. Finally, participants originating from rural areas were more prone to socialization behaviors. Those employees that considered themselves as "country" people were more relaxed, friendly, and more easy going than their urban counterparts and considered it as part of their nature to demonstrate extra role behaviors to deal with labor changes. The differences in behaviors going beyond job requirements have been related to demographic characteristics (Smith et al., 1983).

Task Interdependency

Front office departments are communication hubs; both between the hotel and the guests and between departments or other hotels. In this case, hospitality employees might engage in socialization behaviors not only to work with labor dynamism but also to manage the interrelationships between tasks. Respondents explained that when rotated between departments or tasks, they often engaged in behaviors to create a socialization environment which in turn helped them cooperate with others or enabled them to coordinate and fulfil interdependent activities. Indeed, Organ et al. (2006) argued that task interdependency promotes extra role behaviors such as socialization which become central to a hospitality environment.

Disposable Attitudes

Participants explained that it is important to have dynamic, fluid and disposable attitudes that facilitate the relational alignment of peers. They stress that what is needed is an element of disposability in someone's relational attitude because traditional collaboration moderators such as trust and commitment are not supported through labor movements (Kramar, 2002). This disposable tendency towards relationships may be inherent in some of those who have had a long presence in hospitality, while others use the infinite labor changes of the industry to work towards it (Timo, 2001). Therefore, the certainty and predictability of labor changes does not favour a one size fits all approach.

Safety

Feelings of socialization safety appeared uniform at all levels in the Northern Territory employees interviewed. New employees considered interpersonal relationships important to enable them to blend in with an existing team and to be themselves. This created a feeling of socialization safety that meant that they were more experimental with their work as they did not fear the consequences of trial and error. Indeed, the importance of extra role behaviors in promoting socialization safety was demonstrated in cases where participants felt uncomfortable and not confident with some trainers. Lack of safety made it difficult for employees to relationally align with the trainer and were left with a distaste for the hotel chain, which in turn made them less sociable and less likely to fit in to an existing team. The ability to make a mistake without feeling embarrassed or jeopardising jobs has been argued in the literature (Kahn, 1990).

Socialisation safety was also influenced by "the various unacknowledged characters, or unconscious roles, that individuals assumed" (Kahn, 1990, p. 709). The informal roles assigned to employees in teams created certain dynamism in the group. Indeed when a long standing employee resigned, feelings of discomfort started evolving which in turn influenced employee behavior. Employees were less experimental with their work fearing that if something went wrong their peer would not be there to help them. This was attributed not only to the departing employees' in-depth knowledge but also to the unconscious role (e.g. motherly figure) her peers had assigned to her.

Finally, employees had to "feel relatively secure about those [other] selves" (Gustafson & Cooper, cited in Khan, 1990, p. 715). Socialization security was compromised when there was a sense of lack of trust or a change in one's perceptions for others. For example, when an intimate relationship developed between two peers employed in the same department third parties who socially interacted with them started to withdraw and limited their interaction. Similar actions can result from the over-socialization with peers; in some cases getting to know peers better out of work had a detrimental effect on the team as peers chose not to associate with those they had previously interacted with.

Availability

The socialization availability of peers was influenced by social and emotional energy and the remoteness of the Northern Territory. The ongoing engagement in extra role behaviors to facilitate socialization and adaptation to labor changes had a taxing effect on peers. For some, the constant change made it emotionally laborious

to continue engaging in such behaviors (Hochschild, 1983). Others would become socially unavailable depending on the peers on shift. For example, their peers would not reciprocate or engage in socialization despite the efforts of others. In this case the ones who acted as initiators would disengage temporarily for the duration of the shift and towards those peers. Overall, peers required "…energy, strength and readiness" to "engage in" (Goffman, cited in Kahn, 1990, p. 714) socialization as a way to adapt and continue living and working in a dynamic environment and a transient destination.

The low financial returns of the industry combined with the high rental rates of Darwin made it difficult to find accommodation in central areas close to the town moderated the socialization availability. For example, some would compromise and live in the suburbs, enabling them to save money. Nonetheless it would end up being a double-edged sword for those with no transportation. This would deter them from going into the town and meet up with their colleagues. The inability to do so was detrimental for new employees who could not socially integrate with both the destination and their peers. This is ironic for a place like the Northern Territory renowned for its social lifestyle. Indeed, the Northern Territory was found to be different to the rest of Australia. Its transient nature and tropical culture promoted a social lifestyle that substantially differed to the rest of Australia. Similar findings have been reported in the literature (Hinkin & Tracey, 2000).

Mutuality

Participants in the Northern Territory study commented on the lack of consistency and continuity in the hotel-chains formal procedures and the effect this had on the socialization willingness of peers. For example, the organization promoted values of openness that in practice were unsupported. This drove employees to being reserved and less willing to engage in socialization with peers. Therefore, organizations ought to recognize that they and the employees are mutually responsible for promoting and facilitating socialisation behaviors.

Summary

Depending on the level of focus (individual, intra-group, team, inter-group or organizational), relational flexibility is triggered from a variety of factors. The common denominator between all factors is that they instigate a socialization approach which fits the profile of extra role behaviours (Organ et al., 2006). These extra role behaviours ultimately "lubricate the social machinery of the organization" by repairing the relational break-ups between peers and supporting knowledge management activities in labor dynamic environments (Smith et al., 1983, p. 654).

CONCLUSION

Labor dynamism creates relational disruptions. This research from the hospitality industry of the Northern Territory suggests that hospitality employees cope with labor dynamism through extra role behaviors (Smith et al., 1983). These behaviors help employees learn characteristics of relationships such as people and/or collaboration knowledge and build a relational knowledge base that is people, time and context specific (Borgatti & Cross, 2003). This relational knowledge enables employees to become relationally flexible which in turn helps them work with and within infinitely changing teams to ensure critical performance activities such as knowledge management are not inhibited. Depending on the level of focus, relational flexibility is triggered by factors that make socialization meaningful, safe, available and mutual.

Research and Managerial Implications

From a practitioner's perspective, this book chapter offers insights and directions on what actually happens to infinitely changing teams of hotel employees. Practitioners can benefit from this research by becoming aware that other ways are needed to deal with labor changes that differ from the existing strategies of staff and knowledge retention. Also, this work suggests the need and importance for management to be aware of and take into consideration peer relationships and group dynamics. For example, businesses can potentially promote relational flexibility through their value system or organizational culture or they may use behavioral interviewing to detect employees with desired workplace behaviors. Nonetheless, these measures are no panacea. There can be dissonance between an organizations value system and the manifestation of these values in practice. Businesses need to understand that recruitment tools just like behavioral interviewing are limited to surfacing past behavior. The way employees behaved in the past might be totally different to how they will behave in another workplace. This is because behavior could be relationally influenced depending on the nature and quality of peer relationships which go on to influence behavioral dynamics in a team. Furthermore, although this work is the result of research in the hospitality industry and in particular, hotels, it could also offer insight to other industries challenged by labor changes and consequently infinitely changing teams of employees.

From an academic perspective, this work investigates hospitality businesses operating in dynamic labor environments to "propose theory that is hospitality specific, relevant and useful" (Lucas & Deery, 2004, p. 459). For example, it advances the literature on hospitality flexible labor strategies and staff turnover by proposing an alternative strategy, relational flexibility, to manage and work with labor changes. It also contributes to hospitality knowledge management research by advancing the discussion of the limitations of retaining explicit knowledge. Indeed, relational flexibility is a way towards a more fluid approach towards knowledge sharing that embraces the inevitability of labor changes and recognizes the difficulty to externalize valuable tacit and context specific knowledge. Moreover, the findings suggest that teams of hotel employees cope and adapt to labor dynamism through extra role or OCB behaviors which have traditionally required the presence of sufficient time (Organ et al., 2006). On the contrary extra role or OCB behaviors seem not only to develop in highly transient environments but are also the way employees and teams cope and work with labor dynamism. Finally, empirical findings from the hospitality industry of the Northern Territory add to the declining research interest in Australian human resource related issues (Singh et al., 2007).

Limitations

This book chapter is the result of preliminary research conducted in the Darwin based hospitality industry of the Northern Territory of Australia. the research was limited to a single Australian region and an international hotel chain. Australia's national culture differs from other countries or continents suggesting the need for future research in different culture settings. Also, this research was conducted in a single Australian region (Northern Territory). The Northern Territory constitutes a unique Australian case to study hospitality related issues because of its remoteness and people transient nature. These factors suggest that the Northern Territory is an extreme case to study organizational matters arising from labor changes. Replicating this research in other Australian regions which are not as remote or people transient may yield different results. The research was limited only to the hospitality industry and in particular only one case study of an international hotel-chain. Outcomes might differ should this study be replicated in other hotel settings such

as smaller and those independently owned and managed. Also, future research in other service industries or sectors exposed to frequent labor changes will be useful to confirm the findings reported in this chapter. Finally, with regards to the concept of relational flexibility, it should be noted that it is by no means a panacea. Indeed socialization deriving from peer interaction may have undesirable consequences. For example, there is the threat of over-socialization (e.g. social loafing) that may negatively impact organizational performance (Khalid, 2006).

Future Research

Future hospitality research should focus on human resource management and knowledge management issues in environments characterized by labor dynamism. Despite the plethora of research on hospitality staff turnover and flexible labor strategies, academics and practitioners are still unable to offer an in-depth and holistic account of the consequences of labor dynamism and the ways employees, teams and businesses adapt to them. Similarly, future research in the fields of human resource management and knowledge management should incorporate the labor dynamic features of certain industries (Kramar, 2002). More qualitative and quantitative work on group dynamics will yield results that will inform future practices and create hospitality specific HRM strategies (Lucas & Deery, 2004) while increasing the literature relating to social aspects of knowledge management. Moreover, the idea of relational flexibility will greatly benefit from additional research in different hospitality contexts, destinations, a larger sample of case studies, different industries and cultures.

REFERENCES

Adams, S. (1995). The corporate memory concept. *The Electronic Library*, *13*(4), 309–312. doi:10.1108/eb045380

Adler, P., & Kwon, S. (2002). Social capital: Prospects for a new concept. *Academy of Management Review, 27*(1), 17–40. doi:10.2307/4134367

Atkinson, J. (1984). Manpower strategies for flexible organizations. *Personnel Management*, 28-30.

Australian Bureau of Statistics. (2006). *Labor force survey and labor mobility*. Retrieved on November 10, 2008, from http://www.abs.gov.au

Australian Bureau of Statistics. (2007). *Northern Territory at a glance*. Retrieved on November 10, 2008, from http://www.abs.gov.au

Beltran-Martin, I., Roca-Puig, V., Escrig-Tena, A., & Bou-Llusar, J. C. (2008). Human resource flexibility as a mediating variable between high performance work systems and performance. *Journal of Management, 34*(5), 1009–1044. doi:10.1177/0149206308318616

Borgatti, S. P., & Cross, R. (2003). A relational view of information seeking and learning in social networks. *Management Science, 49*(4), 432–445. doi:10.1287/mnsc.49.4.432.14428

Burgess, J. (1997). The flexible firm and the growth of non standard employment. *Labour & Industry, 7*(3), 85–102.

Burt, R. S. (2001). Structural holes vs. network closure as social capital. In N. Lin, K. Cook & R. S. Burt (Eds.), *Social capital: Theory and research* (pp. 31-56). Sociology and economics: Controversy and integration series. New York: Aldine de Gruyter.

Butler, R. (1998). Seasonality in tourism: Issues and implications. *Tourism Review, 53*(3), 18–24. doi:10.1108/eb058278

Carbery, R., & Garavan, T. N. (2003). Predicting hotel managers' turnover cognitions. *Journal of Managerial Psychology, 18*(7), 649–679. doi:10.1108/02683940310502377

Chalkiti, K., & Carson, D. (2009, in press). Knowledge cultures, competitive advantage, and staff turnover in hospitality in Australia's Northern Territory. In D. Harorimana (Ed.), *Cultural implications of knowledge sharing, management, and transfer: Identifying competitive advantage.* Hershey, PA: IGI Global.

Chapman, J. A., & Lovell, G. (2006). The competency model of hospitality service: Why it doesn't deliver. *International Journal of Contemporary Hospitality Management, 18*(1), 78–88. doi:10.1108/09596110610642000

Chen, X. P., Hui, C., & Sego, D. J. (1998). The role of organizational citizenship behavior in turnover: Conceptualization and preliminary tests of key hypothesis. *The Journal of Applied Psychology, 83*, 922–931. doi:10.1037/0021-9010.83.6.922

Cho, S., & Johanson, M. (2008). Organizational citizenship behavior and employee performance: A moderating effect on work status in restaurant employees. *Journal of Hospitality & Tourism Research (Washington, D.C. Print), 32*(3), 307–326. doi:10.1177/1096348008317390

Cohen, D., & Prusak, L. (2001). *In good company: How social capital makes organizations work.* Boston, MA: Harvard Business School Press.

Cotton, J. L., & Turtle, J. M. (1986). Employee turnover: A meta analysis and review of implications for research. *Academy of Management Review, 11*, 55–70. doi:10.2307/258331

Cross, R., Parker, A., Prusak, L., & Borgatti, S. (2001). Knowing what we know: Supporting knowledge creation and sharing in social networks. *Organizational Dynamics, 30*(2), 100–120. doi:10.1016/S0090-2616(01)00046-8

Dalton, D. R., & Krackhardt, D. M. (1983). The impact of teller turnover in banking: First appearances are deceiving. *Journal of Bank Research, 14*(3), 184–192.

Dutton, J. E., Dukerich, J. M., & Harquail, C. V. (1994). Organizational images and member identification. *Administrative Science Quarterly*, *39*(2), 239–263. doi:10.2307/2393235

Farh, J. L., Christopher, E. P., & Lin, S. C. (1997). Impetus for action: A cultural analysis of justice and organizational citizenship behavior in Chinese society. *Administrative Science Quarterly*, *42*(3), 421–444. doi:10.2307/2393733

Feldman, D. C., & Doerpinghaus, H. I. (1992). Patterns of part-time employment. *Journal of Vocational Behavior*, *41*(3), 282–294. doi:10.1016/0001-8791(92)90030-4

Granovetter, M. (1973). The strength of weak ties. *American Journal of Sociology*, *78*, 1360–1380. doi:10.1086/225469

Granovetter, M. (1985). Economic action and social structure: The problem of embeddedness. *American Journal of Sociology*, *91*, 481–510. doi:10.1086/228311

Gustafson, J. P., & Cooper, L. (1985). Collaboration in small groups. Theory and technique for the study of small-group processes. In A. D. Golman & M. H. Geller (Eds.), *Group relations reader* (pp. 139-150). Washington, D.C: A. K. Rice Institute Series.

Hai-yan, K., & Baum, T. (2006). Skills and work in the hospitality sector: The case of hotel front office employees in China. *International Journal of Contemporary Hospitality Management*, *18*(6), 509–518. doi:10.1108/09596110610681548

Hinkin, T. R., & Tracey, J. B. (2000). The cost of turnover. *The Cornell Hotel and Restaurant Administration Quarterly*, *41*(3), 14–21.

Hjalager, A. M., & Andersen, S. (2001). Tourism employment: Contingent work or professional career? *Employee Relations*, *23*(2), 115–129. doi:10.1108/01425450110384165

Hochschild, A. R. (2003). *The managed heart: Commercialization of human feeling*. CA: University of California Press.

Hohl, A., & Tisdell, C. (1995). Peripheral tourism: Development and management. *Annals of Tourism Research*, *22*(3), 517–534. doi:10.1016/0160-7383(95)00005-Q

Johannessen, J., Olaisen, J., & Olsen, B. (2001). Mismanagement of tacit knowledge: The importance of tacit knowledge, the danger of information technology, and what to do about it. *International Journal of Information Management*, *21*, 3–20. doi:10.1016/S0268-4012(00)00047-5

Jolliffe, L., & Farnsworth, R. (2003). Seasonality in tourism employment: Human resource challenges. *International Journal of Contemporary Hospitality Management*, *15*(6), 312–316. doi:10.1108/09596110310488140

Kalleberg, A. L. (2001). Organizing flexibility: The flexible firm in a new century. *British Journal of Industrial Relations*, *39*(4), 479–504. doi:10.1111/1467-8543.00211

Keenoy, T. (1999). Human resource management as a hologram: A polemic. *Journal of Management Studies*, *36*(1), 1–23. doi:10.1111/1467-6486.00123

Khalid, S. (2006). Organizational citizenship behavior, turnover intention, and abstenteeism among hotel employees. *Malaysian Management Review*, *41*(1), 1–11.

Khan, W. A. (1990). Psychological conditions of personal engagement and disengagement at work. *Academy of Management Journal*, *33*(4), 692–724. doi:10.2307/256287

Knox, A. (2002). HRM in the Australian luxury hotel industry: Signs of innovation? *Employment Relations Record*, *2*(2), 59–68.

Knox, A., & Walsh, J. (2005). Organizational flexibility and HRM in the hotel industry: evidence from Australia. *Human Resource Management Journal*, *15*(1), 57–75. doi:10.1111/j.1748-8583.2005. tb00140.x

Koene, B., & Riemsdijk, M. (2005). Managing temporary workers: Work identity, diversity, and operational HR choices. *Human Resource Management Journal*, *15*(1), 76–92. doi:10.1111/j.1748-8583.2005.tb00141.x

Konovsky, M. A., Ellito, J., & Pugh, S. D. (1994). *The dispositional and contextual predictors of citizenship behavior in Mexico*. New Orleans, LA: Unpublished manuscript, Tulane University.

Krackhardt, D. M., & Porter, L. W. (1985). When friends leave: A structural analysis of the relationship between turnover and stayers attitudes. *Administrative Science Quarterly*, *30*, 242–261. doi:10.2307/2393107

Krackhart, D., & Porter, W. E. (1986). The snowball effect: Turnover embedded in communication networks. *The Journal of Applied Psychology*, *71*(1), 50–55. doi:10.1037/0021-9010.71.1.50

Kramar, R. (2002). Human resource management in Australia: Is it a hologram? *Employment Relations Record*, *2*(2), 80–93.

Kvist, A., & Klefsjo, B. (2006). Which service quality dimensions are important in inbound tourism?: A case study in a peripheral location. *Managing Service Quality*, *16*(5), 520–537. doi:10.1108/09604520610686151

Lai, P. C., & Baum, T. (2005). Just-in-time labour supply in the hotel sector: The role of agencies. *Employee Relations*, *27*(1), 86–102. doi:10.1108/01425450510569328

Lee, C., & Moreo, P. J. (2007). What do seasonal lodging operators need to know about seasonal workers? *International Journal of Hospitality Management*, *26*(1), 148–160. doi:10.1016/j. ijhm.2005.11.001

Lin, N. (2001). *Social capital: A theory of social structure and action*. Cambridge, New York: Cambridge University Press.

Lucas, R., & Deery, M. (2004). Significant developments and emerging issues in human resource management. *Hospital Management*, *23*(5), 459–472. doi:10.1016/j.ijhm.2004.10.005

Lun, J., & Huang, X. (2007). How to motivate your older employees to excel? The impact of commitment on older employees' performance in the hospitality industry. *International Journal of Hospitality Management*, *26*(4), 793–806. doi:10.1016/j.ijhm.2006.08.002

Lundvall, B., & Nielsen, P. (2007). Knowledge management and innovation performance. *International Journal of Manpower*, *28*(3/4), 207–223. doi:10.1108/01437720710755218

Mohsin, A. (2003). Backpackers in the Northern Territory of Australia-motives, behaviours, and satisfactions. *International Journal of Tourism Research*, *5*(2), 113–131. doi:10.1002/jtr.421

Moorman, R. H., & Harland, L. K. (2002). Temporary employees as good citizens: Factors influencing their OCB performance. *Journal of Business and Psychology*, *17*(2), 171–187. doi:10.1023/A:1019629330766

Mu, J., Peng, G., & Love, E. (2008). Interfirm networks, social capital, and knowledge flow. *Journal of Knowledge Management*, *12*(4), 86–100. doi:10.1108/13673270810884273

Nahapiet, J., & Ghoshal, S. (1998). Social capital, intellectual capital, and the organizational advantage. *Academy of Management Review*, *23*(2), 242–266. doi:10.2307/259373

Organ, D. W., Podsakoff, P. M., & MacKenzie, S. B. (2006). *Organizational citizenship behavior: Its nature, antecedents, and consequences*. CA: Sage Publications Inc.

Peters, T. (1987). *Thriving on chaos*. New York: Harper and Row.

Podsakoff, P. M., MacKenzie, S. B., Paine, J. B., & Bachrach, D. G. (2000). Organizational citizenship behaviors: A critical review of the theoretical and empirical literature and suggestions for future research. *Journal of Management, 26*(3), 513–563. doi:10.1177/014920630002600307

Poon, A. (1993). *Tourism, technology and competitive strategies*. UK: C.A.B International.

Portes, A. (1998). Social capital: Its origins and application in modern sociology. *Annual Review of Sociology, 24*, 1–24. doi:10.1146/annurev.soc.24.1.1

Pringle, C. D., & Kroll, M. J. (1997). Why Trafalgar was won before it was fought: Lessons from resource-based theory. *The Academy of Management Executive, 11*(4), 73–89.

Riley, M., & Lockwood, A. (1997). Strategies and measurement for workforce flexibility: An application of functional flexibility in a service setting. *International Journal of Operations & Production Management, 17*(4), 413–419. doi:10.1108/01443579710159996

Robins, G., & Pattison, P. (n.d.). *Multiple networks in organizations*. Retrieved on December 10, 2008, from http://www.sna.unimelb.edu.au/publications/publications.html

Rodwell, J., & Shadur, M. (2000). Management best practices in large firms of the Australian hospitality industry. *International Journal of Employment Studies, 8*(2), 121–138.

Rowley, G., & Purcell, K. (2001). "As cooks go, she went": Is labor churn inevitable? *International Journal of Hospitality Management, 20*(2), 163–185. doi:10.1016/S0278-4319(00)00050-5

Russ, M., & Jones, J. K. (2006). Knowledge-based strategies and information system technologies: Preliminary findings. *International Journal of Knowledge and Learning, 2*(1/2), 154–179. doi:10.1504/IJKL.2006.009685

Russ, M., Jones, J. K., & Fineman, R. (2006). Toward a taxonomy of knowledge-based strategies: Early findings. *International Journal of Knowledge and Learning, 2*(1/2), 1–40. doi:10.1504/IJKL.2006.009677

Singh, N., Hu, C., & Roehl, W. S. (2007). Text mining a decade of progress in hospitality human resource management research: Identifying emerging thematic development. *Hospital Management, 26*(1), 131–147. doi:10.1016/j.ijhm.2005.10.002

Smith, C. A., Organ, D. W., & Near, J. P. (1983). Organizational citizenship behavior: Its nature and antecedents. *The Journal of Applied Psychology, 68*(4), 653–663. doi:10.1037/0021-9010.68.4.653

Taylor, D. W., Jones, O., & Boles, K. (2004). Building social capital through action learning: An insight into the entrepreneur. *Education & Training, 46*(5), 226–235. doi:10.1108/00400910410549805

Timo, N. (2001). Lean or just mean? The flexibilisation of labor in the Australian hotel industry. *Research in the Sociology of Work, 10*, 287–309. doi:10.1016/S0277-2833(01)80030-3

Tsai, W., & Ghoshal, S. (1998). Social capital and value creation: The role of intrafirm networks. *Academy of Management Journal, 41*(4), 464–476. doi:10.2307/257085

Uzzi, B. (1996). The sources and consequences of embeddedness for the economic performance of organizations: The network effect. *American Sociological Review, 61*(4), 674–698. doi:10.2307/2096399

Uzzi, B. (1997). Social structure and competition in interfirm networks: The paradox of embeddedness. *Administrative Science Quarterly, 41*, 35–67. doi:10.2307/2393808

Von Krogh, G., Nonaka, I., & Aben, M. (2001). Making the most of your company's knowledge: A strategic framework. *Long Range Planning, 34*(4), 421–439. doi:10.1016/S0024-6301(01)00059-0

Walsh, J., & Deery, S. (1999). Understanding the peripheral workforce: Evidence from the service sector. *Human Resource Management Journal, 9*(2), 50–63. doi:10.1111/j.1748-8583.1999.tb00196.x

Whitehouse, G., Lafferty, G., & Boreham, P. (1997). From casual to permanent part time: Non-standard employment in retail and hospitality. *Labour & Industry, 8*(2), 33–48.

Wildes, V. J. (2007). Attracting and retaining food servers: How internal service quality moderates occupational stigma. *International Journal of Hospitality Management, 26*(1), 4–19. doi:10.1016/j.ijhm.2005.08.003

Woods, R., Heck, W., & Sciarini, M. (1998). *Turnover and diversity in the lodging industry.* American Hotel Foundation.

Zhang, H. Q., & Wu, E. (2004). Human resources issues facing the hotel and travel industry in China. *International Journal of Contemporary Hospitality Management, 16*(7), 424–428. doi:10.1108/09596110410559122

Zopiatis, A., & Constanti, P. (2007). Human resource challenges confronting the Cyprus hospitality industry. *EuroMed Journal of Business, 2*(2), 135–153. doi:10.1108/14502190710826022

ADDITIONAL READING

Appelbaum, S. H., Iaconi, G. D., & Matousek, A. (2007). Positive and negative deviant workplace behaviors: Causes, impacts, and solutions. *Corporate Governance, 7*(5), 586–598.

Chiang, F. F. T., & Birtch, T. A. (2008). Achieving task and extra-task related behaviors: A case of gender and position differences in the perceived role of rewards in the hotel industry. *International Journal of Hospitality Management, 27*(4), 491–503. doi:10.1016/j.ijhm.2007.08.009

Comeau, D. J., & Griffith, R. L. (2005). Structural interdependence, personality, and organizational citizenship behavior. *Personnel Review, 34*(3), 310–330. doi:10.1108/00483480510591453

DeGroot, T., & Brownlee, A. L. (2006). Effect of department structure on the organizational citizenship behavior-department effectiveness relationship. *Journal of Business Research, 59*(10, 11), 1116-1123.

Dimitriades, Z. S. (2007). The influence of service climate and job involvement on customer oriented organizational citizenship behavior in Greek service organizations: A survey. *Employee Relations, 29*(5), 469–491. doi:10.1108/01425450710776290

Gill, A. S., & Mathur, N. (2007). Improving employee dedication and prosocial behavior. *International Journal of Contemporary Hospitality Management, 19*(4), 328–334. doi:10.1108/09596110710747661

Organ, D. W., & Ryan, K. (1995). A meta-analytic review of attitudinal and dispositional predictors of organizational citizenship behavior. *Personnel Psychology, 48*(4), 775–802. doi:10.1111/j.1744-6570.1995.tb01781.x

Raub, S. (2008). Does bureaucracy kill individual initiative? The impact of structure on organizational citizenship behavior in the hospitality industry. *International Journal of Hospitality Management, 27*(2), 179–186. doi:10.1016/j.ijhm.2007.07.018

Ravichandran, S., Gilmore, S. A., & Strohbehn, C. (2007). Organizational citizenship behavior research in hospitality: Current status and future research directions. *Journal of Human Resources in Hospitality & Tourism, 6*(2), 59–72. doi:10.1300/J171v06n02_04

Singh, V., Vinnicombe, S., & Kumra, S. (2006). Women in formal corporate networks: An organizational citizenship perspective. *Women in Management Review, 21*(6), 458–482. doi:10.1108/09649420610683462

Torlak, O., & Koc, U. (2007). Materialistic attitude as an antecedent of organizational citizenship behavior. *Management Research News, 30*(8), 581–596. doi:10.1108/01409170710773715

Van Emmerik, I. J. H., & Jawahar, I. M. (2005). Lending a helping hand: Provision of helping behaviors beyond professional career responsibilities. *Career Development International, 10*(5), 347–358. doi:10.1108/13620430510615283

Walz, S. M., & Niehoff, B. P. (2000). Organizational citizenship behaviors: Their relationship to organizational effectiveness. *Journal of Hospitality & Tourism Research (Washington, D.C. Print), 24*(3), 301–319. doi:10.1177/109634800002400301

Chapter 3
Agile Alignment of Enterprise Execution Capabilities with Strategy

Daniel Worden
RuleSmith Corporation, Canada

ABSTRACT

Emergent strategy provides for both planned and reactive aspects of strategic planning. It also identifies that strategy as implemented will often have different characteristics than originally anticipated. Today, even traditional, non-knowledge based organizations have adopted comparatively high levels of computerization compared to a decade ago. Enterprises now rely extensively on digital systems for data handling across operational and administrative processes. This chapter maintains that detection and reporting capabilities inherent in information technology (IT) can themselves be exploited as a strategy for managing knowledge. Using feedback loops to describe the dynamics of systems lets an organization capture and communicate intended strategy and emergent characteristics of the actual strategy along with changes in the execution environment. The role of IT as an execution capability required for both business strategy and knowledge management is examined, along with the need to more quickly align the business processes that use IT services to changes in business strategies or priorities. Advances in IT assisting in requirements discovery, system design and development- including use cases, patterns, decision modeling, and aspect-oriented software-are discussed. Techniques to capture and communicate knowledge vital for aligning organizational capabilities with emerging strategies and competing priorities are evaluated. A predicted emergent business pattern as a tool for managing the capture and communication of organizational knowledge is proposed. This includes techniques for defining strategy and decision elements as data about processes that can be used during execution to trigger notification and appropriate handling of exceptional events.

DOI: 10.4018/978-1-60566-348-7.ch003

INTRODUCTION

Knowledge management strategies require effective execution to be successful. Over time, information technology has become a de facto repository for organization knowledge, in the form of business rules and data integrity constraints expressed as computer programs. IT is a requirement for successful execution of a knowledge management strategy.

Even while information systems have become increasingly pervasive across organizations of all sizes and types, their ability to capture and convey knowledge elements has generally been secondary to their intended utility in processing data.

In many cases, these systems are deemed inflexible, expensive to enhance or worse.

As much as organizations have come to rely on information technology to enable their knowledge strategies, change to the computing infrastructure, or the introduction of new systems to support knowledge management carries significant risk. Many enterprises have launched IT initiatives that have failed completely (Santa, Ferrer & Pun, 2007).

Recent innovations in information technology and techniques offer valuable new ways to use information technology to collect and communicate knowledge across organizational lines and functions, while reducing that risk.

The Predicted-Emergent pattern captures a context and motivation for any organizational endeavor, describing both the planned for and actual events that occur. Advanced separation of concerns is used to define relevant scope for each activity. These activities include strategic planning and course correction, and progress through levels of detail down to business process definition and decision management. These in turn can be implemented as adaptive software, which establish thresholds for action and notification through operational parameters.

This approach pulls the discussion of IT solution elements into earlier phases in the organizational planning process. Incorporating a predicted-emergent knowledge management strategy allows the enterprise to more accurately assess events as the plan unfolds, and to communicate priorities more quickly. The net effect is faster reaction and shorter implementation times with the ability to capture significant new knowledge as it arises from organizational experience.

The predicted-emergent approach to knowledge management strategy seeks to enable an agile alignment between enterprise planning and operational systems.

The legacy of traditional systems has given rise to hardened silos of computing, with inflexible data structures, complex program logic, scattered business rules and standard reports designed to serve a fixed set of organizational requirements.

This gap between expectations for and delivery of information system affects and is affected by knowledge management practices. Given that IT frequently fails to deliver basic business operations support, it should come as no surprise that a gap exists between implemented systems and their capabilities for the management of institutional knowledge.

That there is a lack of alignment between information technology departments and enterprise strategies is not a new observation (Chan, Huff & Copeland, 1998). Nor is the notion that IT can and should be an integral part of realized corporate business and knowledge management strategies (Henderson & Venkatraman, 1992). Achieving the goal of pulling those systems into tighter alignment with needs for knowledge management and adaptive organizational strategies lies in the first part with those responsible for defining system requirements.

If the lack of alignment between operational information systems and business strategy is the problem, a solution can be found in creating a faster, more accurate feedback loop between planning and execution. Many IT practitioners have already identified this as an area of focus for their own strategies. That community often refers to the process by the jargon term - agility.

Figure 1. A predicted-emergent feedback loop for business strategies

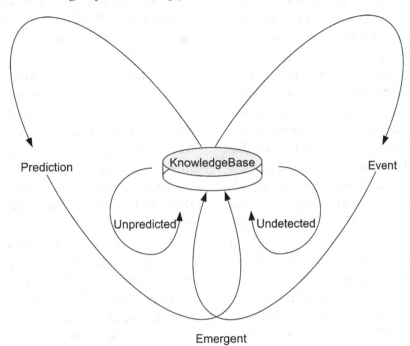

This chapter introduces several techniques that have emerged as part of research and practice of information technology and computer science. These practices have relevance to knowledge management strategies; particularly in support of capture and communication of both requirements and capabilities.

The discussion of techniques and approaches begins with the gathering of requirements to describe the problem domain. Enterprise business and knowledge management strategies are considered included in those requirements. As part of the expression of business requirements, however, several innovative architectural notions from software development will be introduced. The value of expressing the problem within the framework of how the solutions are developed will be considered.

This chapter will describe the linkage of business processes with their operational context as well as how meta-data about the process can be defined, collected and acted upon as part of a dynamic loop, as shown in figure 1. The goal is to outline a set of steps for containing business planning and process models into descriptions grouped by relevant level of detail for both business process owners and solution developers.

Strategic Feedback

Every strategy admits of both assumptions and a lack of certain foreknowledge of events yet to occur. Plans have within them the seeds of achievement and disappointment in similar measure. In keeping with this reality is the need to continually inform business development strategies with events as they actually unfold and the situation as actually exists. Knowledge of these things is a strategic advantage, as it allows an organization to change, refine or bolster a given plan based on how well the assumptions are validated and the ability of the organization to address unanticipated issues that arise. This combination of top-down strategy and bottom-up status reporting creates a feedback loop and represents a dynamic between the planned and the discovered. A systems dynamics model of the overall flow is shown in figure 1.

The diagram depicts the role of the knowledgebase (KB) as central to deriving predictions or making strategic assumptions as well as collecting event information to populate the knowledge base with data. Predictions are essentially known unknowns, with probabilistic values supplied for purposes of decision-making. Detected events are added to the KB as either predicted or unpredicted. Additionally, the diagram shows that there is a class of event that goes undetected and correspondingly uncollected within the knowledgebase. Unpredicted events may occur but remain undetected for some period of time. Agile alignment as a strategy emphasizes the role of event detection to improve predictions or expose areas for strategic evaluation.

Ranges for probable values defined as part of predictions is a key way to ensure the pattern translates into a specification for usable systems dynamics model. By setting minimum and maximum ranges various scenarios can be simulated to determine the effect on other elements in the system.

Describing the Problem to be Solved

There are few truly 'green field' opportunities to define business strategies, plans and projects from scratch. Generally, some version of the activity or system is already in use. In keeping with this reality, assume that some knowledge about the systems and processes will already exist. What is needed then is a strategy for capturing this knowledge in a manner that will make it more suitable for inclusion in enterprise planning and operation.

Use cases have become a commonly used mechanism to capture business requirements and describe systems behaviors. Arising from early software development methodology efforts, they are an example of the practical value IT innovators can provide to business users and management through systems tools and techniques. Clearly, use case models are not in and of themselves sufficient

to define a given organizational problem, but in combination with process models, business plans and budgets, the user view of the problem can be explained this way.

Use case descriptions typically incorporate step-by-step flows of user-system interaction through 'as-is' and 'to-be' versions of the organizations behavior. Use cases are a vitally important tool for the capture of knowledge management, though some care must be paid in how the use cases narratives are structured in order to optimize their applicability to knowledge management in practice.

With the formulation of a use case based approach to requirements gathering, many software project members believe they are effectively capturing 'real' business requirements. However, too often the effort bogs down in degree of detail – either too high or too light – and in an attempt to capture every scenario imaginable.

Employing use case descriptions supports the agile, iterative development process, allowing the design and development to flesh out detail as it is discovered. More important, the focus is on defining what is known and how to handle all other events – whatever they may be- as they arise. Accordingly, capturing all possible scenarios is less important than defining the foreseeable (predictable) states of a process, and identifying the acceptable parameters within which it may operate effectively.

Once the business defines these parameterized processes, the exception handling procedures of an emergent event means that software developers can reasonably rely on coding only those cases that are explicitly specified. They can also ensure those parameters are accessible and modifiable by business users of the software rather than requiring re-coding.

By pulling the definition of exception handling up into the earliest efforts of the requirements gathering, processes can be formalized, reviewed and revised as needed. Test cases that reflect exception handling can be derived concurrently with the use case effort. Programmers can then focus their efforts on automating well-defined scenarios, while throwing all others, predicted or not, into the exception handling processes defined as acceptable to the business.

This offers the promise of increased quality of the delivered product (by alleviating programmers requirement to guess at how the system should behave) as well as making the system more responsive to changes in thresholds, which are administered by those closest to the systems use, specifically the business (Alexander, 2004).

A Strategic Context

Use cases are a relatively low-level artifact within an enterprise knowledge system. Frequently they deal with detail at the process and function level. The motivation of the business for the project or process sponsoring the use cases will be taken as an input or an assumption.

However, as a function of their ability to convey 'as-is and 'to-be' states, Use cases provide a vehicle to capture current capabilities (or challenges) of the current environment to planners, and also to communicate strategic goals or priorities to mid level operations resources.

EMERGENT STRATEGY

Organizational strategies may be deliberate or emergent (Mintzberg & Waters, 1985). The classic vision of the senior leader devising a brilliant plan for the way ahead is the epitome of a deliberate strategy. In contrast the emergent strategy is one that arises out of experience. It is this capture and dissemination of experience that is most relevant to knowledge management. Decision makers and business planners are a key user and constituency of knowledge management systems. They depend on the collection and communication of relevant, timely information that describes the status of the organization and changes in the environment in

which it operates. That information can be aggregated into repeatable patterns that form the basis for organizational knowledge.

However, this tends not to happen effectively when relied on to occur spontaneously.

Part of the difficulty in creating a learning organization that adapts to its environment as changed circumstances or incorrect assumptions are encountered is the human tendency to avoid communicating 'bad news.' The recommended approach to defining exceptions and notification parameters as part of use cases definitions is one way to de-politicize that communication.

Where intended strategy is the deliberate plan, emergent strategy is the plan as realized or implemented. Success is a function of how well and how quickly variances between the two can be identified and reconciled.

The intent of this chapter is to provide specific techniques that can be used to better employ use cases and emergent strategy in knowledge management efforts. One of the techniques that support overlaying business process definition and use cases with strategies for enhancing institutional knowledge management is to separate the concerns.

Advanced Separation of Concerns

In software engineering, the separation of concerns is a principle that allows complexity to be restricted to a certain number of elements related by a given context or purpose (Dijkstra, 1976). The problem and solution domains represented by the business users and IT solution providers can be taken as one example of two separate concerns. Integrating those two is another concern in its own right.

Concerns may be separated into level of detail, for instance where both the problem and solution definitions are being addressed within a single iteration during an agile development project, or along a chain of related processes, as part of an operational or planning exercise. The separation may also occur dynamically as a concern arises, from an audit for example or as non-compliance with a new regulation.

One of the knowledge management strategies advocated in this chapter is to identify knowledge management concerns. Each of these can be rooted in current practice or systems, from which the realized strategy may emerge for validation or review. Alternately, a change in overall direction or priority may be a deliberate strategy that requires implementation to be made effective.

The technique for defining specific processes to be handled by a system and raising exceptions is another example of applying the principle of separation of concerns. By doing so deliberately, the requirements express not only precisely what the process is intended to achieve, but also a mechanism for handling all exceptions that occur outside those pre-defined thresholds. These are the parameterized processes set by the business.

Use cases that reflect these requirements capture the business intent and also better enable the allocation of implementation work to specialists. One resource with suitable background and knowledge to handle the active process can be assigned to requirements, design or programming as appropriate. Others may be given the task of detecting and handling the exceptions.

While business focused practitioners will not be burdened with having to understand the solution design internals, software architects will realize this promotes both agile, iterative development and also sets the stage for an aspect oriented (Kiczales, et al., 1997) solution to be developed.

Knowledge Management Aspects

To this point communication has run from leadership to operational resources and back, and from business users to coders, however, knowledge management concerns are not necessarily hierarchical. In identifying separate concerns, it is also possible to intersect those concerns with an additional concern.

A learning organization may identify a concern for knowledge capture and consolidation into a specified knowledgebase. Given that exception handling is its own concern, so too would this acquisition of knowledge elements. But where an exception handling process might be common to some number, or unique to a single process, knowledge acquisition will cut across a number of processes and domains. It becomes a crosscutting concern or aspect of the system.

Put another way, a knowledge system may not simply exist separate and apart from an operational system. Knowledge systems can also be constructed as aspects of all other systems, with their own unique set of elements included as part of its own knowledge management concern, co-existing with the operational systems in use within the enterprise.

The useful computer science innovation that applies here is AOSD, Aspect Oriented Software Development. Building on the use case definition technique described in this chapter, a knowledge management aspect could be considered to be the requirement for a KM practitioner to be notified of previously un-encountered exceptions, so they can be reviewed for severity, catalogued and handled as predicted scenarios as appropriate.

This approach may prove less technically demanding than might be feared. Trends in software development have been leading towards an emphasis on discovery over rigidly defined specifications. This is consistent with the needs of emergent strategy, as it reflects the reality that environments change, as does knowledge of that change, and it can be used to support organizational learning. Agility in IT terms can become synonymous with enterprise adaptability, enabled by an aspect oriented knowledge management strategy.

ADVICE FOR UN-TANGLING
AND UN-SCATTERING

Using aspects as a fundamental approach to segregating systems concerns was intended to solve a particular problem that arises in object-oriented approaches to software development. As objects are defined as methods or operations that occur on specific data, those operations can be required on many different data sets throughout an information system. As a result, the operations become scattered across the code and the business models used to depict the processes and software solution. Additionally, certain concerns, such as exception handling, cut across many other concerns and so become tangled up with other concerns such as business logic and operational rules.

Where a use case involves several systems components it can be considered to be subject to scattering, and where a component is invoked by several use cases it may be considered to be entangled. The mechanism used in AOSD to encapsulate crosscutting aspects is called 'advice'.

Advice is of particular interest in the context of knowledge management practice. As described earlier, to achieve separation of concerns in software solutions, it is a great benefit to define them as part of requirements. Use cases support this defined separation, but do not force it. By defining and naming certain functions, such as exception handling, or notification as Advice, use cases may simply refer to the function to be called without bogging the effort down in explaining the detailed implementation of the procedure.

Emergent strategy provides a way to capture the differences between strategy and plans as implemented when compared to their original intent. Use cases provide a way to document business requirements that can be used to describe systems to implement solutions for meeting those requirements. Aspects provide a way to separate the concerns into manageable modules and to navigate both the requirements and software solutions along the path relevant to a given purpose.

RE-USE THROUGH
PATTERN LANGUAGE

With their 1995 book *Design Patterns: Elements of Reusable Object-Oriented Software* by Erich Gamma, Richard Helm, Ralph Johnson, and John Vlissides (the famous Gang of Four or *GoF*) translated the architectural concept of Patterns to software design. Their work was inspired by another book, that of an Architect Christopher Alexander – Towns, Buildings, Construction – A Pattern Language. Through their combined insight, design problems and aspects of their solutions can be more efficiently abstracted and communicated from one setting to another.

Design patterns are by definition constituent elements of a solution. These patterns inform the construction of a software solution. The extent to which that solution addresses specific problems depends on how well the design pattern fits within the target problem domain. The solutions as built will only accidentally address the problem better than it was designed to do.

As well as introducing design patterns to the software industry, the GoF went on to create the Unified Modeling Language (UML) and the Rational Unified Process (RUP) for requirements discovery and software development. Their original focus was primarily on the optimal engineering of software solutions. There was somewhat less emphasis on establishing the context in which the solution fits until Jacobson brought his use case emphasis with him when he joined the group in 1995.

A subset of these tools and techniques are applicable to knowledge management systems, particularly some of the patterns for describing problems and solutions.

PATTERNS USAGE IN KNOWLEDGE MANAGEMENT

Design patterns and pattern language have influenced the Information Technology community for more than a decade. The applicability of these concepts, approaches and tools to a knowledge management environment may be less common (Hughes, 2006).

One dictionary definition of the work 'Pattern' is as follows: Anything used as a model or guide for something to be fashioned or made (Dictionary.com, n.d.). As an information or knowledge management system is something to be fashioned or made, it would seem to follow that patterns for the creation of effective solutions should be available. This general definition of the term has been made much more specific as applied to the creation of software solutions. However, the emphasis in this chapter is not solely on the construction of solutions, but rather on the setting of the overall and on-going context in which software solutions must fit.

A pattern language for business concepts, including an enterprise architecture that encompasses its requirements and IT services, is delineated as part of the IBM Enterprise Solutions Structure (McDavid, n.d.). This approach uses patterns to describe situations where IT solutions fill a role. One benefit of this approach is apportioning of the business functions with human and computing resources are intertwined but still contained within discrete blocks. Consistent with advanced separation of concerns, this approach segregates the functions allowing detailed design for both the problem and solution domains while containing the scope into a discrete and manageable size.

The intent behind pattern language was to communicate applicable considerations from one environment to another. As such it is highly suited to adoption as part of a knowledge management strategy. This chapter advocates that pattern descriptions for software solutions be pulled into the requirements definition phase of information systems projects, through the vehicle of use case descriptions. By applying aspect-oriented labels to organizational functions within business processes described during use case development, an optimized level of modularization can be achieved. This modularization contains both requirements and systems support and lends itself to agile and iterative implementation. In turn, this agile approach supports emergent strategies for knowledge management.

The key to successfully applying these patterns is defining the controlling context.

ESTABLISHING CONTEXT

The purpose or goal of any given effort informs all aspects and subsequent implications arising from the endeavor. Decisions regarding priority, resource allocation, scheduling, approval or deferment are frequently the result of comparing the purpose and impact of one endeavor against another.

Every initiative, product, project, campaign or event, has presumably only been launched after at least an informal cost-benefit analysis to define its operating parameters. The initiators often understand the desired outcomes but that definition can become lost to the downstream operators and managers of the tasks required to accomplish it. Additionally, the initiators are aware of the factors under which the endeavor is viable. The states of these factors may change over time.

Knowledge management systems seek to capture and communicate these descriptors but the challenge remains to present a complete subset of data associated with the descriptors that is relevant to a given audience at the point in time they seek it. Meta-data, often summed up as data about data, includes the descriptions of factors and their states. Here the interest is in capturing those factors and states as they were when the endeavor was evaluated and determined to be viable.

At the highest level, the context for an organization can be defined by its mission and boundaries which consist of resources and constraints (Wernerfelt, 1984). The predictive aspect is expressed in strategies, plans, budgets and other forms of defining direction. Environmental issues, such as regulatory compliance requirements or market conditions represent additional constraints on any viable effort.

The IT definition of pattern languages for systems solutions is a necessary part but insufficient to completely describe all of the concerns an organization must address as part of its on-going existence. Similarly, there is no one modeling technique, unified or otherwise, that fully describes the environment, financial implications, business strategy, priorities and other aspects of the problem domain as used by members of any given enterprise.

An overlapping, intersecting and collaborating set of concerns is depicted in Figure 2.

Where IT may maintain object and data models, data dictionaries and flows, operations might be the owner of business process models. Finance views the enterprise in terms of dollars and cents, balance sheets, income statements and cash flow models while leadership often expresses its direction through narrative business plans.

The artifacts generated by each of these constituents are valid within the confines of their own purposes, and frequently might be inputs, outputs or both to the other organizational members. When attempting to create a catalog or model for knowledge of both problems and solutions across the enterprise as a whole, the difficulty of managing dynamic changes with static models arises.

It is here that a pattern for depicting predicted-emergent events offers assistance.

Figure 2. Dimensions of organizational concerns (Ossher & Tarr, n.d.)

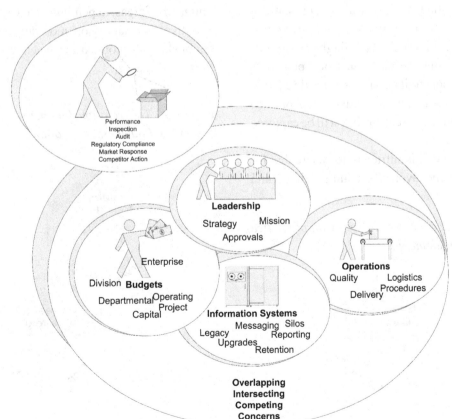

BOXING UP THE MODELS

The first step in aligning the systems solution to a given organizational problem is to isolate what is known. The key consideration for relevance is defined by the endeavor under evaluation. It may be as far-reaching as reorganization or a five-year plan. Alternatively, it may be a departmental initiative. The approach to application of the predicted-emergent pattern related to knowledge management scales in either direction.

As the scope of the endeavor moves towards operational and focused efforts, only the level of detail needs to change. Implementation of a new Financial System (for example) may be only mildly informed by the enterprise mission statement, but to be successful the project requires a plan that addresses the applicable constraints. The relationship of these elements is depicted in figure 3.

This simple diagram is a visual reminder that, for any initiative, both the plan and constraints must be identified. While the diagram is static, it should be noted that not all constraints are known at the time of initiation, accordingly constraints may emerge and the plan must be updated to reflect those constraints. This is a usual function of project management, but attention should be paid to how emerging constraints will be captured and communicated.

At this stage, it is sufficient to ensure that for the particular endeavor, all planning artifacts and

known constraints have been identified. Where knowledge management systems provide a catalog of knowledge assets to their internal users, endeavor contexts for particular projects or initiatives could be linked by name to the published plans, budgets and risk assessment documents.

Such referencing of models across organizational functions can be promoted as a knowledge management specific service, providing clear value to all participants. Equally valuable is the assignment of responsibility for updating the catalog to reflect emergent constraints and potential impact on plans.

BUSINESS MOTIVATION

From a Predicted/Emergent perspective, the business motivation expresses the goals of the plan and incorporates the priorities already set.

Of course, business motivation can cut across a number of areas, depending on the nature of the initiative. For that reason, motivation depends on establishing the context for the endeavor. This is shown in figure 4.

Figure 4. The relationship between endeavor context and business motivation

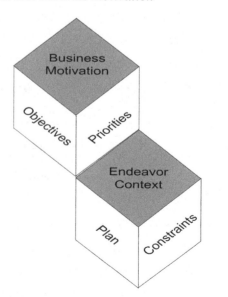

Figure 3. Endeavor context step with predictive and emergent elements

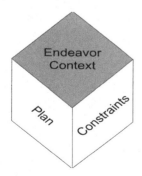

In this slightly more complex depiction, the business motivation applies to a specific endeavor. As already discussed, the endeavor might be as large as the organizations existence or a much smaller, focused initiative. In either case, the predictive aspect includes a plan with specific objectives, and an emergent aspect that allows for priorities to be realigned as the constraints that apply to the endeavor become apparent as the plan unfolds.

A useful methodology and notation neutral definition of business motivation has been adopted by the Object Management Group (OMG) as a standard for Business Motivation Modeling (Object Management Group, 2008).

BUSINESS PROCESSES

The work of any organization is typically conducted through processes. These may be formal or informal, approved or unapproved. They may be aligned with the organizations overall plan and constraints, or they may operate independently. From a knowledge management perspective, the more clearly understood and consistently operated processes are, the better.

The predictive aspects of business processes are the models developed to show them. The emergent aspects are contained in the resources using and used as part of the process. This is shown in relationship with the business motivation and endeavor context in figure 5.

The diagram now shows the relationship between the plan, its objectives and models. These are all related predictive elements for a given endeavor. Additionally, we can see that the constraints and priorities that affect resources within processes are all informed by the applicable context and motivation for the larger endeavor the processes support.

Figure 5. Business process in context

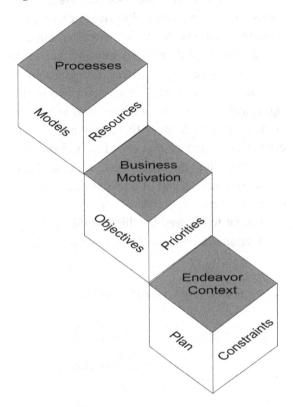

DECISIONS

With the introduction of The Decision Model (Von Halle, et al., 2009), a compelling case has been made for the segregation of decisions and processes. Similar to the isolation of data from business logic and user interfaces in systems design, decisions are discrete elements of processes that can be reused and shared. Decisions are comprised of rule families that in turn are made up of sets of business rules.

From a predicted-emergent perspective, decisions also identify thresholds at which the rules may be triggered. These are set as parameters that are modifiable over time, set by the business to reflect the constraints and priorities of the current state.

The decision definition step is depicted in figure 6.

In this multi-dimensional block diagram, it follows that plans define objectives described in models specifying thresholds. An alternate traversal of the graph describes constraints that result in priorities affecting resources through rules.

The most basic set of steps described in the figure show that every endeavor exists in its own context. The motivation for achieving specific outcomes as part of that endeavor informs the processes within the endeavors context, and that decisions taken as part of a process exist as discrete concerns.

Similar to the way in which AOSD supports a reduction in tangling and scattering of software operations, the use of decision modeling allows segregation of decisions from the processes that invoke and consume them. Decisions may be combined with Advice to perform notifications, or they may themselves be invoked as a named Advice where process owners need not have visibility into the rules that makes up the decision.

SEGREGATING DECISION RESOURCES

It should be noted that some organizational decision models exist in the form of deployed ap-

Figure 6. Decisions related to their endeavor context, business motivation and processes

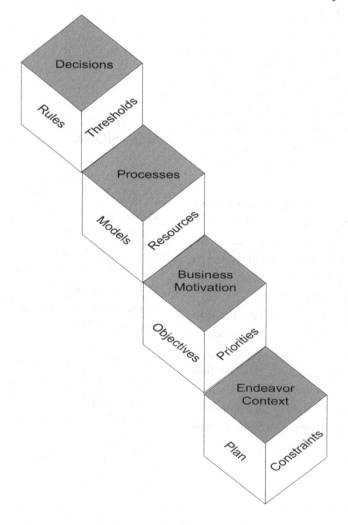

plication code. The expertise may not have been formalized as process models or rule diagrams. In some cases, those decisions access other data or processing resources, such as calls to external systems to validate a credit card, for example.

One of the advantages of detailing decisions separately from process models is the ability to simplify process models. The decision is not represented as part of the process flow; it can be merely shown as an intrinsic part of the process. The decision becomes, in an aspect-oriented sense, a crosscutting concern.

Figure 7 shows how a process diagram could contain decision points without modeling the decision itself.

The black diamond inside the process indicates a named decision. Using a software tool, rather than a printed page, the decision resources details can be accessed when relevant. Since the decision might be used by any number of processes, consolidating the depiction this way reduces visual complexity in the process model and also ensures that decisions are not scattered and tangled within the process model.

Additionally, decisions for notification or exception handling can be treated as advice during the requirements definition phase. Where such decisions are not well understood, the name can be used as a stub or placeholder and fleshed out later during a subsequent iteration.

This technique supports the treatment of knowledge management strategy as a crosscutting concern while enabling an iterative approach to defining requirements, processes and software solutions to address them.

PREDICTED EMERGENT FORCES AND RELATED PATTERNS

One of the principal premises of the predicted-emergent pattern is that the quality of delivered software is a direct function of the quality of the requirements definition; too often those who don't understand what they are building are doing so for those who don't understand what is needed. The chunking of discrete stages of a project frequently

Figure 7. A Process containing a named decision (Worden, 2009)

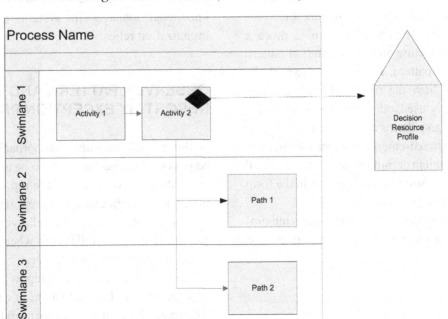

termed 'the waterfall approach' to requirements definition and solution specification has long been identified as a major culprit and cause of disappointment (Royce, 1970). While Agile, iterative and spiral methodologies have been proposed as a viable alternative, they have hardly proved the cure-all solution.

These forces – requirements to integrate computing and business operations more effectively, at less cost and support on-going changes – are not new, but neither have they been resolved. Organizations continue to face these problems regardless of the technologies, hardware or software, and the methodologies, rapid or traditional, they employ.

The predicted-emergent pattern addresses these problems by beginning with what is known, and capturing new events so they can be analyzed, classified and converted into new knowledge. This is in stark contrast to a traditional approach to requirements definition, which emphasizes identification of every possible outcome before deeming the requirements 'complete. With the strategies recommended here, the focus is on decisions, not merely process, on information not data and on usage over technology. The differences are subtle but the implications are remarkable.

The predicted-emergent pattern is more a business architecture and an integration pattern than a design pattern. However, as part of the definition of how the predicted-emergent pattern is properly used, other patterns, specifically software design patterns are incorporated. In this way, the predicted-emergent pattern allows the linkage of problem definitions and organizational requirements to solution descriptions in the form of software design artifacts.

The key to successfully achieving this integration is to focus on detection of emergent events.

DETECTION OF EMERGENT EVENTS

Given that the predicted-emergent pattern is a business architecture and integration pattern, it is necessarily described at a higher level of abstraction than a design pattern, such as those put forward by the GoF. The purpose of applying the predicted-emergent technique is to set a context with a contained scope for the application of design patterns as part of a given solution.

One such useful design pattern is the Observer pattern. This pattern describes how a resource may identify an interest in a particular state or states of a subject. When that states changes, the observer is notified and subsequent action may be triggered by that notification.

A real world example of information as a strategic asset and where the observer pattern is applied can be found in credit history data services. Data aggregators receive notifications of events from credit issuers such as banks and retailers. These transactions report payment amounts and dates, as well as balance and query information to arrive at a credit score. For business decisions that are affected by financial considerations these services often integrate with and form part of the knowledge management systems on which an organization relies.

OBSERVER PATTERN AND THE REPORT BY EXCEPTION PRINCIPLE

Within a predicted-emergent approach for knowledge systems, a best practice to be applied when using the observer pattern is to report by exception. The difference between a report periodically and report only exceptions is relatively slight, but carries significant implications when the requirements are supported by software.

A real world example of a report by exception approach to an observed situation can be found when considering the subject of a credit report. As integral as credit ratings are to many transactions, studies have shown 79% of the records have errors of some kind, with 25% of them significant enough to result in a denial of a credit-based application (National Association of State PIRGs, 2004). Even with such a high percentage of error, many people and business do not actively monitor their scores and data on a periodic basis. When an application for credit is denied, however, that exception can trigger a review and correction.

Clearly, the traditional approach generates a great deal of data. While it may be relevant if fluctuations of recorded credit scores are the subject of investigation, it can generally be taken to simply be a record of data of no particular relevance where the only consideration is whether the score falls below or above a certain set range. For someone with a good credit rating they may range considerably above the floor level of 720 with no effect on their status.

The observer pattern as applied to credit ratings describes the secondary communication of the individuals financial transactions to a third party, in this example, the credit bureaus. As implemented the pattern requires the identification of a triggering event and the third party must be prepared to receive notifications subsequent to activation of the trigger. A report by exception would apply to organizations that decline to share all transaction data, opting instead to report only certain exceptions, such as a closed account.

Whether report by exception presents a strategic opportunity to improve data integrity for credit reporting agencies is a matter for experts in that domain to determine. Instances of the observer pattern can be found in many organizations, and it is predictable that some of those will benefit from applying the report by exception principle.

OBSERVER PERFORMANCE AND RESOURCE CONSUMPTION

The implication to systems people of trapping a value and comparing it to a range is quite differ-

ent than maintaining an on-going log of values. IT considerations such as file sizes, systems performance and so on are dramatically affected. By opting for the report by exception approach, the parameters representing the acceptable values can be changed without resorting to programming alterations. This means that software so designed is more easily maintained and operated by 'the business' where things like the temperature values may need adjustment.

Use case definitions for gathering system requirements and describing business-systems interaction have become a common practice under many methodologies. Expressing use cases using the report-by-exception technique becomes a vital component of capturing emergent events at the requirements level and lends itself particularly well to the definition of exception handling concern.

Anti-Patterns in Predicted-Emergent Environments

Anti-patterns can be thought of as reasonable, attractive approaches to problems that tend to yield poor solutions. Assigning more people to a project that is behind schedule is one example. New people require support to be effective and this tends to take away time available to the project members already assigned. It seems reasonable that more people will result in more work being accomplished in the same period, but overlooking the increased cost of coordination makes this an anti-pattern.

The predicted-emergent approach to defining business process parameters and decision elements such as rules, exceptions and notifications is one way to structure responses to unanticipated events. This becomes especially valuable when systems automate responses and the elapsed time between encountering the new business situation and responding is immediate.

Where the predicted-emergent pattern is applied as a knowledge management strategy, there are two key anti-patterns to avoid. Ascertainment bias describes the tendency for experienced practitioners to discover only what they expect to find. An unwarranted influence describes factors that generate a disproportionate impact during the realization of a strategy.

The use of a knowledge base in a predicted-emergent context provides opportunities to assess and correct for either ascertainment bias or unwarranted influence. A business process or use case may elect to name a decision or call advice at a particular point in its flow. As a distinct procedure, that decision or advice can include provisions to evaluate its context, constraints, motivation or priorities. That evaluation may or may not be automated. In fact, many decision points in new processes may require human intervention before control is returned to the calling software and its execution resumed.

Unwarranted influences are those that have a higher than desired impact on a business process or resource. As shown in the examples, these influences can range from course of dealings and customary practice, to abrupt price changes of inputs. It is neither necessary nor desirable to attempt to predict all influences in advance. Overlaying a predicted-emergent structure on business processes can result in specification of solutions that appropriately trap and handle ANY event that falls outside acceptable predicted ranges.

Ascertainment bias refers to the tendency for investigators or analysts to find supporting correlations in data or results consistent with their expectations. Organizational anti-patterns such as GroupThink (Janis, 1972) can create ascertainment bias, where critical appraisal is not raised as a direct result of the group dynamic. The predicted-emergent loop allows events and actual experience to notify pre-defined monitors as the existence of an anomalous occurrence. Not all ascertainment bias is a result of a failure to speak up or overlooking the obvious. It can also result from a lack of aggregation of knowledge over time.

RESULTS

The Business Motivation model of the Object Management Group (OMG[1]), calls out initiation of any action because of internal or external influence. One pressing problem of business today is to identify acceptable or desirable behaviors as they apply to emergent situations. The key benefit of a quick turnaround in communication to senior managers of relevant new experience and efficiently returned direction is the mitigation of risk.

This is an attractive consequence of good knowledge management strategies, effectively implemented and used within an organization. The application of emergent strategy, defined as separate concerns in both requirements and software solutions, accessing named decisions and notifications as explicit aspects of either manual or automated processes, taken as a whole these represent the predicted-emergent pattern for knowledge management.

By beginning with what is known, and identifying suitable processes for dealing with any unknown event that arises (as opposed to trying to imagine them all), knowledge management sets the operational context for all business processes. Separation of decisions from processes yields the advantages of specialization. Decisions are not scattered and tangled in the process flows, they are called by name, and the parameters of the decisions can be changed to suit the environment of the day as it emerges. This yields the agility and responsiveness decision makers are looking for in their operations

SUMMARY

As this is merely a single chapter, the treatment of emergent strategy, aspect oriented software design, use case development, the rational unified process, pattern language, and decision modeling is necessarily spare. Nevertheless, building on these cornerstone concepts provides a solid basis for an adaptive knowledge management strategy.

As a discipline, knowledge management has a pivotal role in assisting practitioners when aligning operations with business goals and priorities. There are several key underpinning contributors to realizing that alignment.

Emergent strategy supports the definition of organizational plans in a way that does not rely on omniscience or having all required data in advance. Knowledge management can leverage emergent strategy by encapsulating processes, data and rules into decisions for what is known, and by handling exceptional events appropriately as they arise.

Business and design patterns offer a vocabulary and description of reusable practices that can be successfully applied in various settings. These patterns describe effective ways of partitioning the problem and solution domains, as well as the services that link them, into manageable pieces.

Agile and adaptive development methodologies use these patterns to support discovery and allow IT to address changes in requirements in a flexible and responsive way. Use cases are an effective way to collect and express both requirements and solution design, especially where well-understood scenarios are spelled out in detail, and others are relegated to a separate exception handling process, whether manual or automated.

The models and depictions of each concern consume, inform and extend the others. Taken as a whole, the integrated set of models represents an actual knowledgebase of an organization encompassing its operations in all their contexts. Explicit responsibility for creating and maintaining a catalog of these models is a key role for knowledge management practitioners and an effective way to provide value across the organization as a whole.

Aspect oriented software development capabilities enable IT resources to capture and collect data relevant to an identified set of concerns, as well as to automate business operations to the optimum extent and increase productivity through appropriate specialization.

The goal of this chapter was to introduce these approaches and to provide a context for evaluating knowledge acquisition and communication by better exploiting information systems resources. In a predicted-emergent sense, each of these initiatives within information and organizational management has developed from its own impetus. The constructs were predicted as academic exercises to address unexpected problems, and the modeling techniques have emerged in their current forms from actual practice and experience.

By taking stock of these capabilities and using them to more fully express business plans, processes, rules and decisions, knowledge management can take an active role in creating adaptive enterprises. It can be predicted that those who do, will emerge the better for it.

REFERENCES

Alexander, R. (2004). Aspect-oriented technology and software. *Software Quality Journal, 12*(2). doi:10.1023/B:SQJO.0000024109.11544.65

Chan, Y. E., Huff, S. L., & Copeland, D. G. (1998). Assessing realized information systems strategy. *Strategic Information Systems, 6*(4), 273–298. doi:10.1016/S0963-8687(97)00005-X

Dictionary.com. (n.d.). Pattern. In *Dictionary.com unabridged (v 1.1)*. Random House, Inc. Retrieved on June 11, 2007, from http://dictionary.reference.com/browse/pattern

Dijkstra, E. W. (1976). *A discipline of programming*. Prentice Hall. Henderson, J. C., & Venkatraman, N. (1992). Strategic alignment: A model for organizational transformation through information technology. In T. A. Kocham & M. Useem (Eds.), *Transforming organizations*. New York: Oxford University Press.

Hughes. (2006, February). *Journal of Usability, 1*(2), 76-90.

Janis, I. (1972). *Victims of GroupThink.* Houghton Mifflin.

Kiczales, G., Lamping, J., Mendhekar, A., Maeda, C., Lopes, C., Loingtier, J.-M., & Irwin, J. (1997). Aspect-oriented programming. *Proceedings of the European Conference on Object-Oriented Programming, 1241,* 220–242.

McDavid, D. W. (n.d.). A standard for business architecture. *IBM Systems Journal, 38*(1).

Mintzberg, H., & Waters, J. A. (1985). Of strategies, deliberate and emergent. *Strategic Management Journal, 6,* 257–272. doi:10.1002/smj.4250060306

National Association of State PIRGs. (2004). *Mistakes do happen.*

Object Management Group. (2008). *Business motivation model.* OMG document number formal/2008-08-02. Standard document. Retrieved from http://www.omg.org/spec/BMM/1.0/PDF

Ossher, H., & Tarr, P. (n.d.). Multi-dimensional separation of concerns and the hyperspace approach. IBM, T.J. Watson Research Center.

Royce, W. K. (1970, August). In *Proceedings of IEEE Wescon.*

Santa, R., Ferrer, M., & Pun, D. (2007). *Why do enterprise information systems fail to match the reality?* USA: ISRST.

Von Halle, B., et al. (2009). In Auerbach (Ed.), *The decision model.*

Wernerfelt, B. (1984). A resource-based view of the firm. *Strategic Management Journal, 5*(2), 171–180. doi:10.1002/smj.4250050207

Worden (2009). Making the case for the physical decision. In Auerbach (Ed.), *The decision model.*

[1] OMG has been an international, open membership, not-for-profit computer industry consortium since 1989.f

Section 2
Knowledge Management Audit

Chapter 4
KARMA:
Knowledge Assessment Review and Management Audit

Meir Russ
University of Wisconsin - Green Bay, USA

Robert Fineman
Independent Consultant, USA

Jeannette K. Jones
American Intercontinental University, USA

ABSTRACT

Companies tend to start their knowledge management initiatives with a knowledge management audit. A framework used for developing this specific audit, as well as some issues encountered while utilizing the audit, are illustrated. A number of benefits and weaknesses are also identified. Finally, a detailed, open-ended audit tool is introduced, knowledge assessment review and management audit-KARMA.

INTRODUCTION

Throughout our journey in the area of Knowledge Management, we found that very often companies had no clue what kind or types of knowledge they had and what they were lacking. Take for example, a merger of two companies that ended poorly for one line of business. Mergers are very tricky because the process forces the combination of multiple entities. It is relatively easy to combine financial systems and reporting because of the commonality in accounting practice. Since there is no commonality in addressing knowledge issues, assumptions are made. There are

many well documented cases of mergers where one line of business fails or the expected synergies do not meet the initial expectations. In one example the authors are familiar with, cost savings and areas to be kept or discarded were identified. One area that was being kept by the merged company included a $2 million line of business. There was only one person who possessed the tacit knowledge to make the process complete (the People aspect of the triangle discussed earlier in chapter 1). Unfortunately, that individual was let go in the merger process and when he walked out the door, the $2 million line of business walked out with him.

This may be an extreme example, but how many times has a knowledgeable or seemingly

DOI: 10.4018/978-1-60566-348-7.ch004

not-too-knowledgeable employee left an area and presented management with a knowledge void that they never knew existed? How many stories have you heard about someone leaving only to finally be replaced by more than one individual? It's not because the workload for the position increased; it's because the knowledge gap between the new people and the replaced person has a direct impact on productivity. What we call the learning curve, in many instances, is really the process of re-creating all the knowledge that was possessed and never passed on by the person leaving. In these cases, organizations are continually re-inventing the wheel.

This chapter will provide an in-depth discussion of an auditing tool. There are three major aspects of the tool that will be discussed in this chapter. The first will be customization of the tool. In order for KARMA (our audit tool) to be successful, it must be customized to meet the needs of the organization. Here we plan to discuss how the customization will work. For example, a manufacturing business will be different from a service business and the questions of the audit will have to be adjusted to accommodate the type of organization. When we talk about the product/services, for the manufacturing company, the product identification will be relatively straight forward. For the service company, on the other hand, the definition of their service offering might be more complex and difficult to define. Or we might assume there will be more constraints if we are dealing with a defense contractor vs. a financial service company. Not that there aren't secrets in both companies, but the perceptions will be different. We identified early in the process that a good, solid audit was (and still is) a very powerful tool for helping organizations get into the journey of KM. The framework discussed in this chapter has evolved and has been fine-tuned over time and with actual use. Through implementation of audits, we have discovered that a cookie cutter, comprehensive audit approach is not practical. Why? Remember that knowledge is context specific. This means a comprehensive audit that is right for one company might not be appropriate for another company, even within the same industry, at the same point in time. Why? The two companies will probably have different strategies, goals, and game plans. Even for the same company at different points in time, there will be a need for some modification. Again, changes in their strategy, changes in customer needs, etc., will probably force the company to modify its questions.

We also found that there is an interesting dilemma organizations face when dealing with the type of audit they want to conduct. We have found that the open ended questionnaire is a great tool when the company is open to the KM journey and understands the value of the audit. We, our clients, and students have conducted more than 150 audits, and the average time that is required for a high quality audit was more than 80 hours. So, yes, you get a high quality product, BUT there is need for a heavy investment. Our proposed tool is a recommendation. You are encouraged to add, eliminate, or modify the discovery questions to align with your specific needs. The more specific the tool and the better it is tailored to your situation, the more valuable it becomes. But there is more to the audit than just finding where you are in the KM journey. We have found the audit to be an excellent context for beginning to understand some of the concepts we want the key players to understand, absorb and utilize. One area in which this has proved valuable concerns the codification of tacit knowledge. When we talked with one company about the strategic dilemma of codification versus tacit the concepts were clear but their KM team was not able to work with these concepts. At some point, they decided to develop product pages to support their newly recruited sales people. Then they had to go back, and verify what knowledge they had about their products, who had, and who owned that knowledge. In order to do that, they had to develop the process of codification, validation, etc. of that knowledge. They had just started the audit process in one specific area of their company, BUT, the concepts and the dilemmas had become clear in their minds.

Another issue is the knowledge gaps you might have which you might not expect to find. These gaps are another reason why we prefer the open ended qualitative tool. This tool approach also points to another sensitive issue in regard to the open ended version: Who is conducting the audit? If you are not looking for gaps, you will not find them. The assumptions that you have going into the audit, will be, in all probability, validated. On the other hand, if you are willing to leave your assumptions at the door, and be open to gaps, you might be able to find them. In many cases, this is asking the impossible from an internal auditor, which is why companies often have external auditors and auditing.

KARMA enables validation of underlying assumptions about the knowledge an organization has and where that knowledge is located. It also uncovers areas of knowledge that management never knew existed (perhaps an insight that allows entry into a new line of business or the exploitation of a niche in an existing line of business). It is important to acknowledge these assumptions because they are usually anecdotal and not based on factual or empirical data. Therefore, decisions made as a result of assumptions can produce inconsistent, unpredictable, or disastrous results. How many projects have you seen delayed or discarded for no apparent reason? We speculate that a majority of these projects were based on assumptions that had little or no factual basis. KARMA strips out assumptions and biases and gets as close to empirical issues as possible, although we admit that human nature won't allow us to get to the level of 100% objectivity.

AUDIT'S WEAKNESS AND BENEFITS

As stated above, we cannot completely remove bias, and because of that, there are certain inherent weaknesses and risks within the Audit process. We have identified two types of risks to be recognized and considered. If the organization starts with the end in mind or predicts where they want to be in the future, that will bias the audit. Conversely, if the organization uses the audit to define the correct path, the end result will also be biased. You may have a mandate from top management that forces you to predict where you want to be, perhaps the provider of specialized software within a specific manufacturing technology. This will bias the audit and will require analysis of the results to ensure that other avenues are not closed out. You may find that your assumed knowledge base in that niche is much less than you imagined. Now you have the problem of trying to fill the knowledge gap in an area where you don't have expertise. It's not impossible and we have developed tools to deal with those instances, but KARMA may tell you that you are much better aligned to provide the processes that go into building the technology rather than providing the software to make it run. On the other hand, if you don't know where you want to go, the process may take you in many directions that don't provide a clear guidance for strategic planning. Again, we have developed tools that can take you through that process as well (see our discussion in chapters 7 and 9 in this book).

These weaknesses in KARMA can be mitigated by utilizing an independent third party to conduct the audit. This comment may cause some, especially those in the audit community, to take exception, but this observation is not meant to create any bad feelings. On the contrary, we believe this is a flaw that can only be corrected as more knowledge audits are performed. Since there is no external regulatory body to oversee the audit process, or a standard set of guiding principals, such as GAAP, any internal audit could potentially be biased based on cultural norms within the organization. The exception to this is if there is an individual within the organization who has the insight and political power (CIO or CEO) to drive the independence of the process. The inherent weakness in KARMA is based on the assumption that an organization will perform the audit internally. Think of your knowledge audit as being on an equal footing with your financial audits. The Enron's and Tyco's have put a spotlight on reliable third party oversight in the financial arena. We suggest using an independent third party to customize the audit and interpret the final results in the knowledge arena as well.

KARMA was designed to allow you to describe your organization from a knowledge point of view. It can tell you if your strategic plans have been consistent with your available assets. It can even go further and pinpoint the areas where your knowledge base is lacking. It can affirm a decision to move your business in a specific direction or it can let you know that you have potentially made a serious mistake. Bill Gates did this intuitively when he changed the direction of Microsoft in the early 1990's from a company that provided operating system software into a company that provides software solutions for the emerging Internet economy[1]. This was a huge gamble for Microsoft but management inherently understood the strategic direction of the business environment. Since there was little or no knowledge base for the technology that had to be developed, the decision was to either become a leader or follow the pack. KARMA would have shown a huge gap in the knowledge possessed and the knowledge needed. This is somewhat analogous to President Kennedy's directive in the early 1960's to put a man on the moon. A vision and direction were put in place and People, Processes, and Systems were used to create the Knowledge necessary to fulfill that vision.

This chapter will go into the specifics of KARMA but it is useful to understand the benefits of the audit and what it provides. KARMA identifies knowledge assets, both internal and external.

When we discuss knowledge assets, we are talking about People, Processes, and Systems. KARMA breaks down those elements into knowledge areas. You can't ask a system or process what they know, but by talking with the people involved, you can determine where your knowledge assets reside. However, the knowledge auditor must dig deeper into the systems and processes to determine if the knowledge embedded in the system or process is available and how that knowledge is codified. Phil may have designed the system and Mary may have implemented the process. Joe and Amy are the people who run the system. KARMA will identify the possessors of the knowledge. Perhaps Joe and Amy don't have to possess any knowledge because it's embedded in the system and process. Perhaps Joe and Amy are essential because only they possess the knowledge required to run things properly. Perhaps Phil built something into the system that is dependent on the process flow. If you don't know where the knowledge resides, when reconstruction or deconstruction of the process is required, the process will take longer and be more costly. One additional item you can't forget about is your customers. In the example above, we didn't bother looking at the downstream users of the process. They can tell you a lot about what you are doing and how well. KARMA gives you the means to listen to them. The bottom line is that KARMA will allow you to identify where the knowledge resides so when a crisis arises, you can quickly and effectively take the appropriate action.

KARMA also helps you to quantify your knowledge assets and allows you to determine what your assets are worth. There is a story about a company that brought back an engineer from retirement because they had a problem that no one could fix. The engineer walked around the plant and looked and listened to all the machinery. Finally, after a couple of days of tinkering, he took a piece of chalk and put an "X" on the panel of one of the machines. He told the management team that the problem could be solved by fixing the components of the machine where he put the "X". He also presented them with a bill for $10,001. When asked why his bill was so much, the engineer explained that the "X" was worth $1.00, however knowing where to put the "X" was worth $10,000.

KARMA also provides a baseline to track internal and external sources of knowledge with respect to current strategies and actions of the knowledge base. Perhaps its most important benefit is providing a framework to obtain a consensus of opinion regarding the current knowledge management system within your organization and its relationship to business strategy. This allows you to provide all interested parties with an understanding of the knowledge assumptions your organization has made as well as the knowledge assets your organization possesses.

AUDIT FRAMEWORK

While developing the framework for the audit we used a number of tools and ideas found in KM and/or other strategic areas. One widely used tool is the 6 Ws [2], or the 6 Knowledge Ws [3]. Another framework is the life cycle, or in our case the Knowledge Life Cycle (KLC) [4]. The combination of the two tools results in a six by six table (see Figure 1) that allows us to ask many questions. The discussion below will illustrate some of the issues the auditors (or their customers) will face when designing an audit.

An additional tool that can be used is the Constituency (or stakeholders) Analysis [5] which is context dependent. An example of the use of this tool is also illustrated below. The focus of the analysis will shift based on the nature of the entity. Therefore, the following discussion will focus on the questions that frame the answers rather than the specific answers and what they may mean.

Knowledge Creation and What Do You Know?

This aspect of the analysis focuses on the knowledge the entity creates and what they actually know. It must be remembered that creating knowledge and possessing knowledge are two very different things. Knowledge creation is an active process while maintaining possessed knowledge is a relatively passive process. Here you are looking to analyze how created knowledge is maintained within the entities so all the stakeholders are aware of what knowledge has been created and also what knowledge is possessed. As we analyze this aspect, we will focus on customers, suppliers, and competitors. Of these three, the competitor component is unique because there are three sub-divisions which we will discuss. The three subdivisions are known, unknown, and specialized. Known competitors are those that have a relationship with your customers and have the same or similar goods and/or services to sell. Unknown competitors are entities that are "under the radar", start-up entities, or existing

Figure 1. The six knowledge Ws and the knowledge life cycle

	Create	Organize	Formalize	Distribute	Apply	Evolve
Know what						
Know how						
Know where						
Know when						
Know who						
Know why						

non-competitors who are looking to enter the market with the same or similar goods and/or services. Specialized competitors could be any of the two previously mentioned but with a focus that will allow them to differentiate themselves from other suppliers in the market. This could take the form of new technology, an innovative process, or even an un-exploited niche that, once established, can be used as leverage to create additional market share.

Knowledge Creation and What Do You Know (Using Constituency Analysis)?

Customers create knowledge like any other entity but the focus from the Customer-Supplier perspective is usually narrowly defined. Your customers are, for the most part, concerned with what they 'know' about you. What is your product or service? How is it different (better or worse) than any other supplier? Are orders filled in a timely manner? Are the quality standards acceptable? Etc. It is fair to say that customers want suppliers to have products and services available when needed. As an integral part of the supply chain hierarchy, it becomes incumbent upon the customer to broaden their perspective to not only include the supplier in the knowledge creation process, but to partner with the supplier to allow the relationship to maintain or enhance the knowledge sharing process. For example, if the customer requires new products or services, there must be an exchange of knowledge so both parties can plan accordingly. It is also important for the supplier to transfer knowledge to the customer as changes are made so the customer can adapt, if necessary.

It is imperative that the knowledge creation aspects of the Customer-Supplier relationship be maintained at a level where each entity has a firm understanding of the other's needs and abilities. A customer change from one product or service to another may exclude a supplier or group of suppliers because they were not brought into the process and have not had the time to create the knowledge needed to provide the new product or service. From a strategic perspective, this has far reaching implications because long term strategic goals between customers and suppliers may not be consistent with the knowledge created or needed to create the specific product or service deemed necessary by the other entity.

Sharing this strategic knowledge will allow each entity to determine early in the process whether creating the knowledge required will fit into their strategic plan or not. This gives the customer adequate time to secure a supplier with similar strategic goals and it gives the supplier time to either exit the market for that particular product or service or re-tool for another product or service that is consistent with their strategic goals.

Suppliers look at this aspect from the perspective of meeting the customer's needs. Therefore, it is incumbent on the supplier to create knowledge at levels consistent with the strategic goals of the customer. It can be argued that the supplier must exceed the knowledge of the customer and lead the customer based on the customer's strategic goals. Although this is the most advantageous approach, it is also the most difficult and requires both an intimate relationship with the customer and creation of knowledge that is powerful enough to be complementary to their strategic goals. If the goal of the supplier is to maintain the status quo with the customer, they must be in a position that will allow them to create the knowledge required to maintain an equal footing with the customer and utilize that knowledge to make adjustments in their products or services to satisfy customer needs. See more about KM in supply chains in chapter 18.

The competitor situation creates different issues because there is less cooperation between competitors. Much of what you know about a competitor is based on external data. It is difficult, if not impossible, to know how competitors create knowledge. However, it is possible to gain some insight based on what you know about the competition in general. In this example, the competitor is known. They are in a similar line of business and provide similar products and services. What you know about them comes from the knowledge you created based on an understanding of the industry, feedback received from the same or similar customers, as well as the process of providing products and services. Unless some unforeseen event occurs, you know that this competitor has knowledge that is probably consistent with yours and will maintain that level of knowledge. If you both are providing a commodity type product or service, there is good reason to believe that levels of service will remain consistent. If four suppliers have been providing all the needs of a customer for the last ten years with little change in the percentages for each supplier, you know the needs of the customer are static and the volumes you produce for the customer will remain static.

When the competitor is an unknown, the knowledge they possess is unknown although a base knowledge requirement can be inferred because they are in a similar line of business. We will exclude the start-up companies from the .com era as they were special cases that require specialized analysis. Since you have no understanding of their knowledge creation process, you cannot determine what they know or how they know it. However, since all entities have a certain amount of exposure, you can leverage the industry knowledge required for entry into the business along with the background of the key players in the organization to begin the knowledge creation process. Until a product or service is provided, there is nothing to be done. However, once the product or service is public, a reverse engineering process specific to knowledge can be started to determine the level of knowledge the competitor possesses. Since this example is dealing with commodity providers, the product or service can be analyzed by price, quality, time to market, and additional factors specific to the industry. Once known, strategies can be developed to deal with the new competition. However, it must be noted that although you do not have much knowledge

about an unknown competitor, they will have a great deal of knowledge about your organization and other known competitors in the specified line of business.

Specialized competitors are another potential risk that must be analyzed because they can be known competitors developing an innovative process or an unknown entity ready to take market share based on factors new to the specific line of business. Perhaps it is a new manufacturing technique that reduces costs by 20% or a technological service that allows new products to come to market in weeks rather than months. These specialized entities have an extensive understanding of the entire supply chain hierarchy and are using that knowledge to exploit a niche in the current framework, obtain market share and create a new standard of competition, re-defining the landscape of the industry.

Knowledge Creation and How Do They Know it?

How they know what they know is another aspect of the analysis that should be understood. It can be assumed that a customer knows what he knows as a means to stay in business. Customers can actively pursue knowledge and use that knowledge to set strategic goals or maintain or create a competitive advantage, or they can passively create knowledge as it is presented to them.

Actively pursuing knowledge allows an entity to have a multitude of sources for knowledge creation. This allows for a diversity of knowledge upon which to base any analysis and potential strategic planning opportunities. It is obvious that possessing more knowledge and possessing more diverse knowledge will allow for a more useable finished product. Passively creating knowledge may only supply one or two differing points of view where actively looking for knowledge will provide for a variety of points of view as well as subtle differences within those points of view. When the analysis is done, a limited number of inputs will provide a limited number of outputs and the quality of the outputs may be impacted by the quality of the input. Entire areas of analysis may be overlooked because the knowledge needed to understand them is missing.

It is essential to understand what method of knowledge pursuit a customer is using so you have an understanding of how they know what they know. Either method described above can be exploited to your advantage and can guide strategic direction. For customers who have limited knowledge inputs, maintaining the status quo seems to be the most advantageous strategic direction since they seem to be limited in how they approach innovative ideas. Conversely, those customers who are actively seeking knowledge inputs require specialized care to ensure you provide a stream of data that can be used by them for knowledge creation. Used wisely, the inputs given to the customer can be consistent with the strategic goals of your organization.

How suppliers know what they know can also be a useful tool in understanding the environment you are dealing with. Suppliers are in the position where they must know what the customer wants. A supplier that wishes to attain and maintain a competitive advantage is also attempting to understand what the customer will need in the future, even if the customer itself does not know. Therefore, the supplier has a number of options to obtain knowledge, from reactive to proactive. How the acquisition of knowledge is obtained can tell you many things about the supplier and the foundation of the relationship structure. If your supplier is constantly seeking to understand your strategic direction, sharing marketing and economic data, and actively searching for ways to incorporate innovative ideas and technologies into their delivery stream, that indicates that they are an active participant in the knowledge creation process and are taking a proactive approach to knowledge creation. An alternative is the supplier who is only looking to stay a few steps ahead of the delivery cycle. Both of these approaches and all the permutations in between are valid but they

must be balanced with your strategic objectives. If your strategy is to maintain the status quo, it does not require an innovative supplier.

The aspect of how competitors know what they know can be directly related to their actions. Again, there can be competitors anywhere on the passive to aggressive scale. The interesting part of this analysis is not only understanding how they know what they know, but also how they utilize that knowledge. This aspect exemplifies the complexity of the analysis and the fact that one aspect of the equation might be more important than others. A competitor may be aggressive in their acquisition of knowledge but they may not be an aggressive competitor because they have determined that the customer base does not reward that type of behavior. Strategically they may be looking to exit the business or they have determined that the cost of acquiring the knowledge cannot be offset by either long term or short term gains. Just because there is an understanding of how knowledge is acquired does not necessarily give you an understanding of how it will be utilized.

Knowledge Creation and Where is the Knowledge?

Although it may not be apparent at first, an understanding of where knowledge resides may be one of the primary factors in the Customer-Supplier-Competitor relationship. Possessors of knowledge are key players in the equation and it is critical to understand where knowledge dwells not only within your organization, but everywhere within the Customer-Supplier-Competitor relationship. The reason resides in the practical usage of knowledge and it must be remembered that every entity uses knowledge differently. Therefore, understanding where knowledge resides can give you insight as to the structure of an organization as well as lay the foundation to understand how that organization utilizes knowledge strategically.

There are strategic and competitive advantages to be gained from such knowledge as well. If your organization is aware of where specific knowledge resides within a competitor's/supplier's/customer's organization and the competitor/supplier is not aware that the knowledge only resides in a particular area, that piece of knowledge can be leveraged into a meaningful competitive advantage. We see this happen when organizations are unwittingly forced to battle internally because the knowledge base is unknown or structured in such a way that it allows for exploitation by third parties. This can also work as a disadvantage to your organization and as such it is imperative that this knowledge be recognized and understood. Organizationally, an entity may be satisfied with this type of exposure. However, it must be aware that there are advantages and disadvantages that have to be factored into their strategic knowledge equation.

Organizations utilize knowledge in different ways and part of that process is developing an internal structure to understand where knowledge resides. For example, when knowledge is created based on data provided, the provider can track the knowledge to see how it is disseminated within another entity within the organization. If the knowledge stays at the creation point, the organization either does not value a knowledge sharing environment or it is compartmentalized to the point where knowledge does not flow freely between organizational silos. If the company in question is a supplier this might be a clue that the supply chain cannot react quickly to market pressures and therefore has questionable long-term value. However, the silo approach may also become the supplier's competitive advantage because there is no need to internally transfer knowledge to the rest of the organization and this allows the area that controls the knowledge to strategically restructure itself faster than an alternative organizational structure would allow.

As you can see, this understanding can only provide a glimpse of how an organization reacts and is structured. This is one piece of a complex model that provides insight into how organizations react to events as they arise. It is also important to understand the type of business and the changes within the business model that impact the knowledge tracking process. For example, the PC business was initially a high-tech, specialized business that focused on providing computing power to satisfy business, educational and home based applications. Part of that model was software distribution and we still see that with the Apple/PC wars for the home buyer. But that is only an offshoot of the change in the industry from a high-tech industry to a supplier of a commodity. Within the entire supply chain, organizations must be aware of the changes in business that impact the need to understand where knowledge is located. In this example, it was imperative to understand where organizations held their knowledge in order to exploit their competitive advantage although in today's world of commodity PCs, those implications are inconsequential, at least until the next technological breakthrough is discovered and gives at least one provider a potential competitive advantage[6].

Tracking where knowledge goes, and finally where it resides, can also provide insight into the supply chain matrix. Although this seems simple, it is more complex than simply tracking the location of a package. Tracking knowledge assumes that there is a solid understanding of what is being tracked and to a lesser extent it requires a general understanding of the organizational structure within which it is being tracked. Understanding what knowledge is being tracked has potential problems because as knowledge is assimilated it can be modified to suit the needs of the culture of the receiving organization. Therefore, tracking the flow of knowledge must include the insight to be able to adjust to the knowledge modification process and still allow for tracking its core components.

Knowledge Creation and When is the Knowledge Used?

It seems obvious that knowledge will be used when there is a need, but that is not always the case. How many companies have gone out of business because they kept doing the same thing year after year only to find that the knowledge they needed to stay competitive was never created within their organization? In a similar example, how many companies created knowledge and never used it because they didn't understand the signals the market was sending or the key decision makers didn't know the organization possessed the knowledge? Xerox created the first PC but never used that knowledge to bring the product to market. If they had exploited that knowledge, we would be looking at a very different business landscape today[7]. Therefore, it is imperative not only to create the knowledge, but also to be able to identify trends in the market that will allow exploitation of that knowledge. In the 1990's Microsoft transformed itself from a software company into an internet company[8] by being able to identify that the organizational knowledge had to shift direction and in many cases new knowledge had to be created in order to remain competitive.

As we look at competitors, the use of knowledge can be either a sledgehammer or a scalpel. Consideration of the strategic goals of an organization is of the utmost importance in order to leverage the most efficient use of the knowledge. It is also imperative to have a full understanding of the impact of the potential issues involving the use of knowledge. For example, your business is a supplier to a major manufacturing company and you and three competitors get 25% of the orders each for a particular product. If your company creates a process that allows you to cut prices by 30% you will gain a significant advantage over your competitors. However, when and if the knowledge is put into play is of critical importance and it must be considered from many different perspectives. By implementing the process, your organization can realize an immediate increase in profit against the 30% reduction in costs. By most measures, implementing that type of enhancement is a sound strategic move. However, one must be cognizant of the situation in the competitive market. If the process employed allows for a reduction in the workforce of 10%, what signal will layoffs send to the competition and the customer? Does a reduction in both price and staffing signal a reduction in quality or will this be rolled out with an indication, at least to your customer, that the new processes allowed this change to occur. Are your competitors working on similar processes and what is their strategic direction? It is important to remember that actions may be interpreted in many different ways and all possible interpretations must be factored into the rollout process.

Let's continue this example assuming that the process outlined above is in place, and your organization is forecasting an economic downturn in the future. By combining these two different pieces of knowledge, your organization may want to wait until both the customer and competition is feeling the effects of the downturn while internally your organization has been gearing up for additional production. By timing events correctly you will be able to reduce costs to the customer and increase market share. Although oversimplified to a certain extent, understanding when knowledge should be used can provide both short term and long term strategic advantages.

Some additional factors to consider include: What is the relative financial stability of the competition? If this knowledge is used and effectively eliminates one of your competitors, can your organization increase its production by 100% to meet the needs of the customer at the lower price? Are the barriers of entry high enough to make the risk of entering the market a poor investment relative to potential returns? Is the customer comfortable with a diversified supplier base and will the elimination of one or more of the suppliers raise red flags about the long term stability of remaining in that line of business. Is your organization supplying a commodity or a specialized product? As with any strategic decision, there are a great number of factors that must be considered and we propose that factoring knowledge into the equation will provide additional insights to the decision making process.

Of all the touch points relative to knowledge creation, understanding when knowledge is used has the most strategic consequences. It requires a familiarity with internal knowledge creation including what knowledge is possessed, how it got created, where it resides, who owns it, and why the organization has it. Assimilating this is a complex task, but to make the process as effective as possible, this understanding should also be compiled for competitors, suppliers and customers. Understanding your own organization is difficult enough, but adding others into the mix assumes that your organization has the capability to be strategically focused in the decision making process.

Knowledge Creation and Who Owns the Knowledge?

Although touched on above, owners of knowledge or knowledge possessors are a critical part of any organization. We look at knowledge possessors as individuals, groups, departments, or divisions, literally any individual or group of individuals. Organizational knowledge exists although the larger the entity that encapsulates the knowledge the more difficult it is to quantify and define. Consider the fact that Honda has the organizational knowledge to design and build an automobile engine but it would be almost impossible to point to specific individuals within the organization that possess specific pieces of that knowledge. From a knowledge perspective it would be impossible for a competitor to steal the knowledge that Honda has disbursed throughout the organization.[9] However, the type of knowledge ownership that resides at the enterprise level takes a number of years to develop and requires a strategic management vision to employ.

On a day-to-day basis we deal with, for the most part, individuals. It is difficult to conceptualize that the individuals you deal with are part of larger entities that own knowledge. If your immediate group of co-workers consists of five people, that group owns various pieces of knowledge. As knowledge is disbursed within the group, a number of different knowledge sub-sets are created and the utilization of those knowledge assets begins to come into play. Owning the knowledge is one thing but leveraging that knowledge is something quite different. All the knowledge in the world won't make any difference unless there is an internal mechanism within the organization that allows the knowledge to be utilized. Individuals, groups, and various other entities within the organization may use their knowledge but if the use of the knowledge is not consistent with strategic goals, the value of the knowledge decreases from an organizational perspective. Unused knowledge is similar to potential energy however the value of the knowledge can change over time. Like any asset, the potential for an increase in value must be weighed against the different ways knowledge is utilized to create a competitive advantage.

Once knowledge is created, it is owned either by an individual, group, or entity within the organization that can utilize that knowledge. The sales and marketing areas need knowledge that relates directly to the supply chain they are working with. In addition, they need knowledge regarding economic factors, competitors, suppliers, etc. A determination must be made within the organization as to who or what sub-entity within the group will own the knowledge. This situation is analogous to any other asset held by an organization. It must be remembered that the simple fact of understanding who owns the knowledge does not necessarily mean that it will be utilized, it only points to a repository. The factors involved in how the knowledge is utilized constitute another matter altogether.

If one looks to suppliers and customers, knowing the owners of the knowledge that is needed to enhance the business relationship is a crucial aspect of gaining an advantage. The most simplistic example is that any combination of the supplier/customer relationship depends on the supplier knowing what the customer needs. In other words, the supplier owns the knowledge regarding the delivery of the product. It may be a person or team, but there will be a point of contact. This point of contact will inform you of what materials (products) will need to be supplied as well as when they will be delivered. Conversely, the customer must own similar knowledge about the supplier and own the knowledge relative to price, quantity available, etc. As you can see, even in a simple supplier/customer relationship there are complexities that can make the issue more intricate than it may appear. As the relationship between organizations evolves and becomes more and more complex, the knowledge ownership question can become very convoluted.

Mergers fail for a variety of reasons and it can be argued that knowledge ownership plays an important part in the success or failure of any merger/acquisition. One of the reasons mergers/acquisitions occur is because one entity owns knowledge desired by another. If the buying entity understands that the owners of the knowledge are the real assets purchased, there is a greater chance for success than if the knowledge is valued less than the product or service created by the knowledge owners.

Knowledge Creation and Why is the Knowledge Utilized?

Why knowledge is utilized has a rather simple answer. Why the *specific* knowledge is utilized is a much more complex question. Remember, in chapter 1 we said that knowledge is context specific, so which knowledge you use is of crucial importance. Since in many cases we frame the questions in terms of the answers we have, in many cases we use the knowledge we have, not the knowledge that needs to be used. In chapter

9 we illustrate this by suggesting that knowledge strategy should not be limited to the use of the available knowledge base the company has and that the company should have the option of using needed knowledge from the outside. This might be one reason why more and more companies are using external sources of new knowledge.

In a business situation, knowledge owners utilize knowledge in order to obtain an objective. It may be as complex as attempting to gain a strategic advantage over the competition or as simple as winning a contract to supply widgets. The underlying fundamental aspect of all knowledge utilization is to gain some objective. These may be simple or complex, easy or difficult, done over a number of years or completed in a matter of minutes. The essential item to remember is that the old adage, "Knowledge is Power," is true. However, understanding the aspects that lead to new knowledge utilization makes the knowledge more useful and therefore, *more* powerful.

Next, we will introduce our audit instrument.

KARMA

Following is the KARMA framework that we have found to be applicable for most of the organizations we have worked with:

Introduction
Environmental and Administrative
Expectations
Critical External Sources of Knowledge
Customers
Market Trends
Competitors
Suppliers
Critical Internal Sources of Competitive
    Knowledge
Organization's Products and Services
Core Competencies
Competitive Advantage

Value Adding Activities
Best Practices
Organization's Strategy
Organization's Goals
Knowledge Management Strategy (Explicit or
    Implicit)
Company Strategy/Knowledge
KM Strategic Issues
Levers of KM
KM Challenges
Culture
Knowledge Leadership
Knowledge Roles and Skills
Intellectual Capital
Knowledge Processes
Knowledge Mapping
Infrastructure
Security
Intellectual Property
Knowledge Projects/Initiatives
Summary
Methodology

The result of the audit is a database (or a benchmark) of the knowledge assets of an organization at a single point in time.

The following is the current version of the open ended KARMA. You will find below an introduction letter to the auditor as well as the list of the open ended questions. The next chapter is presented as a case study that will illustrate the use of KARMA as an audit tool for a not-for-profit organization.

KM AUDIT

Introduction Letter

This audit is designed to be a comprehensive tool for assessing where your organization is in regard to Knowledge Management. As such, you might find some redundancies in the audit. This was done by design.

While starting the audit you will be asked to define the entity you will be doing the audit for, as well as your expectations. The decision about which unit of analysis to do the audit for is seen as critical. You may want to consider the following aspects while thinking about the scope of the audit. The entity must be significant, large, and abundant enough to be considered as a unit for the audit, while not TOO complex and impossible to manage. You might want to reflect on the following as criteria:

a. Relatively clear organizational boundaries
b. Clear set of inputs and outputs
c. Relatively cohesive culture
d. Availability of required information sources

You will need to utilize a number of sources within and outside the entity and conducting an interview utilizing the open questionnaire provided is seen as critical. You will have to talk to a number of people about each issue for validity purposes. You also will have to utilize secondary resources, such as manuals, for the same purpose. You are encouraged to keep a log of your interactions during the audit. The last part of the audit will ask you to document your methodology.

The audit will start analyzing the use of knowledge between the entity and its external constituencies. This will be followed by understanding the value knowledge is creating within your entity. Next, specific aspects of Knowledge Management will be analyzed, concluding with your summary. Good luck ☺

1. Introduction

1.1 Describe briefly the entity and its environment.
1.2 Describe the expected benefits of the audit

2. Critical External Sources of Knowledge

2.1 Customers

2.1.1 Who are the key customers, segments?

2.1.2 What do we know about their current, future needs?

2.1.3 What data/information/knowledge do we have about the mentioned above?

2.1.4 Where is this data/information/knowledge stored?

2.1.5 Who is collecting, storing, managing, diffusing this data/information/knowledge?

2.1.6 How are we collecting, storing, managing, diffusing this data/information/knowledge?

2.1.7 Who are the users of this data/information/knowledge?

2.1.8 How, when, and where is this data/information/knowledge utilized?

2.1.9 What are the key knowledge issues?

2.2 Market Trends

2.2.1 What market trends, regulations, etc. are seen as critical to follow?

2.2.2 What data/information/knowledge do we have about the mentioned above?

2.2.3 Where is this data/information/knowledge stored?

2.2.4 Who is collecting, storing, managing, diffusing this data/information/knowledge?

2.2.5 How are we collecting, storing, managing, diffusing this data/information/knowledge?

2.2.6 Who are the users of this data/information/knowledge?

2.2.7 How, when, and where is this data/information/knowledge utilized?

2.2.8 What are the key knowledge issues?

2.3 Competitors

2.3.1 Who are the key competitors?

2.3.2 What do we know about their current and future strengths, weaknesses, and strategies?

2.3.3 What data/information/knowledge do we have about the mentioned above?

2.3.4 Where is this data/information/knowledge stored?

2.3.5 Who is collecting, storing, managing, diffusing this data/information/knowledge?

2.3.6 How are we collecting, storing, managing, diffusing this data/information/knowledge?

2.3.7 Who are the users of this data/information/knowledge?

2.3.8 How, when, and where is this data/information/knowledge utilized?

2.3.9 What are the key knowledge issues?

2.4 Suppliers

2.4.1 Who are the key suppliers?

2.4.2 What do we know about their current and future strengths, weaknesses, and strategies?

2.4.3 What data/information/knowledge do we have about the mentioned above?

2.4.4 Where is this data/information/knowledge stored?

2.4.5 Who is collecting, storing, managing, diffusing this data/information/knowledge?

2.4.6 How are we collecting, storing, managing, diffusing this data/information/knowledge?

2.4.7 Who are the users of this data/information/knowledge?

2.4.8 How, when, and where is this data/information/knowledge utilized?

2.4.9 What are the key knowledge issues?

3. Critical Internal Sources of Competitive Knowledge

3.1 Own product and/or services

   a.   Identify all products and services that are delivered by the entity that are considered important.

   b.   For each one, answer the following:

3.1.1 Identify the data/information/knowledge required for each one of the specific products/services for its successful development, management and delivery.

3.1.2 Who is collecting, storing, managing, diffusing this data/information/knowledge?

3.1.3 How are they collecting, storing, managing, diffusing this data/information/knowledge?

3.1.4 Where is this data/information/knowledge stored?

3.1.5 Who are the users of this data/information/knowledge?

3.1.6 How, when, and where is this data/information/knowledge utilized?

3.1.7 What are the key knowledge issues?

3.2 Core Competencies

    a.   Identify all core competencies of the entity.

    b.   For each one, answer the following:

3.2.1 Identify the data/information/knowledge required for each one of the specific core competencies for its successful development, management and implementation.

3.2.2 Who is collecting, storing, managing, diffusing this data/information/knowledge?

3.2.3 How are they collecting, storing, managing, diffusing this data/information/knowledge?

3.2.4 Where is this data/information/knowledge stored?

3.2.5 Who are the users of this data/information/knowledge?

3.2.6 How, when, and where is this data/information/knowledge utilized?

3.2.7 What are the key knowledge issues?

3.3 Competitive Advantage

    a.   Identify all competitive advantages that are considered critical for the entity. You can use the following list as examples:

Quality; Patents; Production flexibility; Research capabilities; Operation/cost; Advertisement/PR; Product development (variety, customer responsiveness, timeliness); Distribution/logistics; Price; Brand name; Sales force; etc.

    b.   For each one, answer the following:

3.3.1 Identify the data/information/knowledge required for each one of the specific competitive advantages for its successful development, management and implementation.

3.3.2 Who is collecting, storing, managing, diffusing this data/information/knowledge?

3.3.3 How are they collecting, storing, managing, diffusing this data/information/knowledge?

3.3.4 Where is this data/information/knowledge stored?

3.3.5 Who are the users of this data/information/knowledge?

3.3.6 How, when, and where is this data/information/knowledge utilized?

3.3.7 What are the key knowledge issues?

3.4 Value Adding Activities

    a.   Identify all critical value-adding activities for the entity. You can use the following list as examples:

Research; Development; Raw materials; Input processing; Intermediate processing (e.g. subassembly); Final processing, Marketing; Sales; Distribution; Customer service; IT; HR; etc.

    b.   For each one, answer the following:

3.4.1 Identify the data/information/knowledge required for each one of the specific value-adding activities for its successful development, management and implementation.

3.4.2 Who is collecting, storing, managing, diffusing this data/information/knowledge?

3.4.3 How are they collecting, storing, managing, diffusing this data/information/knowledge?

3.4.4 Where is this data/information/knowledge stored?

3.4.5 Who are the users of this data/information/knowledge?

3.4.6 How, when, and where is this data/information/knowledge utilized?

3.4.7 What are the key knowledge issues?

3.5 Best Practices

a. Identify all critical best practices for the entity.

b. For each one, answer the following:

3.5.1 Identify the data/information/knowledge required for each one of the specific best practices for its successful development, management and implementation.

3.5.2 Who is collecting, storing, managing, diffusing this data/information/knowledge?

3.5.3 How are they collecting, storing, managing, diffusing this data/information/knowledge?

3.5.4 Where is this data/information/knowledge stored?

3.5.5 Who are the users of this data/information/knowledge?

3.5.6 How, when, and where is this data/information/knowledge utilized?

3.5.7 What are the key knowledge issues?

3.6 Organization's Strategy

a. Identify the strategy of your organization.

b. Identify the relevant strategies of your entity that support the mentioned above.

c. For each one, answer the following:

3.6.1 Identify the data/information/knowledge required for each one of the specific strategies for its successful development, management and implementation.

3.6.2 Who is collecting, storing, managing, diffusing this data/information/knowledge?

3.6.3 How are they collecting, storing, managing, diffusing this data/information/knowledge?

3.6.4 Where is this data/information/knowledge stored?

3.6.5 Who are the users of this data/information/knowledge?

3.6.6 How, when and where is this data/information/knowledge utilized?

3.6.7 What are the key knowledge issues?

3.7 Organization's Goals

a. Identify the goals and Key Success Indicators (KSI) of your organization. Are they balanced?

b. Identify the goals and KSI of your entity that support the mentioned above. Are they balanced? Do they support those at 3.7.a?

c. For each one, answer the following:

3.7.1 Identify the data/information/knowledge required for each one of the goals and KSI for its successful development, management, implementation and measurement.

3.7.2 Who is collecting, storing, managing, diffusing this data/information/knowledge?

3.7.3 How are they collecting, storing, managing, diffusing this data/information/knowledge?

3.7.4 Where is this data/information/knowledge stored?

3.7.5 Who are the users of this data/information/knowledge?

3.7.6 How, when, and where is this data/information/knowledge utilized?

3.7.7 What are the key knowledge issues?

4. Knowledge Management Strategy

4.1 Company Strategy and Knowledge

4.1.1 Is your industry knowledge intense? In what areas?

4.1.2 What specific areas of knowledge are extremely important to your company? Why? To your organization/entity? Why?

4.1.3 What are (might be) your company's key benefits of active Knowledge Management? Which benefits are critical for your company's success?

4.1.4 What are (might be) your organization's/entity's key benefits of active Knowledge Management? Which benefits are critical for your organization's success?

4.2 Knowledge Management strategic issues
Identify and describe how your entity is:

4.2.1 Developing strategy to exploit new knowledge.

4.2.2 Leveraging knowledge at all levels.

4.2.3 Integrating knowledge from various areas.

4.2.4 Integrating Knowledge Management with the overall business plan of the company.

4.2.5 Improving knowledge of company goals at all levels.

4.2.6 Identify SWOT of knowledge areas.

4.3 Levers of Knowledge Management

Identify and describe the following:

4.3.1 Knowledge of people, processes and technology used currently as Core Competencies.

4.3.2 Knowledge of people, processes and technology to be used in the future as Core Competencies.

4.3.3 Knowledge of people, processes and technology used currently as Competitive Advantages.

4.3.4 Knowledge of people, processes and technology to be used in the future as Competitive Advantages.

4.3.5 Information Technology tools/platforms enhancing the organization's knowledge base.

4.3.6 Is the organization well organized to generate new knowledge? To share and diffuse existing knowledge?

4.3.7 Perceived value of:

4.3.7.1 Formal knowledge offices.

4.3.7.2 Organizational knowledge base.

4.3.7.3 Demonstrable knowledge leadership.

4.3.8 Are there formal knowledge offices? If yes, identify.

4.3.8.1 Are there good communication and working relations between knowledge offices and other offices?

4.3.8.2 Are knowledge offices able to plan profitability and effectiveness or only projects and expenses?

4.3.8.3 Is there a need for more training, motivation or evaluation for any of the knowledge offices/officers?

4.4 Knowledge Management Challenges

Identify and describe the:

4.4.1 Biggest obstacles/challenges in your organization to knowledge transfer; to acquisition of external knowledge.

4.4.2 Biggest obstacles/challenges in your organization to disseminate knowledge; to create new knowledge.

4.4.3 Culture of the organization as challenge/ supportive.

4.4.4 Measures of success as creating value/cost oriented.

4.4.5 Major risks in your organization to managing knowledge.

4.5 Culture

Identify and describe how your organization is:

4.5.1 Developing a sharing culture.

4.5.2 Developing and implementing appropriate behaviors.

4.5.3 Developing and implementing appropriate reward systems.

4.5.4 Supporting informal networks.

4.5.5 Developing a continuous learning environment.

4.6 Knowledge Leadership

4.6.1 Does your organization have an explicit vision for Knowledge Management? If yes, what is it?

4.6.2 What is the framework (if any) for the knowledge agenda?

4.6.3 Do people understand Knowledge Management?

4.6.4 Describe the commitment of your organization's top executives to Knowledge Management.

4.6.5 Identify the knowledge champions.

4.6.6 Do you have a knowledge team/s? If yes, describe.

4.7 Knowledge Roles and Skills

Identify and describe how your organization is (if any):

4.7.1 Developing and implementing new knowledge specific roles at the following levels:

4.7.1.1 Individual.

4.7.1.2 Team.

4.7.1.3 Organizational.

4.7.1.4 Inter-organizational.

4.7.2 Developing and implementing new knowledge specific skills at the following levels:

4.7.2.1 Individual.

4.7.2.2 Team.

4.7.2.3 Organizational.

4.7.2.4 Inter-organizational.

4.8 Intellectual Capital

4.8.1 Describe the ways your organization identifies/quantifies the value of knowledge.

4.8.2 Describe the ways your organization links knowledge to the bottom line.

4.8.3 Describe how your organization invests/allocates resources that increase its knowledge base in a measurable way.

4.9 Knowledge Processes

Describe the systematic approaches your organization has to:

4.9.1 Create new knowledge.

4.9.2 Acquire new knowledge.

4.9.3 Codify knowledge.

4.9.4 Warehouse knowledge.

4.9.5 Diffuse knowledge.

4.9.6 Measure knowledge.

4.9.7 Protect knowledge.

4.9.8 Exploit knowledge.

4.9.9 Disseminate knowledge.

4.9.10 Describe the use of Knowledge Management in your organization's decision making.

4.10 Knowledge Mapping

Identify and describe how your organization is:

4.10.1 Developing a classification for existing knowledge.

4.10.2 Developing a classification for desired knowledge.

4.10.3 Identifying and mapping knowledge gaps.

4.10.4 Identifying and mapping gaps in knowledge strategy.

4.10.5 Building knowledge repository.

4.11 Infrastructure

Identify and describe how your organization is:

4.11.1 Developing IT/IS/KBS systems to support knowledge management.

4.11.2 Developing IT/IS/KBS structures to support knowledge management.

4.11.3 Budgeting for KBS.

4.11.4 Allocating time for knowledge management.

4.12 Security

Identify and describe how your organization is:

4.12.1 Securing knowledge when restructuring/transferring personnel.

4.12.2 Securing knowledge when involved in alliances.

4.12.3 Securing knowledge when involved in Electronic Commerce.

4.13 Intellectual Property

Identify and describe how your organization is:

4.13.1 Identifying its Intellectual Property and its value.

   a.   Brand Name.

   b.   Reputation.

   c.   Trademarks.

   d.   Patents.

   e.   Copyrights.

   f.   Topography rights.

   g.   Rights in protectable data bases.

   h.   Regulatory approval and authorizations.

   i.   Trade secrets.

4.13.2 Managing the value (and the taxation) of its Intellectual Property.

   a.   Brand Name.

   b.   Reputation.

   c.   Trademarks.

   d.   Patents.

   e.   Copyrights.

   f.   Topography rights.

   g.   Rights in protectable data bases.

   h.   Regulatory approval and authorizations.

   i.   Trade secrets.

4.13.3 Protecting, managing the risk and insuring its Intellectual Property.

a. Brand Name.
b. Reputation.
c. Trademarks.
d. Patents.
e. Copyrights.
f. Topography rights.
g. Rights in protectable data bases.
h. Regulatory approval and authorizations.
i. Trade secrets.

5. Knowledge Projects/Initiatives

5.1 Describe current (if any) initiatives your organization is developing and/or implementing.

5.2 Identify the roles/positions currently leading those initiatives.

5.3 Describe the most difficult aspect of these projects.

5.4 How management is/will be assessing the outcomes of these projects.

5.5 What knowledge projects are planned for the near future?

5.6 What knowledge training efforts are planned for the near future?

6. Summary

6.1 Conclusions

6.1.1 The current stage of your organization's experience with knowledge management is?

6.1.2 The current status of knowledge management offices is?

6.1.3 The most valuable aspects for your organization, of knowledge management are?

6.1.4 The critical gaps in knowledge strategy are?

6.1.5 Other most important findings are?

6.2 Implications

Where and when should your organization go from here, in regards to:

6.2.1 Knowledge strategy.
6.2.2 Knowledge processes.
6.2.3 Knowledge value measures/Intellectual Capital.
6.2.4 Leadership/roles/skills.
6.2.5 Culture.
6.2.6 Infrastructure/KBS.
6.2.7 Resource allocation.
6.2.8 Intellectual Property.
6.2.9 Security.
6.2.10 Knowledge Initiatives.

6.3 What else did you learn? What other suggestions, proposals might you have?

6.4 What would you add or change in this audit?

7.0 Methodology

7.1 Define Scope
7.2 Resources used:
7.2.1 Interviews
7.2.2 Secondary sources
7.3 Vocabulary/dictionary

The following chapter (by Phillip Mattek) is an example of how the audit process can be used and will illustrate the potential value created by such a process.

ACKNOWLEDGMENT

The first author wishes to acknowledge the Frederick E. Baer Professorship in Business for partial financial support. The authors wish to thank Kelly Anklam for her assistance in editing this chapter.

REFERENCES

Bresnahan, T., Greenstein, S., & Henderson, R. (2006, October). *Making waves: The interplay between market incentives and organizational capabilities in the evolution of industries.* Paper presented at Harvard Business School Strategy Conference, Retrieved on June 25, 2009, from http://mba.tuck.dartmouth.edu/digital/Programs/ Seminars/HendersonPaper.pdf

Bryson, J. M. (2004). *Strategic planning for public and nonprofit organizations* (3rd ed.). San Francisco, CA: Jossey-Bass.

Chapman, C. B., & Ward, S. C. (2003). *Project risk management: Process, techniques, and insights* (2nd ed.). Chichester, UK: John Wiley and Sons.

Nissen, M., Kamel, M., & Sengupta, K. (2000). Integrated analysis and design of knowledge systems and processes. *Information Resources Management Journal, 13*(1), 24–43.

Prahalad, C. K. (1993). The role of core competencies in the corporation. *Research in Technology Management, 36*(6), 40–47.

Russ, M., Jones, J. G., & Jones, J. K. (2008). Knowledge-based strategies and systems: A systematic review. In M. Lytras, M. Russ, R. Maier & A. Naeve (Eds.), *Knowledge management strategies: A handbook of applied technologies* (pp. 1-62). Hershey, PA: IGI Global.

Schilling, M. (2002). Technology success and failure in winner takes all markets: The impact of learning orientation, timing, and network externalities. *Academy of Management Journal, 45*(2), 387–398. doi:10.2307/3069353

Smith, D. K., & Alexander, R. C. (1988). *Fumbling the future: How Xerox invented then ignored the first personal computer.* New York: William Morrow & Co.

Szu, H., Jenkins, J., Hsu, C., Goehl, S., Miao, L., Cader, M., & Benachenhou, D. (2009). Digging for knowledge. In H. Szu, J. Jenkins, C. Hsu, S. Goehl, L. Miao, M. Cader & D. Benachenhou (Eds.), *Independent component analyses, wavelets, neural networks, biosystems, and nanoengineering VII.* Proceedings of the SPIE (Volume 7343, pp. 734304-734304-17). Retrieved on May 19, 2009, from http://adsabs.harvard.edu/ abs/2009SPIE.7343E..26S

ENDNOTES

[1] See example at Bresnahan, Greenstein and Henderson. 2006.

[2] See for example the discussion of the 6 W's and some great examples of the use of this framework in Chapman and Ward (2003), ISBN: 0-470-85355-7.

[3] See for example" Digging for knowledge" by Szu, et al., 2009.

[4] Used by Russ and Jones, 2008, based on and slightly modified (definitions) from Nissen, Kamel and Sengupta (2000).

[5] See for example Bryson, 2004, pp.107-113, ISBN: 0-7879-6755-6.

[6] See example at Schilling, 2002.

[7] See example at Smith and Alexander, 1988.

[8] See endnote 1.

[9] See example at Prahalad, 1993.s

Chapter 5
The Green Bay Chamber of Commerce:
Foundation's Foundation

Philip Mattek
University of Wisconsin-Green Bay, USA

ABSTRACT

Knowledge management is many things to different people. Within complex organizations, this reality needs to be acknowledged. For an organization to utilize and enhance knowledge for competitive advantages, systems and culture need to be analyzed within the context of an organization's strategy. Once analyzed, an honest appraisal of the knowledge systems in place and those needed to fulfill the strategic goals of the organization will have to be performed. For everyone within an organization to be able to "pull in the same direction" and achieve maximum value from a knowledge management system, that system will have to mean the same thing to all. If a knowledge management system is to be central in maintaining a competitive advantage for organizations, it will engulf the organization. To understand financial systems, audits are undertaken to ensure that systems provide the information as expected. It is well understood that for financial information to be meaningful, it must be understood. To be understood, it must be logically prepared and presented in a manner useful and timely to the end user. Through an audit process of this nature performed on knowledge management systems within the context of business strategy and culture, an organization learns what is needed to get their divergent individuals on the same page, as it were, to fulfill the promise of enhancing its most valuable resource in a competitive world. This chapter examines how to systematically conduct a knowledge management audit. By design, the audit was simplified and designed around a single specific issue. By breaking apart where the organization needs to go and combining it with a study of what it will take to get there from a knowledge management systems standpoint, individuals can come together to build the framework literally from the ground up. Companies can use this framework to assess how they plan with knowledge management as the central, differentiating factor in their business strategy.

DOI: 10.4018/978-1-60566-348-7.ch005

BUSINESS ISSUE

The business world is increasingly global. Local ownership of companies is diminishing. With this comes the diminishing ability of local management to affect decisions made in a community. Many local foundations rely on the generosity of companies located in their areas for funding their missions. This isn't as easy as it used to be. In today's business world, it may take months for a decision of any funding request. Getting a decision to fund a foundation request is usually a matter of personal contact. This is all the more difficult in the absence of local ownership. Turnover at either the foundation or corporate level adds to the complexity of maintaining personal contact information. Foundations can be funded from many different parts within an organization. Some companies have foundations of their own which support other foundation activities. Others rely on internal public affairs or relations budgets. Others support foundation activities through marketing departments. Identifying and keeping track of these avenues and leveraging this knowledge to increase funding is also complex. The business issue for foundations is to identify ways to raise more money in this environment. They need to do it more efficiently and with fewer resources.

KNOWLEDGE MANAGEMENT AUDIT INTRODUCTION

The Green Bay Chamber of Commerce – Foundation was begun in 1982. It is broken down into two major programs. These are its economic development initiatives and its education and leadership initiatives. The majority of the funding needed to run these programs is raised primarily through private business contributions. For the Foundation to be able to fulfill its mission, these contributions not only must continue but increase.

This is increasingly becoming more difficult due to the business environment described above. Companies with local ownership and decision making capabilities are increasingly declining. The art of local networking for success is diminishing. With it is the ability to just "pass that knowledge along."

Currently there is no system in place that adequately addresses fundraising across the organization. This has created an information void in the Foundation's fundraising. More importantly, the knowledge that is currently being learned while individuals in these groups are fundraising is never recorded, analyzed and used to enhance the probability of future success. Many organizations fund both Foundation initiatives and are openly asking the programs to justify why that should be so. To make matters worse, competition for funds has increased with the introduction of New North – a regional entity with many of the same goals as the chamber's foundation programs.

Knowing there are issues and knowing what to do with them are usually two different things. Assuming that the chamber's Foundation can go forward in a "business as usual" manner will surely fail. Moving forward, however, should not be through happenstance. It is expected that a thorough analysis of the current ways of fundraising tied to current best practices will enable the organization to record, analyze and enhance its ability to raise valuable funding resources. Passing that knowledge throughout the organization will help ensure success moving forward in this ever-changing business environment. It is anticipated that the building blocks of data within the context of the Foundation will be used to create information which will allow staff to take fundraising action which will add value to the foundation. The following sections, A-E, are components of a staff audit of the foundation's knowledge management as it relates to the foundation. It is followed by a summary of findings.

A) Knowledge Types

Gottschalk (2002) gives us basic definitions of categories and levels of knowledge. They are supplied below.

- **Administrative Knowledge (p. 82):** Includes all the nuts and bolts information about firm operations, such as company policies, invoicing data, and system sign-on and use.

- **Declarative Knowledge (p. 82):** Includes specific knowledge of economic development, leadership and education professionals. This knowledge is acquired through educational opportunities in the specific area of interest. This is typically described as what people know and declarative knowledge is the starting point for procedural knowledge and any subsequent actions.

- **Procedural Knowledge (p. 82):** Is the "know how" of the individuals within the organization. Individuals use this knowledge to interact with their environment through action.

- **Analytical Knowledge (p. 82):** Results from analyzing declarative knowledge as it applies to a particular fact setting. As it relates to the Foundation, this knowledge should be applied to assist the interaction of the organization with its environment.

- **Core Knowledge (p. 81):** Is the basic knowledge required to stay in business. This type of knowledge can create efficiency barriers for entry of new competitors. The foundation must have this type of knowledge.

- **Advanced Knowledge (p. 81):** This knowledge makes the foundation competitively visible and active. It allows the foundation to differentiate itself from its competitors.

- **Innovative Knowledge (p. 81):** This is knowledge which allows the foundation to lead in a way that clearly differentiates it

from anybody else. From a fundraising perspective, this knowledge can clearly tie the foundation program's mission to the funding sources most appropriate. It can also identify new sources of competitive programming and the funding that will most likely result from the new programming.

Following are two knowledge matrixes of the foundation[1]. The first matrix (Table 1) represents the current situation of the organization and the second (Table 2) represents the desired state of where the organizational knowledge of fundraising should be.

Knowledge can be a funny thing within an organization. The Wissenmanagement Forum (2003) notes the unique role of organizational culture when it states

culture can be described as the declarative knowledge of an organization, since it provides the meaning and guidelines for behavior and thus forms the basis of all actions. Consequently, the organizational learning process follows comparable phases to its human counterpart, whereby any changes in structure can be seen as procedural learning and changes in culture as declarative learning in an organization (p. 14).

In effect, both procedural and declarative learning will always interact. The foundation must have trust, commitment internal communication, and commitment to the funding success of all programming as core cultural components. The Wissenmanagement Forum (2003) also stated that "from a strategic point of view, it would appear wise to build up the core knowledge an organization requires to remain competitive internally, and only draw supplementary knowledge from free markets" (p. 20). Understanding how core knowledge is tied to each program's mission and that mission's tie ultimately to funding, limited resources will need to be applied wisely and funneled directly towards areas that strengthen core knowledge.

Table 1. Knowledge management matrix (current situation)

Levels / Categories	Core Knowledge	Advanced Knowledge	Innovative Knowledge
Administrative Knowledge	Accounting Knowledge / E-Mail Knowledge / Member Partner Lookup / Microsoft Office Products (Word, Excel) / Sign-on for system work	Web Site Manipulation / Query Member Partner / Billing Preparation / Fundraising Preparation / Identification of Key Decision Maker in Funding Request	
Declarative Knowledge	Foundation IRS Status / Foundation Tax Reporting / Electronic Economic/Education/Leadership sources / Budgets/Minutes	Economic Statistics / DWD Statistics / US Census / Education Statistics / Leadership Statistics / Business Leaders / Government Leaders / Education/Leadership Leaders / "Value" of Funding	Community Solutions to Issues
Procedural Knowledge	Accounting Procedures / Database update and additions procedures / Bylaws of Foundation / Plan of Action	Governmental Budgeting / School/Education Law / Billing Timing / Fundraising Process with Volunteers	
Analytical Knowledge	Spreadsheets / Graphics / Flowcharting / Site Maping	Economic Interpretation / Education Interpretation / Education Achievement Statistics / Leadership Interpretation	Fact Book / Truancy Statistics / Workforce Preparedness

Table 2. Knowledge management matrix (desired situation)

Levels / Categories	Core Knowledge	Advanced Knowledge	Innovative Knowledge
Administrative Knowledge	Accounting Knowledge / E-Mail Knowledge / Member Partner Lookup / Microsoft Office Products (Word, Excel) / Sign-on for system work / *Office Automation / Electronic Case Entry*	Web Site Manipulation / Query Member Partner / Billing Preparation/ Billing Timing / Fundraising Preparation / Identification of Key Decision Maker in Funding Request / *Mobile Information*	*Funding Request Timing / Funding Source Identification w/in Targeted Organization / Shared Best Practices*
Declarative Knowledge	Foundation IRS Status / Foundation Tax Reporting / Electronic Economic/Education/Leadership sources / Budgets/Minutes / *Donations-Specific Data Base*	Economic Statistics / DWD Statistics / US Census / Education Statistics / Leadership Statistics / Business Leaders / Government Leaders / Education/Leadership Leaders / "Value" of Funding / *Customer Use Base*	Community Solutions to Issues / *Tie Back of Knowledge to Funding Source / (Corporate Hot Button) / Personnel Change Reporting Base*
Procedural Knowledge	Accounting Procedures / Database update and additions procedures / Bylaws of Foundation / Plan of Action / *Donations Planning System / Foundation Funding Request Standards*	Governmental Budgeting / School/Education Law / Fundraising Process with Volunteers / *Electronic Library of Corporate Head Offices*	*Work Flow System for Fundraising / Intuitive, Open Query Function of Systems / Knowledge Base Analysis of Funding Results*
Analytical Knowledge	Spreadsheets / Graphics / Flowcharting / Report Preparation / Presentation Preparation / Site Mapping / PowerPoint / *Query*	Economic Interpretation / Education Interpretation / Education Achievement Statistics / Leadership Interpretation / *Tie of Donor Type to Funding Option Selected*	Fact Book / Truancy Statistics / Workforce Preparedness / *New Donor Identification / Multi Data Source Query / Forecasting Fundraising Success*

B) Knowledge-Based-Systems

The foundation is in a unique situation where the groundwork for a knowledge-based-system has already begun. The organization recently updated both its information and communication technologies. These technologies offer valuable support for the foundation's current and desired knowledge management activities. Gottschalk (2000) discusses the different levels of knowledge management and breaks them down in a table between levels of knowledge and the tasks needed to achieve these levels. The levels of knowledge begin with any knowledge as simply an end-user tool, progress to knowing who know what, finding out what individuals know and finally using a system to find out what individuals think. The tasks of knowledge are to distribute, share, capture and ultimately apply it. From this table, it is estimated that the foundation's ability to utilize its IS/IT is somewhere close to the point of Capture Knowledge and What They Think. This is not the ultimate goal, however, as Knowledge Application in the fundraising activity is needed. Following are two tables showing the current desired IS/IT knowledge management matrix (Table 3) and the software supporting the current and desired IS/IT situation of the organization. (Table 4)

The hardware infrastructure of the organization has been set up for information sharing. Citrix software allows for the secure sharing of organizational data from any location. Technology should always be seen as something that enables staff to not only do its job, but record, share and use the data in ways to further create value within the organization. Since any knowledge management initiative should not be primarily technology driven, software should be applied to specific needs as resources are available. Human resources are critical and applying technology that nobody can use or has the ability to learn only makes the current situation worse. Because the foundation needs to focus on creating, organizing, integrating and transferring of knowledge, the focus of the technology tools needed should be content generation, formats and standards, document management, communication technologies in an e-learning environment.

C) Culture, etc.

The Green Bay Chamber of Commerce Foundation culture appears to be somewhat of a cross between a Power-Driven and Role-Driven culture. The attitude towards knowledge management is largely not formalized and is at best, departmentalized. Following is a list of questions and answers. (Table 5) (Table 6) (Table 7) The questions were developed by Russ et al. (2010a; see previous chapter) and help to explain the reasoning behind the culture comments above.

The chamber has functionally organized departments and any knowledge services are for all practices, project teams and staff. These are characteristics of a central KM strategy and that is borne out in the manner the organization has developed its IT structure – the current determinant of the organization's knowledge management.

D) Business Strategy, etc.

3.1 **Own products and/or services**
   a. Identify all products and services that are delivered by the entity that are considered important:
      - Economic Development Attraction/Retention (Table 8)
      - Business Incubation (Table 9)
      - Education/Corporate collaboration to address education issues affecting business and impacting economic development (Table 10)
      - Leadership Development: Teen through adult (Table 11)

From a fundraising perspective, it is clear that the customers and potential funders for all of the

Table 3. Knowledge management matrix IS/IT desired situation

Levels / Categories	Core Knowledge	Advanced Knowledge	Innovative Knowledge
Administrative Knowledge	Accounting System - 2 / E-Mail - 6 / Member Partner - 4 / Word Processing - 6 / Spreadsheets - 2 / Databases – 2 / Phone systems – 4	Internet - 5 / File Maintenance - 3	Information Merge- 2 / Communications Convergence – 2 / Electronic Billing-0
Declarative Knowledge	Electronic Census Sources -4 / Electronic Education Sources - 4 / Electronic Foundation Sources - 2	State/Local Economic Statistics Databases - 5 / DWD Statistics Databases - 4 / US Census Databases - 3 / Education Databases - 2 / Leadership Databases - 2 / Government Databases-1	E-Mail Newsletter -3 / Electronic Fact Book (Publishing)-3 / Web Site – 1 / On-Line Externalization-1 / Combination Categorization - 0
Procedural Knowledge	Accounting Procedures-6 / Database update and add / Procedures - 3 / Document Standards - 4 / Document Templates – 3 / Contribution Meta-Data Definition - 0	Electronic Contribution Follow-up/reminder-2 / Web Meeting-Schools-2 / Group E-Mail Maint.- 3 / Committee Management-2	On-Line Contributions – 0 / Web Site Updates-1
Analytical Knowledge	Corporate Statistics on Member Partner-2 / Pledge Source on Member Partner-2	Member Partner Contribution Tracking-2 / Database Tracking-2	Mission Tie to Funding Source-2 / Advanced Web Search-0 / Advance Database Query-1 / On-Line Internalization - 1

Extent of Usage Scale: 1=Low 6=High 0=Desired

Table 4. Knowledge management matrix for software supporting desired IS/IT situation

Levels / Categories	Core Knowledge	Advanced Knowledge	Innovative Knowledge
Administrative Knowledge	MAS90 - 6 / Microsoft Outlook - 6 / Member Partner - 3 / Microsoft Word - 4 / Microsoft Excel - 3 / Microsoft Access / Oaisys NetPhone – 2	Microsoft Internet Explorer – 4 / Windows Browser – 2 / Windows 2003 – 4 / DoubleCheck Spam/ / Virus Protection-3 / Symantic Antivirus/Backup - 6	Internet Explorer- 4 / Citrix – 5 / Adobe 8.1 - 4 / *PDA/Palm* / *Intranet* / *Visual FoxPro* / *Microsoft Netmeeting*
Declarative Knowledge	Member Partner - 2 / NCES Website-2 / USCensus GoSoftware-3 / NEA Website-2 / Microsoft Access-4	Internet Explorer – 6 / Search Engines - 6 / Member Partner Pledge Module-0 / http://www.foundationsearch.com / *Customer Use Base*	Microsoft FrontPage - 3 / SBA Web – 4 / BuildMyOwnSite.com - 2 / *SBA Survey*
Procedural Knowledge	Microsoft Word – 4 / Microsoft Outlook-6 / Document Templates – 3 / *Donations Planning System* / *Microsoft Office InfoPath*	Member Partner - 4 / Microsoft Word – 6 / Microsoft PowerPoint – 3 / Microsoft Outlook – 6 / *Electronic Library of Corporate Head Offices* / *Query Tool*	*Microsoft Office InfoPath* / *Open Query Function of Systems* / *Knowledge Base* / *Analysis Tool/Report Writer*
Analytical Knowledge	Microsoft Visio-1 / Microsoft PowerPoint - 4 / Adobe Writer Suite-4 / Microsoft Word-4 / *Query*	Member Partner Contribution Tracking-2 / Database Tracking-2 / Microsoft Exchange - 4 / NetPhone Chat-1 / Google-4 / *Query Tool/Report Writer*	Microsoft Access-2 / *Webmine* / *Matchmaker*

Italics denotes Desired Software or Software Capability

Table 5.

4.5 Culture: Identify and describe how your organization is:		
4.5.1	Developing a sharing culture	• Bi-weekly staff meetings • Bi-weekly leadership meetings • One Centralized system • Groupware – Member Partner • Shared hard drive space for file sharing – available to all staff • Web site and common publications • In-house Microsoft Exchange server • Sharing financial results
4.5.2	Developing and implementing appropriate behaviors	• Plan of Action • Strategic planning and reporting to boards • Bi-weekly leadership meetings to discuss behaviors and work towards solutions • Working on areas of trust This is an area where the foundation in particular struggles. Programs have multiple locations making this issue even more difficult. Development of appropriate behaviors is also difficult because the strategic alignment of outside partners to each of the foundation programs actually can clash.
4.5.3	Developing and implementing appropriate reward systems	• Mostly done on the basis of program funding success – making the trust issue paramount. • This system does not lend to the process of sharing data – quite the opposite, it leads to one of territory and "departmentalization"
4.5.4	Supporting informal networks	This is an area the organization works quite well with its infrastructure. It was designed to take from a central date source and assist the entire organization in the identification of its members and their overall support of the entire organization. Included in that data source is the company and personal information needed to assist in the fundraising process. It also works to assist in volunteer and committee management. These network supports can be either formal or informal and the communication with them is also set up to automatically be saved for future reference
4.5.5	Developing a continuous learning environment	Here is an issue that is hardly addressed internally for various cultural and financial reasons. Culturally, management hasn't been appraised of solutions which can be backed to fill the sharing and learning void. Also, the current culture has issues of trust, role power plays and lack of employee buy-in. The buy-in is particularly acute in areas where cutbacks have put a strain on personnel time to the point that any new learning is not viewed as that but rather additional work. Other financial issues in training or education dollars. Here, they compete with scarce programming dollars and usually lose out to the "community" good.

Table 6.

4.6 Knowledge Leadership		
4.6.1	Does your organization have an explicit vision for Knowledge Management? If yes, what is it?	No
4.6.2	What is the framework (if any) for the knowledge agenda?	The framework is basically the setup of the IT infrastructure. Be sure to be tied to the outside world and allow for the free-flow of information in and out.
4.6.3	Do people understand Knowledge Management?	Not to the extent of understanding how it could be of value organizationally. It is understood that there needs to be a departmental methodology of organizing data but to put that into the context of the entire organization and then to understand how it may be used to create value is not a point of consciousness for most of the staff.
4.6.4	Describe the commitment of your organization's top executives to Knowledge Management.	Top management understands the need for computer networking and for utilizing e-mail, the internet and current data sources for maintaining contact between departments and with the community at large. The role knowledge management could play has not been a topic for strategic discussion.
4.6.5	Identify the knowledge champions	Philip Mattek / Marilyn Heim / Sara Dodge / Cindy Gokey / Amy Mattek / Nan Nelson / Lori Lodes / Lisa Schmelzer
4.6.6	Do you have a knowledge team/s? If yes, describe.	There are no knowledge teams

Table 7.

4.7 Knowledge Roles and Skills Identify and describe how your organization is (if any):		
4.7.1	Developing and implementing new knowledge specific roles at the following levels:	
4.7.1.1	Individual	The organization recognizes the need for additional support in the foundation fundraising process. To that end, it has worked with support staff and the VP of Finance to work through training in: • Member Partner Training • Fundraising for foundation programs These programs and this additional knowledge will be used to supplement the tacit knowledge of the program managers.
4.7.1.2	Team	The organization currently does not have a knowledge team. An organizational leadership team and individual program teams substitute for the knowledge teams of the organization. This is a culture issue as the organization has previously run in this manner. A knowledge team for this project would be a new measure.
4.7.1.3	Organizational	Leadership meetings fit the culture but leave the knowledge developed as tacit. This project would take one aspect of the organization and attempt to codify the knowledge related to fundraising.
4.7.1.4	Inter-organizational	To accomplish the goal of being able to utilize outside data, a fundraising data repository would need to be created. Currently, there is no formal inter-organizational linkage or new learning in this regard.
4.7.2	Developing and implementing new knowledge specific skills at	
4.7.2.1	Individual	On an individual level, management encourages training where it seems there are specific needs. Currently this includes: • MMA Course • Member Partner training • Program specific training
4.7.2.2	Team	There is no team current team knowledge specific skill development occurring on a formal basis. Knowledge creation/brainstorming/data mining are done in staff meetings with new knowledge skills remaining in the tacit repository of the individual.
4.7.2.3	Organizational	N/A
4.7.2.4	Inter-organizational	Program managers' mark and note outside knowledge-specific skills either through the internet or e-mail. Knowledge repositories are not codified on an organizational level and again, this has been the culture of the organization to leave all knowledge at a program specific, tacit level.

programs listed above are potentially the same. This could be quite a complex mess to those who are actually funding the foundation. Why wouldn't one contribution be sufficient for all programming? In effect, this puts the programs in not only competition for funds with the rest of the community at large but with each other.

3.2 **Core Competencies:** Each of the foundation programs is incredibly complex and fairly well developed. Defining, organizing, implementing a program for and reporting on community needs in the areas identified in section 3.1 require multiple competencies. The scope of this audit is on the aspects directly relating to fundraising

and it is from that perspective which will drive the responses to follow.

a. Identify all core competencies of the entity.
   ▪ "Customer tracking" (Table 12)
   ▪ Volunteer and committee management. (Table 13)

The heart of the issue in fundraising occurs here. Something which should be a core competency is being left to chance in the mind of the individual. The knowledge would leave should the individual leave. Worse yet, even while employed, the organization is not taking advantage of the information available to actually analyze and expand fundraising in a systematic manner.

Table 8.

3.1.b Foundation Services – Economic Development Attraction/Retention		
3.1.1	Identify the data/information/knowledge required for their successful development, management and delivery	For this information you would need to understand the local business environment and all the players of local government. That data is stored in multiple locations and is developed by the governmental affairs department of the chamber, advance staff and outside experts. They must also be able to relay information to organizations and create "sales" packets of statistical data of the community and oftentimes compare it to a competing outside location.
3.1.2	Who is collecting, storing, managing, diffusing this data/information/knowledge	Advance staff – particularly Cindy and Barb – collect, store, manage and diffuse this information.
3.1.3	How are they collecting, storing, managing, diffusing, this data/information/knowledge	They post contacts onto a Lois data base and also use the internet and governmental websites to collect information. A sites and buildings data base is also maintained. The information is stored on the chamber's fileservers and on web-based programs. The data is usually compiled into reports and shared with the company, local elected officials or volunteers who actually help with the process. Currently, Advance is also doing an e-wire to investors and other strategic partners to point out the activity which is being done within the community.
3.1.4	Where is this data/information/knowledge stored	The knowledge is stored at the various sites listed above but primarily on the chamber's file servers
3.1.5	Who are the users of this data/information/knowledge	The users of this data are elected local officials, the companies requesting help in a location/relocation and also the companies who are being called on locally. Advance uses the data for fundraising as proof of the work being performed for the community.
3.1.6	How, when and where is this data/information/knowledge utilized	It is used for community reports, grant writing, municipal reporting. It is also used by companies who are looking to locate in the community. The retention committee uses it to help the companies they call on with issues that are uncovered on the retention call.
3.1.7	What are the key knowledge issues	Organizing the data into easily usable formats for fundraising. The data should point to successes for the community that are directly attributable to Advance and the foundation.

Table 9.

3.1.b Foundation Services – Business Incubation		
3.1.1	Identify the data/information/knowledge required for their successful development, management and delivery	The data/information/ and knowledge are primarily in the marketing and financial maintenance of a business incubator. They need to track new business startups, past tenant success and also work towards developing the current tenants. All this with a minimal budget and staff that still must effectively manage the facilities with multiple partners. Knowledge of the community is important along with networked resource contacts.
3.1.2	Who is collecting, storing, managing, diffusing this data/information/knowledge	Incubator staff – particularly Lori, Jen and Connie – collect, store, manage and diffuse this information.
3.1.3	How are they collecting, storing, managing, diffusing, this data/information/knowledge	The majority of the data is being stored in spreadsheets, data bases or word documents on the chamber's file servers. Also, outlook keeps the staff in constant contact with its network of experts and maintains a contact database for assisting in all facets of data/information/knowledge.
3.1.4	Where is this data/information/knowledge stored	The D/I/K is stored primarily on the chamber's file servers but also on local drives of the remote desktops at their site on the NWTC Campus.
3.1.5	Who are the users of this data/information/knowledge	The users of this data are elected local officials, the companies requesting help in incubation/business plan development. Advance uses the data for fundraising as proof of the work being performed for the community. The chamber's accounting function also used the data financial statement preparation.
3.1.6	How, when and where is this data/information/knowledge utilized	It is used for community reports, grant writing, municipal reporting. It is also used by companies who are looking to locate in the community. The retention committee uses it to help the companies they call on with issues that are uncovered on the retention call.
3.1.7	What are the key knowledge issues	Organizing the data into easily usable formats for fundraising. The data should point to successes for the communities that are directly attributable to Advance and the foundation. The community should also have a resource of incubation successes to assist new or aspiring entrepreneurs.

Table 10.

3.1.b Foundation Services – Education/Corporate collaboration to address education issues affecting business and impacting economic development		
3.1.1	Identify the data/information/knowledge required for their successful development, management and delivery	For this information you would need to understand the local education environment and all the players in local school districts. Of vital importance is the added component of linking educational issues to economic development outcomes. That data must be gleaned from multiple locations and is developed by the PIE staff, volunteers and outside experts. They must also be able to relay community and program information to outside stakeholders. There is also the technical issue of operating a youth apprenticeship program. This requires additional knowledge and information in human resources, personal taxation, insurance, employment law and payroll processing.
3.1.2	Who is collecting, storing, managing, diffusing this data/information/knowledge	PIE and Administration staff – particularly Nancy, Melinda, Amy, Lisa and Elizabeth – collect, store, manage and diffuse this information.
3.1.3	How are they collecting, storing, managing, diffusing, this data/information/knowledge	Staff uses multiple software programs for collecting, storing and diffusing their work. Much of the educational information comes from data housed outside of the chamber's computer information and is typically retrieved either through mail, e-mail, internet searches or direct contact with professionals. The information is stored on the chamber's fileservers and on web-based programs or in paper files for items that directly pertain to the youth apprentice students. The data is usually compiled into reports and shared with the companies, local elected officials, school district employees or volunteers who actually help with the process.
3.1.4	Where is this data/information/knowledge stored	The knowledge is stored at the various sites listed above but primarily on the chamber's file servers or in paper files.
3.1.5	Who are the users of this data/information/knowledge	The users of this data are elected local officials, school district employees and the companies who are funding the work being done. Also, other community stakeholders with interests in educational issues use this information. Students, parents, workforce coordinators are the primary users of the youth apprentice payroll data. Granting agencies also use the data as proof of grant dollars.
3.1.6	How, when and where is this data/information/knowledge utilized	It is used for community reports, grant writing, school district information, governmental reporting and community award programs. The PIE and chamber boards also use the information to ensure the ties to the overall mission of the chamber and the foundation.
3.1.7	What are the key knowledge issues	Organizing the data into easily usable formats for fundraising. The data should point to successes for the community that are directly attributable to PIE and the foundation.

3.3 **Competitive Advantage:** Each of the foundation programs is incredibly complex and fairly well developed. Defining, organizing, implementing a program for and reporting on community needs in the areas identified in section 3.1 require that somehow a competitive advantage is maintained. The scope of this audit is on the aspects directly relating to fundraising and it is from that perspective which will drive the responses to follow.

a. Identify all the competitive advantages that are considered critical for the entity.
- Organizational leadership. (Table 14)
- Community knowledge. (Table 15)

3.4 **Value-Adding Activities:** Each of the foundation programs is incredibly complex and fairly well developed. Defining, organizing, implementing a program for and reporting on community needs in the areas identified in section 3.1 require that somehow a value added activity can be shown. The scope of this audit is on the aspects directly relating to fundraising and it is from that perspective which will drive the responses to follow.

a. Identify all critical value-adding activities for the entity.
- Economic prosperity advocacy. (Table 16)
- Community resource hub. (Table 17)

Table 11.

3.1.b Foundation Services – Leadership Development		
3.1.1	Identify the data/information/knowledge required for their successful development, management and delivery	Must know leadership techniques and community areas for exposing potential leaders. Have to understand people and how leadership training is tied to personal and professional growth and success. Have to coordinate and remain in contact with many people who are not only in the current classes but who have been through the programs.
3.1.2	Who is collecting, storing, managing, diffusing this data/information/knowledge	Leadership staff – Jeanne, Brian and Rebecca.
3.1.3	How are they collecting, storing, managing, diffusing, this data/information/knowledge	Staff uses multiple software programs for collecting, storing and diffusing their work. Much of the leadershipl information comes from data housed outside of the chamber's computer information and is typically retrieved either through mail, e-mail, internet searches or direct contact with professionals. The information is stored on the chamber's fileservers and on web-based programs or in paper files for items that directly pertain to the individuals. The data is usually compiled into reports and shared with the companies, employees or volunteers who actually help with the process.
3.1.4	Where is this data/information/knowledge stored	The knowledge is stored at the various sites listed above but primarily on the chamber's file servers.
3.1.5	Who are the users of this data/information/ knowledge	The users of this data are individuals or companies requesting help in leadership training. The leadership programs use the data for fundraising as proof of the work being performed for these individuals and the community. Granting agencies also use the data as proof of work performed and results shown.
3.1.6	How, when and where is this data/information/ knowledge utilized	It is used for community reports, grant writing, school district information, governmental reporting and community award programs. The Leadership and chamber boards also use the information to ensure the ties to the overall mission of the chamber and the foundation.
3.1.7	What are the key knowledge issues	Organizing the data into easily usable formats for fundraising. The data should point to successes for the community that are directly attributable to Leadership and the foundation.

Table 12.

3.2.b Foundation Core Competency – Customer Tracking		
3.2.1	Identify the data/information/knowledge required for their successful development, management and delivery	The data and information needed in this core competency are primarily individual and company demographics and baseline information. To be really successful, this should also include an area for "motivation." Also, funding source department is needed to be tracked.
3.2.2	Who is collecting, storing, managing, diffusing this data/information/knowledge	While the organization provides a centralized data base for the tracking of this information called Member Partner, all staff are responsible for these tasks to varying success. Supplemental databases in Microsoft Access, Excel, Word and Outlook are also used by all staff.
3.2.3	How are they collecting, storing, managing, diffusing, this data/information/knowledge	Contacts are primarily recorded and stored in Microsoft Outlook. Accounting information is recorded on Member Partner and specialty reporting is prepared by support staff or program managers to supplement the others.
3.2.4	Where is this data/information/knowledge stored	The knowledge is stored in the various program files listed above but primarily on the chamber's file servers. Some information is stored on local pc hard drives as well.
3.2.5	Who are the users of this data/information/ knowledge	The primary users are staff responsible for securing the funding of the programs. This is usually the program manager. Finance and executive leadership also use the information. Volunteer committees also use the information stored when assisting with fundraising.
3.2.6	How, when and where is this data/information/ knowledge utilized	The data is used primarily to track payments and make new funding requests.
3.2.7	What are the key knowledge issues	The key knowledge issues are to analyze what is occurring to minimize internal competition and expand the source of funding to other donors in areas that benefit can be proved.

Table 13.

3.2.b Foundation Core Competency – Volunteer and Committee Tracking	
3.2.1	Identify the data/information/knowledge required for their successful development, management and delivery	The data and information needed in this core competency are primarily individual information at the company level. This requires demographics and baseline information on both. To be really successful, this should also include an area for "motivation." Also, personal contacts or "spheres of influence" should be known about the individuals working with foundation programs.
3.2.2	Who is collecting, storing, managing, diffusing this data/information/knowledge	While the organization provides a centralized data base for the tracking of this information called Member Partner, all staff are responsible for these tasks with varying levels if success. Supplemental databases in Microsoft Access, Excel, Word and Outlook are also used by all staff.
3.2.3	How are they collecting, storing, managing, diffusing, this data/information/knowledge	Contacts are primarily recorded and stored in Microsoft Outlook. Accounting information is recorded on Member Partner and specialty reporting is prepared by support staff or program managers to supplement the others. Personal contacts of volunteers and their "spheres of influence" are either not collected, managed and diffused or are informally collected in unknown places and diffused by chance.
3.2.4	Where is this data/information/knowledge stored	The knowledge is stored in the various program files listed above but primarily on the chamber's file servers. Some information is stored on local pc hard drives as well. Much of the personal contact and spheres of influence is stored in the minds of program managers.
3.2.5	Who are the users of this data/information/ knowledge	The primary users are staff responsible for securing the funding of the programs. This is usually the program manager. Finance and executive leadership also use the information. Volunteer committees also use the information stored when assisting with fundraising.
3.2.6	How, when and where is this data/information/ knowledge utilized	The data is used primarily to track payments and make new funding requests.
3.2.7	What are the key knowledge issues	The key knowledge issues are to analyze what is occurring to minimize internal competition and expand the source of funding to other donors in areas that benefit can be proved. Also, the information stored in the minds of program managers needs to be codified so that analysis of that data can be accomplished as well.

Table 14.

3.3.b Foundation Competitive Advantage – Organizational Leadership	
3.3.1	Identify the data/information/knowledge required for their successful development, management and delivery	This starts with the basic training and education levels applicable to each program and extends into leadership influence sphere that can actually raise the funds required. Here, the ability to absorb all of the community information is critical. This occurs not only at the codified level but also through face-to-face exchanges of tacit information.
3.3.2	Who is collecting, storing, managing, diffusing this data/information/knowledge	Staff records minutes of meetings and also compiles strategic plans to be implemented. This is sent out to committees and other staff via e-mail and shared files.
3.3.3	How are they collecting, storing, managing, diffusing, this data/information/knowledge	Most of this data is diffused through staff meetings. The culture of the organization is not conducive to data collection of this type. Individuals are expected to absorb this ever-changing data and use it to lead.
3.3.4	Where is this data/information/knowledge stored	Most leadership data is stored with the individual. The influence sphere is nominally tracked through e-mail contact lists.
3.3.5	Who are the users of this data/information/ knowledge	Funders of programs use this data as a measure of how much they can "trust" the organization to accomplish the task that money is being asked for. Committees and volunteers also use this information in determining their use of time within the organization.
3.3.6	How, when and where is this data/information/ knowledge utilized	The data/information is utilized in marketing materials, information pieces, press releases, and other public relations areas of the organization. It is also used in grant writing and funding requests.
3.3.7	What are the key knowledge issues	The key knowledge issue is the understanding that the information is related to the person and no attempt has been made by the organization to codify, analyze and expand the scope of its influence in a systematic manner.

Table 15.

3.3.b Foundation Competitive Advantage – Community Knowledge		
3.3.1	Identify the data/information/knowledge required for their successful development, management and delivery	This starts with community demographics in all areas of the foundation's scope and continues intimate knowledge of individual business entities within the community. Governmental and school district knowledge is also needed as well as resource identification throughout the community.
3.3.2	Who is collecting, storing, managing, diffusing this data/information/knowledge	Each program manager and their support staff are collecting, storing, managing and diffusing this information. It is being done in independent files throughout the system.
3.3.3	How are they collecting, storing, managing, diffusing, this data/information/knowledge	They are accomplishing this mostly through the paper, internet, personal meetings and e-mail.
3.3.4	Where is this data/information/knowledge stored	Most of this information is stored in personal files throughout the chamber's file server. Very little is stored in the central data base. Some is available on the chamber's web page.
3.3.5	Who are the users of this data/information/knowledge	Outside funders, government agencies, granting agencies, school districts, volunteers, committees, community stakeholders all use this data.
3.3.6	How, when and where is this data/information/knowledge utilized	This is used for fundraising, showing program effectiveness, recruiting business/individuals to the community and for identifying need.
3.3.7	What are the key knowledge issues	The key knowledge issues are maintaining this knowledge and actually finding what you need when you need it. Old knowledge needs to be eliminated and updated constantly for the ever-changing nature of the community.

Table 16.

3.4.b Foundation Value-Adding Activities – Economic Prosperity Advocacy		
3.4.1	Identify the data/information/knowledge required for their successful development, management and delivery	The data is diverse and from all sources within the community. Most comes from census and school district data but others are internally generated in entrepreneurship figures and leadership positions assumed. The knowledge needed is to find, assemble and analyze it to show the economic benefits of programs so that economic prosperity for business translates to economic prosperity for all within the community.
3.4.2	Who is collecting, storing, managing, diffusing this data/information/knowledge	Program heads and their support staff do all the data collection, storing and diffusion with the help of a communications department.
3.4.3	How are they collecting, storing, managing, diffusing, this data/information/knowledge	Most of this is done through staff research and task force participation. Strategic planning assists in identifying the most "valuable" advocacy positions. It is tracked through progress reports and diffused through newsletters, the web site and e-mails.
3.4.4	Where is this data/information/knowledge stored	This information is stored in annual reports, strategic plans, web pages, committee reports and official meeting minutes. It is stored electronically on the chamber's file servers but in individual files throughout.
3.4.5	Who are the users of this data/information/knowledge	Those who fund the foundation programs are most concerned with this data. Also, those who are looking to start or locate businesses in the community need this also. Individuals looking to move to the community use this information as well.
3.4.6	How, when and where is this data/information/knowledge utilized	It is used to underscore the relative success of the programming being performed by the foundation. It is also used in fundraising and economic development discussions throughout municipalities and school districts in the county.
3.4.7	What are the key knowledge issues	The key knowledge issues are primarily defining the metrics to show this is occurring. Once identified, it is the continuous maintenance of this data. Also, getting this information out in a timely and useful manner is difficult. Communication of this value-added activity is also very difficult. Not so much from the ability to do it, but communicating in a meaningful manner. There is also no search for outside users to access this data on their timeframe.

Table 17.

3.4.b Foundation Value-Adding Activities – Community Resource Hub		
3.4.1	Identify the data/information/knowledge required for their successful development, management and delivery	Business, government, school and other influential community individuals need to be known. Tying people, business, schools, and government to resources needed is critical. Knowing where the resources are in the community – especially the personal resources is a value added in the foundation.
3.4.2	Who is collecting, storing, managing, diffusing this data/information/knowledge	All staff is responsible for collecting this data. Program heads are primarily responsible for the diffusing of the data with the assistance of the chamber's communication's department. Many volunteers and committee members also collect this data for the chamber.
3.4.3	How are they collecting, storing, managing, diffusing, this data/information/knowledge	The data is collected in meetings and stored in minutes of those meetings. It is also collected via surveys, phone calls, e-mails and from web sources. It is diffused in much the same manner with the addition of newsletters. It is stored by happenstance at best throughout the organization.
3.4.4	Where is this data/information/knowledge stored	Most of this information is stored as tacit knowledge by the individuals who run into it. The organization is small and "experts" are known. Most staff knows who to ask to get an answer.
3.4.5	Who are the users of this data/information/knowledge	Those who fund the foundation programs are most concerned with this data. Also, those who are looking to start or locate businesses in the community need this also. Individuals looking to move to the community use this information as well. Companies within the community use it as a shortcut for finding solutions to issues they may have. Marketers use some of the codified information to purchase mailing lists. The community at large uses it for business and community related questions.
3.4.6	How, when and where is this data/information/knowledge utilized	This information is used to solve specific issues. It is often utilized to save time and it is always used for the betterment of those within the community.
3.4.7	What are the key knowledge issues	There is no central repository proving that this is occurring. Without that, it is hard to market this value-added process unless you stumble across it. It is also difficult to retain this knowledge if a person should leave. This is a "word-of-mouth" value and its value can be limited due to who is answering the question.

Table 18.

3.5.b Foundation Best Practices – Program Value Proposition		
3.5.1	Identify the data/information/knowledge required for their successful development, management and delivery	This information comes from primarily tracking program outcomes and measuring against key metrics for success. Additional sources come from advertising agencies and proposed value of donor exposure. Communications information and knowledge are utilized to develop program-specific marketing and fundraising materials.
3.5.2	Who is collecting, storing, managing, diffusing this data/information/knowledge	Program heads and their support staff do all the data collection, storing and diffusion with the help of a communications department.
3.5.3	How are they collecting, storing, managing, diffusing, this data/information/knowledge	Most of this is done through staff research and tracking. Strategic planning assists in identifying the most critical aspects of the program's value proposition. It is tracked through progress reports and diffused through newsletters, the web site and e-mails, direct mailings and phone and face-to-face meetings.
3.5.4	Where is this data/information/knowledge stored	This information is stored in annual reports, strategic plans, web pages, committee reports and official meeting minutes. It is stored electronically on the chamber's file servers but in individual files throughout.
3.5.5	Who are the users of this data/information/knowledge	Those who fund the foundation programs are most concerned with this data. Also, staff doing the funding requests, rely on the data being accurate and up-to-date. Media also use the data in feature stories about the programs.
3.5.6	How, when and where is this data/information/knowledge utilized	It is used to underscore the relative success of the programming being performed by the foundation and to allow foundation staff an ability to propose a ROI to a prospective donor or granting agency. It is also used in fundraising and economic development discussions throughout municipalities and school districts in the county.
3.5.7	What are the key knowledge issues	The key knowledge issues are primarily defining the metrics that tie a "ROI" to a particular donor. Once identified, it is the continuous maintenance of this data. Also, getting this information out in a timely and useful manner is difficult. Communication of this value proposition is also very difficult. Not so much from the ability to do it, but communicating in a meaningful manner. There is also no search for outside users to access this data on their timeframe. This type of knowledge is "customized" to the donor ad as such, requires an ability of chamber staff to make needed adjustments to existing data to fit the need. There is limited ability to accomplish this quickly from the stored information. This process is too time consuming.

Table 19.

3.5.b Foundation Best Practices – Fundraising Strategy		
3.5.1	Identify the data/information/knowledge required for their successful development, management and delivery	This knowledge is primarily a leadership best practice. The data, information, knowledge needed is internal operating and program procedures. Sources of funding are identified and knowledge is gained on who to contact, what they will fund, when their funding cycle and decision process is, where they are located and can meet, and why an organization will fund a program. The same process is used with grant preparation. Volunteers and staff must know this information when making an ask. Staff is constantly discussing the possibilities of referrals or personal contacts with potential donors. Paul Jadin and his knowledge of the business, governmental and educational communities is an invaluable resource.
3.5.2	Who is collecting, storing, managing, diffusing this data/information/knowledge	Program heads and their support staff do all the data collection, storing and diffusion with the help of an accounting department.
3.5.3	How are they collecting, storing, managing, diffusing, this data/information/knowledge	Most of this is done through staff research and tracking. Web searches and readings of papers and periodicals also help. Information comes from the chamber's current Member Partner database and personal contact lists. Volunteer input, suggestions and contacts are actively requested. Most of the high-level information and data is stored in the tacit knowledge of the program managers and Paul Jadin. It is typically diffused through face-to-face contacts or meetings. Other ways are through internal e-mails and phone conversations.
3.5.4	Where is this data/information/knowledge stored	This information is stored in strategic plans, committee reports and official meeting minutes. It is stored electronically on the chamber's file servers but in individual files throughout. It is also stored as a component of the organization's overall intelligence. Mainly, it is stored in program manager and Paul Jadin's tacit knowledge.
3.5.5	Who are the users of this data/information/knowledge	Staff doing the funding requests, rely on the data as do volunteers who are utilizing personal contacts or other tacit information they may have about a potential donor. Accounting uses the data to also track receivables and payments.
3.5.6	How, when and where is this data/information/knowledge utilized	The data is used between program managers and Paul Jadin. It is also used in program planning and budget preparation. Fundraising committees also use it to make calls on behalf of the foundation.
3.5.7	What are the key knowledge issues	The key knowledge issues here are taking the information, knowledge and data from the minds of program heads and Paul Jadin and somehow get it codified. Once accomplished, regularly updating and analyzing the data are important. There will be the strategic issues of using the data for expanding the funding sources database. Somehow, information known will have to be combined with data from outside sources to bring this all to fruition.

Table 20.

3.6.c Organization Strategy – Fundraising Committees		
3.6.1	Identify the data/information/knowledge required for their successful development, management and delivery	Tacit information of the volunteers. Financial goals responsible for as an organization. Company/individual data. Program goals and objectives. Program successes. ROI statistics for community and company if applicable.
3.6.2	Who is collecting, storing, managing, diffusing this data/information/knowledge	Program staff collects stores and manages this information. Departmental managers work with volunteers to ensure they have all the information needed.
3.6.3	How are they collecting, storing, managing, diffusing, this data/information/knowledge	Most of this is done through staff research and tracking. Strategic planning assists in identifying the most critical aspects of the program's value proposition. It is tracked through progress reports at regularly scheduled meeting dates and times.
3.6.4	Where is this data/information/knowledge stored	This information is stored in annual reports, strategic plans, web pages, committee reports and official meeting minutes. It is stored electronically on the chamber's file servers but in individual files throughout.
3.6.5	Who are the users of this data/information/knowledge	Primarily program heads are the users of this data. They use it to track success and adjust as needed.
3.6.6	How, when and where is this data/information/knowledge utilized	It is used to track the relative success of the fundraising efforts and that in turn points directly to programming success in those areas of the foundation. Feedback from meeting and requests are tracked in meetings, phone calls and e-mails.
3.6.7	What are the key knowledge issues	The key knowledge issues are ease of retrieving data and once disseminated, tracking results. Follow-up with volunteers is critical in this effort and outside communications with e-mail and phone service are primarily what is used.

Table 21.

3.6.c Organization Strategy – Centralized IT infrastructure and billing		
3.6.1	Identify the data/information/knowledge required for their successful development, management and delivery	This requires the individual/company raw data to be continually updated. Individuals must be able to get information from the chamber's Member Partner program.
3.6.2	Who is collecting, storing, managing, diffusing this data/information/knowledge	All staff has access to this program and is encouraged to utilize the features of the program. Updates to the data occur continually and are the responsibility of Marilyn and Sara. While departmental staff has the ability to create invoicing, the accounting department does much of this for the departments. All staff has access to billing records and outstanding amounts for any organization.
3.6.3	How are they collecting, storing, managing, diffusing, this data/information/knowledge	Updates to the individual/corporate record are routed to Marilyn or Sara primarily via e-mail. Others come from individuals calling and requesting that their records be updated. Some of the corporate records are also changed from written notes on returned invoices. Annually, the corporate record with the individuals associated with that company is e-mailed to the organization and updates are requested.
3.6.4	Where is this data/information/knowledge stored	This is stored on the chamber's file servers.
3.6.5	Who are the users of this data/information/knowledge	All staff uses this information at some level.
3.6.6	How, when and where is this data/information/knowledge utilized	This data is used for any interaction with an organization that includes a financial transaction. It is also used to populate the member portion of the web site. Updates are automatic to the web site when made. Staff utilizes it to break out business by industry. The data is also sold as lists to members. As the data hold e-mail and fax addresses, it is used for electronic "blasts" to members. A non-member portion tracks donors who are not chamber members as prospects. Lookup is a component of this program and electronic communications with members is tracked automatically. There is a "contacts" site in this database which is used sporadically. That section would be beneficial for the inclusion of tacit knowledge about individuals/companies that is not currently codified.
3.6.7	What are the key knowledge issues	The key knowledge issues are primarily regularly updating the data, retrieving the data and analyzing the data. While the organization has done a pretty good job at systematically ensuring that the data is up-do-date, data retrieval and analysis is lacking. Query is difficult and typically requires a more than passing knowledge of the process. Reports are not written by chamber staff and need the help of the program's staff in Oklahoma. With so much and such diverse data held in one place, understanding the structure of the entire data base and what might be out there takes time. There is limited staff time for training new or inexperienced staff on the intricacies of the program. Because of the retrieval and analysis issues, much of the tacit knowledge the system should be collecting is not occurring. Program heads do not see the value connection of inputting the data if there is not an adequate and almost instantaneously available output.

3.5 **Best Practices:** Each of the foundation programs is incredibly complex and fairly well developed. Defining, organizing, implementing a program for and reporting on community needs in the areas identified in section 3.1 require that best practices are implemented. The scope of this audit is on the aspects directly relating to fundraising and it is from that perspective which will drive the responses to follow.

a   Identify all critical best practices for the entity.

- Program Value Proposition. (Table 18)
- Fundraising strategy. (Table 19)

3.6 **Organization's Strategy:** Each of the foundation programs is incredibly complex and fairly well developed. Defining, organizing, implementing a program for and reporting on community needs in the areas identified in section 3.1 require that organizational funding strategies are implemented.. The scope of this audit is on the aspects directly relating to fundraising

Table 22.

3.6.c Organization Strategy – Leadership Staff Fundraising Strategy Face-to-Face Sessions		
3.6.1	Identify the data/information/knowledge required for their successful development, management and delivery	Tacit information of the staff. Financial goals responsible for as an organization. Company/individual data. Program goals and objectives. Program successes. ROI statistics for community and company if applicable.
3.6.2	Who is collecting, storing, managing, diffusing this data/information/knowledge	Currently nobody is collecting or storing the tacit knowledge. The program goals and objectives are collected by program heads and their staff. Company information is collected through Member Partner in the manner previously discussed. For donor information not on that data base, web information is usually the source and that is collected by staff.
3.6.3	How are they collecting, storing, managing, diffusing, this data/information/knowledge	These are face-to-face meeting sessions held every other week. They can also be meetings with Paul Jadin, sales staff or any other staff that may have knowledge related to a certain company the foundation is looking to receive donations from. Diffusion is through face-to-face or e-mail follow-up. Sometimes phone conversations are also used.
3.6.4	Where is this data/information/knowledge stored	Some is stored in e-mail but the majority remains with the program heads or in the minds of staff. Some of the information is written down and stored in paper files of the company.
3.6.5	Who are the users of this data/information/knowledge	Department heads use the information in fundraising. Volunteers also use this information.
3.6.6	How, when and where is this data/information/knowledge utilized	The data and knowledge is used to match the ask with the appropriate individual/company or department of the potential donor. It is also used to understand granting requirements or even granting agencies.
3.6.7	What are the key knowledge issues	The key knowledge issue that this information remains tacit knowledge with limited ability for retrieval and analysis.

Table 23.

3.7.c Organization Goals – IT and Phone Infrastructure Continually Operational and Robust Enough for Foundation Informational Needs.		
3.7.1	Identify the data/information/knowledge required for their successful development, management and delivery	Outside professional IT and phone support. Of vital importance is the internet bandwidth issue. Knowledge of IT/phone systems a must. Use patterns of staff and program managers needed and changes in these industries has to be monitored.
3.7.2	Who is collecting, storing, managing, diffusing this data/information/knowledge	Amy keeps track of the IT/phone vendors as well as the internet service provider. IT/phone vendors are responsible for capturing system specific knowledge. New products/updates are also the vendor's responsibility with the expectation that a ROI will be required for any expenditures made by the chamber. Staff updates Phil on issues or needs for additional new products/services. Also, face-to-face meetings occur with the technicians where updated information is passed along.
3.7.3	How are they collecting, storing, managing, diffusing, this data/information/knowledge	Amy stores the contact information in the shared drive of the chambers file servers. Receptionists also have paper copies of this data. Most of the product update/new product information is retained with the vendor and utilized in solution presentations as needed. Phil retains much of the information as tacit knowledge. Staff is surveyed on current situation/needs basis. Budget process includes capital and system needs.
3.7.4	Where is this data/information/knowledge stored	The data, information and knowledge is stored on the chamber's file servers. Vendor knowledge is stored at their locations. New product/services are stored in e-mails, phone calls, as tacit knowledge or in paper files.
3.7.5	Who are the users of this data/information/knowledge	The users of the data are primarily the technicians in conjunction with Phil and Paul Jadin in the expenditure decision making process.
3.7.6	How, when and where is this data/information/knowledge utilized	The data is used to weigh the benefits with costs and compatibility of existing systems. The pace and quantity of change in this environment requires continuous monitoring. Being able to communicate with a diverse customer base is also a challenge. Ensuring network security and limiting outside exposure is also a main consideration.
3.7.7	What are the key knowledge issues	Being able to keep up with this information bombardment when it is not a primary function of anybody on staff is incredibly difficult. Vendor choice is critical. IT choice for compatibility and financial strength (staying power) are very important criteria. Understanding how different components of the infrastructure work in tandem and sometimes against each other is also a challenge.

Table 24.

3.7.c Organization Goals – Accounting/Member Partner and Budgetary Support.		
3.7.1	Identify the data/information/knowledge required for their successful development, management and delivery	Mas90 and Member Partner knowledge along with ability to incorporate the information from Microsoft Excel and Word documents. Query ability and database manipulation needed. Report writing and analysis work is vital.
3.7.2	Who is collecting, storing, managing, diffusing this data/information/knowledge	Primarily this is being done by the accounting staff and Marilyn. Program managers also use their knowledge in the preparation of base data.
3.7.3	How are they collecting, storing, managing, diffusing, this data/information/knowledge	Information is collected and diffused from written reports and e-mail primarily. Phil also uses socialization to extract tacit information from program heads. That information is usually hand written onto worksheet documents. Phone is also used. Information to volunteers and other interested community parties is usually diffused through e-mail and the inclusion of appropriate attachments.
3.7.4	Where is this data/information/knowledge stored	The data/information/knowledge is primarily stored on the chamber's file servers. However, much of the socialized information is in binders in the form of hand written notes. Tacit knowledge at the program level or at the executive level remains in their domain.
3.7.5	Who are the users of this data/information/knowledge	The users of the data are primarily the program heads, Paul Jadin, volunteers, donors, granting agencies, auditors, and boards.
3.7.6	How, when and where is this data/information/knowledge utilized	This is primarily used in budgetary times but also it is used on a monthly basis in comparing budgets to actual performance. Due to the lack of query and analysis tools, it is not being used to expand the funding base. Volunteers use it to track the financial performance of the programs and granting agencies use the information for their own purposes for disbursing and awarding funds.
3.7.7	What are the key knowledge issues	One of the biggest issues, surprisingly, is the definition of the meta-data. Accounting and the program managers must understand what it is exactly they are looking at. Capturing tacit knowledge is also quite difficult. To be of any value, query and analysis must occur. There are system limitations on those levels. Also, data must be timely and accurate.

and it is from that perspective which will drive the responses to follow.

a. Identify the strategy of your organization.
- Tie program to funding source to maximize overall fundraising success.

b. Identify the relevant strategies of your entity that support the strategy mentioned above.
- **Fundraising committees (Table 20)**
- **Centralized IT infrastructure and billing (Table 21)**
- **Leadership staff fundraising strategy face-to- face sessions (Table 22)**

3.7 **Organization's Goals:** Each of the foundation programs is incredibly complex and fairly well developed. Defining, organizing, implementing a program for and reporting on community needs in the areas identified in section 3.1 require that organizational goals are implemented and met. The scope of this audit is on the aspects directly relating to fundraising and it is from that perspective which will drive the responses to follow.

a Identify the goals and key success indicators (KSI) of your organization. Are they balanced?
- Annual program budgetary goals – Success indicator is meeting/ exceeding budget.
  1. These are directly related to the financial needs of the program in any given fiscal year.
  2. Because they are based on annual budgetary needs of the program, they are balanced.
- Program funding stabilization

Table 25.

3.7.c Organization Goals – Strategic Planning at Program and Organizational Level.		
3.7.1	Identify the data/information/knowledge required for their successful development, management and delivery	Program statistics. Community and company demographics. Volunteer information. Competitor information. Internal process and procedures.
3.7.2	Who is collecting, storing, managing, diffusing this data/information/knowledge	Program managers and their staff are doing this collection, storing, managing and diffusing of data. Administrative staff assists with overall organizational information and support.
3.7.3	How are they collecting, storing, managing, diffusing, this data/information/knowledge	Most of the data is collected from outside web sources, e-mails, phone conversations or through socialization interactions in the community or with staff. Official minutes are kept at committee or board meetings and strategic planning documents are prepared annually for each functional program. These documents are put on the web site, handed out in meetings, e-mailed or mailed.
3.7.4	Where is this data/information/knowledge stored	The data, information and knowledge is stored on the chamber's file servers or individual hard drives. The combined organizational strategic plan is in the organization's shared drive and available to all staff. Supporting data or tacit knowledge are diffused throughout the organization and are not systematically cataloged.
3.7.5	Who are the users of this data/information/knowledge	The users of this data are all program managers, staff responsible for budgeting, volunteers and committee members, potential donors, actual donors, granting agencies, governmental and educational entities and interested community stakeholders. External auditors also use this data in determining the foundation's relative staying power.
3.7.6	How, when and where is this data/information/knowledge utilized	It is used for determining the availability of funding for any given year. As budgets are developed, the programs can expect to accomplish the strategies with the funding available. This also helps to prepare any program ROI and ultimate "fundability." Much of what these documents contain is used by volunteers and staff in the fundraising quest. Granting agencies need this information in their decision-making process. Auditors use it, as was stated above, to make a determination of a foundation's relative staying power. They also use it to ensure that the foundation remains within its stated purpose for IRS and donor purposes.
3.7.7	What are the key knowledge issues	The key knowledge issues are finding relevant and reliable data sources. Information needed must then be analyzed and put into an absorbable format. As with any information, it needs to be up-to-date and timely. The organization will need to find new information to help support the long-term funding issues. That information will need to be defined, codified, sorted, analyzed and finally used.

E - KM Strategy, etc.:

goals – Program reserves or Endowment Fund established for the program's ongoing operations.

1. These goals are needed to ensure the continuation of the program and move program managers from the primary role of "fundraiser" to program execution.

2. These goals are not clearly defined and as such, remain unbalanced.

b Identify the goals and KSI of your entity that support the mentioned above. Are they balanced? Do they support those at 3.7.a?

- **IT and phone infrastructure continually operational and robust enough for foundation informational needs. (Table 23)**

1. These goals are as balanced as they can be given the constraints of staff, time and money. These goals also work in the realm of

Table 26.

4.1.1	Is your industry knowledge intense? In what Areas

The programs of the foundation rely entirely on knowledge. The end product is service and accomplishment of goals as determined by community need. The continuation of funding requires that knowledge needs to be developed, analyzed, stored, utilized and disbursed. The intensity of the knowledge relates to the following areas:
  • Change – this occurs continually in both the community and foundation program.
  • Technology – Sources of new knowledge are continually being developed. This is most acute at the state, local and federal government level. These changes make it imperative to have the latest data sources and most up-to-date information. Also, being a data source and having the ability to communicate electronically with donors is very important not only for identifying and asking for funding, but also for ensuring that the funding continues over the life of a program.
  • Business and people – This is continuous change and having the data as up-to-date as possible is the most important component in getting fundraising sources identified and utilized.
  • Economic Environment – Fundraising is dependent.

4.1.2	What Specific Areas of knowledge are extremely important to your company? Why?

Collective Knowledge – From a fundraising perspective, this knowledge becomes vital in ensuring that the same source is not used for multiple purposes. All must be able to possess this knowledge for this process. Because the programs encompass such a variety of issues and are funded by such a broad range of possible organizations and governmental entities, no one person can hold all of this knowledge.
Procedural Knowledge – for the reasons stated under collective knowledge, staff has to have and follow procedures in this area in order to be successful. No analysis could be performed on the collective knowledge if procedures weren't in place for its capture.
Declarative Knowledge – This is the "know what" of knowledge and program heads must possess this knowledge to communicate issues, solutions and successes. This is critical in building a case for an entity to fund a program.
Explicit Knowledge – This knowledge is needed for analysis purposes. Too many "asks" from the same source will result in less actually received for the foundation. Not understanding who and which departments within companies is actually funding which program will result in less success for all as well. Information on these points gained at the tacit level needs to be made explicit in order for this analysis to occur.
Tacit Knowledge – The organization relies on this knowledge type too extensively. While the culture, change, technology environment and pragmatic budget considerations will always make this a very important knowledge area, for fundraising, it would be better if this knowledge were used less than it currently is.

4.1.3	What are (might be) your company's key benefits of active Knowledge Management? Which benefits are critical for your company's success?

  • Increased fundraising effectiveness
  • Increased fundraising efficiency
  • Increased sharing of data
  • Increased trust among staff
  • Better relations with funding organizations
  • Improved employee morale
  • Improved program effectiveness
While all of the above benefits would be improvements to the organization, it is critical that fundraising effectiveness and efficiency are met. No money, no mission – and little money, little mission. Once the benefits of the KM initiative can be shown, the other benefits can have a chance to occur. The foundation has survived without this initiative but the real issue is "can it thrive."

4.1.4	What are (might be) your organization's/entity key benefits of active Knowledge Management? Which benefits are critical for your company's success?

Here again, fundraising at the company and organization/entity level have the same key benefits. Correspondingly, the critical benefits would also be identical.
  • Increased fundraising effectiveness
  • Increased fundraising efficiency
  • Increased sharing of data
  • Increased trust among staff
  • Better relations with funding organizations
  • Improved employee morale
  • Improved program effectiveness
While all of the above benefits would be improvements to the organization, it is critical that fundraising effectiveness and efficiency are met. No money, no mission – and little money, little mission. Once the benefits of the KM initiative can be shown, the other benefits can have a chance to occur. The foundation has survived without this initiative but the real issue is "can it thrive."

Table 27.

4.2.1	Developing strategy to exploit new knowledge

The organization continuously looks at new methodologies for exploiting new knowledge. Meetings of both internal staff and external volunteers are the most common method for developing strategy and the inception of this fundraising KM project has been done in much the same manner. Informal/formal meetings, e-mail and phone contacts are being used to determine strategy for this new knowledge. Ultimately, the new knowledge is tied to strategic objectives. Practically speaking, the base strategies of collaboration, trust, and sharing of data – culture change – are being developed to further exploit this new knowledge.

4.2.2	Leveraging knowledge at all levels?

This question goes back to 4.1.4. The organization is leveraging knowledge in the fundraising arena by taking advantage of the potential benefits to their fullest extent.
- Increased fundraising effectiveness
- Increased fundraising efficiency
- Increased sharing of data
- Increased trust among staff
- Better relations with funding organizations
- Improved employee morale
- Improved program effectiveness

With limited staff, these areas will be left less to chance and the skill of an individual and more to culture and process.

4.2.3	Integrating knowledge from various areas?

Currently, the organization integrates knowledge in a very haphazard manner. Because knowledge resides within programs and personnel knows who typically owns or has the most accurate tacit knowledge on a subject, integration for any specific purpose is done on an as-needed basis. The organization does facilitate shared systems and communications tools on its file servers for integrating knowledge when needed. The organization also encourages use of a common data base – Member Partner – for company/individual data. When outside sources of knowledge are needed, they are mainly found electronically at the outside source and copied into employee-specific files. Again, these can be shared but they are not systematically cataloged, tagged, verified or otherwise identified as knowledge that can be integrated. The web site is currently the main area where the organization integrates knowledge from various areas. Other areas include financial data, internal human resource data, strategic planning documents and board and committee meeting minutes.

4.2.4	Integrating Knowledge Management with the overall business plan of the company?

The organization began this process in the previous year when it went through the computer and phone upgrades needed to its infrastructure. This integration of systems was considered imperative to achieving the goals of the strategic plan. The organization plan included the goals of:
- Shared services
- Shared information
- Seamless integration of data into existing sources of knowledge
- Increased productivity of staff in goal accomplishment
- Increased funding for all programming
- Better customer information sources
- Improved customer sharing of data at reduced costs
- Sharing of information at any location

Where the organization is lacking in this regard is a common best-practices or community of practice as it relates to getting the funding portion of all programs accomplished. Collecting, recording, analyzing of fundraising data in an agreed upon manner is the step which must be tied back to the overall business plan of the company.

4.2.5	Improving knowledge of company goals at all levels

The organization is making a conscious effort to improve the knowledge of company goals at all levels. This is primarily being done through the strategic planning and budgeting process. The organization has adopted benchmarks which are in the early stages of being defined and reported. These are not only used at the programming level, but are reported to the chamber board on a quarterly basis throughout the year. The leadership team of the organization is responsible for the reporting of the benchmarks. Budgetary goals are reported to staff with budgetary responsibility on a monthly basis to budget and against forecasts after six months of the fiscal year. Boards, committees, volunteers and staff review financial results and goal results on a monthly basis. While reports are systematic, most of the knowledge is passed along and retained at a tacit level.

continued on following page

Table 27. continued

4.2.6	Identify SWOT of knowledge areas	
Strengths: • High level of competency of current individuals - • Centralized IT infrastructure – for backups and storage issues • Mobile access to data • Internet infrastructure is good with speed and e-mail • Filtering of incoming e-mails	**Weaknesses:** • Mobilization and conversion of tacit knowledge • Analysis of existing knowledge • Resources – staff time and dollars • Query of all knowledge sources • Staff training in knowledge areas • Use of knowledge areas in strategy development	
Opportunities: • Identification of key knowledge areas that can ease burden on human resources and increase resources of money and consequently – staff • Codification of tacit knowledge • Query tools • Staff training in use of knowledge areas to achieve program strategies • Analysis of knowledge for fundraising opportunities	**Threats:** • Staff turnover/depletion • Too much systems/programming knowledge in the tacit domain of too few individuals • Knowledge obsolescence • Knowledge competition	

Table 28.

4.3.1	Knowledge of people, processes and technology used currently as core competencies.
The chamber and, consequently, the foundation are currently *Intuitive Utilization organizations*. They focus on exploiting their currently existing knowledge while keeping this knowledge tacit. Again, keeping this focused on the fundraising portion of the equation, raw, demographic and informational knowledge of people are utilized via the chamber's Member Partner database and Microsoft Outlook. The core competency is fundraising and communications. Lists are maintained of possible interested donors. These are accomplished with Outlook, Word or the Member Partner database. Procedures are relatively non-existent until billing or accounting is involved. Technology is used both to push and pull data on the programs and also to push and pull data on the donors. Personal face-to-face is typically required to secure the funding.	
4.3.2	**Knowledge of people, processes and technology to be used in the future as Core Competencies**
This is where the entire concept of Knowledge Management as it relates to the fundraising process takes the core competency to the next level. Here, processes of consolidating data for the dissemination after analysis makes the knowledge more valuable and efficient. Housing the data in one, centrally acceptable database with pre-defined meta-data and query definition makes the process something that can be done in the context of existing staff. The project isn't so large as to be over-burdensome on any one department but the results are such that all who need the information benefit. The procedures needed to do this will insure that data is accurate and timely. The query and meta-data definitions will help avoid confusion. Staff will learn to trust each other and the system needed to encourage growth. Company and individual analysis before an ask is made will become common practice. If a company is asked to give to multiple programs, timing and department identification will be considered on top of just pushing data and competing with other foundation programs.	
4.3.3	**Knowledge of people, processes and technology used currently as Competitive Advantages**
Currently, personal knowledge of people and process in the funding of programs is utilized either at a program manager or volunteer level. Personal, tacit knowledge of a prospective donor is always considered a competitive advantage when fundraising. Letters through snail mail, e-mails, phone conversations and face-to-face meetings are all included as methods for maintaining this advantage. Staff keeps in regular contact with funding sources through newsletters, minutes, reports and web site.	
4.3.4	**Knowledge of people, processes and technology to be used in the future as Competitive Advantages.**
In the future, the personal touch will continue to be a competitive advantage. However, to expand fundraising, analysis as to what has been successful will be utilized expand into other funding sources. Being able to identify industries, foundations, granting agencies will be facilitated with such analysis. Having an up-to-date data source on personal contacts will be used to identify funding hot-buttons and possible additional fits for companies that otherwise wouldn't have been thought of. Query and electronic reporting as well as procedures to ensure the capture and use of the data will be needed. Either the existing Member Partner data base will be expanded or a new, central repository will need to be identified. Tacit knowledge previously unknown will be more readily available and easily shared.	

continued on following page

Table 28. continued

4.3.5	Information Technology tools/platforms enhancing the organization's knowledge base.
The organization is pretty well situated from an IT perspective to implement this item of its knowledge base. The tools needed are query tools and analysis tool. Also, linking tools to external data sources will be required once the tacit knowledge is codified. The goal will not only be to increase the information but then to use what is known to find additional organizations that fit our donor profiles. Analysis tools will also be looking for "close fits" as well.	
4.3.6	Is the organization well organized to generate new Knowledge? To share and diffuse existing knowledge?
The organization is well organized to generate new knowledge. Because each program is so different, multiple perspectives on similar issues are always popping up. The issue is resources and trust to share and diffuse existing knowledge. The current systems limitations make this difficult and limitations of funding and knowledge personnel to facilitate the sharing and diffusing of knowledge are difficult obstacles to overcome.	
4.3.7	Perceived value of:
4.3.7.1 – Formal knowledge offices - There would be limited perceived value of this office. The organization shares administrative services and this would be considered overhead that simply could not be absorbed by foundation programming any further than is already being incurred.	
4.3.7.2 – Organizational knowledge base – The perceived value of this for fundraising would be high. Frustrations mount whenever there is a feeling of competition for dollars amongst staff and this would be one area that transparency could not only show the programs aren't competing, but also that administrative help in the identification and expansion of funding sources would be appreciated.	
4.3.7.3 – Demonstrable knowledge leadership – Each program manager understands the value of leadership throughout the organization so for this function, demonstrable knowledge leadership would be greatly valued.	
4.3.8	Are there formal knowledge offices? There are no formal knowledge offices in the foundation or the chamber as a whole.

change and compatibility which both require continuous balancing and re-balancing.

2. These goals are critical to the overall support of the goals mentioned in 3.7.a.

- **Accounting and Member Partner support. (Table 24)**

1. These goals have been the focus of staff since implementation of the systems and remain a priority of the organization supported from Paul Jadin down. They are balanced to the extent of budgetary and time constraints. Reporting and analysis goals are the areas that currently are the least balanced. Unfortunately, this is causing the most severe issue in staff perception of need to capture tacit knowledge.

2. The accounting and Member Partner support goals work better in the support of Annual program budgetary goals. Because of the reporting and analysis issues in this goal being unresolved, they are not supporting to their capability the program funding stabilization goals.

- **Strategic planning at program and organizational level. (Table 25)**

1. These goals are incredibly balanced in the annual program budgetary goals as that has been the focus of leadership over the past 4 years. Because of the culture and nature of the organization, program funding stabilization goals have not been a driven strategy and thus are not balanced.

Table 29.

4.4.1	Biggest obstacles/challenges in your organization to knowledge transfer; to acquisition of external knowledge

The foundation's biggest challenges to knowledge transfer are cultural. Quite honestly, this hasn't been an area of high priority and certainly not a strategic issue. If knowledge transfer were really important, compensation would be tied at least somewhat to this area. As it is, the closest we have is the expectation that coworkers will at least respect each other. While this allows for a somewhat collegial working environment, it doesn't enable the organization to get to the next level in its needs. As for the acquisition of external knowledge, these challenges are much different. The organization doesn't have a filtering mechanism outside of individual program manager socialization that addresses this issue. Because so much external knowledge is brought to the organization, the issue of knowledge overload becomes almost paralyzing. Because everything seems "possible," everything seems important. Filtering incoming knowledge to targeted areas for maximum results is a very large challenge.

4.4.2	Biggest obstacles/challenges in your organization to disseminate knowledge; to create new knowledge

The biggest challenges to the foundation for disseminating knowledge are:
- Trust of the new knowledge
- Time to absorb and use the new knowledge to its potential
- Reporting new knowledge in a manner that is easily understood and applied
- Tying knew knowledge to real programming need
- The development of common meta-data and categories between programs

Much of these areas relate to the transfer of knowledge and are impediments to actual knowledge generation program occurrence.

4.4.3	Culture of the organization as challenge/supportive

The organization's culture has been a topic of many of the previous sections of this audit. Challenges of the power-driven/role-driven culture – which the foundation is – include the following:
- Do not have many rules and regulations
- Depend on telepathy for effectiveness – quite difficult when discussing knowledge management
- Talk rather than write
- Are essentially autocratic and bureaucratic at the same time – a very confusing and frustrating aspect for new members of the team in particular
- Learn by trial and error

In short, getting agreement, teamwork, and any knowledge codified is an extremely difficult proposition. This is further exacerbated due to the fact that the compensation system is in no way tied to knowledge management.

This doesn't mean the culture is without its merits. Paul Jadin does encourage and support fast individual decision-making. This has been very helpful in an ever-changing environment. He does encourage stability so not much tacit knowledge of value is lost amongst his top foundation program management team. Because both the role and the individual are valued within this cultural taxonomy, independence in knowledge acquisition is encouraged.

4.4.4	Supporting informal networks.

This is what the organization, with its culture, is good at. Part of the role each program manager accepts is to be a creator of informal networks. The socialization between the community and all program managers simply makes informal networks a byproduct of activity. This can lead to new funding sources but at the end of the day, it is a hit-or-miss proposition with no real ability to duplicate and expand. It does, however, ensure a steady, ever-renewing flow of external knowledge.

4.4.5	Major risks in your organization to managing knowledge.

The biggest risk to managing fundraising knowledge in the foundation is the potential misappropriation of responsibility. In the under funded and understaffed environment of the foundation as it exists today, something of this importance could be assumed to be the responsibility of the "knowledge manager." The logic goes something along the line of "if you want that information, you do it. I don't have any time." And with that attitude, responsibility is shifted not only for the creation of knowledge, but also the results anticipated from any knowledge management initiative. Because compensation is not tied to performance along these lines, another risk is that it will be done in a less than stellar manner. While leadership would like to see managing knowledge done to a higher level, with the staffing and funding as it is today, leadership loss is always an issue. One last issue is that managing knowledge means that it continues to keep knowledge fresh and useful. This cannot be an excuse to stop doing what is successful today. Knowledge management must be an enhancement to today's activities and an insurance policy for tomorrow's success.

Table 30.

4.9.1	Create new knowledge

Because of the culture of the organization, much of the creation of new knowledge is systematically gained through socialization. Meetings, phone calls and to an extent e-mail are all utilized in creating new knowledge. This is particularly true in the fundraising approach of the foundation. While this may not seem "systematic," these activities are all planned with expectations transferred it a program's plan of action.

4.9.2	Acquire new knowledge

As in the creation of new knowledge, much knowledge is acquired for the organization in much the same manner. Add to this the internet, news sources and other statistical and business oriented publications and that are subscribed to and you are filling in how the organization acquires new knowledge. The organization also systematically partners with other local, state and national foundations and programs to acquire knowledge specific to the programs. Again, brochures and publications along with examples of best practices are oftentimes cited and included in the knowledge base of the organization and employees.

4.9.3	Codify knowledge

Hit or miss. There is no real systematic methodology although newsletters, e-newsletters and program brochures are all areas where program knowledge is codified. The business database of Member Partner is systematically updated by identified individuals and further updates are encouraged of all staff. The only real systematic approach other than this is through formal minutes of meetings. While chamber board minutes are on the shared drive and accessible to all, others are not. Also, none of the minutes are in a format for easy cross-reference.

4.9.4	Warehouse knowledge

Outside of the care and feeding of program manager brains, warehousing of codified knowledge that does exist is quite systematic and planned. Systems were designed to include mobile access, unlimited sharing and nightly backup. Security of these systems was considered paramount and thus Citrix was used to overlay access to the data. Also, antivirus and spam filtering occur on two levels. Firewall protection of file servers along with a DMZ file server help to ensure unwanted access to the knowledge servers.

4.9.5	Diffuse knowledge

Computing and internet advances have assisted this process for the organization in many systemized ways. Formal mailing and e-mail lists are maintained and scheduled dates of "knowledge diffusion" are important components of all program managers. This is enhanced through shared calendars of all staff. Setting up meetings for the socialization process to occur for diffusing knowledge is also systematic and was designed to integrate with a recipient's calendar software as well. Planned press conferences and releases via e-mail and (God help us) faxes diffuse knowledge to the general public. These lists are also systematically maintained in the communications department and are a part of the codified knowledge that is retained even through turnover. The system was designed to diffuse any "program specific" knowledge in as seamless a manner possible. All files under the domain of an individual who leaves are automatically transferred to the domain of the individual who is brought on board. Also, e-mail contact lists and calendars are also set up from the old to the new.

4.9.6	Measure knowledge

The only real systematic approach the organization has in measuring knowledge is really in the dollars raised programmatically. This isn't really a knowledge measurement but rather an outcome measure of the entire process. The organization has begun reporting on benchmarks and this process is evolving throughout. Because measuring knowledge has not been a part of the culture in the organization, it is by no means a competence. This will have to evolve into a competence as the culture evolves with knowledge measurement as a goal.

4.9.7	Protect knowledge

The codified knowledge of the organization is protected in the manner discussed in warehousing. Security of these systems was considered paramount and thus Citrix was used to overlay access to the data. Also, antivirus and spam filtering occur on two levels. Firewall protection of file servers along with a DMZ file server help to ensure unwanted access to the knowledge servers. However, because so much of the knowledge the organization needs to currently protect is tacit, special consideration is given to benefits that the organization offers employees. The health plan is geared towards a healthy lifestyle with rewards offered for not only health status but also for healthy lifestyle choices. The organization doesn't consider vesting in its 401K but rather show the value of the benefit from acceptance into the plan. Sick days are unlimited with a reward of 3 additional vacation days if fewer than 3 are used in any year. Life insurance, long and short-term disability is also carried for staff. Staff are encouraged to use all vacation days earned. Outside activities and interests are also encouraged. Basically, the human resource approach to knowledge management helps to ensure the protection of the tacit knowledge.

4.9.8	Exploit knowledge

There is very fine line between the diffusion of knowledge and the exploitation of it. The foundation uses one (diffusion) to accomplish the other (exploitation). The IT infrastructures as well as applications software purchased all were systematically chosen to enable the efficient exploitation of knowledge. However, as is the case with most knowledge in the organization, it remains tacit. Systematic training of the individuals on the software and in the systems of the organization is not occurring. However, socialization – that which works in the culture present – is highly encouraged and actually, most staff is very willing to work with each other in sharing ways to exploit the knowledge of the systems and programs. Formal, systematic exploitation of fundraising knowledge needs to be accomplished in order to be expanded.

continued on following page

Table 30. continued

4.9.9	**Disseminate knowledge**
	Dissemination of knowledge is done in much the same manner as was discussed in Diffusion and exploitation of knowledge. In addition to electronic and socialization means, however, the organization does publish a bi-weekly newsletter as well as a bi-monthly magazine. Each scheduled event is also systematically promoted according to our best event practices. One crucial aspect is the systematic dissemination of knowledge between staff. Again, this is only "systematically" done at regularly scheduled socialization events – staff/leadership meetings. This does not, however codify and make the tacit knowledge explicit.
4.9.10	**Describe the use of Knowledge Management in your organization's decision making**
	Knowledge management isn't in the current lexicon of the organization's culture. The culture relies more on face-to-face knowledge in coming to organizational decisions. Programs use these individual bases on an as-needed bases and rely on the abilities of staff to "pull together" the information required at any given time. The foundation is a knowledge intensive organization in which knowledge is the key asset that needs proper consolidation. There is a de facto community of practice surrounding fundraising. New knowledge needs to be continuously created for the organization to survive. These facts point to the need for interaction with the people of the organization to make decisions. The knowledge and instincts of the program managers coupled with specialized internally or externally created reports and information is how the typical decision making of the foundation is achieved. Little if any quantitative indicators in Knowledge Management are used or found.

Table 31.

4.8.1	**Describe the ways your organization identifies/quantifies the value of knowledge**
	The organization identifies knowledge in fundraising primarily from a business listing perspective. As most queries are tacit and handled through socialization, knowledge is only quantified at the outputs end.
4.8.2	**Describe the ways your organization links knowledge to the bottom line**
	Program knowledge is directly related to program fundraising. Fundraising dollars raised drive program goals. Program goals and fundraising are incorporated into overall budget processes. The actual amounts raised are reported against budget on a monthly basis. The success or failure is consistently known and tracked.
4.8.3	**Describe how your organization invests/allocates resources that increase its knowledge base in a measurable way**
	The organization does invest in employee training through conferences and memberships in statewide and national organizations of similar types. This allows for the accumulation of tacit knowledge in best practices in other similar organizations. The resources are allocated on a programmatic basis through the budgeting process and include the lodging and travel costs associated with such training. The organization also pays management fees to its Member Partner vendor for updates and improvements to the data base of organizations and individuals. These investments are made on a prospective basis with intended future benefits expected and anticipated. Resources are also allocated through the budget process with the business case for both tacit and system expenditures expressed either through written or verbal exchange.

2. These goals directly relate and support the goals in section 3.7.a. No money, no mission. The strategic planning goals ensure the programs are tackling the most pressing issues of the community related to the foundation's mission and that adequate financial resources are in place to do that. Due to the changing nature of any community, programs must adapt and adjust as well. Economic and community development don't just happen, they require constant care. The goal of the organization and ultimately its supporters is to move from a year-to-year funding mentality to a longer-term sustainable funding base. Currently, the planning does not support this long-term approach.

4.1 **Company Strategy and Knowledge** (Table 26)

4.2 **Knowledge Management Strategic Issues** (Table 27) Identify and describe how your entity is.

Table 32.

4.13.1	Identifying its Intellectual Property and its value
a.	Brand Name – Currently attempting to enhance with radio marketing – no valuation
b.	Reputation – Identifying through brand but no valuation
c.	Trademarks – Have logos trademarked – no valuation
d.	Patents – N/A
e.	Copyrights – Web-based copyright laws otherwise not identified or valued
f.	Topography Right – N/A
g.	Rights in protectable data bases – Through Licensing – not valued
h.	Regulatory approval and authorizations – Through granting agencies – value of grants
i.	Trade Secrets – N/A
4.13.2	**Managing the value (and taxation) of its Intellectual Property**
a.	Brand Name – The organization has begun radio marketing. Publications, web site and family of logos are used to manage the value of the organization. N/A
b.	Reputation – This is being done through the quality of the staff and its leadership. Also, programming and events are managed value fo the organization
c.	Trademarks – this is being managed through the family look of all program logos.
d.	Patents – N/A
e.	Copyrights – Managed through review of web-based law and in conjunction with Build My Own Site.com.
f.	Topography rights – N/A
g.	Rights in protectable data bases – Managed through annual contracts with data base vendor.
h.	Regulatory approval and authorizations – Internally, staff manages the entire granting process from application through payment and final closure
i.	Trade secrets – N/A
4.13.3	**Protecting, managing the risk and insuring its Intellectual Property**
a.	Brand Name – Officers and Directors Liability insurance for volunteers. The organization also utilizes hiring practices that help to ensure quality hiring. Personnel policies are also in place to protect the brand. Staff review and accountability practices are also used in the protection of the brand name.
b.	Reputation – This is protected and managed in much the same manner as brand name with the addition of legal action against those threatening harm to the reputation of the organization. For this, the organization carries additional insurances.
c.	Trademarks- Trademarks are registered and infringements are met with legal challenges. Close to trademarks are domain names. These are registered with national registers as well and maintained for the benefit of the organization.
d.	Patents – N/A
e.	Copyrights – Most of this is protected through web-based copyright protections of Buildmyownssite.com
f.	Topography rights – N/A
g.	Rights in protectable data bases – Business insurance is included for this protection and the IT infrastructure set in place to protect the data includes firewalls, Citrix overlay and a DMZ file server. All access to database materials is also password protected with varying levels of accessibility based on position and job duties.
h.	Regulatory Approval and Authorizations – To maintain a foundation and receive donations or grants, certain IRS regulations need to be met. The organization authorized an independent outside financial audit for these purposes. Tax returns are prepared in conjunction with audit duties.
i.	Trade Secrets – N/A

Table 33.

6.1.1	The current stage of your organization's experience with knowledge management is?

For as small as the organization is, it is actually quite phenomenal how much planning has gone into the knowledge management aspects without any formal recognition of knowledge management. IT and phone infrastructure are in place based on an understanding that the sharing of information at any location amongst the organization's staff and volunteers is quite valuable and needed for not only survival, but expansion of operations. Of the three taxonomies identified by Russ et al. (2010b see chapter 7), the organization is an intuitive utilization, Internal Utilization and External Tacitness. The characteristics of these point to an organization that:

- exploits current existing knowledge while keeping this knowledge tacit
- Tries to sustain new product development to improve present products and services
- Tends to have lower product effectiveness and lower process effectiveness
- Focuses on exploiting currently existing knowledge while focusing on developing most of the knowledge needed internally
- Focuses on close relationship within the company
- Focuses on keeping core capability knowledge tacit and using knowledge and capabilities from the outside as much as possible for everything else
- Seems to be the least effective of the four strategies represented in each of the three taxonomies

This has been the knowledge plan to date and it has created the culture within the organization as it exists. Because the organization is in such a high-knowledge industry, this points to a need for change in strategy. Since the previous strategy caused the culture as it exists, it will be difficult to implement strategy that changes both the experience with knowledge management and the culture required for that change.

6.1.2	The current status of knowledge management offices is?

The currently does not exist any formally identified knowledge management office within the organization.

6.1.3	The most valuable aspects for your organization, of knowledge management are?

There are two primary aspects are the tacit knowledge of fundraising and donors which is resident with staff and the organization's data base within its IT infrastructure. This is made valuable because of the leadership within the organization. These combinations have enabled the organization to at least maintain the status quo from a fundraising standpoint over the past decade.

6.1.4	The critical gaps in knowledge strategy are?

The largest gaps in the current knowledge strategy are:

- Not having a formal knowledge strategy concerning fundraising
- Allowing for the majority of fundraising knowledge to remain tacit
- Too little procedural knowledge for capturing tacit knowledge and converting into explicit knowledge
- Very little analytical definition and activity regarding fundraising
- Limited query capability of internal and external data bases
- Unable to tie multiple data sources together within organizations systems
- Cultural gaps that could move current knowledge strategy to one of "most effective" in the taxonomies identified by Russ et al. (2006)
- Not tying compensation systems to the acquisition, documentation and sharing of knowledge throughout the organization

6.1.5	Other most important findings are?

Outside of the gaps, important findings of this audit are that a lot of the groundwork for developing and implementing a knowledge strategy are in place. The IT infrastructure is in place, leadership is strong and staff tacit knowledge is something that could be collected on many levels. What remain critically lacking are the resources to accomplish what needs to be done from both a financial and personnel standpoint. Time and money should not be critical impediments but the organization does need a plan to overcome them. Leadership backing of a knowledge initiative of this sort will be critical for success.

Table 34.

6.2.1	Knowledge strategy

The organization should work throughout the current planning cycle to identify and hammer out plans to implement a knowledge strategy concerning fundraising for fiscal 2009. They will need to identify:

- People responsible
- Project scope
- Major stakeholders
- Information needed
- Sources of knowledge
- Systems needed
- Processes agreed upon
- Resources allocable – financial, systems, human
- Goals and objectives
- Outcomes/Measurements

continued on following page

Table 34. continued

6.2.2	**Knowledge Processes**

This will need to begin and be nurtured with leadership from the top. Once that has been accomplished, a clear understanding of the concepts of knowledge management is going to have to be inferred upon staff in order to come to a common understanding of what is being done, why it is being done and how it will tie to the organizational goals of increased fundraising. A knowledge strategy will need to be developed that incorporates the items listed above. Timelines will be developed but a small project should be worked on initially so success and momentum of the process can occur.

6.2.3	**Knowledge value measures/Intellectual Capital**

Value measures should be discussed in the strategy-setting part of the project but continually refined and adjusted as the process moves forward. Initially, getting the knowledge codified will be the focus and this will require value measures on that data. These can be tracked as the process progresses. Particularly insightful Intellectual Capital should be acknowledged throughout the collection process. Once up, utilization value measures should be identified with success factor targets met. The intellectual capital needed in the extraction and analysis of the data combined with new reporting methodologies will then need to become a part of the process.

6.2.4	**Leadership/roles/skills**

Leadership will need to take on this issue as soon as is practically possible. Once identified as an organization priority by Paul Jadin (the chamber President), the leadership team will need to identify project leaders/team members and ensure that the skills needed from a knowledge perspective and the resources required are in place.

6.2.5	**Culture**

In analyzing the taxonomies of Russ et al. (2006), it became apparent that the culture of the organization is a direct result of its strategy. Because the strategy will need to be changed in order to accomplish anything resembling a "most effective" knowledge strategy, culture will also need to change. Information sharing will need to be a norm. Codifying knowledge will need to be a priority and trust issues will need to be overcome. These will need adjustments to compensation systems and that should occur simultaneously with the implementation of the new knowledge initiative.

6.2.6	**Infrastructure/KBS**

A study will need to commence regarding tools that can assist the knowledge team in query, search and reporting of both internal and external sources of knowledge. The majority of a sharing and open infrastructure and KBS is in place with the exception of these much needed tools to assist in the fundraising for the foundation's programs.

6.2.7	**Resource allocation**

Time, people and money resources were identified as items that were impediments to the knowledge initiative. Leadership will have to decide where and when these resources need to be available and where they will ultimately come from. This analysis should begin immediately as eliminating as many barriers to successful completion as possible is critical.

6.2.8	**Intellectual Property**

The organization should at a minimum begin to understand and track its intellectual property. Much of the product developed by staff could be copyrighted and new ideas used to further enhance other intangible assets such as the overall brand and standing of the human capital within the community and industry. Ultimately, leveraging these will also help in the fundraising aspects of the foundation programs.

6.2.9	**Security**

This was one area that the organization took great pains to implement in the latest IT and phone upgrades. Web-based security and e-mail security continue to be challenging areas in the organization and documented, planned upgrades need to be planned. While most of the software upgrades are set to occur automatically and external IT support is contract for regularly scheduled maintenance, centralized and documented procedures and actual work performed should be recorded.

6.2.10	**Knowledge Initiatives**

This is a knowledge initiative that should be undertaken by the organization. This audit pointed to areas where adjustments need to be made and where there were gaps to implementing a knowledge initiative. Educating the leadership of the organization in knowledge management, working up a pilot project of this minimal magnitude and then planning for continued initiatives as resources permit are clearly in the organization's best interest.

4.3 **Levers of Knowledge Management** (Table 28) Identify and describe the following.

4.4 **Knowledge Management Challenges** (Table 29) Identify and describe the:

4.9 **Knowledge Processes** (Table 30): Describe the systematic approaches your organization has to:

IC AND SUMMARY

4.8 – Intellectual Capital (Table 31)

4.13 – Intellectual Property (Table 32)

Identify and Describe how your organization is:

SUMMARY

6.1 Conclusion (Table 33)

6.2 Implications (Table 34)

Where and when should your organization go from here, in regards to:

6.3 What else did you learn? What other suggestions, proposals might you have?

Aligning an organization's Knowledge Management with its strategic objectives and goals is an incredibly thought provoking and in many instances, controversial process. It isn't enough to know that something may or may not be in the interests of an organization, one also has to be able to justify and convince others of the need. Once the need is established, to have others take responsibility for KM activities is no small task. The KM Manager cannot be driving an initiative for his or her own sake, it must be aligned appropriately with strategic objectives and those objectives must remain the responsibility of the appropriate individuals. It cannot be something just for "someone who has the time," it must be a cultural shift in thinking and then process for the continued competitiveness and survival in the business environment of today.

Change is never easy and I doubt most in my organization will take the time to read something this long, much less try to absorb and understand what KM truly is and how it can assist in achieving strategic objectives. Knowing this makes me realize that I am going to have to work out a plan to deal with the truly most forceful barrier to KM – our own employees. I know we discussed that it is critical to have support from the top and that leadership in these initiatives is crucial but the only suggestion I would have is to identify by name those who are going to need to understand what is being proposed and have a plan to effectively pass this knowledge on to them and deal with them before the process begins.

6.4 What would you add or change in this audit?

As I move forward with this initiative, I will be looking to add visuals that help explain the concepts, timelines, strategy, goals, implementation, and ultimately flow processes that tie KM to the organization's strategic objectives and show KM as a vital core competence moving forward.

REFERENCES

Gottschalk, P. (2000). Knowledge management systems: A comparison of law firms and consulting firms. *Information Science*, 3(3), 117–124.

Gottschalk, P. (2002). Toward a model of growth stages for knowledge management technology in law firms. *Information Science*, 5(2), 79–123.

Russ, M., Fineman, R., & Jones, J. K. (2010a). KARMA-Knowledge assessment review and management audit. In M. Russ (ed.) *Knowledge Management Strategies for Business Development*. Hershey PA: IGI Global.

Russ, M., Fineman, R., & Jones, J. K. (2010b). C³EEP taxonomy: Knowledge based strategies. InM. Russ (ed.) *Knowledge Management Strategies for Business Development.* Hershey PA: IGI Global.

Russ, M., Jones, J. K., & Fineman, R. (2006). Toward a taxonomy of knowledge-based strategies: Early findings. *International Journal of Knowledge and Learning, 2*(1&2), 1–40. doi:10.1504/ IJKL.2006.009677

Wissensmanagement Forum. (2003). *An illustrated guide to knowledge management.* Graz Austria. Retrieved on February 14, 2008, from http://www.wm-forum.org/files/Handbuch/ An_Illustrated_Guide_to_Knowledge_Management.pdf

ENDNOTE

[1]   Based on Gottschalk, 2002.

Chapter 6
A Model for Knowledge Management and Intellectual Capital Audits

Carolina López-Nicolás
University of Murcia, Spain

Ángel L. Meroño-Cerdán
University of Murcia, Spain

ABSTRACT

Due to contradictory results obtained in knowledge management (KM) initiatives, a model of audit is presented. The main action in the international project "Strategi" is the development and application of a model to diagnose and propose suitable recommendations concerning the management of knowledge and intellectual capital of a firm. A brief description of the model is presented after the exposition of its key scientific assumptions.

INTRODUCTION

In the last decade, the importance of knowledge has been highlighted by both academics and practitioners (Hislop, 2003; Braganza, 2004). Nowadays, knowledge is the fundamental basis of competition (Zack, 1999) and, particularly tacit knowledge, can be a source of advantage because it is unique, imperfectly mobile, imperfectly imitable and non-substitutable (Ambrosini & Bowman, 2001). However, the mere act of processing knowledge itself does not guarantee strategic advantage (Zack, 2002); instead, knowledge has to be managed. Skyrme (2001) defines Knowledge Management

DOI: 10.4018/978-1-60566-348-7.ch006

(KM) as the explicit and systematic management of vital knowledge - and its associated processes of creation, organization, diffusion, use and exploitation. This conceptualization concerns about three basic ideas. Firstly, organizations need to have a clear attitude and constant efforts to KM. Secondly, companies have to focus on managing core knowledge (both explicit and tacit) due to limited resources. Finally, KM is a process composed by a set of different knowledge activities, which need to be properly managed.

From academic perspective, KM principles have been studied and implemented in every organizational discipline (Chourides et al., 2003) and related to many aspects, including strategy (Snyman & Kruger, 2004), human resources (e.g. Bierly &

Daly, 2002), quality (e.g. Adamson, 2005), information technology (IT), and marketing (Tsai & Shih, 2004). This diversity has contributed to the rapid advance of the field (Argote et al., 2003), but also to a lack of integration of ideas (Scholl et al., 2004) and terminology (Clarke & Turner, 2004). In this situation, there are several challenges to establishing KM as a separate discipline (Nonaka & Peltokorpi, 2006). As a result, there is not a clear model about the factors that may enable or disable companies to adopt KM or about the variables which KM may have a significant impact on.

From practice perspective, firms are noticing the importance of managing knowledge if they want to remain competitive (Zack, 1999) and to achieve performance improvement (King et al., 2008). Thus, many companies everywhere are beginning to actively manage their knowledge and intellectual capital (DeTienne et al., 2004): most large companies in the USA, and many in Europe, have some sort of KM initiative in place (Davenport & Völpel, 2001). Nevertheless, many KM systems have been unsuccessful (Tsui, 2005; Schultze & Boland, 2000), with Storey & Barnett (2000) reporting failure rates of over 80%, due to diverse reasons, such as an overfocus on IT, inappropriate organizational culture and KM strategies, or ignorance of KM consequences.

Literature is consistent in the idea that KM audits can play a significant role in the solution of many of the failures in KM programs (Hylton 2002). By discovering what knowledge is possessed, it is then possible to find the most effective method of storage and dissemination. (Liebowitz et al., 2000). Thus, these audits must be the first part of any KM strategy (Henczel, 2000). Yet it has not been sufficiently recognized as being of supreme importance to every KM undertaking (Perez-Soltero et al., 2006). Thus, the purpose of present chapter is to contribute to the advance of KM research from a strategic point of view, by analyzing the importance of KM audits, and by proposing a model to implement a consis-

tent methodology for auditing knowledge. Our contribution may help organizations to put into practice such a complex and confusing concept as KM (De Long & Seemann, 2000; Firestone & McElroy, 2005).

LITERATURE ON KM AUDITS

Prior research agrees in that KM audits are paramount to the success of any KM program (Hylton, 2002). Many of the mistakes of both earlier and more recent adopters of KM can be traced to the serious oversight of not including the knowledge audit in their overall KM strategies and initiatives (Burnet et al., 2004). Generally a KM audit will help to identify: the knowledge needs of the organization; what knowledge assets are available and where they are located; if knowledge gaps or bottlenecks exist; and the knowledge flow within the organization. KM audits are considered as the first part of any KM strategy (Henczel, 2000), since by discovering what knowledge is possessed, it is then possible to find the most effective method of storage and dissemination. (Liebowitz et al., 2000). More recently, Cheung et al. (2007) conclude that many KM programs failed because the companies themselves lacked the knowledge on KM and their knowledge organization. The practical implementation of the systematic approach for knowledge auditing allows an organization to reveal its KM needs, strengths, weaknesses, opportunities, threats and risks. Hence, appropriate KM strategy can be derived for better managing its knowledge.

There are many benefits in applying a KM framework or methodology to audit knowledge: offers legitimacy, provides consistent language, outlines a process, provides a checklist, offers a source of ideas and addresses non-technical aspects (Robertson, 2002). Specifically, benefits of KM audits include: 'identifying what knowledge is needed to support overall organizational goals and individual and team activities; it gives tangible evidence of the extent to which knowledge is being effectively managed and indicates where improvements are needed; provides an evidence-based account of the knowledge that exists in the organization and how that knowledge moves around in and is used by the organization; provides a map of what knowledge exists in the organization and where it exists revealing both gaps and duplication; reveals pockets of knowledge that are not currently being used to good advantage and therefore offer untapped potential; it provides a map of knowledge and communication flows and networks, revealing both examples of good practice and blockages and barriers to good practice; it provides an inventory of knowledge assets allowing them to become more visible and therefore more measurable and accountable and giving a clearer understanding of the contribution of knowledge to organizational performance; and it provides vital information for the development of effective KM programs and initiatives that are directly relevant to the organization's specific knowledge needs and current situation' (National Electronic Library Health, 2001).

Despite its potential benefits, KM audits have not been sufficiently recognized as being of supreme importance to every KM undertaking (Perez-Soltero et al., 2006) and few studies focus on the analysis of KM audit implementation. A reason for this situation may lay on the fact that researchers on the topic will frequently encounter references to reputable consulting enterprises that own proprietary knowledge audit methodologies. Such methodologies are not publicly available but can be acquired for a fee, if one wishes to implement KM within an enterprise. This may not always be an economically viable option for an enterprise, nor does it provide any opportunities for the client to compare the suitability of each technique. Despite the lack of published accounts that precisely detail how to execute a standard KM audit methodology, it is possible to extract sufficient insight from existing literature to de-

velop a basis for the creation of a knowledge audit methodology (Schwikkard & Du Toit, 2004).

Methodology in a KM Audit

In general knowledge audits consist of various phases: the identification of knowledge needs through the use of questionnaires, interviews and focus groups; the development of a knowledge inventory mainly focusing on the types of knowledge available; where this knowledge is located; how it is maintained and store, what it is used for and how relevant it is; analysis of knowledge flows in terms of people, processes and systems; and the creation of a knowledge map (National Electronic Library Health, 2001).

Phases of a KM Audit

A knowledge audit will consist of two major tasks, each of which can be done without the other (Stevens, 2000). The first, often called knowledge mapping, involves locating repositories of knowledge throughout the organization. This effort is primarily technological and usually prepares the way for creating a knowledge database. The knowledge mapping process is relatively straightforward. It takes an inventory of what people in the organization have written down or entered into information systems, as well as identifying sources of information employees use that come from the outside (such as public or university libraries, Web sites or subscription services). Finding and organizing all that data may be time-consuming, but it is not conceptually difficult. The second, more intensive category of audit task attempts to capture the patterns of knowledge flow in the organization. This knowledge flow audit examines how people process information that ultimately determines how well an organization uses and shares its knowledge (Stevens, 2000).

The specific detail of each phase is different depending on the methodology under study.

Although many researchers proposed different approaches of knowledge audit, some are either too theoretical or have limitations in practical value. Thus, a systematic methodology for KM audits, the Strategi model, is presented later as a solution for both academics and practitioners in this area.

Next, more salient models for performing KM audits are presented: KeKma-Audit Road-Map by Hylton; knowledge auditing model by Cheung et al. (2007); the KM audit model by Hadzic et al. (2008); the knowledge audit by Sharma & Chowdhury (2007); the KM audit by Biloslavo & Trnavc̆evic (2007); the knowledge audit by Liebowitz et al. (2000); and the knowledge audit tool by Hull et al. (2000).

The KeKma-Audit Road-Map by Hylton

The ©KeKma-Audit method (http://www.kekma-audit.com/) provides a comprehensive Knowledge Audit, from start to finish. From the starting point of Research, Consultation, Assessments and Training, then to Questionnaire Survey and Interviews, and on to the Knowledge Inventory, and then to the final stage of Knowledge Mapping. The method is a Knowledge Audit system and tool designed to help an organization, in any industry, sector or business, know and assess its current knowledge assets focusing on the quantity, quality, use and value of existing corporate knowledge.

The Knowledge Auditing Model by Cheung et al. (2007)

Cheung et al. (2007) present a systematic approach for knowledge auditing which is composed of a number of stages with the focus on the establishment of an overall framework and customized tools for knowledge auditing. Their method consisted of eight phases: orientation and background study, cultural assessment, in-depth investigation, building knowledge inventory and

knowledge mapping, knowledge network analysis and social network analysis, recommendation of KM strategy, deploying KM tools and building collaborative culture, and continuous knowledge re-auditing. This KM audit involves a complete analysis and investigation of the company in terms of what knowledge exists in the company, where it is, who owns it and how it is created.

The model is trial successfully implemented in a railway company and results show that the method yields a number of benefits that include the identification of the critical knowledge and the subsequent recommendations can be derived for better managing the knowledge in the railway company.

The KM Audit Model by Hadzic et al. (2008)

Hadzic et al. (2008) propose a KM audit model to assist organizations to obtain an accurate picture of their knowledge-based assets and the strategies used to manage that knowledge across the organizations. The model, consisting of the analysis of KM drivers, KM contingencies (socio-technical enablers, knowledge processes and knowledge stocks) and KM outcomes, also serves as a means for assessing how well the identified assets and strategies meet organizational business goals and strategies. The practical application of the model is illustrated in the local government environment.

The Knowledge Audit by Sharma & Chowdhury (2007)

Their research outlines the construction and utilization of a diagnostic tool for performing what they call a material knowledge audit in an enterprise of medium complexity. The tool was developed by adapting some of the more applicable techniques suggested in the literature by practitioners. Their method composed of four phases: knowledge needs analysis, knowledge inventory analysis, knowledge flows analysis, and knowledge mapping. It was then put on trial in five organizations – a library, an it consulting firm, a research institute, a telecommunications service provider, and a media agency – which were involved in knowledge intensive business activities. Their results reveal the dearth of such diagnostic tools as well as the need to continually refine knowledge audit techniques so that the practice evolves from an art into a science.

The KM Audit by Biloslavo & Trnavcevic (2007)

In contrast to other methods for KM assessment, Biloslavo & Trnavcevic (2007) propose a KM audit consisted of two phases. In the first stage, the focus is on providing insights into the present situation concerning KM in the organization, by means of a 'snapshot' of a number of crucial processes and preconditions. In the second stage, the stress is on providing strategies and tactics for the further development of KM in the organization, by positioning the organization along the KM development path. Moreover, they consider that besides gaining some insights about the nature of its own KM practices, an organization can use a KM audit as an external and internal benchmarking tool. As an external benchmarking tool, a KM audit can help the organization to collect and transfer best practices from different industries. As an internal benchmarking tool, a KM audit can reveal internal best practices that have been overlooked and support their transfer to other parts of the organization. Since these best practices are also in a constant state of flux, the KM audit can be used in an ongoing way to continuously represent the changing profile of the organization's KM competencies.

The Knowledge Audit by Liebowitz et al. (2000)

They view the knowledge audit as being the business needs assessment, cultural assessment, and an examination of what knowledge is needed, available, missing, applied, and contained. Their focus is on the third strand of the knowledge audit described above, namely determining what knowledge is needed, what is available and missing, who needs this knowledge, and how it will be applied.

The Knowledge Audit Tool by Hull et al. (2000)

They develop a knowledge audit tool for analysing and improving the various forms of KM activity within the Innovation processes of companies. It is addressed principally to those companies with well-developed and sophisticated units for innovation, such as R&D departments. The main operational element of this Audit Tool is in the form of a questionnaire, which aims to act as both a discovery mechanism and as a prompt to further reflection on the specific KM activities within innovation processes. The questionnaire consists of some 80 questions, each in the form of a description of a specific KM practice (namely, knowledge processing characteristics, knowledge domain, format of the practice, and perceived contribution to unit performance) these having been derived from the case studies and additional desk research.

THE STRATEGI MODEL FOR KM AUDITS

As previously highlighted, many researchers proposed different approaches of knowledge audit. Yet, some are either too theoretical or have limitations in practical value. Thus, a systematic methodology for KM audits, the Strategi model, is presented here as a solution for both academics and practitioners in this area.

The prominence of concepts and applications in the KM field has leaded some Region of Murcia (Spain) social agents to devise a mechanism to spread new management principles across businesses (Sabater et al., 2003). The Strategi project is formed by the following European regions: Murcia (Spain), Wien (Austria) and Aveiro (Portugal) and is funded by the European Commission (European Social Fund). The project consists of the following main actions:

1) **Awareness Campaign:** Two awareness activities about the importance of introducing KM concepts and initiatives have been done in each participant country. The first activity was a mailing where KM concepts and benefits were explained, and at the same time, the performance of a series of public conferences about the Strategi project was announced. Conferences, three in each participant country, were structured as follows: a well-known national expert, an international one, and, finally, a round table with firms possessing experience in Knowledge Management program implementation Candidates met in the third conference so that the project was explained in detail and firms' commitment was shown.

2) **KM and Intellectual Capital (IC) Audit Among 36 Companies from the Three Countries:** According to different criteria, such as innovation grade, geographical decentralization and industry, on the one hand, and interest and commitment, on the other hand, the participant firms were selected. Their membership consists of, first, attending specific training about KM and IC, and second, being audited as explained below. The aims of training are related to the subsequent

audit: to create a common language with common concepts, to make firms aware of the need for audits and, finally, to provide companies with resources so that they can manage themselves in the future, as they will have learnt from audit. This part of the project is where we are going to focus our attention in the next pages of this chapter.

3) **Portal Web:** This action has a transverse nature and serves during the project as a communication tool among public, the participant firms and the auditors.

Background for the KM Audit in the Strategi Model

The purpose of audits is to diagnose and propose some recommendations for improving KM and Intellectual Capital (IC) measurement systems. The reasoning behind the Strategi methodology for implementing KM audits is based on two theoretical assumptions.

1. Simultaneous Consideration of KM and IC

We consider that the value of a firm's IC is a stock variable, whereas KM is a flow variable. So, we will follow one of the KM kind of projects named by (Davenport et al., 1998] as "KM as an asset". Although this alternative is in a minority (Almansa et al. 2002), we suspect being especially useful the link between KM Plan and the use of IC indicators. Bontis (1999) points that the real problem of KM is related to its measurement. Managers need a methodology to identify and value their KM efforts.

Being aware of initiatives such as APCQ (Lopez, 2001) especially interesting in the starting stages of implementing KM programs, our proposal deals with linking KM efforts and variables selected to measure intangible assets. Once practices have been chosen and KM programs came into operation, the attention is in linking its use

Figure 1. *Intellectual Capital and KM Audit Strategi Model*

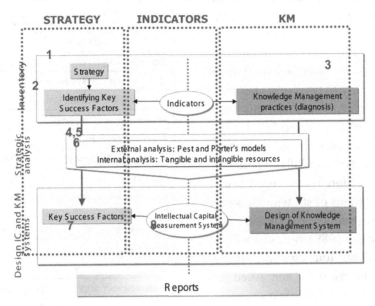

(measured by a set of indicators) to the evolution of measurement IC system components.

Similarly, Iazzolino & Pietrantonio (2005) propose an innovative Knowledge Audit Approach (KAA) which has been particularly developed basing on two main fundamentals: first, the Balanced Scorecard classification scheme of the business objectives and goals; and second, an Intellectual Capital (IC) representation model.

2. Categorizing KM Approaches according to Strategy

IC measurement models ask for the need to adaptation to the specific reality of each firm. However, there is no enough evidence of how to do it. Mainly according to Hansen et al. (1999), Hahn & Subramani (2000), Gray & Chan (2000), and Zack (1999), we want to analyze links between the firm strategy and KM strategy. Besides strategy, the very selection of the participant companies has been made in order to know about the influence of national culture, industry, innovation level, geographical distance and other variables.

Phases of the KM Audit in the Strategi Model

In order to perform the IC and KM audit, the following phases must be followed. Those stages are presented in Figure 1. The three main phases (inventory, strategic analysis and design of KM and IC systems) are further consisted of various steps (numbers in Figure 1) related to strategy, indicators and KM.

Inventory

The objective of this phase is to know about the initial state of the firm's intangible assets and KM practices. This inventory is considered as the initial step of the auditing process in the Strategi model. This position contrasts to the proposal by Hylton (2002), since inventory is not the starting point in her KeKma-Audit Road-Map. Instead, we consider that a first stage in a KM audit must provide insights into the present situation of a company in terms of KM, as Biloslavo & Trnavčevic (2007) also state.

A set of questionnaires has been made to obtain information concerning:

- Strategy at the business level (step 1 in Figure 1). To measure business-level strategy a diversity of typologies has been used in literature. Among them, this study tries to measure the more widely accepted and extended ones: Miles & Snow's (1978) and Porter's (1980) typologies. Two basic procedures were used. First, nominal descriptions of strategies. As previous literature (Snow & Hebriniak, 1980; Zajac & Shortell, 1989) we used written descriptions of the four strategies in the Miles and Snow typology and asked top managers to classify their own organization. The second way we used to measure strategy was a multi-item scale containing different competitive variables considered the basic elements of two generic strategies (Dess and Davis, 1984; Segev, 1992; Kotha & Vadlamani, 1995), as shown in Table 1.

- For identifying key success factors (step 2 in Figure 1) a set of questionnaires has been made from the literature revision (Edvinsson, 1996; Bontis, 1996; Brooking, 1996; Roos & Roos, 1997; Euroforum, 1998). Companies must assess the

Table 1. Inventory of Strategy at business level

Cost Leadership	Differentiation
Competitive pricing	Specialise in geographical segments
Concern for cost reduction	New product development
Operating efficiency	Influencing distribution channels
Manufacturing process innovation	Customer service capability
Experienced personnel	Innovation in marketing techniques and methods
	Brand identification

Table 2. Inventory of key success factors

Key Success Factors: Human Capital
Employees' satisfaction
Type of employees (age, contract, …)
Knowledge an skills of employees
Employees with abilities to motivate others
Innovativeness of employees
Teamwork abilities

Key Success Factors: Structural Capital
Shared vision
Making processes of design, definition and revision of strategy regularly
Clear assignment of tasks, responsibilities and decision making
Patents and licenses
Production and sales activities
Complementary activities (HR management, finance, …)
Products/services design and development
Mechanisms for information and knowledge capturing
Mechanisms for information and knowledge sharing
Use of ICT
Making innovation processes regularly
Organizational culture

Key Success Factors: Relational Capital
Be aware of the type of customers
Customers' loyalty
Reputation
Customers' satisfaction
Customer service and attention
Be aware of changes in customers' tastes and needs
Brand awareness
Collaborative relationships with customers
Collaborative relationships with competitors
Collaborative relationships with suppliers
Collaborative relationships with other stakeholders
Actions oriented towards attracting new profitable customers

importance of each factor to the success of the firm (Table 2).

- KM practices used by the companies in order to increase their Intellectual Capital are examined (step 3 in Figure 1). A generic view of practices has been used partly based on Hahn & Subramani (2000) and Gray & Chan (2000). The final list includes: Individual Learning, Teams/Communities of Practices, Training, External Sources of Knowledge, Knowledge Transferring Mechanisms, Business Computing Applications, Repositories and Electronic Communication Systems. Every KM practices focus either on a codification strategy or a personalization strategy (Hansen et al., 1999). The codification strategy focuses on codifying knowledge using a 'people-to-document' approach: knowledge is extracted from the person who developed it, made independent of that person, and reused for various purposes. Codification firms invest heavily in IT. This strategy allows many people to search for and retrieve codified knowledge without having to contact the person who originally developed it, since knowledge is stored in documents, manuals, databases, electronic repositories, and so on. That opens up the possibility of achieving scale in knowledge reuse and thus of growing the business. Hence, codification creates intellectual capital, by converting individual knowledge into structural capital. On the other hand, the personalization strategy focuses on dialogue between individuals, not knowledge objects in a database. It is a person-to-person approach where knowledge is shared not only face-to-face, but also over the telephone, by e-mail and via videoconferences, thus building networks of people. Examples of KM practices included in the inventory phase are shown in Table 3.

• Finally, auditors will search for the indicators used by the firm to monitor IC factors and KM.

Table 3. Inventory of KM practices

Codification Strategy	Personalization Strategy
Decision Support Systems	Spontaneous knowledge transfer initiatives
Groupware	Mentoring
Document repositories	Teams/Communities of Practice
Knowledge maps	Groupware
Workflow	Video conferencing
Shared databases	Yellow pages
	Discussion forums

Strategic Analysis

The context in which firms act conditions their present and future strategy and, therefore, the base of Intellectual Capital and knowledge that they should develop. Therefore, a Strategic Analysis is carried out distinguishing:

• EXTERNAL ANALYSIS. Its purpose is to identify those factors that may influence the firms but are not under their control. External analysis has two major components: the general and the industry environment analysis. The general environment (step 4 in Figure 1) is composed of elements that can influence an industry and the firms within it (Fahey & Narayanan, 1986). To identify the key success elements derived from the general environment, we asked their top managers to assess the influence on their own company of 25 demographic, socio-cultural, economic, technological and political/legal elements. The second component of external analysis is industry environment, which is the set of factors that more directly influences the firms in a particular industry (step 5 in Figure 1). Companies have to assess the expected influence of each environmental factor in the sector. Porter's Five Forces Framework (Porter, 1980) is used to analysis industry environment. To measure the importance of the five forces two questions were included. In the first one we asked the top managers to asses the threat of each force. To complete this information in a second question we asked the top managers to assess 15 variables which are considered determinants of the five competitive forces. All the measures are shown in Table 4.

- INTERNAL ANALYSIS. It has been carried out based on resource-based view of the firm (Grant, 1992). According to this view, the internal resources and capabilities of firms are their main source of competitive advantage (Barney, 1991; Grant, 1991; Amit & Schoemaker, 1993). Although the main sources of competitive advantage are capabilities, the basic units of analysis

Table 4. External strategic analysis

General Environment
Political situation in the country will have a positive (negative) effect on the companies operating in my sector
Regional economic law will have a positive (negative) effect on the companies operating in my sector
National economic law will have a positive (negative) effect on the companies operating in my sector
EU economic law will have a positive (negative) effect on the companies operating in my sector
Fiscal law will have a positive (negative) effect on the companies operating in my sector
An important increase (decrease) in product demand is expected
The expected situation of production factors (human labor, capital, raw materials, ...) will have a positive (negative) effect on the companies operating in my sector
National economic policy will have a positive (negative) effect on the companies operating in my sector
The expected situation of the labor market will have a positive (negative) effect on the companies operating in my sector
The expected social unrest will have a positive (negative) effect on the companies operating in my sector
Trade union activities will have a positive (negative) effect on the companies operating in my sector
The existence of social groups will have a positive (negative) effect on the companies operating in my sector
The existence of ethnic groups will have a positive (negative) effect on the companies operating in my sector
The existence of religious groups will have a positive (negative) effect on the companies operating in my sector
Values, attitudes, life rules and beliefs (culture) will have a positive (negative) effect on the companies operating in my sector
Movements to defend consumers will have a positive (negative) effect on the companies operating in my sector
R&D national policy and budget will have a positive (negative) effect on the companies operating in my sector
Innovation in production processes will have a positive (negative) effect on the companies operating in my sector
The development of new technologies will have a positive (negative) effect on the companies operating in my sector
Policies supporting new technologies will have a positive (negative) effect on the companies operating in my sector
Expected scientific and technical knowledge will have a positive (negative) effect on the companies operating in my sector
The existence of scientific and technical infrastructure will have a positive (negative) effect on the companies operating in my sector
Specific Environment
New firms can easily establish in the sector
Competitiveness among the firms in the sector is high
Customers show higher bargaining power than firms in the sector
Suppliers show higher bargaining power than firms in the sector
Products similar to the product sold in the sector are created easily

are resources (Grant, 1991). Therefore, in this phase (step 6 in Figure 1) 13 tangible and intangible resources of each firm are assessed in comparison to their competitors´ resources, asking top managers to do it (Table 5). To complete strategic analysis, we used opened questions to ask top managers about the information of internal and external context that they systematically search and have into account to take decisions.

Design of Intellectual Capital and KM Measurement Systems

The objective of this phase is to design a system which will allow the firm to know the state of intangible assets and KM practices that lead the company to aim its strategy. This is such a creative process that each company has to put all its efforts (and employees) together in order to effectively design the system. The following stages must be followed:

- Identifying the firm's future strategy and assessing key success factors (steps 7 and 8 in Figure 1). A set of perspectives (human, organizational, relational and financial) will be considered from some Intellectual Capital models: Edvinsson (1996), Bontis (1996), Brooking, (1996), Roos & Roos (1997), Euroforum (1998) and the Balanced Scorecard (Kaplan & Norton, 1992). For each perspective, there will have to search for factors that are considered as essential to achieve the selected strategy, as well as the casual-effect links between selected factors. Finally, a set of indicators will be proposed in order to monitor the degree of accomplishment of the selected corporate objectives.
- Defining KM practices (step 9 in Figure 1). As mentioned earlier, the KM practices proposal will be based on firm strategy. Finally, a set of indicators has to be proposed in order

Table 5. Internal strategic analysis

Internal Analysis
Debt capacity
Capacity to obtain benefits
Aiming economies of scale
Plant location
Technological resources
Plant flexibility
Equipment flexibility
Employees' experience
Employees' adaptability
Employees' loyalty and commitment
Patents
Resources for innovation
Reputation

to assess the state of those KM practices. KM indicators, along with those concerning main Key Success Factors, will make up IC measurement and control proposal.

Organizations which adopt the Strategi method to perform KM audits will achieve their auditing objectives in a systematic way.

Application of the Strategi Model for KM Audits in Spanish Companies

The Strategi model has been implemented in diverse companies in Spain to test its applicability in real organizations. The target firms are SMEs (from 15 to 50 employees) because they are the most and, above all, because they have special features in the implementation of KM programs: different needs and less available resources. Obviously, to obtain firms participation is crucial to project success. That's why EU finances training and audits. Even being for free, companies must dedicate time and energy to the project. What's more, the novelty of concepts and their being so abstract could be an obstacle to firms without previous contact with the application of KM concepts. So, an important part of the project has been to communicate the benefits of taking part in the project to firms. In the initial conferences, the project was publicized and application forms distributed. Furthermore, due to the importance of firms' commitment, mediating role of business promotion institutions and auditors are determinant to obtain reliable candidates.

The application of the proposed model for KM auditing in the Spanish companies has revealed significant issues:

1. All the firms agree in the importance and need for auditing KM. However, the number of workers involved in the audit differs from one company to another, with some organizations having up to 9 employees participating actively in each phase of the process while other firms hardly had one member involved. This situation can be seen as an indicator of the different implication and support of diverse companies in the adoption and implementation of KM principles.
2. The companies are fully aware of the significance and role of each phase in the KM audit model.
3. The inventory and strategic analysis happened to be considered as the easiest phases in the KM audit, whereas most firms had to deal with some problems and difficulties in completing the last phase, that referring to the design of future systems.
4. Firms where the Strategi auditing model was applied agree in the idea that a KM audit must be a step in the process of managing knowledge prior to the deployment of any knowledge strategy. Previous research also highlights the need for a KM audit in order to later develop a KM strategy (Biloslavo & Trnavcevic, 2007; Cheung et al., 2007).

Our experience, as presented in this chapter, may help academics and practitioners in their attempts to further develop and implement

methodologies to perform KM audits. They are now aware of the real difficulties researchers and managers must deal with in the application of KM auditing methods in real companies.

FUTURE DIRECTIONS

This chapter deals with important issues regarding KM audits, as previously observed. Although a method for auditing knowledge is proposed and applied, further research may be still needed. Literature in this area is still in its infancy, thus showing some inconsistencies and impracticalities. These shortcomings for the development of KM audit research may be reduced or even eliminated by further studying new methodologies.

On the other hand, the model proposed here has been trial implemented in diverse organizations. However, testing the KM audit method in other contexts (public sector, educational companies, healthcare organizations and so on) may be interesting. Also, differences in the validity and applicability of the Strategi model may arise due to firms' characteristics as size, geography or age. Analyzing this possibility may be of interest in the near future.

Moreover, as learnt from the application of the proposed model for KM auditing in Spanish companies, the support corporate managers give to KM programs and audits is essential for their success. Future research should focus on the factors which may influence a positive behavior and an active support to KM initiatives in organizations. Besides, the implementation experience shows us that most firms faced to some problems and difficulties in designing their future KM systems and strategies. This task needs for a creative process which is seen somehow unfeasible by some managers. Further studies are needed in order to assist practitioners in performing the different tasks of that creative process and provide them with appropriate tools.

As seen in this chapter, KM audits are seen as a first step in the process of managing knowledge, prior to the deployment of any KM strategy. Future researchers may be interested in analyzing the process of planning and implementing a KM strategy consistent with the results of the KM audit and the measurement of its outcomes. A longitudinal study should be carried out since KM is thought to be a long-term concern with an impact on future performance. Also, it may be interesting to analyze companies in different periods of time in order to observe their advances in KM and the existence of a KM implementation lifecycle. Initially, different levels of formalization and KM strategy are expected over time.

Finally, organizational learning, sometimes considered as a part of a greater phenomenon called KM, is acknowledged as a key issue on strategic management. However, a detailed analysis of OL exceeds the purpose of this chapter, needing further research in future investigations. Also, the interplay of IT, human resources and organizational design may have an impact on KM strategy and its study may be of interest for research.

CONCLUSIONS

Nowadays, knowledge is the fundamental basis of competition. However, the mere act of processing knowledge itself does not guarantee strategic advantage; instead, knowledge has to be managed. Firms are noticing the importance of managing knowledge if they want to remain competitive and to achieve performance improvement and they are beginning to actively manage their knowledge and IC. Nevertheless, many KM systems have been unsuccessful due to diverse reasons. KM audits can play a significant role in the solution of many of the failures in KM programs (Hylton 2002). By discovering what knowledge is possessed, it is then possible to find the most effective method of storage and dissemination. (Liebowitz et al., 2000). Thus, these audits must be the first part of any KM strategy (Henczel, 2000). Yet it has not been sufficiently recognized as being of supreme

importance to every KM undertaking (Perez-Soltero et al., 2006).

Despite being of paramount importance in the deployment of KM strategies and, in turn, in today firms' survival, KM audits are slowly implemented in companies and scarcely studied by academics. The purpose of present chapter has been to contribute to the advance of KM research from a strategic point of view, by analyzing the importance of KM audits, and by proposing a model to implement a consistent methodology for auditing knowledge.

From the literature review, one may draw the conclusion that although many researchers proposed different approaches of knowledge audit, some are either too theoretical or have limitations in practical value. In order to overcome this situation, we propose the Strategi model as a systematic and practical methodology for performing KM audits. Practitioners can easily advance along the different phases in the audit process as they have the questionnaires to do it. This may constitute the main practical contribution of the chapter as most prior studies hardly provide with specific questions to perform KM audits.

Our experience, as presented in this chapter, may help academics and practitioners in their attempts to further develop and implement methodologies to perform KM audits. The application of the Strategi model for KM audits in diverse Spanish companies reveals that firms agree in the importance and need for auditing KM, as well as in the idea that a KM audit must be a step in the process of managing knowledge prior to the deployment of any knowledge strategy. These companies are fully aware of the significance and role of each phase in the KM audit model, and the inventory and strategic analysis happened to be considered as the easiest phases in the KM audit, whereas most firms had to deal with some problems and difficulties in completing the last phase, that referring to the design of future systems.

In sum, managers and researchers are provided with a systematic model for performing KM audits (Strategi model) that has been developed by revising prior research in the area and considering previous experiences in the field. As the Strategi model has been applied in diverse companies, academics and practitioners are more aware of the real difficulties they may face to and deal with in the application of KM auditing methods in real companies.

REFERENCES

Adamson, I. (2005). Knowledge management: The next generation of TQM? *Total Quality Management and Business Excellence, 16*(8-9), 987–1000. doi:10.1080/14783360500163177

Almansa, A., Andreu, R., & Sieber, S. (2002). *La gestión del conocimiento en España-2001*. Cap Gemini, Ernst & Young.

Ambrosini, V., & Bowman, C. (2001). Tacit knowledge: Some suggestions for operationalization. *Journal of Management Studies, 36*(6), 811–829. doi:10.1111/1467-6486.00260

Amit, R., & Schoemaker, P. (1993). Strategic assets and organizational rent. *Strategic Management Journal, 14*(1), 33–46. doi:10.1002/smj.4250140105

Argote, L., McEvily, B., & Reagans, R. (2003). Managing knowledge in organizations: An integrative framework and review of emerging themes. *Management Science, 49*(4), 571–582. doi:10.1287/mnsc.49.4.571.14424

Barney, J. (1991). Firm resources and sustained competitive advantage. *Journal of Management, 17*(2), 99–120. doi:10.1177/014920639101700108

Bierly, P., & Daly, P. (2002). Aligning human resource management practices and knowledge strategies: A theoretical framework. In C. W. Choo & N. Bontis (Eds.), *The strategic management of intellectual capital and organizational knowledge*. Oxford University Press.

Biloslavo, R., & Trnavcˇevic, A. (2007). Knowledge management audit in a higher educational institution: A case study. *Knowledge and Process Management, 14*(4), 275–286. doi:10.1002/kpm.293

Bontis, N. (1996). *Intellectual capital: An exploratory study that develops measures and models*. WP 96-11. Canada: Richard Ivey School of Business.

Bontis, N. (1999). Managing organizational knowledge by diagnosing intellectual capital: Framing and advancing the state of the field. *International Journal of Technology Management, 18*(5-8), 433–462. doi:10.1504/IJTM.1999.002780

Braganza, A. (2004). Rethinking the data–information–knowledge hierarchy: Towards a case-based model. *International Journal of Information Management, 24*(4), 347–356. doi:10.1016/j.ijinfomgt.2004.04.007

Brooking, A. (1996). *Intellectual capital, core asset for the third millennium enterprise*. International Thomson Business Press/ London.

Burnet, S., Illingworth, L., & Webster, L. (2004). Knowledge auditing and mapping: A pragmatic approach. *Knowledge and Process Management, 11*(1), 25–37. doi:10.1002/kpm.194

Cheung, C. F., Li, M. L., Shek, W. Y., Lee, W. B., & Tsang, T. S. (2007). A systematic approach for knowledge auditing: A case study in transportation sector. *Journal of Knowledge Management, 11*(4), 140–158. doi:10.1108/13673270710762774

Chourides, P., Longbottom, D., & Murphy, W. (2003). Excellence in knowledge management: An empirical study to identify critical factors and performance measures. *Measuring Business Excellence, 7*(2), 29–45. doi:10.1108/13683040310477977

Clarke, J., & Turner, P. (2004). Global competition and the Australian biotechnology industry: Developing a model of SMEs knowledge management strategies. *Knowledge and Process Management, 11*(1), 38–46. doi:10.1002/kpm.190

Davenport, T., De Long, D., & Beers, M. (1998). Successful knowledge management projects. *Sloan Management Review, 39*(2), 43–57.

Davenport, T. H., & Völpel, S. C. (2001). The rise of knowledge towards attention management. *Journal of Knowledge Management, 5*(3), 212–221. doi:10.1108/13673270110400816

De Long, D., & Seemann, P. (2000). Confronting conceptual confusion and conflict in knowledge management. *Organizational Dynamics, 29*(1), 33–44. doi:10.1016/S0090-2616(00)00011-5

Dess, G. G., & Davis, P. S. (1984). Porter's (1980) generic strategies as determinants of strategic group membership and organizational performance. *Academy of Management Journal, 27*(3), 467–488. doi:10.2307/256040

DeTienne, K. B., Dyer, G., Hoopes, C., & Harris, S. (2004). Toward a model of effective knowledge management and directions for future research: Culture, leadership, and CKOs. *Journal of Leadership & Organizational Studies, 10*(4), 26–43. doi:10.1177/107179190401000403

Edvinsson, L. (1996). Knowledge management at Skandia. *The Knowledge Challenge Conference*, MCE, Brussels, 30-31.

Eisenhardt, K. M. (1989). Building theories from case study research. *Academy of Management Review, 14*(4), 532–550. doi:10.2307/258557

Euroforum. (1998). *Medición del capital intelectual: Modelo intelect*. Madrid: Instituto Universitario Euroforum Escorial.

Fahey, L., & Narayanan, V. K. (1986). *Macroenvironmental analysis for strategic management*. St. Paul: West Publishing Company.

Firestone, J. M., & McElroy, M. W. (2005). Doing knowledge management. *The Learning Organization, 12*(2), 189–212. doi:10.1108/09696470510583557

Gold, A., Malhotra, A., & Segars, A. (2001). Knowledge management: An organizational capabilities perspective. *Journal of Management Information Systems, 18*(1), 185–214.

Grant, R. M. (1991). The resource-based theory of competitive advantage: Implications for strategy formulation. *California Management Review, 33*(3), 114–135.

Grant, R. M. (1992). *Contemporary strategy analysis: Concepts, techniques, application*. Basil Blackwell/Cambridge.

Gray, P., & Chan, Y. (2000). *Integrating knowledge management practices through a problem-solving framework*. Queen's Centre for Knowledge-Based Enterprises, WP 00-03.

Hahn, J., & Subramani, M. (2000). A framework of knowledge management systems: Issues and challenges for theory and practice. *Proc. of the 21st International Conference on Information systems* (pp. 302-312).

Handzic, M., Lagumdzija, A., & Celjo, A. (2008). Auditing KM practices: Model and application. *KM Research & Practice, 6*(1), 90–99. doi:10.1057/palgrave.kmrp.8500163

Hansen, M. T., Nohria, N., & Tierney, T. (1999). What's your strategy for managing knowledge? *Harvard Business Review, 77*(2), 106–116.

Henczel, S. (2000). The information audit as a first step towards effective KM: An opportunity for the special librarian. *Inspel, 34*(3/4), 210–226.

Hislop, D. (2003). Linking human resource management and knowledge management via commitment: A review and research agenda. *Employee Relations, 25*(2), 182–202. doi:10.1108/01425450310456479

Hooff, B., & Ridder, J. (2002). Knowing what to manage: The development and application of a knowledge management Scan. *European Conference Organisational Knowledge, Learning & Capabilities, Athens.*

Hylton, A. (2002). A KM initiative is unlikely to succeed without a knowledge audit. Retrieved from KnowledgeBoard.com

Iazzolino, G., & Pietrantonio, R. (2005, November). Auditing the organizational knowledge through a balanced scorecard-based approach. *International Conference on Knowledge Management in Asia Pacific (KMAP 2005).*

Kaplan, R., & Norton, D. (1992). The balance scorecard-measures that drive performance. *Harvard Business Review, 70*(1), 134–147.

King, W. R., Chung, R., & Haney, M. (2008). Knowledge management and organizational learning. *Omega, 36*(2), 167–172. doi:10.1016/j.omega.2006.07.004

Kotha, S., & Vadlamani, L. (1995). Assessing generic strategies: An empirical investigation of two competing typologies in discrete manufacturing industries. *Strategic Management Journal, 16*(1), 75–83. doi:10.1002/smj.4250160108

Krogh, G., Nonaka, I., & Aben, M. (2001). Making the most of your company's knowledge: A strategic framework. *Long Range Planning, 34*(3), 421–439. doi:10.1016/S0024-6301(01)00059-0

Liebowitz, J., Rubenstein-Montano, B., McCaw, D., Buchwalter, J., Browning, C., Newman, B., & Rebeck, K., & theThe Knowledge Management Methodology Team. (2000). The knowledge audit. *Knowledge and Process Management, 7*(1), 3–10. doi:10.1002/(SICI)1099-1441(200001/03)7:1<3::AID-KPM72>3.0.CO;2-0

Lopez, K. (2001). How to measure the value of knowledge management. *Knowledge Management Review,* March/April.

Miles, R., & Snow, C. H. (1978). *Organizational strategy, structure, and processes.* New York: McGraw-Hill.

Moffett, S., McAdam, R., & Parkinson, S. (2002). Developing a model for technology and cultural factors in knowledge management: A factor analysis. *Knowledge and Process Management, 9*(4), 237–255. doi:10.1002/kpm.152

Moffett, S., McAdam, R., & Parkinson, S. (2003). An empirical analysis of knowledge management applications. *Journal of Knowledge Management, 7*(3), 6–26. doi:10.1108/13673270310485596

National Electronic Library Health. (2001). *Conducting a knowledge audit.* Retrieved from http://www.nelh.nhs.uk/knowledge_management/km2/audit_toolkit.asp

Nicolas, R. (2004). Knowledge management impacts on decision making process. *Journal of Knowledge Management, 8*(1), 20–31. doi:10.1108/13673270410523880

Nonaka, I., & Peltokorpi, V. (2006). Objectivity and subjectivity in knowledge management: A review of 20 top articles. *Knowledge and Process Management, 13*(2), 73–82. doi:10.1002/kpm.251

Perez-Soltero, A., Barcelo-Valenzuela, M., Sanchez-Schmitz, G., Martin-Rubio, F., & Palma-Mendez, J. (2006). Knowledge audit methodology with emphasis on core processes. *European and Mediterranean Conference on Information Systems (EMCIS),* Alicante, Spain.

Porter, M. E. (1980). *Competitive strategy.* New York: Free Press.

Robertson, J. (2002). Benefits of a KM framework. Retrieved on January 12, 2002, from http://www.intranetjournal.com/articles/200207/se_07_31_02a.html

Roos, G., & Roos, J. (1997). Measuring your company's intellectual performance. *Long Range Planning, 30*(3), 413–426. doi:10.1016/S0024-6301(97)90260-0

Scholl, W., König, C., Meyer, B., & Heisig, P. (2004). The future of knowledge management: An international delphi study. *Journal of Knowledge Management, 8*(2), 19–35. doi:10.1108/13673270410529082

Schultze, U., & Boland, R. J. (2000). Knowledge management technology and the reproduction of work practices. *The Journal of Strategic Information Systems, 9*(2-3), 193–212. doi:10.1016/S0963-8687(00)00043-3

Schwikkard, D. B., & Du Toit, A. S. A. (2004). Analyzing knowledge requirements: A case study. *Aslib Proceedings, 56*(2), 104–111. doi:10.1108/00012530410529477

Segev, E. (1989). A systematic comparative analysis and synthesis of two business level strategies typologies. *Strategic Management Journal, 10*(4), 487–505. doi:10.1002/smj.4250100507

Sharma, R., & Chowdhury, N. (2007). On the use of a diagnostic tool for knowledge audits. *Journal of KM Practice, 8*(4), 1–11.

Skyrme, D. (2001). *Capitalizing on knowledge: From e-business to k-business.* Butterworth-Heinemann, Oxford.

Snow, C. C., & Hrebriniak, L. G. (1980). Strategy, distinctive competence, and organizational performance. *Administrative Science Quarterly, 25*(2), 317–336. doi:10.2307/2392457

Snyman, R., & Kruger, C. J. (2004). The interdependency between strategic management and strategic knowledge management. *Journal of Knowledge Management, 8*(1), 5–19. doi:10.1108/13673270410523871

Stevens, L. (2000). Knowing what your company knows: A knowledge audit is a necessary precursor to a new KM initiative. Retrieved on January 12, 2006, from http://www.destinationcrm.com/km/dcrm_km_article.asp?id=475

Storey, J., & Barnett, E. (2000). Knowledge management initiatives: Learning from failure. *Journal of Knowledge Management, 4*(2), 145–156. doi:10.1108/13673270010372279

Tsai, M. T., & Shih, C. M. (2004). The impact of marketing knowledge among managers on marketing capabilities and business performance. *International Journal of Management, 21*(4), 524–530.

Tsui, E. (2005). The role of IT in KM: Where are we now and where are we heading? *Journal of Knowledge Management, 9*(1), 3–6. doi:10.1108/13673270510584198

Zack, M. H. (1999). Developing a knowledge strategy. *California Management Review, 41*(3), 125–145.

Zack, M. H. (2002). Developing a knowledge strategy: Epilogue. In N. Bontis & W. Choo (Eds.), *The strategic management of intellectual capital and organizational knowledge: A collection of readings.* Oxford University Press.

Zajac, E. J., & Shortell, S. M. (1980). Changing generic strategies: Likelihood, direction, and performance implications. [f]. *Strategic Management Journal, 10*(3), 413–430.

Section 3
Organizational Knowledge Management Strategic Dilemmas

Chapter 7
C³EEP Typology and Taxonomies:
Knowledge Based (KB) Strategies

Meir Russ
University of Wisconsin-Green Bay, USA

Robert Fineman
Independent Consultant, USA

Jeannette K. Jones
American Intercontinental University, USA

ABSTRACT

This chapter proposes the C³EEP typology as a framework of knowledge management strategies by using six knowledge based strategic dilemmas. A number of graphic presentations of the complete typology are reported. Based on the typology, nine taxonomies of knowledge management (KM) are proposed and are followed by a framework that uses the six dilemmas and the knowledge levers as leading dimensions for the development of organization's knowledge management strategy. The proposed typology and taxonomies are closing a gap in academic knowledge management and strategic management literatures.

INTRODUCTION

Have you ever used a map to chart the route for an important destination? How about getting directions off the Internet? Maybe you have used a travel agent to plan a trip or called upon AAA to create a trip ticket. Regardless of the method you may have used, the first step in creating your route is determining your beginning location. Without a clear starting point and desired destination, plotting a course is next to impossible. The same is true when charting a path toward KM goals. You have to determine your Knowledge Base (KB) (Chapter 4). You have to determine your desired destination and you have to plot your course or a game plan (Chapter 9). You also will need to have a map. This is what this chapter is about.

DOI: 10.4018/978-1-60566-348-7.ch007

"ARE WE THERE YET?"

If you are going to use a map to plot your course, you might look at the mileage numbers, route numbers, or the legend for the information you need to make your decision. If you use a travel agent, he/she might volunteer the shortest or most interesting route, explain costs, and provide brochures so you can make your decision. If you use MapQuest, you might select the shortest distance or maybe the shortest time. The important factor is that you trust the information the map, agent, or Internet is providing. By using a map, you are expressing your confidence that the people who created the map were skilled in the area of map making. In addition, you rely on the expertise of your travel agent and even the accuracy of an Internet directions tool. Bottom line, you trust the tool you have chosen to use or you wouldn't have made the choice. Ultimately, you know your trip will be successful because the resources you used to make your trip plans and plot your course were timely and reliable.

Well, now you are beginning a KM journey. You know your starting point and you know your destination, all you need now is to decide the route. To do that you need to gather the information necessary to make directional decisions and that requires the use of a resource you can trust. Like the creation of a map or the use of an expert, you want a tool that is reliable, valid, and created by skilled practitioners. You want a resource that has been tested in the field and has a history of success. The *C³EEP Taxonomy* is just such a tool. Need proof? See our academic supporting research (Russ et al., 2005; 2006, and Russ and Jones 2006; 2008; forthcoming). After all, we are practitioners turned academics so we love sharing our years of work with you. We will start with an introduction of the dimensions of the map (the typology). Then, using these dimensions we will identify and describe the different types of KM strategies an organization might have (the taxonomy).

C³EEP TYPOLOGY

In chapter 1, we talked about strategic thinking on a global level. In chapters 4, 7 and 9 we focus on strategic thinking coming into play for the organization. As mentioned in chapter 1, we have developed a matrix that requires management to focus on the types of knowledge it possesses or would like to possess and guides management toward making the most appropriate decisions based on where they want the organization to go. The *C³EEP Typology* is a way to interpret six possible strategic dilemmas so an organization can chose a direction to follow toward their desired KM destination. As mentioned in the introduction of the book, *C³EEP Typology* stands for:

Codification-Tacitness
Complementary-Destroying
Concealment-Transparent
External Acquisition-Internal Development
Exploration-Exploitation
Product-Process

Specifically, our research has determined that there are six strategic dilemmas/questions that organizations will face when it comes to determining their KM goals:

1. "Should the company focus on codifying the knowledge or would it be better off leaving the knowledge tacit[1]?
2. Should the company focus on developing knowledge that is complementary to its current KB or would it be better off developing new knowledge even if this destroys the existing KB[2]?
3. Should the knowledge be transparent or would the company be better off keeping the knowledge concealed[3]?
4. Should the company focus on getting the most from its existing knowledge or would the company be better off experimenting with new knowledge[4]?

5. Should the knowledge be developed internally, or would the company be better off acquiring the knowledge from external sources[5]?

6. Should the company focus on the KB that is supporting the process and creating the value, or should the focus of value creation and the KB supporting this be the product/service[6]?" (Russ et al., 2006, pp. 3-4).

Our research and experience has also found that these six dilemmas are independent. In other words, an organization can decide to respond to each one of the six choices independently since they are not related. Therefore, we took them individually and created the *C³EEP Typology* for your use. So let's take a moment to review each of the six strategic dilemmas. For a more formal, academic discussion of this subject see Russ and Jones (forthcoming).

Codification (Explicit) vs Tacitness

Does the organization want to codify all of its knowledge or keep it tacit? Basically, write everything down and have it codified within the processes and systems or let the people maintain the knowledge. This is not a black and white decision. Most companies fall somewhere in the middle ground where a portion or different aspects of knowledge are codified and the remainder is kept at the tacit level. As with every decision point, there are advantages and disadvantages to every resolution. But that also has to be based on your industry, your culture, your risk management philosophy regarding knowledge, patent protection, industrial espionage, etc. This decision will guide management to invest in specific systems or processes or people.

Tacitness might nourish competitive advantage by making it more intricate for competitors to imitate a company's knowledge. On the other hand, by codifying knowledge and making it explicit (or embedded), the company can speed up the distribution of knowledge throughout the company more effectively than the competition. The application at this level is on the internal processes, tools, and controls of the company. The Tacitness strategy centers on the culture and routines necessary to share, protect, and control knowledge, while the Codification strategy converges on codifying the knowledge for internal sharing.

Tacit-explicit knowledge is a choice opportunity that companies have either implicitly or explicitly. Specifically, for example, it is the company's strategic choice that will determine if it will invest in knowledge-base systems to encourage employee's knowledge sharing or if it will sponsor employee travel for the purpose of personal interaction. Based on the strategic choices made, the company will conclude whether and how to remunerate employees for using databases. Knowledge might be in a tacit form, but the company might choose to transfer it into an explicit/codified setting. Marriott, for example, made such a conversion with its operating procedures[7] at significant expense, with the intent that it will also increase the value of the knowledge. Such a codification is becoming less problematic and cheaper as the price of IS technologies drops and performance improves. Tacit-codification choices made are NOT dichotomous but continuous[8]. It is believed that there is a continuum of range or balance and it is the company's choice (and strategy) as to where on this continuum it wants/intends to situate itself.

Here is an example that will illustrate to you why such a balance and/or a right choice of which knowledge to use can be important. NASA invested a lot of money in codification of knowledge plus IS/KBS just to find that the most valuable knowledge they had was large scale project management. NASA found that the risk assessment and management aspect of the project was most valuable and that this tacit knowledge could only be transferred by either the cheap way (learning by observation, mentoring, consulting fees to retired experts) or by the expensive way (trial and error). Unfortunately, the lesson was not learned until a few major disasters occurred and the agency became a famous case study in management failure[9].

Complementary vs Destroying

Does the organization want to develop knowledge that is compatible and complimentary with its existing knowledge base or does it want to build or acquire new knowledge that will destroy the current knowledge base to gain a competitive advantage? Again, this is a strategic question that will guide the decision-making process. At first it may seem counterintuitive to destroy or undermine the value of your current knowledge base. However, if that knowledge is obsolete, or will be obsolete in the future, you have to calculate the value of maintaining the status quo against the costs and potential income stream of replacing that knowledge with a new knowledge/technology. If KARMA (see chapter 4) told you that this was soon to be obsolete or this knowledge was solidly implanted within your organization, it might be an indication that the knowledge is useless, or it may also be the driver to fill a niche in a market that does not currently exist.

Complementary strategy can be depicted as a strategy based on using and developing only knowledge that is well-matched to the currently existing knowledge base within an organization. Such knowledge could even be "new to the world" innovation, but be connected and accommodating of the obtainable knowledge base of the company. Or, the knowledge could merely be a recombination of existing knowledge. The Destroying strategy can be portrayed as a strategy focused on mounting a new knowledge base while destroying the value of the existing knowledge base in order to cultivate a unique competitive advantage permitting the company to revolutionize the industry.

The traditional academic thought regarding disruptive technologies is that established companies have great difficulty developing and/or absorbing innovations. It is a rare occurrence (an outlier) that an incumbent firm is successful in such an attempt. Companies are changing this pattern of behavior as more and more of them become aware of the risks they might be taking by avoiding/underestimating innovations. A rising number of established companies are, therefore, embarking on incorporating (at least some) aspects of destroying strategies[10].

Concealment (Secrecy) vs Transparency

Does the organization want to conceal its knowledge or does it want to let everyone know what is being done? This can be very tricky since it combines legal and regulatory issues, depending on the industry, as well as trade secrets, patent availability, etc. Pharmaceutical companies have to be fully transparent about new drugs going through the clinical trial process, but that is because of the law. It should also be noted that the law also rewards these companies for their transparency by granting patents to protect the investment. Microsoft is very careful to conceal the inner workings of its operating system and has gained a competitive advantage because of that secrecy. Only in recent years has Microsoft lost some of that advantage due to the latest court and regulatory rulings.

Research in international accounting recognized secrecy and transparency as distinguishing values for a country's accounting system. Secrecy was recognized as a value that denotes leaning toward confidentiality, disclosure within the legal confines only to constituencies that are the most directly involved with finance and management on a need-to-know basis. Transparency was recognized as being overtly open and accountable. The Anglo-Saxon accounting system was acknowledged as the most transparent and the Less-Developed Latin system as the most secretive.

Research in the subject matter of patent law recognized two distinct frameworks for the purpose and effects of intellectual property laws. One contemplates patents as a means for privatizing information, and the second proposes looking at the patents as a means for validating and publishing information. Consistent with the former framework, research established that companies exploit patenting as grounds to build bargaining power[11]. When companies deem their original patents are susceptible, they tend to rely on litigation. For example, research insinuates that early secrecy might result in harming an asset protection plan, while transparency might result in an improved position as a preemptive effort in case of later litigation[12]. In a similar vein, Lev (nd) found that information revelation by pharmaceutical companies in the vicinity of the time of FDA approval had a significant positive effect on a company's stock value above and beyond the value consequential from the approval itself. Also, research established that the type of information being released had a dissimilar impact on the company--quantitative data producing a more positive influence than qualitative data[13].

But, does this distinction persist also in other managerial areas? We know that knowledge can, at the same time, be both leaky (transparent) and sticky (tacit). This may imply another feature of knowledge, one that might be associated with the practice of knowledge. One example is in the subject matter of value formation and supply chain management. IS technologies are altering the associations between suppliers and customers and imposing partnerships and transparent relationships between partners. Research insinuates that companies are making a deliberate choice with respect to their level of transparency as well as the type of transparency employed internally and externally[14]. Another example is in the subject matter of strategic alliances, where learning and knowledge have been recognized as a critical matter. For example, research recognized the issue of how shielding the partners of their knowledge as an essential aspect of the knowledge acquisition process between partners[15]. For instance,

the choice that Toyota made in relation to being more transparent than one would be expecting with its partner/competitor (GM) because it was not troubled by GM's abilities to make use of this knowledge effectively in a timely manner.

Research identified three reasons why companies may want to share knowledge with competitors: receiving inputs into their planning, formation of industry standards, and getting acceptance into professional networks[16]. One major implication is that companies should direct their employees about suitable behavior in the area as well as what and how knowledge can be shared. Another implication is that companies may want to have employees sign a confidentiality agreement in order to guard knowledge embedded in their systems, for example in a revenue management system thus utilizing trade secrets as a concealment mechanism. But, there is more to knowledge fortification than patents and employees' conduct policies, since knowledge has a number of distinctive characteristics that make protecting it different from protecting tangibles. Recently, Tapscott and Ticoll (2003) took this discussion one step further, suggesting that companies should see transparency not as a threat but as an opportunity to build trusting relationships with both internal and external constituencies. The premise for this dimension, in our opinion, is that companies might be better off balancing the need for transparency and concealment.

Exploration vs Exploitation

Does the organization want to be innovative or does it want to exploit existing knowledge to gain an advantage? This decision can be based on the knowledge that resides within an organization. KARMA will tell an organization a lot about how knowledge is created. You may have an environment that fosters innovative ideas. You may be in a company that uses its knowledge base to exploit existing technologies to gain its advantage. However, if you are planning to move into a new line of business, KARMA will allow you to assess what knowledge is available for this purpose. KARMA may also show you that exploration may work in one division and exploitation may work in another division. This is especially true in larger organizations but it can also be found in small companies.

The Exploration strategy can be portrayed as a strategy typically using inventions and innovation in order to create new knowledge. An Exploitation strategy of knowledge assets can be portrayed as a strategy established on routinely using and refining accessible knowledge. There is also a distinction in regard to time frames; Exploitation usually focuses on the short term - which may generate long term risks, while Exploration concentrates on the long term - which may generate short term risks. The application of learning mechanisms is also different--the Exploration learning is variation -seeking and reconfiguration of new resources while the Exploitation learning is midpoint -seeking and reconfiguration of existing resources. The culture, information systems, and reward systems that will be most valuable for each strategy might be different. For example, IS are fairly ineffective in advancing the innovation and creativity that are important for Exploration, but can be very cost-effective for sharing obtainable knowledge that is important for Exploitation.

Companies infrequently use the genuine style of the archetypes. For example, some companies can balance Exploration and Exploitation by using obtainable knowledge as an opening position for developing new knowledge. Harmonizing the two is seen as essential in new service development, dynamic capabilities development, research and development, organizational adaptation, and innovation implementation in high technology manufacturing, and many other business applications. Such balancing can be challenging because of the "failure trap" and the "success trap." The "failure trap" does not permit companies to experiment with new products, markets, etc, because delaying uncertain profits may be costly and not-beneficial.

The "success trap" keeps the company within a narrow (existing) variety of products, markets, etc. since the company is content with the present profitability (and low investments and risk taking), which comply with its short-term goals. Such a strategy, however, generates long-term risks by creating rigidities. An additional complexity in having a thriving balance between exploration and exploitation is organizational. The activities supporting the strategies seem to have contradictory processes and striking a balance might not be straightforward.

External Acquisition vs Internal Development

Does the organization want to buy knowledge or develop it internally? Again, KARMA provides a baseline to help determine if the organization is better at assimilating knowledge from outside sources or creating the knowledge in-house. There is another element that could influence this and that is timing. If there is a limited window of opportunity for development of knowledge, you may determine that buying the knowledge is the better strategic fit even though your organization is better at creating its own knowledge. Remember, if you only acquire the processes and systems and not the people, there will still be an abbreviated "learning curve" to create the required knowledge.

Developing technologies for innovative new processes or new products can either be accomplished internally or acquired from outside the company by means of inter-organizational provisions. For example, research indicates that since the mid-1990s pharmaceutical companies located in the UK, viewed such an R&D option as another "make or buy" alternative. [17] The same choice dilemma can be recognized in other aspects of knowledge management in companies, for example, marketing, new product development, production, etc.

There is a widespread academic body of research indicating that large companies are obtaining new knowledge from the outside, mostly from small, innovative and entrepreneurial companies. This is achieved by using a number of alternative means with differing extent of interaction between the partnering companies. Such acquisitions may account for an increasing proportion of these companies' R&D portfolios. For example, a partnership between an equipment supplier and buyer, in which the supplier extracts the engineering knowledge from their customer and the customer, on the other hand gains an early peak into the potential of the technology, will illustrate the use of external sources of knowledge. This early peak affects the future equipment performance and gives a preview of new process technologies.

Research implies that companies contemplate strategic outsourcing for value propositions (not for cost saving purposes only), professing that companies might use such outsourcing arrangements to intensify their innovation, intellectual depth and worldwide reach.[18] Research also recognizes a number of concerns that companies need to be alarmed with, for example, entirely losing skill sets, difficulty in precisely identifying expected outcomes, opportunistic risks, etc. This may propose why companies might want to balance their dependence on external sources with their internal development. Companies that are seriously engaged in external knowledge acquisition (or exchange) need to attain an "alliance learning capability" or, in other words, acknowledge a learning curve in managing the relationship with the external partners, what some[19] call collaborative experience. Such capability might in fact include the capacity to understand, assimilate, and apply external knowledge, all of which are ingredients of the company's absorptive capacity. Also, the relationships that the employees have with external constituencies, specifically customers, could be seen as an important knowledge transfer mechanism by assimilating a knowledge-based indicator into the performances of the sales force.

The premise for this dimension, in our opinion, is that companies might be better off balancing the need for internal development and external acquisition. For example, research mentions two options of external sources for acquisition--within the industry and outside the industry, each having a different impact on new knowledge development.[20]

Take, for example, Kroger. The retailer is competing with Wal-Mart on price, with Whole Foods on differentiation, and with Trader Joes on differentiation and price. Kroger should be losing, right? Not exactly. Using analytics and customer loyalty cards supplied by a British company (Dunnhumby) the company is able to survive and show a profit[21]. But there must be more to the story than incorporating knowledge, in this case a system, plus software, plus results. For one, there is tacit knowledge exchange. Dunnhumby's American headquarters is in Cincinnati, OH which is also the location of the Kroger headquarters. Actually, Kroger brought Dunnhumby to the US, even though they happen to be a division of a competitor (Tesco). But really, there is more to it. The abilities of different stores to respond to the unique circumstances they are in (Best Buy; another example of using the same software and systems) can only result from the freedom that store managers have to tailor their offerings to the identified needs PLUS the ability of corporate distribution to deliver systematically the needed goods on time and in price. No wonder few companies can match this set of capabilities. Of course, knowledge management was not mentioned in the article or in related stories even once, but the reality is that it is all about putting the knowledge in action and creating value.

One additional aspect that must be mentioned here is that managing the acquisition of external knowledge as well as incorporating/integrating it into the organization and meshing/melting it with the internal knowledge is far from simple or routine. In all actuality, it is a skill/capability that organizations have to learn. In other words, there is a learning curve in acquiring knowledge from the outside, like in learning how to establish and manage successful strategic alliances, or how to merge or acquire another company. Such a capability can be learned and some companies do, but many do not or even do not realize that they lack the skill. Even worse, many organizations have the capability but lack the awareness or have not realized that the knowledge is within one person and when s/he leaves the company, the knowledge and the capability are gone.

Product vs Process

Does the organization want to produce a product or does it want to be the driver to produce the product better? Is the organization better at production or re-engineering and streamlining the process and outsourcing the production? Again, KARMA provides the critical data that can be used to guide your answer.

The early 1990s brought a number of realizations: 1) The productivity paradox - despite spending great amount of capital in IS technology companies could not demonstrate positive returns or productivity improvements; 2) Continuous quality improvements were not adequate to bring the needed cost cutbacks necessary to be successful against intense global competition; and, 3) The majority of reengineering programs failed or at best, the results were ambiguous.[22] These realizations made it apparent that companies need to manage all of their processes considerably better; hence process innovation, dynamic capabilities, value stream reinvention, six sigma, and BPM-Business Process Management among other processes. These processes exemplify the companies' recognition that the "what" they produce could be as important as, the "how." Indeed, recently there have been a number of endeavors to incorporate process management with KM. Another explanation of why process management came to the front is the relative intensification of the service sector and the (relative) decay of the

manufacturing sector. Services can be described as an interaction between human actors, processes, and physical elements. Such a definition of the service economic sector is increasing the need to better appreciate and manage processes. Also, increasingly, manufacturing companies are broadening their offerings by adding, or by bundling services as part of their product/service offerings.

What are the choice dilemmas offered by this dimension? One can be demonstrated by firms losing their innovative capacity and as a result, starting to concentrate on value creation through process efficiencies, or in a reciprocal cause and effect direction, and/or obtaining innovative ideas from small companies.[23] In other words, new ideas that generate value for customers can be either a better new product or a cheaper product, or what we describe in strategy as "differentiation" and "low cost" strategies. For example, when a product is mature, it is much more complex to achieve product innovation, while competitor's pressure and customer demands press for cost cutbacks by means of process development. A different type of choice dilemma is suggested by research which reveals that for companies, the selection of a specific product design is joined with a choice of a specific process in a reciprocal relationship.[24] For example, a tightly designed product will necessitate a process that is intensively synchronized. Also, research established that when the life cycle of the product is short, process knowledge has a positive effect on the company's performance.[25]

THE COMPLETE C³EEP TYPOLOGY

Now, we have to remind you that what we described above are the dilemmas companies have to resolve. Rarely will such resolution or choice be a decision to adopt the extreme anchor as an alternative strategy. In the majority of the cases, companies will choose some kind a balance be-

Figure 1. Four SBUs' profiles based on the C³EEP typology

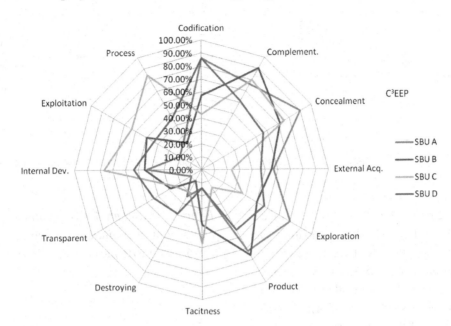

tween the two anchors (for each one of the six choices). Taken together, the choices describe a space (typology[26]) in which companies are making decisions. Actually, the company may find that different SBUs, divisions, or functions might be better served if their choice of a specific balance is different. Our early research supports this conclusion. For example we found that within one company, four different SBUs were making different choices. See their different profiles below in Figure 1.

An alternative way to describe the profile of the strategy is described below by comparing the data of different industries. The average of all the companies participating in our earlier study is illustrated by the star and the average of the service industries illustrated by the octagons. As one would expect, the service companies tend to be more process oriented and tend to codify those processes as well as keep them more transparent than the average company. They also seem to be more innovative (both more exploratory and destroying) as well as they rely more heavily (than

the average company) on external development of new knowledge. (see Figure 2)

Next we will discuss some alternative strategies companies are using when making different choices for the dilemmas we discussed.

C³EEP TAXONOMIES: THE STRATEGIES

Our early research (e.g. Russ et al., 2005, 2006) findings of the significant relationship between KB strategies and outcomes suggest that three of the six dimensions mentioned above might be the most important when considering specific strategies. The possible KB strategies based on those dimensions will be discussed below.

Codification-Tacitness and Exploration-Exploitation Strategies

Our earliest research suggested that Codification-Tacitness and Exploration-Exploitation strategic

Figure 2. Industries C³EEP profile

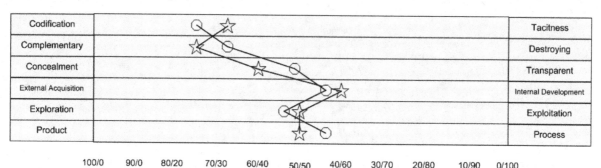

dilemmas might be of the most importance.[27] Four alternative strategies that companies can use when managing their KM assets (see Figure 3) were proposed within Taxonomy A. As part of this and later research[28] we were also able to relate outcome effectiveness to the strategies identified[29]. Only in the case of this taxonomy, do we have definite conclusions.

Type (I) companies employ the Structured Utilization strategy. Structured Utilization companies concentrate on exploiting their currently existing knowledge while also codifying that knowledge. The "Structured Utilizers" use codification and exploitation strategies concentrating on codification of knowledge when sustaining their new product development efforts to improve their existing products, and the servicing of their existing clients to achieve higher process effectiveness. Such a strategy choice results in lower (within Taxonomy A) product effectiveness than the exploration alternative (Type III has a higher product effectiveness than type I) and in higher process effectiveness than the tacitness alternative (Type I has a higher process effectiveness than type II) based on our research results. Take for example NASA. NASA invested heavily in KM and in codification of knowledge and the appropriate IS/KBS systems. These strategies allow them to keep delivering on their mission, while reducing their budget and downsizing. BUT, the price of this strategy was significant system and mission failures, and learning that the most

Figure 3. Taxonomy A: Codification-tacitness and exploration-exploitation strategies (Russ et al., 2006. Used with permission. ©Inderscience)

	Codification	Tacitness
Exploitation	Structured Utilization **I**	Intuitive Utilization **II**
Exploration	Structured Innovation **III**	Intuitive Innovation **IV**

valuable knowledge they have is tacit and that they don't know how to capture or manage that tacit knowledge[30].

Type (II) companies employ the Intuitive Utilization strategy. Intuitive Utilization companies concentrate on exploiting their currently existing knowledge while maintaining this knowledge as tacit. The "Intuitive Utilizers" rely on tacitness and exploitation strategies, concentrating on maintaining the knowledge as tacit and focusing on sustaining their advantage in new product development to enhance their contemporary products, and the servicing of their existing markets. Such a strategy choice results in lower (within Taxonomy A) product effectiveness than the exploration alternative (Type IV has a higher product effectiveness than type II) and in lower (within Taxonomy A) process effectiveness than the codification alternative (Type I has a higher process effectiveness than type II). This seems to be the least effective strategy (out of the four mentioned here) based on our research results. Take for example a small sized iron casting company located in Northeast Wisconsin. The company had been very successful in the past and has a core of knowledgeable employees that are very good at what they do. A number of them are getting ready to retire, and the HR director has started the process of succession planning. To her surprise, she found that the most valuable knowledge of those middle level managers is not codified, as well as there are no individuals trained to replace those individuals when the time comes. Her first step was mapping alternative replacements as well as skills and competencies needed by the potential replacements.

Type (III) companies employ the Structured Innovation strategy. Structured Innovation companies concentrate on exploring new knowledge to the extent that it is feasible while codifying this knowledge. The "Structured Innovators" use codification and exploration strategies that concentrate on codification of new knowledge as sustaining new innovative product development and/or servicing new markets to attain higher process and product effectiveness. Such a strategy choice results in higher (within Taxonomy A) product effectiveness than the exploitation alternative (Type III has a higher product effectiveness than type I) and higher (within Taxonomy A) process effectiveness than the tacitness alternative (Type III has a higher process effectiveness than type IV). Out of the four mentioned here this seems to be the most effective strategy based on our research results. Take for example the company that adopted an Enterprise Resource Planning (ERP) system[31] to improve on their process efficiency and effectiveness. The company was able to successfully implement the new software (and process) by modifying and adjusting its processes as required by the software and codifying them appropriately. Interestingly enough, during the implementation, the need to adjust the software to the processes

and the need to tailor the training to the people and culture, suggested that significant aspects of knowledge were tacit and that caused some issues during the early stages of implementation.

Type (IV) companies employ the Intuitive Innovation strategy. Intuitive Innovation companies concentrate on exploring new knowledge as much as they can while maintaining this knowledge as tacit. The "Intuitive Innovators" use tacitness and exploration strategies that focus on developing contemporary innovative products and/or servicing novel markets while keeping their knowledge tacit. Such a strategy choice results in higher (within Taxonomy A) product effectiveness than the exploitation alternative (Type IV has a higher product effectiveness than type II) and in lower (within Taxonomy A) process effectiveness than the codification alternative (Type III has a higher process effectiveness than type IV) based on our research results. Take for example the heavy manufacturer and engine producer, which realized that their company needed to incorporate a new to the company, electronic, engine control technology. In order to accelerate the process, the company acquired that knowledge from an external partner (see strategy C below). Originally, there was a complete misunderstanding of and underestimation of the complexity of the technology. The first round was a complete failure. The second round was a successful process, but the product was not in par with the market. Only in the third attempt did the company find the right partner and had the right process in place to integrate the external knowledge into their product. Compare that with the Chinese car manufacturer that realized it was embarking on a quantum leap technological and social change and was able to bridge the gap by recruiting the right managerial and technological leadership and by acquiring the knowledge by using an appropriate intermediary that was rewarded appropriately.[32]

Exploration-Exploitation and External Acquisition-Internal Development Strategies

Our research findings (Russ et al., 2006 and Russ and Jones, 2006) suggest that the combination of the Exploration-Exploitation and of the External Acquisition-Internal Development dimensions is also significant (see Taxonomy B in Figure 4).

Type (A) companies employ the External Utilization strategy. External Utilization companies concentrate on exploiting their presently obtainable knowledge while focusing on their core activities and utilizing knowledge and capabilities from the outside to the extent that it is feasible for everything else. The "External Utilizers" employ external acquisition and exploitation strategies concentrating on their core capabilities to enhance their existing products and the servicing of their existing markets while concentrating on developing close relationships with external constituencies. This seems to be the least effective strategy in terms of product effectiveness (out of the four mentioned in Taxonomy B) based on our research results. This might suggest that outsourcing strategies might not be the most effective when "product based outcomes" (for example new product development outcomes) are the focus of the strategy. However, this may not prevent this strategy from being the most appropriate with regard to process efficiencies (for example, cost cutting).

Type (B) companies employ the Internal Utilization strategy. Internal Utilization companies concentrate on exploiting their currently existing knowledge while focusing on developing most of the knowledge they need internally. The "Internal Utilizers" employ internal development and exploitation strategies concentrating on internally developing the knowledge they need to improve their existing products and the servicing of existing markets while concentrating on developing close relationships within the company.

Figure 4. Taxonomy B: Exploration-exploitation and external acquisition-internal development strategies (Russ et al., 2006. Used with permission. ©Inderscience)

	External Acquisition	Internal Development
Exploitation	External Utilization **A**	Internal Utilization **B**
Exploration	External Innovation **C**	Internal Innovation **D**

Type (C) companies employ the External Innovation strategy. External Innovation companies concentrate on exploring new knowledge focusing on their core activities while acquiring the rest of the knowledge from external sources. The "External Innovators" employ external acquisition and exploration strategies that concentrate on supporting new innovative product development and/or servicing new markets while centering their attention on developing close relationships with external constituencies.

Type (D) companies employ the Internal Innovation strategy. Internal Innovation companies concentrate on exploring new knowledge to the extent that it is feasible while developing most of the knowledge they need internally. The "Internal Innovators" employ internal development and exploration strategies that concentrate on internally embracing the new knowledge needed to support new innovative product development and/or the servicing of new markets to achieve higher product effectiveness. This seems to be the most effective strategy (out of the four mentioned in Taxonomy B) based on our research results.

Codification-Tacitness and External Acquisition-Internal Development Strategies

The findings of our earlier research (Russ et al., 2006, and Russ and Jones, 2006) also suggest that the combination of the Codification-Tacitness and that of the External Acquisition-Internal Development dimensions might be of importance (see Taxonomy C in Figure 5).

Type (1) companies employ the External Codification strategy. External Codification companies concentrate on codifying their core activities and utilizing knowledge and capabilities from the outside to the extent that it is feasible for everything else. The "External Codifiers" employ external acquisition and codification strategies focusing on their core capabilities to enhance their products and the servicing of their markets.

Type (2) companies employ the Internal Codification strategy. Internal Codification companies concentrate on codifying the majority of their knowledge while developing most of the knowledge they need internally. The "Internal Codifiers" employ internal development and codification strategies that concentrate on internally embracing the new knowledge needed to support new product development and/or the servicing of their markets to realize higher product effectiveness. This appears to be the most effective strategy (out of the four mentioned in Taxonomy C) based on our research results.

Type (3) companies employ the External Tacitness strategy. External Tacitness companies concentrate on maintaining their core capabilities knowledge as tacit and utilizing knowledge and capabilities from the outside as much as feasible for everything else. The "External Intuitives" use external acquisition and tacitness strategies focusing on their core capabilities to enhance their products and the servicing of their markets while focusing their attention on developing close relationships with external constituencies. This appears to be the least effective strategy (out of

Figure 5. Taxonomy C: Codification-tacitness and external acquisition-internal development strategies (Russ et al., 2006. Used with permission. ©Inderscience).

	External Acquisition	Internal Development
Codification	External Codification 1	Internal Codification 2
Tacitness	External Tacitness 3	Internal Tacitness 4

the four mentioned in Taxonomy C) based on our research results.

Type (4) companies employ the Internal Tacitness strategy. Internal Tacitness companies concentrate on maintaining their knowledge as tacit as much as they can while developing most of the knowledge they need internally. The "Internal Intuitives" use internal development and tacitness strategies that concentrate on internally embracing the knowledge needed to enhance new product development and/or the servicing of their markets while concentrating on developing close relationships within the company.

Our recent study (Russ et al., 2008) suggested that the Product-Process dilemma might also be of significance. Below we describe the feasible taxonomies resulting from the combination of this dilemma with the other three dilemmas used above.

Product-Process and External Acquisition-Internal Development Strategies

The next taxonomy describes a combination of the Product-Process and that of the External Acquisition-Internal Development dimensions (see Taxonomy D in Figure 6).

Type (α) companies employ the External Product strategy. External Product companies concentrate their core activities on developing and managing their product strategies externally and using knowledge and capabilities from the outside to the extent that it is feasible for everything else. The "External Product" companies employ external acquisition to improve and/or develop their new products concentrating on their core capabilities to service their markets while making sure that their reward system is consistent and supportive of such activities.

Type (β) companies employ the Internal Product strategy. Internal Product companies concentrate on developing most of the product knowledge they need internally, while using as little knowledge and capabilities as possible from the outside for everything else. The "Internal Product" companies concentrate their core capabilities on internal development to improve and or develop their new products and use external partners to develop and service their markets, while making sure that their reward system is consistent and supportive of such activities.

Type (γ) companies employ the External Process strategy. External Process companies

concentrate on maintaining their products and focusing their core capabilities knowledge on process improvement by using knowledge and capabilities from the outside as much as possible. The "External Process" companies use external acquisition and process improvement strategies concentrating on their core capabilities to improve their processes and the servicing of their markets

while centering their attention on developing close relationships with external constituencies and while making sure that their reward system is consistent and supportive of such activities.

Type (δ) companies employ the Internal Process strategy. Internal Process companies

concentrate on improving the process knowledge they need internally, while using as little knowledge and capabilities as possible from the outside for everything else. The "Internal Process" companies use internal development that focuses on internally embracing the knowledge needed to support new process development and/or the servicing of their markets while focusing on developing close relationships within the company while making sure that their reward system is consistent and supportive of such activities.

Product-Process and Codification-Tacitness Strategies

The next taxonomy describes a combination of the Product-Process and that of the Codification-Tacitness dimensions (see Taxonomy E in Figure 7).

Type (א) companies employ the - Codified Product companies concentrate on codifying their knowledge of product development and management focusing on their core capabilities to improve their products and servicing their markets. The "Codified Product" companies sustain their process development efforts to improve their

Figure 6. Taxonomy D: Product-process and external acquisition-internal development strategies

	External Acquisition	Internal Development
Product	External Product α	Internal Product β
Process	External Process γ	Internal Process δ

Figure 7. Taxonomy E: Product-process and codification-tacitness strategies

	Codification	Tacitness
Product	Codified Product א	Tacit Product ב
Process	Codified Process ג	Tacit Process ד

products and the servicing of their clients and achieve higher product effectiveness by using the most appropriate source of knowledge and using the appropriate IT systems to support their core capabilities as needed.

Type (ב) companies employ the Tacit Product strategy. Tacit Product companies concentrate on maintaining their knowledge of product development and management as tacit, focusing on their core capabilities to improve their products, and servicing their markets. The "Tacit Product" companies sustain their process development efforts to improve their products and the servicing of their clients and achieve higher process effectiveness by using the most appropriate source of knowledge and using the appropriate IT systems to support their core capabilities as needed.

Type (ג) companies employ the Codified Process strategy. Codified Process companies concentrate on codifying their process knowledge as much as possible. The "Codified Process" companies employ codification strategies that concentrate on internally embracing the most appropriate source of knowledge and using the appropriate IT systems to support their core capabilities that will result in higher process effectiveness.

Type (ד) companies employ the Tacit Process strategy. Tacit Process companies concentrate on maintaining and developing their process knowledge as tacit as much as they can. The "Tacit Process" companies use tacitness strategies that focus on internally embracing the knowledge and the use of appropriate IT systems to support process development and/or the servicing of their markets while focusing on developing close relationships within the company.

Product-Process and Exploration-Exploitation Strategies

The next taxonomy describes a combination of the Product-Process and that of Exploration-Exploitation dimensions (see Taxonomy F in Figure 8).

Type (١) companies employ the Product Utilization strategy. Product Utilization companies concentrate on exploiting their currently existing product knowledge while servicing their existing and/or new markets. The "Product Utilization" companies employ existing and/or new processes concentrating on their core capabilities to enhance their product strategies, focusing on their core activities and using knowledge and capabilities to the extent that it is feasible for everything else.

Type (ب) companies employ the Product Innovation strategy. Product Innovation companies concentrate on exploring new knowledge focusing on new product development activities while utilizing their existing knowledge for the non core activities. The "Product Innovation" companies employ product and exploration strategies that concentrate on supporting new innovative product development and/or the servicing of new markets while centering their attention on delivering those products to their customers.

Type (ت) companies employ the Process Utilization strategy. The "Process Utilization" companies employ process and exploitation strategies concentrating on utilizing their currently existing process knowledge while also focusing on improving their process strategies and the servicing of existing markets.

Type (ث) companies employ the Process Innovation strategy. Process Innovation companies concentrate on exploring new process knowledge to the extent that it is feasible. The "Process Inno-

Figure 8. Taxonomy F: Product-process and exploration-exploitation strategies

	Exploitation	Exploration
Product	Product utilization ١	Product innovation ب
Process	Process Utilization ت	Process innovation ث

vation" companies employ internal and/or external resources for development of new processes to service their markets while improving on their process strategies.

There are two additional dimensions of the C³EEP typology that were not yet used for KM strategy taxonomies (Complementary-Destroying and Concealment-Transparent). We suspect that these two dilemmas will become more and more important due to recent Information and Communications Technology (ICT) trends. The question raised here is, which of the nine plausible combinations that the two dilemmas are adding in combination with the previously mentioned four are of more importance (if there is any difference in importance)?

One answer would be to look into the number of levers (see Table 1) shared by any two dilemmas. Interestingly, the one that has the most (three) is also one that is very intriguing to us as well as one that is probably one of the less understood by the popular and academic literature.

Complementary-Destroying and Exploration-Exploitation Strategies

The next taxonomy introduced in this chapter is the Complementary-Destroying and the Exploration-Exploitation dimensions (see Taxonomy G in Figure 9).

Type (あ) companies employ the Complementary Utilization strategy. Complementary Utilization companies concentrate on exploiting their currently existing product and process knowledge while servicing their existing markets. The "Complementary Utilization" companies employ existing processes concentrating on their core capabilities to enhance their product strategies, focusing on their core activities and using knowledge and capabilities to the extent that it is feasible for everything else. Such a strategy can be very successful in the short term but since no options for responding to future changes are acquired, the company is taking on significant risk for the medium and long terms.

Figure 9. Taxonomy G: Complementary-destroying and exploration-exploitation strategies

	Exploitation	Exploration
Complementary	Complementary utilization あ	Complementary innovation い
Destroying	Destroying Utilization う	Destroying innovation え

Type (い) companies employ the Complementary Innovation strategy. Complementary Innovation companies concentrate on exploring new knowledge focusing on new product and process development activities while adding this knowledge to its existing knowledge base and enhancing its value. The "Complementary Innovation" companies employ product and exploration strategies that concentrate on supporting new innovative product development and/or the servicing of new markets while centering their attention on delivering those products to their current and new customers. Such a strategy might create some short term risks, but if successful, could provide for mid term success. In long and mid term product life cycle (PLC) industries, this might even be successful long term. In industries that have short PLC, this strategy might be risky long term.

Type (う) companies employ the Destroying Utilization strategy. The "Destroying Utilization" companies employ counter intuitive strategy since they utilize some existing aspects of their knowledge base while destroying the value of it in other aspects. For example, a company can utilize their currently existing process knowledge while at the same time moving to a completely new product market, where it will need to develop new knowledge to serve new customers. Under this strategy, the transition is slow, and the new product market must be close to the old one, see for example the GM strategy of penetrating the

Table 1. KM strategy framework (Based on and modified from Russ et al., 2006)

KM Levers/Outcomes	Codification *vs* Tacitness	Complementary *vs* Destroying	Concealment *vs* Transparency	External Acquisition *vs* Internal Development	Exploration *vs* Exploitation	Product/Service *vs* Process
Product/Service Development-strategy		Taxonomy G			Taxonomies A, B, F, G	Taxonomies D, E, F
New Product developed in the last two years-weight		Taxonomy G			Taxonomies A, B, F, G	
Market-Scope		Taxonomy G			Taxonomies A, B, F, G	
Customers	Taxonomies A, C, E	X				
Technology	Taxonomies A, C, E			Taxonomies B, C, D		
Processes-Capabilities				Taxonomies B, C, D		
Employees utilization	Taxonomies A, C, E, I		Taxonomy I			Taxonomies D, E, F
Rewards		X	Taxonomy H	Taxonomies B, C, D, H		
The role of IT			X			
Use of IT and Data	Taxonomies A, C, E, I		Taxonomy I			Taxonomies D, E, F
Product Effectiveness			Taxonomy H	Taxonomies B, C, D, H		
Process Effectiveness	Taxonomies A, C, E					

Chinese market[33]. Such a strategy might create some short term risks, but if successful, could provide for midterm success. In long and midterm product life cycle (PLC) industries, this might even be successful long term. In industries that have short PLC, this strategy might also be risky long term, but on the other hand, the transition into a new product market could provide a valuable option for the future.

Type (え) companies employ the Destroying Innovation strategy. Destroying Innovation companies concentrate on exploring new product and process knowledge to the extent that it is feasible, while also destroying the value of their current knowledge base. The "Destroying Innovation" companies employ internal and/or external resources for development of new processes and products to service new markets. An example here would be Corning which in the late 1990's and early 2000's, moved completely away from its kitchenware markets into the fiber communication, high-tech glass markets. The company invested heavily and successfully in R&D of new technologies and products taking significant technological risks and facing financial markets criticism for years of poor performance. Luckily, long term success paid off for the risk taken[34]. Such a strategy will create high short term risks, and also could provide for midterm risks. In industries that have short PLC, this strategy might provide the only option to survive while creating a valuable alternative for the company.

The last two taxonomies introduced in this chapter were selected using similar criteria to the one used earlier (number of levers, see taxonomy G).

Concealment-Transparency and External Acquisition-Internal Development Strategies

The next taxonomy describes a combination of the Concealment-Transparency and the External Acquisition-Internal Development dimensions (see Taxonomy H in Figure 10).

Type (甲) companies employ the External Con-

cealment strategy. External Concealment companies concentrate their core activities on effectively developing and managing their product strategies internally, and using knowledge and capabilities from the outside to the extent that it is feasible for everything else. The "External Concealing" companies employ external acquisition to improve and or develop their new processes concentrating on their core capabilities to service their markets while making sure that their relationships with their customers are protected.

Type (乙) companies employ the Internal Concealment strategy. Internal Concealment companies concentrate on developing most of the product knowledge they need internally, while using as little knowledge and capabilities as possible from the outside for everything else. The "Internal Concealing" companies concentrate their core capabilities on internal development to improve and/or develop their new products and use external partners as little as possible to develop and service their markets, while making sure that their relationships with their suppliers and customers are protected.

Type (丙) companies employ the External Transparency strategy. External Transparency companies concentrate on maintaining their products and focusing their core capabilities knowledge on process improvement by using knowledge and capabilities from the outside while being transparent as much as possible. The "External

Figure 10. Taxonomy H - Concealment-Transparency and External Acquisition-Internal Development Strategies

	External Acquisition	Internal Development
Concealment	External Concealment 甲	Internal Concealment 乙
Transparency	External Transparency 丙	Internal Transparency 丁

Transparency" companies use external acquisition and process improvement strategies concentrating on their core capabilities to improve their processes and the servicing of their markets while centering their attention on developing close relationships with external constituencies and making sure that they are transparent with their suppliers and customers as much as possible, protecting only those aspects that are absolutely necessary.

Type (⊤) companies employ the Internal Transparency strategy. Internal Transparency companies concentrate on improving the process knowledge they need internally, while using as little knowledge and capabilities as possible from the outside for everything else. The "Internal Transparency" companies use internal development that focuses on internally embracing the knowledge needed to support new process development and/or the servicing of their markets while focusing on developing close relationships within the company, making sure that they are transparent with their suppliers and customers as needed while protecting only those aspects that are absolutely necessary.

Concealment-Transparency and Codification-Tacitness Strategies

The next taxonomy describes a combination of the Concealment-Transparency and the Codification-Tacitness dimensions (see Taxonomy I in Figure 11).

Type (⌐) companies employ the Codified Concealment strategy. Codified Concealment companies concentrate on codifying their knowledge of product and process development and management, focusing on their core capabilities to improve their products and processes and servicing their markets. The "Codified Concealment" companies sustain their process development efforts to improve their products and the servicing of their clients to achieve higher product effectiveness by using the most appropriate codified source of knowledge while concealing the knowledge both

Figure 11. Taxonomy I: Concealment-transparency and codification-tacitness strategies

	Codification	Tacitness
Concealment	Codified Concealment ⌐	Tacit Concealment ∟
Transparency	Codified Transparency ⊏	Tacit Transparency ⊐

internally and externally and using the appropriate IT systems to support their core capabilities as needed.

Type (∟) companies employ the Tacit Concealment strategy. Tacit Concealment companies concentrate on maintaining their knowledge of product and process development and management as tacit, focusing on their core capabilities to improve their products and processes and servicing their markets. The "Tacit Concealment" companies sustain their process development efforts to improve their products and the servicing of their clients to achieve higher process effectiveness by using the most appropriate tacit source of knowledge, while concealing the knowledge both internally and externally and using the appropriate IT systems to support their core capabilities as needed.

Type (⊏) companies employ the Codified Transparency strategy. Codified Transparency companies concentrate on codifying their product and process knowledge as much as possible, while making it available both internally and externally as much as needed. The "Codified Transparency" companies employ codification strategies that concentrate on internally embracing the most appropriate source of knowledge and using the appropriate IT systems to support their core capabilities sharing this knowledge as needed and resulting in higher process effectiveness, protecting only those aspects that are absolutely necessary.

Type (⊇) companies employ the Tacit Transparency strategy. Tacit Transparency companies concentrate on maintaining and developing their product and process knowledge as tacit as much as possible, while making it available both internally and externally as much as they can. The "Tacit Transparency" companies use tacitness strategies that focus on internally embracing knowledge and the use of appropriate IT systems to support process development and/or the servicing of their markets while focusing on developing close relationships within and outside the company, protecting only those aspects that are absolutely necessary.

Conclusion

Our own research as well as that of others[35] would suggest that companies are using a combination of the nine taxonomies mentioned above, and that there are more synergies between some of them than others. For example, the "Internal-Codifier-Innovator" strategy ("2" * "III" using our taxonomies notation) seems to be the most valuable in terms of product and process effectiveness (in our research, Russ et al., 2006). On the other hand, the "External-Intuitive-Utilizer" strategy ("3" * "II" using our taxonomies notation) strategy seems to be the least effective strategy. Miller et al. (2007) found within manufacturing firms that product strategies and exploration strategy together with a focus on radical innovation seem to work hand-in-hand as do process strategies and exploitation strategy with a focus on incremental innovation; which in our taxonomy translates into Product- Innovator-Destroyer and Process-Utilizer-Complementer. Questions of interest can be raised here. Will some industries provide a more fruitful environment for different combinations than others? Will different sized companies have a tendency to use or avoid specific strategies and combinations of strategies? Also, what different key success indicators aspired to by the companies might be supported by different combinations of strategies? For example, outcomes of profitability and earnings might show different results.

KM STRATEGY FRAMEWORK

If the six C³EEP strategic dilemmas describe above are combined with the KM strategic levers and outcome measures identified in our earlier research[36], a possible framework for KM strategy emerges (see Table 1 below). This framework can help your company in developing a detailed KM strategy. The specific levers that were found to be of significance in regard to the strategic dilemmas as well as the outcome indicators in our earlier research are marketed with an "X" or with the specific typology identified in this chapter under each strategic dilemma.

This framework should provide KM practitioners with advice as to what to focus their attention on and where and how to allocate resources. For example, companies that are investing greatly in IS technology and are utilizing the Codification strategy, are recommended to verify that their reward systems and employee utilization strategy (as well as culture) are aligned. Or, for example, companies that utilize the Exploration strategy should have an external market focus. Companies that have Product (versus Process) focus, are advised to ensure that their reward systems and their data and IT systems are aligned suitably with their strategy. Companies are also advised not to neglect the need to balance this internal focus with the necessity to expand new product development as part of the Exploration strategy.

FINAL CONCLUSIONS

This framework should provide KM practitioners, as well as academic researchers, with guidelines as to where to focus their attention, and where to focus resource allocation when considering alternative business and KM strategies and their alignment.

For example, our early research confirmed that Codification strategy sponsored by a KM supportive culture is effective when the center of attention is on the process outcomes, while the "Exploration-Codification-Internal Development" strategy is more effective when the center of attention is on the product outcomes. One possible explanation for this is that for processes to be effective, their codification might make it easier to manage and measure, while for New Product Development to be effective, discovering new needs and new customers might be more relevant. There is intricate academic literature corroborating the importance of innovation and new product development for sustaining competitive advantage. On the other hand, there is very little research done on process management and the importance of codifying tacit knowledge in processes, especially in the service sector. Such research should have major consequences since the productivity of services (at least some of them) is comparatively low, and since the service sector represents about 70% of the developed economies GDP.

As mentioned in our earlier research, we would like to remind the reader, that there is a crucial need to incorporate the aspects of organizational culture and the technology aspects of KBS in each KM strategy discussion, which unfortunately is rarely done.

ACKNOWLEDGMENT

The first author wishes to acknowledge the Frederick E. Baer Professorship in Business for partial financial support. The authors wish to thank Kelly Anklam for her assistance in editing this chapter.

REFERENCES

Abernathy, W. J. (1978). *The productivity dilemma.* Baltimore: John Hopkins University Press.

Appleyard, M. M. (1996). How does knowledge flow? Interfirm patterns in the semiconductor industry. *Strategic Management Journal, 17*(Special Issue-Winter), 137–154.

Appleyard, M. M. (1998). *Cooperative knowledge creation: The case of buyer-supplier codevelopment in the semiconductor industry.* Working Paper No. 98–06. Darden Graduate School of Business Administration. Retrieved on December 26, 2003, from http://papers.ssrn.com/abstract=287855

Barley, S. R. (1986). Technology as an occasion for structuring: Evidence from observations of CT scanners and the social order of radiology departments. *Administrative Science Quarterly, 31*, 708–808. doi:10.2307/2392767

Bierly, P., & Chakrabarti, A. (1996). Generic knowledge strategies in the U.S. pharmaceutical industry. *Strategic Management Journal, 17*(Special Issue-Winter), 123-135.

Bloodgood, J. M., & Salisbury, W. D. (2001). Understanding the influence of organizational change strategies on information technology and knowledge management strategies. *Decision Support Systems, 31*, 55–69. doi:10.1016/S0167-9236(00)00119-6

Bower, J. L., & Christensen, C. M. (1995). Disruptive technologies: Catching the wave. *Harvard Business Review, 73*(1), 43–53.

Casillas, J., Crocker, P., Jr., Fehrenbach, F., Haug, K., & Straley, B. (2000). *Disruptive technologies: Strategic advantage and thriving in uncertainty.* Kellogg TechVenture 2000 Anthology (pp. 203–229).

Claycomb, C., Droge, C., & Germain, R. (2001). Applied process knowledge and market performance: The moderating effect of environmental uncertainty. *Journal of Knowledge Management, 5*(3), 264–277. doi:10.1108/13673270110401239

Cohen, W. M., Nelson, R. R., & Walsh, J. P. (2000). *Protecting their intellectual assets: Appropriability conditions and why U.S. manufacturing firms patent (or not)*. NBER Working Paper No. 7552.

Conner, K. R., & Prahalad, C. K. (1996). A resource-based theory of the firm: Knowledge vs. opportunism. *Organization Science*, 7, 477–501. doi:10.1287/orsc.7.5.477

Davenport, T. H. (1993). *Process innovation: Reengineering work through information technology*. Boston, MA: Harvard Business School Press.

Davenport, T. H. (1995). The fad that forgot people. *Fast Company*, 1(1), 70–75.

DeTienne, D. R., & Koberg, C. S. (2002). The impact of environmental and organizational factors on discontinuous innovation within high-technology industries. *IEEE Transactions on Engineering Management*, 49, 352–364. doi:10.1109/TEM.2002.806719

Fjeldstad, O. D., & Haanaes, K. (2001). Strategy tradeoff in the knowledge and network Economy. *Business Strategy Review*, 12(1), 1–10. doi:10.1111/1467-8616.00160

Fleming, L. (2001). Recombinant uncertainty in technological research. *Management Science*, 47, 117–132. doi:10.1287/mnsc.47.1.117.10671

Gray, S. J. (1988). Toward a theory of cultural influence on the development of accounting systems internationally. *Abacus*, 8(1), 1–15. doi:10.1111/j.1467-6281.1988.tb00200.x

Gupta, A., & Govindarajan, V. (2000). Knowledge management's social dimensions: Lesson from Nucor steel. *Sloan Management Review*, Fall, 41(1), 71–80.

Hansen, M. T., Nohria, N., & Tierney, T. (1999). What's your strategy for managing knowledge? *Harvard Business Review*, 77(2), 106–116.

Hill, C. W., & Rothaermel, F. T. (2003). The performance of incumbent firms in the face of radical technological innovation. *Academy of Management Review*, 28, 257–274.

Holden, N. (2001). Knowledge management: Raising the spectre of the cross-cultural dimension. *Knowledge and Process Management*, 8(3), 155–163. doi:10.1002/kpm.117

Inkpen, A. (1998). Learning and knowledge acquisition through international strategic alliances. *The Academy of Management Executive*, 12(4), 69–80.

Jones, O. (2000). Innovation management as a post-modern phenomenon: The outsourcing of pharmaceutical R&D. *British Journal of Management*, 11, 341–356. doi:10.1111/1467-8551.00177

Jones, P. (2002). When successful product prevent strategic innovation. *Design Management Journal*, 13(2), 30–37.

Katila, R. (2002). New product search over time: Past ideas in their prime? *Academy of Management Journal*, 45, 995–1010. doi:10.2307/3069326

Kluge, J., Stein, W., & Licht, T. (2001). *Knowledge unplugged*. New York: Palgrave.

Lamming, R. C., Caldwell, N. G., Harrison, D. A., & Phillips, W. (2001). Transparency in supply relationships: Concepts and practice. *The Journal of Supply Chain Management*, 37(4), 4–10. doi:10.1111/j.1745-493X.2001.tb00107.x

Lanjouw, J. O., & Schankerman, M. (2001). Characteristics of patent litigation: A window on competition. *The Rand Journal of Economics*, 32(1), 129–151. doi:10.2307/2696401

Leonard-Barton, D. A. (1995). *Wellsprings of knowledge*. Boston, MA: Harvard Business School Press.

Lev, B. (nd). *Communication knowledge capabilities*. Retrieved on December 23, 2003, from http://pages.stern.nyu.edu/~blev/communicating.doc

Levinthal, D. A., & March, J. G. (1993). The myopia of learning. *Strategic Management Journal, 14*, 95–112. doi:10.1002/smj.4250141009

Li, A., Oppenheim, J., Chaplain, C., Dinkelacker, D., Elgas, J., Ramos, J., et al. (2002). *NASA, better mechanisms needed for sharing, lessons learned.* Washington, D.C.: GAO Report, GAO.

March, J. G. (1991). Exploration and exploitation in organizational learning. *Organization Science, 2*, 71–87. doi:10.1287/orsc.2.1.71

Martin, J. (1995). *The great transition.* New York: AMACOM.

McGrath, R. G. (2001). Exploratory learning, innovative capacity, and managerial oversight. *Academy of Management Journal, 44*, 118–131. doi:10.2307/3069340

Miller, B. K., Bierly, P. E., & Daly, P. S. (2007). The knowledge strategy orientation scale: Individual perceptions of firm-level phenomena. *Journal of Managerial Issues, 19*(3), 414–435.

Olla, P., & Holm, J. (2006). The role of knowledge management in the space industry: Important or superfluous? *Journal of Knowledge Management, 10*(2), 3–7. doi:10.1108/13673270610656584

Parikh, M. (2001). Knowledge management framework for high-tech research and development. *Engineering Management Journal, 13*(3), 27–33.

Paxton, L. J. (2006). Managing innovative space missions: Lessons from NASA. *Journal of Knowledge Management, 10*(2), 8–21. doi:10.1108/13673270610656593

Pitt, M., & Clarke, K. (1999). Competing on competence: A knowledge perspective on the management of strategic innovation. *Technology Analysis and Strategic Management, 11*, 301–316. doi:10.1080/095373299107375

Powell, T. C. (1995). Total quality management as competitive advantage: A review and empirical study. *Strategic Management Journal, 16*, 15–37. doi:10.1002/smj.4250160105

Quinn, J. B. (1999). Strategic outsourcing: Leveraging knowledge capabilities. *Sloan Management Review, 40*(4), 9–21.

Radebaugh, L. H., & Gray, S. J. (1997). *International accounting and multinational enterprises* (4th ed.). New York: John Wiley and Sons, Inc.

Russ, M., Jones, J. G., & Jones, J. K. (2008). Knowledge-based strategies and systems: A systematic review. In M.D. Lytras, et al. (Eds.), *Knowledge management strategies: A handbook of applied technologies* (pp. 1-62). Hershey, PA: IGI Global.

Russ, M., & Jones, J. K. (2006). Knowledge-based strategies and information system technologies: Preliminary findings. *International Journal of Knowledge and Learning, 2*(1&2), 154–179. doi:10.1504/IJKL.2006.009685

Russ, M., & Jones, J. K. (forthcoming). Knowledge management's strategic dilemmas typology. In D.G. Schwartz and D. Te'eni (Eds.), *Encyclopedia of knowledge management* (2nd ed.). Hershey, PA: IGI Reference.

Russ, M., Jones, J. K., & Fineman, R. (2005). Knowledge-based strategies: A foundation of a typology. *International Journal of Information Technology and Management, 4*(2), 138–165. doi:10.1504/IJITM.2005.006764

Russ, M., Jones, J. K., & Fineman, R. (2006). Toward a taxonomy of knowledge-based strategies: Early findings. *International Journal of Knowledge and Learning, 2*(1&2), 1–40. doi:10.1504/IJKL.2006.009677

Russ, M., Jones, J. K., & Jones, J. G. (2004). Knowledge-based strategies, culture, and information systems. *International Journal of Knowledge. Culture and Change Management, 4*, 427–452.

Sanchez, R., & Mahoney, J. T. (1996). Modularity, flexibility, and knowledge management in product and organization design. *Strategic Management Journal, 17*(Special Issue-Winter), 63–76.

Schultz, M., & Jobe, L. A. (2001). Codification and tacitness as knowledge management strategies: An empirical exploration. *The Journal of High Technology Management Research, 12*, 139–165. doi:10.1016/S1047-8310(00)00043-2

Simonin, B. L. (1997). The importance of collaborative know-how: An empirical test of the learning organization. *Academy of Management Journal, 40*, 1150–1174. doi:10.2307/256930

Smith, P. G., & Reinertsen, D. G. (1998). *Developing products in half the time*. New York: Van Nostrand Reinhold.

Spender, J. C. (1996). Making knowledge the basis of a dynamic theory of the firm. *Strategic Management Journal, 17*(Special Issue-Winter), 45–62.

Steensma, H. K. (1996). Acquiring technological competence through inter-organizational collaboration: An organizational perspective. *Journal of Engineering and Technology Management, 12*(4), 267–286. doi:10.1016/0923-4748(95)00013-5

Stock, G. N., & Tatikonda, M. V. (2004). External technology integration in product and process development. *International Journal of Operations & Production Management, 24*(7), 642–665. doi:10.1108/01443570410541975

Stringer, R. (2000). How to manage radical innovation. *California Management Review, 42*(4), 70–88.

Subramaniam, M., & Venkatraman, N. (2001). Determinants of transnational new product development capacity: Testing the influence of transferring and deploying tacit overseas knowledge. *Strategic Management Journal, 22*, 359–378. doi:10.1002/smj.163

Sullivan, J. E. III. (2000). The often overlooked role of disclosure in asset protection planning: Part 1. *Asset Protection Journal, 2*(1), 1–14.

Tapscott, D., & Ticoll, D. (2003). *The naked corporation: How the age of transparency will revolutionize business*. New York: Free Press.

von Furstenberg, G. M. (2001). Hopes and delusions of transparency. *The North American Journal of Economics and Finance, 12*, 105–120. doi:10.1016/S1062-9408(01)00040-7

Zack, M. H. (1999). Developing a knowledge strategy. *California Management Review, 41*(3), 125–145.

ENDNOTES

[1] e.g., Conner and Prahalad, 1996; Hansen et al., 1999; Leonard-Barton, 1995; Schultz and Jobe, 2001; Spender, 1996; Subramaniam and Venkatraman, 2001.

[2] e.g., Barley, 1986; Bower and Christensen, 1995; Fleming, 2001; Hill and Rothaermel, 2003.

[3] e.g., Gray 1988; Inkpen, 1998; Lamming et al., 2001; Radebaugh and Gray, 1997; von Furstenberg, 2001.

[4] e.g., Bloodgood and Salisbury, 2001; Fjeldstad and Haanaes, 2001; Levinthal and March, 1993; March, 1991; McGrath, 2001; Pitt and Clarke, 1999.

[5] e.g., Appleyard, 1998; Bierly and Chakrabarti, 1996; Jones, 2000; Parikh, 2001; Pitt and Clarke, 1999; Steensma, 1996; Zack, 1999.

[6] e.g., Abernathy, 1978; Jones, 2002; Smith and Reinertsen, 1998.

[7] Gupta and Govindarajan, 2000, p. 79.

[8] e.g., Holden, 2001, Kluge et al., 2001; Russ et al., 2004; Russ et al. 2005.

[9] See for example Li et al., 2002, Paxton, 2006 and Tammy Joyner. (2005, July 3).

Boomer expertise heads to retirement U.S. companies face loss of valuable experience and skills that can't be passed to new generation in textbooks, seminars:[Home Edition]. The Atlanta Journal - Constitution,p. B.1. Retrieved June 25, 2009, from ProQuest Newsstand database. (Document ID: 862150571).

10   e.g., Casillas et al., 2000; DeTienne and Koberg, 2002; Stringer, 2000.

11   Lanjouw and Schankerman, 2001; Cohen et al., 2000.

12   Sullivan, 2000.

13   Lev (nd).

14   Lamming et al., 2001.

15   Inkpen, 1998.

16   Appleyard, 1996.

17   Jones, 2000.

18   Quinn, 1999.

19   Simonin, 1997.

20   Katila, 2002.

21   WSJ, December 24, 2007, pp. B1, B3.

22   Davenport, 1993, p.1; Martin, 1995, p. 32; Davenport, 1995; Powell, 1995.

23   Jones, 2002; Abernathy, 1978.

24   Sanchez and Mahoney, 1996.

25   Claycomb et al., 2001.

26   See a more academic discussion in Russ and Jones (forthcoming).

27   Russ et al., 2005.

28   Russ et al., 2006 and Russ and Jones, 2006.

29   Russ et al., 2006 and Russ and Jones, 2006.

30   e.g., http://km.nasa.gov/pdf/182783main_Gibson_Lessons_Learned.pdf; http://www.csc.com/aboutus/leadingedgeforum/knowledgelibrary/uploads/CSC%20Papers%202007%20-%20Lessons%20Learned%20-%20A%20Case%20Study%20from%20NASA_MDA_GMD.pdf and Olla and Holm, 2006.

31   Stock and Tatikonda, 2004.

32   'In Chine, Chery Automobile drives an industry shift.' WSJ, December 4, 2007; pp. A1 and A17; by Gordon Fairclough.

33   See for example: Robert L. Simison. (1999, October 26). Buick Succeeds in China by Laying Stress on Quality --- GM's Approach In Difficult Market Is Yielding Growth. Wall Street Journal (Eastern Edition), p. A18. Retrieved June 25, 2009, from ABI/INFORM Global database. (Document ID: 45798488).

McGregor, Richard. (2002, December 12). These cars are fast movers: MOTOR INDUSTRY by Richard McGregor: Growth of 40 per cent may not last, but the market is still likely to expand rapidly:[Surveys edition]. Financial Times,p. 08. Retrieved June 25, 2009, from ABI/INFORM Global database. (Document ID: 262573451).

Karby Leggett and Todd Zaun. (2002, December 13). Peeling Out: World's Car Makers Race to Keep Up With China Boom --- As Sales Surge, Firms Roll Out New Models, Cut Prices; Looming Capacity Glut --- A Minivan Called Sunshine. Wall Street Journal (Eastern Edition), p. A.1. Retrieved June 25, 2009, from ABI/INFORM Global database. (Document ID: 264312951).

Katie Merx. (18 May). Chinese buyers give Buick a second wind. Knight Ridder Tribune News Service,1. Retrieved June 25, 2009, from ProQuest Newsstand database. (Document ID: 1273405651).

34   See for example: Sandra Ward. Corning Goes Prime Time. *Barrons*. April 6, 2009. http://online.barrons.com/article/SB123880713385288961.html Kelic, A. (2005). Networking Technology Adoption: System Dynamics Modelling of Fiber-to-the-Home, Ph.D. Thesis, MIT. Available at: http://esd.mit.edu/people/dissertations/kelic_andjelka.pdf

Mahmud Awan. (2006) The Comparative Success of Disruptive Innovations in the

Fiberoptic Industry http://www.techmaninc. com/downloads/disruptive%20innovations%205-06.pdf

[35] e.g., Miller et al., 2007.

[36] e.g., Russ et al. 2005, 2006, and Russ and Jones, 2006.

Chapter 8
Linking Exploration and Exploitation Capabilities with the Process of Knowledge Development and with Organizational Facilitators[1]

César Camisón-Zornoza
Jaume I University, Spain

Montserrat Boronat-Navarro
Jaume I University, Spain

ABSTRACT

Knowledge management is a fundamental capability in today's evolving markets. Management needs to understand which organizational processes are necessary to trigger each of the stages in knowledge development. The objective of this study is to outline the main concepts and stages in the process of knowledge development in organizations and the organizational activities that have a positive influence on those stages. A conceptual framework is proposed which combines the model of knowledge development proposed by Nonaka (1994) with the concepts of exploration and exploitation initially described by March (1991). Information systems are seen to play a fundamental role in supporting this process, especially in activities related to exploitation capability.

INTRODUCTION

The aim of this research is to go a step further in this direction. The Knowledge-Based View (or KBV) is taken as a starting point, but with the addition of concepts and lessons from the perspective of

Organizational Learning (or OL), because the two views can be considered to be closely related, as described in the next section. The intention of this research is to take a closer look at the concepts of exploration and exploitation, which still stir controversy about their real meaning. Here, it is claimed that these are two capabilities which together will enable organizational knowledge to develop. An

DOI: 10.4018/978-1-60566-348-7.ch008

analysis to determine which processes activate these capabilities will make it possible to associate them with different phases of one of the most popular models of knowledge creation—that proposed by Nonaka (1994).

The main goal of this paper is to examine the activities and phases involved in the development of organizational knowledge, with special attention paid to determining which organizational activities make up this process. This conceptual analysis can then be used to draw conclusions about the organizational capabilities and activities that must be fostered by managers to develop knowledge.

After this introduction, the paper continues with a description of those ideas from the KBV literature that the authors consider to be most relevant to the present analysis. It also deals with some concepts that were initially put forward in the OL perspective. These two approaches claim that the capability to enable knowledge and organizational learning to evolve has become the most important capability for organizations. The main body of the paper begins with an analysis of the meanings of the concepts of exploration and exploitation, with brief comments on the controversy in the literature regarding their meanings. The knowledge creation model proposed by Nonaka (1994) is then described in detail, but as a model divided into several phases. Later, the concepts of exploration and exploitation are associated with the different phases of the knowledge creation process. The discussion concludes with a comprehensive description of the organizational processes that are involved in both the exploration and the exploitation of knowledge. These organizational processes are the ones that will enable knowledge to develop. In the fourth section, some future lines of research are proposed, and the conclusions that have been drawn are discussed.

BACKGROUND

The importance of the creation, exploitation, and transfer of knowledge has been emphasized to the point where it now constitutes a body of theory in its own right, i.e., the KBV (Grant, 1996a, b; Nonaka, 1994; Nonaka & Takeuchi, 1995; Spender, 1996a, b). The KBV considers knowledge to be the most important strategic asset within an enterprise (Grant, 1996b; Quinn, 1992). Companies are increasingly investing in knowledge management systems to develop and exploit it (Sarvary, 1999). There are various classifications of knowledge management strategies (Choi, Poon, & Davis, 2008). The first of these categorizes strategies according to their focus. On the one hand, tacit-oriented strategies involve a personalized approach in which socialization processes are encouraged through individual contact and communication among organization members (Zack, 1999). On the other hand, an explicit-oriented strategy refers to the codification and reuse of organizational knowledge (Hansen, Nohria, & Tierney, 1999). This latter type of strategy is concerned mainly with the development and application of new information technologies to capture, store, and distribute the organization's explicit knowledge (Zack, 1999). The two strategies are based on the difference between the explicit and tacit dimensions of knowledge, which is explained below. The need for organizations to obtain a balance between the two types of strategy has been stressed in several studies (Choi & Lee, 2003; Choi, Poon, & Davis, 2008). Integrating the two approaches should lead to higher performance. In this paper, these two strategies are linked with the entire process of knowledge development, and as will become apparent, activities included in both kinds of strategy are necessary to obtain new knowledge. Therefore, this study agrees with the line of research that advocates complementary use of both strategies.

Claycomb, Dröge, and Germain (2001) identify five characteristics that distinguish knowledge from tangible resources: it is not easily divisible, it is not easily appropriable, it is not inherently scarce, it is essentially regenerative, and its value can increase with use. These distinguishing features of knowledge explain why it contains many of the requisites for being a strategic asset, including specificity, difficulty of transfer, difficulty of codification, high complexity (Kogut & Zander, 1992), and dependence on the history of the company (Cohen & Levinthal, 1990). Thus, according to this approach (Grant, 1996a, b; Nonaka, 1994; Nonaka & Takeuchi, 1996; Spender, 1996), the reasons for the heterogeneity of companies and the dynamic sources of competitiveness are to be found in knowledge and learning as essential intangible assets. Furthermore, the enterprise is seen as a single base where organizational knowledge can be developed.

To clarify the concept of knowledge, several authors have taken ideas and classifications from other branches of science. In the epistemological dimension of knowledge, a distinction has traditionally been made between explicit, or formal, knowledge and tacit knowledge (Polanyi, 1958; Winter, 1987). The importance of tacit knowledge (Polanyi, 1962) provides the foundation for later prominent studies, such as those by Nelson and Winter (1982) and Nonaka (1994). In an attempt to clarify the difference between tacit and explicit knowledge, Spender (1996b) speaks of explicit knowledge as knowing, theoretical knowledge, knowing what or knowledge of or about, in contrast to tacit knowledge, described as know-how, knowledge in a practical sense, knowing how to do, or knowledge of acquaintance. Grant (1996b) also clearly associates "knowing how" with tacit knowledge and "knowing about" with explicit knowledge.

Different classifications of knowledge have been produced by combining this epistemological dimension with the ontological dimension. Thus, Spender (1996a, b) obtains four differ-

ent types of knowledge using the categories of explicit, implicit (tacit), individual, and social. Conscious knowledge is that which is explicit and individual; combining individual and implicit knowledge results in automatic knowledge; the explicit knowledge category combined with the social level gives us objective knowledge, and lastly, collective knowledge is the term used to describe knowledge which is implicit and social. For the enterprise, the most important of these four types will be the collective type (Spender, 1996a, b), because the fact of its being embedded in the organization will make it more difficult to imitate and strategically the most important, and it will lead to gaining what are known as Penrose rents (Spender, 1995). Nevertheless, the four types of knowledge, as well as the interactions among them, will all exist within the enterprise. These interactions are precisely what will help the collective knowledge to grow. The company is no longer seen as a set of resources (Spender, 1996a), but instead as a community of practice (Brown & Duguid, 1991; Lave & Wenger, 1991) in which this collective knowledge is embedded. This last level is the most interesting because, in line with Grant (1996b), the main role of the enterprise is considered to be the integration of knowledge.

Nonaka and Takeuchi's (1995) model furthers our understanding of how the individual level can facilitate the growth of collective knowledge. It does so by taking as its foundation the different combinations of knowledge conversion that are possible if we consider the features of explicit and tacit knowledge. The ideas posed by these authors and by Spender (1996b) are therefore similar, because the interaction between the different types of knowledge is what fosters their development. This distinction between explicit and tacit knowledge is therefore the main characteristic that has opened up the way to the creation of different models to explain how knowledge develops.

In their overview survey and as one of the paths to be followed to examine the KBV in greater depth and endow it with more meaning, Eisenhardt and

Santos (2002) highlight the importance of focusing more on the process of knowing and not so much on knowledge itself. The dynamic conditions of the market make the ability to integrate or apply new knowledge, rather than just possessing it, the capability that can provide competitive advantages (Eisenhardt & Santos, 2002). In a Schumpeterian world, these advantages will be temporary, but achieving successive temporary competitive advantages will make it possible to reach higher performance. Organizations need to handle increasing complexity and high-velocity change in today's environments to compete and even to survive (McGrath, 2001).

This discussion refers to the capability to create knowledge. This capability will rest on the skill that the organization has to develop processes for creating, storing, distributing, and interpreting knowledge, as well as on the progress made in building systems for gathering information and the skills needed to transform it into knowledge that is valuable for the organization. Knowledge management skills and R&D together make up the infrastructure that is needed to carry out these processes so that new knowledge can be generated. The capacity for managing this infrastructure is embedded within certain routines and organizational processes that constitute internal mechanisms of knowledge transmission, as well as in elements to facilitate the wide-ranging and effective application of the knowledge that already exists in the organization.

This approach, which stresses the importance of the process of knowing, over and above the possession of knowledge as a resource, is linked with the OL perspective. OL is part of the foundation that supports the thinking of the KBV (Eisenhardt & Santos, 2002); at first it was studied at the individual level, but was later conceptualized on the social level as a key process in adapting the organization to the environment (Argote, 1999).

By considering them from a constructivist perspective, KBV and OL are brought closer together by the emphasis that is placed on the social construction of learning and knowledge. In this research, KBV and OL concepts will be addressed from this perspective because this study focuses more on the process of knowledge creation than on knowledge as a resource, as we show in Figure 1. Here, dynamic capabilities are understood to be those that enable the enterprise to integrate and reconfigure internal and external competencies to guide, and hence cope with, rapid changes in the environment (Teece, Pisano, & Schuen, 1997). Therefore, the development of organizational knowledge is, or can be, a dynamic capability that enables continuous organizational learning and favors the development of knowledge assets (Tsoukas & Mynolopoulos, 2004).

Two of the concepts proposed in the OL perspective are exploitation and exploration. Strategic decisions are closely related to the choice of how much to invest in different activities, and each of these approaches—exploration and exploitation—may require different resources, processes, skills, and even organizational structures. In his seminal paper, March (1991) suggests that exploration is the activity related to searching, experimenting with new alternatives, and taking risks, whereas exploitation refers to refining, efficiency, implementation, and selection. The change that is proposed from the OL perspective is the need to strike a balance between the two activities (Bontis, Crossan, & Hulland, 2002), rather than forcing the organization to choose to channel more resources towards one activity or the other.

On the basis of this review, the next section will explain what is understood by exploration and exploitation. A more thorough analysis will be performed of one of the knowledge creation models that has exerted a strong influence in the literature, associating it specifically in this case with the terms *exploration* and *exploitation*. Understanding the processes that are implicit in the two concepts will help determine which activities can help management foster the development of organizational knowledge. Particular attention will also be given to the importance of informa-

Figure 1. Combination of two approaches (Source: Developed by authors)

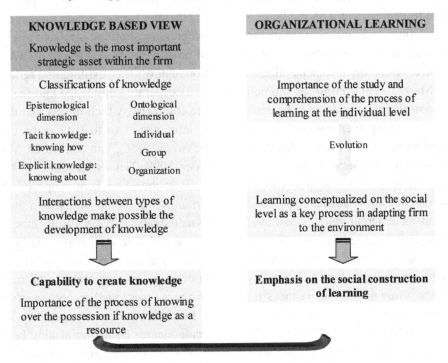

tion technologies, especially in one of the phases of the process.

EXPLORATION AND EXPLOITATION AND THE ORGANIZATIONAL PROCESSES THAT ACTIVATE THEM

Issues, Controversies, Problems

The Meaning of Exploration and Exploitation

Although the terms *exploration* and *exploitation* have been widely used in the literature on strategy, they are not always given the same meaning. The question of what each of them really represents remains unanswered (Gupta, Smith, & Shalley, 2006). There is a fair degree of agreement about the term *exploration*, as referring to the pursuit and acquisition of new knowledge, but this is not the case with *exploitation*, and this has been one

of the main issues needing resolution ever since March (1991) used both of these terms in relation to organizational learning. The main discussion is about whether or not new knowledge can be considered to be produced in exploitation, and therefore about whether or not exploitation can be seen as a dynamic capability. However, confusion also arises as a result of applying the terms on different conceptual levels: at the capabilities level, the results level, or as an adjective applied to other activities (e.g., alliances, innovation).

This research starts from the idea that the two concepts are part of the dynamic capabilities construct. Many studies that use the two concepts corroborate the hypothesis that learning and acquisition or generation of new knowledge take place in both exploration and exploitation. These same studies also distinguish between these concepts on the basis of whether or not that learning follows the same technological trajectory that the enterprise is already using. In the present case, as in Gupta, Smith, and Shalley (2006), the starting point is the idea that both concepts entail learning, a notion which is in full agreement with the logic of March's (1991) definition. This author argues that organizational learning requires both exploration of new paths and exploitation of what has already been learned (March, 1991). From the moment organizational learning is considered to be made up of the two concepts together, both of them are then considered to involve a certain degree of learning. Moreover, even when the company is doing nothing more than replicating past actions, some new learning and knowledge are produced, albeit in only an incremental manner, and even though they serve only to reduce variability in the performance of actions that the organization already performs (Gupta, Smith, & Shalley, 2006). Repetition through routines reduces the time needed to carry out a given activity, but it also increases reliability in the performance of the activity, because variability in its implementation is reduced (Benner & Tushman, 2002; Levinthal & March, 1993; March, 1991). Thus, the distinction between exploration and exploitation does not lie in whether or not new learning is produced, but rather in what type of knowledge or learning is generated. Any other way of looking at it would fail to analyze many activities related to replication as new learning—something that does not make sense because in social systems there is no such thing as perfect replication without some variation in the learning taking place.

As in March (1991), exploration is therefore defined as experimentation with new alternatives, and exploitation is the refinement and extension of existing competencies, paradigms, and technologies. It must also be made clear that both concepts entail new knowledge and learning, and that the difference between them lies in the type of knowledge and the extent to which it is produced. In this regard, Helfat and Raubitschek (2000) propose two systems of learning which they associate with March's (1991) distinction between exploration and exploitation. They also distinguish the system that they call *step functional learning* from the

incremental learning system, the difference being that the former entails fundamental changes. Whereas exploration is related to a higher degree of novelty because it has to do with the generation of new ideas, exploitation reflects the ability to incorporate knowledge into the operations of the enterprise, which means that the knowledge is internalized so that it can be used (Lyles & Schwenk, 1992; Van den Bosch, Volberda, & de Boer, 1999; Tiemessen et al., 1997).

It is therefore here proposed that the term *exploitation* should be used to mean a kind of dynamic capability, because together with exploration, it will generate the organizational knowledge creation process. From the moment organizational knowledge is considered to be made up of the two processes together, both are then considered to be kinds of dynamic capability. The concept is made clearer by distinguishing between simply exploiting the capabilities that the organization already has and exploiting the knowledge that has just been created. In this work, exploitation is understood in this latter sense, in line with Nonaka (1994), who considers the process of generating knowledge as a continuum on which the newly created concepts must crystallize and become internalized for use to complete the process of knowledge generation. Some studies understand exploitation as referring only to organizational routines that enable different organizational processes to be carried out, but the definition used here will omit this sense because the authors consider it to refer to certain functional or coordinating capabilities and not to exploitation in the sense of refinement and incorporation of new knowledge. This conceptual sense also implies that exploration and exploitation should be considered as two complementary concepts which can occur at the same time inside the organization, in spite of the contradictory processes driving them.

The idea that both concepts imply learning and development of new knowledge is underlined in the definitions of dynamic capabilities that are proposed in the Competence-Based Approach

(CBA). Zollo and Winter (2002) claim that dynamic capabilities emerge and evolve when enterprises are capable of adopting a set of processes related to both cognitive and behavioral aspects, and this then favors the development of knowledge in a cycle in which exploration and exploitation follow each other. Dynamic capabilities are based on the exploitation of current resources, on technologies to improve efficiency, and on the generation of new possibilities through exploration (Benner & Tushman, 2002; March, 1991; Rosenkopf & Nerkar, 2001; Teece, Pisano, & Shuen, 1997). Both exploration and exploitation, therefore, should be classified as dynamic capabilities because these capabilities are based on both exploration and exploitation activities (Benner & Tushman, 2003).

Process of Knowledge Creation

Nonaka (1994) does not speak in terms of the tension that exists between exploration and exploitation, but he does mention both in his explanation of knowledge creation. In this process, different contexts can be distinguished: acquisition, generation, exploitation, and the accumulation of knowledge. Focusing on the analysis of what this process of knowledge creation is—as described in Nonaka (1994)—will help define the mechanisms in the organization that make it possible to carry out exploration and exploitation. This paper is a valuable contribution as a meeting place between the OL and the KBV literature and can serve as a foundation for a line of reasoning that will make it possible to distinguish between exploration and exploitation. The holistic and integrative approach of Nonaka's (1994) papers, together with some of the ideas proposed in the works of Bontis, Crossan, and their colleagues (Bontis, Crossan, & Hulland, 2002; Crossan, Lane & White, 1999), will serve as the basis for the model to be developed here. There is no intention to confirm Nonaka's model by itself, but rather to use it as a basis for theoretical development.

The spiral model of organizational knowledge creation proposed by Nonaka (1994) is based on a joint treatment of the epistemological and ontological dimensions. While the former distinguishes between tacit and explicit knowledge, the latter refers to the level of analysis (individual, group, organizational or inter-organizational) in the creation of organizational knowledge.

The characterization of knowledge on the first dimension, tacit versus explicit, is based on the premises stated by Polanyi (1966), who defined explicit knowledge as that which, when codified, is transmissible by a formal, systematic language, whereas tacit knowledge, which the literature has analyzed as more important, is based on action and experimentation and is difficult to formalize and communicate. This second type of knowledge has both cognitive and technical elements (Nonaka, 1994) and therefore includes the paradigms and beliefs that enable individuals to form their own vision of the world and also the know-how and skills that can be applied to certain contexts. The distinction between tacit and explicit is similar to the division of knowledge into procedural and declarative types (Anderson, 1983).

The transformation or growth of already-existing knowledge into new knowledge takes place through interaction among the four different types of conversion at the ontological level. This produces an expansion of the process into a kind of spiral of knowledge through social interaction among the individuals in the organization. Although each mode of conversion entails knowledge creation on its own, only the convergence of the four at the same time gives rise to organizational knowledge creation. The modes of conversion reflect the transformation of knowledge, taking into account its nature as either tacit or explicit.

First, the conversion of tacit knowledge among individuals in the organization, through the interactions that take place among them, is called *socialization*. The experience shared by members of the organization and the interaction that occurs among them enable them to acquire knowledge without having to do so explicitly. The author cites, as an example of this mode of conversion, what happens with the traditional apprentice in a trade who learns from his mentors or masters by watching and imitating. In contrast, the mode of conversion called *externalization* requires language to make explicit the tacit knowledge possessed by individuals. Nonaka (1994) claims that the use of mechanisms such as metaphors, analogies, and dialogues favors this mode of conversion. These mechanisms are necessary because of the difficulties involved in making tacit knowledge explicit, because it is a personal kind of knowledge based on one's own way of seeing the world and on action-based know-how. These two modes of knowledge conversion (socialization and externalization) are linked mainly with the transformation of explicit knowledge and therefore with tacit-knowledge-oriented strategies, as it is shown in Figure 2.

As for the other two modes of knowledge creation, so-called *combination* involves conversion within the explicit dimension, while *internalization* entails the transformation of explicit into tacit knowledge. *Combination* is performed by reconfiguring different bodies of explicit knowledge through the use of computer systems or other social processes that are traditionally studied in the literature on information systems. Documenting existing knowledge will make it easier for the concepts that are developed to be condensed in a more concrete form (Nonaka, 1994: 20). *Internalization* refers to a traditional learning concept, because it requires the interiorization of explicit knowledge, thus turning it into tacit knowledge. This is why action and experimentation are important for this mode of conversion to take place. Here the explicit dimension is more important, and this is then linked with explicit-oriented strategies.

The distinction between the two environments is interesting for the present line of reasoning.

In the next section, the modes of *socialization* and *externalization* will first be discussed in rela-

Figure 2. Four modes of knowledge conversion (Source: Developed by authors, based on Nonaka, 1994)

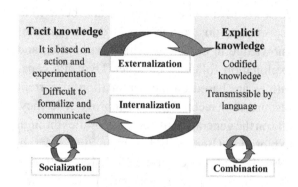

tion to the overall process by which knowledge is generated within the organization (Nonaka, 1994). The modes of *combination* and *internalization* will then be discussed, also in relation to this process. This will make it possible to associate the various phases of the knowledge creation process with the concepts of exploration and exploitation and also to determine the processes and organizational activities that activate each.

SOLUTIONS AND RECOMMENDATIONS: THE KNOWLEDGE CREATION PROCESS AND ITS RELATION TO EXPLORATION AND EXPLOITATION

Associating the Concepts of Exploration and Exploitation with the Various Phases of the Knowledge Creation Process

To propose a conceptual framework that helps to identify the processes that activate exploration and exploitation in each case, it is important to consider that the socialization and externalization modes of conversion, in particular, require fluent interaction among the individuals in an organization. In this context, the mechanisms associated with shared experience, dialogue, and organizational culture will play a key role. Although no specific line of research in organizational theory has specifically addressed the case of externalization, according to Nonaka (1994) the topic of socialization has traditionally been dealt with by the literature associated with organizational culture. In the authors' opinion, organizational capabilities associated with mechanisms that facilitate dialogue and fluent interaction will favor both types of conversion. The idea that a flatter, nonhierarchical organizational environment working through self-organizing teams fosters the socialization and externalization modes is also in line with the authors' views.

Taking these concepts as his starting point, Nonaka (1994) develops the process in which knowledge is generated within the organization, a process which involves combining the modes of knowledge conversion and expanding them from individual knowledge to organizational knowledge. Individual tacit knowledge is expanded in this process thanks to the variety of individual experience, which gives rise to an increase in the amount of tacit knowledge that is obtained over time. This knowledge is enlarged and articulated by the social interaction that takes place among members of the organization. Here, teams can also play a decisive role in endowing the organization with the degree of flexibility it needs to create new ideas, problems, and solutions. The self-organizing group enables a buildup of mutual trust among its members, and this facilitates the creation of a shared perspective and creative dialogue.

The author discusses self-organizing teams because they enable the creation of a more richly linked common knowledge base where new ideas flow through the interaction among their members. Nevertheless, this idea can also be applied to all members of the organization. In other words, although it is true that work teams (Nonaka, 1994) can work more autonomously, with a shared vision that is closer than the one they may have with other members of the orga-

nization, and with a common goal of creating knowledge, this idea can also be expanded to include the other members of the organization. Working in teams in a flat structure and sharing a culture focused on learning and innovation can favor the processes of socialization and externalization more strongly than would be the case in an organization that is hierarchically and functionally organized. Furthermore, Nonaka (1994) also refers to this idea of extending knowledge creation to all members of the organization when he states that *the interactions between tacit knowledge and explicit knowledge will tend to become larger in scale and faster in speed as more actors in and around the organization become involved*. For the organization to be able to create a new concept, the process of externalization must take place to convert the tacit knowledge of the group members into explicit concepts. Socialization must also be performed by sharing the mental models among the members of the group. This will enable the process of conceptualization, or articulation of concepts, to be carried out.

The modes of *internalization* and *combination* will now be discussed. The process of *internalization* is essential for crystallization, that is, for turning the new concepts that have been created into a real application, such as a new product or system in the enterprise (Nonaka, 1994). Furthermore, it is clear that the main element involved in this process is *combination*, because when transforming an idea into a real application, documenting and articulating the knowledge will make it easier to implement and apply, as pointed out by Nonaka himself when defining combination. The process of crystallization also typically requires the involvement of several organizational departments and functions to put the idea into practice. To do this, there must be redundancy of information (Nonaka, 1994: 20), because this will enable any member of the organization with access to the information and knowledge to use it in his or her field or specialty. However, *combination* does not refer only to the knowledge that is needed at any given time, but also to having easy access to more extensive information that will enable more connections among different concepts and therefore will accelerate crystallization. Crystallization is the next step after conceptualization in the process of organizational knowledge creation, although the process is circular, with no definite start or end point. Nevertheless, for the process of knowledge creation to continue, there has to be a convergence and a proof that the knowledge that has been created is in fact useful and necessary. This process is what Nonaka (1994) calls *justification of the quality of knowledge*, and it must be achieved by integrating the concept into the enterprise's knowledge base (knowledge network), thus giving rise to a reorganization of existing knowledge.

The transformation required to produce crystallization occurs when various departments in the enterprise confirm the possibility of implementing and applying the concept that has been created. Therefore, if the two forms of knowledge conversion that are mainly involved in this part of the process, i.e., *combination* and *internalization*, are considered together, the organizational capabilities involved will be those related to mechanisms for internally evaluating and applying knowledge, its integration within the enterprise, and the actions that drive individual development and learning in organization members.

Analysis of socialization and externalization, on the one hand, and internalization and combination, on the other, also follows the logic of distinguishing between different contexts in the process of knowledge creation. Each of these contexts, here called acquisition, generation, exploitation, and accumulation, has its own requirements (Nonaka, 1994). This makes it possible to establish the parallelism shown in Figure 3.

The socialization and externalization modes, which are involved mainly in the conceptualization phases, will be active in the acquisition and generation contexts because conceptualization entails the creation of a new concept or idea, that is, new knowledge. However, the internalization and combination modes, which are more involved in the crystallization phase, enable this new knowledge to be applied, that is, implemented. The new knowledge is therefore related to the contexts of implementation, exploitation, and accumulation.

The conceptual proposition to be presented here will be based on these distinctions, considering that the capabilities needed to carry out socialization and externalization processes will reflect knowledge exploration, while knowledge exploitation will be represented by capabilities that can activate internalization and combination modes. Even though Nonaka (1994) makes no specific reference to the distinction between exploration and exploitation, he in fact refers to it when he speaks of the various contexts of knowledge creation. Furthermore, in the process that he proposes for creating organizational knowledge, these two concepts are clearly reflected, either through the creation of a new concept, in the case of exploration, or through putting it into practice, in the case of exploitation.

Therefore, on the one hand, exploitation entails mainly the use of explicit knowledge bases and their combination and internalization (Figure 3) (Nonaka, 1994). On the other hand, exploration entails the use of tacit knowledge bases so that new concepts are developed by socializing and externalizing them (Figure 3). This will make it possible to deal with new trends that are latent in the environment by creating innovative technologies and gaining access to new markets (Lubatkin et al., 2006).

Although the concepts presented here are based on this line of reasoning and the various measures that have been proposed in the literature for the concepts of exploration and exploitation, the intention of this study is to approach this conceptualization from a different angle. The conceptual proposition presented here associates the capabilities for exploration and exploitation with those dynamic capabilities which are capable of producing a constant evolution within the organization, thus

Figure 3. Parallelism between the different modes of knowledge conversion and the different phases of knowledge creation related to exploration and exploitation. (Source: Developed by authors, based on Nonaka, 1994)

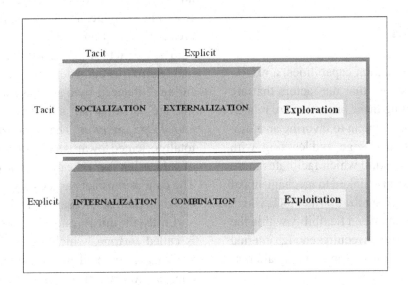

generating innovations and encouraging both the development of existing capabilities and the creation of new capabilities.

Processes that Make Up Exploration and Exploitation

It has already been said that exploration and exploitation capabilities can activate both parts of a process aimed at generating knowledge within the enterprise. More specifically, exploration refers to the use of mainly tacit knowledge bases by members of the organization, so that if this knowledge is socialized and externalized, new ideas and trajectories can be developed and conceptualized, thereby enabling the enterprise to address new trends in the market. However, in exploitation, mainly explicit knowledge is combined and internalized, so that the new idea that has been created can crystallize and be incorporated into the functioning of the enterprise, thereby making it possible to develop existing trajectories further.

Exploration capabilities therefore reflect the skill of the organization in enabling a fluent interaction among its members through shared experience, dialogue, and the organizational culture. This skill will determine whether or not it is possible to perform socialization (in which mental models are shared among individuals) and externalization to turn the tacit knowledge of group members into explicit concepts. The conceptualization of new knowledge cannot be understood without taking into account both processes (Nonaka, 1994). Exploitation capabilities, on the other hand, consist of those processes that enable the reconfiguration of different bodies of knowledge to favor combination, and of those that favor individuals' interiorization of the knowledge that has been developed, in other words, its internalization. Both of these sets of processes will trigger the crystallization of knowledge (Nonaka, 1994).

These capabilities are embedded in organizational processes and must be seen in terms of structures and managerial processes (Teece, Pisano, & Shuen, 1997). The processes that make up exploration and exploitation are what is understood here as facilitators, that is, processes that form and activate these capabilities.

EXPLORATION

In the case of exploration capabilities, a review of the literature shows that the factors that are capable of activating these processes are related to leadership's commitment to favoring an atmosphere of innovation, change, and learning, with an organizational culture which facilitates these activities. They are also linked to mechanisms of combination among organization members which encourage participation and flexibility within the organization. Exploration requires enough internal variety so that people can propose many alternatives and search for new ideas and approaches (McGrath, 2001). The factors that activate the processes making up these exploration capabilities are precisely those that are related to shared experience and dialogue (Nonaka, 1994). The papers of Nonaka (1994), Crossan, Lane, and White (1999), Bontis, Crossan, and Hulland (2002), and Zollo and Winter (2002) are especially useful for defining the processes that make up exploration.

The first facilitators discussed here reflect the essential role played by management in generating an atmosphere which encourages individuals in the organization to share experiences (Nonaka, 1994). The importance of management staff as catalysts and drivers of knowledge creation is confirmed by the literature (de Boer, van den Bosch, & Volberda, 1999; Grant, 1996a, b; Ichijo, von Krogh, & Nonaka, 1998; Kusunoki, Nonaka, & Nagata, 1998; McGrath, 2001; Nonaka, Toyama, & Nagata, 2000), which acknowledges that, essentially, organizational knowledge generation cannot take place if it does not begin at the individual level, and that management must encourage individuals to participate. Managers should promote a goal and grant supervisory autonomy to working groups in their organizations to allow greater latitude and

heterogeneity, and therefore higher variability, in the proposals and ideas which the groups generate (McGrath, 2001). Management must promote an atmosphere that favors change and learning by fostering dialogue, sharing of experience, and a creative orientation.

The extent to which this culture of innovation and learning is embedded in the organization is further enhanced by a second set of facilitators that are part of what is called here a *culture of knowledge creation*. The organization must be totally oriented towards a way of working and a set of values that favor the generation of knowledge. The culture thus acts as a catalyst for individual activity (Bontis, Crossan, & Hulland, 2002).

Lastly, the third group of factors is part of what is called *linkage*, which reflects the organization's capability to design processes and achieve coordination among organization members to favor the atmosphere needed to share experiences and facilitate dialogue. The relevance of routines related to linkage mechanisms has been highlighted in a number of studies (Bontis, Crossan, & Hulland, 2002; Grant, 1996a, b; Hult, Snow, & Kandemir, 2003).

Thus, the three essential components that are needed to carry out exploration capabilities have been identified: leadership, culture, and processes which foster the creation of an appropriate atmosphere for facilitating dialogue and sharing experience. Table 1 shows the literature that supports each of these components, together with the capabilities where each of them appears.

EXPLOITATION

The factors that are capable of activating the processes of combination and internalization involved in the exploitation capabilities are related to experimentation, "learning by doing," and processes that favor documentation (Nonaka, 1994). A literature review revealed three facilitating factors related to the integration of knowledge within the

Table 1. Factors and specific capabilities making up knowledge exploration and the authors who analyze each

Facilitator	Specific capabilities that activate it	Authors
Knowledge leadership	Rejecting tradition and fostering change Fostering initiative Promoting self-criticism Mobilization of middle management Dialogue approach Entrepreneurial approach Focus on opportunities Creative approach Goals with supervisory autonomy Focus on learning	Nonaka (1994) Crossan, Lane, & White (1999) Bontis, Crossan, & Hulland (2002) Grant (1996a, b) Un & Cuervo-Cazurra (2004) De Boer, van den Bosch, & Volberda (1999) Hult, Snow, & Kandemir (2003) Ichijo, von Krogh, & Nonaka (1998) McGrath (2001)
Culture of knowledge creation	Group learning Stimulating continuous improvement Self-responsibility Incorporating ideas	Nonaka (1994) Crossan, Lane, & White (1999) Bontis, Crossan, & Hulland (2002) Un & Cuervo-Cazurra (2004) De Boer, van den Bosch, & Volberda (1999) Bontis, Crossan, & Hulland (2002) Hult, Snow, & Kandemir (2003)
Linkage	Intelligence incorporated into processes Flexibility in processes Stimulating dialogue Wide range of tasks	Nonaka (1994) Crossan, Lane, & White (1999) Bontis, Crossan, & Hulland (2002) Zollo & Winter (2002): knowledge articulation Grant (1996a, b) Un & Cuervo-Cazurra (2004) Bontis, Crossan, & Hulland (2002) Hult, Snow & Kandemir (2003)

Source: Developed by the authors.

enterprise, as well as to its evaluation, distribution, and application, and to the interiorization of this knowledge by individuals. This review included Crossan, Lane, and White's (1999) concept of the feedback processes involved in exploitation and the concepts of accumulation of experience and codification of knowledge as described by Zollo and Winter (2002).

The first group of factors reflects the organizational skills needed to drive the processes and resources that are best suited to directing the new concepts towards a particular purpose in the enterprise and integrating them within the organizational strategy. The process of knowledge creation is not completed if ideas do not crystallize in specific applications within the organization (Nonaka, 1994), and to achieve this, resources have to be directed towards achieving this goal.

Furthermore, the organization must have suitable processes for articulating and documenting knowledge (Nonaka, 1994). Redundancy of information and easy access to the knowledge that has accumulated in the enterprise make it easier for each individual to use the knowledge in a particular area. These factors create favorable conditions for establishing connections between different concepts, thus enabling knowledge to be combined. These skills and organizational processes have been included in the second group of factors. This is where the company's information systems can play a crucial role. Corporate intranets can act as a mechanism for agglomerating and quickly updating relevant experience and information. Information systems help collect data and information from a variety of sources and systematize and distribute them so that individuals from different functional areas or different fields of knowledge can access and use the information. This favors and speeds up access to the knowledge accumulated by the organization. Nonaka (1994) also refers to this when he points out the need for information redundancy in the process of knowledge creation. Information systems facilitate the creation of an abundance of data so that individuals have more information than they really need at any given time, and therefore they are relevant to promoting the development of new knowledge (Camisón et al., 2009). Literature on explicit-oriented strategies has contributed mainly to understanding the importance of information systems in enabling the storage and distribution of the explicit knowledge of the organization (Zack, 1999). This is essential for applying and articulating the new concepts that have been created. This redundancy of information enables the members of the organization to share more distinct ideas, and moreover, access to the new concepts is not limited just to those who generated them or to individuals belonging to a specific functional area. It is precisely the sharing of different visions and mental models that facilitates the development of new knowledge.

The third group of factors is called here *integration of individual learning* because it includes the creation of conditions suitable for stimulating the interiorization of knowledge by individuals in the organization. All actions aimed at boosting knowledge development and individual learning will be necessary if the concepts and ideas generated within the organization are to be applied (Bontis, Crossan, & Hulland, 2002; Hurley & Hult, 1998; Nonaka, 1994). Unless individuals are able to interiorize knowledge, they will not be able to apply it to their respective responsibilities. This integration completes the sequence of processes that is necessary for knowledge exploitation.

Table 2 shows the literature sources used to develop each of the facilitating factors.

Specifically, the importance of information systems in the case of exploitation has been discussed here because these systems will make it easier to apply and distribute knowledge. Furthermore, the process of knowledge creation requires interaction among individuals in the organization, as described by Nonaka (1994). New knowledge is specific to the context in which it is created; in other words, the goal that is reached will depend on the individuals, the place, and the space where it is created. Nonaka, Toyama, and Nagata (2000) call the shared context of cognition and action that determines the creation of new knowledge "ba." "Ba" is the shared place where information is exchanged, takes on meaning, and, through interaction, finally becomes new knowledge. However, this idea does not necessarily entail interaction within a physical space. The space can also be a mental or virtual place (Nonaka, Toyama, & Nagata, 2000: 9). Virtual interaction is characterized by different properties from those of interaction among individuals in the same physical space, and it can be more or less appropriate than in-person interaction in certain contexts. Nevertheless, what should be emphasized here is that virtual interaction can also favor the development of new knowledge, more particularly in the exploitation phase. At this point, it is also necessary to highlight the importance of information and communications systems as a vehicle for favoring virtual interaction. In both socializing and internalizing knowledge, this type of interaction is becoming more important. The virtual and collective interactions facilitated by information technologies using online networks or shared databases provide a collaborative environment which enables information to be exchanged easily (Nonaka, Toyama, & Konno, 2000). Furthermore, simulation programs or written handbooks which represent codifications of existing knowledge can also be made more readily available thanks to these new technologies. Moreover, information which is communicated by means of virtual media provides a context that favors the internalization of knowledge (Nonaka, Toyama, & Konno, 2000).

Table 2. Factors and capabilities making up knowledge exploitation and the authors who analyze each.

Facilitator	Specific capabilities that activate it	Authors
Knowledge integration	Integration of financial resources Integration of human resources Control of R&D&I (research, development, and innovation) Integration of R&D&I Integration with experts Analysis of existing processes Coordination of processes with knowledge development Focus on integration	Nonaka (1994) Crossan, Lane, & White (1999) Bontis, Crossan, & Hulland (2002) Zahra & George (2002)
Application and Distribution	Group distribution of knowledge Written distribution of knowledge Technology-based transmission Integration and documentation systems Assimilation and distribution of suggestions	Nonaka (1994) Crossan, Lane, & White (1999) Bontis, Crossan, & Hulland (2002) Zollo & Winter (2002) Grant (1996a) Grant (1996b) De Boer, van den Bosch, & Volberda (1999) Hult, Snow, & Kandemir (2003) Zahra & George (2002)
Integration of individual learning	Needs assessment Development and training Fostering competencies through tasks Fostering competencies through communication	Nonaka (1994) Crossan, Lane, & White (1999) Bontis, Crossan, & Hulland (2002) Zollo & Winter (2002) Bontis, Crossan, & Hulland (2002) Zahra & George (2002)

Source: Developed by the authors.

FUTURE DIRECTIONS

The association between exploration and exploitation capabilities and the different phases of the knowledge creation process is a starting point for the construction of measurement scales that can capture the wide range of organizational processes making up exploration and exploitation. It is, however, necessary to be more specific about the indicators which serve as the foundation for measuring exploration and exploitation. To achieve this, the various measurement scales described in the literature should be analyzed. There are confusion resulting from the use of different terms means that each author measures his or her variables in very different ways. In some studies, the concepts of exploration and exploitation have been measured by analyzing them as an outcome (e.g., Benner & Tushman, 2003). In

other cases, they have been measured as inputs, but through proxy variables or substitute quantitative measurements such as spending on R&D (e.g., Auh & Menguc, 2005). In other research, the terms *exploration* and *exploitation* are not discussed directly, but they are defined and the dynamic capabilities measured in a similar way. Other authors have focused on the creation of an environment that favors dialogue, sharing of experience, and individual learning, which are all processes relevant to the concept of exploration and exploitation capabilities as developed here (e.g. Hult, Snow, & Kandemir, 2003; Hurley & Hult, 1998). Although these studies provide only a partial view of the capabilities according to the concepts developed here, they can also be very useful for generating indicators. Bontis, Crossan, and Hulland (2002) provide definitions closer to those used in this study. Their scales measure various flows of learning related to how learning is transformed as it moves from the individual level up to the organizational level (feedforward) and how the learning embedded in the organization affects individual behavior (feedback). These flows are associated here with exploration and exploitation respectively, which means they can also be very useful. The measurement of both concepts will make it possible to introduce them into more complex causal models.

Furthermore, a more complete framework requires an analysis, not only of the specific processes that make up these capabilities, but also of the underlying circumstances that must be fostered in the organization to have a positive influence on the two capabilities. Raisch and Birkinshaw's (2008) recent review of underlying circumstances, outcomes, and moderators of the implementation of both exploration and exploitation in the enterprise provides an analytical framework for investigating which underlying circumstances can have a positive effect and which ones have still not been effectively capitalized upon (taking into account the extant literature on the subject). Such an analysis will be important for extracting lessons of interest to management about how to direct and promote the development of organizational knowledge.

Lastly, this study has highlighted the importance of information and communications systems, more particularly in one of the phases of knowledge creation. Future research must analyze more specifically the role played by these information systems in replicating organizational knowledge in large enterprises which are divided into different operating units. The line of research that analyzes explicit-oriented strategies should contribute to this task. Investment in this kind of system in large enterprises with different locations is essential to facilitate transmission of what has been learned in one part of the organization to the rest of the enterprise. A number of authors have analyzed the importance of replication of knowledge within organizations (e.g., Jensen &

Szulanski, 2004; Szulanski & Jensen, 2006; Winter & Szulanski, 2001), but there is still a need for a more detailed analysis of the key role played by information systems in this type of internal knowledge transmission.

CONCLUSION

In an environment as complex and dynamic as the present, the capability to create knowledge becomes essential for competitive success, because knowledge is precisely the asset that possesses all the properties and characteristics needed to be strategic. Knowledge management within the enterprise requires an understanding of which processes and organizational activities are capable of activating the whole process of generating and developing knowledge. This is why this study has focused on a detailed analysis of which processes shape and drive this overall process of knowledge generation.

More specifically, this study has analyzed the different phases of one of the most widely used models of knowledge creation, but with the addition of a new perspective, associating these phases with the concepts of exploration and exploitation. Exploration is defined as the capability that enables new concepts to be generated, whereas exploitation constitutes the application of these concepts. New ideas need to be crystallized in a real application within the organization before organizational knowledge can be said to have evolved. Exploration and exploitation thus become the two necessary and complementary phases of the development of organizational knowledge. This research has therefore furthered our understanding of these two concepts, which still cause some confusion in the literature, by taking into consideration theoretical contributions from both KBV and OL.

All this has provided a deeper comprehension of the organizational processes that activate the two phases. It has been suggested that exploration is activated by the existence of a knowledge leadership, by fostering an appropriate organizational culture, and by organizational systems which provide a high degree of flexibility for the exchange of ideas among individuals in the organization. Exploitation, on the other hand, is favored by an adequate integration of all organizational resources to foster the evolution of knowledge, by systems that facilitate the application and distribution of knowledge, and by an atmosphere which promotes interiorization or individual learning. A review of the literature made it possible to determine which of these capabilities are the most specifically involved in each of these processes. All these capabilities should be fostered in the enterprise to achieve effective knowledge management.

Furthermore, this analysis has shown how information and communications systems can be essential for the effective exploitation of knowledge. Written handbooks represent a codification of knowledge and can be distributed easily with the help of new technologies. Access to this codified knowledge is important to bring about a replication of best practices throughout the whole organization. Information systems also provide a framework for integrating existing knowledge and distributing it easily to a large number of individuals in the organization. Ready access to this codified knowledge by all the members of the organization provides more information than is explicitly necessary for the particular activities of each individual. This favors the discovery of new applications by individuals in functional areas other than those where the codified knowledge originated. In a similar manner, new technologies enable virtual and collective interactions and provide a collaborative environment in which information can be easily exchanged. Such exchanges are essential for knowledge creation to take place. In enterprises with multiple physical locations, the new information and communications systems play a key role in putting different members of the organization virtually in touch with one another, thus enabling them to share ideas that may ultimately crystallize in new knowledge.

New technologies have proved to be fundamental in facilitating the process of generating new knowledge as well as the replication of best practices within a single organization which consists of different, physically remote spaces. The advantages of information and communication systems for geographically dispersed companies are even clearer than for single-site organizations. A repository system provides knowledge storage, which in turn facilitates access by all organization members to this explicit knowledge. Management must therefore bear in mind that investment in information systems is essential to favor the development of organizational knowledge.

Nevertheless, practitioners should keep in mind that the role of information use should not be confused with that of knowledge development. Knowledge development is an organizational capability which entails a complex combination of processes, as has been stressed in this study. Information management provides a way of facilitating knowledge development, but information per se is only one resource among many in the organization, and only the capability to develop new knowledge is a dynamic capability which offers superior competitive advantage to companies. Knowledge needs to be transformed and distributed to provide organizational success.

As this study has shown, managers need to address knowledge development through a variety of approaches which reflect a combination of tacit-oriented and explicit-oriented strategies. First, the transformation of individual knowledge into organizational knowledge requires that managers promote and emphasize communication between individuals and groups and the interchange of different interpretations and ways of doing things. Therefore, managers should strive to institutionalize in their organizations practices related to sharing information, meetings, sharing conflicting views, and working in groups to develop novel ideas.

Second, managers should facilitate access to the information and knowledge that the organization already has, by codifying it in the form of manuals and information systems. They must promote and encourage the use of communication and information systems because these systems facilitate information sharing by all organization members.

Finally, managers must promote internalization by organizational members of new ideas and of the knowledge generated by fostering individual competencies and by promoting development and training for their human resources. All these actions should work in favor of organizational knowledge development, knowledge which in turn should be transformed into innovations which give competitive advantage to their companies.

This study leads therefore to the conclusion that in knowledge management, managers must find a balance between tacit-oriented strategies, which are more focused on a social approach that advocates an emphasis on facilitating interaction between individuals in the organization, and explicit-oriented strategies, which are centered on the importance of information systems which help the organization to store and distribute the knowledge which has already been created in the company.

REFERENCES

Anderson, J. R. (1983). *The architecture of cognition*. Cambridge, MA: Harvard University Press.

Argote, L. (1999). *Organizational learning: Creating, retaining, and transferring knowledge*. Berlin: Springer.

Auh, S., & Menguc, B. (2005). Balancig exploration and exploitation: The moderating role of competitive intensity. *Journal of Business Research, 58*(12), 1652–1661. doi:10.1016/j.jbusres.2004.11.007

Benner, M. J., & Tushman, M. (2002). Process management and technological innovation: A longitudinal study of the photography and paint industries. *Administrative Science Quarterly, 47*, 676. doi:10.2307/3094913

Benner, M. J., & Tushman, M. L. (2003). Exploitation, exploration, and process management: The productivity dilemma revisited. *Academy of Management Review, 28*(2), 238–256.

Bontis, N., Crossan, M. M., & Hulland, J. (2002). Managing an organizational learning system by aligning stocks and flows. *Journal of Management Studies, 39*(4), 437–469. doi:10.1111/1467-6486. t01-1-00299

Brown, J. S., & Duguid, P. (1991). Organizational learning and communities-of-practice: Toward a unified view of working, learning, and innovation. *Organization Science, 2*(1), 40–57. doi:10.1287/orsc.2.1.40

Camisón, C., Palacios, D., Garrigós, F., & Devece, C. (Eds.). (2009). *Connectivity and knowledge management in virtual organizations: Networking and developing interactive communications*. Hershey, PA: IGI Global.

Choi, B., & Lee, H. (2003). An empirical investigation of KM styles and their effect on corporate performance. *Information & Management, 40*, 403–417. doi:10.1016/S0378-7206(02)00060-5

Choi, B., Poon, S. K., & Davis, J. G. (2008). Effects of knowledge management strategy on organizational performance: A complementarity theory-based approach. *Omega, 36*, 235–251. doi:10.1016/j.omega.2006.06.007

Claycomb, C., Dröge, C., & Germain, R. (2001). Applied process knowledge and market performance: The moderating effect of environmental uncertainty. *Journal of Knowledge Management, 5*(3), 264–277. doi:10.1108/13673270110401239

Cohen, W. M., & Levinthal, D. A. (1990). Absorptive capacity: A new perspective on learning and innovation. *Administrative Science Quarterly*, *35*(1), 128–152. doi:10.2307/2393553

Crossan, M. M., Lane, H. W., & White, R. E. (1999). An organizational learning framework: From intuition to institution. *Academy of Management Review*, *24*(3), 522–537. doi:10.2307/259140

De Boer, M., Van den Bosch, F. A. J., & Volberda, H. W. (1999). Managing organizational knowledge integration in the emerging multimedia complex. *Journal of Management Studies*, *36*(3), 379–398. doi:10.1111/1467-6486.00141

Eisenhardt, K. M., & Santos, F. M. (2002). Knowledge based view: A new theory of strategy? In A. M. Pettigrew, H. Thomas & R. Whittington (Eds.), *Handbook of strategy and management* (pp. 139-164). London: Sage Publications.

Grant, R. M. (1996a). Prospering in dynamically-competitive environments: Organizational capability as knowledge integration. *Organization Science*, *7*(4), 375–387. doi:10.1287/orsc.7.4.375

Grant, R. M. (1996b). Toward a knowledge-based theory of the firm. *Strategic Management Journal*, *17*(Winter Special Issue), 109-122.

Gupta, A. K., Smith, K. G., & Shalley, C. E. (2006). The interplay between exploration and exploitation. *Academy of Management Journal*, *49*(4), 693–706.

Hansen, M., Nohria, N., & Tierney, T. (1999). What's your strategy for managing knowledge? *Harvard Business Review*, *72*(2), 106–116.

Helfat, C. E., & Raubitschek, R. S. (2000). Product sequencing: Coevolution of knowledge, capabilities, and products. *Strategic Management Journal*, *21*(10-11), 961–979. doi:10.1002/1097-0266(200010/11)21:10/11<961::AID-SMJ132>3.0.CO;2-E

Hult, G. T. M., Snow, C. C., & Kandemir, D. (2003). The role of entrepreneurship in building cultural competitiveness in different organizational types. *Journal of Management*, *29*(3), 401–426.

Hurley, R. F., & Hult, G. T. M. (1998). Innovation, market orientation, and organizational learning: An integration and empirical examination. *Journal of Marketing*, *42*(July), 42–54. doi:10.2307/1251742

Ichijo, K., von Krogh, G., & Nonaka, I. (1998). Knowledge enablers. In G. Von Krogh, J. Roos & D. Kleine (Eds.). *Knowing in firms. Understanding, managing, and measuring knowledge* (pp. 173-203). London: Sage Publications.

Jensen, R., & Szulanski, G. (2004). Stickiness and the adaptation of organizational practices in cross-border knowledge transfers. *Journal of International Business Studies*, *35*(6), 508–523. doi:10.1057/palgrave.jibs.8400107

Kogut, B., & Zander, U. (1992). Knowledge of the firm, combinative capabilities, and the replication of technology. *Organization Science*, *3*(3), 383–397. doi:10.1287/orsc.3.3.383

Kusunoki, K., Nonaka, I., & Nagata, A. (1998). Organizational capabilities in product development of Japanese firms: A conceptual framework and empirical findings. *Organization Science*, *9*(6), 699–718. doi:10.1287/orsc.9.6.699

Lave, J., & Wenger, E. (1991). *Situated Learning: Legitimate peripheral participation*. Cambridge, MA: Harvard University Press.

Levinthal, D. A., & March, J. G. (1993). The myopia of learning. *Strategic Management Journal*, *14*(Special Issue), 95–112. doi:10.1002/smj.4250141009

Lubatkin, M. H., Simsek, Z., Ling, Y., & Veiga, J. F. (2006). Ambidexterity and performance in small- to medium-sized firms: The pivotal role of top management team behavioral integration. *Journal of Management, 32*(5), 646–672. doi:10.1177/0149206306290712

Lyles, M. A., & Schwenk, C. R. (1992). Top management, strategy, and organizational knowledge structures. *Journal of Management Studies, 29*(2), 155–174. doi:10.1111/j.1467-6486.1992.tb00658.x

March, J. G. (1991). Exploration and exploitation in organizational learning. *Organization Science, 2*(1), 71–87. doi:10.1287/orsc.2.1.71

McGrath, R. G. (2001). Exploratory learning, innovative capacity, and managerial oversight. *Academy of Management Journal, 44*(1), 118–131. doi:10.2307/3069340

Nelson, R. R., & Winter, S. G. (1982). *An evolutionary theory of economic change.* Boston, MA: The Belknap Press of Harvard University Press.

Nonaka, I. (1994). A dynamic theory of organizational knowledge creation. *Organization Science, 5*(1), 14–37. doi:10.1287/orsc.5.1.14

Nonaka, I., Toyama, R., & Konno, N. (2000). SECI, Ba, and leadership: A unified model of dynamic knowledge creation. *Long Range Planning, 33*(1), 5–34. doi:10.1016/S0024-6301(99)00115-6

Nonaka, I., Toyama, R., & Nagata, A. (2000). A firm as a knowledge creating entity: A new perspective on the theory of the firm. *Industrial and Corporate Change, 9*(1), 1–20. doi:10.1093/icc/9.1.1

Polanyi, M. (1958). *Personnal knowledge: Towards a post-critical philosophy.* Chicago: University of Chicago Press.

Polanyi, M. (1962). *Personnal knowledge: Towards a post-critical philosophy, 2nd edition.* Chicago: University of Chicago Press.

Polanyi, M. (1966). *The tacit dimension.* London: Routledge & Kegan P.

Quinn, J. B. (1992). *Intelligent enterprise: A knowledge and service based paradigm for industry.* New York: Free Press.

Raisch, S., & Birkinshaw, J. (2008). Organizational ambidexterity: Antecedents, outcomes, and moderators. *Journal of Management, 34*(3), 375–409. doi:10.1177/0149206308316058

Rosenkopf, L., & Nerkar, A. (2001). Beyond local search: Boundary-spanning, exploration, and impact in the optical disc industry. *Strategic Management Journal, 22*(4), 287–306. doi:10.1002/smj.160

Sarvary, M. (1999). Knowledge management and competition in the consulting industry. *California Management Review, 41*(2), 95–107.

Spender, J. C. (1995). Organizations are activity systems, not merely systems of thought. In P. Shrivastava & C. Stubbart (Eds.), *Advances in Strategic Management* (Vol. 11, pp. 151-172). Greenwich, CT: JAI Press.

Spender, J. C. (1996). Making knowledge the basis of a dynamic theory of the firm. *Strategic Management Journal, 17*(Winter Special Issue), 45-62.

Spender, J. C. (1996a). Organizational knowledge, learning, and memory: Three concepts in search of a theory. *Journal of Organizational Change Management, 9*(1), 63–78. doi:10.1108/09534819610156813

Szulanski, G., & Jensen, R. (2006). Presumptive adaptation and the effectiveness of knowledge transfer. *Strategic Management Journal, 27*(10), 937–957. doi:10.1002/smj.551

Teece, D. J., Pisano, G., & Shuen, A. (1997). Dynamic capabilities and strategic management. *Strategic Management Journal, 18*(7), 509–533. doi:10.1002/(SICI)1097-0266(199708)18:7<509::AID-SMJ882>3.0.CO;2-Z

Tiemessen, I., Lane, H. W., Crossan, M., & Inkpen, A. C. (1997). Knowledge management in international joint ventures. In P. W. Beamish & J. P. Killing (Eds.), *Cooperative strategies: North American perspective* (pp. 370-399). San Francisco, CA: New Lexington Press.

Tsoukas, H., & Mylonopoulos, N. (2004). Introduction: Knowledge construction and creation in organizations. *British Journal of Management, 15*(Supplement 1), 1–8. doi:10.1111/j.1467-8551.2004.t01-2-00402.x

Un, C. A., & Cuervo-Cazurra, A. (2004). Strategies for knowledge creation in firms. *British Journal of Management, 15*(Supplement 1), 27–41. doi:10.1111/j.1467-8551.2004.00404.x

Van den Bosch, F. A. J., Volberda, H. W., & de Boer, M. (1999). Coevolution of firm absorptive capacity and knowledge environment: Organizational forms and combinative capabilities. *Organization Science, 10*(5), 551–568. doi:10.1287/orsc.10.5.551

Winter, S. G. (1987). Knowledge and competence as strategic assets. In D. J. Teece (Ed.), *The competitive challenge: Strategies for industrial innovation and renewal* (pp. 159-84). New York: Ballinger.

Winter, S. G., & Szulanski, G. (2001). Replication as strategy. *Organization Science, 12*(6), 730–743. doi:10.1287/orsc.12.6.730.10084

Zack, M. H. (1999). Managing codified knowledge. *Sloan Management Review, 40*(4), 45–58.

Zahra, S. A., & George, G. (2002). Absorptive capacity: A review, reconceptualization, and extension. *Academy of Management Review, 27*(2), 185–203. doi:10.2307/4134351

Zollo, M., & Winter, S. G. (2002). Deliberate learning and the evolution of dynamic capabilities. *Organization Science, 13*(3), 339–351. doi:10.1287/orsc.13.3.339.2780

ENDNOTE

[1]   This research was financially supported by various research programs financed by the Generalitat Valenciana (ACOMP06/240, ARVIV/2007/077, GVPRE/2008/054), and the Universitat Jaume I / Fundació Bancaixa 2007 Research Promotion Plan (P1-1B2007-20).

Section 4
Knowledge Management Strategy

Chapter 9
How Do We Get There?
Strategy Action Framework–"Action Engine"

Meir Russ
University of Wisconsin-Green Bay, USA

Robert Fineman
Independent Consultant, USA

Riccardo Paterni
Professione Lavoro®, Italy

Jeannette K. Jones
American Intercontinental University, USA

ABSTRACT

The chapter will describe a comprehensive planning framework for developing a company's knowledge management strategy. The framework includes the goals and game plans of the strategy and the use of three enablers supporting such a strategy: levers, processes, and systems. This is complemented by the development of an action plan while considering the resources needed and the constraints present. The framework also includes the discussion of aligning the knowledge management strategy with the company's business strategy as well as with the organization's knowledge base and core competencies. The chapter uses two cases to illustrate some of the aspects discussed.

INTRODUCTION

We described in chapter 7 the six strategic dilemmas that frame the KM strategic conversation. It is now time to put theory into practice and get right to work. The following pages will describe the KM strategic framework and how to use the specific tools of the

detailed KM strategy. This framework will include a number of tools that can be employed independently or as part of a complete package. Strategic thinking is not new to business. In fact, a significant number of frameworks, taxonomies, and typologies are described in the academic and popular literature, and there are plenty of established tools that are used by business practitioners. However, the framework that

DOI: 10.4018/978-1-60566-348-7.ch009

we are proposing has the added benefits of being user friendly and being supported by successful implementation results. The basic framework includes outcomes (or goals), levers, processes, systems, resources, constraints, game plans, and action plans (see Figure 1). In order to apply the framework, we always start with the goals of the KM strategy. The established goals must align the business strategy and the KM strategy. Once the alignment is identified, then the selected strategy is described using the appropriate levers, processes, and systems needed to support the devised game plan. We also identify the resources needed and constraints identified under which the goals and the game plan were devised and the action plan will be implemented. The implications of the strategies are translated into action plans that will allow you to combine your business strategy with your KM strategy, while putting to work not only your knowledge base, but also your core competencies. Even though the building blocks of the framework seem simple, and putting the framework to work seems straight forward, our experience suggests that implementation is not without some challenges since few companies apply the entire process successfully.

As an example, Dell in 2002 had the largest market share in the PC business. The company had a unique business model that was well protected and was on its way to crushing its competition, especially Hewlett Packard (HP). At the same time, HP was on crutches and barely limping along. HP had lost a charismatic leader, failed in the acquisition of Compaq, and was falling into a decline. So Dell decided to go for the kill and to expand its product offerings to include printers[1], realizing that printers were the cash cows allowing HP to survive. Guess what? Dell was not successful as

Figure 1. KM strategic framework – The complete planning framework

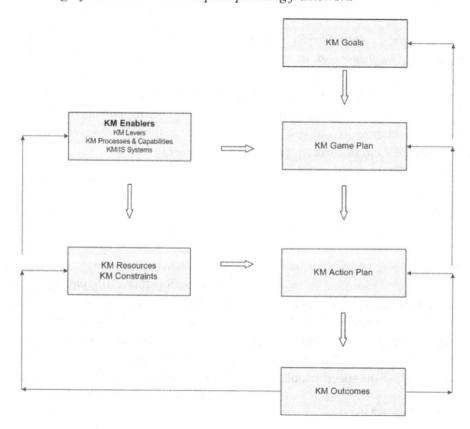

it was unable to take its current competencies and transfer them to the printer market which was a new marketplace for Dell. This was particularly surprising to Dell as the new market seemed similar, if not the same as the PC market and even the skills and capabilities needed for success seemed the same. However, Dell, the leader in the PC market and a very successful company, was not able to transfer the skills and capabilities. As a result of this change in focus Dell lost a percentage of its market share advantage in the PC market to HP (as of the end of 2007[2]).

Mastering a framework for knowledge management decisions would have given Dell an opportunity to review potential approaches in order to penetrate new markets by utilizing existing competencies or developing new ones when needed. Two frameworks that provide such a resource will be presented in this chapter (see Figure 1 and Figure 3). Both are developments and a recombination of our own and others[3] academic work and one of the authors, Dr. Russ, used them extensively in his consulting practice in developing strategic plans for KM and other (IS, manufacturing) consulting projects and assignments. A partial illustration of this framework is provided later in the next chapter by two of his students that proposed the implementation of this framework at Aurora Health Care, in Green Bay, WI.

But there is more to it. We are living in economically and socially fascinating and uncertain times. New paradigms are sweeping society and the business environment. Companies are refocusing their attention from their tangible assets to intangible assets based on knowledge and information systems (IS). The experience based economy is increasing in importance. The economy is alternating from boom to bust in a matter of a few short months. The emergence of the global economy on one hand, and the surfacing of new economic powers in transition on the other hand, the need to resolve both the environmental and human poverty crisis simultaneously, and the increased importance of global electronic networks and communications at the same time as face to face contact and regional clustering is gaining importance and creating a new landscape for knowledge management and business strategies. At the same time, knowledge management itself as a managerial practice is transitioning from being IS driven to being driven by the human-IS interaction, and is seen as a socio-technical phenomenon. The shrinking half life of knowledge and product life cycle is adding pressure on business and knowledge management strategists. Some of the questions that top executives and managers are dealing with are: can the same set of tools or strategies serve SMEs and large corporations? Service oriented and manufacturing companies? Companies for profit, not for profit organizations, and/or governmental agencies? Can they (the tools and strategies) satisfy internal and external users? Are the needs of different generations of users in different economies different? We think that Knowledge Management Strategy in the Age of Paradox and Transition[4] has some new characteristics and requires some new tools. These will be presented later in this chapter.

Following is an introduction to the components of the KM strategy, which include as mentioned above, goals, levers, processes, systems, resources and constrains.

GOALS

The first thing you must do is decide on the specific goals of your strategy. This is the stage where you align the gap analysis (see chapter 1) with the business strategy. What is it you want to accomplish in the KM arena that will support/drive your business strategy? Increase the value of your brand? Increase your intellectual capital? Improve your processes or develop new products (or both)? This is also where the six strategic dilemmas described earlier (see chapter 7), will come to fruition, since the choices you will make regarding which goals to actually use will relate directly to the conclusion of your preferences for the different choice of alternatives you made earlier, or will reflect on these choices.

When determining your goals, be selective and stick initially with a reasonable number. If you identify too many goals up front, you may find that some of them might contradict each other and you do not have all the necessary resources (people, time, money, etc.) to pursue all of them at once. Strategy is about choices, what you decide to do and what you decide not to do. The essence of a successful KM strategy is to focus on the choices and allow those choices to guide you through the process. We found that limiting the goals can be the most difficult aspect of strategy making. Therefore, having some metric or rule of thumb like "we need between 3-5 goals" can be very helpful. Also, what is extremely helpful is the strategic discussion that leads to the choices made, especially the part about those goals that didn't make the final list.

Figure 2 illustrates some options you might have available to you. For example, we identified increase in intellectual property, sales, earnings, profits, liability or risk reduction, delivery performance improvements, cost reduction, quality improvements, flexibility, agility improvements, innovation, learning, savings, and responsiveness, as some of the most important goals companies tend to focus on. This is by no means a comprehensive list and you would not want to try and create goals for them all, but it will give you a place to start. Once you have developed your goals, it will be necessary to identify measurable Key Success Indicators (KSI) for each one of those goals. You will have to be careful choosing the goals and the indicators, because, assuming you will reward the people the right way to achieve

Figure 2. KM strategic framework – Goals and enablers

KM Goals/Outputs

Intellectual Property | Sales, Earnings, etc. | Liability | Delivery, Performance | Cost, Savings | Quality | Flexibility, Agility, Responsiveness | Innovation | Learning

KM Levers
HR Policies
Reward (formal & informal) System
Cross Functional Collaboration
Core Competencies

Top Management Support
External Relationships
Culture/Tolerance of Risk
....

Game plan

KM Processes and Capabilities
Communities of practice
Products Domains
Functional Units

Project Teams
Informal Networks/Clubs
....

Game plan

KM/IS Systems
KM/IS Architecture
KM/IS Hardware

KM/IS Software
KM/IS Policies
Security
....

Game plan

them, you might realize them (or as some say, be careful what you wish for, because you may get it). For example, you may wish to increase sales from new products. You might do so, but at the same time, the increased sales may cause a lowering of your profits, or increase your dependencies on external sources of knowledge that helped you to develop your new products.

Of course you know that the discussion you will have about which goals to use, how to measure them, and what are specific (measurable Key Success Indicators, KSI) outcomes you want to accomplish is as important as what you will agree upon. Keep in mind that the first discussions will likely just be the beginning of your dialog, since you may have to revisit the list a number of times. You may find that after the planning for implementation phase, the constraints identified will not allow you to achieve all your goals at the same time. Putting aside some of your goals may have beneficial long term effects because organizationally, you will create knowledge that should speed the process when you are able to revisit the goals that were excluded from the first phase. However, remember to keep these goals in a repository that can and will be accessed on a regular basis. If the goals are viable you will want to keep them in the forefront of your future analysis and have them ready for either the next phase of the process or use them to bolster current goals.

For example, acquiring new leading clients might be part of a goal that can drive your KM strategy. How will that be accomplished given the constraints that have been identified? Here is an example. In 1998, one of the authors, Dr. Russ, while consulting with a steel processing company in the Mid-West suggested that the company diversify their client base and try to penetrate the Japanese car companies--specifically, Toyota and Honda. The response was that the company had not had the relationships nor the knowledge of the culture in order to approach such customers and they were more than happy with their current Detroit based customers. Years later, the company

was less than happy with its local customer base, but luckily, through acquisition was able to acquire access to an alternative customer base which was local and easier (similar culture) to penetrate. The same difficulties the company had in penetrating the US based Japanese producers seem to haunt the company while trying to penetrate the Asian new markets and the company found itself lagging in such markets.

Once you have the overall goals and KSI, now you have to translate them into divisional, functional, project team, and individual goals. Some examples of goals at the individual or team level might be challenging assignments[5] or at the individual, team (sales) or organizational level might be acquiring leading clients[6]. Individual/team challenging assignments might feed organizational goals of increasing intellectual property or improving competitive positioning, for example, by increasing the number of patents in an area that is critical to the success of the company. The FIAT case (see below) will illustrate how creating business vision and tying the appropriate business goals to existing design and engineering knowledge allows the company to achieve turn-around in a relatively short time frame.

FIAT CASE:KM AND BUSINESS VISION

In 2004 FIAT, with over one hundred years of history in car making, was considered by analysts and the general public to be close to an unavoidable end. During the preceding five years the company had piled up losses of $12 billion and it seemed bound to be moving toward a crushing insolvency. For years the company had been losing market share to European and Japanese competitors, unable to compete on both pricing and overall quality of its cars. During the late 1980s and early 1990s top management had chosen to diversify its business into non car related investments, mainly banking and insurance, and the lack of a committed focus on research and development in the car business had begun to show its consequences. FIAT Panda, a small sized car kept basically unchanged in its design and key features for over 20 years, from 1985 through 2005, became a symbol of the stalling situation. Year after year it became clear that the money the company was losing on its car business was not balanced by the profits made by its diversified investments.

In 2004 the key shareholders realized that it was time to take control of the situation. They came to this decision after realizing that their latest attempt to sell the car business to General Motors was not going through. GM had bought 10% of FIAT stock in previous years, and also signed a put (buying) option that obliged the American company to buy the remaining 90% if FIAT wanted to sell. Now, GM (itself in serious financial trouble) was no longer in a position to execute its put option and FIAT had to find a way out of its trouble by itself. A new CEO was hired with the clear goal to bring back profitability to the car business in order to outline a path to a lasting financial recovery.

Sergio Marchionne (a Swiss-Italian manager trained in Canada) was the man selected for the task. Marchionne had no experience with the car business but had a successful track record in bringing faltering companies back to profitability. His plan was clear: first find a solution to the pending put option issue with GM and buy time from banking creditors; then focus on a business plan leveraging upon the key assets of design and engineering that had once characterized the winning appeal of FIAT, mainly within the Italian and European market.

The first part of the plan was accomplished in February 2005 when Marchionne convinced GM to clear their contractual put option obligations by paying $2 billion, and showing to banking creditors a business plan in which the car business became once again the main focus (investments in banking and insurance were either considerably reduced or totally dismissed in order to readily increase cash flow for business development). Marchionne clearly stated that FIAT was going to tap back into the roots of its former success: innovative, practical, user- friendly engineering, and most of all unique, distinguished Italian car design. According to Marchionne this was the only way to gain back a "passion for the business" within factories and dealerships; passion that for too long had been faltering. He acknowledged that FIAT had become "old and bureaucratic" and, as a consequence, out of touch with the changing market needs and demands. Most of all, FIAT had become unable to foster and enable a full appreciation for the design and manufacturing engineering talent that had characterized the successes of the brand during its hundred year old history.

Since the mid 1990's FIAT cars began to be considered by the market still mechanically dependable (as it was the tradition for the brand) yet of little appeal due to their outdated design and lack of affordable, driver-friendly features and frills made popular by aggressive European competitors (mainly the French Peugeot and Renault, and the German Volkswagen) and Japanese ones (Toyota and Nissan). All of this had progressively created a low morale within factories and dealerships (no real hope for future improvements since management had shown no commitment for the development of the car business) contributing to the market perception of FIAT as old, outdated and bound to end as a brand, a brand that for over one hundred years had been the pride and joy of Italian creative, innovative and stylish engineering brought to mass market products.

The fact was that underneath the hoods, such innovative design and manufacturing engineering was still very much present. For example in the mid 1990's FIAT engineering had created the jet-stream turbo-diesel system (JTD) that had made diesel engines ever more efficient in fuel consumption yet ever more powerful and even more fun to drive than a traditional gasoline engine car. Unfortunately, due to dire cash flow needs, the JTD technology was sold to the German car component company, Bosch, and through Bosch, readily utilized by all of FIAT's main competitors. The majority of car drivers and buyers never realized that the revolutionary JTD system was FIAT's creation; it was a given that such innovation was born in Germany and mainly developed by Bosch. The whole issue contributed to fuel and deepen the low morale that had spread within FIAT. People and suppliers close to the factory headquarters as well as factory workers and unions had started to comment that many FIAT managers were doing nothing for the future of the company and actually they were undermining the expression of the engineering talents that the company had hired and trained in the past. The feeling was that there was a lot of wasted know-how and talent in FIAT and the dire financial situation was considered proof of it.

Marchionne was determined to end these dynamics making sure that all of the knowledge and talent present within the company was not only fully utilized but also properly developed to better serve the market. A radical change in the mindset of top management was necessary: several top managers within the organization were asked to leave and were replaced by younger, more dynamic and attuned to the market, managers. For the first time in the history of the company people in their late thirties and early forties became part of top management. This was quite a shock within the traditionally seniority based cultural dynamics of Italian companies and under the direct, informal culture, Marchionne has become popular even on the pages of Italian gossip magazines for leading board meetings wearing a shirt and dark blue sweater doing away with the traditional stylish ties and jackets. At the same time, Marchionne set focused, clear goals for growth and profitability and monitored the implementation of this strategy by his top management.

Making design a key feature of FIAT cars' appeal was one of the goals. In 2005 Marchionne hired from Ferrari (FIAT still owned the majority of the sport car maker's shares even after having

to sell a portion of the shares to a banking consortium for cash flow needs) its top designer: the Norwegian-Spanish Frank Stephenson. The design goals were set, once again, to leverage upon the know-how based on FIAT's past successes making new models resembling the designs that supported the creation of the FIAT brand during the booming 1950's and 1960's as well as tapping into the sporty, dashing style of Ferrari itself. These goals were to be accomplished by making sure to efficiently utilize the mechanical and electronic engineering technology that was already performing and dependable on FIAT cars; in other words making sure to find a way to make the market fully appreciate and value all the best that the company engineering had been able to create in the past and the present: to redirect present technical ideas and talents to market focused solutions.

The strategy was readily put into practice: the new, key, small sized car, Punto, and the mid sized Bravo models were totally new in their design while retaining 60% of the components of previously unsuccessful models that the company already had in place. The new cars were also set to reduce manufacturing costs by sharing structural platforms with several models (belonging to different market segments depending upon size and comfort levels) and sharing components with other car manufactures (for example Ford, Suzuki, Tata) with which Marchionne had set focused partnership manufacturing agreements. For all of this to happen it was essential to accomplish a proper flow of information and knowledge within all of the company's departments and factories. No longer were seniority-based political games and personal agendas going to rule business decisions; market focus and actual merit and competence were clearly stated and practiced as the cornerstone of FIAT's revival.

No longer was engineering isolated from marketing; technology topics were put back into marketing campaigns to leverage upon and boost the traditional "Italian passion" for car innovation and style. End users were invited to share ideas, through customized web sites, about ways they would have liked to see new versions of classic FIAT successes (for example the small FIAT 500). Similar internet tools and campaigns were utilized to understand what drivers and passengers actually wanted to experience during their driving. Traditionally, FIAT had been the company "teaching the rules of the business" to the market and competitors. Now the focus was more on "learning the new rules" and putting them readily into practice.

The new mindset was also set to affect the way a key market player did his part of the job: the dealerships. Marchionne and his new top management team realized that the company had to be closer, much closer to its customers, and dealerships were the vital links in the relationship. New dealerships were opened all over Europe and concrete ways to better engage feedback sharing were identified and practiced. Each dealership was financially encouraged to participate in any attention drawing local event. The focus was on making sure that the "bring back the Italian passion" theme was shared not only within the company but also with clients and prospects.

All of these changes also affected the traditionally uneasy relationship between FIAT's management and its factory workers. Once FIAT workers and relevant unions understood that the company was really getting back to focus on the car business with actual investments (letting go of other activities: banking, insurance) it was possible for Marchionne and his team to get workers to cooperate (more hours worked for the same pay) leveraging upon reestablishing "FIAT passion and pride" also within the workforce. For years workers were pointing out wasted resources on outdated strategies and models (the 1985-2005 Panda previously mentioned was once again a symbol of the situation) and complaining about the poor working conditions of factories that until the early 1990's were considered to be "world class". Progressively, investments were made to improve the situation and workers were happy to

make cars that, once again, anyone could recognize as Italian just by looking due to their unique, appealing style. This was exactly what Marchionne had envisioned within his company recovery strategy. A vision that, not only for management and workers, but also for customers, has become a reality. In 2007 workers were awarded for their renewed commitment to FIAT with a substantial pay increase.

After all of these changes (many of them set to create a powerful link between the glories of the past and the appealing innovations of the present and the future) FIAT once again scored profits in 2006 and 2007, with financial results listed among the very best of the more than one hundred year history of the company. Both in Italy and Europe the market share gains were considerable: even a plus 20% over the previous year within a slowing down market. The new FIAT 500 was awarded with the "2008 Car of the Year" Award in Europe and its market demand exceeded FIAT's expectation at the time of the new car presentation (July 2007) by 70,000 units.

On April 24th, 2008 the reputable financial journal, *The Economist,* featured a Leader article by the title "The miracle of Turin" subtitle: "the lessons that other car makers can learn from the fixing of FIAT". Two key suggestions inspired by Marchionne's work were noted in the articles aimed mostly at the troubled US carmakers: 1) get back to focusing on the primary business, car making, without getting strategically and operationally sidelined by focusing on higher margin smaller markets such as pick up trucks; 2) address directly, rapidly, and with determination the operational and product line problems. As we have described, FIAT leveraged and developed the knowledge and talent present within the organization and largely neglected in the struggling years prior to Marchionne's arrival.

The global car market remains difficult and it is actually getting worse. During the first half of 2008 its overall demand has been rapidly decreasing due to the oil prices surge and the unfolding global financial crisis. In July 2008 FIAT announced that it had to lay off workers at four of the six Italian plants for three one week periods during the coming fall due to the slowing demand for some popular models in Italy. At the same time, FIAT announced the signing of a Memorandum of Understanding with BMW laying out a strategic and operational cooperation regarding the manufacturing (and sale in the US market) of the Mini (owned by BMW) and Alfa Romeo (owned by FIAT) brands in the profitable market of compact fashionable cars. This was the 35th strategic and operational alliance with other car makers signed by Marchionne since his arrival at FIAT in 2004. The alliance with the prestigious (and always profitable) BMW points out the fact that FIAT has gotten back to inspiring a sense of trust and dependability for its future. Without the new course the company has taken during the last few years, it is quite possible that the current market crisis would have sealed the end of its independence and the end of its ability to show the 'unique Italian feel' Marchionne has so determinately sought back. Nowadays FIAT seems to be back on track, taking full advantage of its know-how within a market that is still difficult and challenging for all the car manufacturers. By using the new vision of the future the company can now envision a brighter future.

As we finalize this chapter, a new fascinating chapter in FIAT history is developing, one that provides for an interesting perspective on value of knowledge. FIAT is negotiating the receipt of about 30% of Chrysler stock value in exchange for access to FIAT's knowledge of the design and manufacturing of small, fuel efficient cars. Not only that, FIAT also will have immediate access to the American market through its alliance with Chrysler, and its network of dealers. If such intent is materialized, it will be a wonderful illustration and example of the value of knowledge and leadership (what we call intellectual, and more specifically human capital).

Once you have chosen the expected outcomes

(see also our earlier discussion of goals in chapter 1) your strategic KM plan will focus on, now you have to identify the enablers: the levers, processes, and systems you need to have in place in order to achieve them. For example, you have identified as an outcome that you want to increase your sales of new products. For that you might need more sales people with the knowledge base to sell the products (lever) or you might need to have a Customer Relationship Management (CRM) system in place that will allow you to support the sales people (see chapters 15 and 16 in this book for discussion) and you will need some product sites to complement the data and knowledge that they might need (systems). You also might need to have a process of hiring and training the sales people (option A) and/or a process of developing and updating the product sites (option B) as you go. The point is that in order to arrive at the outcome you want; you will need some enablers that will allow your people to achieve them.

* * *

ENABLERS: LEVERS, PROCESSES AND SYSTEMS

We will now describe the enablers, the second part of our framework. We have found that executives and managers like to think in terms of the three categories we have identified, even though they may use different terms for them.

KM Levers

Think about the lever as a multiplier of force for whatever strategy or action you put in place in order to arrive at the outcome. Our experience suggests that the following levers should be considered: Human Resources (HR) Policies, Reward (formal & informal) System, Cross Functional Collaboration, Core Competencies, Top Management Support, External Relationships, and Culture/Tolerance of

Risk. By no means is this a comprehensive list. Feel free to add, eliminate, or modify the levers that we have proposed. In any case, be sure that you truly have in place the levers you think you have and that they are appropriate for the use you intend. Take for example, internal collaboration. You may take it for granted that the two units you need to collaborate on sharing the knowledge in order to share best practices will do so. But, you may be surprised to learn that: the two units have contradicting reward systems, or, there is no shared policy that allows them to easily exchange the data/information they need to share in order to have effective collaborations. Or, you may learn that the heads of the two units don't talk, or they talk, but cannot agree on anything because of conflicting agendas and time horizons. Or take for example what some people call "knowledge bridges." Knowledge bridges can be individuals or units that provide their organizations with knowledge boundary spanning roles, between different, independent organizations or subunits. They go beyond gatekeeping since they connect and share knowledge. This can be done through a formal arrangement, like patent licensing (for codified knowledge) or by intentionally moving the tacit knowledge by moving the person in which the tacit knowledge is embodied[7].

Next we will discuss the specific levers we suggest you consider.

HR Policies

HR policies cover the areas of recruiting, selecting, hiring, training, developing, and rewarding new and current employees at all levels. Here are some illustrations of the ties between HR policies as levers for KM strategy (rewards will be discussed separately since we believe they deserve special attention).

Hiring, training, retaining, etc. is seen by many as talent management and to be different from knowledge management. We agree that they are different, but we claim that they are intensely/ heavily related, and that talent (one result of having the appropriate HR policies) is one of the most important, if not the most important lever needed for your KM strategy.

For example, one of the key positions companies have to develop for successful KM strategies are gatekeepers that have the capacity to bridge across disciplines. This unique set of skills can be either groomed internally or acquired from the outside, but the HR policies must allow for gatekeepers to survive, improve, flourish, and perform their function effectively.

We have also found that diversity is crucial to support creativity. One hiring policy that can increase cross fertilization and creativity is hiring people with different backgrounds, e.g. ethnicity, culture, complementary (but different) technical skills. Having the appropriate policies for that in place might seem natural in the US, but this is not necessarily the case in other countries and societies. As globalization becomes more and more common in business, this strategy may have far reaching consequences. Diversity takes on new meaning when dealing with personnel with inherently different cultures, and goes beyond gender, race, age, etc.

Reward (Formal & Informal) System

Appropriate reward systems are crucial for the success of any strategy and KM is not an exception. The discussion below will illustrate some of the issues and complexities of this lever.

Pay for Performance

Individual pay for performance might be contradictory to new knowledge creation or to existing knowledge sharing behavior. Take for example a lawyer that is rewarded by billable hours and the profit for her firm resulting from getting new clients. Would she be spending time on developing new services for the firm and sharing them and her knowledge with her colleagues? Probably not. So how about team based rewards based on profits?

This might work if the team or organization has a strong culture, but if this is not the case you might be facing free riding (knowingly or unknowingly) by some individuals. If you are dealing with tacit knowledge and the organizational culture is not open, the knowledge that must be shared may not be released to the individuals who need it and it may be hoarded by those who have the tacit knowledge. If the knowledge that needs to be shared is codified it will be easier to detect, even if the company reward system is positioning the different units as competing for the pool of rewards. However, tacit knowledge is much too easy to hide. This might explain why copying best practices within the firm is so difficult. First, the best practice that might work in one place will probably have to be slightly modified because of local conditions, regulations (if it is a different state or country), etc. Second, the knowledge provider might not be aware of some of the tacit knowledge assumptions that are taken for granted at his/her location. And lastly, the reward system based on the profits in the specific business unit will probably not be rewarding him/her if it is based on a profit at the other business unit.

On the other hand, delayed payment, or payment that results from a relatively long period/tenure, may be effective in promoting the appropriate behaviors that support KM strategy implementation.

Promotion

Promotion (or tenure in the academic environment) might be used more effectively to promote new knowledge creation and/or knowledge sharing. For example, McKinsey created a special promotional track for their "knowledge experts"[8]. Those experts are promoted based on their ability to develop new knowledge that is then incorporated and judged by other internal users as part of their consulting assignments.

A problem with promotion is that it might be more subjective and as such create/play into internal politics.

Intrinsic Rewards

Intrinsic rewards are seen by some as the most appropriate but the most difficult to create and sustain. Some specific examples used to support KM strategies are: increasing the visibility (e.g. "best seller" advice) of an expert[9] or being nominated as a mentor, or being sent to conferences to represent the organization.

This might be even more effective, but requires the right culture (for example a team spirit), and leadership, and it is also easy to ruin.

Issues with Reward Systems

1. Be careful with putting in place a simplistic system, one that might encourage people stealing others' ideas to be submitted by a due date to avoid being penalized; see example in Samsung.[10]

2. Ask questions such as: What is the appropriate level of aggregation (unit of analysis) for KM reward systems? Are individual's goals and rewards the appropriate units or should it start with teams or departments?

Cross Functional Collaboration

Cross functional collaboration is seen as a Key Success Factor (KSF) for successful KM strategy implementation. Here are some issues and illustrations.

Cross functional collaboration is a KSF for new product innovation (new knowledge creation) in large high tech companies. For example, marketing collaborating with other functions might be crucial in some cases more than others. Learning from failures or from successes presents challenges for KM in a fast changing and uncertain environment. So, in this context a strategic question will be how to structure the cross functional team (composition) and how much autonomy and flexibility the team should have in making strategic and tactical/operational decisions. This also requires coordination with the nature of the knowledge (codified versus explicit) and the systems supporting the team activities.[11]

Another question will be how to break the barriers between the internal or external silos, when true collaboration between people is needed but language barriers, organizational (intra and inter) authority lines, functional responsibilities, etc. make true dialogue difficult if not impossible. And since the collaboration seems to be dependent on effective dialogue and the majority of the knowledge is tacit[12], can IT systems help? What about virtual cross functional teams? How do you develop a dialogue when you also have to cross culture and time zone boundaries? How do you allow gatekeepers to operate effectively?

Some of the most interesting aspects revolve around sales people and their integration into cross functional teams, due to their unique nature, potential for turnover and critical role.

The stickiness of the knowledge in question will be an issue as well. For example, if the knowledge is highly technical, the collaboration might require mechanisms appropriate for sharing tacit knowledge, while if the knowledge is codified (or codifiable) the collaborative mechanisms that will be appropriate will be more IT systems based.

The other issue we identified that is relevant here is that in many cases the function of KM is siloed (under/owned) by either the IT function or by the HR function. If this is the case in your organization then the cross functional collaboration may be tainted by turf wars.

You have to allow redundancies within your organizational design, since assuming that only formalized and planned processes will work is wrong. So for example, some companies have organized idea fairs, some have halls covered with posters that promote ideas (supply) or needs (demands) sharing so people can randomly interact.

How can you determine if you actually do or don't have cross functional (formal or informal) collaboration? The British Council provides an example of using a relatively simple tool of social network analysis to identify the communication within a globally dispersed organization. For those teams to be effective, they can not operate in a vacuum. The British Council uses this tool as complementary to their use of KM audits. It also has a formal KM strategy and formal KM roles within the organization.[13]

Core Competencies

We use the following definition of organizational core competencies: the key processes that allow the organization to deliver its product/services to its customers better than any of its competitors, and which result in its sustainable competitive advantage. Those processes are unique, hard to copy[14], and cut across multiple units (function, business units, layers/levels, etc.). As such, they depend significantly on company culture and are not based on (but use) information systems. They are the result of a complex process of organizational learning and an accumulation of multiple teams' learning, and as such are very difficult to manage, codify, or copy.

Core competencies can operate as levers since they are the center of the organization's business model. As such, they should be the lenses through which the organization concentrates its efforts, and the required knowledge support, updates, reconfiguration of existing knowledge, etc. Being such a magnate for knowledge is a great advantage, but when the environment changes, or when the company may want to change its strategy significantly, this might be a huge burden.[15] It is crucial to understand that managing existing core competencies and developing new competencies requires a different set of organizational skills and leadership to say the least (more on that later in this chapter).

Top Management Support

Top management support (or lack of) is crucial as in any other major organizational change or strategic initiative. It can create a powerful lever by providing the appropriate environment, e.g. budget, people, time, establishing appropriate performance indicators and reward systems, as well as providing the vision and leadership needed, as illustrated by the Fiat case.

In some cases, gaining top management support might not be easy, since KM might have a negative connotation, sound like another buzz word, or is seen as just another way IT is trying to increase their budget, by sneaking in a fancy technology. Since KM requires time, top management might see it as a significant drain on their attention and time, especially if the outcomes are not quantified. On the other hand, the Top Management Team might see KM as a tool for gaining control over labor, as it may allow for a better knowledge of what labor does (CRM allows more transparency of the performance of a sales person than end-of-month sales figures; GPS on a truck not only allows for better management of inventory but also lets you know what the driver does every second) and in this way allows for de-skilling of the human asset as well as lowering cost, etc.[16]

Top management support is not static. The lenses through which the top executives test the value of KM are dynamic, and can be modified. One example of when the lens of KM will change will be due to government regulation, or when a government body like the FDA, introduces new legislation or a new standard. Another way to change the lens of KM and to gain support of top management is by aligning KM vision and mission with organizational vision and mission, which is why the goals are on top of our matrix.

Top management support, is not synonymous with control. Actually in the KM case they contradict. The more control you have, the less support you are showing, since KM requires the soft touch of management.

One word of caution, having strong top management support is crucial, but not sufficient. The role of middle management in KM is one of the least understood and studied aspects, even though it is clear that middle management plays a crucial role in successful implementation of both. For example, Bontis and J. Fitz-enz, (2002) found that middle management's experience (tenure) had a positive impact on revenue and income growth. In other words, you will need to ensure the support and commitment of your middle management as well.

External Relationships

More and more companies depend on external sources of knowledge. As there is a greater need to react quickly to environmental issues and the ever-changing market, it becomes apparent that knowledge creation not only must be fostered from within, but companies should always be ready to discover additional external sources of knowledge. One variable in the equation is time. Although we have not explicitly quantified time within the knowledge creation process, it is evident that organizations are required to streamline this process. Knowledge creation can be a relatively slow process and one way to accelerate it is to utilize outside knowledge. There will be rare occasions when all the knowledge required by an organization will be available in one or few individuals and even then the cost of such knowledge can be relatively expensive. However, understanding what knowledge is required and how that knowledge can be used for a particular set of circumstances can greatly impact the time needed. For example, it can reduce the time-to-market of a new product or service.

It may seem contradictory to discuss the length of time it takes to create knowledge when discussing external relationships, but time is one of the primary factors that must be considered when analyzing the overall requirements for knowledge creation. Knowledge will be exchanged when external relationships are fostered. It is both an advantage and disadvantage depending on your perspective. However, the ultimate cost of knowledge loss or additional risk acquired, assuming it is a value to the organization, must be weighed against the perceived gain of creating knowledge at a faster pace than creating it from within, which is why more and more companies, even the larger and successful, use external sources of knowledge extensively[17].

Remember this is not a "cure all" and there are many obstacles that could inhibit the dissemination of knowledge from the resource that "owns" the knowledge. It will not be a one-to-one (knowledge to need) relationship but it can be a significant lever for advantage if managed correctly.

The Toyota-Formula One case provides many examples of external knowledge sources. It also provides examples of how collaboration with suppliers can result in an improved design of a new product as well as lower the cost of supply chain management. As you can see, these items are all inter-related and focusing on one aspect, although important, can take you away from the overall picture.

Some other issues to consider when discussing external relationships include utilizing customer relationships as a trigger for new product/service development. You can never assume that you have a complete understanding of the market and where it may be going. You must recognize that your customers may be telling you there is a need for a new product or service that you can provide. However, that need must be weighed against strategic direction as well as the ability to ramp up and bring the new product or service to market in a timely and cost efficient manner. Inherently, customers with intimate relationships will know if the product or service is something that is within your organization's scope but decisions of that scope must be made by you, based on the strategic direction in which the organization is planning to move. Customers, like individuals are selfish and are only looking to their own needs and strategic direction. They will endeavor to push their agendas and the coercion of their requests may look like a lucrative niche is developing. The reality is that there may be a new market opening and you may

have the knowledge to fill that need. However, if the direction is contrary to your organization's strategic direction, there may be dire consequences when what seems like a good fit runs against the direction the organization is taking.

Acquiring knowledge from external resources may also allow for a recombination with internal knowledge and creating a new knowledge/product/ service. Some capabilities are more relevant than others depending on the expected outcomes and strategies. For example, for exploitation purposes, strategic alliances and affiliation with Venture Capital might be more appropriate, while for exploration purposes embracing a broad scope of human capital skills supported by previously engaging in more challenging explorations might be more appropriate. [18]

Development of alliances and or joint ventures with one or more partners or participation with competitors in the development of industry standards or as part of a consortium is another way to acquire knowledge from external sources. The issue here is the transfer of knowledge to manage the relationships and understand what proprietary knowledge may be shared with others. If that knowledge is part of an organization's competitive advantage or core competency, steps must be taken to ensure that the newly shared knowledge is leveraged and any strategic decisions made because of that knowledge are reviewed. In this case, a strategic decision may be compromised because proprietary knowledge is no longer contained within the organization's domain.

All that is required to formalize the process of developing alliances is the capacity to develop and manage external relationships. This is more complex that it sounds, especially in the knowledge intensive context. For example, some of this participation may require signing a contract. In the context of developing new knowledge, writing the contract too early will be impossible; you will not know what knowledge outcome is possible and when. Even when the outcome uncertainty is reduced later on, customer expectations might not be clear enough to estimate value. But even if a signing a contract is not an issue, developing the relationships (taking risks of sharing exposing knowledge and opportunity costs) and managing the relationships have their risks and costs. One of these risks is being 'locked' into a "strong tie" relationship with a 'wrong' customer or supplier. Meaning, the customer was right at first, but when circumstances changed, they may turn out to be a wrong customer. Or, the supplier was appropriate for the first product line, but 'wrong' for a very different product line (see example in the *Toyota-Formula One case* below). In another words, one aspect of managing relationships, is to know when to disconnect/detached from a wrong partner, customer, or supplier, while one aspect of developing relationships is to write a contract that will allow for such detachment.

Culture/Tolerance of Risk

As in all things, there will be failures experienced as organizations work through the knowledge management strategy development and implementation processes. Indeed, many of the organizational failures experienced today could have their roots in KM. It must be remembered that building a culture or enhancing the present culture that will accept failure is of critical importance. As employees and partners see that the organization will accept failure, an implicit trust will be developed that will foster individual efforts to enhance internal knowledge. Much of this reasoning is implicitly understood, but consider the differences between the quantification of knowledge and the quantification of, for example, a sales quota.

Just as setting sales quotas for individuals and groups is important to help drive business and forecast revenue, similar quotas should be set for knowledge creation. However, guidelines for not meeting the knowledge quota should be defined during the goal setting process. One problem that may be discovered is the quantification of the goal. Although these technical issues must be addressed,

one important aspect to remember is that failure in one aspect of KM may not necessarily be a failure in another aspect of KM or business strategy. If a quota was set for a division to acquire a specific domain of knowledge and that goal was not reached, analysis is required to determine if any knowledge was created. Although the specific goal was not attained, different knowledge may have been created that will enhance the organization's knowledge base, or, the business using external feedback, is communicating the possibility that such knowledge is not needed at this time.

These are not simple concepts to grasp at first but it should be remembered that knowledge creation is an active process and the creation of any knowledge requires active participation by all the parties involved. So as you look at the cultural aspects of accepting failure, you must also look at the willingness the organization has to accept and live with a moderate risk factor of not creating the knowledge it wants to create.

Like failure, risk is another factor that must be addressed. The amount of risk an organization is prepared to accept when dealing with KM should be consistent with the amount of risk the organization can culturally accept. You cannot expect an organization that is culturally risk-averse to be non-risk averse when dealing with knowledge issues. An organization that accepts a high level of risk will usually understand that the risk resulting from the interchange of knowledge with other entities is something they will live with based on the potential benefits that can be achieved later. Indeed, the high-risk taking companies that flourished during the internet boom seemed to thrive, not only on risk, but on sharing as much knowledge as possible in order to gain even the smallest competitive advantage. Of course as the companies matured and their knowledge base became solidified, the amount of knowledge risk they would accept changed because the paradigm governing knowledge of the organization changed from creators of technology (or new knowledge) to keepers of products (sustaining existing knowledge). In any case, as the recent economic crisis illustrated, most companies lack the ability to manage their risks and are not prepared for negative (e.g. black swans) or positive contingencies. From the KM perspective this is extremely risky today because of the shrinking knowledge life cycle, the accelerated pace of new knowledge developed causing both faster knowledge depreciation and a shorter half life of knowledge.

These issues did not emerge in a vacuum. Especially in the knowledge creation process, sharing knowledge must be rewarded and hoarding that knowledge should be penalized. At the macro level, consider the difference between Apple computer and Microsoft. Apple 'hoarded' its proprietary operation system while Microsoft "shared" its operating system and allowed it to be used on a variety of hardware platforms. Although both companies navigated the rough waters of the technology boom, from an operating system market share perspective, it is obvious that Microsoft is clearly dominant. If this argument is narrowed to a micro level, it is consistent that the more knowledge is shared, the greater the possibilities available for benefiting from knowledge exchanged.

The final item on the subject of culture is the level of trust an organization is willing to put in its knowledge base. It is fair to say that any organization that is risk-averse and culturally "closed" will have a difficult time managing the knowledge creation process. Inherently, knowledge creation thrives on the ability to share, experiment, and fail. Creating knowledge is difficult but managing the creation and exploitation of that knowledge requires managers to grant a level of trust that may go counter to the culture of an organization and its constituent parts. The most impressive example of this is a playground of small children. They freely share knowledge, experiment, fail, and succeed. Rarely, if ever, does the child in the corner grow as much as the ones fully engaged with others.

KM Processes and Capabilities

Our experience also suggests that the following KM processes and capabilities (see Figure 2) should be considered: Communities of Practice, Product Domains, Functional Units, Project Teams, and Informal Networks/Clubs. Again, this is not a comprehensive list. Below we elaborate and illustrate some of the important aspects. What makes these processes and capabilities different from the levers (mentioned earlier) is that they are KM specific based and NOT organization wide based.

Communities of Practice

McKinsey initially used an open market system to clean and validate the knowledge within their data systems within a community of practice; this was followed by creating a position of "practice coordinators"[19]. Every organization has these types of structures but because they are not formalized they do not get the recognition they deserve. By setting apart specific organizational units, possibly a microcosm of the organization or division, the company is allowing the area in question to focus on a specific domain. We see this all the time in companies that geographically separate divisions and departments into smaller, more manageable units. The difference is that when specialized individuals or groups are allowed to focus on specific responsibilities and work in peer groups, the knowledge sharing possibilities begin to grow internally.

People and teams in similar positions and similar disciplines begin to communicate for the common good and interpersonal relationships begin to emerge for the betterment of the organization as a whole and not for individual advancement. These relationships are less focused on specific goals and more on providing better means of doing business within a domain. As the network of these relationships grows, knowledge is shared on a variety of levels. Out of these "siloed" environments come best practices that are fostered by institutional experience and shared knowledge. Because the competitive nature of division vs. division is not in place, inter-relational knowledge sharing becomes the norm. Once different areas within an organization have more than a financial reason to share resources, the best resources in the organization can be put to work where they can be used to their best advantage. The end result is gaining and maintaining a strategic advantage because there is a common goal rather than competitive in-fighting. Part of structuring an organization in this manner is the ability to create, maintain, and utilize a common set of tools that can be shared with others in similar situations. These tools may, by design, be position or discipline specific to enable the end users to accomplish their individual goals without changing the status quo of the organization. Similar networking structures, schemas, metadata, etc., all combine to provide an organic resolution to problems that cross functional lines and reduce the need for re-inventing the wheel every time a new project is undertaken.

Product Domains

Product domains are another area where knowledge is created, utilized, and maintained for the common good. There is great similarity between communities of practice and product domains. Consider these domains as somewhat smaller communities of practice but instead of encompassing knowledge at the macro level, products put limits on the macro view as they focus more sharply on the functional parts of the practice.

Product domains are still broad in their scope, but they are more narrowly focused than the practice level. Product domains may be comprised of one product or a number of products that work either independently or in concert to provide an output for the end user. They are also knowledge creation tools as individuals and teams develop, maintain, and support existing products.

Of course, how customer feedback is solicited will have a great impact on how new knowledge will be created within the organization. As the support mechanisms for the products are developed, internal structures must be developed to maintain and support the knowledge base that is required to sustain the organizational understanding of the domain. This is a broad concept and the next step down is the understanding of the functional units that are created to maintain the domains.

Functional Units

Functional units are created to support the product domains. They may grow organically out of need or they may be intentionally developed by organizations that have a strong strategic plan and direction. As you can imagine, these functional units are a level lower than Product Domains. These units, although not the lowest level we will discuss, can be considered the fundamental baseline for knowledge creation. These are however the lowest level at the formalized organizational structure. We do not discount knowledge creation at lower levels, in fact we have found that lower level knowledge creation can be a more significant factor but organizationally these levels are difficult, if not impossible to manage and informal low-level knowledge creation at the project team level should be brought to the functional level to enable more rapid dissemination throughout the organization.

Functional units are small enough to allow knowledge creation on a one-to-one basis and large enough to ensure diversity within the units to allow for a wide ranging environment for knowledge creation. The assumption regarding these units is that the same or similar work is being performed by groups or teams but within formalized structures, geographical boundaries for example. Perhaps your organization provides consulting services and within the United States, the functional units are broken down geographically to better serve your customer base. Ideally, these functional units will incorporate best practices and the services provided will be formalized to a point where all the consultants have a standard way to provide the services. However, things happen and the unexpected always occurs.

These types of issues are, or certainly should be, the basis for any organization's knowledge creation strategy. At the functional level, the knowledge created can easily be quantified and added to the knowledge base.

Project Teams

Project Teams feed the Functional Units. The reason we exclude these teams from the formalized organizational levels is due to the transient nature of Project Teams. This is not to say that they don't provide an excellent platform to create knowledge, but the dynamics involved in, do not create the atmosphere for a long term knowledge creation base. It must also be recognized that Project Teams could, and often do, provide a springboard for knowledge creation especially because they are constantly interacting with internal and external stakeholders. They are on the front lines and are doing the day-to-day work that allows knowledge to be shared and disseminated to other areas within the organization.

Because the nature of projects is short-term and finite, organizations cannot look to project teams to provide long-term knowledge creation. Since the knowledge created will be project specific, and knowledge sharing must be formalized within the functional units to analyze the knowledge and determine the most appropriate area for the knowledge to be utilized in. This is not to say that the knowledge created at the project level cannot be used to the advantage of the entire organization but transferring knowledge from a project team to an organization is complex, and as such the majority of the knowledge transferred is in the tacit format, embodied in employees, unless the organization created a specific mechanism for such transfer.

It is suggested that Project Teams be used as

inter-disciplinary teams that work together to share the knowledge created and provide the basis for internal knowledge creation and for creating processes, either tacit or explicit, to develop knowledge. This will go a long way to establish a detailed knowledge base as well as to establish best practices that can be used for multiple project teams. We look at this as an informal knowledge creation process that becomes formalized as knowledge is shared and as formalized processes become the norm. It should also be remembered that as multiple project teams are sharing newly created knowledge and formalizing the project approach, the functional units will begin to see cohesive knowledge bases that can be utilized for ensuring consistency among multiple project teams.

Informal Clubs and Networks

Informal clubs are similar to project teams but with much less formality. We look at these clubs at the organizational level as similar to sub-conscious knowledge creation at the individual level. It is established that we create knowledge at the conscious and sub-conscious level. We have all had experiences where once we set aside a problem and stop actively trying to solve the problem an epiphany occurs and suddenly we "know" the answer. Because of the informal nature of these clubs and the lack of formalized organizational structure, these clubs bring knowledge to the organization that is based on individuals who are dedicated to the process and have an intrinsic affinity to the process and to creating knowledge for that process.

The potential problem that may arise from these clubs is the lack of codification of knowledge created at this level. Since there is no formal structure to share knowledge between the clubs and project teams, any knowledge created may not be available to the organization at any level. Although this is an extreme case, we are confident that individuals who are drawn to these clubs will also bring that knowledge to their project teams. Therefore, although difficult to codify and quantify, knowledge created at these levels will eventually become available to the organization although it might take longer to manifest that knowledge.

If one looks at the social networking sites available to anyone with access to the internet, you can see the power of informal networks. However, do not be misled by the seemingly unstructured organization of these types of networks. There is much to be gained by individuals and teams that gather in this type of environment. The knowledge might not be easily codified and its value quantified and it is certainly based on the individual entity but there is a much to be gained from this type of interaction at both the individual and organizational levels.

Systems

Finally, you also want to add the systems you need to have in place to make the outcomes happen. Systems in our case are not limited to IS. We are suggesting of course to include KM/IS Architecture, but you also should consider the KM/IS Security Policies. Here is another example where the strategic dilemmas discussion (see chapter 7) will come back. But you have to be careful here. Just to have the systems in place might not be sufficient. For example, you might have the IS in place, and you also might collect the data that you need, BUT the data might not be valid or reliable. We have found more than once, that companies assume they have the valid and reliable data they need to support their decision makers, but are surprised badly when they put it to test. And even when they have the data, the data may not be available where and when needed because of security policies. Think about a sales person in the field collaborating online with a client at a third location, connecting with a mobile PDA and needing access to a secured data base, and you will begin to see the complexities.

KM/IS Architecture

It is fair to say that technology will become even more pervasive than it is today. Organizations must be diligent to understand that without information systems, knowledge management systems are useless. Every day the workforce grows more and more reliant on computers and communication networks to access their workday needs. If the IT infrastructure and systems are not built along with the knowledge base that an organization is looking to expand and foster, the process will be doomed to failure.

What these systems will look like and how they will be accessed in the future is almost anyone's guess. What is clear is that a knowledge repository is not a collection of documents. It has to be an easy to use intuitive set of tools that can quickly allow someone to create the knowledge they need to complete the tasks assigned. In addition, it must also allow for the analysis of how something was done and if the results were satisfactory. The fast growing importance of analytics as a business intelligence tool is just one illustration of the trend (see below).

Knowledge Embedded in Systems

So if connecting the dots is difficult, even having events and reward policies (for example) is not enough, since the organization is spread in multiple locations, across time zones, etc. Can KBS systems and policies help? Sometimes it might. For example, a mix of knowledge capturing structured interviews, with a mind mapping technique (and data aggregation and interrogation engine software-Crossbow) to capture the knowledge visually is described by Nousala et al, 2005[20]. Such interviews not only capture the knowledge (to a degree of course) but also might precondition the individual to share their knowledge later, at the appropriate time (of course if the right reward system is present).

KM/IS Security Policies and Reporting Systems

As mentioned in the sections above, the transfer of knowledge could/should be free flowing in the appropriate cultural environment. Organizations must put some security constraints on the transfer and sharing of knowledge but this is a very difficult aspect to manage. If the security restrictions are too stringent and do not allow for the sharing of knowledge both internally and externally then the company creates the possibility of becoming too insular and defeating many of its goals before they can be achieved. The same is true for KM systems within the IS infrastructure. If accessing data is difficult, cumbersome, or restrictive due to security policies, people will not use the systems. The difficulty is managing what is available against what can be disseminated to individuals outside the organization. If the systems are too secretive, individuals will create their own domains and the organization will have created multiple KM domains with no inter-relationships. The knowledge will not be shared because the barriers for sharing are too high.

Reporting is similar but has at least one additional facet, it must be relevant. Of course before that question can be answered, an analysis of what is being reported must be addressed. Just like a financial database, a knowledge database will have a wide variety of data but that data may or may not be useful depending on the structure and audience. If an organization is only interested in the quantification of knowledge then the reporting will go in one direction. If it is interested in providing the reporting as a means to create additional knowledge then reporting will go in another direction. Regardless of the direction, the organization must tie the reporting to the security policies to ensure that the entities that need the data can access it in a useable and secure format.

Business Intelligence and Analytics

Business intelligence in this context deals with the knowledge and data on the interface/boundary of the organization. Focusing on the KM aspect, the knowledge should help the organization to understand and respond better to its customers, end users and suppliers as well as better manage its competition (current and potential) and its macro-environment. Any system that is the repository of data requires that the data be available in a number of forms to serve multiple heterogeneous users, for applications not always anticipated in advance. Understanding the basics of the business and the data that is housed within its systems is the beginning of understanding what the business needs, as output, in order to prosper.

Business intelligence isn't a knowledge creation function; on the contrary, it is an output of the knowledge creation process. As long as systems are in place to capture organizational data, there will be a need to formalize that data into specific outputs that enhance the business process. It is critical here to understand the business process and how it has changed in the past along with the expectations of changes in the future. It makes no sense to create output that is mired in historical attitudes and formats. Outputs are essential but they must be designed so all potential users can understand the value of the output as well as have access to it. In today's decentralized environment, paper reports are quickly becoming obsolete but we really don't know what form the next generation of output will have. It may be a web site generated knowledge or based on internal algorithms specific to sub-sets of data within a data warehouse. We just don't know. However we must be aware that output must be channeled to users in a fashion that is realistic, timely, and useable. Some of that is depicted by systems, what some people call Analytics[21] but the most complex and fuzzy aspects of business intelligence are still managed tacitly by organizations, which is why it is critical to allow for flexibility in outputs to accommodate currently unknowable future needs.

How to Use Levers, Processes and Systems (LPS) to Achieve the Goals

Now we need to tie the Levers, Processes and Systems to the goals and how to achieve them.

Be sure to consider a number of alternatives, before deciding finally on the goals you like. Remember, the decisions you make here are not set in stone. Once you begin to move forward you must constantly review your decision and determine if what you want to achieve is a valid outcome of what you are doing.

It is a very complex task to reflect on all the Levers, Processes and System that should be part of the design process but such a reflection should be addressed on a regular basis. It is a simple matter to get off track because of a business necessity or market forces that steer you away from the matter at hand. You have to remember that these are long term goals and it may take a very long time for them to be achieved. However, focus must be placed on the process. This will be something that requires constant attention and should have a significant place in the status reporting of the organization. For example, the economic crisis that started to develop in late 2007 with the decline of the housing market would have to be analyzed in conjunction with the other Levers, Processes, and Systems to determine how to proceed based on your original goals. To be specific, let's assume that your organization made the decision to purchase a new Human Resources system but economic factors delayed or cancelled the project. The conditions surrounding the Process and Systems involved with the delay/cancellation would have to be analyzed based on the goals that were part of the reasons to purchase the new system.

Simply because you have created a set of goals you cannot forget that all the variables that went into the decision making process must be addresses on a continual basis. You have to be in the position to understand the current situation and factor in any changes from when you made the initial decision. Based on that, a re-assessment of all the Levers, Processes, and Systems has to be an on-going process to remain on course and account for any circumstances that will impact the final goals.

There is a holistic element to tying the LPS together as a cohesive unit. The critical aspect is ensuring that the three work in tandem and do not contradict or interfere one with another. This is a highly complex balancing act because these elements are constantly changing and the relationship and balance between them might be shifting. Even a slight, almost non-existent shift may have undue consequences on the other factors. Another aspect to remember is the need to tie the goals and LPS to capabilities and competencies (see Figure 3). Your KM strategy needs to support the short-, mid- and long-term goals of the organization (see Figure 5 in chapter 1).

There is one additional reason for your KM strategy to be cohesive and that is support for the building of internal capabilities and competencies. Although the process may seem overly complicated, if these items are not considered and addressed, your organization will have a very difficult time creating the necessary tools to become a knowledge-based entity. Further, if these items are not addressed and there is a modicum of success from the process, that process will be replicated and the amount of work that is put into creating knowledge will be inconsistent with the relatively meager results.

You also must allow for some ambidexterity[22] here, meaning, create a variety of capabilities, levers, etc. so if the external environment requires resources that are not in your core, you still will be able to acquire them in a timely fashion with minimal effort.

Figure 3. KM strategic framework: the big picture

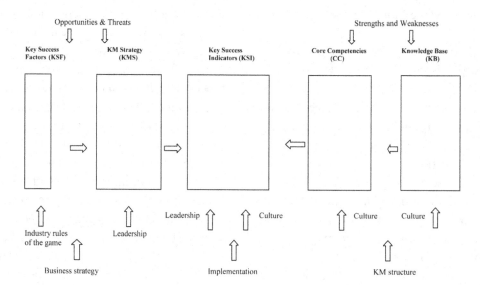

KM STRATEGY

Now you should create your KM strategy and put it in place. This should be done by matching your goals with the levers, processes and systems. Following that, you will develop an action plan and match that to your resources and constraints.

Here are some ideas[23] you may want to think about. The current business environment is extremely volatile and creates paradoxical, contradictory forces on any organization. For one, change is not the only constant; it is the increasing pace of change that is constant[24]. Next, organizations need to be able to respond to conflicting pressures, for example centripetal and centrifugal competing forces, or the need to attract young, Y-generation employees while still being attractive to older and "not retiring any time soon" older employees. So, how can the company have a strategy responding to such environment, or what Stacey (1992) identified as the need for strategic decision making when the future is unknowable. His advice was to use outcomes and feedback to detect the environment, not only to control for the effectiveness of the strategy. He also recommended for the organization to strive for being in the most

innovative state, which is bounded instability that should allow the organization to determine its own future, which is what others called the Blue Ocean Strategy.[25] Others suggested that organizations should create such an innovative capacity by increasing their action's requisite variety[26] and increasing their anticipatory memory[27], as well as using indicators for developing anticipatory, positive, non-linear (but within limits) feedback mechanisms. We would strongly recommend also to develop your human capital, even though we don't know how to measure it, and reward them appropriately and consistently with your goals, all the while being open to good and bad surprises (Black Swans[28] and others).

There is very little more we can add here. For one, check chapter 7 for strategic choices you can make. Also, since your strategy will be (hopefully) unique to you, you will have to figure out how to match your goals while using the LPS to achieve them. There is no cookie cutter solution for that, sorry ☹ .

Next you have to think about implementation and communication.

The most effective way to address these issues is to be open minded about not only what you are doing but the results you expect to achieve. This is consistent with what we have studied and the outcomes lend themselves to an open discourse about how the implementation should be completed as well as how the communications process should be managed. As with everything, the platform and the content used to disseminate the data should be geared toward the user. How they are going to use the data is the important aspect, not the form the data takes. However, it should be noted that the data should be controlled in some sort of repository, a data warehouse for example, and that might be a determining factor in how the final data is presented and utilized.

KM CONSTRAINTS AND RESOURCES

The obvious constraints are the current resources that you have, and/or that are available for any initiative, project, activity, etc. Budget, time, and staff are major among them, and like in any strategic planning or thinking you must take them into consideration in your planning process.

But this will not suffice.

Basically, any existing levers can be a constraint due to limited availability or due to a change in circumstances/conditions. For example, your current culture, norms and leadership (support, commitment) are constraints. Your current IS/KB systems are constraints. Your current policies, procedures, etc. are constraints. Your current capabilities and people skills (or lack of) are constraints. You must take them all into account and consideration in your planning process.

Also, like in any major change initiative, internal politics must be taken into account and addressed. Organizationally, you must take a critical look at where you want to go with the understanding that the journey must be mapped out based on how the organization works. Analysis must be done to evaluate where the roadblocks will come from and how the organization will be

able to navigate around any unforeseen problems. Is the commitment from management there? Will funding be cut off in the future? We invite you to review the *Toyota-Formula One case* and see the issues they faced and what they did to overcome obstacles.

This can be a difficult exercise but it is required preparation to give you an understanding of how you will manage the process going forward. In some areas you will succeed and in others you will fail. However, failure should not be looked at as defeat, it is a learning experience so you can gain the knowledge required to make furthers attempts successful.

Early research[29] in KM suggested that time (and not money) is the major constraint people face in their jobs. So, smart KM companies allow their employees 10-15% of their weekly hours to use for whatever they choose. This may seem counter intuitive, but if you look at the way the workforce has changed in the last 20 years, you can see that managing time efficiently is no longer the driving force behind work. When most jobs were based on an assembly line of some sort, it was relatively easy to understand the relationship between workers (time) and output (product). A factory manager needed only to know how many workers it took doing a week's work to produce x number of widgets. Based on orders and forecasts, staffing the correct number of workers was a fairly simple process. Of course this did not leave any time for the workers to learn anything more than the job they were assigned. There was no need for a line worker to understand the marketing strategies of the company since there was no correlation between those functions. In today's environment, it is fair to say that Apple could never have gotten the iPod to market with that type of mindset.

Learning and training (new knowledge development) is one of the first things that companies cut when economic downturn occurs. This is because they do not have a solid, valid set of tools for quantifying the value of ROI on human capital development. Imagine when times are most difficult and companies are trying to get the most out of every dollar, they begin cutting the very essence of their future. However, it is not a difficult call to make for a CEO. They have fiduciary responsibilities to the shareholders and maintaining the status quo will, it is hoped, allow them to maintain predefined levels of output and quality. The problem is that once the cycle starts to ramp back up, they are not in a position to learn from the mistakes they might have made. They are in a position where a decision has to be made to either move forward with training and new knowledge development or they can, if their business model allows for it, become a commodity producer in the market. Most companies are somewhere in the middle and are in a constant state of flux with relation to their new knowledge creation. It is very similar to the yo-yo diet effect and like that, without any clear direction, knowledge creation takes a back seat and there is no great material gain or loss. However, in the long term, these companies are doomed to fail because the failure of companies to create critical new knowledge and/or maintain existing knowledge and disseminate it throughout the workforce creates an environment where the status quo is the only goal, at best.

Action Plans and Planning Constraints and Resources

Now you are ready for the next step and reality check (see Figure 1). You will now list the specific steps/action plans as well as the all the resources needed for the strategy to happen, and all the constraints you will be facing when implementing it. Again, here, the devil is in the details. The more specific you are and the better and accurate your data and planning is, the higher the probability that you will be able to accomplish your goals. We have found (unfortunately) that in many cases management is clueless about the details needed for such planning, but at the same time they are not willing to involve the people at the bottom

of the ladder that have the knowledge needed for such detailed planning.

That is not to say that this is an exercise that will go unnoticed. At this point it is vital to bring in resources at all levels to ensure that you can actually perform the steps/activities based on the game plan and achieve the goals you have formalized. Management must realize that this cannot be done in an ivory tower and disseminated top-down to the employees like another policy. If you look at the thought process behind the structured process we have provided, it is imperative to ensure all the appropriate people are in place to formalize the process and provide the necessary input that allows management to make the correct decisions.

If you go through this process assuming that the management team has all the knowledge to set the correct goals you may be misguided. No select group of individuals can possess all the knowledge needed to drive this process forward. The premise we use is to bring in as many different opinions as we can to detail the activities, to identify the resources needed, as well as the constraints, and to establish the correct goals. Once this is done, you are well on your way to providing a roadmap that has an excellent chance of success.

An integral part of the process is creating a Risk Analysis that encompasses the resources, constraints, and goals. Specifically, a major risk in this type of environment is to understand that the major players are constituents in the process and losing any of them might adversely affect the KM proposition as a whole. It must be remembered that the people in the forefront have already created a vast amount of knowledge and the management may not understand the level of expertise these people bring to the process. Conversely, losing one or two key players in the process can adversely impact the KM implementation process timeline but if the participants have been utilizing the structured approach we outlined, the amount of organizational knowledge or in this case team knowledge, will more than compensate for the loss of individual participants as long as there is a strategy for transferring the team knowledge to the new participants.

Although at this point there is much to be said for keeping individuals within the process, it is also important to understand the importance of reviewing risks associated with the defined constraints. Since business is a fluid process, constraints will change throughout the KM strategy formulation and implementation lifecycle and these must be addressed on a periodic basis as the process moves forward. Do not discount the possible ramifications of addressing this step. It is of critical importance that the risks be updated so all possible scenarios can be analyzed. Look at the recent financial crisis where real estate values plummeted substantially and an organization was funding a number of initiatives based on the relative values of that real estate, a 20% or 30% devaluation of the company's assets could have an adverse effect on the funding available for the KM initiative. Although it would be difficult for most organizations to forecast that type of event and add it to their risk scenarios, it is an example where constant re-evaluation of all constraints, not just the ones that have a direct impact, is vital to the long term success of the KM initiative.

MANAGING CORE COMPETENCIES

Now you are ready for the big picture. We will now connect the concept of core competencies and the KM strategy to indicators and to other traditional tools for strategic thinking. There are a couple of reasons for this, but the most important one is that we know from our experience that companies have a very difficult time knowing how to manage their core competencies. They also have no clue how to develop new ones when they are needed (for example Sony[30]) or when they are restructuring (for example Thomson-France[31]), or when they have a need to use them in another product/market (Dell). So here is a framework that might just help (see Figure 3).

Core Competencies (CC), is a sound academic construct that makes sense for management intuitively, but we found it extremely difficult to put to use as a rigorous, formalized process that can be used effectively and efficiently by management. We found examples to be helpful in explaining the concepts, but it is almost impossible to get management to truly comprehend it and more than that, to put it to use. Most interestingly, even when a company developed a competency at one point in time, when they need to change it, or when they need to "re-engineer" it, they have no clue how to do that. Which would suggest to us, then, rather than referring to the development of the competency in the first place, we should refer to it as stumbled into it?

The framework described in Figure 3 builds on the original work of Roos and Roos (1997) but adds building blocks as well as identifies which aspects in the environment of the organization have stronger impact on which components of the framework.

First the basic framework; there are couple of reasons for the arrangement (from left to right in Figure 3) KSF-KMS-KSI-CC-KB in this order. From the right, we are consistent with Figure 2 in Chapter 1 and with the need for the KB to support CC resulting in KSI. From the left we need the external environment to have an effect on the KM strategy, which will also result in KSI, hopefully the same indicators and outcome, as mentioned earlier. Now obviously, there is a KB-KM strategy relationship, but separating them is intentional, since we do not want to limit the KM strategy to our own KB. We want to allow for strategies that utilize external sources of knowledge (see C^3EEP, in chapter 7) as from acquisitions or open sources, as mentioned also earlier in this chapter.

We start again with the outcomes. On one hand we identify the KSF that we need to have (resulting from the industry you are in) within our context to get to them, and we identify the business strategy that will provide for them. On the other hand, we identify the core competencies, activities, processes we need to have to arrive to them and we identify the knowledge base and the KM strategy that will get us there. Please note that there are a number of internal forces here you need to take into account, such as, culture and leadership; and external forces, such as industry's "rules of the game". By the end of the day, it is the implementation that makes the difference, and that causes the achievement of the expected outcomes. Why is this framework different? First it requires to "spelling out the guts" of the competency. What specific activities, and processes you have (or need to have) in place for this competency to work. Second, it is framed by outcomes and knowledge bases, which will make this connection explicit, and also will allow you to verify that indeed you have the "right" competency in place. And lastly it will connect it both to your strategy and to your industry, again explicitly, so you can verify that the connections, relationships and ties make sense.

You will also notice that the SWOT factors are placed in specific positions to help illustrate where in the process they come into play. Opportunities and Threats directly influence Key Success Factors and KM Strategy. In a similar fashion, Strengths and Weaknesses are directly influence Core Competencies and the company's Knowledge Base. We attempted to place the analysis factors with the most direct influence on the areas that they are impacting. As you move to the bottom of Figure 3 you see the relationship come full circle as, for example, Strengths and Weaknesses influence Core Competencies and the Knowledge base in a direct relationship and that directly influences Culture and the corporate KM Strategy. All of these factors have a vertical influence from top to bottom but they also influence the other items in the framework as you move from side to side. There are no stand alone items in the framework. Everything has some influence on other items. The difference is how directly the items are influenced.

KM OUTCOMES

Outcomes should be consistent with goals, so our discussion in chapter 1 and in this chapter (goals) should cover that, but keeping the 80/20 rule in mind as well as surprises, we must allow for new learning to happen, meaning we must be able to account for some unplanned outcomes to create value. Even in continually updated plans, the unexpected can (and will) happen, with both positive and negative results and/or consequences.

This also may encourage your organization to experiment and to be open to the unexpected, or re-invent itself partially, or completely. What we are really saying here is that there will always be new and unexpected events that will require you to re-think, re-do, and even re-invent what has already transpired. Knowledge is vibrant and multifaceted but more importantly, knowledge is dynamic. The factors we have defined as influencing knowledge are a sub-set of all the factors that directly influence the knowledge creation process. This sub-set has specific meaning in the business environment and provides a guide to maneuver through the knowledge creation process.

As we have discussed, the process is complex and there are no simple answers. In fact, you may be surprised by some of the answers you will get throughout the process. It is a simple thing to say that organizationally, you want to make changes and start moving toward a knowledge-based organization, however actually making that change involves considerable work and buy-in at all levels of the organization.

We have said that it is critical to review the process and the specific steps within the process on a continual basis and that is also true of reviewing the outcomes. An interesting exercise to perform is, when the process is complete, look back at the initial drivers that led to the decision to go forward with a KM initiative and look at the differences between what was accomplished and the expectations. You will see that the initial expectations, at a high level, have not changed that much because the vision is supported by the process. However, as you look into the specifics of the process, we are sure that you will find many of your initial assumptions were incorrect and that the process required you to make more changes than you thought you would have to, because of the dynamics of the process.

Don't be surprised by this. It is not inconsistent with the knowledge creation process. We all make internal assumptions and try to fit our world view into those assumptions. The process simply allows you to take an objective look at the assumptions and fit them into the business process to create value. The journey is long and hard but the benefits speak for themselves.

KM CONTROLS (CLOSING THE LOOPS)

Now that the process has come to a close and the KM strategy development initiative is over, you cannot stop. Maintenance is critical to ensure the process continues and provides for learning and knowledge creation on an ongoing basis. To do that, controls have to be established and stakeholders and other interested parties should be brought into discussions regarding the organization's vision, mission, and goals. Consistent with this, the strategy, levers, and constraints of the KM initiative should be reviewed on a periodic basis to ensure the baseline has not changed. These controls will allow the organization to completely understand the implications of both internal and external factors that impact how business is done and the external environment. This is actually a mini KM initiative with one difference: since most of the hard work has already been done, this simply keeps everything that has been accomplished on track.

Another way to view this is to understand that once a KM initiative has been completed, especially a successful one, it can quickly become a model for other areas within the organization. By

maintaining controls, the newer initiatives will have a great advantage over the previous ones as the process becomes defined and the errors made in earlier attempts become laboratories for new learning and knowledge creation.

We need to add here one additional aspect, and this is the question of the self identity of the organization. In our research[32] and consulting we found that in more and more cases, one of the stumbling blocks or barriers for change, or for understanding the environment, is the definition of self identity. Organizations take their old identity for granted so much that they never realize how this is limiting their strategic options and alternative futures. So, to summarize, be sure that you are aware of this issue, and allow yourself to question the need for change as part of your control, closing the loop process.

Finally, below, you find a case describing how a very successful company, despite being a world leader as a learning organization, had difficulty with transferring its core competency to a very different product market, and how its definition of self identity and early successes are limiting its ability to succeed in an environment foreign to them.

TOYOTA AND FORMULA ONE

Toyota: celebrated 'best world manufacturer', a global model of exemplary efficient and effective management of resources (both material and human). Formula One: the world's greatest expression of car technology brought to the extreme level of research & development, tested on the most challenging tracks in the world and a powerful global marketing tool. The match between Toyota and Formula One makes a lot of sense on both technological and marketing fronts. This is why Toyota has "spent more than 20 billion yen ($170 million) a year competing in Formula One races since its entry in 2002, for a cumulative total of over $1 billion in 2007."[33]

Through Formula One the Japanese company competes with many of the key manufacturers it has aggressively and successfully challenged in the global car market: BMW, Ferrari (Fiat), Honda, Mercedes, Renault (Nissan). Unfortunately the successes in the marketplace have not been matched by the results of the Toyota Formula One (www.toyota-f1.com) team to date: no wins, a handful of podium finishes, only one pole position on the starting grid and many frustrating and humiliating experiences (even on the home track in Suzuka, Japan owned by Toyota itself!).

Over six years of trying; over $1 billion spent (Toyota Formula One yearly overall budget equals, some say exceeds, that of the top winning teams Ferrari and McLaren-Mercedes); the top engineering, technical and driving expertise money can buy yet few results to show for it and little progress year after year. The top management of the company in Japan's headquarters has been increasingly under pressure either to come up with results or quit the Formula One program altogether. Why is this happening? What is Toyota doing wrong?

Many Formula One insiders are very skeptical that Toyota Formula One will be able to succeed any time soon. The key reason for this skepticism is related to the roots of the company's Formula One program and the way Toyota has been managing and developing knowledge in the unique, fast paced, ever changing Formula One environment. Let's analyze these issues further.

Formula One historically has been a European centered sport in terms of component manufacturers, team locations (the sport rules require each participating team to design and manufacture its own original chassis, the engine can be manufactured or purchased from a different manufacturer) and tracks. For these reasons Toyota realized that Formula One operations could not be based in Japan, they had to be based in Europe. They decided to utilize the facilities and expertise of the Toyota Team Europe, which was set up and managed by the Swedish former rally driver Ove

Andersson. Andersson founded the team (originally named Andersson Motorsport) in Cologne, Germany in the early 1970's and has been very competitive in the World Rally Championship ever since. In 1993 Toyota decided to purchase the team in order to further affirm the racing competitiveness of its cars on a global scale (the Rally World Championship features cars based upon commercial models). Toyota Team Europe was made up of 300 professionals coming from 17 nations. In 1997 it became the first motorsport business to be awarded the ISO 9001 label for the quality of its operations. Thanks to Andersson's work Toyota won the Rally World Championship as manufacturer in 1990-91-92-93-94-98 and 1999. These successes and the high level of professionalism and determination shown by Andersson and his people convinced Toyota headquarters to stop the Rally program and utilize the facilities and people in Cologne to enter the Formula One program. In 1999 Toyota headquarters officially presented their plans to begin competing in Formula One at the start of the 2002 racing season as engine and chassis manufacturer, developed and managed by its own team. The proper budget was set in order to involve Formula One experienced engineers and technical personnel, who left their positions at top Formula One teams lured by lavish compensation and the ambitious plans of the Japanese manufacturer famous for the reliability of its cars. They trusted Toyota not to jeopardize the worldwide reputation it had built with Formula One failures.

Since the beginning of the Formula One project in Cologne, Toyota aimed to make the sport headlines for its efficient organization based upon its very own celebrated Toyota Way. It prided itself on the multicultural origins of its people (more than 20 countries represented) managed the "Japanese way" with "German discipline" and aided by sophisticated operations management "American software". The software helped to gear operations toward a Business Service Model (BSM) allowing for an overall integrated

(End-to-End) vision of the manufacturing, testing and racing processes. Within this model all of the processes are integrated upon the improvement and feedback of the end user (for this specific case, the drivers detailed technical feedback from the track which is crucial for effective car development). On paper it is a flow of information and actions that are supposed to, at least, keep the pace (if not lead) in the rapid technological changes in Formula One where a three month old component is often already technologically obsolete.

Theoretically the organizational model should work but the results on the track have been disappointing given the amount of resources and expertise invested in the project. Since 2002 the team has changed many drivers (ruining in the process the career of at least a couple of them who had, until their arrival in Cologne, shown substantial racing and testing skills), it has changed several lead designers (one every year, by average) and it has also changed the top management: Ove Andersson (recently deceased in a vintage rally crash in South Africa) was sidelined from his lead role in 2003 due to the lack of results (officially he retired and remained linked to the team as a consultant). He was replaced by John Howett, former VP of Marketing and Sales for Lexus, who was supported by Japanese executives focusing on day-to-day and strategic operations. Many changes were made, but still no concrete and consistent results were realized.

Formula One insiders link the lack of results to two key aspects: the location of the team operations in Cologne and the lack of a step-by-step technical development continuity. Cologne is an issue because traditionally, Formula One manufacturers of both engines and chassis, have been located in Surrey (South East England) and specifically in areas such as Woking and Guildford (the World Championship started in 1950). Through the decades those areas have hosted small and midsize companies specialized in developing Formula One components and able to keep up with and stimulate the many technological changes (for example the

shift from metals to carbon fiber materials). In order to tap into this knowledge base and expertise many Formula One teams have been founded and still are located in this area and even Formula One newcomers have bought-out teams located here (for example the current official Honda Formula One was founded years ago by purchasing the 1970s World Champion Tyrrell team). There are some successful exceptions like Ferrari, located in Maranello, Italy or the former Sauber team (now BMW-Sauber) located in Hinwill, close to Zurich in Switzerland. It should be noted that through the years both teams have had active technological links with England. For example Ferrari, during the late 1980's and early 1990's, implemented a technological design and aerodynamics center in Guilford, England directed by the then top Formula One designer, John Barnard. Barnard agreed to leave his employer (several times World Champion McLaren team) and work for Ferrari only if the Italian company was willing to finance the center. This was certainly a radical change for the Italian manufacturer always proud to point out that everything in a Ferrari Formula One car was 'Made in Maranello' (Ferrari's historical headquarters are close to Modena). According to Barnard, it was not going to be possible to design and manufacture a winning Formula One chassis without tapping into the know-how and skills present in England. Ferrari Formula One wins in 1990 and 1991 (after almost a decade of struggling performances) proved him right even if political tensions within Ferrari eventually lead Barnard to leave the company and the Guilford center to be closed. The Toyota Formula One team has missed out on this knowledge base. They felt empowered by the Rally World Championship successes and by the far reaching knowledge base of Toyota. Knowledge and work methodology that have been proven over and over to be effective in making commercial cars yet the results at hand were not fully suitable for the nimble (compared to the global Toyota operations) but constantly changing Formula One world.

The location has not been the only contributing factor to the lack of success. The other key contributing factor has been the talent base on which the team was founded and the way that such talent has been managed ever since. During the last 25 years Toyota has been the only manufacturer to begin Formula One operations starting from zero, in other words without buying-out existing Formula One teams (Mercedes, Honda, BMW have all done that). The purchased teams were on a competitive downslide caused by lack of funds or by the fading inspiration and determination of aging visionary founders. Still, all of them had a knowledge base (in terms of people, infrastructure, tools and experiences) upon which to build renewed, better funded and better focused operations. For example the current successes of Mercedes (purchasing the historic McLaren team) and BMW (purchasing the small but experienced Sauber team) were dependent upon these factors.

Toyota Formula One has tried to compensate for this initial lack of specific technological know-how (involving design and engineering for both chassis and engines) and organizational know-how (involving the most efficient and effective way to obtain the best performance on track) by hiring experienced professionals. Yet the lack of results has caused the Japanese top management to keep changing the lead chassis engineers hoping to find better results. This has caused a lack of continuity in development of the knowledge base. Every new lead chassis engineer has chosen to start the overall design project almost anew, often taking into little consideration the expertise developed by the team until then. It is to note that instead on the engine side (lead since 1999 by the Italian engineer Luca Marmorini, a former Ferrari Formula One team professional) the step-by-step continuity has built upon technical advances over the years and the Toyota Formula One engine has been rated one of the most dependable and powerful ones over the last few years, an engine so effective as to place the Williams chassis manufacturer and

team, that has been utilizing the Japanese engine during the last two seasons, quite often ahead of the official all Toyota team.

These days, more than ever, winning in Formula One is a matter of technological effectiveness matched by organizational efficiency. Formula One has become one of the most challenging technological and organizational arenas not only in competitive motor sports but also in terms of the overall competitive global industry. Present and future successes in the sport depend upon specific expertise that cannot be improvised nor artificially acquired. Real experience with all its successes and failures is needed.

Only time will tell if Toyota will have the patience, bureaucratic and political inner dynamics, and resources to fill the knowledge base gap it has started its Formula One operations with and to implement a real overall step-by-step incremental approach, season after season, to making a more consistently performing and dependable car. To many Formula One fans its global image depends upon this.

* * *

ACKNOWLEDGMENT

The first author wishes to acknowledge the Frederick E. Baer Professorship in Business for partial financial support. The authors wish to thank Kelly Anklam for her assistance in editing this chapter.

REFERENCES

Ashby, W. R. (1956). *An introduction to cybernetics.* London: Chapman and Hall.

Barney, J. B. (1991). Firm resources and sustained competitive advantage. *Journal of Management, 17*(1), 99–120. doi:10.1177/014920639101700108

Bontis, N., & Fitz-enz, J. (2002). Intellectual capital ROI: A causal map of human capital antecedents and consequents. [from http://www.leighbureau.com/speakers/nbontis/essays/intel.pdf]. *Journal of Intellectual Capital, 3*(3), 223–247. Retrieved on June 25, 2009. doi:10.1108/14691930210435589

Cheuk, B. W. (2006). Using social networking analysis to facilitate knowledge sharing in the British Council. *International Journal of Knowledge Management, 2*(4), 67–76.

Davenport, T. H., & Harris, J. G. (2007). *Competing on analytics: The new science of winning.* Boston, MA: Harvard Business School Press.

Dodgson, M., Gann, D., & Salter, A. (2006). The role of technology in the shift towards open innovation: The case of Procter & Gamble. *R&D Management, 36*(3), 333-346. Retrieved on June 25, 2009, from http://espace.library.uq.edu.au/eserv/UQ:78772/RADM_03603002-2.pdf

Ghosh, T. (2004). *Creating incentives for knowledge sharing.* Retrieved on June 25, 2009, from http://myoops.org/twocw/mit/NR/rdonlyres/Sloan-School-of-Management/15-575Spring-2004/72ACA0F6-3943-4C1F-AB7F-0013602D7A61/0/tanu_15575.pdf

Henderson, R., & Clark, K. B. (1990). Architectural innovation: The reconfiguration of existing product technologies and the failure of established firms. *Administrative Science Quarterly, 35*, 9–30. doi:10.2307/2393549

Hsu, D. H., & Lim, K. (2005). Knowledge bridging by biotechnology startups. *The Wharton School Working Paper Series* (pp. 1-32). Retrieved on June 25, 2009, from http://knowledge.wharton.upenn.edu/papers/1320.pdf

Hsu, D. H., & Lim, K. (2007). *The antecedents and innovation consequences of organizational knowledge brokering capability.* Mimeo. Wharton School, University of Pennsylvania.

Huston, L., & Sakkab, N. (2006). Connect and develop: Inside Procter and Gamble's new model for innovation. *Harvard Business Review, 84*(3), 58–66. Retrieved on June 25, 2009 from http://randgaenge.net/wp-content/uploads/hbr-connect-and-develop.pdf

Kim, C. W., & Mauborgne, R. (2005). *Blue ocean strategy: How to create uncontested market space and make competition irrelevant.* Boston, MA: Harvard Business School Press.

Kurzweil, R. (2005). *The singularity is near: When humans transcend biology.* New York: Viking Adult.

Luca, L. M. D., & Atuahene-Gima, K. (2007). Market knowledge dimensions and cross-functional collaboration: Examining the different routes to product innovation performance. *Journal of Marketing, 71*(1), 95–112. doi:10.1509/jmkg.71.1.95

Miltenburg, J. (2005). *Manufacturing strategy: How to formulate and implement a winning plan.* Portland, OR: Productivity Press.

Nousala, S., Miles, A., Kilpatrick, B., & Hall, W. P. (2005, November 28-29). Building knowledge sharing communities using team expertise access maps (TEAM). *Proceedings from KMAP05: Knowledge Management in Asia Pacific, Wellington, NZ.* Retrieved on June 25, 2009, from http://www.orgs-evolution-knowledge.net/Index/DocumentKMOrgTheoryPapers/NousalaEtAl-2005KnowledgeSharingCommunitesExpertiseMapping.pdf

Osono, E., Shimizu, N., Tackeuchi, H., & Dorton, J. K. (2008). *Extreme Toyota. Radical contradictions that drive success at the world's best manufacturer.* Hoboken, NJ: John Wiley and Sons Ltd.

Raisch, S., & Birkenshaw, J. (2008). Organizational ambidexterity: Antecedents, outcomes, and moderators. *Journal of Management, 34*(3), 375–409. doi:10.1177/0149206308316058

Raisch, S., Birkinshaw, J., Probst, G., & Tushman, M. L. (2009). Organizational ambidexterity: Balancing exploitation and exploration for sustained performance. *Organization Science* (in print).

Roos, G., & Roos, J. (1997). Measuring your company's intellectual performance. *Long Range Planning, 30*(3), 413–426. doi:10.1016/S0024-6301(97)90260-0

Russ, M. (2008, January 28-30). *Do we need a new theory or a conceptual model to explain SME internationalization or do we need to apply existing theories and conceptual models by using a different epistemology?* Paper presented in the International Business Symposium at the International Academy of Management and Business Conference in San Diego, CA.

Russ, M. (2009, April 15-17). Knowledge management strategy in the age of paradox and transition. In *Proceedings of the Annual ISOneWorld Conference.* R. Hackney (Ed.), *Emergent challenges in IS/IT.* Washington, D.C.: Information Institute Publishing. ISBN: 978-1-935160-05-2.

Russ, M., & Jones, J. K. (2009, May 28-30). *International virtual industry clusters and SMEs: Early content and process policy recommendations.* Paper presented at the 40th MCRSA Annual Conference, Milwaukee, WI.

Russ, M., & Jones, J. K. (forthcoming). Knowledge management's strategic dilemmas typology. In D.G. Schwartz & D. Te'eni (Eds.), *Encyclopedia of knowledge management* (2nd ed.). Hershey, PA: IGI Global.

Schwartz, P. (1991). *The art of the long view.* New York: Doubleday.

Skjølsvik, T., Løwendahl, B. R., Kvålshaugen, R., & Fosstenløkken, S. M. (2007). Choosing to learn and learning to choose: Strategies for client co-production and knowledge development. *California Management Review, 49*(3), 110–128.

Spender, J. C. (2006). Getting value from knowledge management. *The TQM Magazine, 18*(3), 238–254. doi:10.1108/09544780610659970

Stacey, R. D. (1992). *Managing the unknowable: Strategic boundaries between order and chaos in organizations.* San Francisco, CA: Jossey-Bass.

Storey, J., & Barnett, E. (2000). Knowledge management initiatives: Learning from failure. *Journal of Knowledge Management, 4*(2), 145–156. doi:10.1108/13673270010372279

Taleb, N. N. (2007). *The black swan: The impact of the highly improbable.* New York: Random House.

Tushman, M. L., Anderson, P. C., & O'Reilly, C. (1997). Technology cycles, innovation streams, and ambidextrous organizations: Organization renewal through innovation streams and strategic change. In M. L. Tushman & P. C. Anderson (Eds.), *Managing strategic innovation and change: A collection of readings* (pp. 3-23). New York: Oxford University Press.

von Hippel, E. (1986). Lead users: A source of novel product concepts. *Management Science, 32*(7), 791–805. doi:10.1287/mnsc.32.7.791

ADDITIONAL READING

"A pinch of retro spices up Fiat's classic Italian recipe" by Bill Patton, New York Times, September 17, 2006.

"A tu per tu con Giancarlo Minardi tra passato, presente e futuro" Racingworld.it, December 18, 2007.

"At Last! Something Toyota isn't good at" by Angus MacKenzie, Motor Trend, May 16, 2007.

"Cosi' abbiamo guarito la Fiat dalla crisi peggiore" by Paolo Griseri, L'Espresso, August 1, 2008.

"Creativity And Innovation Driving Business" Toyota's Innovation Factory, October 17, 2006.

"Extreme Toyota. Radical Contradictions That Drive Success at the World's Best Manufacturer" by Emi Osono, Norihiko Shimizu, Hirotaka Tackeuchi with John Kyle Dorton, 2008, Wiley.

(2008). "Fiat Extreme Makeover" by Sergio Marchionne . *Harvard Business Review*, (December): 1.

"Fiat profit more than doubles on higher vehicle sales" by Alessandro Torello, International Herald Tribune, June 25, 2007.

(2006). "Fiat's comeback - is it for real?" by Gail Edmonson . *Business Week*, (July): 25.

"How do you solve a problem like Toyota?" F1Fanatic.co.uk, January 22, 2007.

"Il motore pulito e' la carta segreta del Lingotto" by Piero Bianco, La Stampa, May 20, 2009.

(2009). "Man in the news: Sergio Marchionne" by John Reed in Detroit and Vincent Boland in Milan . *Financial Times (North American Edition)*, (January): 23.

"Marchionne Has Dual Task of Reviving Chrysler, Keeping Fiat Fit", by Sara Gay Forden, June 11, 2009. http://www.bloomberg.com/apps/news?pid=20601087&sid=aOH_sOx3V85M

"Marchionne plays lead role in Chrysler cliffhanger", Financial Times, By Paul Betts, Published: April 17, 2009. http://www.ft.com/cms/s/0/7ec658d0-2ae6-11de-8415-00144feabdc0.html

(2008). Rebirth of a carmaker . *The Economist*, (April): 24.

"Resurgent Fiat sets sights higher" by Alessandro Torello, International Herald Tribune, June 18, 2007.

(2005). Saving FIAT . *The Economist*, (December): 1.

"Scommessa grande Fiat" by Maurizio Maggi, L'Espresso, May 13, 2009.

"Strategia Marchionne" by Stefano Livadiotti, L'Espresso, August 1, 2008,

(2008). The miracle of Turin . *The Economist*, (April): 24.

"Toyota F1: Savvy Marketing, Crappy Performance" Sports Guru, December 22, 2007.

"Toyota F1: Ultimate Incompetance?" FastMachines The Motorsports Weblog, December 5, 2004.

(2004). "Toyota's man has designs on the top" by James Allen . *Financial Times (North American Edition)*, (February): 16.

"Will Toyota ever win an F1 race?" by Nick Trott, Top Gear Blogs – Motorsports, January 22, 2007.

"Winless Toyota Formula 1 Chief Calls It Quits" Edmunds InsideLine, April 26, 2007.

ENDNOTES

[1] Gartner, March 25, 2003, available at http://www.gartner.com/resources/113900/113972/113972.pdf accessed October 3, 2008

[2] http://www.computerworld.com/action/article.do?command=viewArticleBasic&taxonomyName=laptops&articleId=9049999&taxonomyId=76&intsrc=kc_top; accessed October 3, 2008

[3] The first one (figure 6.1 and detailed in 6.2 is mostly based and modified for KM strategy

from John Miltenburg's "Manufacturing Strategy: How to Formulate and Implement a Winning Plan", 2005. The second (figure 6.3) is based on Roos and Roos, 1997 "Measuring your company's intellectual performance", published in Long Range Planning, 30(3), 413-426 and significantly modified.

4   Russ, M. (2009).Knowledge Management Strategy in the Age of Paradox and Transition, In proceedings of the Annual ISOne-World Conference. Hackney, R. "Emergent Challenges in IS/IT". April 15-17, 2009. DC: Information Institute Publishing. ISBN: 978-1-935160-05-2.

5   Skjølsvik et al. 2007, CMR 49(3): 110-128.

6   Von Hippel, 1986; see http://web.mit.edu/evhippel/www/papers/Lead%20Users%20Paper%20-1986.pdf

7   see Hsu and Lim, 2005, for discussion.

8   Tanu Ghosh, draft dated May 3, 2004; Creating Incentives for knowledge sharing; downloaded from the Internet, p. 11; http://myoops.org/twocw/mit/NR/rdonlyres/Sloan-School-of-Management/15-575Spring-2004/72ACA0F6-3943-4C1F-AB7F-0013602D7A61/0/tanu_15575.pdf

9   McKinsey-Ghosh, 2004, see endnote 8.

10   J-C. Spender; 2006; page 242; Getting value from knowledge management. The TQM Magazine. Vol. 18 No. 3, 2006. pp. 238-254;. http://www.jcspender.com/uploads/Getting_value_TQM06.pdf

11   Luigi M. De Luca & Kwaku Atuahene-Gima, 2007.

12   Knowledge management in manufacturing, Economist, June 2007. Retrieved May 22, 2008.http://www.ugs.com/products/nx/docs/wp_knowledge_management_web.pdf

13   Cheuk, B.W. (2006). Using social networking analysis to facilitate knowledge sharing in the British Council, *International Journal of Knowledge Management* 2(4); 67-76.

14   See Barney, 1991 Barney JB. 1991. Firm resources and sustained competitive advantage. *Journal of Management, 17*(1): 99–120.

15   See for example: Henderson and Clark, 1990 or Tushman, Anderson and O'Reilly, 1997.

16   Spender, 2006; page 248.

17   See for example the use by P&G of external sources of knowledge for New Product Development in Dodgson, M., Gann, D. and Salter, A. (2006). http://espace.library.uq.edu.au/eserv/UQ:78772/RADM_03603002-2.pdf and Huston, L. and Sakkab, N. (2006) http://randgaenge.net/wp-content/uploads/hbr-connect-and-develop.pdf

18   Hsu and Lim, March 2005, "Knowledge Bridging by Biotechnology Start-ups."

19   Tanu Ghosh, draft dated May 3, 2004; Creating Incentives for knowledge sharing; downloaded from the Internet, p. 11.

20   Nousala et al., 2005; "building Knowledge sharing Communities using Team Expertise Access Maps (TEAM) 17/11/2005. 21 See example Competing on Analytics: The New Science of Winning", Thomas H. Davenport and Jeanne G. Harris (2007), Harvard Business School Press.

22   See discussion in S Raisch, J Birkinshaw - Journal of Management, 2008; and in S Raisch, J Birkinshaw, G Probst, ML Tushman - *Organization Science*, 2009.

23   Russ, M. (2009). Knowledge Management Strategy in the Age of Paradox and Transition, In proceedings of the Annual ISOne-World Conference. Hackney, R. "Emergent Challenges in IS/IT". April 15-17, 2009. DC: Information Institute Publishing. ISBN: 978-1-935160-05-2.

24   See The Singularity Is Near: When Humans Transcend Biology. by Ray Kurzweil (2005)

published by Viking Adult.

[25] See Blue Ocean Strategy: How to Create Uncontested Market Space and Make Competition Irrelevant: W. Chan Kim, Renée Mauborgne (2005) Harvard Business School Press.

[26] Ashby, 1956.

[27] Schwartz, 1991.

[28] See The Black Swan. The Impact of the Highly Improbable. New York: Random House, 2007, by Nassim Nicholas Taleb.

[29] See for example John Storey, Elizabeth Barnett (2000). Knowledge management initiatives: learning from failure. 2000. *Journal of Knowledge Management, 4*(2): 145-156.

[30] See for example: http://money.cnn.com/magazines/fortune/fortune_archive/2007/06/11/100083454/?postversion=2007060116http://www.sonyinsider.com/2006/01/30/sonys-software-czars-big-challenge/http://bits.blogs.nytimes.com/2007/08/16/sony-v-microsoft-with-helmets-the-sequel/ http://g4tv.com/thefeed/blog/post/694922/Sonys-Peter-Dille-Acknowledges-The-Companys-Poor-Marketing.html?utm_source=g4tv&utm_

medium=rssfeeds&utm_campaign=TheFeed http://digg.com/tech_news/Will_the_PS3_save_Sony,_or_be_its_death_knell_

[31] see for example:http://www.tradingmarkets.com/.site/news/Stock%20News/1778925/ http://papers.ssrn.com/sol3/papers.cfm?abstract_id=1146528http://www.mngt.waikato.ac.nz/ejrot/cmsconference/2001/Papers/Management%20Knowledge/Hislop.pdf

[32] Russ, M., & Jones, J. K. (2009). "International Virtual Industry Clusters and SMEs: Early content and process policy recommendations", Paper presented at the 40th MCRSA Annual Conference, Milwaukee, May 28-30, 2009.

[33] "Extreme Toyota. Radical Contradictions That Drive Success at the World's Best Manufacturer" by Emi Osono, Norihiko Shimizu, Hirotaka Tackeuchi with John Kyle Dorton - 2008 - Wiley (p.11).

Chapter 10
Aurora Health Care:
A Knowledge Management Strategy Case Study

Thomas Ginter
Aurora BayCare Medical Center, USA

Jane Root
Aurora Medical Group, USA

ABSTRACT

Aurora Health Care, Wisconsin's largest employer and healthcare provider faces intense competition, consolidation, and reform. Its choice is to view these challenges as opportunities instead of problems. A key component to realizing Aurora's opportunities is an aggressive knowledge management system. They understand that to maximize their potential, they must get the most out of their knowledge management. The purpose of this chapter is to present to you a case study of knowledge management applications in the healthcare industry through the many lenses of Aurora Health Care. First we will describe the background of this accomplished healthcare provider. We will then look at their business and knowledge management strategies. Next will be a review of the major components: core competencies, knowledge base, culture, implementation, and key success indicators.

INTRODUCTION

Successful healthcare providers will employ robust knowledge management systems that promote positive clinical outcomes, align clinical business aims, and enable effective assistance to the surrounding communities. This chapter will describe Aurora Health Care's knowledge management strategy. We will explain Aurora's history with a SWOT analysis completed by the authors. Then we will show the organization's business and knowledge management strategies. This is followed by communicating Aurora Health Care's knowledge management strategy and its major components: core competencies, base, culture, implementation, and key success indicators.

AURORA HEALTH CARE'S HISTORY

In 1984, Aurora Health Care, a not-for-profit Wisconsin integrated health care provider, was created

DOI: 10.4018/978-1-60566-348-7.ch010

around one idea: there is a better way to provide health care. This concept has been a hallmark of the organization and central to its vision. Aurora Health Care believes there is a better way for:

- people to get the care they need in settings that are convenient and comfortable;
- families to receive the services and support they need to lead healthier lives;
- physicians to offer the latest technology and treatment options to their patients;
- talented people working in health care to fulfill their professional callings;
- employers to provide for the health care of their employees, more cost-effectively;
- building healthy communities.

Aurora simplifies the translation of this belief for its employees through a motto of their *#1 Priority*, "Our patients deserve the best care. When we achieve top performance in our clinical quality, patient satisfaction and caregiver engagement, patients receive a better care experience than they can get anywhere else," (Aurora Health Care, 2009a).

Aurora Health Care serves a large geographic base with sites in more than 90 communities throughout eastern Wisconsin, including 13 hospitals, more than 100 clinics and over 130 community pharmacies. In excess of 3,400 physicians are affiliated with Aurora Health Care, including more than 700 who comprise Aurora Medical Group. The many strategic business units that form Aurora Health Care are dedicated to enhancing organizational knowledge. A portion of the Aurora Health Care mission statement is as follows: "We are committed to improving the quality of health care and health outcomes for people today, through the rapid and broad application of current knowledge," (Aurora Health Care, 2009b).

AURORA KNOWLEDGE MANAGEMENT SWOT

An analysis of knowledge management strategy begins with a SWOT analysis to identify if Aurora Health Care is getting the most out of its knowledge management system. Table one represents a knowledge management SWOT analysis of Aurora Health Care.

Strength: Leadership

As identified in their mission statement, Aurora recognizes that organization knowledge is critical to improving the quality of healthcare and health outcomes. Leadership's ability to manage knowhow will help ensure effective performance. Examples of this begin at the top. Aurora has established several multidisciplinary councils to provide leadership and input on strategy, policy,

Table 1. SWOT Analysis of Aurora Health Care, prepared by Tom Ginter and Jane Root, May 2009.

Strengths	Opportunities
• Leadership • Financial Assets • Human Assets • Training • IT Infrastructure • Human Resources & Compensation • Centralized Decision Control	• Innovation • Access to Knowledge • Customer Service • Knowledge Reward System
Weaknesses	**Threats**
• Varied Business Unit Processes • System Interface • Knowledge Management Focus & Control • Best Practices	• Competition • Knowledge Loss • Poor Patient Outcomes

clinical operations, and Care Management initiatives to Aurora Health Care senior leaders. In addition, the councils provide system-wide clinical leadership through collaboration with other senior leadership teams, along with identifying, sharing, and rapidly adopting best practices system-wide around quality, patient loyalty, employee engagement, and financial performance. These councils are the Physician Leadership Council, The Hospital Administrative Council, Aurora Nursing Leadership Council, and One Aurora Team.

To ensure future leaders have a base built upon best practices and value knowledge management, the organization established the Aurora Leadership Academy. This program aims to prepare Aurora's next generation of leaders from among current staff. During a 15-month period, the participants experience a series of leadership and skill-building opportunities. These activities are enhanced through a one-on-one relationship with an individually assigned mentor and through formal networking opportunities.

Strength: Financial Assets

Aurora's total net service revenue grew from $3.2 billion in 2007 to $3.5 billion in 2008. Revenue from inpatient services decreased 2.1% while revenue from outpatient hospital visits and visits to clinics rose 25.5%.

Strength: Human Assets

A good healthcare organization has a mix of highly mobile skilled, unskilled, and professional employees to perform care giving functions. Aurora Health Care is Wisconsin's largest employer. These employees have a strong corporate identity that operates in diverse business units. Leadership has defined a concept called "*Responsible Freedom*" for staff to maximize problem solving to enhance patient care and experience. Responsible freedom supports better ways to provide exceptional, patient centered experience. Each employee needs to know how to take independent action that benefits the customer and organization. Expectations for staff are to learn on a continual basis, be team players, respect diversity, and utilize cross-business unit, cross-cultural experience.

Strength: Training

Aurora Health Care as a whole is committed to continuous learning. The educational resources within the system are vast—and available to all employees. New hires are encouraged to create a "*Learning Plan*" with their immediate supervisor, which validates their scheduled class/educational event activities for the upcoming calendar year. All newly hired leadership positions (supervisor and higher) are required to attend the "Aurora Quest" program. This program is a series of sessions to expose new leaders in the organization to fundamentals as well as enhanced knowledge regarding leadership skills.

A learning culture has been established for staff to optimize best practice applications. The group responsible for this implementation is the Employee and Organizational Development (E&OD) department. The mission of E&OD is to be the collaborator with leaders and staff to identify and respond to training and development needs. This is accomplished by providing the following services:

- Leadership orientation and development programs
- Educational Assistance Program Administration
- In-service Recording Program Administration
- Title IV, U.S. Office of Education Student Financial Aid Program administration for Aurora schools
- Staff orientation and training programs with emphasis in the areas of:
  - Clinical patient care
  - Life Support Education

- ◦ Office Professional Services
- ◦ Service
- ◦ Quality improvement
- ◦ Diversity and cultural competence
- Internal consulting and executive coaching to leadership in the areas of:
  - ◦ Leadership and employee training
  - ◦ Service management
  - ◦ Workforce planning
  - ◦ Career development
  - ◦ Organization development, including:
    - ▪ Caregiver (Employee) Engagement
    - ▪ Team and partnership building and development
    - ▪ Change and conflict management

Strength: IT Infrastructure

Aurora seeks to lead in *the innovative use of IT in the health care market*. In support of this goal, Aurora Information Services works closely with the business groups to define and implement the Information Technology (IT) infrastructure component of Aurora's business strategy. In addition to the major IT projects, linked directly to the Aurora strategy, Information Services supports a large number of regional and departmental projects, and provides key infrastructure and operational support including: system operation and backup, the Aurora network, the help desk, user access and security, and desktop support. The Information Services website serves as a key source of information on many of these activities for both business and staff.

An overview of the electronic tools and technology used across Aurora:

- *Aurora iConnect:* the internal intranet that links all caregivers to information.
- *Employee Connection:* a link that allows individuals access to personalized information regarding compensation, benefits, emergency notification.
- *Learning Connection:* the link that monitors mandatory and elective education and training programs.
- *My Aurora:* the mechanism allowing electronic communication between patients and caregivers. This can be accessed both internally and externally.
- *Web Budgeting:* the electronic application that monitors budget trends and variances.
- *Web Management Reporting:* the electronic financial application with specific access parameters to information.
- *Brass Ring:* software application program that manages employment postings, applications and the applicant review process.
- *Cerner (Electronic Medical Record):* the patient medical record; includes numerous applications, security clearance levels and defined processes.
- *IREQ:* software application program that manages supply and services expense item purchases.
- *Authorization for expenditure (AFE):* software application program that manages capital item purchases.
- *Data Warehouse:* electronic application that collects different data sources through a repository.
- *Biorepository:* electronic application that processes the distribution of all biological products and related clinical information for clinical research and genetic knowledge enhancement.

Strength: Human Resources & Compensation

As with any successful business, Aurora relies on its mission, vision, and values to establish human resource and compensation philosophies. The philosophy supports hiring and retaining qualified and motivated employees to ensure appropriate patient care while managing human resources responsibly. Further elements involve accurate job descriptions, job analysis and evaluations, pay grades with established pay ranges, with individual incentive through performance measures based on merit. Individual workers receive pay incentive through a merit pay program conducted on an annual basis. Employees receive merit increases to their compensation when they meet or exceed job expectations. The annual performance through merit program will occur during scheduled performance evaluations that concentrate on employee general competency for organization, job specific standards, accomplishment on agreed upon goals, and skill competencies.

Strength: Centralized Decision Control

Aurora Health Care strives to mitigate varied business unit practices and ensure consistent best practices are uniformly used across the organization. Their motivation is to:

- Integrate care for patients.
- Standardize and support common practices that benefit patients.
- Constantly challenge one another to find better ways to achieve the highest quality and service for patients without competing with one another for patients and revenue.
- Work together to give people the care needed - when, where, and how patients want to access it.

Centralized decision control due to the enormity of Aurora's geographic span of services is sometimes hindered through centralized decision making. The time and energy to access decision authorities can mitigate how nimble decisions are made in local markets.

Weakness: Varied Business Unit Processes

With strategic business units spread over a large geographic base with sites in over 90 communities throughout eastern Wisconsin, including more than 28,000 employees and over 3,500 physicians, it is easy to appreciate the risk of varied business unit process. The organization works to mitigate mediocre know how by becoming *One Aurora*. This long-term strategy sets the vision to move from common practices partially applied to *Best Care Everywhere*. The vision and mission statements of the organization are well known to the general employee base. What is less known is the specific application for those statements to the everyday work environment. Application of best practices can at times be fragmented.

Weakness: System Interface

Within a large organization, it can be logistically challenging to make the necessary connections between departments and teams. It is essential to include representation from all appropriate entities that could impact any specific initiative. With a broad, comprehensive approach, there is less likely to be unintended consequences on effected departments. To maximize resources, it is important to align work and allow opportunity for various entities input to help support the strategies and initiatives.

Patients have provided feedback to Aurora Health Care that they want health care to be simple. Aurora has designed an integrated health delivery system work to make this possible. Offering a full range of care services, Aurora professionals include physicians, nurses, behavioral health therapists, pharmacists, social workers and other experts, working together to achieve the best outcomes for patients. The goal is to coordinate care across a broad spectrum of services and patient needs.

Weakness: Knowledge Management Focus & Control

The challenge of establishing knowledge management focus and control throughout a large healthcare provider in an industry that evolves daily is challenging. Knowledge management operations such as codification, knowledge oversight, selective encoding, and knowledge purging are typically problem prone.

Weakness: Best Practices

As with most complex organizations Aurora struggles with how to decide the benefit of exploiting known best practices or continuing the investment of further exploration and experimentation.

Opportunity: Innovation

Innovation is used to develop ideas, new opportunities and build the capacity to innovate within the Aurora organization. Aurora's strategic positioning as the premier innovator in the delivery of healthcare mandates that its staff have the capacity to innovate, develop new and better ways and recognize opportunities as they arise. Leadership understands that without new perspectives and a set of tools to help, idea generation can be difficult or even impossible. The innovation process uses a systematic approach that helps overturn beliefs that hinder, uses trends to identify emerging opportunities and evaluates and develops ideas into actionable opportunities.

Aurora Health Care has established innovation tools for idea generation by getting rid of old ideas and helping to get new ideas in play. The tools help employees remove barriers that hold them back when using traditional brainstorming techniques. A common approach and language for idea development help all understand what innovation is and how Aurora Health Care takes action based on a deep understanding of established strategy

and goals. Decisions, once made, are implemented in a flawless manner. Aurora permits the use of creative tension and healthy debate to facilitate change. They know that the best ideas likely come from the organization's employees caring for customers every day. Innovation is ongoing and Aurora constantly measures and improves. To ensure a high level of performance, best practices are reviewed continuously. While patient needs change rapidly, the organization works to anticipate and change with them.

Opportunity: Access to Knowledge

Review of patient, financial and employee data is continuous. Leadership is expected to play an active role in this data review. The opportunity that exists involves the overwhelming amount of data required for collection, analysis, review, communication, and action.

Opportunity: Customer Service

Aurora Health Care has chosen and works toward a care model and philosophy that provides patient-centered care. This patient–centered concept comes in the form of individualized and personalized care developed from the patient's point of view and designed around what patients need to heal.

Opportunity: Knowledge Reward System

Front line staff has expressed the feeling of detachment from knowledge management reward measures. This connection is an opportunity for improvement.

Threat: Competition

Healthcare is very competitive, and the healthcare organization that does not value knowledge, risks loss of market share and efficient operations. Aurora Health Care has competition in each community it provides service.

Threat: Knowledge Loss

Failure to rapidly adapt "One Aurora" may lead to ineffectual encoding, fragmentation and ultimately mediocre know how. To mitigate this risk the organization works to effectively *on-board* new employees. This provides new staff with the necessary information, tools, and resources as they begin work with the organization. A good start for new employees is believed to make a big difference in how effective employees are on the job.

Threat: Poor Patient Outcomes

The healthcare industry is knowledge intense for several reasons. One reason is that the value associated with an individuals' health is of vital importance. It is therefore a tremendous expectation that those within the health industry do whatever necessary to positively contribute to maximizing healthcare delivery. In the focused review of the care management, the primary value is centered on patient outcomes. These patient-centered outcomes translate into the quality of care for the specific physician, entity and system. A subset of the patient condition outcome is patient loyalty. This *loyalty index* is another key component of the knowledge necessary for business success.

KNOWLEDGE MANAGEMENT STRATEGY

Next, the authors will describe in detail, the knowledge management strategy that is currently in place for Aurora Health Care. The strategy is focused on codification and internal development opportunities, along with an effective balance between exploitation and exploration (Russ et al., 2006).

Focus is Long Term

Aurora Health Care as a not-for-profit provider strives to maximize long-term societal benefits of activities and services. This requires a focus on disease prevention and treatment. They are Wisconsin's largest provider of charity care providing more than $25 million in community outreach and free preventive services. Their communities count on them and they feel the obligation to look ahead, preparing themselves, their programs and their facilities to meet the health care needs of tomorrow.

A Complex Knowledge Balancing Act

The identified challenges and responsibilities combine to make the delivery of health care services a complex and delicate balancing act. To address these challenges, the organization invests resources in developing knowledge through information systems that will put patient records at physicians' fingertips to help improve clinical outcomes. It means directing the energies of thousands of caregivers into finding and applying best practices to reduce the human and financial burden of illness. It also involves working with high schools and colleges to introduce and prepare young people for careers in health care. This action helps to alleviate personnel shortages that will cripple health delivery services in the decades ahead.

Addressing the challenges of today and tomorrow requires investing in clinical research and ensuring Aurora is on the forefront of applying new medical knowledge to the prevention and treatment of disease. Aurora Health Care also must enable the benefits from its economies of scale, and expanding services to provide people with the right care in the right place at the right time. It also calls for investing in the renovation and construction of facilities for tomorrow, even in the face of criticism that these investments contribute to today's health care cost burden.

Being a not-for-profit health care organization means Aurora Health Care must strive to balance what's in the long-term best interest of the people they serve, just as a doctor would for a patient.

Knowledge Codification

As stated, Aurora Health Care will only be satisfied when they give patients better access, better service, and better results than they can get anywhere else. They believe that working together, the people of Aurora will find a better way. This consistent approach reinforces and allows:

- Rapid adaptability
- Flexibility and efficient change
- Improved communications through common language

Aurora Health Care believes a consistent approach allows innovation, generates ideas to find better ways, overturns beliefs that hinder success, and uses trends to identify opportunities. Planning includes structured approaches and tools to design or establish processes. Data and IT tools are used to improve processes and reduce or eliminate waste. Control can also be used to detect and reduce or eliminate sporadic problems.

Internal Knowledge Development

Internal knowledge development is a key element toward the knowledge management strategy for Aurora Health Care. The organization has developed knowledge role definitions for leaders. They have created a structure for shared learning to drive improved results. This is accomplished by identifying subject champions; linking system teams to site teams to share results and lessons learned; establishing a team of experts as a problem solving resource; and developing and communicating feedback mechanisms on specific indicators.

They have also developed 60-day rapid action plans to improve outcomes, process, and efficien-

cies. Sites in the organization identify issues. A team is formed to review and provide feedback on the identified opportunities. Once the 60-day action plans are developed, the plans are made visible within the organization and system.

Balanced Knowledge Exploration/Exploitation

Aurora Health Care maintains a structured utilization/innovation scheme that applies focus on exploring new knowledge and exploiting knowledge that exists while codifying that knowledge. This knowledge is used to support new servicing of markets to achieve higher process and product effectiveness.

Next, the frameworks for connecting the business and KM strategies with the organization's core competencies and key success indicators (figure 1) will be described.

BUSINESS STRATEGY

The first building block described will be Aurora's business strategy.

Business Objectives Support Community Benefit

As a not-for-profit health care provider, Aurora has one overriding goal and that is to provide community benefit. They set a variety of business objectives to meet that goal. These objectives fall into two broad categories: finding better ways to work, and creating better value to offer patients, caregivers and communities. As they identify and achieve specific objectives in these areas, they succeed in generating the margin they need to fulfill the mission. At the same time, they keep moving closer to fulfilling the vision of providing people with better access, better service and better results than they can get anywhere else. They come full circle from mission to margin, and back again to

Figure 1. Aurora framework connection for business knowledge management (Source: by authors, prepared in May 2009, based on Russ et al., 2010).

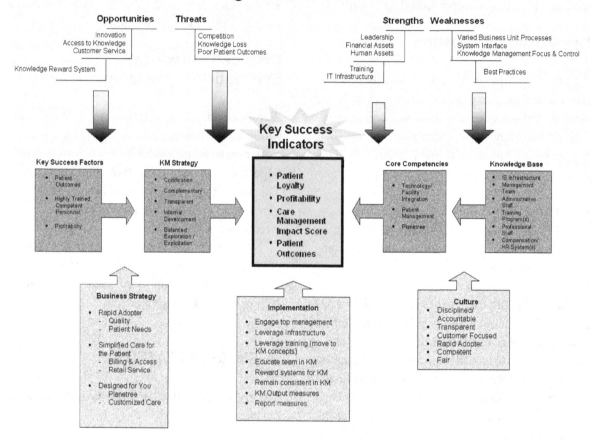

the reason they exist, which is to improve the well being of the communities they serve.

Aurora Health Care's 2007 Strategic Plan defines their first key actions to successfully accomplish their strategy in the years to come:

- Advance Care Management
- Become One Aurora
- Develop a Patient Point of View
- Continue to Strengthen Aurora's Financial Performance

Three of these key actions have been mapped to their Long-term Strategy roadmap. Financial performance provides the foundation to achieve

their Long-term Strategy. Strategic objectives come directly from Aurora Health Care's new Long-term Strategy:

- Simplified Care for the Patient
- Designed for the Customer
- Rapid Adopter

First Key Action: Advance Care Management – Integrate Care Management across Care Continuum and achieve their #1 Priority

Measure top performance in quality – their #1 Priority – in the following ways:

- The Premier clinical performance measures, a database of the top performing hospitals in the country, provide Aurora Health Care with both quality and cost data for nine major diagnoses. Although a hospital-based measure, they will only be successful in achieving top quartile performance by utilizing the care continuum of their integrated delivery system and by everyone reducing costs.

- Aurora Health Care continues to track Care Management Impact Score. Similar to a school report card, each of their Care Management initiatives, their safety efforts, and their quality improvement efforts are scored as an "A", "B", "C", or "F" which, like a grade point average, earns points of 4, 3, 2, or 0.

- In addition to the #1 Priority measures, Aurora Health Care will provide a single accurate medication list to all Aurora care providers to improve patient safety and to simplify care for their patients.

Second Key Action: Become "One Aurora," with 3 Areas of Focus

- Integrate clinical service lines across the system
- Simplify and design care for their patients
- Adopt clinical innovation into clinical practice

The first area of focus under becoming "One Aurora" is to integrate clinical service lines across the system. Currently Aurora Health Care's clinical service lines have been developed from a facility, market or regional perspective. At times, this has resulted in best practices being partially applied, fragmented care, confusion for patients, and differing prioritization or competition within the system.

The second area of focus under becoming "One Aurora" is to simplify and design care for patients. During the discovery phase of Aurora Health Care's Long-term Strategy work, they obtained hundreds of insights from their patients. Aurora Health Care heard how they could simplify and design their processes to better meet their patients' needs and selected the first five (5) system processes to improve in 2007:

- Patient billing
- Patient registration
- Managing resources responsibly (specific focus to be determined)
- Medicare length of stay
- Appropriately utilizing their diagnostic and inpatient resources

The third area of focus under becoming "One Aurora" is to adopt clinical innovation into clinical practice. Aurora Health Care will continue to integrate their clinical research to support the discovery and adoption of new knowledge within clinical service lines.

Third Key Action: Develop a Patient Point of View, with 3 Areas of Focus

- Adopt and embrace Planetree
- Provide care to a defined patient group in a way that meets their needs
- Integrate retail into care delivery locations to better meet patients' needs

The first area of focus under developing a patient point of view is to adopt and embrace Planetree (a philosophy of patient-centered care in a healing environment). Aurora Health Care will measure success by:

- Increasing the percent of people who would recommend Aurora Health Care to family and friends (patient loyalty index).
- Increasing the percent of their patients who perceive that they received care in a

coordinated, simple, and easy to use way.
- Increasing the system-wide employee engagement index by 5%.

The second area of focus under developing a "patient point of view" is to provide care to a defined patient group in a way that meets their needs. Health care typically groups patients based on their demographics (age – senior services, sex – women's health, etc.) or by their medical diagnosis (oncology, orthopedics, cardiac, etc.). An additive way of understanding their patients is by addressing their needs, behaviors, or preferences. Aurora Health Care is experimenting with new models of care delivery that include the focus on the needs of their patients, starting with offerings specifically asked for by very busy (time-starved) families. They will measure if these offerings make a difference in patients choosing Aurora for their needed services.

The third area of focus under "Develop a Patient Point of View" is to integrate retail into care delivery locations to better meet their patients' needs. How to integrate retail: Aurora Health Care's patients' experiences do not stop at their doors – they need to re-define and expand concepts of patient care beyond the hospital or physician visit. At times, patients and their families need to acquire retail products to support the care they provided. Consistent with their Long-term Strategy, they need to ensure the patient's experience in acquiring these products is as easy and convenient as possible.

Fourth Key Action: Continue to Strengthen Aurora's Financial Performance

Aurora Health Care will improve profitability by increasing the operating margin by 0.1% in 2009 from base operations excluding start up facilities.

Next the core competencies will be described.

Core Competencies

Specific core competencies vary by position and job code. The general competencies for many caregivers include: understanding of clinical conditions, data collection, financial processes, medical records, use of information systems and communication skills. Intensity and level of expertise can be defined via the specific job standards associated with each defined role within the organization. As an example, a core competency within the Care Management is the ability to utilize the large amount of data they have exposure to and add value to it for the patients they serve.

The Planetree philosophy of care that is unique to Aurora Health Care (within business markets) can provide advantages as well. Planetree is a philosophy and model of personalizing, humanizing, and demystifying healthcare. This connection with a patient-centered focus allows capturing loyalty via the sharing of best practices through this international organization. All caregivers throughout the system, regardless of their actual direct patient contact, are accountable for knowledge and understanding regarding the Planetree philosophy.

Additionally, there is opportunity to capture a business lead on utilization of a *Just Culture* approach to patient safety. This approach focuses on investigation of the true cause of any error—individual, process, or system failure. Highlighting this as a cultural shift would be seen as a positive step. Even though many organizations can validate their processes for patient safety, this cultural focus sets the tone for significant system impact.

KNOWLEDGE BASE

In the complex environment of healthcare, a solid base to support administrative, declarative, procedural, and analytical knowledge is necessary. Aurora Health Care satisfies these base requirements through developing an intense information

Table 2. Aurora Health Care IT/IS knowledge management systems (Source: Developed by the authors in May 2009, based on Gottschalk, 2002)

Categories	Core Knowledge	Advanced Knowledge	Innovative Knowledge
Administrative Knowledge	-Microsoft Word -Microsoft Excel -Microsoft Office -IDXware -Lotus email -Accounting System -Capital Expense System	-Press Ganey Patient Loyalty Database -The Joint Commission Website	-National Committee for Quality Assurance Benchmark Database -Risk Management Database -Employee Injury Database
Declarative Knowledge	-Cerner PowerChart Office -Center for Medicare and Medicaid website -Wisconsin Administrative Code website -Wisconsin Department of Regulation and Licensing website -The Joint Commission on Healthcare Accreditation Standards -OSHA Codes	-Cerner patient database -Cerner report writer -Wisconsin Collaborative for Healthcare Quality website -National Committee for Quality Assurance website -American Medical Association website -Code Libraries -Aurora Health Care Experts	External Best Procedures
Procedural Knowledge	-Aurora iConnect internal website -Aurora Policy and Procedure website link	-Wisconsin Collaborative for Healthcare Quality website -National Committee for Quality Assurance website -American Medical Association website -CINAHL (Cumulative Index to Nursing and Allied Health Literature)	-Up-to-date -Zynx -Center for Disease Control website
Analytical Knowledge	-Lotus Sametime -Care Management AHC system database	-Institute for Healthcare Improvement website -Cancer, Trauma and Perinatal Registry databases	-Premier clinical performance website -Micromedex

system infrastructure, and providing for a vision, understanding, and commitment to building a solid knowledge-base, as well as, with a firm development of knowledge roles and skills.

IS Infrastructure

A review of the information technology and systems utilized by the organization clearly indicates that Aurora Health Care relies heavily on both internal and external knowledge-based-systems. In the highly regulated environment of healthcare, the sharing of electronic information (data and meta-data) is a business necessity. The reimbursement system alone mandates compliance with electronic sharing of information. A positive impact of these requirements is that

healthcare organizations can identify actions and opportunities for improved care and processes. When the opportunities promote action, there is value created for the patient and organization through knowledge management.

IT / IS Knowledge Based Systems

Knowledge Management Vision

The vision of Aurora Health Care is centered on the single idea: there is a better way to provide health care. The following segment of the vision describes their knowledge management philosophy:

"We are committed to improving the quality of health care and health outcomes for people today,

through the rapid and broad application of current knowledge. We are also engaged in the education of health care professionals, and the ongoing quest for new knowledge through medical research, in order to contribute to the quality of health care in the future," (Aurora Health Care, 2009a).

Knowledge Management Understanding and Commitment

Within the employee base of the Aurora Health Care there is a strong understanding of the need for data and information review. There is continued assessment of the value this knowledge brings even when it is not commonly referred to or understood as Knowledge Management. Messages come from senior leadership for constant improvement and to maintain steady progress. This information is shared throughout every segment of the organization. The organization has identified knowledge champions that manage knowledge. These champions are the Chief Information Officer (CIO) and Vice President of Quality and Research. These two individuals lead the system teams that organize the work within many departments, specifically the technology and quality areas. Although very high-ranking employees, they are accessible and available to nearly every employee. From a clinician point of view they are well known. Another knowledge champion would be the Chief Financial Officer (CFO). This person is responsible for assisting all leadership with availability and understanding of financial data. The system also has established knowledge teams who collect and sort through data and processes involved in analyzing knowledge information for codification. There are local business unit teams for various initiatives that feed into larger regional or system teams.

Knowledge Roles and Skills

Development and implementation of new knowledge specific roles occur at the following levels:

The Individual
The development of new knowledge specific roles is truly based on individual motivation and interest. Every employee has the opportunity to identify areas in which they desire growth. This could be basic computer skills, to advanced analysis and interpretation of data. Based off of specific job duties and responsibilities, an employee is challenged to create their "Learning Plan" to improve their knowledge and skill set.

Team
Team development of new roles would be visible when a new initiative is identified. There would be opportunity to engage and lead the effort to establish protocols and processes regarding the identified initiative. There is significant support to have teams bring forward new ideas and share "best practices." There is recognition and support when an idea or process that has positive impact to the patient and/or organization is identified. These sharing opportunities can originate at the local and regional level, but are often taken to system teams.

Organizational
As information technology and quality initiatives continue to expand, so does the organization's need to respond to those challenges. The new perspective that comes with new leadership can quickly help the entire organization review old ways of thinking. This pause for review does not require sweeping change; it may only validate the right path.

Inter-Organizational
Within Aurora Health Care there is opportunity to network and engage in collaboration both inside

and outside of the system. The system has both hospital and clinic based entities, which create opportunities for unique collaboration, learning and sharing. As a large health care organization, there is also the availability to work with outside systems for comparison and learning. This type of knowledge is limited due to the industry's reliance on regulatory agencies. Much of the data and information collected is subject to their review. This includes quality data and also financial data that impacts the business at all levels.

KNOWLEDGE MANAGEMENT CULTURE

Knowledge Philosophy

Within Aurora Health Care, there is significant effort to standardize and share best practices. Becoming "One Aurora" means that care will be integrated, with the goal of exceptional results for the patient. This is part of the long-term strategy that every employee receives training and education.

The philosophy of care is *patient-centered*. This means that all staff actions can be linked to the impact to the patient. Considerable time is focused on the specific quality outcomes employees are charged with obtaining. The focus on those outcomes and goals supports established behavioral expectations. The behaviors relate not only to individual expectations, but the expectations of departments, and strategic business units. The entities are established within various markets and regions as well as the overall system.

Knowledge Management Reward System

The reward system for achievement of knowledge management goals is seen at various levels. An example is the *Care Management Impact Score* which is a measure that combines both hospital and clinic based measures into one score. This score is part of the performance review of every employee within the Aurora Health Care system. The final score has an impact on the merit increase of an employee on an annual basis. This financial tie to initiatives places significant emphasis on achievement of the goals. Published accomplishments can be viewed on the Aurora internal website as well as in numerous mailings and publications.

Knowledge Networks

There is significant corporate support of informal networks. Staff at all levels is encouraged to connect and interact with peers in other regions and outside of the Aurora Health Care system. There are routine system based meetings, which promotes internal relationship building. It is a frequent event for staff to check with other internal and external parties for ideas on processes, solutions, or validation of an identified problem. These calls, emails and exchanges with colleagues are seen as value added.

KNOWLEDGE MANAGEMENT IMPLEMENTATION

The healthcare industry is knowledge intense for many reasons. Primarily, the public values individual health and the expectations for those within the healthcare industry are to positively contribute to healthcare delivery. This expectation requires effective implementation of knowledge.

Levers that Support Knowledge Management

Top Management Engagement

An expectation defined by Aurora Health Care leadership is that caregivers will continue to work together, taking responsibility for their actions, fulfilling their promises and helping one another to do their best work for their patients, because they believe in accountability, teamwork and respect. This value statement includes the following core beliefs:

- People are their greatest asset
- Aurora Health Care embraces their promise to their employees
- They are accountable to each other, to their patients, and to their communities
- They work with each other and with their patients and their families
- They welcome diversity of ideas and opinions
- They respect their patients' wishes. They effectively work with their patients and with each other within the context of cultural beliefs, behaviors and needs (cultural competence)

The organization has defined key expectations of its leadership team:

- Instill confidence, creativity and passion in others by
  ○ Building my own credibility, meaning: walking the walk, keeping promises, practicing the golden rule, treating staff fairly and equitably
  ○ Accentuating the positives in people's ability, and not dwelling on weaknesses
  ○ Praising employees for their efforts
  ○ Providing opportunities for growth - special projects, etc.
- Provide a vision with defined expectations and time frames
  ○ State clear expectations
  ○ Provide the "why" when outlining responsibilities
  ○ Challenge staff to go beyond their expected potential
  ○ Provide guidance in times of uncertainty

- Provide feedback regularly and hold employees accountable
  ○ Let staff know you are there and that you are interested in them
  ○ Seek to find times when staff are doing things right
  ○ Use informal coaching and just–in-time feedback
  ○ Give consistent, timely feedback
- Be fair and apply established practices consistently when addressing employee relation issues
  ○ Don't play favorites – apply rules and expectations to all staff
  ○ Don't assume guilt or fault during investigations – consider all sides until it's time to evaluate
  ○ Listen to all staff and all sides
- Treat others with dignity and respect by
  ○ Separating the behaviors from the individual – poor or inappropriate behavior does NOT give one license to treat the employee in a disrespectful or degrading manner. Disciplines and even "for cause" terminations should be delivered with dignity.
  ○ Remember the Aurora Promise to their employees. Aurora Health Care will provide them with the tools and resources to have them be successful in their jobs, to provide feedback and to be fair.

Highly Trained, Competent Personnel

As an organization, the employees, referred to as caregivers, are considered Aurora's greatest asset. To help define the commitment to the caregiver, a *"Promise"* was developed. It reads as follows:

"We promise to listen to and implement better ideas, recognize and reward contributions, offer competitive pay and benefits, and continue

building a wide range of career opportunities. We pledge to explain business issues and strategies, to anticipate and respond to change, and to provide needed technology and information. We will use resources wisely, operate cost-effectively, and maintain a sound financial base so we will be able to make investments in the future — improving health care for all of us. Together, we find new ways to deliver health care, from the simplest of preventive services to the most advanced, life-saving treatments. Every day each of us needs to use our knowledge, experience and creativity to find better ways of doing things. We improve current ways of providing care, combining science with common sense, and embrace best practices — setting new standards for quality care. Aurora's strength stems from the teamwork and collaboration among a talented and diverse group of professionals. That's why it's critical that Aurora continue to attract, keep and motivate talented people. Aurora provides the tools and resources we need to find better ways, and recognizes our successes. Working together, the people of Aurora can challenge conventional wisdom, solve problems through teamwork, develop innovative ideas, and implement best practices. Each caregiver is part of a leading-edge organization, doing important work for people and their families. We're passionate about caring, we're striving to provide better service, and every day...we find better ways," (Aurora Health Care, 2009a).

Human Resource Promise and Rewards

As an organization, everything Aurora does must be focused on providing the best patient care experience, which includes creating an engaging environment for their staff. The Aurora Pulse survey provides caregivers the opportunity to tell leadership how they are meeting this expectation. By asking caregivers to take the survey, leadership makes an implied contract that those results will be used to make Aurora a best place to work and to achieve great results for patients. They have committed to an annual survey and using the four-step *Making a Difference* process to provide:

- leaders with feedback and insight on how well caregivers think Aurora Health Care is doing in living the values, achieving the mission and vision, and following the strategy.
- caregivers with the opportunity to share their opinions regarding topics such as communication, recognition, and personal growth.
- caregivers with an opportunity to become engaged in discussions regarding survey results and development of action plans to improve and enhance current processes.

Caregivers have a chance to impact their day-to-day operations as they follow-through on the action plans and see the results of their activities.

Each Aurora Health Care caregiver has the opportunity to identify specific individual goals they can strive to accomplish per the corporate performance review process. Goal selection and accomplishment can be related to personal growth (learning) as it pertains to their specific role and job function. In addition, there are performance goals that are set via the department, region and system levels. There can be a monetary reward based on accomplishment.

From a recognition perspective, there is an established employee recognition program that allows acknowledgement of exemplary service or work. This program allows for the caregiver to be acknowledged in a setting of their peers, with specifics as to their accomplishment. In addition, there is a lapel pin called the Aurora Star that can be worn as a constant reminder.

Team recognition is often highlighted in the corporate messaging that occurs via the internal intranet system. The reward systems for achievement of care management goals are seen at various levels. The system *Care Management Impact Score* is a measure that combines both hospital and clinic based measures into one score. That score is part of the performance review of every employee within the Aurora Health Care system. The final system score has an impact on the merit increase on an annual basis. This financial tie to the initiatives places significant emphasis on achievement of the goals.

Other recognition for achievement is noted for individual physicians as well as regional and market teams. The published accomplishments can be viewed on the Aurora internal website as well as in numerous mailings and publications. Whenever possible, most leaders seek to publicly praise and recognize individuals for their contributions during meetings with peers.

A criticism of the reward system by front line staff is that they do not always feel they can have a significant direct impact on some of the measures. The clinical specifics involved in many of the initiatives are physician led. If the practitioner makes decisions that could change the overall goal achievement, front line staff feels disempowered. The leadership message that has helped to overcome this criticism is that every employee has the opportunity to contribute in some way to each and every goal.

Report Measures

Healthcare is ever changing. As most industries deal with technology changes, the research involved in disease management and cures is significant in meeting patient expectations to have the latest diagnostics and treatments available. This requires Aurora to maximize the ability to turn data and information into value-added knowledge.

A subset of the patient condition outcome is patient loyalty. The *Loyalty Index* is another key component of knowledge the organization requires for business success.

Another key benefit for the organization is financial stability. When Aurora Health Care manages the current patient population with a best practice approach, they have maximized that patient encounter and delivered the right care at the right time. This also translates to resources used wisely. Minimizing waste would be seen as a contribution toward future investments in strategies for continuous improvement.

Exploiting New Knowledge

Aurora Health Care is constantly being challenged to maintain the highest level of clinical care knowledge and standards. For the patient, this translates into high-end care within their local environment. To maximize this message, they rely on supporting technologies. To be considered "innovative" and "cutting edge" requires people, processes and equipment.

Leveraging Knowledge at All Levels

Nearly all teams within Aurora, feel that information can come from many sources and levels—the patient, the employee, the system and externally. The size of Aurora Health Care provides connectivity that is difficult to quantify. The organization has the opportunity to study a massive patient population base along with its employee group. They can look for value in small, intricate details, or large system processes.

Integrating Knowledge From Various Areas

The integration of knowledge for Care Management is founded in the structure. With the regional teams, there is clear flow of data/information and subsequent knowledge to the system and from the system. Aurora Health Care improved knowledge of company goals at all levels by linking each employee to the email system. This was a major success factor in improving the sharing of information. The corporate strategies, goals and initiatives are part of that knowledge. Although every employee does not have access to their own computer, they do have computer access close to their work environment. The cultural adjustment in this initiative involved clarifying the expectation that electronic communication was a standard, not an option.

Knowledge Used as Competitive Advantage

The organization's large patient base provides a tremendous amount of data and information. If used effectively, that information can provide significant advantages in looking at what a large number of patients want. Aurora Health Care was not the first healthcare entity to embrace LEAN principles to gain leverage over competition. Maximizing operational efficiency can be impressive for the patients—they see organization, communication and connectivity.

PROCESSES TO IMPLEMENT KNOWLEDGE MANAGEMENT

Key Points for Success

- Engage top management in knowledge management concepts and practices.
- Increase knowledge management awareness – begin small – utilize high priority project.
- Leverage existing infrastructure and identify hardware/software and information gaps.
- Leverage current training and consolidate to knowledge management concepts.
- Select Implementation team (provide education on knowledge management concepts).
- Create a CoP for small project.
- Adjust culture and knowledge management strategies through incentive and rewards.

- Utilize consistent approach.
- Allocate the resources and define the time-frame for the project.
- Have knowledge management outputs related to:
  - Quality – Performance
  - Financial improvement
  - Liability reduction
- Validate and report the results.
- Develop a pool of experts necessary for knowledge management applications at Aurora. Examples include the following:
  - **Six Sigma:** Six Sigma is a disciplined and rigorous analytical approach to quality improvement. It is typically used to decrease variation and eliminate defects for key business processes. Six Sigma is a proven methodology for improving the quality and financial performance of businesses.
  - **Flawless Implementation:** The Flawless Implementation model is used to help ensure that Aurora Health Care's opportunity to succeed is not by chance but rather by consistently and appropriately applying a disciplined management process. The Flawless Implementation model focuses on identifying and sharing lessons learned and best practices, ultimately improving quality in all that they do. The model has a well-defined cycle of four phases that include Plan, Brief, Implement and Debrief.
  - **Tools for Innovation:**
    - **Closely held beliefs:** All industries have closely held beliefs about, "how things are done here." The beliefs tool helps to view Aurora Health Care's organization from the customers' perspectives in order to identify the deeply held beliefs and conventions that drive their

behavior. By identifying the belief, they can "flip" it to see what other facets emerge and what opportunities exist with a fresh eye.

- **Trends and Convergences:** Trends can affect what will happen to a business today and in the future. When more than one trend converges with others, it can create even greater changes. The trends tool helps them to learn how to recognize and take advantage of trend convergences and generate opportunities with the new insights.

- **Idea Generation:** Combining multiple insights and discoveries generates ideas. By exploring the intersection of various insights, Aurora Health Care begins to see things with new eyes and new opportunities emerge. By clustering related ideas, larger domains of opportunities emerge.

- **Idea Elaboration:** Not all ideas are good ones. By taking an idea "through the wringer" it helps to more clearly define the idea and its scope and to assess the risks and benefits of the idea before implementing it. The idea elaboration tool guides an idea through the evaluation process to determine if it is worthwhile.

- **Statistical Process Control (SPC):** Once Innovation and/or Quality Planning and/or Quality Improvement work has been accomplished it is critical that the new process(s) are managed so that they are safe, stable, predictable and capable of meeting customer requirements. Statistical Process Control (SPC) is used to determine how a process is performing. Statistical Process Control, through the use of control charts, serves to reveal the "Voice of the Process," a term used to describe what the process is telling them. Time-ordered sequence data is used to objectively and statistically determine how a process is performing.

- **Baldrige Criteria** (Malcolm Baldrige National Quality Award) Baldrige is a business model used to evaluate an organization's approaches to addressing key business processes and their connection to results achieved. Consistent approaches provide for the alignment of resources to improve communication through a common language, productivity and effectiveness in achieving strategic goals. The criteria are intended to ensure that the strategies used are balanced among customers, objectives or goals.

The Baldrige criteria are not prescriptive in what tools an organization uses or how they are deployed. In other words, it does not say that an organization needs to use Six Sigma or Plan Do Study Act. The selection of tools, techniques and systems usually depends on factors such as size, organizational relationships, staff capabilities and responsibilities. What the criteria look for is systematic approaches used consistently throughout the organization that achieve the desired or expected results.

- **LEAN**

  The purpose of LEAN is to identify and eliminate waste in order to facilitate process improvement and ensure that all activities create value to the customer. LEAN is a process used to create customer value – goods and services with higher quality and fewer errors or defects. This includes creating and/or improving value to customer, eliminating non-value added activities (waste), increasing efficiency and reducing cost, standardizing processes, reducing hand-offs, and improving quality and cycle time.

- **Plan Do Study Act** (PDSA)

  The PDSA process is a defined process for improvement. Through a series of steps each change is analyzed using data to assess outcomes in achievement of desired results.

KNOWLEDGE MANAGEMENT KEY SUCCESS INDICATORS

The Patient Loyalty Index

Today's health care consumer is much more savvy than ever in the history of health care delivery. They have certain expectations and it's our job to understand what those expectations are and work to exceed those expectations. The most important reason Aurora Health Care believes in increasing loyalty is that it's just the right thing to do. Aurora is in the business of caring for people. Each employee is considered a caregiver, as Aurora

Health Care strives to personalize, humanize and demystify the patient's experience.

When Aurora can provide this patient-centered experience, it means they are providing the patient and their loved ones with what they need during their healing process. This results in loyal patients who trust their care. Patients use more of their services and they tell others about Aurora Health Care.

The benefits of patient loyalty are numerous and include:

- Increased revenue
- Positive word of mouth
- More donations to hospital
- Increased referral behavior
- Resistance to competition
- Increased use of other Aurora services

Aurora measures loyalty via review of key questions on their patient satisfaction survey. The Loyalty Index is the mean score of the *likelihood to recommend* Aurora Health Care to their family and friends on the Press Ganey surveys or *definitely yes* on the Hospital Consumer Assessment of Healthcare Providers and Systems (HCAHPS) survey. The mean score is closely monitored because research indicates that it is a good predictor of loyalty.

PROFITABILITY

As with most business entities, financial objectives are established. The big-picture focus within Aurora is to generate enough margin to accomplish its not-for-profit mission. The impact of effectively managing resources is a direct tie to its knowledge management. The immediate benefit of active knowledge management is the direct impact to each patient. The organization can see "results" when processes, protocols and guidelines are followed. This translates into a better quality of life for the patient as well as fiscal accountability for the organization. When resources are managed well, Aurora Health Care is able to focus funds on future opportunities such as disease prevention and research. Prudent financial management also allows capital fund availability to support high-cost IT and medical equipment technology needs.

Care Management Impact Score

As identified in early portions of this chapter, the commitment to quality care is evident throughout Aurora Health Care. A measurement of the outcomes related to quality initiatives is demonstrated via an assigned score. How that score is calculated is as follows:

Each of the twenty-seven (27) care management initiatives, safety efforts, and the quality improvement efforts are scored as an A, B, C, or F based on performance. If Aurora meets national targets, it is graded a B, if it is better than national targets, it is graded an A. If it is less than internal targets, it is graded a C or F. Like a grade point average, they earn 4 points for an A, 3 points for a B, 2 points for a C, and 0 points for an F. All points are summed and then divided by the number of initiatives to equal a care management impact (grade point average).

The care management impact score is like a grade point average for performance on clinical improvement and safety efforts. National targets/averages are set at a "B" level or a 3.0 grade point average. Their objective is to be at a 3.1 level or higher. The stretch objective is to be at a 3.4 level or higher.

Aurora believes that continuous support of a learning environment will support continued scores higher than the national targets.

PATIENT OUTCOMES

Care management is the philosophy of improving patient care through prevention, early detection and disease management. The purpose of care management is to keep patients healthy and out of the hospital. If hospitalization is required, patients can be assured that the care received will be safe and efficient. Successful implementation requires a focused, coordinated approach to delivering health care in the right place, at the right time, for the right price and with the best possible results.

Aurora's care management is unique. In its integrated health care system, patient care can be fully coordinated among many different providers, facilities, and services on an on-going basis. Aurora's care management provides staff with knowledge management tools and immediately accessible information they need to obtain the best results for patients by employing the best practices in medical care and treatment.

The Care Management approach to patient care is the foundation of how the Aurora system measures patient outcomes. The continuous monitoring of key indicators allows adjustment and reaction to achieve the best possible outcome. Comprehensive data is available at individual physician, site, and department levels. This allows for customized analysis, which promotes continuous learning.

Each Care Management initiative has specific goals. These goals are based on research-proven best practices from around the country. They regularly keep track of progress in achieving these goals. A number of national organizations focus on healthcare quality measures. They report Aurora Health Care results along with those of other participating hospitals and health care systems.

SUMMARY

Aurora Health Care's business strategy is based on objectives to support its benefit to the community. These objectives translate into key actions of advanced care management, aligning business practices across its organization, conducting business from a patient's point-of-view, and strengthening its financial performance. These key actions are mapped into a long-term strategy of simplified care for the patient, service designed by the customer, and rapid adoption of best practices.

The knowledge management strategy is structured to provide knowledge balance, codification, and internal development opportunities, along with effective exploitation and exploration. As a not-for-profit healthcare provider, Aurora Health Care strives to maximize long-term societal benefits of activities and services. This requires a long-term focus on disease prevention and treatment. A complex knowledge-balancing act of identified challenges and responsibilities is structured to ensure the best long-term interest of the people they serve. They believe that working together the people of Aurora will "find a better way." A consistent knowledge codification approach reinforces this belief and allows them to rapidly adopt innovation, be flexible with efficient change, and use common language to improve communication. Internal knowledge development is a key element toward knowledge management strategy at Aurora Health Care. The organization has developed knowledge roles and functions for leaders. They have a structure for shared learning to drive results. Aurora maintains a structured utilization/innovation scheme that applies focus on exploring new knowledge and exploits knowledge that exists while codifying that knowledge.

Core competencies are important to any knowledge management system. Aurora Health Care ensures core competencies that relate to operations, customer service, and safety. Specific core competencies vary by position and job code. Among the general competencies for many Aurora employees are: understanding clinical conditions, data collection, financial processes, medical records, use of information systems, and common communication skills. Aurora Health Care utilizes a philosophy of care that makes a connection with a patient-centered-focus. This supports capturing patient loyalty via the shar-

ing of best practices in customer service. Aurora also uses a "just culture" method toward patient safety. This approach focuses on investigation of the true cause of any error made by an individual, process, or system.

In the complex environment of healthcare, a solid base system that supports administrative, declarative, procedural, and analytical knowledge is necessary. Aurora Health Care satisfies these base requirements through an intense information system infrastructure, knowledge, vision, understanding, and commitment, with a firm development of knowledge roles and skills. Aurora relies on both internal and external knowledge based systems. The sharing of electronic information (data and meta-data) is a must in healthcare. Knowledge management is identified in Aurora Health Care's Vision Statement. This vision is centered on the single idea: there is a better way to provide healthcare. The organization has instilled a strong understanding of the need for data and information review. Aurora's senior leadership requires constant improvement ensuring that the organization maintains steady progress. This message is shared throughout every segment of the organization. Knowledge roles and skills development, and implementation of new knowledge occurs at the individual, team, organization, and inter-organizational levels.

Knowledge management culture is an important ingredient to the strength of Aurora Health Care. Knowledge management philosophy, reward system, and networking, support the knowledge management culture. Aurora seeks exceptional results for its patients. All employees receive training on how to standardize and share best practices throughout the organization. Employees are incentivized toward knowledge management as a part of their annual merit increase. Knowledge management key success indicators are incorporated into each employee's annual performance review. This formal tie places significant emphasis on achievement. Staff at all levels are encouraged to connect and interact with peers inside and outside of Aurora.

The healthcare industry is knowledge intense for many reasons. Primarily, the public values individual health and the expectation for those within the healthcare industry is to positively contribute to healthcare delivery. This expectation requires the effective implementation of knowledge. Aurora Health Care knowledge management implementation begins with its levers that support knowledge. Top management has expectations for all staff regarding teamwork, responsibility of actions, fulfilling promises, and helping one another to do their best work for the patient. Human resource policies and practices support implementation through formal employee feedback and recognition of exemplary service and work. Aurora Health Care is constantly challenged to maintain the highest level of clinical care knowledge and standards. To meet this challenge, they rely on supportive technologies. Employees within Aurora feel that information can come from many sources and levels, such as the patient, employee, organization, and outside the organization. It is imperative to have the knowledge management systems that leverage this information into actual implementation. They use many tools to process and implement knowledge. Examples include Six Sigma, flawless implementation, tools for innovation, statistical process control, Baldrige Criteria, LEAN principles, and Plan-Study-Do-Act.

ACKNOWLEDGMENT

The authors wish to thank Philip Mattek for his work on the Aurora Framework Connection for Business KM Source (Figure 1), displayed on page 12.

Thank you to Patrick Falvey, Ph.D., Senior Vice President & Chief Integration Officer for Aurora Health Care for his support of this project.

The authors also wish to thank Kim M. Stencil for her assistance in editing the aforementioned information.

The authors wish also to thank Kelly Anklam for her assistance in editing this chapter.

Finally, a special thank you goes to the editor of this book for his thorough feedback and insightful comments.

As always, the authors take the responsibility for any mistakes.

REFERENCES

Aurora Health Care (2009). *2007 Strategic Plan.* Retrieved from https://iconnect.aurora.org/ DotNetNuke/Default.aspx?tabid=2324

Aurora Health Care (2009). *2009-2011 Strategic Plan Chart.* Retrieved from http://heiwebaz031. aurora.org/DotNetNuke/portals/216/2009-2011_ Strategic_Plan_Chart%20Final.pdf

Aurora Health Care (2009). *Aurora and the quality of health care.* Retrieved from http://www. aurorahealthcare.org/aboutus/quality/details/ default.aspx

Aurora Health Care (2009). *Aurora at a Glance.* Retrieved from http://iconnect.aurora.org/ portal/ default.do?appId=EB416

Aurora Health Care (2009). *Aurora Health Care – 2008 Report to the Community.* Retrieved from http://www.aurorahealthcare.org/aboutus/annualreports/2008/financial_ stewardship.html

Aurora Health Care (2009). *Aurora Health Care's Mission.* Retrieved from http://www.aurorahealthcare.org/aboutus/mission.asp

Aurora Health Care (2009). *Aurora Pulse.* Retrieved from http://iconnect.aurora.org/ portal/ default.do?appId=EB109

Aurora Health Care (2009). *Aurora Service – Aurora Star.* Retrieved from http://ahcweb03. aurora. org/aurora_service/aurora_star.htm

Aurora Health Care(2009). *Care Management/Quality*. Retrieved from http://iconnect. aurora. org/portal/default.do?appId=EB084

Aurora Health Care (2009). *Content Search "Aurora's Promise to Caregivers."* Retrieved from https://iconnect.aurora.org/portal/default.do?appId=EBGOO&appParam=q%3Dpromise

Aurora Health Care (2009). *Content Search "Aurora Quest."* Retrieved from http://iconnect.aurora.org/portal/default.do?appId=EBGOO&appParam=q%3Daurora%20quest

Aurora Health Care (2009). *Content Search "Innovative use of IT in the healthcare market."* Retrieved from https://iconnect.aurora.org/portal/default.do?appId=EBGOO&appParam=q%3Dthe%20innovative%20use%20of%20IT%20in%20the%20health%20care%20market

Aurora Health Care (2009). *Content Search, "Just Culture."* Retrieved from http://iconnect. aurora.org/portal/default.do?appId=EBGOO&appParam=q%3Djust%20culture

Aurora Health Care (2009). *Content Search "Learning Plans."* Retrieved from https://iconnect. aurora.org/portal/default.do?appId=EBGOO&appParam=q%3Dlearning%20lesson%20plan

Aurora Health Care (2009). *Content Search "loyalty index."* Retrieved from https://iconnect.aurora.org/portal/default.do?appId=EBGOO&appParam=q%3Dloyalty%20index

Aurora Health Care (2009). *Content Search "on boarding resources."* Retrieved from https://iconnect.aurora.org/portal/default.do?appId=EBGOO&appParam=q%3Donboarding%20process

Aurora Health Care (2009). *Content Search "Planetree Demystifying HealthCare."* Retrieved from http://iconnect.aurora.org/portal/default.do?appId=EBGOO&appParam=q%3D planetree%20 demystifying%20healthcare

Aurora Health Care (2009). *Operating Principles*. Retrieved from http://iconnect.aurora.org/ DotNetNuke/LinkClick.aspx?link=Operating+Principles+(formerly+Leadership)+FINAL.doc&tabid=1630

Aurora Health Care (2009). *Patient Stories*. Retrieved from http://www.aurorahealthcare.org/aboutus/stories/stories.asp

Aurora Health Care (2009). *Responsible Freedom*. Retrieved from http://www.aurora healthcare.org/jobs/why-aurora/respfreedom.asp

Aurora Health Care (2009a). *Number One Priority*. Retrieved from http://iconnect.aurora.org/portal/default.do?appId=EB416

Aurora Health Care (2009b). *Aurora Health Care fact sheet*. Retrieved from http://www.aurora-healthcare.org/aboutus/media/factsheet.asp

Gottschalk, P. (2002). Toward a model of growth stages for knowledge management technology in law firms. *Information Science*, 5(2), 79–123.

Hospital Consumer Assessment of Healthcare Providers and Systems. (2009). *HCAHPS – Facts Page*. Retrieved from http://www.hcahpsonline.org/facts.aspx

Press Ganey. (2009). *Home|Press Ganey*. Retrieved from http://www.pressganey.com

Russ, M., Fineman, R., & Jones, J. K. (2010). How do we get there: Strategy action framework– "Action Engine."

Russ, M., Jones, J. K., & Fineman, R. (2006). Toward a taxonomy of knowledge-based strategies: Early findings. *International Journal of Knowledge and Learning*, 2(1&2), 1–40. doi:10.1504/IJKL.2006.009677

All web sites used in this case study were accessed between January 3, 2009 and June 30, 2009.

Chapter 11
Strategic Alliances and Knowledge Management Strategies:
A Case Study

Mario J. Donate-Manzanares
University of Castilla-La Mancha, Spain

Fátima Guadamillas-Gómez
University of Castilla-La Mancha, Spain

Jesús D. Sánchez de Pablo
University of Castilla-La Mancha, Spain

ABSTRACT

Managing organizational knowledge in alliances implies establishing the best possible strategic design to create, acquire, maintain, transfer, and apply organizational knowledge developed between the partners (or acquired from partners) in order to achieve competitive goals. In this chapter, the role of knowledge management strategy (KMS) in strategic alliances is analyzed in a technology-intensive company. Focusing on this, the importance of alliances for technological companies and the necessity of designing suitable KMSs in alliances–in terms of establishing objectives, knowledge management tools, and support systems–are explained first of all. This is followed by the analysis of a case study of KMS in the strategic alliances of a company currently developing different businesses in technological settings. Finally, a number of conclusions are discussed, based on how the implementation aspects concerning KMS in strategic alliances have been managed and the way they have contributed to the attainment of the company's objectives and goals.

DOI: 10.4018/978-1-60566-348-7.ch011

1. INTRODUCTION

The growth of alliances has generated considerable interest in this topic among both academics and practitioners. Strategic management literature has recognized alliances as a source for firms to acquire and improve their knowledge-based capabilities in current innovation-intensive environments (Oxley and Sampson, 2004). Thus, alliances can act as mechanism for firms to develop a competitive advantage over their rivals, outperforming them by means of the company's proven access to economies of scope and scale, complementary capabilities and knowledge, the possibility of competing in new markets, the improvement of their learning capacity, or the sharing of costs and risks of R&D projects, among other reasons (Saxton, 1997; Ireland, Hitt and Vaidyanath, 2002; Luo, 2008).

Knowledge Management Strategy (KMS) constitutes one of the main factors in order for firms to achieve these objectives and build collaborative advantages through strategic alliances. Managing organizational knowledge in alliances involves working on the best possible strategic design to create, acquire, maintain, transfer and apply organizational knowledge developed or acquired amongst the partners in order to achieve competitive goals (Guadamillas, Donate and Sánchez de Pablo, 2006).

A clear relationship exists between strategic alliances and the KMS of firms. Lane and Lubatkin (1998) and Stuart (2000) contend the main objective of partners in a technological alliance is the inter-organizational learning, as a consequence of the difficulty faced by each partner in terms of solving their environmental problems internally. Inter-organizational learning is based on the absorptive capacity of the company, which represents its ability to value, assimilate and use the external (acquired) new knowledge (Cohen and Levinthal, 1990; Lane and Lubatkin, 1998). Absorptive capacity depends on the path-dependent investment in R&D and technology developed

by the company, so the more innovative the firm is, the more likely it is to invest in alliances with a view to inter-firm learning. However, in order for such learning to take place, an adequate KMS has to be developed in order to effectively manage and exploit the flow of knowledge that is produced in the strategic alliance (Grant and Baden-Fuller, 2004). In doing so, this will speed up the development of innovation, thus making its implementation over a short period of time possible, ultimately leading to important advantages for the firm whilst encouraging a superior level of learning at the same time (Stuart, 2000).

It is also important to remark on certain key organizational and technical aspects related to the role of KMS in the management of strategic alliances: the use of information technology (IT) and the systems that make the access to knowledge easier, the organizational culture that fosters innovation development and ethical and responsible behavior, and human resources (HR) practices. All of these make the establishment of a coherent structure for knowledge management in strategic alliances a complicated issue (Schmaltz, Hagenhoff and Kaspar, 2004).

Furthermore, there are other kinds of problems that arise in strategic alliances which make the effective development of collaborative activities and knowledge sharing complex. The first problem is both the specificity and tacitness of knowledge, meaning its effective storage and transfer are difficult. Moreover, the distrust between partners and the cultural barriers in respect of collaboration imply certain reluctance on the part of companies to participate in alliances (Lane and Lubatkin, 1998; Ireland et al., 2002). Excessive technological and knowledge diversity (or similarity), for example, can be problematic insomuch as it gives rise to difficulties in terms of learning from partners (Lane and Lubatkin, 1998). Finally, the organizational form and the governance structure of the strategic alliance should be adapted to accomplish the alliance objectives and specific requirements of the companies involved.

In this chapter, we attempt to analyze the KMS of companies involved in strategic alliances, and in particular, a number of aspects related both to the sharing and transmission of knowledge from the knowledge-based view of the firm. Thus, the role of technical and organizational factors in these processes will be analyzed in relation to culture, HR practices and the management of IT systems. The chapter will be structured as follows: first of all, the importance of KMS for individual companies in alliances in order to develop a collaborative advantage and obtain important returns on their R&D investment will be explained; secondly, we shall analyze the importance of organizational and strategic aspects that are involved in this process, stressing those factors that make the effective transmission and sharing of knowledge difficult.

Finally, the role of KMS oriented towards innovation in strategic alliances will be analyzed in a Spanish company within a technology-intensive industry. This firm maintains cooperation agreements considered as being essential for knowledge creation and innovation development. Thus, the manner in which implementation aspects concerning KMS in strategic alliances have been managed and the way they have contributed to the attainment of their strategic objectives shall be explained.

2. KNOWLEDGE MANAGEMENT STRATEGIES IN STRATEGIC ALLIANCES

As Inkpen (2000) points out, learning in a strategic alliance consists of gaining access to the partner's knowledge in order to combine it with the particular assets of the firm to be used in business activities. Moreover, Inkpen and Beamish (1997) contend that while the establishment of an alliance permits access to knowledge between partners, the transfer of knowledge which enables learning will only occur when certain conditions that make

this possible are in place. Furthermore, owing to tacit and non-observable knowledge being more valuable in terms of strategic content (Spender, 1996), firms may establish specific mechanisms to acquire this kind of knowledge, all of which is difficult and costly when put into practice.

Hamel (1991), Khanna, Gulati and Nohria (1998), Lane and Lubatkin (1998) and Stuart (2000) argue that the main objective of partners in strategic alliances is inter-organizational learning as a consequence of the difficulties faced by firms when attempting to internally resolve problems of differing natures for which specific knowledge is required. Hence, learning can be based on a wide variety of aspects such as market characteristics, operational problems, technological capabilities, management abilities and so on. On the other hand, the formal alliance structure can be considered as a "laboratory" for the organizational learning of each partner where the firm's knowledge pool is created and developed (Inkpen, 1998). In order to make this possible, learning has to be an important aspect of the strategic intention of partners who should also have skills to learn and integrate the new knowledge into their current knowledge base.

In addition to this, certain elements are required to make the advantages that have been gained through learning and knowledge transfer effective for partners. Mesquita, Anand and Brush (2008) point out the following: (1) knowledge transfer has to be agreed; (2) assets and capabilities have to be specifically developed through the alliance; (3) a suitable governance structure has to be developed in order to protect specific assets and coordinate the use of complementary resources and capabilities.

Firms establish different kinds of objectives and they can try to attain them through the development of diverse types of strategic alternatives. The KMS of a firm is based on the best possible strategic design in order to create, maintain, transfer and apply organizational knowledge to achieve competitive goals (Earl, 2001; Maier and Remus,

2002; Choi and Lee, 2003; Garavelli et al., 2004; Donate and Guadamillas, 2007). The development of a KMS includes all the operations related to the creation, acquisition, integration, storage, transmission, protection and application of knowledge (Day and Wendler, 1998). In relation to strategic alliances, KMS is oriented to manage those flows of knowledge which are linked to exploitation and exploration processes, depending on the goals and scope of the established cooperation agreement. Based on the works of Donate and Guadamillas (2007) and Earl (2001), four dimensions make up the KMS of a company: (1) Knowledge management (KM) conception; (2) KMS objectives; (3) KM practices and tools; (4) KM support systems, all of which shall be analysed next.

KM Concept

Strategic alliances enable the firm to acquire and/or exploit the knowledge of one or more partners in order to attain specific objectives and goals. In general terms, the KM concept refers to the company's strategic orientation in respect of knowledge, which is reflected in the way the board of directors understand the potential contribution of KM for the firm. For example, they could understand that KM is just related to the use of information technologies or, conversely, be aware that it is a wider concept that includes both human and technical aspects (Huplic, Pouloudi and Rzevski, 2002). In relation to strategic alliances, it would express the main role that KM plays in the inter-organizational system. Obviously, the KM concept should be consistent with the alliance objectives because the more coherent they are, the more effective the final result of the cooperation agreement will be.

KMS Objectives

This dimension could be understood as a company's orientation towards the solution of the knowledge "gap" in different operative and

strategic areas within the organization: quality problems, efficiency searching, new product development, solutions to customer service failures, etc. (Zack, 1999; Earl, 2001: 229). In general, organizations attach greater importance to the accomplishment of certain objectives over others. Moreover, managers will consider that KS can contribute towards the fulfilment of this to a greater or a lesser degree. This fact can influence the way KM tools are designed and used in order to accomplish these objectives (Davenport, DeLong and Beers, 1998). In relation to alliances, objectives are established to acquire, explore or exploit partner knowledge, thus influencing the KM tools, the governance structure of the alliance and its implementation support systems. Clearly, all these aspects will differ depending on the alliance goals, as pursuing the improvement of technological capabilities as an objective is not the same as improving the level of the efficiency in the manufacturing area, for example.

KM Tools

These are the specific methods or initiatives used by the organization to support the creation, transfer, storage, retrieval and application of knowledge, and they can include technical as well as human components (Alavi and Leidner, 2001; Alavi and Tiwana, 2003). As Davenport et al. (1998: 44-45) point out, these KM initiatives specifically seek to create knowledge repositories, to improve knowledge access and transfer or manage knowledge as an asset –including its protection. In addition, the organization could focus on several procedures in a comprehensive manner, or on using some of its tools in a specific way. In an alliance, the main method for a partner to generate knowledge is through its acquisition, either on a voluntary basis or through learning by doing. Once the knowledge is created, mechanisms may be established to transfer knowledge from one location to another. Moreover, the storage of explicit knowledge can constitute a necessity, for which IT-based instruments built on a common basis could be very useful. Some initiatives might also be developed to apply the alliance knowledge, such as interdisciplinary teams or specific instruments based on IT, such as expert systems (Alavi and Tiwana, 2003). Finally, knowledge protection in the alliance is an important issue, although in some cases partners can protect their knowledge by establishing clauses in contracts, designing specific mechanisms (e.g. passwords, firewalls) or relying on the establishment of cooperation agreements in the future (Inkpen, 1998).

Implementation Support Systems

These are organizational aspects that should make the development of KM processes easier, such as a "knowledge-focused" culture, HR practices, flexible structures, and technical systems. Culture should promote knowledge exchange and sharing in order to allow for continual innovation and change (Nonaka, 1994).

Moreover, there are a number of essential changes that KM initiatives imply in HR practices to make implementation possible. Thus, those related to the promotion of access to or availability of the knowledge of experts, the development of work teams and communities of practices, or incentive methods for monitoring and controlling process systems, among others, stand out as important elements in accomplishing the strategic –knowledge– objectives of alliance partners. The implementation of a KMS should also be supported by a suitable structure, which encourages the attainment of objectives and the development of knowledge processes in the co-operation agreement. Finally, technical systems refer to IT-based tools used for developing (and making easier) certain knowledge processes, such as data bases, e-learning tools, intranets or other communication instruments among partners. In general, the promotion of inter-dependence among partners is an essential aspect in order to improve the impact of the KMS on the alliance

performance. Thus, inter-dependence has a key role by promoting cooperation (Dyer, 1997), generating synergies (Saxton, 1997), encouraging reciprocity, and leveraging commitment to and trust in the alliance[1].

One of the most relevant aspects in the KMS development process is the design of the implementation support systems, which are referred to technical, human and organizational elements of KM in relation to the management of the alliance. Owing to their importance, all these aspects will be analyzed in more detail next.

3. TECHNICAL AND ORGANIZATIONAL ASPECTS OF KMS IN STRATEGIC ALLIANCES

3.1. Culture

Culture can be understood as a collective thinking that identifies members in a group or category (Hofstede, 1991; Rodríguez and Wilson, 2002). In order for knowledge transfer that is produced among partners to generate learning, it is necessary that a certain difference between their knowledge bases exists (Lane and Lubatkin, 1998). At the same time, the relationship has to be close enough so for an appropriate transfer of knowledge to take place (Mowery et al., 1998). Thus, for learning to be effective, a balance concerning these two aspects has to be achieved; when the cultural distance is greater, the novelty in terms of knowledge also increases albeit this also impacts on the communication capacity to transfer that information or knowledge by reducing it. Therefore, as learning is being developed, partners capacities tend to converge and knowledge transfer is considered to be a critical aspect.

As the alliance evolves, a common culture based on shared values is created which generates trust and supports mutual learning among partners through which new knowledge and shared capabilities are created, all of which increases the alliance value (Inkpen, 1998). That said, culture is related to trust, as cultural rules and values influence its development over the course of time. In this sense, it is necessary to understand the partner's culture, by trying to identify which values are more beneficial to the alliance, along with those aspects that require a greater level of control. Moreover, trust and cultural adjustment are both interdependent elements, as poor cultural adjustment may produce suspicions among companies and form a significant barrier in the way of building up mutual trust (Sampson, 2005).

Another important aspect concerning culture in strategic alliances is its link with HR management. In this sense, HR has to contribute in building a shared culture that strengthens the alliance and encourages employees to accept common objectives in addition to mutual identification with a common project, making the coordination and control processes easier in the domain of the cooperation agreement. This common culture reduces uncertainty, promotes the endeavors of partners, creates respect for the basic values of each partner, generates interdependence and facilitates conflict resolution (Guadamillas et al., 2006). In order to make this possible, information sharing, transparency, trust and leadership –people acting as an intermediary, managing information flows– are necessary (Sampson, 2005).

3.2. HR Management

Quinn, Anderson and Finkelstein (1996) point out a number of changes that KM implies for HR management. Thus, practices that support the development of knowledge processes stand out, such as the development of teams and communities of practice, control based on the assessment of processes instead of results, or the incentives (monetary and non-monetary) that are designed in order to share knowledge.

HR practices in an alliance may have a significant influence on its success because it can contribute to making the adjustment between corporate partners' cultures and specific HR practices of the companies easier (the establishment of common objectives and practices), offer more effective control mechanisms, promote inter-organizational learning, and encourage the selection and development of teams that are able to share knowledge and work in an effective manner for the organization through collaboration. Thus HR management could contribute towards increasing productivity of the alliance and improve the abilities of partners in order to maximize the value of the cooperation agreement.

In addition, an effort must be made within the parameters of the alliance to offer employees the kind of in-house training that cannot be obtained within the labor market, so as not to distract from the main objective at the heart of the agreement, knowledge transfer (Mesquita et al., 2008). In general terms, capabilities which must be learnt should be incorporated into specific inter-organizational government mechanisms or covered under special modes of knowledge transfer (Mesquita et al., 2008).

HR management should, therefore, be designed to make the knowledge transfer among alliance partners easier, improve communication and promote trust, especially in terms of the partner-partner relationship (in which the search and selection processes for a partner are included), partner-alliance relationships (which seeks a coherent and structural integration of knowledge) and the search for an optimal management of the asymmetries of the partners in relation to culture, vision and values. The main HR practices that promote knowledge transfer and organizational learning are: strategy and procedures training; development of a common culture for the alliance; promotion of the work teams; development of employees' careers; programs which cater for increased work experience at various locations, functions and countries through the transfer of explicit knowledge; development of handbooks for employee training; development of specific databases and electronic systems to gather, share and apply knowledge in the alliance domain.

The most important aspects of HR practices in the different stages of the development of a strategic alliance shall be addressed next.

The search for an alliance partner. The main objective is to identify potential partners in keeping with the objectives of the KMS –exploration or exploitation, depending on the knowledge gaps the company wishes to cover– and analyze the partner/s strategic reasons in wanting to establish the cooperation agreement. Thus, certain aspects have to be considered in relation to partners, such as cultural and management style differences, their objectives and motives, the capabilities and resources they will contribute to the alliance and their previous alliance experience and results. The main HR issue in this previous stage will be the planning of HR practices in relation to KMS objectives for the strategic alliance.

Alliance development. The main aspects to analyze at this stage are the physical site of the alliance, the design of the alliance structure and the recruitment and selection of the alliance managers in line with goals and objectives. In the most complex alliance types (for example, a joint venture), negotiation among partners will be necessary to design the HR policies. In more simple alliances (for example, an alliance established through a contract) responsibilities are better defined, making it is easier for each partner to design their own policies concerning the alliance (recruitment, selection, contracting and job specification).

Alliance implementation. At this stage, vision, mission, values, strategies and structures have to be assessed. Partners also need the support and development of suitable HR mechanisms that allow them to learn, share and exploit knowledge in keeping with goals and objectives that have been established under the KMS. They should design specific actions such as: persons in charge of tasks, abilities and skills necessaries to carry out those tasks, assessment and monitoring systems,

career planning, support to employees, training and incentives for knowledge sharing.

Control and assessment. Finally, the control and assessment of the attainment of knowledge objectives is necessary in order to evaluate whether the alliance is producing benefits (and/or problems) for all the alliance partners. An individual (company) assessment also has to be made to evaluate the contribution and pay-offs that have been obtained by the company. Good results from the alliance will imply that partners have been capable of learning from each other and social capital and new knowledge will have been created. If problems arise, a new perspective will be required in which KMS objectives, KM concept, tools and implementation systems will have to be aligned to ensure that flows of knowledge go in the right direction.

Effective HR management should, therefore, contribute to the improvement of learning processes, create and exploit synergies and efficiency, and support the development of knowledge processes. In order to accomplish these objectives, critical aspects and potential HR issues derived from the cooperation agreement that the firm has to consider in relation to its KMS are:

1. Employees are reluctant to changes. In this sense, problems will depend on the alliance type (obviously, some agreements will imply more changes than others) and motives for the companies to establish the cooperation agreement (e.g., exploration vs. exploitation). Some motivation systems and information transparency are required in order to make the implementation and acceptance of changes easier.

2. Owing to the independence that each firm maintains, partners should make the HR strategy that is developed in individual companies compatible with the HR strategy which is applied to the alliance, because some problems could arise in relation to employees, such as:

a. Company employees might perceive that the treatment given to employees connected with the alliance is better concerning certain HR practices: incentives, salary, social benefits, etc.

b. Alliance employees might consider that the HR strategy is better for them than the strategy which is applied in their companies. Thus, when the alliance finishes or his/her role has finished and the employee returns to the company, a period of adjustment will be necessary to ensure that the employee's performance is not affected by such changes.

c. Lack or difficulties of adaptation to new work tasks that are developed in the ambit of the alliance, mainly as a consequence of cultural differences in relation to individual companies.

3. In some cases certain situations could arise, in which company executives might perceive their jobs as being threatened if there is a possibility of substituting certain tasks (e.g., outsourcing) by carrying them out in the ambit of the cooperation agreement. Therefore, a feeling of insecurity might creep in and motivation could drop, all of which would affect firm performance.

4. Owing to the temporary nature of alliances, HR managers have to make an effort to motivate employees involved with the alliance to ensure they work properly. In this stage, the generation of an atmosphere that encourages innovation and knowledge exchange is an essential aspect; all the employees should know the objectives and meaning of the agreement and the positive and negative effects on their current situation.

5. The assignment of executives to the alliance. The rotation of executives linked to the agreement is a sensible manner in which to operate, not only on the basis of organizational learning but also by way of avoiding excessive dependence of a specific person in certain aspects of the KMS for the strategic alliance.

6. Recruitment and selection of the rest of employees involved in the alliance. Personal recruitment may be carried out by each of the companies (partners) or jointly, taking into account the alliance features. Sometimes the personnel selected for the alliance are not suitable or some employees might be disappointed by the fact that they have not been selected to form part of the alliance personnel.

7. Controversies over reward and salary systems. Incentive systems should be the same for the employees who are participating in the alliance, irrespective of what company they come from and whether they are working exclusively on the agreement or not. Nevertheless, certain problems related to rewards and incentives, such as justice and equity, could arise. In an attempt to avoid issues such as these, the design and establishment of a committee made up of members from all of the partnerships is advisable in order to ensure that the incentives are paid as a result of the contribution to the alliance objectives without considering personal aspects (e.g., hierarchical position).

3.3. IT Systems

IT can play a critical role as a supportive tool in alliances and they can be said to help to explain the fast growth of networks in the last few years (Gulati et al., 2000). The utility of IT can be considerable in the management of some of the more important tasks of the agreement, such as the transmission and storage of knowledge and the outcome of monitoring of activities.

Strategic alliances reduce transaction hazards because of trust generated among partners. In this sense, IT tools permit the storage of information about partners and thus, diminish organizational

Figure 1.

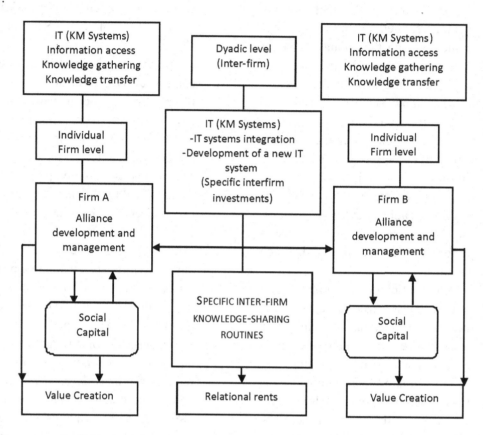

asymmetries. In addition to this, they reduce the loss of information resources in the network (Clemons and Row, 1992). At the same time, IT tools also contribute to leverage the value created in alliances through partners' joint use of design, engineering or computer assistance tools in production. In this case, logic is a by-product of the advantages of synergy gained through the concentration of each partner on their core resources and capabilities –i.e., areas that they know how to make better.

IT tools are a critical aspect of the activites of organizational knowledge management –knowledge and information access, transfer, sharing and storage. IT tools play a critical role in the management of the organizational knowledge owing to the fact that knowledge, under certain conditions (i.e., codification), can be treated as an object that can be divided up in modules (structured), gathered

and transferred (Zander and Kogut, 1995; Sanchez and Mahoney, 1996).

Thus, knowledge management and the advantages of IT application in alliances and networks are, in the first instance, related to the management of the firm's social capital as an intensive resource in knowledge and information. Secondly, they are critical for the building, improvement and use of valuable inter-firm specific knowledge-sharing routines that are difficult to imitate and substitute (Dyer and Singh, 1998).

IT tools are critical for enabling and supporting information and knowledge sharing processes among partners that permit the creation of specific routines and the possibility of obtaining relational rents (Dyer and Singh, 1998). In most cases, these routines make partners an important source of information and ideas, which result in an innovative stream for the firm. However, organizational differences, knowledge bases and IT structure among partners influence on the way knowledge is managed in the alliance with the objective of leveraging the experience and competencies of the participants (Schmaltz, Hagenhoof and Kaspar, 2004). Figure 1 shows how IT can support the alliance development and management, within the context of a knowledge management system at firm and alliance level (considering two firms):

As the model shows, alliance advantages can occur on two different levels: (1) individual, through value creation during the interaction process between alliances management and social capital in each firm; (2) dyadic, through the creation and improvement of specific inter-firm knowledge-sharing routines. They can be defined as "*a regular pattern of inter-firm interactions that permits the transfer, recombination or creation of specialized knowledge*, (…) and these are institutionalized inter-firm processes that are purposefully designed to facilitate knowledge exchanges between alliance partners" (Dyer and Singh, 1998: 665).

Two issues arise in relation to knowledge transfer among alliance partners that affect IT tools and their use and effectiveness in supporting the creation and improvement of inter-firm routines and the potential for obtaining relational rents. First, IT tools are required for knowledge codification processes. In doing this, knowledge can be transferred across firm boundaries and can be understood among partners –including the development of a common code shared by firms in the cooperative relationship (Kogut and Zander, 1992) which could even constitute an advantage for partners (Oliveira, 1999). In addition to this, IT tools can improve the absorptive capacity of each alliance partner, based on the support for the development of overlapping knowledge bases and the interaction between routines.

In general terms, the establishment of a coherent structure for the development of knowledge management in strategic alliances implies solving some technical problems and taking decisions about what information technologies to use, along with the design and implementation of the knowledge management system.

4. COOPERATION ISSUES RELATED TO KMS

In some cases, alliances fail or their results fall short of what was expected owing to problems in the sharing of knowledge between the firms involved. The main difficulty is to face two potential concerns: to maintain an open knowledge exchange to achieve collaborative advantages and to control knowledge flows to avoid the unintended leakage of valuable technology (Oxley and Sampson, 2004).

Firms often erect barriers that make the effective development of collaborative activities, knowledge sharing and transmission in alliances difficult. The main problems discussed in this section will be: (1) the specificity and complexity of knowledge; (2) distrust between partners; (3) technological knowledge diversity; and (4) the organizational form or governance structure of alliances (Guadamillas et al., 2006).

The Specificity, Complexity and Tacitness of Knowledge

In order to carry out the alliance objectives successfully, it is essential for a certain amount of specific knowledge to be shared between the participating partners. There are some difficulties in relation to knowledge transmission and sharing, especially when knowledge is specific, complex and tacit. This kind of knowledge is difficult to keep and transmit because it depends on the context, experience, language and previously accumulated knowledge (Grant, 1996; Oliveira, 1999). Tacit knowledge is difficult to share and transfer to other people (Nonaka and Takeuchi, 1995). The same problem arises with knowledge that is specific to a context or culture (Zander and Kogut, 1995). Transferring tacit and specific knowledge is a very costly and lengthy process. When knowledge is explicit, it is easier to share and to transfer, but it has a smaller strategic value than tacit knowledge (Zander and Kogut, 1995). Acquiring the latter kind of knowledge can be the main reason to participate in an alliance.

Protection of Strategic Knowledge

One of the main risks of strategic alliances is the difficultly in protecting certain types of essential knowledge (Oxley and Sampson, 2004: 727): hints and ideas about strategy orientation, directions and partial results of technological research; competitive benchmarking data; codified knowledge contained in formulas, design and procedures; tacit knowledge involved in skills and routines and the essential competences of key employees that can be hired when the alliance is finished. The risk of the partner developing an opportunistic behaviour in the alliance and appropriating this kind of strategic knowledge is one of the main factors that discourage firms from participating in an alliance. On the other hand, sometimes the sharing of some strategic knowledge is necessary for achieving alliance objectives. Trust between participants is required in order to make this possible.

Mutual Distrust Among Partners

Firms are especially reluctant to share knowledge with companies that may become competitors in the future. Mechanisms and systems to reduce distrust and opportunism and to improve collaboration between partners are very important. The common space created in an alliance allows partners to share their tacit and explicit knowledge, their abilities and productive processes. Furthermore, if an adequate level of trust is attained it is possible to create and exchange new knowledge, especially that which is tacit, generated in the agreement and which afterwards is absorbed and assimilated by firms, leading them to improve their capabilities

(Inkpen, 1998). Therefore, it is possible to affirm that the last goal of a cooperation agreement, carried out to access the partner's knowledge, is the internalization of this knowledge and also of that generated in the alliance. In this case, cooperation is a tool that makes organizational learning easier.

Alliance Organizational Form or Governance Structure

The lack of common routines, clear lines of authority and limited hierarchical organizational forms can make cooperation difficult, along with the sharing of knowledge and learning for the members of the alliance. Although all organizational forms have disadvantages, partners must implement that which is optimal according to the nature of the agreement (joint ventures, alliances, joint equity ventures, etc.). The more hierarchical the organizational forms are the more they facilitate the control of processes and performance, albeit they also imply higher costs and more bureaucracy (Oxley and Sampson, 2004).

5. CASE STUDY ANALYSIS: KMS IN TECNOBIT STRATEGIC ALLIANCES

5.1. Introduction

In general, a case study aims to examine a "contemporary phenomenon within its real-life context" (Yin, 1994: 13). As a research method, it is viewed as improving our knowledge of individual and organizational phenomena (Van Maanen, 1979; Yin, 1994). Case studies primarily involve researchers undertaking an in depth study of a particular organization with a wide variety of information being collected as a result. In our case, we collected multiple data and information from interviews with one of the company's main directors and other company documents. In interviews, questions were kept unrestricted

Table 1. Main figures (evolution) in Tecnobit

Concept*	2005	2006	2007	%Δ (2006-2007)
Equity	25.3	28.6	33.5	17.13
Incomes	40.7	50.4	57.3	13.69
EBITDA	10.4	12.2	14.7	20.49
Net profit	2.6	3.5	4.9	40
Clients' portfolio	144.2	159.4	162.9	2.19
*Million of €				

in order to encourage the manager to converse freely (Maykut and Morehouse, 1994). Extracts from internal reports, the company's web page and other relevant documentation were also used to make up the case study.

The company analyzed has been chosen because it has developed its growth strategy based on new knowledge created internally but especially through strategic alliances. The company was founded in 1976 as *DOI-Associate Engineers*. Located in Madrid (Spain) its main activity centred on the control of industrial processes. In 1981, an industrial plant was created in Valdepeñas (Ciudad Real, Spain) and the company's name was changed to Tecnobit. Over the next decade, the company's development took place: in 1983, an important contract was signed with the Spanish Ministry of Defence; in 1987, the command and control activities began; in 1992, the first EF-2000 contracts (avionics) were obtained; in 2000, the Tecnobit Group was created; and in 2003, companies that made up the Tecnobit Group were melted into a single legal entity. The current name for the company is Tecnobit S.L., and its shareholders are: CCM Corporation (48%), IT Deusto (48%) and other shareholders (4%).

Tecnobit develops five activity lines, with the following sales income distribution (2007): Avionics (49%); command and control systems (21%); simulation systems (14%); optronics (8%) and IT systems (8%). It has two plants, Alcobendas (Madrid, Spain) and Valdepeñas (Ciudad Real, Spain), with a total extent of 20.300 m². It has 330

employees, of which 60% have a university degree in engineering or computer sciences. In respect of financial data, in 2007 Tecnobit improved on the (good) results of 2005 and 2006. (Table 1)

Tecnobit has also devoted, on average, 8.5% of sales income to R&D (in 2007 €4.9 million was invested). Moreover, in the last few years it has improved its efficiency due to the reduction of commercial and general expenses, achieve through functional and organizational restructuring, all of which is reflected in the financial performance of the company.

What is especially interesting about the evolution of the company is how it has diversified its business lines, beginning with its main activity of aviation electronics (avionics) spreading to new simulation and training projects within the same industry[2], as well as towards the IT field, through the creation of command and control systems, the development of software, and knowledge management projects. The diversification has been carried out via internal development and knowledge acquisition through cooperation agreements and the purchase of certain companies. With the newly acquired companies, Tecnobit extended its activities beyond the electronics industry, to provide maintenance and technical support to other companies within the industry. During 2003-2007, Tecnobit furthered its expansion strategy, incorporating a new computer services company into the business, and currently continues to consolidate its position and growth in related industries. One important point worth mentioning here is the company's effort towards its international expansion, which has resulted in international sales by the firm representing an increasing proportion of its total sales income, as a consequence of its reputation and the consolidation of its brand image.

Industries in which this company operates are rapidly changing because they are technology-intensive, and there is an increasing trend towards industrial concentration to gain advantages derived from size. In this setting, and to face these competitive conditions and the innovation challenge, Tecnobit has designed a dynamic and aggressive growth strategy, with the objective of generating synergies (essentially based on taking advantage of the knowledge that it possesses) and improving the value of the company through internal development and related diversification. Thus, Tecnobit has based its diversification pattern on the application of available resources, and its expertise and knowledge in IT, internally developed or acquired, for the development of new products and services.

Additionally, Tecnobit attaches great importance to internal IT systems, and it tries to manage them in order to take advantage of the great potential which, from a strategic and organizational viewpoint, these technologies can offer in relation to certain critical activities for knowledge management –to ease the access to and the transfer and storage of knowledge and information within the firm and in strategic alliances as well.

5.2. Strategic Alliances in Tecnobit

Tecnobit has successfully developed a growth strategy through diversification involving related businesses representing the aviation electronics and IT industries. This strategy was based on the application of its accumulated knowledge, which was internally developed by the organization or obtained and integrated in its knowledge base as a result of its external acquisition in strategic alliances and the purchasing of companies.

KMS applied to its strategic alliances and their management (IT systems, governance structure or HR practices) has played a fundamental role in this process.

Strategic alliances and the purchase of companies have been used by Tecnobit to acquire knowledge that the company did not possess and that would have been difficult and costly to develop internally. Sometimes, the acquired knowledge has been complementary to existing knowledge, with which it has been successfully integrated, bearing in mind that the firm has a good level of absorptive capacity (Cohen and Levinthal, 1990), and occasionally, such knowledge has directly been used to break into new markets.

Alliances have been developed by Tecnobit to cover different objectives, both to exploit and explore knowledge in different areas (Grant and Baden-Fuller, 2004; Rothaermel and Deeds, 2004). Alliances frequently present themselves as an option for Tecnobit to grow technologically because they involve less financial risk compared to other alternatives, such as company acquisitions. They are also appropriate when technological capabilities are too difficult to develop internally and the firm would spend too much time in doing this[3]. Tecnobit, apart from technological alliances, has entered into cooperation agreements with other firms and institutions in financial, commercial, service, manufacturing and industrial domains[4]. Sometimes, these firms have important differences to Tecnobit in aspects such as size, sectors or countries, but they are always characterised by complementary knowledge and a compatible culture which have enabled alliance objectives to be accomplished.

Some cooperative agreements entered into by Tecnobit have particular significance, even if they are of a very different nature. On the one hand, in the avionics area, it has established an *exploration* alliance with the Israeli company, *Rafael DM,* on the joint development of a laser indicator[5]. It has also been working with the American companies *Lockheed Martin* and *Cubic Defence Electronics,* in the development of diverse simulators. It is trying, for example, to adapt Cubic's air simulator (in which this company is the world's technological leader) to the terrestrial domain, such as in combat cars. Moreover, co-operative agreements have been developed with public institutions, such as the *University of Castilla-La Mancha*, for the development of various technological projects. On the other hand, Tecnobit has signed an agreement with the German firm *Hyperwave* for the *exploitation* of its computer tool –also referred to as Hyperwave, as previously point out– through commercialization in Spain and Latin America. In general, Tecnobit is satisfied with all these alliances, in terms of objectives attainment, acquisition of complementary technological knowledge through learning, and the possibilities this gives to Tecnobit of growing through the exploration and exploitation of new markets and products[6]. Moreover, Tecnobit has channelled some of its cooperative agreement projects through its participation in official R&D programs[7], for which it has received financial support. For example, it has participated in the *Technological Aeronautic Plan II*, which includes important financial support for carrying out these investment projects. It also maintains collaboration projects in technological matters with other government research centers, such as the *R&D Army Center* (CIDA).

In some cases, and due to the difficulties of incorporating certain capabilities and tacit knowledge into the organization through strategic alliances or other means (imitation, hiring of technical experts, etc.), technology-intensive firms that had the required capabilities were directly acquired. Essentially, the explanation for these acquisitions is based on the knowledge characteristics to be transferred; that is to say, due to problems of causal ambiguity, high specificity and context-dependency, which would have made the transfer or replication of knowledge and capabilities difficult to carry out otherwise (DeCarolis and Deeds, 1999; Grant, 1996; Reed and DeFillipi, 1990).

5.3. KMS for Alliances in Tecnobit

In this section, Tecnobit's KMS in strategic alliances is exposed, distinguishing in turn its objectives and KM conception, KM tools and the most significant aspects of the implementation support systems.

Objectives and KM Conception

As has previously been pointed out, objectives for KMS in alliances combine exploitation and exploration issues. On the one hand, depending on the exact nature of these goals, cooperation agreements have ranged from joint ventures in the case of exploration objectives in order to pool knowledge and other kinds of resources with the partner company, to contractual agreements and informal structures when the exploitation of the partner's knowledge and resources has been necessary. For Tecnobit, the more exploratory the alliance is, more innovative the final aim of the cooperation agreement will be. Obviously, the structure of the alliance will be different in relation to tools and systems because the problems that need to be solved are different as well. On the other hand, the perspective of Tecnobit's managers concerning KM conception is clear: the company employees should bear in mind that the human and cultural component is as important as IT tools in the development of projects, and KM should not only be centered on information management but in trying to promote interaction and knowledge sharing among employees, and employees-partners in strategic alliances.

IT Tools and Systems for KM

Tecnobit's current IT tools for knowledge management, apart from being oriented towards external markets, are widely used in the internal organization as well as strategic alliances. They are based on the use of web technologies in open and multi-platform systems, jointly with the development of applications and content with international standards through the use of document management and content tools. In terms of KM tools based on IT, the following stand out as being the most important: information and control systems, document management tools, storage systems and other data and information archive systems. Overall, these tools have been designed to assist in the creation, storage, retrieval, transfer and application processes of knowledge management, permitting the development of these processes in order to attain the company and alliance objectives in the ambit of KMS.

KMS Support Systems

Tecnobit considers that one of the main success factors in an alliance is the trust between partners. For this reason, it considers it necessary to develop a shared culture with its alliance partners in order to generate trust and an efficient HR strategy. To achieve this aim, an optimal alliance plan is necessary, in which the search for a partner and the understanding of the partner′s culture are key issues. Consequently, Tecnobit selects partners that will complement their culture in the search for common goals.

With the objective of enhancing efficiency and integration even further whilst providing greater flexibility to its innovative activities and change, the organization has been structured in terms of projects. The decision-making process is, therefore, decentralized, on the basis that the closer the decision unit is to the decision taken, the better qualified they are to do this. This kind of flexible structure is applied in some exploration alliances under which the integration of employees from different companies is required. Tecnobit has developed a policy whereby employees are continuously moving between projects, thus increasing flexibility. In doing so, communication between employees and knowledge transfer becomes easier.

A high level of flexibility exists because the employees are assigned to diverse projects within different lines of activity to cover the alliance needs, thus attempting to develop a "concurrent engineering" where employees "can think about everything", by having a global vision of the company's projects. As a result, the employees move within all lines of activity, which promotes the sharing of knowledge and ideas, and stimulates creativity (Nonaka and Takeuchi, 1995). This organizational structure also allows Tecnobit to rapidly respond to changing customer needs and preferences, which ultimately enables it to adjust to the dynamic and complex conditions of its competitive environment.

The main HR practices of Tecnobit that support the KM processes in alliances are:

- The design and implementation of extensive training practices. It is important to highlight that the knowledge generated in an alliance cannot be used easily by other competing firms –i.e., it is highly specific to the alliance.

- The use of teamwork. The firm considers that teamwork is the best option in order to achieve its alliance goals. The interaction between employees from different firms increases shared knowledge, making the development of learning processes possible. In teamwork it is important to select the most suitable employees to achieve the common objectives. Moreover, a continual negotiation process should be carried out between partners to immediately solve the problems which may arise.

- The specific contracting of highly qualified external employees.

- The identification of internal employees with the best abilities, skills and qualifications to work in each activity of the alliance. HR policies can contribute to the alliance success if managers are able to identify employees with the ability to form better interpersonal relationships, on the basis that they have more highly developed social abilities and are able to learn and transfer knowledge more easily. Moreover, the knowledge generated in alliances for these workers will be integrated into the firm more efficiently, thus making them the most suitable employees to work in the alliance. During the last year, certain exploratory studies have been carried out in Tecnobit in order to identify the most suitable employees from a learning perspective in terms of its intra-organizational learning network. With this knowledge in mind, managers can better develop reward systems and motivational schemes for their employees and adjust their management style to the existing conditions (Sánchez de Pablo et al., 2008).

- The design and implementation of various incentive systems to promote specific aspects in the alliance, such as knowledge sharing or the extensive use of IT.
- The development of a shared culture between partners. The importance of a shared culture has been analyzed previously but it is necessary to emphasize that Tecnobit fosters a shared culture which encourages employees to accept a common vision. Thus, more benefits can be obtained by making the coordination and control of common activities easier; (control must be carried out on two levels: individual and inter-organizational).
- The design of employees' careers. Usually, alliances are of a temporary nature, that is

Table 2. KMS in Tecnobit's strategic alliances

Dimensions	Explanation	
KM Concept	To obtain knowledge and integrate it to achieve exploration or exploitation objectives, bearing in mind that KM is not only related to IT management but that cultural and human factors are also very important for alliance success.	
KMS Objectives	Exploitation of partners' technologies and resources to gain in respect of quality, efficiency or service to clients.	
	Exploration of partners' knowledge in order to improve innovation capabilities and learning.	
KM Tools	Knowledge creation	Socialization and sharing of knowledge through formal and informal meetings, teamwork and tools based on IT.
		Interdisciplinary teams with university researchers
	Knowledge storage	Databases for each common project
	Knowledge protection	Confidentiality and non-concurrence agreements in contracts
Implementation support systems	Culture	To establish principles and values based on the transfer and sharing of knowledge among partners in relation to alliance goals
		To develop inter-organizational knowledge networks through cooperative projects
	HR Practices	Promotion of access to databases
		Rewards given to employees who suggest new ideas and share their knowledge
		To assign key employees to the alliance
	Structure	Work teams, joint ventures, contracts or informal structures, depending on the alliance objectives (exploration vs. exploitation)
	Technical Systems	Databases, data-mining, data warehousing
		Collaborative systems based on networking

to say, their time span is limited. To avoid uncertainty among employees who work in the alliance, Tecnobit has developed well-established career plans in order for employees to be able to perceive their future possibilities in the firm.

- The development of a balanced remuneration plan within the alliance. Its main objective is to avoid situations of unfair financial compensation on either side of the alliance.
- The use of electronic databases and other specific IT solutions.

Finally, it is important to also note that these practices allow for some degree of individual and group autonomy while ensuring the achievement of the goals of the cooperation agreement.

As a result of this analysis, a table (Table 2) has been drawn up, which details Tecnobit's KMS in relation to its strategic alliances.

6. CONCLUSION

In this chapter, we have analyzed KMS in alliances as an instrument for achieving the objectives of partners by establishing the company's orientation towards KM, tools and instruments to develop knowledge processes and systems to support the KMS implementation, amongst which HR practices and flexible alliance structures are included. Organizational problems in alliances concerning knowledge management have also been addressed. Finally, the way in which an innovation-intensive company establishes its KMS in order to attain objectives, based around alternatives of knowledge exploration or exploitation in alliances, has been discussed.

In general, although each alliance implies the development and implementation of a specific KMS considering its own circumstances and objectives, the analysis of this case shows how, in order to face the strong competitive requirements of the current environment, the coherence of the KMS in relation to the aim of the strategic alliance has to be taken into account. Certain aspects concerning the exploration or exploitation of the knowledge that is generated, shared and applied also have to be analyzed by each partner, such as: the exclusivity and complementary domains of strategic knowledge, the creation of new knowledge, and finally, the appropriation of profits derived from these, through the establishment of mechanisms which permit the protection of each partner's knowledge domain while the knowledge sharing among them is maximized. Thus, managers should ask themselves certain questions concerning the structure and governance of the strategic alliance, such as: how can we develop new knowledge and what are the factors that influence this process? For each factor considered, what kinds of mechanisms are available for the company and how can we use them to make knowledge management easier? In this sense, is the existing organizational alliance flexibility adequate? How can we make better use of IT tools to manage knowledge in the alliance? What kind of HR practices would facilitate the sharing of knowledge, minimizing the risk of undue appropriation of our strategic knowledge?

The response to all these questions implies the design of adequate KMS's for the firm's alliances, wherein objectives, the vision of managers in relation to KM, the KM tools and the implementation systems must be coherent and support the overall strategy of the organization. Particularly, it is especially important to manage cultural elements and deal with human aspects in cooperation agreements. In doing so, the transfer of knowledge is made possible, both to exploit and explore the knowledge of another partner(s). As the case of Tecnobit has shown, in technological settings, where knowledge is in a state of constant development, single companies operating by themselves come up against difficulties in terms of developing all the necessary knowledge in order to grow, enter into new markets and be technologically innovative in respect of products and processes, meaning that alliances and cooperation agreements are essential to gain access to important knowledge for the firm. Companies also have to search for technological solutions in order to store, create and transfer knowledge effectively in the alliance, whilst protecting their most valuable knowledge from imitation. In this sense, it is more difficult for a partner to imitate tacit knowledge over explicit knowledge, which should be protected from unwanted appropriation through some kind of specific mechanism. In any case, for a firm to be able to assimilate and exploit a partner's knowledge, it requires a certain amount of absorptive capacity, which ultimately depends on its internal innovative path (Cohen and Levinthal, 1990).

Finally, it should be pointed out that trust is the key factor in the success of a cooperation agreement, because it is the link between responsible behavior and knowledge sharing in the alliance. Trust needs to be generated between partners in cooperation agreements, in order for a firm to develop its business activities and achieve its strategic objectives.

REFERENCES

Alavi, M., & Leidner, D. (2001). Knowledge management and knowledge management systems: Conceptual foundations and research issues. *MIS Quarterly*, *25*(1), 107–136. doi:10.2307/3250961

Alavi, M., & Tiwana, A. (2003). Knowledge management: The information technology dimension. In M. Easterby-Smith & M. A. Lyles (Eds.), *Organizational learning and knowledge management* (pp. 104-121). London: Blackwell Publishing.

Chan, K., & Liebowitz, J. (2006). The synergy of social network analysis and knowledge mapping: A case study. *Int. J. Management and Decision Making*, *7*, 19–35. doi:10.1504/IJMDM.2006.008169

Choi, B., & Lee, H. (2003). An empirical investigation of knowledge management styles and their effect on corporate performance. *Information & Management*, *40*, 403–417. doi:10.1016/S0378-7206(02)00060-5

Clemons, E. K., & Row, M. C. (1992). Information technology and industrial cooperation: The changing economics of coordination and ownership. *Journal of Management Information Systems*, *9*(2), 9–28.

Cohen, W. M., & Levinthal, D. A. (1990). Absorptive capacity: A new perspective on learning and innovation. *Administrative Science Quarterly*, *35*, 28–152. doi:10.2307/2393553

Davenport, T., DeLong, D., & Beers, M. (1998). Successful knowledge management projects. *Sloan Management Review*, *39*(2), 43–57.

Day, J. D., & Wendler, J. C. (1998). Best practices and beyond: Knowledge strategies. *The McKinsey Quarterly*, *1*, 19–25.

Donate, M., & Guadamillas, F. (2007). The relationship between innovation and knowledge strategies: Its impacts on business performance. *International Journal of Knowledge Management Studies*, *1*(3/4), 388–422. doi:10.1504/IJKMS.2007.012532

Dyer, J. H. (1997). Effective interfirm collaboration: How transactors minimize transaction costs and maximize transaction value. *Strategic Management Journal*, *18*(7), 535–556. doi:10.1002/(SICI)1097-0266(199708)18:7<535::AID-SMJ885>3.0.CO;2-Z

Dyer, J. H., & Singh, H. (1998). The relational view: Cooperative strategies and sources of interorganizational competitive advantage. *Academy of Management Review, 23*(4), 660–679. doi:10.2307/259056

Earl, M. (2001). Knowledge management strategies: Toward a taxonomy. *Journal of Management Information Systems, 18*(1), 215-233.

Garavelli, C., Gorgoglione, M., & Scozzi, B. (2004). Knowledge management strategy and organization: A perspective of analysis. *Knowledge and Process Management, 11*(4), 273-282.

Grant, R. M. (2002). *Contemporary strategy analysis. Concepts, techniques, and applications* (4th ed.). Boston: Blackwell Publishers.

Grant, R. M., & Baden-Fuller, C. (2004). A knowledge accessing theory of strategic alliances. *Journal of Management Studies, 41*(1), 61-79.

Guadamillas, F., Donate, M., & Sánchez de Pablo, J. D. (2006). Sharing knowledge in strategic alliances to build collaborative advantage. In S. Martínez-Fierro, J. A. Medina-Garrido & J. Ruiz-Navarro (Eds.), *Utilizing information technology in developing strategic alliances among organizations* (pp. 99-122). Hershey, PA: IGI Global.

Gulati, R., Nohria, N., & Zaheer, L. (2000). Strategic networks. *Strategic Management Journal, 21*, 203–215. doi:10.1002/(SICI)1097-0266(200003)21:3<203::AID-SMJ102>3.0.CO;2-K

Hamel, G. (1991). Competition for competence and interpartner learning within international strategic alliances. *Strategic Management Journal, 12*, 83–103. doi:10.1002/smj.4250120908

Hofstede, G. (1991). *Cultures and organizations: Software of the mind*. New York: McGraw-Hill.

Huplic, V., Pouloudi, A., & Rzevski, G. (2002). Towards an integrated approach to knowledge management: 'Hard,' 'soft,' and 'abstract' issues. *Knowledge and Process Management, 9*(2), 90–102. doi:10.1002/kpm.134

Inkpen, A. C. (1998). Learning, knowledge acquisitions, and strategic alliances. *European Management Journal, 16*(2), 223–229. doi:10.1016/S0263-2373(97)00090-X

Inkpen, A. C. (2000). A note on the dynamics of learning alliances: Competition, cooperation, and relative scope. *Strategic Management Journal, 21*, 775–779. doi:10.1002/1097-0266(200007)21:7<775::AID-SMJ111>3.0.CO;2-F

Inkpen, A. C., & Beamish, P. W. (1997). Knowledge, bargaining power, and the instability of international. *Joint Ventures Academy of Management Review, 22*(1), 177–202. doi:10.2307/259228

Ireland, R. D., Hitt, M. A., & Vaidyanath, D. (2002). Alliance management as a source of competitive advantage. *Journal of Management, 28*, 413–446. doi:10.1177/014920630202800308

Khanna, T., Gulati, R., & Nohria, N. (1998). The dynamics of learning alliances: Competition, cooperation, and relative scope. *Strategic Management Journal, 19*, 193–210. doi:10.1002/(SICI)1097-0266(199803)19:3<193::AID-SMJ949>3.0.CO;2-C

Kogut, B., & Zander, U. (1992). Knowledge of the firms, combinative capabilities, and the replication of technology. *Organization Science, 3*(3), 383–397. doi:10.1287/orsc.3.3.383

Lane, P. J., & Lubatkin, M. (1998). Relative absorptive capacity and interorganizational learning. *Strategic Management Journal, 19*(5), 461–477. doi:10.1002/(SICI)1097-0266(199805)19:5<461::AID-SMJ953>3.0.CO;2-L

Liebowitz, J. (2007). Developing knowledge and learning strategies in mobile organisations. *International Journal Mobile Learning and Organizations*, *1*(1), 5–14. doi:10.1504/IJMLO.2007.011186

Luo, Y. (2008). Structuring interorganizational cooperation: The role of economic integration in strategic alliances. *Strategic Management Journal*, *29*(6), 617–637. doi:10.1002/smj.677

Maier, R., & Remus, U. (2002). Defining process-oriented knowledge management strategies. *Knowledge and Process Management*, *9*(2), 103–118. doi:10.1002/kpm.136

Mesquita, L. F., Anand, J., & Brush, T. H. (2008). Comparing the resource-based and relational views: Knowledge transfer and spillover in vertical alliances. *Strategic Management Journal*, *29*, 913–941. doi:10.1002/smj.699

Mowery, D. C., Oxley, J. E., & Silverman, B. S. (1998). Technological overlap and interfirm cooperation: Implications for the resource-based view of the firm. *Research Policy*, *27*, 507–523. doi:10.1016/S0048-7333(98)00066-3

Nonaka, I. (1994). A dynamic theory of organizational knowledge creation. *Organization Science*, *5*(1), 14–37. doi:10.1287/orsc.5.1.14

Nonaka, I., & Takeuchi, H. (1995). *The knowledge-creating company*. New York: Oxford University Press.

Oliveira, M. (1999). Core competencies and the knowledge of the firm. In M. A. Hitt, et al. (Eds.), *Dynamic strategic resources: Development, diffusion, and integration* (pp. 17-41). New York: John Wiley and Sons.

Oxley, J. E., & Sampson, R. C. (2004). The scope and gobernance of international R&D alliances. *Strategic Management Journal*, *25*, 723–749. doi:10.1002/smj.391

Rodríguez, C. M., & Wilson, D. T. (2002). Relationship bonding and trust as a foundation for commitment in U.S.-Mexican strategic alliances: A structural equation modeling approach. *Journal of International Marketing*, *10*(4), 53–76. doi:10.1509/jimk.10.4.53.19553

Sampson, R. C. (2005). Experience effects and collaborative returns in R&D alliances. *Strategic Management Journal*, *26*, 1009–1031. doi:10.1002/smj.483

Sanchez, R., & Mahoney, J. T. (1996). Modularity, flexibility, and knowledge management in product and organization design. *Strategic Management Journal*, *17*, 63–76.

Sánchez de Pablo, J. D., Guadamillas, F., Dimovski, V., & Škerlavaj, M. (2008). Exploratory study of organizational learning network within a Spanish high-tech company. *Proceedings of Rijeka Faculty of Economics Journal of Economics and Business*, *26*(2), 257–277.

Saxton, T. (1997). The effects of partner and relationship characteristics on alliances outcomes. *Academy of Management Journal*, *40*(2), 443–461. doi:10.2307/256890

Schmaltz, R., Hagenhoff, S., & Kaspar, C. (2004, April 2-3). *Information technology support for knowledge management in cooperation*. Paper presented at the Fifth European Conference on Organizational Knowledge, Learning, and Capabilities, Innsbruck, Austria.

Spender, J. C. (1996). Making knowledge the basis of a dynamic theory of the firm. *Strategic Management Journal*, *17*, 45–62.

Stuart, T. E. (2000). Interorganizational alliances and the performance of firms: A study of growth and innovation rates in a high-technology industry. *Strategic Management Journal*, *21*, 791–811. doi:10.1002/1097-0266(200008)21:8<791::AID-SMJ121>3.0.CO;2-K

Zack, M. (1999). Developing a knowledge strategy. *California Management Review, 41,* 125–145.

Zander, U., & Kogut, B. (1995). Knowledge and the speed of transfer and imitation of organizational capabilities: An empirical test. *Organization Science, 6,* 76–92. doi:10.1287/orsc.6.1.76

ENDNOTES

[1] Luo (2008) points out that inter-dependence is basically based on resource interdependence, strategic links and relational and structural aspects. He also stresses the importance of economic integration, defined as the interdependence which is created by partners in relation to resources that have been jointly generated and their future use.

[2] Some examples are: electro-optical sensors, command systems, naval control and aviation operations control systems.

[3] Joint ventures, for example, have been occasionally used by Tecnobit in order to reduce risk and generate new technology in a short period of time.

[4] Obviously, in order to develop these alliances, the firm must have alliance government abilities, because the success of the alliance, in terms of objectives achievement strongly depends on this (Ireland, Hitt and Vaidyanath, 2002)

[5] In this sense, the enlargement of Tecnobit's facilities to appropriately face the cooperative projects with this company has actually been carried out.

[6] Interview with Tecnobit's plant Manager (Valdepeñas, Spain, 2007).

[7] Among these programs we can highlight ATICA, PATI, CEDETI and PROFIT.

Chapter 12
Creating and Delivering a Successful Knowledge Management Strategy

Jiming Wu
California State University, USA

Hongwei Du
California State University, USA

Xun Li
Nicholls State University, USA

Pengtao Li
California State University, USA

ABSTRACT

Over the past decade, the rapid proliferation of knowledge management (KM) has been one of the most striking developments in business. Viewing KM as a key driver of competitive advantage, we attempt to provide managers with important guidance on how to create and deliver a successful KM strategy. Specifically, we develop a framework of three factors that are vital to KM success: top management support, a culture of organizational learning, and effective measures of KM performance. To offer a better understanding of the factors, their multiple facets are further investigated and discussed.

INTRODUCTION

In the past decade, knowledge management (KM) has increasingly become a vital strategic practice that enables organizations to operate more efficiently and gain competitive advantage in the marketplace. As pointed out by Bill Gates (1999), the co-founder of software giant Microsoft, KM is of great strate-

gic importance because it will ultimately lead to a higher corporate IQ – an enhanced ability needed by a company to get the best collective thoughts and actions. Indeed, prior research suggests that effective KM initiatives can bring important strategic consequences to organizations by enhancing innovation, promoting firm productivity, increasing agility, maximizing market share, fostering customer loyalty, boosting product/service quality and variety, and so forth (Holsapple & Wu, 2008b).

DOI: 10.4018/978-1-60566-348-7.ch012

Although KM has been widely recognized as a main driver of competitive advantage, there is little well-developed guidance for managers on how to create and deliver a successful KM strategy. As Russ and Jones (2005) argue, creating and delivering an effective KM strategy is an important first step for organizations to develop a shared knowledge base that is required to increase process management efficiency and to improve their competitive positions. They thus suggest the need to build a comprehensive framework that focuses on the key factors critical to the development and delivery of a successful KM strategy. We think such a framework will assist both researchers and practitioners in understanding not only how to apply KM initiatives in ways that lead to competitive advantage, but also why some firms are better at converting their KM investments into superior KM performance.

This study contributes to such framework. More specifically, the objective of this chapter is to identify factors important to the success of a KM strategy and to discuss their roles in supporting and sustaining effective KM initiatives. In particular, we contend that KM strategies and initiatives are less likely to be successful without such key elements as top management support, a culture of organizational learning, and effective measures of KM performance. Previous research suggests that these factors are critical because they all play significant roles in facilitating an organization to expand, cultivate, and apply available knowledge in ways that add value to its products and services (Wu, 2008). Next, we will discuss these factors in the context of KM.

TOP MANAGEMENT SUPPORT

Management support that starts at the top level in the hierarchy is one of the primary factors that strongly influence the success of a KM strategy. Prior research suggests that top management support is essential because the implementation of KM initiatives is resource intensive (Holsapple & Wu, 2009). Substantial financial, human, and material resources are necessary to carry out KM initiatives: sufficient budget is allocated to KM activities; eligible employees are assigned to perform those activities; and adequate facilities are employed to do the job. Such resources are more likely to be available when KM initiatives receive support from top management (Wu, 2008).

In addition, significant and visible top management support contributes to the legitimacy of KM initiatives. Legitimization indicates the validation of employees' particular activities and beliefs in an organization. As an important signal from executives, top management support is often used as a normative template to ensure employees about the organizational legitimacy of activities and beliefs. Therefore, top management support for KM initiatives will encourage employees' adoption of, and commitment to, the initiatives.

Emphasizing the importance of KM through organizational mission and goals also reflects the supportive role of senior management. By using organizational mission and goals to emphasize an organization's commitment to KM, top management credits KM initiatives with high priority, captures the attention of employees, and sets up the notion that KM initiatives are important to the success of the company.

Top management support for KM can be translated into a company structure that, by itself, sends a strong message to staff in terms of the significance of KM. For example, to respond to the business environment in which KM needs more respect and support, an organization may create a new management position – Chief Knowledge Officer (CKO). Job responsibility of a CKO may include "leveraging knowledge content," "developing a knowledge strategy," and "promoting awareness of KM" (McKeen & Staples, 2003).

Another important approach to show top management support is to link reward and personnel evaluation structures to desired KM behaviors

Figure 1. Facets of top management support

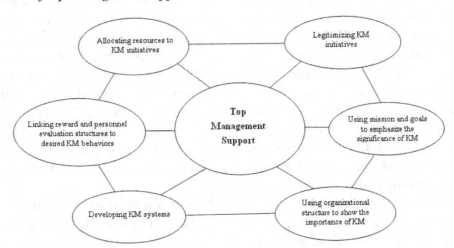

(Jennex & Olfman, 2004). Reward and punishment standards set by top management help define acceptable behavior because they usually specify what activities are encouraged and what are prohibited. Thus, by incorporating desired KM behavior into annual performance evaluation, top management supports KM initiatives via encouraging such KM behaviors as knowledge creation, sharing, and application.

Finally, top management can also support KM through developing and implementing KM systems (KMS). Alavi and Leidner (2001) define KMS as "a class of information systems applied to managing organizational knowledge. That is, they are IT-based systems developed to support and enhance the organizational processes of knowledge creation, storage/retrieval, transfer, and application" (p. 114). Organizations can use KMS to better leverage its knowledge resources by applying IT-based tools for knowledge creation, codifying and storing knowledge for reuse, and employing electronic communication channels for knowledge sharing.

In summary, this chapter identifies six important facets of top management support for KM (as shown in Figure 1). To provide more insights into these facets, we discuss each in further detail below.

ALLOCATING RESOURCES TO KM INITIATIVES

Wernerfelt (1984) conceptualizes resources broadly to include anything that may be thought of as a strength or weakness of a given firm. Based on this conceptualization, he defines resources as all tangible and intangible assets that are closely tied to an organization and can be used by the organization to create value. Similarly, Holsapple and Wu (2008a; 2008b) regard resources as various necessary production inputs that are owned or controlled by a firm. They assert that resources can bring a competitive advantage to an organization when they are rare or difficult to imitate, have no direct substitutes, and enable companies to pursue opportunities or avoid threats. In other words, resources must have some value that can be utilized by an organization to compete against its industry rivals.

Past research has attempted to categorize resources into different types. Barney (1991) contends that resources can be classified into three categories: physical, human, and capital. Grant (1991) adds three types of resources to the classification: finance, technology, and reputation. Based on a Delphi study, Holsapple and Joshi (2003) find that organizational resources can be categorized into four classes: financial, material, human, and knowledge. Grounded on Wernerfelt's definition of resources, Grant (1991) identifies three resource modes: tangible, intangible, and personnel-based. Tangible resources involve financial capital and physical assets such as facilities, equipments, and materials. Intangible resources include assets such as patents, trademarks, and copyrights. Finally, personnel-based resources consist of technical know-how and other knowledge assets that are rooted in organizational culture, employee training, employee education, etc. To create and maintain a competitive advantage, an organization must make different types of resources work together to create organizational capabilities.

To make KM initiatives a success, an organization needs to ensure that proper resources are brought to bear at appropriate times and that they appropriately relate to each other during the conduct of KM activities. This requires management to ensure that KM initiatives are provided with sufficient funding, that KM activities are performed by eligible employees, and that adequate materials and facilities are employed for the KM activities (Wu, 2008). However, these cannot be realized without the commitment of top executives, because it is their support that sets the tone and provides the resources.

LEGITIMIZING KM INITIATIVES

Legitimacy can be defined as a generalized perception or assumption that the actions of an organization's members are desirable and appropriate within the organization's structured system of mission, values, goals, norms, policies, and regulations (Suchman, 1995). Legitimizing KM initiatives can be viewed as processes in which employees are encouraged to formulate general perceptions that the KM initiatives are necessary and proper.

Previous research suggests that top management support plays a significant role in the legitimacy of KM initiatives. For example, Emmanuelides (1993) asserts that top management support can secure required legitimacy of business activities. Similarly, Weaver and colleagues (1999) also argue that top management support contributes to enhanced legitimacy. In summary, legitimization makes employees believe that KM initiatives are useful in their work processes and task activities, and thus facilitates employees' tendencies to welcome and embrace the initiatives.

Using Mission and Goals to Emphasize the Significance of KM

Mission and goals are recognized as the core purpose of an organization—what it wants to accomplish in the future (Sathe & Smart, 1997). Usually, mission and goals not only describe the business that an organization is in, but also provide the rationale for its current existence. Setting a clear target and timetable can make mission and goals more concrete because it provides near-sighted milestones to keep the organization moving in the right direction at the right time (Sathe & Smart, 1997). In addition, the statements of mission and goals should be meaningful, memorable, and communicative to all members of the organization so that its units and members can establish their own objectives that fully conform to the organization's core purpose.

Members' appreciation for the mission and goals of an organization plays an important role in encouraging coordination efforts and supporting organizational objectives (Desouza, 2005). To help employees achieve an intrinsic understanding of an organization's mission and goals, management should do the following. First, it should turn the statements of mission and goals into actions. As Desouza (2005) indicates, actions speak louder than words. To make employees appreciate its core purpose, an organization not only needs to rely solely on pronouncements and directives, but also needs to exhibit concrete actions that highlight its mission and goals. Second, it should live the organization's mission and goals by setting examples that encourage employees to incorporate them into their daily work as guiding principles. This can be further realized by publicizing the statement of mission and goals as widely as possible (e.g., webpage, informational handouts, newspaper articles), keeping employees engaged in the discussions of organizational mission and goals, and linking their daily work to the overall goal of the organization.

Many important organizations have leveraged their mission and goals to emphasize the significance of KM and strategic use of knowledge. For example, part of the mission statement of Fuji Xerox is that "we, the Fuji Xerox Group, will strive to build an environment for the creation and effective utilization of knowledge" (Fuji Xerox, 2002, p. 3). Here, the mission statement focuses on the necessity of knowledge creation and application. Another example, which highlights the strategic use of knowledge, is from Buckman Laboratories: "We... will excel in providing measurable, cost-effective improvements in output and quality for our customers by delivering customer-specific services and products, and the creative application of knowledge" (Buckman Laboratories, 2005, p. 1). Meanwhile, as a leading consulting firm, KPMG has a similar mission statement that emphasizes leveraging knowledge for value creation: "KPMG is the global network of professional advisory firms whose aim is to turn knowledge into value for the benefit of its clients, its people and its communities" (KPMG, 2002, p. 2). These examples indicate that KM is widely recognized by organizations as an essential ingredient for striving to achieve and maintain a competitive advantage.

Using Organizational Structure to Show the Importance of KM

Organizational structure refers to an organization's internal degree and pattern of integration among its members: whether they are primarily atom-

ized as individuals, integrated through relationship networks, or separated by formal divisions (Brickson, 2000). Past research identifies three main dimensions of organizational structure, each of which appears to have substantial implications for organizational strategic decision making and conduct of business activities.

The first is the dimension of centralization, which refers to the degree to which decision making and activity evaluation authority is concentrated (Fry & Slocum, 1984). In a centralized organization, decisions are usually made by very few managers at the top level and thus organizational decision making is relatively easy to be controlled and coordinated (Geisler, 2001). However, it is often the case that top managers in such an organization are not well positioned for making effective decisions, because they suffer from limits in cognitive capacity due to the lack of detailed knowledge that are necessary for quality decisions (Mukherji et al., 2004).

The second is the dimension of formalization, which refers to the degree to which organizational behaviors are prescribed by the rules, procedures, regulations, and policies (Hall, 1977). An organization with high level of formalization usually involves many standardized operations and business behaviors, and enforces a relatively high degree of control over its members and even its stakeholders (Geisler, 2001). Such an organization receives the benefit of eliminating role ambiguity, but limits members' decision making discretion (Mukherji et al., 2004).

The third is the dimension of complexity, which refers to the degree to which an organization is differentiated by the skills, functions, and occupations of its members and units (Mukherji et al., 2004). Hall (1977) argues that there are three types of complexity: horizontal differentiation, vertical differentiation, and spatial dispersion. Horizontal differentiation refers to the degree to which units are differentiated at the same level of an organization's hierarchy, while vertical differentiation refers to the number of hierarchic levels in the organization (Geisler, 2001). Spatial dispersion refers to the degree to which the organization's functions and units are distributed in different locations. An organization that simultaneously has many units at one hierarchy level, multiple hierarchical levels, and several geographic locations is considered to be highly complex.

Many organizations intuitively realize that they are not able to leverage knowledge resources to full potential unless decision making and activity evaluation authority for KM are concentrated at top level. That is, they need to change their organizational structures by creating a top-level position like Chief Knowledge Officer (CKO), who is in charge of KM initiatives and reports directly to the CEO. Moreover, a CKO can also efficiently and effectively deal with organizational structure complexity and thus ensure smooth implementation of new KM initiatives. Translating the strategic importance of KM into organizational structure has evolved further in leading companies. For example, it has been estimated that about one-fifth of the Fortune 500 companies have the position of CKO, even though some positions are not titled as CKO (Wu, 2008). In addition, Watt (1997) finds that with the big consulting firms leading the way, the approach of using organizational structure to emphasize KM has been adopted by many firms since the early 1990s.

A CKO should be a strategist, with the ability to see the big picture in the mind of the CEO and to put it into action by formalizing the rules, procedures, regulations, and policies for KM. According to McKeen and Staples (2003), an organization can leverage knowledge into tangible business benefits through the efforts of a CKO designed to: (1) set knowledge management strategic priorities, (2) establish a knowledge database of best practices, (3) gain senior executives' commitment to support a learning environment, (4) teach knowledge seekers to ask better and smarter questions in using intelligent resources, (5) put in place a process for managing intellectual assets, (6) obtain customer satisfaction information in near real-time, and (7)

globalize knowledge management. John Peetz, the first CKO of Ernst and Young, summarizes his job in three separate roles: evangelizing about the importance of sharing knowledge, running and supporting projects that find, publish, and distribute knowledge, and managing his staff (Wu, 2008). In short, realigning organizational structure with the importance of KM is an important step to the success of KM initiatives.

Developing Knowledge Management Systems

KMS allow organizations to leverage their knowledge resources by using computer-based technologies. Prior research identifies two models of KMS: the repository model and the network model (Wu, 2008). These two models are also known as integrative architecture and interactive architecture, respectively.

The repository model involves a codification strategy that allows knowledge to be carefully codified and digitally stored so that it can be accessed and used easily by anyone in the organization (Hansen et al., 1999). Thus, this approach focuses on knowledge reuse through knowledge codification and storage. One important technical component for repository model is an electronic knowledge repository (EKR) that involves technologies such as Lotus Notes, Web-based intranets, and Microsoft's Exchange, and that is usually enhanced by search engines, document management tools, and other tools that support editing and access (Wu, 2008).

The network model involves a personalization strategy that helps people transfer knowledge in a geographically distributed business environment by using computer networks (Hansen et al., 1999). Thus, this approach focuses on knowledge sharing among people through computer-based communication channels. Important technical components for network model include electronic mail, which provides users with one-to-one and one-to-many communication channels, and groupware which allows people in the same group to have topic-based discussions and collaborative interchanges.

According to Jennex and Olfman (2004), two different approaches can be employed to develop a knowledge management system: the process approach and the infrastructure approach. The process approach focuses on the use of knowledge in a business process and aims to make the process more efficient. When using this approach, developers must recognize knowledge needs in the process: what type of knowledge is required, who needs the knowledge, and when it is needed. Because this approach is business-process-based and users of the system usually know how to exploit the knowledge, the approach places minimal demands on the system to capture knowledge context and application guidelines.

The infrastructure approach differs in two ways. First, it focuses on the use of knowledge within and across a whole organization and aims to allow all the units of the organization to take advantage of the knowledge codified into the system. Second, the approach captures a great deal of knowledge context and application guidelines in order to explain the codified knowledge and the technical details needed to help users identify, retrieve, and utilize the knowledge. Thus, this approach emphasizes strong network capacity facilitating fast knowledge transfer, well-developed database structure enabling efficient knowledge storage, and appropriate knowledge classification differentiating various kinds of knowledge. To create comprehensive KMS, an organization can use both approaches: with the process approach facilitating the development of KMS for a specific business activity and infrastructure approach fostering the integration of the process-based KMS into a single comprehensive system that can be leveraged by the entire organization instead of just a single functional department (Jennex & Olfman, 2004).

LINKING REWARD AND PERSONNEL EVALUATION STRUCTURES TO DESIRED KM BEHAVIORS

Reward and personnel evaluation programs are important not only because they give management a clear picture of employees' performance, but also because they motivate employees to perform in accordance with management's expectations. Generally, the objective of a reward and personnel evaluation program is to improve firm performance and to make a fair judgment about employees' performance that can be used for decision making. According to Levinson (1987), a reward and personnel evaluation program provides managers with five major benefits: (1) an opportunity to learn about employee expectations, fears, potential, and goals, (2) a chance to learn more about their managerial style and how it impacts employees' performance, (3) clues into the informal day-to-day life of the organization, (4) a formal approach to reward and motivate employees and to reinforce effective performance, and (5) trustworthy information that can be used to make decisions about compensation, promotions, and job design.

Reward and personnel evaluation structures have been recognized as one of the most important determinants of desired KM behaviors. Using rewards as a means to encourage critical KM behaviors has already been adopted by many organizations. For example, to create a knowledge-sharing environment in the World Bank, management of the organization makes knowledge-sharing activities as part of the annual performance evaluation. Similarly, the incentive and promotion systems at McKinsey & Company are designed to recognize and reward employees who create and share knowledge (Ghosh, 2004). This knowledge creation and sharing is facilitated by creating a Practice Development

Network (PDNet), which allows employees to codify and select knowledge from repositories. Also, to ensure that the knowledge sharing is not skewed towards sharing between experts, McKinsey assigns experts to its client studies so that everyone on the study can share the expertise (Ghosh, 2004). Another example is that rewards are used to promote organizational learning. For instance, at one consulting company, employees are required to document what they have learned about what works and what does not, and they are partially compensated based on how often their documentation is accessed by others (Wu, 2008). As these examples reveal, reward and personnel evaluation can play an important role in guiding KM behaviors of employees.

A CULTURE OF ORGANIZATIONAL LEARNING

Organizational Culture

Organizational culture refers to "the set of shared, taken-for-granted implicit assumptions that a group holds and that determine how it perceives, thinks about, and reacts to its various environments" (Schein, 1985, p. 238). Thus, culture can be viewed as a shared mental model that influences how individuals interpret behaviors and behave themselves (Saxena & Shah, 2008). The management literature suggests two different levels of organizational culture: deepest level and observable level. At the deepest level, organizational culture comprises values, which are inherent preferences about what an organization wants to pursue and how to achieve it (Kayworth & Leidner, 2003). At an observable level, organizational culture includes norms and practices that stem from underlying values (Delong & Fahey, 2000).

As the personality of an organization, culture is holistic, historically determined, and socially constructed (Ajmal & Koskinen, 2008). It exists at various levels in the organization and manifests

itself in virtually all aspects of organizational life. Generally, different organizations have distinctive "personalities", i.e., distinctive cultures at work. In other words, culture may serve as a label of the identity of an organization – "who we are," "what we do," and "how we operate" (Wu, 2008). It determines, through the organization's legends, rituals, beliefs, conventions, values, norms, and practices, the way in which "things are done around here" (Saxena & Shah, 2008). According to Ajmal and Koskinen (2008), organizational culture also serves as a foundation for management style and structure. Because it provides norms regarding the "right" and "wrong" methods of operation, organizational culture guides the ways a company manages business processes and reacts to external environmental changes. That is, organizational culture determines how to achieve business objectives, how business decisions are made, and how employees should behave in particular situations.

Organizational Learning

Organizational learning refers to the ways that organizations build, supplement, and structure knowledge and routines around their activities and within their cultures, and develop organizational efficiency by improving the use of the broad skills of their workforces (Dodgson, 1993). The term "routines" includes not only the structure of codes, beliefs, values, and frameworks that shape and define the firms, but also the forms, policies, procedures, conventions, and strategies under which firms are constructed and operated (Wu, 2008).

To enrich the concept of organizational learning, researchers have described it in detail via its attributes: existence, breadth, elaborateness, and thoroughness (Huber, 1991). Existence of organizational learning refers to the assumption that an organization learns if any of its departments (no matter how many) obtain knowledge that is relevant and valuable to the organization. Breadth

Figure 2. Developing a culture of organizational learning

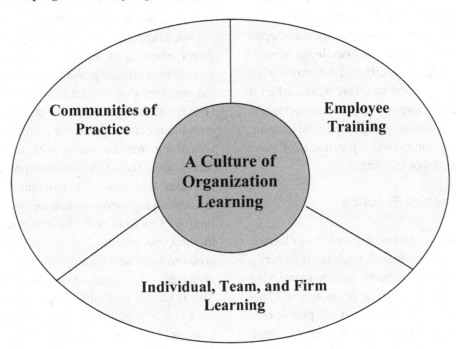

of organizational learning refers to the assertion that more organizational learning occurs when more of the organization's departments acquire the knowledge and regard it as relevant and valuable. Elaborateness of organizational learning refers to the claim that more organizational learning occurs when more varied interpretations are derived. Finally, thoroughness of organizational learning refers to the statement that more organizational learning occurs when more departments of the organization uniformly comprehend the various interpretations.

Learning in an organization has three levels: individual, team (i.e., learning in small or large groups), and firm. All these levels of learning are necessary for an organization to possess the requisite knowledge for strategic business objectives. From a business strategy perspective, all levels of learning are critical, and should be nurtured and made a natural part of organizational culture; this is because organizational learning reflects a company's capacity to acquire or generate the

knowledge necessary to survive and compete in its environment (Bennet & Bennet, 2003). This perspective is in keeping with that advanced by Friedlander (1983, p. 194): "the crucial element in learning is that the organism be consciously aware of differences and alternatives and have consciously chosen one of these alternatives. The choice may be not to construct behavior but, rather, to change one's cognitive maps or understandings."

A culture of organizational learning can have a strong impact on individual, team, and firms' pursuit of knowledge and skills. More specifically, the culture influences organizational learning through values, norms, and practices (Delong & Fahey, 2000). From a KM perspective, a culture of organizational learning is an integral part of KM strategy and reflects an organization's capability in undertaking effective KM initiatives. Prior work suggests that such an organizational culture is of great importance to KM success because it fosters activities of generation, storage, sharing, and application of knowledge (Kayworth & Leidner, 2003). Particularly, it facilitates knowledge sharing by encouraging peer collaboration and open communication; it promotes knowledge generation through helping specify and determine what should be created, why to create it, and when it should be created. Two very important components of developing a culture of organizational learning are building communities of practice (CoP) and providing employee training.

Communities of Practice

A CoP refers to a group of people who have a common interest and work together informally in a responsible, independent fashion to promote learning, solve problems, or develop new ideas (Storck & Hill, 2000). Within a CoP, people collaborate directly, learn from each other, and share knowledge and experience; all these activities foster a culture of organizational learning. Moreover, the creating, learning, sharing, and using of knowledge in a CoP are usually spontaneous because the community has a focus on the open sharing of ideas and best practices (Bennet & Bennet, 2003). Groups are important to both what people learn and how they learn. Wegner (1999) observes that knowledge, traveling on the back of practice, is readily shared among community members. Similarly, Brown and Duguid (2000) argue that a community enables its members to generate, share, and deploy highly esoteric knowledge.

In general, a community facilitates both single-loop and double-loop learning. Single-loop learning often takes place when problems are solved by changing actions or approaches for achieving a desired outcome, but without changing the underlying theory or assumptions about those actions (Bennet & Bennet, 2003). Focusing on a specific field, a community provides a thought test-bed for creating and sharing better ways of taking actions, developing new processes and approaches, and

applying new management ideas. In this way, a CoP fosters single-loop learning.

Sometimes, the open exchange of ideas and direct interactions among members of a community may challenge the underlying theory and assumptions about the actions and the approaches (Bennet & Bennet, 2003). In other words, when a problem occurs and never seems to be solved, something may be wrong with the underlying theory about the actions and the approaches. This indicates that when the environment changes, the underlying theory or assumptions need to be improved to work with the new settings. When this happens, an entirely new understanding of the problem and the difficulty of solving it must be reviewed and a new theory needs to be developed. This is known as double-loop learning.

A CoP also plays a critical role in double-loop learning, because a community encourages the exchange of ideas, experiences, and assumptions that open its members to new ways of understanding a problem as well as to new theories of tackling the problem. Since a CoP facilitates both single-loop and double-loop learning, it has been recognized as one of the most important elements of any organization that strives to construct and deliver a successful KM strategy. In addition, a CoP can serve as a bridging mechanism that cuts across regional, divisional, and geographic boundaries within an organization. This bridging role enhances the function of the action-oriented and knowledge-based CoP in fostering a culture of organizational learning.

Employee Training

Training is a means to develop specific useful skills through learning. Employee training is crucial to the development of a culture of organizational learning because it improves employees' knowledge processing capabilities and thus motivates them to learn more. Lee and colleagues (1995) suggest that formal training in an organization fosters a culture of learning due to the factor that training significantly influences employees' skills and job performance. In a study of the relationship between individual difference and skill in end-user computing, Harrison and Rainer (1992) also indicate that training plays a key role in facilitating a culture of organizational learning.

Having clear training goals is an important ingredient in employee training success. In order to be measurable, training goals should clearly describe what skill will be developed, what related knowledge will be learned, and what type of job behavior will be changed as a result of training. In addition, training goals should also state how the training will contribute to employees' career growth: from where they are today to where they will be in the future (Roberts et al., 2005). Setting clear training goals not only helps managers evaluate a training program, but also motivates employees to participate in it.

Training can be conducted in different types of environments and two of them are classroom-based environment and virtual learning environment. In a classroom-based environment, learners usually sit in a real classroom and have instructors give lectures. In such a training environment, learners and instructors form a learning community and can easily communicate face-to-face with each other to achieve optimal learning outcome. A virtual learning environment is a collection of computer-based tools that allow real-time interactions among participants and provide access to a wide range of resources. In this training environment, learners can access the training materials independently through computers, study at their own pace at times that fit their schedules, and use different material displays based on their individual needs (Piccoli et al., 2001). Because a virtual learning environment is usually built upon a well-established network infrastructure, it fosters communities of learners and encourages electronic interactions and discussions. In the environment, the learning process is thus no longer an isolated individual effort, but a particular course of many-to-many collaborations among learners and with instructors (Piccoli et al., 2001). The most important difference between virtual learning and classroom-based learning is the interaction style. In a classroom-based learning environment, face-to-face interaction is the main communication method for students and instructors, while in a virtual learning environment, they all use computer-mediated communication and hence, cannot really see each other.

Measuring training effectiveness is critical because it helps managers identify progress toward training goals. In addition, showing training results can encourage management to support training programs because managers are more willing to undertake or sponsor a program that will yield a return on investment. As a pioneer training and education researcher, Kirkpatrick (1998) proposes that training programs can be evaluated at four levels: reaction, learning, behavior, and result. The first measures the satisfaction of learners with the training material, instructor, lecture, schedule, and environment. The second measures the percentage of skills learned by learners through comparing their newly acquired skills with the skills defined by the training goals (Roberts et al., 2005). The third measures the effect of training on learners' job performance. At the fourth level, the effect of training on overall organizational performance is measured. Any discrepancies identified during these evaluations should be noted and necessary adjustments should be made to the training program to make it meet specified goals (Roberts et al., 2005).

EFFECTIVE MEASURES OF KM PERFORMANCE

The inherently intangible characteristic of KM makes its measurement difficult (Ahn & Chang, 2004). However, to make KM strategy a success, it is essential to effectively measure KM performance (Holsapple & Wu, 2008b). Well-designed, reliable measures are necessary for managers to assess KM progress, improve KM initiatives, and achieve valid comparisons with other companies. It is also widely accepted that effective measures of KM performance are indispensable to encourage further organizational investment in knowledge management. Although there is little one-size-fits-all guidance on measuring KM performance, some useful approaches emerge after reviewing prior studies.

To identify leading organizations in the knowledge-based economy, Teleos and KNOW Network have conducted the internationally recognized *Most Admired Knowledge Enterprise* (MAKE[sm]) study (Holsapple & Wu, 2008a). Teleos is an independent KM and intellectual capital research company based in the United Kingdom; the Web-based KNOW Network is operated by Teleos and aims to help practitioners achieve the best possible levels of KM performance. To measure KM performance, the MAKE[sm] study employs eight criteria that are deemed primary elements of KM success: (1) ability to develop and deliver knowledge-based goods/services, (2) top management support for managing knowledge, (3) success in establishing an enterprise knowledge culture, (4) effectiveness in creating an environment of knowledge sharing, (5) success in maximizing the value of the enterprise's intellectual capital, (6) effectiveness in managing customer knowledge to increase loyalty and value, (7) success in establishing a culture of continuous learning, and (8) ability to manage knowledge in ways that create shareholder value (Holsapple & Wu, 2009).

In developing a "knowledge value chain" (KVC) framework, Lee and Yang (2000) argue that it is difficult to evaluate KM initiatives via financial ratios and thus propose two kinds of non-financial assessments: operating performance measures and learning measures. Examples of the former include lead times, customer satisfaction, and employee productivity, while the latter involves the numbers of participants in CoP, of employees trained, and of customers benefited

by the implementation of KM initiatives. They further argue that these non-financial measures are all key indicators of KM competence.

Understanding the difficulty of measuring business benefits of KM, de Gooijer (2000) has introduced a framework for measuring KM performance and another for measuring KM behaviors. The former employs a scorecard to assess the degree to which KM objectives are achieved in six key result areas: (1) KM strategy, (2) products and services, (3) IT infrastructure, (4) business processes, (5) relationships among stakeholders, and (6) organizational culture. The latter involves seven levels of people's skills in adopting and using KM resources: (1) awareness but non-use of KM tools or practices, (2) seeking information about KM, (3) personal experimentation with KM tools and practices, (4) personal implementation of KM practices, (5) engagement with impacts and consequences of KM behavior, (6) active collaboration in all aspects of work, and (7) refocusing KM skills on new business opportunities. The framework also shows some typical behaviors of managers and the roles they play in relation to individuals at each level.

Emphasizing the need for metrics to assess the effectiveness of KM initiatives, Lee and colleagues (2005) propose a knowledge management performance index (KMPI) defined as a logistic function involving five major KM activities: knowledge creation, accumulation, internalization, sharing, and utilization. Multiple constructs are further developed to measure each of these five contributors to KMPI. More specifically, knowledge creation is assessed by using two constructs: knowledge creation by task understandings and knowledge creation by information understandings; knowledge accumulation includes three constructs: database utilization, systematic management of task knowledge, and individual capacity for accumulation; knowledge internalization depends on three constructs: capability to internalize task-related knowledge, education opportunity, and level of organization learning; knowledge sharing

Table 1. KM performance measures

Researcher	KM Performance Variable	KM Construct
Bogner and Bansal (2007)	KM capability	(1) New knowledge development, (2) internal KM, and (3) KM capture.
Choi, Poon, and Davis (2008)	KM strategy	(1) KM focus and (2) KM source.
Chuang (2004)	KM capability	(1) Structural KM resource, (2) cultural KM resource, (3) human KM resource, and (4) technical KM resource.
Darroch (2005)	KM orientation	(1) Knowledge acquisition, (2) knowledge dissemination, and (3) responsiveness to knowledge.
Decarolis and Deeds (1999)	Organizational knowledge	(1) Knowledge stocks and (2) knowledge flows.
Marques and Simon (2006)	KM practices	(1) Orientation towards the development, transfer, and protection of knowledge, (2) continuous learning in the organization, (3) an understanding of the organization as a global system, (4) development of an innovative culture that encourages R&D projects, (5) approach based on individuals, and (6) competence development and management based on competences.
Tanriverdi (2005)	KM capability	(1) Product KM capability, (2) customer KM capability, and (3) managerial KM capability.
Wiklund and Shepherd (2003)	Knowledge-based resources	Knowledge position (i.e., measuring procedural knowledge).

involves two constructs: core knowledge sharing and common knowledge sharing; and knowledge utilization also consists of two constructs: degree of knowledge utilization in organization and knowledge utilization culture.

In addition to the above studies, other prior work on the relationship between KM performance and firm performance also offers some valuable solutions to the measurement problem. Table 1 summarizes these solutions.

CONCLUSION

Over the past decade, the rapid proliferation of KM has been one of the most striking developments in business. Regarding KM as a primary driver of competitive advantage, this chapter suggests that organizations must develop a clear strategy for making their KM initiatives a success, rather than merely have some form of KM practice. The chapter provides important guidance for managers on how to create and deliver a successful KM strategy. Specifically, we propose a framework that identifies three factors critical to the success of

the strategy: top management support, a culture of organizational learning, and effective measures of KM performance. Multiple facets of these factors are advanced to cover more of the subject and gain a better understanding of the three factors. This study contributes to practice by giving managers a clear picture of why top management support is vital to the success of KM initiatives, what needs to be integrated into an organizational culture, and how to directly and effectively measure KM performance.

REFERENCES

Ahn, J. H., & Chang, S. G. (2004). Assessing the contribution of knowledge business performance: The KP3 methodology. *Decision Support Systems*, *36*(4), 403–416. doi:10.1016/S0167-9236(03)00029-0

Ajmal, M. M., & Koskinen, K. U. (2008). Knowledge transfer in project-based organizations: An organizational culture perspective. *Project Management Journal*, *39*(1), 7–15. doi:10.1002/pmj.20031

Alavi, M., & Leidner, D. E. (2001). Review: Knowledge management and knowledge management systems: Conceptual foundations and research issues. *MIS Quarterly, 25*(1), 107–136. doi:10.2307/3250961

Barney, J. (1991). Firm resources and sustained competitive advantage. *Journal of Management, 17*(1), 99–120. doi:10.1177/014920639101700108

Bennet, A., & Bennet, D. (2003). The rise of the knowledge organization. In C. W. Holsapple (Ed.), *Handbook on knowledge management 1: Knowledge matters*. Berlin: Springer Verlag.

Bogner, W. C., & Bansal, P. (2007). Knowledge management as the basis of sustained high performance. *Journal of Management Studies, 44*(1), 165–188. doi:10.1111/j.1467-6486.2007.00667.x

Brickson, S. (2000). The impact of identity orientation on individual and organizational outcomes in demographically diverse settings. *Academy of Management Review, 25*(1), 82–101. doi:10.2307/259264

Brown, J. S., & Duguid, P. (2000). *The social life of information*. Boston, MA: Harvard Business School Press.

Buckman Laboratories. (2005). Retrieved from http://www.buckman.com/eng/AR/Buckman_AR_2005.pdf

Choi, B., Poon, S. K., & Davis, J. G. (2008). Effects of knowledge management strategy on organizational performance: A complementarity theory-based approach. *Omega, 36*(2), 235–251. doi:10.1016/j.omega.2006.06.007

Chuang, S. (2004). A resource-based perspective on knowledge management capability and competitive advantage: An empirical investigation. *Expert Systems with Applications, 27*(3), 459–465. doi:10.1016/j.eswa.2004.05.008

Darroch, J. (2005). Knowledge management, innovation, and firm performance. *Journal of Knowledge Management, 9*(3), 101–115. doi:10.1108/13673270510602809

de Gooijer, J. (2000). Designing a knowledge management performance framework. *Journal of Knowledge Management, 4*(4), 303–310. doi:10.1108/13673270010379858

Decarolis, D. M., & Deeds, D. L. (1999). The impact of stocks and flows of organizational knowledge on firm performance: An empirical investigation of the biotechnology industry. *Strategic Management Journal, 20*(10), 953–968. doi:10.1002/(SICI)1097-0266(199910)20:10<953::AID-SMJ59>3.0.CO;2-3

DeLong, D. W., & Fahey, L. (2000). Diagnosing culture barriers to knowledge management. *The Academy of Management Executive, 14*(4), 113–127.

Desouza, K. (2005). Vital dimensions of mission-critical organizations. *KM Review, 8*(3), 28–31.

Dodgson, M. (1993). Organizational learning: A review of some literatures. *Organization Studies, 14*(3), 375–394. doi:10.1177/017084069301400303

Emmanuelides, P. A. (1993). Towards an integrative framework of performance in product development projects. *Journal of Engineering and Technology Management, 10*(4), 363–392. doi:10.1016/0923-4748(93)90029-I

Friedlander, F. (1983). Patterns of individual and organizational learning. In S. Srivastva & Associates (Eds.), *The executive mind: New insights on managerial thought and action*. San Francisco: Jossey-Bass.

Fry, L. W., & Slocum, J. W. (1984). Technology structure and workgroup effectiveness: A test of a contingency model. *Academy of Management Journal, 27*(2), 221–246. doi:10.2307/255923

Fuji Xerox. (2002). Retrieved from http://www.fujixerox.com/eng/company/ecology/report2002/2002e-01.pdf

Gates, B. (1999). *Business @ the speed of thought: Using a digital nervous system.* New York: Warner Books, Inc.

Geisler, E. (2001). Organizing for e-business: The implementation of management principles in electronic commerce. Retrieved from http://www.stuart.iit.edu/faculty/workingpapers/geisler/organizin g%20for%20e-business.pdf

Ghosh, T. (2004). Creating incentives for knowledge sharing. Retrieved from http://ocw.mit.edu/NR/rdonlyres/Sloan-School-of-Management/15-575Spring-2004/72ACA0F6-3943-4C1F-AB7F0 013602D7A61/0/tanu_15575.pdf

Grant, R. M. (1991). The resource-based theory of competitive advantage: Implications for strategy formulation. *California Management Review, 33*(3), 114–135.

Hall, R. H. (1977). *Organizations: Structure and process.* Englewood Cliffs, NJ: Prentice-Hall.

Hansen, M. T., Nohria, N., & Tierney, T. (1999). What's your strategy for managing knowledge? *Harvard Business Review, 77*(2), 106–116.

Harrison, A. W., & Rainer, R. K. (1992). The influence of individual differences on skill in end-user computing. *Journal of Management Information Systems, 9*(1), 93–111. doi:10.1080/10580539208906858

Holsapple, C. W., & Joshi, K. D. (2003). A knowledge management ontology. In C. W. Holsapple (Ed.), *Handbook on knowledge management: Vol.1, knowledge matters* (pp. 89-124). Berlin/Heidelberg: Springer-Verlag.

Holsapple, C. W., & Wu, J. (2008a). Does knowledge management pay off? In *Proceedings of 41ˢᵗ Hawaii International Conference on System Sciences,* Hawaii.

Holsapple, C. W., & Wu, J. (2008b). In search of a missing link. *Knowledge Management Research & Practice, 6*(1), 31–40. doi:10.1057/palgrave.kmrp.8500170

Holsapple, C. W., & Wu, J. (2009). *An elusive antecedent of superior firm performance: The knowledge management factor.* Working paper.

Huber, G. P. (1991). Organizational learning: The contributing processes and the literatures. *Organization Science, 2*(1), 88–115. doi:10.1287/orsc.2.1.88

Jennex, M. E., & Olfman, L. (2004). Assessing knowledge management success/effectiveness models. *Proceedings of the 37ᵗʰ Annual Hawaii International Conference on System Science.* IEEE Computer Society Press.

Kayworth, T., & Leidner, D. (2003). Organizational culture as a knowledge resource. In C. W. Holsapple (Ed.), *Handbook on knowledge management, volume 1: Knowledge matters* (pp. 235-252). Berlin/Heidelberg: Springer-Verlag.

Kirkpatrick, D. (1998). *Evaluating training programs.* San Francisco: Berrett-Koehler Publishers.

KPMG. (2002). Retrieved from www.kpmg.com/aci/docs/aci_uk.doc

Lee, C. C., & Yang, J. (2000). Knowledge value chain. *Journal of Management Development, 19*(9), 783–793. doi:10.1108/02621710010378228

Lee, K. C., Lee, S., & Kang, I. W. (2005). KMPI: Measuring knowledge management performance. *Information & Management, 42*(3), 469–482. doi:10.1016/j.im.2001.09.001

Lee, S. M., Kim, Y. R., & Lee, J. (1995). An empirical study of the relationships among end user information system acceptance, training, and effectiveness. *Journal of Management Information Systems, 12*(2), 189–202.

Levinson, D. (1987). Making employee performance evaluations work for you. *Nonprofit World, 5*(5), 28–30.

Marques, D. P., & Simon, F. J. G. (2006). The effect of knowledge management practices on firm performance. *Journal of Knowledge Management, 10*(3), 143–156. doi:10.1108/13673270610670911

McKeen, J. D., & Staples, D. S. (2003). Knowledge managers: Who they are and what they do. In C. W. Holsapple (Ed.), *Handbook on knowledge management: Vol. 1, knowledge matters* (pp. 21-41). Berlin/Heidelberg: Springer-Verlag.

Mukherji, A., Kedia, B. L., Parente, R., & Kock, N. (2004). Strategies, structures, and information architectures: Toward international gestalts. *Problems and Perspectives in Management, 3*(1), 181–195.

Piccoli, G., Ahmad, R., & Ives, B. (2001). Web-based virtual learning environments: A research framework and a preliminary assessment of effectiveness in basic IT skills training. *MIS Quarterly, 25*(4), 401–426. doi:10.2307/3250989

Roberts, G., Seldon, G., & Roberts, C. (2005). *Human resources management.* Retrieved from http://www.sba.gov/library/pubs/eb-4.doc

Russ, M., & Jones, J. K. (2005). A typology of knowledge management strategies for hospital preparedness: What lessons can be learned? *International Journal of Emergency Management, 2*(4), 319–342. doi:10.1504/IJEM.2005.008743

Sathe, V., & Smart, G. H. (1997). Building a winning organization: The mind-body diagnostic framework. *Journal of Management Development, 16*(6), 418–427. doi:10.1108/02621719710174570

Saxena, S., & Shah, H. (2008). Effect of organizational culture on creating learned helplessness attributions in R&D professionals: A canonical correlation analysis. *Vikalpa, 33*(2), 25–45.

Schein, E. H. (1985). *Organizational culture and leadership.* San Francisco, CA: Jossey-Bass Publishers.

Storck, J., & Hill, P. (2000). Knowledge diffusion through 'strategic communities.'. *Sloan Management Review, 41*(2), 2000.

Suchman, M. C. (1995). Managing legitimacy: Strategic and institutional approaches. *Academy of Management Journal, 20*(3), 571–610.

Tanriverdi, H. (2005). Information technology relatedness, knowledge management capability, and performance of multibusiness firms. *MIS Quarterly, 29*(2), 311–334.

Watt, P. (1997). Knowing it all. *Intranet,* 17-18.

Weaver, G. R., Trevino, L. K., & Cochran, P. L. (1999). Integrated and decoupled corporate social performance: Management commitments, external pressures, and corporate ethics practices. *Academy of Management Journal, 42*(5), 539–552. doi:10.2307/256975

Wenger, E. (1999). *Communities of practice: Learning, meaning, and identity.* New York: Cambridge University Press.

Wernerfelt, B. (1984). A resource-based view of the firm. *Strategic Management Journal, 5*(2), 171–180. doi:10.1002/smj.4250050207

Wiklund, J., & Shepherd, D. (2003). Knowledge-based resources, entrepreneurial orientation, and the performance of small and medium-sized businesses. *Strategic Management Journal, 24*(13), 1307–1314. doi:10.1002/smj.360

Wu, J. (2008). *Exploring the link between knowledge management performance and firm performance.* Unpublished doctoral dissertation, University of Kentucky.f

Chapter 13
Aligning Business and Knowledge Strategies:
A Practical Approach for Aligning Business and Knowledge Strategies

Lars Taxén
Linköping University, Sweden

ABSTRACT

The alignment of business and knowledge strategies necessarily includes the individual and the organizational perspectives. A major problem in this context is to reconcile these perspectives into a common framework for alignment. To this end, an intermediate level is introduced–the activity domain. The activity domain is a canonical structure comprising all kinds of organizational units, irrespective of size and organizational level. The organization is regarded as a constellation of activity domains, each having a capability to produce an outcome that the organization needs in order to fulfill its goals. Alignment is defined as the management of dependencies between capabilities such that these capabilities fit the business's strategic intents. As a consequence, business and knowledge strategies can be linked to the same target–the activity domain. Practical guidelines and alignment targets for these strategies are suggested.

INTRODUCTION

The quintessence of alignment is how to bring various elements of an organization to work in concert in order to maximize its overall performance. Achieving and maintaining fit between these elements is a necessity for survival in a changing economy. For example, aligning IT and business is still the number one concern for information technology (IT) executives (Luftman & McLean, 2004). In the era of globalization, ever escalating turbulence of the market, and increasing complexity of products, alignment pose immense challenges (e.g. Chan, 2002; Earl, 1996; Hackney, Burn, Cowan, & Dhillon, 2000; Opdahl, 1997; Regev & Wegmann, 2003). Some of the difficulties are:

- There is an ambiguity of how to define alignment, and how to decide which elements are relevant for alignment. Common elements

DOI: 10.4018/978-1-60566-348-7.ch013

mentioned in connection with alignment are externally oriented ones such as strategies, goals, market needs, and internally oriented ones such as IT, business processes and knowledge.

- Central concepts in alignment such as "business goal", "business structure", "informal organization structure", "strategy", etc., are inherently vague (Chan, 2002).

- Alignment spans across the boundaries of several organizational units. With increased organizational dynamics such as outsourcing, alliances formation, etc., both intra- and inter-organizational aspects need to be considered. Outsourcing, for example, implies that the control of alignment concerning the outsourced functions is lost.

- Alignment includes not only technical issues but also social ones such aligning different informal structures and organizational cultures (Chan, 2002).

- There is an apparent lack of theories that can provide an integrative, socio-technical foundation for alignment (e.g. Martinsons & Davidson, 2003).

Since IT is an indispensable part of organizations, it is not surprising that alignment of business and IT has been in focus for many years. Approaches, i.e., constellations of methods, processes and implementation strategies for achieving business/IT alignment, are often referred to as Strategic Information System Planning (SISP). According to Earl (1996), SISP approaches can be categorized from the particular underpinning assumptions driving the approach:

- *Business led* maintains that business aspects should lead information system (IS) implementations: "current business direction or plans are the only basis upon which IS plans can be built and therefore business planning should drive SISP" (Earl, 1996, p. 141).

- *Method driven* assumes that SISP "is enhanced by, or depends on, use of a formal technique or method" (ibid., p. 143). This approach focuses on the "best" method and is often executed with the aid of consultants.

- *Administrative* insists that the aims of SISP can be reached by formal procedures for allocating IS resources. Business units submit IS development proposals to committees who examine "project viability, common system possibilities, and resource consequences" (ibid., p. 144).

- *Technological* claims that "an IS oriented model of the business is a necessary outcome of SISP and therefore analytical, modeling techniques are appropriate" (ibid., p. 145). The emphasis is on deriving architectures for the organization. The end product is a business model, and formal methods – often supporter by CAD-tools – are used to define activities, processes, and data flows of the business. The model tends to become complex and hard to make sense of for others than those directly involved in the modeling effort.

- *Organizational* is based on "IS decisions being made through continuous integration between the IS function and the organization". This approach eschews long-term plans and focuses on continuous decision-making activities shared by business and IS. Organizational learning about business problems and opportunities of business and IT are emphasized. A distinguishing feature is the concentration on one or a few "themes" in the organization as targets for alignment, such as service level, product development, or low-cost administration. These themes are then pursued for several years.

Although all approaches have pros and cons, it appears that the organizational one is superior, contrary to espoused wisdom:

[Both] qualitative and quantitative evidence suggest that the organizational approach is likely to be the best SISP approach to use. The organizational approach is perhaps the least formal and structured. It also differs significantly from conventional prescriptions in the literature and practice. (Earl, 1996, p. 153)

The results indicate that an evolutionary, step-by-step, and exploratory approach is more effective in achieving alignment than more rational, formalistic and pre-planned approaches. This view is underpinned by Ciborra (1997), who claims that prevailing planning approaches to alignment in the IS literature do not mirror actual, everyday practices in organizations. Alignment occurs more or less ad-hoc through improvisation and tinkering, if it occurs at all:

[Alignment] does not obtain because strategy is not such a clear concept or practice, since due to various, turbulent and unpredictable circumstances, managers are busy muddling through, betting and tinkering. Furthermore, the use of the technology itself is characterized by improvisations of various sorts [...] and by many unexpected outcomes. (Ciborra, 1997, p. 72)

The advantages of the organizational approach, and the ways implementation of alignment are carried out in practice, indicate that knowledge and learning are immanent aspects of alignment. This perspective was reinforced with the surge of knowledge management (KM) beginning in the mid 1990s (e.g. Wilson, 2002). Organizations began to see knowledge as an asset that should be subject to strategic considerations in line with other assets like capital, equipments, buildings, machinery, etc.

However, with the inclusion of knowledge, the challenges of alignment took on a new dimension. Knowledge does not easily lend itself to management. Indeed, some scholars claim that KM is not possible:

I don't believe knowledge can be managed. Knowledge Management is a poor term, but we are stuck with it, I suppose. "Knowledge Focus" or "Knowledge Creation" (Nonaka) are better terms, because they describe a mindset, which sees knowledge as activity, not an object. It is a human vision, not a technological one. (Sveiby, 2001, reported in Wilson, 2002, p. 9)

The picture that emanates from the current state of alignment can reasonably be described as a confused one, based on a fragile and detached foundation of nebulous concepts, including the fundamental issue of knowledge. It is not surprising that practical results of alignment endeavors are scarce.

It appears that alignment cannot be preplanned; it is an ongoing, continuous and evolutionary process where learning and findings "on the way" are vital elements. At the same time, everything cannot be floating around, and efforts cannot be pursued ad-hoc. This calls for some stable structure guiding alignment endeavors. Moreover, it is obvious that business goals, business strategies, processes, organizational structure, information technology, knowledge, and other elements relevant for alignment are interdependent in various ways. Unless we understand the whole picture, alignment efforts are bound to have marginal effects and may sometimes even produce counterproductive results. Stated differently, there is a need for some kind of architecture that provides a skeleton or backbone of alignment.

To this end, I will recast alignment from a particular perspective that I call the *activity domain approach*. The activity domain can be conveniently thought of as any organizational unit where people work together on some object of work in order to produce something that the organization needs. So, for example, in a car industry, the work contexts that gravitate around developing the chassis, the motor, the brake system, the software applications, and so on, can be considered as activity domains. Activity domains may coincide with organizational functions found in organizational plans. However, as we shall see, the activity domain is meant to be a far more fundamental construct; its intention is to capture the essential features of coordinated, socially oriented activity in general and not only in organizations. In the context of alignment, the activity domain provides a common, integrating mechanism for aligning business and knowledge strategies.

Accordingly, the purpose of this chapter is to discuss how alignment might benefit from the activity domain approach. The focus is on practical achievements. However, in order to appreciate the implications of the approach, I will give a brief account of the theoretical background of the activity domain[1]. A theory is a necessary instrument for guiding practical activities; a kind of searchlight by which we can orient ourselves in a chaotic world and take appropriate actions. As the sociologist Kurt Lewin once said: "there is nothing so practical as a good theory" (Lewin, 1997, p. 288).

The outline of the chapter is as follows. First, some basic points of departure are stated: the definition of business and knowledge strategies, the work object as the determinant of knowledge in organizations, the issue of knowledge versus knowing, and the dispersed nature of knowledge. It is absolutely necessary to be explicit about how knowledge fits into the whole picture, how to characterize knowledge, and which aspects of knowledge are relevant for alignment. Basically, my attitude is one of deflection: rather than getting absorbed in esoteric discussions about knowledge, I will use the closely related concept of "capability", which can be equally applied to humans, means and organizations in a way that knowledge cannot. So, for example, we can talk about a capable software programmer, a computer capable of running Windows Vista, and a capable consultants firm. In this way, I want to stress the close relatedness between purposeful human actions, the means used to perform actions, and the social context in which these actions are carried out.

In the next section, I outline the structure of the activity domain as a core organizational construct. This section is the most demanding one in the chapter, and it should be possible to appreciate the practical guidelines that follow without brooding too heavily about the theoretical intricacies. I discuss five "dimensions" constituting the domain:

- *Contextualization:* the formation and scope of the activity domain.
- *Spatialization:* how relevant information is structured.
- *Temporalization:* how valid actions are ordered.
- *Stabilization:* what routines, norms, standards, etc., guide valid actions.
- *Transition:* how the domain interacts with other domains.

These dimensions, which are called *activity modalities*, as well as their interdependencies, make up an integrated, scaffolding architecture of the domain that needs to be attended in alignment.

With the activity domain in place, it is possible to conceptualize the organization as a constellation of activity domains, where each domain provides a certain capability that the organization needs in order to supply products or services to its clients. Two types of capabilities are needed in every domain: *transformative* ones, which are used to transform the work object into the desired outcome; and *coordinative* ones, which are used to coordinate transformative actions. The alignment task can, in essence, be formulated as *managing the dependencies* between capabilities such that these capabilities fit the business's strategic intents.

This idea is elaborated into practical guidelines for alignment, making use of two diagrams: the *capability dependency map*, and the *information interaction model*. With these two diagrams on hand, alignment stakeholders will have their disposal instruments by which various actions related to alignment can be taken. The chapter concludes with a discussion of possible targets for aligning business and knowledge strategies.

In summary, what I propose is not a ready-made recipe from which alignment follows if adhered to. Rather, the approach suggested shall be seen as an attempt to "break-out" from espoused conceptions about how to conceive alignment; an approach that may open up for alternative ways of achieving alignment in practice.

POINTS OF DEPARTURE

In this section, some points of departure for the activity domain approach are presented. These points are cornerstones from which alignment can be further elaborated.

Strategies

The first cornerstone concerns the definition of the terms "business strategy" and "knowledge strategy". A business strategy is a plan that directs a business to achieve its goal in the most efficient manner. The strategy determines "the basic long-term goals and objectives of an enterprise and the adoption of courses of action and the allocation of resources necessary for carrying out these goals" (Chandler, 1966, p. 16). Thus, it can be seen that resources are vital elements of a business strategy. Moreover, a business strategy is unique to an organization, sometimes unique in time, and always shaped by the cultural values of stakeholders, constituencies, the communities the organization serves, and marketplace considerations (Bishoff & Allen, 2004).

Knowledge strategies are concerned with the linking of "knowledge-oriented processes, technologies, and organizational forms to business strategy" (Zack, 1999, p. 126). The term

"knowledge strategy" appeared in response to the observation that knowledge management initiatives seldom were correlated with business strategy initiatives (Callahan, 2002). Knowledge strategies can therefore be seen as an aspect of business strategy that takes into account the intellectual resources and capabilities of the organization (ibid.). Thus, a knowledge strategy can only make sense in the context of a business strategy, since the knowledge in the organization is imperative in implementing the business strategy. Business and knowledge strategies are tightly intertwined and cannot be developed in isolation from each other. This view squares well with the perspective presented in this contribution.

The Work Object and the Motive

What is knowledge in organizations about? This apparently straightforward question seems to have disappeared in the heated debates about knowledge and KM. The primary role of the organization is in the "application of existing knowledge to the production of goods and services" (Grant, 1996, p. 112). This position is also emphasized by Burstein & Linger (2003), who maintain that knowledge must be seen in relation to the task at hand. Instead of focusing on a philosophical discussion of the nature of knowledge, where the target of inquiry is "knowledge" in general, the foremost question to ask should be: "What kind of knowledge is needed in order to produce whatever the organization produces?" Organizations are intentionally created to fulfill social needs, and consequently, knowledge in organizations is derivative from this purpose:

Organizations are not basically knowledge systems, but systems that produce something of value to the society. [...] Only when the knowledge-creation process is set into the context of an organization's activities, does the understanding of the knowledge processes help us understand organizational learning. (Virkkunen & Kuutti, 2000, p. 297)

This view is foregrounded in Activity Theory, the main theoretical inspiration for the activity domain approach. In this theory, the object of human activity – the *work object* – is emphasized as the main constituent of the activity (e.g. Kaptelinin & Nardi, 2006) together with the *motive* for the activity. Work objects can be material or intangible things as long as they can be shared for manipulation and transformation. These two things, the work object and the motive, determine the kind of knowledge needed for achieving something, and, consequently, the work context in which the activity is taking place. Cutting down a tree requires quite a different kind of knowledge than flying an airplane. Similarly, if the motive of the cutting down a spruce is to get a Christmas tree or just some wood for a bonfire, the activity will differ in terms of what tree to look for, how to transport it out of the forest, and so on.

These observations may seem trivial. Nevertheless, it is important to state that every discussion of knowledge must start from the nature of the work object and the motive of the activity to which the knowledge is pertinent.

Knowledge vs Knowing

The debate on the nature of knowledge is an everlasting one. The literature on knowledge in organizations still "presents sharply contrasting and at times even contradictory views of knowledge" (Brown & Duguid, 2001, p. 198), and traditional assumptions about knowledge "offer a compartmentalized and static approach to the subject" (Blackler, 1995, p. 1021). It is common to see knowledge as "*embodied embedded, encultured* and *encoded*" (ibid., p. 1021, italics in original). This is quite evident in the KM crusade; knowledge can be parceled and treated as a "thing" that can be stored in KM systems:

[KM] processes must [...] be present in order to store, transform, and transport knowledge throughout the organization. (Gold, Malhotra, & Segars, 2001, p. 187)

Sometimes this view takes on rather bizarre forms:

Download knowledge directly to the brain! Today the actual learning process takes too long. In the future we will download knowledge directly to the brain. Connect in to something which contains specific know-how and transfer it over. (Framed statement hanging on the wall at Corporate IT, Ericsson™, July 2000)

However, as Wilson (2002) points out, this view is based on a confusion of knowledge with information. Information can indeed be subject to management and transformed into knowledge, if that information makes sense to a knowing individual. Knowledge is something that goes on "between the ears", and can simply be defined as "that which we know":

[Knowledge] involves the mental processes of comprehension, understanding and learning that go on in the mind and only in the mind, however much they involve interaction with the world outside the mind, and interaction with others. (Wilson, 2002)

It is also becoming increasingly clear that knowledge, if taken as something that cannot be detached from the individual, does not provide a solid ground for management endeavors:

Knowledge is a concept far too loose, ambiguous, and rich, and pointing in far too many directions simultaneously to be neatly organized, coordinated, and controlled. (Alvesson & Kärreman, 2001, p. 1012)

In order to approach a management perspective on knowledge, it is clear that we have to base this perspective on something else than knowledge itself. The first step is to move away from the commodity view of knowledge towards "knowing", which emphasizes action aspects of knowledge. Knowledge is seen as *"mediated, situated, provisional, pragmatic* and *contested"* (Blackler, 1995, p. 1021, italics in original). A similar position is advocated by Orlikowski (2002) who proposes to use "organizational knowing" instead of "organizational knowledge" to emphasize that knowing is *enacted* in practice:

Knowledgeability or knowing-in-practice is continually enacted through people's everyday activity; it does not exist "out there" (incorporated in external objects, routines, or systems) or "in here" (inscribed in human brains, bodies, or communities). Rather, knowing is an ongoing social accomplishment, constituted and reconstituted in everyday practice. (Orlikowski, 2002, p. 252)

By focusing on knowing rather than knowledge, the detachment of the knower and the known is retracted. Knowing is something that occurs close to practice and the particular situation where actions take place. In this way, the task of including knowledge as an element in alignment becomes a matter of investigating the concrete circumstances in which knowing occurs:

Knowledge, or better the activity of knowing, can only be understood through its practice and not as an abstract, disembodied phenomenon. (Lanzara & Patriotta, 2001, p. 966)

Dispersed Knowledge

Another cornerstone concerns what has been called the "dispersed nature of organizational knowledge" (Becker, 2001, p. 1037). Every or-

ganization, except for the one-man firm, needs to make a division of labour. Some people are specialized in a particular task such as accounting, while others are engaged in product development, manufacturing, sales efforts, and so on. As soon as there is a division of labour, various knowledge bases are bound to emerge in the organization, simply because different work contexts need different kinds of knowledge in order to produce their outcomes:

Knowledge, in particular tacit knowledge, is by its nature constituted by the context in which it is created and shared. (Mylonopoulos & Tsoukas, 2003, p. 140)

Enactment in different work contexts brings about the existence of multiple ways of apprehending reality as manifested in everyday life. The way of thinking and acting, which actions are counted as valid ones and which are not, what means are appropriate to achieve results, the work context language; each contribute to forming separate, but not necessarily incommensurable "thought worlds":

A thought world is a community of persons engaged in a certain domain of activity who have a shared understanding about that activity. Microbiologists, plumbers, opera buffs, and organizational departments all can be viewed as thought worlds. (Dougherty, 1992, p. 182)

The emergence of different thought worlds is a consequence of the division of labour and ultimately determined by the work object and motive of the work context. Thus, an organization has to live with multiple realities; in fact these are necessary for the organization to achieve its outcome. As Grant notes, the organization is a kind of a paradox:

The benefit of knowledge integration is in meshing the different specialized knowledge of individuals - if two people have identical knowledge there is no gain from integration - yet, if the individuals have entirely separate knowledge bases, then integration cannot occur beyond the most primitive level. (Grant, 1996, p. 116)

In organizations today it is not uncommon to strive for enforced commonality. This trend is no doubt fuelled by the adoption of Enterprise Resource Management (ERP) systems. However, if not carefully orchestrated to pay heed to the multivocality of the organization, the efficiency of these systems may be severed:

In assuming that a universal consensus of human understanding is possible through rational devices, current information technologies neglect to consider knowledge workers as constituting distinct communities socialized into specialized language games with their unique theories of meaning and their referent interpretations of words, concepts and the world. (Tenkasi & Boland, 1996, p. 80)

Thus, on the one hand the existence of the organization depends on different kinds of knowledge. On the other hand, some measure of commonality must exist that makes it possible to integrate various knowledge bases into something that benefits the organization as a whole.

Capabilities

The view of knowledge as enacted implies that actions are carried out with the aids of various means: tools, instruments, ISs, processes, business rules, work context specific languages, and so on. This brings in yet another aspect of knowledge; actions are always *mediated* by some means. Means may be essentially material, such as hammers and axes, or essentially communicative, such as commanding persons, requesting things to be done or

simply declaring things: "We appoint you to the vice president of the company!" ISs take on a middle position in the sense that their dual nature of being material (runs on hardware) and communicative (provide communication services) is quite evident. In essence, however, all mediational means show such a dual character. For example, spoken words or written texts are based on material substrates (sound waves and paper) in spite of their dominant communicative nature.

By focusing on the mediational aspects of knowledge, the concept of "capability" is near at hand. Someone acting with mediational means is easily conceived of as a capable person. Enactment indicates that it is the joint capabilities of humans and means that enable actions. So, for example, the action of felling a tree implies that the lumberjack is capable of using the chainsaw in a proper and safe way. Moreover, he must make a series of judgments concerning the strength and direction of the wind, how to transport the cut tree out of the forest, how to take proper actions if something goes wrong, etc. It is virtually inconceivable how to characterize the activity of felling a tree without taking into account the joint and indivisible capabilities of the lumberjack and his chainsaw. The use of "capabilities" rather than "knowledge" indicates a deliberate intention to include mediational means as parts of actions. Means and actions are so deeply intertwined that it is more appropriate to speak of "individual(s)-acting-with-mediational-means" rather than individual(s) alone when referring to the agent of action (Wertsch, 1991).

However, the joint capability is useful only in the particular activity taking shape around the work object (a tree) and the motive (to get cut wood for heating or building purposes). In another work context such as painting a wooden house, the lumberjack and his chainsaw would be utterly useless. Thus, capabilities of persons and means become resources only in relation to the context where these capabilities make sense. Still another aspect of capabilities is that they are inherently social in character. This is of course most evident when it comes to language; we cannot cooperate unless there is a common understanding about the particular language in a work context. Terms like "spanker", "jib boom" and "brace up" make sense only to those engaged in square rigged sailing vessels.

The capability view of knowledge can be conveniently thought of as a view where meaning and sense-making are brought to the fore. Mediational means, whether essentially material or symbolical in nature, must stand out as meaningful. A tool, which no one recognizes as a tool, is as useless as a term that no one understands. In the most profound sense, managing the alignment task is a problem of managing meanings:

Words may look similar but the referent meanings associated with apparently similar words can be vastly different. There is a need for elaborating differentiated meaning systems as a basis for dynamic integration. Exploring diversity in knowledge intensive firms is, we propose, a new frontier for the development of information technologies. (Tenkasi & Boland, 1996, p. 80)

In summary, the position I advocate towards knowledge can be described as follows. An organization is a system purposefully created to deliver something of value. This is achieved by people performing various actions directed towards work objects. Since work objects may be of different kinds, dissimilar work contexts emerge around the work objects. These work contexts evolve over time into separate thought worlds, in which particular ways of performing actions are enacted, including work context specific languages. Individuals become capable of carrying out purposeful actions in their everyday interaction with mediational means. Thus, knowledge cannot be separated from the knower and her means. Knowledge is an ongoing process in work contexts aiming at transforming the world.

THE ACTIVITY DOMAIN: THE KERNEL OF THE ORGANIZATION

From the considerations in the preceding section it is clear that the notion of "work context" is central. In order to elaborate this rather vague notion into something that can be used in practical alignment efforts, the construct of the *activity domain* has been suggested by Taxén (2007, 2007b). The central idea behind the activity domain is to find a way to express relevant features of any organizational unit, regardless of the level and size of that unit. Thus, a team, a business unit, an entire organization, and an extended enterprise in the form of inter-organizational cooperation would all be considered as activity domains. With such a "kernel" organizational construct, the ubiquitous manifold of organizational forms can be reduced to a more basic level, from which various organizational phenomena can be explicated; much like the diversity of living organisms ultimately can be traced back to the DNA molecule.

The Structure of the Activity Domain

In order to clarify the structure of the activity domain, I will make use of an example of musical performance. Suppose a person, let's call him Lars, wants to play guitar in a guitar quartet with the ultimate purpose of giving a concert:

In order to carry out his part in the musical activity, Lars must of course be capable of playing the score. This is achieved by a long and arduous practice in which Lars acquires the capability to read the notes in the score, and to make use of the capabilities of the guitar. As time goes by, Lars and his guitar may become so interweaved that they form a unity; the player becomes "one" with his instrument, as illustrated by the following quotation from the cellist Mstislav Rostropovich:

There no longer exist relations between us. Some time ago I lost my sense of the border between us.... I experience no difficulty in playing sounds....

Figure 1. A guitar quartet (Lars second from left)

The cello is my tool no more. (In Zinchenko, 1996, p. 295)

This, I believe, nicely expresses the futility of talking about storing, transforming, and transporting knowledge. Together, the player and his mediating instrument make up a capability of playing in which the knower and known cannot be sensibly separated from each other.

From the very moment Lars decides that he wants to give a concert together with his guitar friends, he is immersed in a social context where the work object is the concert. The motive for engaging in this activity could, for example, be to amuse an audience and convey a musical experience. Of course, the motive might also be to make money by playing for a paying audience, in which case the activity would be structured somewhat differently (for example, by charging a price of admission). The work object – the concert – remains the same.

When interacting with his quartet in practicing for the concert, a context of meaningful phenomena and relationships will emerge around the work object and the motive. Within this work context, only things relevant to "guitar-concert" are entered into the consciousness of the performers: guitars, the musical program, practicing sessions, musical interpretation, and a multitude of other things. These things become, so to speak, visible over the "guitar-concert" horizon of relevance. Other things will not enter into this zone: what Lars had for dinner yesterday, which schools his grandchildren should choose, what colors are included in the Japanese flag, and whatever else. Such things may be relevant in other contexts but not for guitar playing; they are below the relevance horizon.

The faculty to contextualize around a work object and motive – *contextualization* – is one of several fundamental dimensions characterizing the coordination of organized human activity; dimensions which I have coined *activity modalities*. The origin of the activity modalities is deeply anchored in the cognitive apparatus of humans, which is the reason why all activity domains have a similar structure (Taxén, 2006). Human activity leaves modality-specific imprints in each domain. For example, contextualization may be recognized in organizational charts, denotations of organizational units, a sense of "belonging to" for those working in a domain, etc. Thus, imprints are manifested both as tangible artifacts in the domain, and as intangible traces in the minds and bodies of people.

Another modality concerns the interaction between activity domains. The guitar Lars plays on has presumably been manufactured in another domain; that of the guitar maker. Here, the work object is of course the guitar:

In order for the guitar to be playable a common understanding must exist between the two activity domains of making the guitar and playing the guitar. This understanding concerns things like the number of strings (which are manufactured in still another domain), the number of frets, the distance between the frets, and so on. However, there is no need for Lars to know the intricacies of guitar crafting, or for the guitar maker to be a guitar master. In every domain, there are capabilities that make sense only in that specific domain, and therefore are irrelevant in other domains. Such capabilities that enable collaboration between activity domains are associated with the modality *transition*. Thus, transition makes it possible for domains with different work objects and motives to cooperate.

Other modalities are indicated by the score:

First, there is an obvious temporal dimension of the score manifested by the sequence of notes. Each note signifies a certain time interval as indicated by the stems and dots. By learning the temporal aspects of notes, capabilities along the *temporalization* modality are enacted. Correspondingly, the vertical positions of notes in the score indicate a

spatial dimension (above, below, distance, etc.). This is the *spatialization* modality, which concerns how things are spatially related to each other. Furthermore, the various signs in the score – the *mf* indicating mezzo forte, the ? signifying the F-clef, the # showing that the key is e-minor, etc. – are commonly understood signs signifying norms that must be adhered to when playing. These norms have a stabilizing function; hence there is a *stabilization* modality in every activity.

The coordination of the different players in the quartet is now made possible by a common score that the players have enacted in a consorted way:

Figure 2. An acoustic bass guitar

Figure 3. A part of a score for the acoustic bass guitar

All the elements of the activity domain are interdependent. The score does not make sense outside the context of musical performance; the temporal, spatial, and stabilizing character of the score cannot be separated from each other; and the transition between the guitar maker and the player will include elements of all modalities. For example, the distances between frets must correspond to the spatial distance between the notes in the score.

In summary, activity domains are contexts that emerge around particular work objects and motives. In activity domains, people perform actions using mediational means to transform work objects into outcomes. Activity domains are constituted along five interdependent activity modalities – contextualization, temporalization, spatialization, stabilization, and transition – which are found in every domain.

An Example from Ericsson™

I will close this short expose of the activity domain by an illustrative example from the telecom company Ericsson™, a supplier of telecom systems and mobile phones worldwide. In this company, there will be activities concerned with software development, hardware development, mechanical design, selling activities, production, service, and so on. On a high level, the overall structure of the company can be illustrated as in Figure 5:

Ericsson™ may be considered as an overall activity domain that provides products such as third generation (3G) mobile systems to customers. In order to do so, the capabilities of a number of other domains are mobilized: Market & Sales, Research & Development, Supply & Implementation, and Service Support. These domains work with different work objects according to Figure 5.

The temporalization modality in the Ericsson™ domain may be manifested by a business process such as the one in Figure 6:

Figure 4. The common score

Figure 5. An activity domain view of Ericsson™

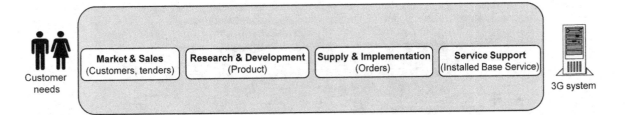

A common expression of the spatialization modality in product development companies is the product structure, which shows what parts a product consists of. In Figure 6, this is only perceptible as the top level "Product".

Concerning the stabilization modality, this is most noticeable in the way companies denote product identities and revisions. Other common examples of stabilization are acronyms of organizational units, which in most cases are completely unintelligible for outsiders.

The transition modality, finally, can be clearly recognized in the transition between domains. In Figure 7 the transitions between the Ericsson™ domain and the domains for hardware design and production are shown:

In hardware design, certain states (DS-, DS1, etc.) are used to indicate the progress of the design. The production of the hardware is progressing according to its own set of states: PR-, PR1, PR2, PRA, and PRB. Simultaneously, the product in the Ericsson overall domain advances through the specific states enacted in this domain (SC3, SC4, etc.)

As the progress of transforming the work object continues, the states used in the different domains need to be synchronized. For example, the DS1, PR-, and SC3 indicate that the product model is approved in the Ericsson™ domain (SC3), preparations for manufacturing have started (PR-), and the design specification is ready (DS1). Thus, it can be seen that there is a need to interpret and map/translate domain specific state values across

domain borders. The rules for how to do this are examples of transition capabilities.

A CAPABILITY CENTRIC ARCHITECTURE OF THE ORGANIZATION

As stated in the introduction, alignment is about bringing various elements of the organization to work in concert to achieve business goals. In order to conceptualize how these elements interact, there is a need for an "organizational architecture" in which these elements can be put into the larger picture of the entire organization. In this section, I will suggest such an organizational architecture based on the activity domain and *dependencies between capabilities*.

The starting point is the division of labor in the firm: "Ultimately, all differences between companies in cost or price derive from the hundreds of activities required to create, produce, sell, and deliver their products or services, such as calling on customers, assembling final products, and training employees" (Porter, 1996, p. 62). An immediate consequence of the distribution of activities is that "the fundamental task of the organization is to coordinate the efforts of many specialists" (Grant, 1996, p. 113). This indicates that alignment is closely related to coordination. If we are able to coordinate the activities in such a way that goals set in the business strategy are fulfilled, then we may say that the elements of the

Figure 6. An example of a business process from Ericsson™

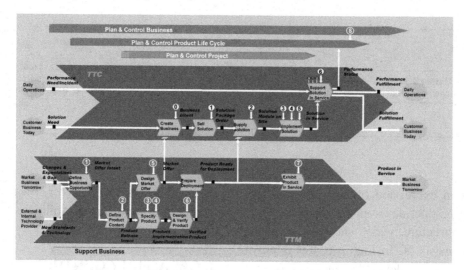

Figure 7. A close-up at hardware development

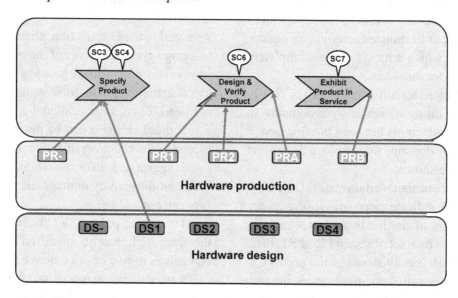

organization are working in concert. However, refocusing alignment to coordination brings about another problem:

Although widely addressed, organization theory lacks a rigorous integrated, well developed and widely agreed theory of coordination. (Grant, 1996, p. 113)

This is where the activity domain comes in. I propose that the activity domain perspective on the organization provides an alternative way of apprehending coordination as follows.

Transformative and Coordinative Capabilities

Malone & Crowston have suggested a commonly quoted definition of coordination:

[Coordination is] managing the dependencies between activities. (Malone & Crowston, 1994, p. 90)

I will elaborate on this definition, starting with the assumption that "activities" are apprehended as activity domains, each with its particular work object and motive, and structured according to the activity modalities. In the activity domain, two basic types of capabilities are needed: capabilities to perform transformative actions by which the work object is transformed into an outcome, and capabilities to coordinate transformational actions. Consider, for example, an activity domain where several developers jointly develop a software application. Each developer may work on a particular software module (transformative actions), which must be integrated together with modules developed by other designers (coordinative actions).

In order to distinguish between these two kinds of capabilities, the activity domain may be seen from two interrelated perspectives: the *transformative* and the *coordinative* ones. These perspectives represent two different focuses; one where the transformation of the work object is in focus – the transformative mode – and one where coordination of transformative actions is in focus – the coordinative mode. Sometimes it is convenient to regard these perspectives as two intertwined domains – the transformation and coordination domains respectively – however, with the transformative one as the primary, since this mode is directly related to the work object. Consequently, coordination is seen as an activity in itself:

Thus, by entering into cooperative work relations, the participants must engage in activities that are, in a sense, extraneous to the activities that contribute directly to fashioning the product or service and meeting requirements. That is, compared with individual work, cooperative work implies an overhead cost in terms of labor, resources, time, etc. The obvious justification for incurring this overhead cost and thus the reason for the emergence of cooperative work formations is, of course, that workers could not accomplish the task in question if they were to do it individually. (Schmidt, 1990, in Schmidt & Bannon, 1992, p. 8)

An example may clarify the relation between the transformative and coordinative modes. Let's consider a requirement on a car. The content of such a requirement may be: "The car shall consume less than 0.5 liters per 10 km at a cruising speed of 100 km per hour". The work object – the car – must fulfill this requirement. In addition there might be a multitude of other requirements on form, safety, exhaust limits, and the like. In order to coordinate the actions in the transformative mode, there is a need to keep track of all the requirements, preferably in a requirement management tool. To achieve this, certain coordinative capabilities must be enacted such as unique identifiers for each requirement; a set of states indicating what state a requirement is in (for example, whether the requirement is fulfilled or not); attributes characterizing the requirement; relations to other items such as requirement issuers/customers and the product the requirements are directed to, and so on. In the coordinative mode, only such coordinative aspects of requirements are relevant, not the actual content of a requirement. The content, on the other hand is of course relevant in the transformative mode. Thus, in the coordinative mode certain aspects of the activity domain are veiled.

Figure 8. The two modes of the activity domain

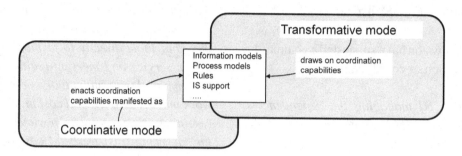

What kind of things do we find in the coordinative mode? How can we characterize these? This is where the activity modalities enter the stage. If, as I propose, the coordination of human activity is organized along the modalities, we should find imprints of these in the coordination mode. This is also the case in practice. When people are struggling to enact coordinative capabilities – possibly using mediational means such as ISs – these capabilities will be manifested as information models showing what entities are relevant for coordination (spatialization); process models showing dependencies between actions (temporalization); rules, standards and norms indicating how to perform actions (stabilization); and elements enabling the cooperation between domains (transition). All of these capabilities are needed to be in full command of coordination[2]. In the transformative mode, coordinative capabilities are utilized to coordinate transformative actions transforming the work object. Thus, the activity domain unfolds through an ongoing focal shift between the coordinative and transformative modes. This is illustrated in Figure 8.

Strategic Implications

Although this elaboration of coordination in organizations seems complicated enough, it is a necessary step on the way towards an integrated view of aligning business and knowledge strategies. In order to clarify this, let's take a look at a common enough situation: two persons decide to spend a nice evening together. The strategy for doing so is to meet at a restaurant to have dinner. In order for this to occur, several things need to be coordinated. First, the persons have to agree on a restaurant and consequently, on a particular place. This is an example of spatialization that could, for example, be manifested by pointing in a map. Both persons need to understand the map in the same way; that is, they must both have enacted the capability to use this means.

Next, our couple must agree to meet at a certain time, which means that another modality has to be engaged: temporalization. Moreover, they must have a common understanding of the time unit and the synchronization of time; examples of the stabilization modality. The coordination will fail if the persons use local time in different time zones without realizing this. Furthermore, both persons must be capable of reading the time off their watches; means for manifesting the temporalization modality.

The individual actions for arriving to the restaurant may take different paths. One person might use the map to walk to the meeting place, while the other may use her car and a GPS equipment to find the place. Again, both interact with different means that they must be capable of using. Also, they must plan when to start in order to arrive at the agreed time. In this way, the modalities – spatialization, temporalization, and stabilization – are all intertwined in the coordination to achieve a common goal.

When arriving at the restaurant, our couple need to interact with another activity, that of the restaurant. Here, the transition modality becomes manifest. Both the guests and the restaurant employees must have a common understanding about the menu, the temporal sequence of ordering, preparing the meal, eating and paying. Furthermore, several aspects of stabilization need to be mutually understood, such as the norm for giving tips, what happens if one does not pay for the meal, and so on. In contrast, the internal workings of the restaurant are in general of no concern to the guests (unless a cockroach suddenly comes running over the floor!).

In this way, the "business strategy" for having a nice evening is inextricably intertwined with the capabilities – "knowledge strategies" – in various modalities in order to fulfill the goal. Suppose now that something occurs that makes it necessary to change the strategy. If, for example, it turns out that the restaurant is closed at the agreed time, another strategy must be invoked. Such strategies could be to find another restaurant, go to the cinema together, postpone the meeting to another day, or simply to prepare a meal at home. For each strategy, quite new capabilities come into play.

Dependencies Between Capabilities

Organizations can indeed be conceptualized as complex systems; they have many parts that interact to form a whole, the whole exhibit features that parts do not have in isolation, and they can be characterized as emergent and self-organizing systems. If we want to manage such systems, it is necessary to conceptualize them in a simpli-

Figure 9. A capability dependency map of Ericsson™

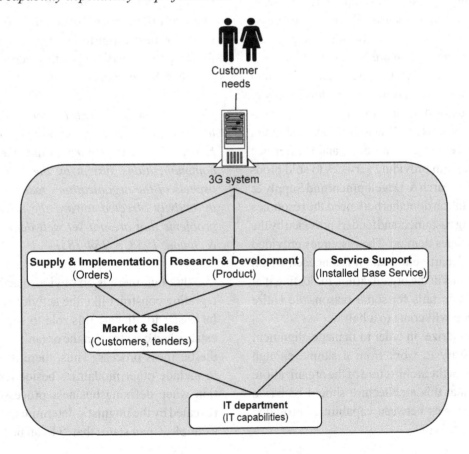

fied way, however without overlooking essential features of the systems.

When struggling with coordinating complex telecom development projects at Ericsson™, it was gradually realized that the most efficient conceptualization was to see the system as *dependencies between capabilities* (Taxén, 2003); the reason being that if such dependencies are not known or erroneously conceived, the system being developed might not work. Take, for example, an ordinary computer. All parts of the computer, the processor, the screen, the DVD-player, the network controller, and so on, depend on one single capability: the one provided by the power-on button. If, for some reason, this button does not work, nothing else will work. The same goes for a car; if you mislay your car key, you cannot evoke of any of the latent capabilities provided by the car such as cruising at a comfortable speed, listening to the radio, switching on the head lights, and so forth.

The same reasoning can be applied to organizations. For example, the overall view of Ericsson as shown in Figure 5 can be illustrated as the dependency map in Figure 9:

The map shows that the 3G system fulfilling the customer's needs is realized by the Supply & Implementation domain providing order management resources, the Research & Development domain developing the product, and the Service Support domain providing services to sold products. The Research & Development and Supply & Implementation domains both need the resources of managing customers and tenders provided by the Market & Sales domain. The resources provided by the IT department domain are needed by all other domains in the organization, indicating that if this domain fails for some reason, the entire organization will come to a halt[3].

To summarize: in order to manage alignment it is necessary to work from a simple enough conception of the architecture of the organization. I suggest that this architecture should be based on dependencies between capabilities provided by activity domains.

THE PRACTICAL TURN

With the activity domain, the activity modalities, and the capability dependency architecture of the organization in place, it is possible to devise a practical approach for aligning business and knowledge strategies as follows.

Identifying the Activity Domains

The first step is to characterize the organization in terms of activity domains. This seemingly straightforward step can be quite arduous, since it brings about a new way of apprehending the organization. A major obstacle is to make unfamiliar terms such as "activity domain" and "activity modalities" part of the organizational language. During 2002, I participated in a project at Ericsson™, the purpose of which was to reconceptualize the way product data was managed in the organization. I put forward a proposal to base new way on the concept of activity domains. This, however, turned out to be exceedingly difficult for the project participants to accept. As already March & Simon noted:

[It] is extremely difficult to communicate about intangible objects and nonstandardized objects. Hence, the heaviest burdens are placed on the communications system by the less structured aspects of the organization's tasks, particularly by activity directed toward the explanation of problems that are not yet well defined. (March & Simon, 1958, p. 184-185)

Although there is an obvious need for an integrating construct like the activity domain, it is far easier to allocate this role to some existing, established construct in the organization, usually the business process. Thus, there is a tendency to include other modalities beside temporalization when defining business processes. This is revealed by the linguistic determination used. For example, Chan states that "IT can be an initiator, a facilitator, and an enabler *in* [emphasis added] a business process" (Chan, 2000, p. 235). Other expressions, such as "coordination in the process", "information in the process", both abundant on the Internet, indicate a similar shift in meaning. This "modality compression" veils the specific character of each activity modality as well as the interdependencies between them.

The tendency to submerge non-temporal things under the auspices of business processes implies that such processes become proxies for activity domains. Thus, a good starting point for identifying domains is the existing business process in the organization (see the example in Figure 10):

TTC stands for "Time To Customer" and expresses the delivery from order to installed solution without the need for developing new products; a fast configuration of existing product variants. TTM stands for "Time To Market" and involves the development of new products.

Candidates for activity domains are those organizational units that have distinct work objects and motives. For example, in Figure 10, the activities "Specify Product" and "Design & Verify Product" have easily recognized work objects (the product) and motives (specify, design and verify the product). On the other hand, the unit "Product Management" appears to denote an administrative area of responsibility, since it includes a number of seemingly disparate units: "Define Business Opportunity", "Define Product Content", "Design Market Offer", "Prepare Deployment", and "Exhibit Product in Service". Thus, "Product Management" would presumably not be considered an activity domain.[4] The ambiguity of elements as shown in Figure 10 is typical for most business processes.

In order to get a firm basis for alignment efforts, each identified domain should be documented along the following lines:

Figure 10. An example of a business process from Ericsson™ (Taxén & Svensson, 2005. Used with permission. ©Inderscience).

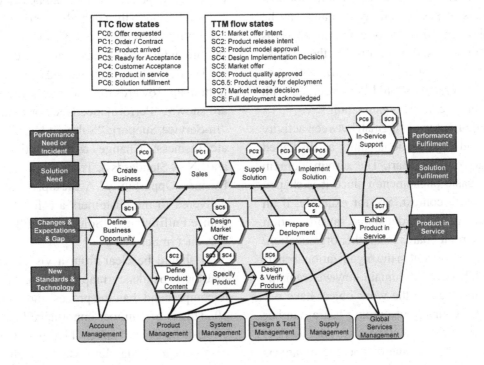

- *Overall characterization of the domain:* The motive and work object of the domain; prerequisites and outcomes; the type of roles involved in the domain; capabilities needed to carry out transformational actions; means used: tools, ISs, etc.
- *Manifestations of spatialization:* Relevant information entities in the domain; attributes used to characterize the entities; information models showing how entities are related to each other.
- *Manifestations of temporalization:* Activities carried out in the domain; process models illustrating the dependencies between activities; state sets indicating progress.
- *Manifestations of stabilization:* Standards used, business rules, methods, norms, and so on.
- *Manifestations of transition:* Means used to interact with other domains, in particular, relations between state sets in different domains.

For practical reasons, there is a limit for how many levels of nested activity domains can be reasonably attended to. A good compromise seems to be two or at most three levels. For the purpose of alignment, this should to be sufficient, since the business strategy should be concerned with the "big" picture of the organization.

It is important to distinguish between activity domains and organizational units as displayed in an organizational chart. The activity domain is a more basic phenomenon since it is shaped around a work context. So, for example, if an organization decides to outsource, say production of printed circuit boards to another organization, the corresponding unit in the organizational chart is removed. The activity domain, however, remains since the motive and the work object have not changed. Of course, outsourcing has a number of implications that will impact how the work is carried out: people in the outsourced organiza-

tion may have to enact capabilities to work with different kinds of circuit boards from various customers; they might need to learn new rules for naming the boards; contracts have to be written to regulate the business transactions between the two organizations, and so on.

It should also be noted that the organization itself is to be regarded as an activity domain with its own work object and motive. The motive is usually veiled in the business idea or slogan. For example, Ericsson's slogan "Taking you forward" illustrates "Ericsson's vision of being the prime driver in an all-communicating world" (Ericsson™, 2008), to which Nokia™ retorts with "Connecting People" (to which some witty person added: "Disconnecting Families" due to the high work load on employees).

Defining the Dependency Map

The next step towards managing alignment is to define the dependencies between capabilities. Again, the business process provides a suitable point of departure. From Figure 10, the following capability dependency map can be derived:

In addition to the capabilities provided by the activity domains, examples of some basic capabilities are indicated at the bottom of the figure.

The dependency map should be read from the bottom up. Towards the bottom, the prerequisites are shown: "Performance Need or Incident" for "In-Service Support; "Solution Need" for "Create Business; "Changes & Expectations & Gap" and "New Standards & Technology" for "Define Business Opportunity". At the top, the capabilities delivered to the customers are found: "Performance Fulfillment", "Solution Fulfillment", and "Product in Service".

It should be clear from a visual inspection that the dependency map in Figure 11 is easier to comprehend than the process model in Figure 10. This is of outmost importance in alignment efforts where many stakeholders need to establish a common understanding. Moreover, the focus on dependencies makes it easier to imagine the consequences of taking or not taking certain actions. The absence and presence of a certain capability becomes immediately discernible. For example, the capability "Business rules" is indicated as a fundamental capability for all domains. An example of such a capability might be the "Ericsson-way of identifying products". Placing this capability at the very foundation indicates that all domains must use the same rules for identifying products. Such rules are always organization specific parts of the organizational language, quite unintelligible for outsiders, but nevertheless of fundamental importance for stabilizing the organization.

The dependency map is a living document. Depending on the issues at hand certain parts may be "zoomed in" and further detailed. In addition, it is important to realize that the map is a social achievement; it reflects the view of the persons that defines it. In this sense, the map should not be regarded as a more or less true representation of the "real world", whatever that is. Rather, it is a means towards achieving alignment. With the map at hand, alignment efforts can be planned and executed.

Figure 11. A capability dependency map derived from the business process in Figure 10

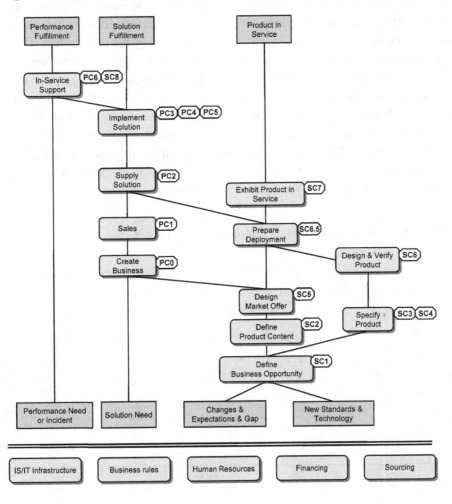

Specifying Information Management Capabilities

Today, IT based information systems are indispensable for organizations. As a consequence, major efforts have been directed to the alignment of IT and business, as is evident from the many SISP approaches reported earlier. In order to address this issue, suppose that an organization has decided to introduce an ERP system in order to enhance its information management capabilities. Such a system would be conceived of as having certain built-in capabilities that might or might not be useful in the organization. In order for these capabilities to become resources, the joint capabilities of the ERP system and the users working with the system must be enacted. The ERP system as such is useless without the enactment process; just installing the system on the computers in the organization is not enough.

With the dependency map in Figure 11 as a basis, the logical step towards the ERP implementation is to focus on the information managed. Almost all of the activities are phrased in the form "do something with something", for example, "Specify Product", "Design Market Offer", and so on. From an information management point of view, it is natural to concentrate on the nouns, which indicate information entity candidates to be managed in the ERP system.

In order to model the evolution of the entities, a model called the Information Interaction Model (IIM) may be used. This kind of process model was used extensively at Ericsson™ during the 1990s to illustrate various processes. In essence, the IIM shows an information oriented view of the activity domain; a complement to the capability dependency map. An example of such a model, derived from the dependency map in Figure 11, is given in Figure 12:

The information entities are lined up vertically to the left, and the activity domains are lined up horizontally at the bottom. The interaction between these is expressed in the "score" diagram showing the prerequisites and outcomes of each domain.

The appealing property of IIMs is that they provide a clear and easily comprehendible separation of information entities and activities to be supported by the ERP system. Thus, the IIMs can be used to define a comprehensive specification of information management capabilities that the ERP system must provide, such as defining, storing, searching for, and changing the state of information entities. Additional management capabilities may be needed like implementing rules for naming entities, workflow support, report generation, and so on.

Figure 12. An information interaction model of the activity domain

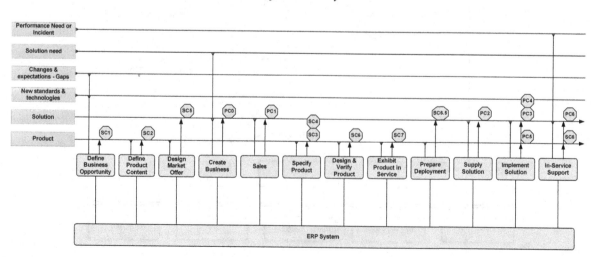

When the activity domains have been identified in the organization, it is (at least in principle) a straightforward task to analyze these in terms of IIMs, and consolidate all information management capabilities needed across all domains. These capabilities, which might be specified by scenarios, task cards, or other means, need the vendor's ERP platform, the structure of the product, and various other capabilities provided by investigations, personnel, review teams, and more. The whole approach is sketched in Figure 13.

Starting from organizational capabilities, the focus is gradually moved to information management capabilities. Business capabilities are related to IS capabilities through the capability dependency map and the IIMs, which implies that these two diagrams are means to align business and IS/IT; an alternative SISP approach so to speak.

Alignment Targets

The view of alignment as a continuous and evolutionary process implies that alignment cannot

be carried out as a planning phase followed by an implementation phase. Rather alignment should be seen as an ongoing initiative where certain "knobs" are adjusted and manipulated to maintain fit. Based on the view of the organizational architecture as dependencies between capabilities, a tentative definition of alignment would be as follows:

Alignment is the management of dependencies between capabilities such that these fit the business's strategic intents.

What does this mean for alignment of business and knowledge strategies? A first observation is that business and knowledge strategies, however defined, both relate to the same construct – the activity domain. Thus, business strategies cannot be separated from knowledge strategies. Rather, these should be seen as intertwined facets of a common whole. With this scope in mind, a tentative set of alignment targets can be identified as follows:

Figure 13. The implementation of the ERP system

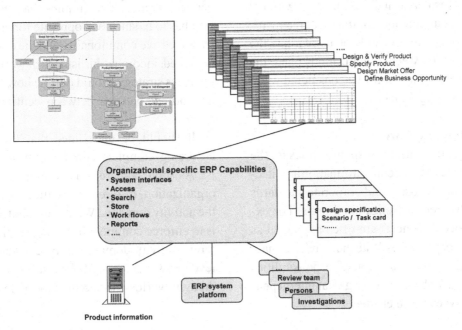

Business Oriented Targets

The Constellation of Activity Domains

This target concerns the constellation of activity domains involved in producing the outcome of the organization. The main issue is to decide which domains are needed to fulfill the strategic intents of the organization, and how these domains depend on each other. For example, suppose that a product line has become outdated due to obsolete technology, and a new product line based on new technology shall be established. This means that some domains working with the old technology must be phased out, and new ones must be established for the new technology. It follows that a strategic decision has to be taken whether the new domains shall be part of the core competence of the company, or outsourced to another company.

Such strategic decisions may be informed by the capability dependency map. For example, if many domains depend on an potentially outsourced domain, this is easily recognized in the map. Such a dependency may expose the organization for too high a risk, especially if the outsourced domain cannot be easily replaced. Other strategic issues that may influence outsourcing decisions are translations between different organizational languages, assignments, contracts, agreements, responsibilities, etc. Such elements regulate the co-operations between organizations, and the cost for enacting these must be considered when out- or insourcing domains.

Domain Responsibility

In most organizations, the responsibilities for the business processes, the core information architecture, the main ISs used, and corporate standards reside in different organizational units. For example, "process owners" are often appointed as responsible for processes. With the activity domain in mind, such a differentiation of responsibilities implies a high risk of neglecting vital interdependencies between these elements.

The activity domain approach suggests quite a different responsibility structure: managers should be assigned in line with the constellation of activity domains. Each domain should have a responsible person. Such a responsibility would include all transactional and coordinative capabilities needed to produce the outcome of the domain.

Business Level Coordination

Another conceivable target for alignment is the coordination of activity domains. The prime strategic issue here is the dependencies between domains at the top-level of the organization. In particular, points of transition between the activities must be considered. For example, if the mapping between synchronization states as illustrated in Figure 7, p. 12, is not attended, the coordination at the organizational level will fail.

Central vs Local Control

The dispersed nature of knowledge emerging in different activity domains directly brings another strategic issue to the fore. Each domain enacts a unique worldview; a certain way to conceive reality. However, the coordination of activity domains calls for some common understanding across domains. This implies that the organization has to balance two opposite forces: the drive for excessive commonality and the emergence of detached, incompatible islands of work. Thus, the business strategy should outline how to maintain an optimal balance between central and local control.

It should be underlined that the option of enforcing complete commonality does not exist. As soon as there is a division of labor in the organization, different capabilities are needed in the activity domains. What is imperative, though, is to enforce commonality to the level where different activity domain can be coordinated. This level, however, can only be a subset of the entire thought worlds enacted in activity domains.

Core Capabilities

Commonality implies that certain capabilities are valid throughout the organization for all domains. One example is the stabilizing modality as manifested by business rules for identification of products, core concepts, correct ways of working, etc. Other core capabilities may be provided by the human resources (HR) domain, financing, sourcing of components, etc., that is, such organizational units that in traditional business language are denoted "support business processes". The strategic aspect here is to identify these fundamental capabilities and provide the necessary means for upholding these.

The IS/IT Architecture

Obviously, the IS/IT architecture is a crucial capability for the organization. A tentative architecture based on the activity domain may be conceived as follows.

The general principle is to push the capabilities of ISs and tools[5] as much as possible towards commonality, but not beyond the point where they become counterproductive in the domains. For example, an ERP system is useless when it comes to supporting the development of software code. The primary capabilities in each domain are those used in transforming the work object into an outcome. Thus, there will always be domain-specific tools that are directly involved in transformational actions. For example, an activity domain developing ASICs (application specific integrated circuits) will need tools to describe the circuit in a hardware-oriented language such as VHDL (2008) or Verilog (2008), tools for synthesizing the lay-out of the ASIC, tools for automatic testing of the ASIC, and so on. The capabilities these tools provide are potential resources only in domains with ASICs as work objects. The commonality aspect here is that all domains working with ASICs should use the same tools from the same vendor. Moreover, it makes good sense to synchronize new releases of the tools such that all domains work from the same set of capabilities.

Besides the transformational capabilities needed in each domain, coordinative capabilities must be enacted. Here, the limits for commonality are more diffuse. To start with, it is quite clear that ISs used for coordinative purposes should be based on the same IS platform from the same vendor. However, it would be a mistake to enforce commonality of coordinative capabilities for all domains. Observations and experiences from using the Matrix PLM (Product Lifecycle Management) system (MatrixOne, 2008) at Ericsson™ indicate that domains involved in developing similar kinds products would benefit from the same coordinative capabilities (Taxén, 2003). One approach might be to align coordinative capabilities with product families or product lines:

What is crucial in a global development organization is that all development locations working in one product line use the same processes, methodology, and terminology even when changes occur. (Ebert & De Neve, 2001, p. 67)

So, for example, in Ericsson™ all domains concerned with developing mobile phones would use the same coordinative capabilities, while those domains developing switches and processor would use another set of coordinative capabilities. Moreover, it probably makes good sense to enact a common set of coordinative capabilities for the "support" domains: HR, financing, sourcing, etc. Such capabilities can preferably be provided by an ERP system. In addition, all ISs and tools should of course use common IT platform capabilities such as the intranet, back-up services, web-servers, and the like. A principal dependency sketch of the IS/IT architecture along these lines is shown in Figure 14.

The ideal picture is seldom an option due to the legacy systems already in use in the organization. Such system cannot be ruled out easily since they have usually been enacted over long periods into useful resources. The introduction of a new IS enforces dismantling of capabilities acquired

Figure 14. The IS/IT architecture

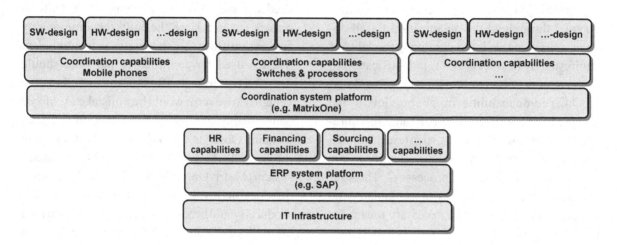

(including the human ones!) and reorientation towards capabilities based on the new IS.

Knowledge Oriented Targets

Transformative Capabilities

This target concerns the capabilities for transformative actions directed towards the work object in each domain. Given the available means, individuals must acquire the skills to use these efficiently. Obvious ways of achieving this are on the job training, master–apprentice arrangements, instructional material, and the like. The strategic aspect here is to secure available means for enacting the necessary transformational capabilities.

Coordinative Capabilities

The knowledge aspect here concerns how to enact common understanding about how coordination should be carried out. In Taxén (2007), a strategy for achieving this is described. The basic idea is to start with a small group of people that iteratively constructs coordination capabilities, which eventually are refined and expanded to include the entire domain. This way of working presumes that a strategic decision has been taken to allow different coordination domains to be constructed on the same IS platform (see Figure 14). This in

turn is dependent on another strategic principle: that a balance should be upheld between central and local control.

Capability Gaps

Obvious targets for knowledge strategies are to identify and remedy capability gaps in the organization. Since capabilities are considered as jointly achieved by humans and means, capability gaps can either be related to humans or means. The first case can be characterized as "we have access to this magnificent tool in our domain, but we don't know how to use it". This gap can be filled in several ways. For example, someone working with the tool in another domain with the same work object may be consulted to teach people how to use the tool. Another way is the converse; to send some people as trainees to domains where the tool is used. A third possibility is to establish a community of practice (Lave & Wenger, 1991) where individuals working within the same kind of work objects and tools meet regularly to exchange findings and spread the word: "this is how we did it!" [6].

The second case can be characterized as "I know how to use this magnificent tool we urgently need here, but unfortunately we do not have access to that tool". This is a gap in means, which quite naturally could be filled by providing the means to the domain in question. Regardless of whether gaps appear in humans or means, however, it is important not to detach these from each other. A capability should always be seen as totality where both humans and means are included.

Knowledge Management Systems

It has been noted that the predominant use of KM systems is to capture, store and transmit "commodified knowledge" in the form of patents, documents, experiences, etc. (e.g. Hildreth & Kimble, 2002). However, in order for such information to become capabilities, the KM systems should rather be seen as a means for communication:

[Information] systems for knowledge management and organizational memory should be seen as media that is used as an interpersonal cognitive artifact. A critical factor in designing such artifacts is to consider those knowledge stocks that are needed to make sense of the information stored in the system. (Tuomi, 1999, p. 9)

This means that the demarcation line between ISs used in the activity domains and dedicated KM systems become blurred. When used for manipulating the work object, the domain specific systems contribute to the "knowledge stock" in that domain. As communicative artifacts, such systems should be designed to facilitate the construction of common understanding. This implies, for example, that the semiotic aspects of the systems should be given a high priority when designed. The action character of cues, symbols, help texts, and so forth, should be made as evident as possible.

It is possible to conceive of how information structured from an activity domain perspective can be managed in dedicated KM systems. Some capabilities of such systems may be:

- Keeping a list of activity domains.
- Storing descriptions of activity domains.

- Keeping track of the dependencies between activity domains.
- Matching activity domains where people with similar capabilities may be found; a yellow-pages function.
- Listing individuals with expert knowledge related to a particular domain.

Such systems would most certainly be classified as strategic ones since they would support the business oriented aspects of alignment.

CONCLUDING REMARKS

The reality meeting everyday practitioners in large organizations is complex, fragmented, contradictory, and in constant motion. Alignment is about bringing all elements of this reality to work in concert with the organization's strategic intents. Needless to say, this is awesome task. The gist of the approach suggested here is that alignment presumes some kind of framework by which you can simplify matters and become aware of critical interdependencies. Unless you can put elements like IS/IT, organizational units, business processes, information, strategic plans, people, and so on, into a coherent whole, you are lost. You need, so to speak, to dwell below the surface of the immediately given and direct alignment effort towards the essence of the organization – human activity as such.

This sounds reasonable enough. The question is, however: how should we conceive human activity in such a way that we can make alignment happen in practice? The answer proposed in this contribution is to base alignment on the *activity domain*. There are several reasons for this. First, the activity domain captures features that can be found in every organized activity: a motive for the activity, a work object that is transformed into an outcome, actors/individuals doing the work, coordination of their actions, means by which they transform the work object, and cooperation with other activities. Thus, the activity domain provides a single conception of any intra- or interorganizational unit. Although different on the surface, such units can all be described as activity domains. As a consequence, the myriads of organizational forms can be reduced to the same construct, which greatly simplifies the burden of making sense of a fragmented world. By looking through the activity domain glasses, you see patterns that otherwise will remain veiled.

Second, the activity domain defines the context within which capabilities of individuals and means are turned into resources. What is counted as a resource is ultimately tied to the motive and work object of the domain. Knowing how to skate and make use of a hockey stick is not relevant if you are on stage singing Celeste Aida in Verdi's opera Aida. Capabilities include not only obvious means such as information systems, but also common understanding about how to use these means. Thus, the activity domain frames the way individuals experience their reality and make sense of it.

Third, the organization can be conceived as a constellation of activity domains, each providing a capability that the organization needs in order to fulfill its goals. In this way, an intermediate level is introduced that makes it possible to focus alignment efforts on the activity domain, rather than on individuals, IS/IT or the organization in isolation.

Fourth, the activity domain approach makes it possible to device means for achieving alignment in practice. The overall capability of the organization can be illustrated in a capability dependency map, showing how the various capabilities of the domains depend on each other. From this map it is possible to derive information management capabilities and illustrate these in an information interaction model for each domain. These models can be consolidated over all activity domains into specifications for information systems such as ERP systems or PLM systems. In this way, a

practical path for including IS/IT in alignment efforts is suggested.

Finally, strategic targets for business and knowledge can be stated with the activity domain in mind. Business oriented targets include the constellation of activity domains, business level coordination, responsibility distribution, balancing central versus local control, and identifying core organizational capabilities. In the same manner, knowledge oriented targets include what capabilities are needed in different activity domains, how missing capabilities can be remedied, and which knowledge management systems capabilities can be reasonably made use of.

In conclusion, by placing the activity domain in the center of alignment efforts, a viable approach of aligning business strategies, knowledge strategies, and IT is suggested. Some elements of this approach – the capability dependency map and the information interaction models – have already been proven in the demanding practice of developing telecom systems. No doubt, however, many details still need to be worked out. Nevertheless, I propose that the activity domain approach represents an alternative vantage point of alignment – a perspective that may open up new ways of achieving alignment in practice.

REFERENCES

Alvesson, M., & Kärreman, D. (2001). Odd couple: Making sense of the curious concept of knowledge management. *Journal of Management Studies*, *38*(7), 995–1018. doi:10.1111/1467-6486.00269

Becker, M. C. (2001). Managing dispersed knowledge: Organizational problems, managerial strategies, and their effectiveness. *Journal of Management Studies*, *38*(7), 1037–1051. doi:10.1111/1467-6486.00271

Bishoff, L., & Allen, N. (2004). *Business planning for cultural heritage institutions*. Washington, D.C.: Council on Library and Information Resources.

Blackler, F. (1995). Knowledge, knowledge work, and organization: An overview and interpretation. *Organization Studies, 16*(6), 1021–1046. doi:10.1177/017084069501600605

Brown, J. S., & Duguid, P. (2001). Knowledge and organization: A social-practice perspective. *Organization Science, 12*(2), 198–213. doi:10.1287/orsc.12.2.198.10116

Burstein, F., & Linger, H. (2003). Supporting post-Fordist work practices. A knowledge management framework for supporting knowledge work. *Information Technology & People, 16*(3), 289–305. doi:10.1108/09593840310489395

Callahan, S. D. (2002). Crafting a knowledge strategy. In *ACT Knowledge Management Forum (ActKM) Conference*, Canberra (ActKM). Retrieved on January 2, 2009, from http://www.anecdote.com.au/papers/CallahanCraftingKnowledgeStrategy.pdf

Chan, S. (2000). Information technology in business processes. *Business Process Management Journal, 6*(3), 224–237. doi:10.1108/14637150010325444

Chan, Y. (2002). Why haven't we mastered alignment? The importance of the informal organization structure. *MIS Quarterly Executive, 1*(21), 76–112.

Chandler, A. (1966). *Strategy and structure*. Garden City, NY: Doubleday & Company.

Ciborra, C. U. (1997). De profundis? Deconstructing the concept of strategic alignment. *Scandinavian Journal of Information Systems, 9*(1), 67–82.

Dougherty, D. (1992). Interpretive barriers to successful product innovation in large firms. *Organization Science, 3*(2), 179–202. doi:10.1287/orsc.3.2.179

Earl, M. J. (1996). An organizational approach to IS strategy making. In M. J. Earl (Ed.), *Information management-the organizational dimension* (pp. 136–170). Oxford: Oxford University Press.

Ebert, C., & De Neve, P. (2001). Surviving global software development. *IEEE Software*, (March/April): 62–69. doi:10.1109/52.914748

Ericsson.™ (2008). Retrieved on January 2, 2009, from http://www.ericsson.com/ericsson/press/releases/20050215-980794.shtml

Gold, A. H., Malhotra, A., & Segars, A. H. (2001). Knowledge management: An organizational capabilities perspective. *Journal of Management Information Systems, 18*(1), 185–214.

Grant, R. (1996). Toward a knowledge-based theory of the firm. *Strategic Management Journal, 17*(Winter Special Issue), 109-122.

Hackney, R., Burn, J., Cowan, E., & Dhillon, G. (2000). Challenging assumptions for strategic information systems planning: Theoretical perspectives. [CAIS]. *Communications of the Association for Information Systems, 3*(9), 2–24.

Hildreth, P. M., & Kimble, C. (2002). The duality of knowledge. *Information Research, 8*(1). Retrieved on May 2, 2006, from http://informationr.net/ir/8-1/paper142.html

Kaptelinin, V., & Nardi, B. (2006). Acting with technology-activity theory and interaction design. Cambridge, MA: The MIT Press.

Lanzara, G. F., & Patriotta, G. (2001). Technology and the courtroom: An inquiry into knowledge making in organizations. *Journal of Management Studies, 38*(7), 943–971. doi:10.1111/1467-6486.00267

Lave, J., & Wenger, E. (1991). *Situated learning: Legitimate peripheral participation*. Cambridge: Cambridge University Press.

Lewin, K. (1997). *Resolving social conflicts: Field theory in social science*. Washington, D.C.: American Psychological Association. Original work published in 1943.

Luftman, J., & McLean, E. R. (2004). Key issues for IT executives. *MIS Quarterly Executive, 3*(2), 89–104.

Malone, T., & Crowston, K. (1994). The interdisciplinary study of coordination. *ACM Computing Surveys, 26*(1), 87–119. doi:10.1145/174666.174668

March, J. G., & Simon, H. A. (1958). *Organizations*. Cambridge, MA: Blackwell Publishers.

Marjanovic, O. (2005). Towards IS supported coordination in emergent business processes. *Business Process Management Journal, 11*(5), 476–487. doi:10.1108/14637150510619830

Martinsons, M. G., & Davidson, R. (2003). Cultural issues and IT management: Looking ahead. Guest editorial . *IEEE Transactions on Engineering Management, 50*(1), 3–7. doi:10.1109/TEM.2003.808299

MatrixOne. (2008). Retrieved on February 2, 2005, from http://www.matrixone.com/index.html

Mylonopoulos, N., & Tsoukas, H. (2003). Technological and organizational issues in knowledge management. *Knowledge and Process Management, 10*(3), 139–143. doi:10.1002/kpm.174

Opdahl, A. L. (1997, June). A model for comparing approaches to IS-architecture alignment. In B. Irgens, K. Ellingsen, E. Mathisen, N. M. Nielsen & Z. Uddin Quazi (Eds.), *Proceedings of "Norsk konferanse om organisasjoners bruk av IT"* (pp. 67-79). Bodö/Norway.

Orlikowski, W. (2002). Knowing in practice: Enacting a collective capability in distributed organizing. *Organization Science, 13*(3), 249–273. doi:10.1287/orsc.13.3.249.2776

Porter, M. (1996). What is strategy? *Harvard Business Review*, (November-December): 61–78.

Regev, G., & Wegmann, A. (2003). Why do we need business process support? Balancing specialization and generalization with BPS systems. Introductory note to the *4th BPMDS Workshop on Requirements Engineering for Business Process Support*. Velden, Austria.

Schmidt, K. (1990). *Analysis of cooperative work. A conceptual framework*. Risø National Laboratory, DK-4000 Roskilde, Denmark, [Risø-M-2890].

Schmidt, K., & Bannon, L. (1992). Taking CSCW seriously: Supporting articulation work. *Computer Supported Cooperative Work, 1*(1-2), 7-40. Retrieved on April 4, 2008, from http://citeseer.ist.psu.edu/schmidt92taking.html

Sveiby, K. E. (2001). *Frequently asked questions*. Brisbane: Sveiby Knowledge Associates. Retrieved on July 16, 2001 from http://www.sveiby.com.au/faq

Taxén, L. (2003). *A framework for the coordination of complex systems' development*. Dissertation No. 800. Linköping University, Dep. of Computer &Information Science. Retrieved on January 4, 2009, from http://www.ep.liu.se/smash/record.jsf?searchId=1&pid=diva2:20897

Taxén, L. (2006). Cognitive grounding of activity modalities. In *Proceedings of Action in Language, Organisations, and Information Systems (ALOIS 2006)* (pp. 75-93). Borås, Sweden: University College of Borås. Retrieved on January 8, 2009, from http://www.vits.org/?pageId=317

Taxén, L. (2007). Activity modalities–a multidimensional perspective on coordination, business processes, and communication. *Systems, Signs, & Actions, 3*(1), 93–133. Retrieved on January 4, 2009, from http://www.sysiac.org/?pageId=36

Taxén, L. (2007b). The activity domain theory– informing the alignment of business and knowledge strategies. In E. Abou-Zeid (Ed.), *Knowledge management and business strategies: Theoretical frameworks and empirical research* (pp. 253-280). Hershey, PA: Information Science Reference.

Taxén, L., & Svensson, D. (2005). Towards an alternative foundation for managing product life-cycles in turbulent environments. [IJPD]. *International Journal of Product Development, 2*(1-2), 24–46. doi:10.1504/IJPD.2005.006667

Tenkasi, R., & Boland, R. J. (1996). Exploring knowledge diversity in knowledge intensive firms: A new role for information systems. *Journal of Organizational Change Management, 9*(1), 79–91. doi:10.1108/09534819610107330

Tuomi, I. (1999, January 5-8). Data is more than knowledge: Implications of the reversed knowledge hierarchy for knowledge management and organizational memory. In *Proceedings of the 32nd Hawaii International Conference on System Sciences* (pp. 1-12). Volume Track 1.

Verilog. (2008). Retrieved on January 2, 2009, from http://www.verilog.com/

VHDL. (2008). Retrieved on January 2, 2009, from http://en.wikipedia.org/wiki/VHDL

Virkkunen, J., & Kuutti, K. (2000). Understanding organizational learning by focusing on "activity systems." . *Accounting, Management, and Information Technologies, 10*, 291–319. doi:10.1016/S0959-8022(00)00005-9

Wertsch, J. V. (1991). *Voices of the mind: A sociocultural approach to mediated action*. Cambridge, MA: Harvard University Press.

Wilson, T. D. (2002). The nonsense of "knowledge management." *Information Research, 8*(1), paper no. 144. Retrieved on December 3, 2008, from http://InformationR.net/ir/8-1/paper144.html

Zack, M. (1999). Developing a knowledge strategy. *California Management Review, 41*(3), 125–145.

Zinchenko, V. (1996). Developing activity theory: The zone of proximal development and beyond. In B. Nardi (Ed.), *Context and Consciousness, Activity Theory, and Human-Computer Interaction* (pp. 283-324). Cambridge, MA: MIT Press.

ENDNOTES

[1] Theory-focused accounts for the activity domain are given in Taxén (2007; 2007b).

[2] Thus, it can be seen that the definition of coordination proposed by Malone & Crowston (1994) only comprises one of the activity modalities: temporalization.

[3] Due to ease of reading, the direct dependencies from the IT department to Supply & Implementation and Research & Development are suppressed in the diagram. These dependencies are indirectly present through the Market & Sales domain.

[4] It is of course possible to group activity domains into other constellations for various reasons, for example, book-keeping purposes. Such constellations, however, should not be confused with activity domains.

[5] I will use "information systems" and "tools" indiscriminately without going into what might distinguish them. The important aspect here is that they both provide some capability that is useful in an activity domain.

[6] It can be noted that communities of practice and activity domains are two different things. In communities of practice the individual is, so to speak, on leave from her daily work in

the activity domain, and gather together with peers in an exchange of ideas and experiences that in turn may be useful when back "at home".

Section 5
Knowledge Management Functional Strategies

Chapter 14

SMEs and Competitive Advantage:
A Mix of Innovation, Marketing and ICT—The Case of "Made in Italy"

Eleonora Di Maria
University of Padova, Italy

Stefano Micelli
Ca' Foscari University, Italy

ABSTRACT

The global economy is transforming the sources of the competitive advantages of firms, especially for firms embedded in local manufacturing systems. Based on the theoretical contributions to knowledge management and industrial districts, this chapter describes alternative firm's strategies and upgrading options by exploring the relationships among innovation, marketing, and network technologies. Starting from the analysis of the Global Competitiveness Report and the European Innovation Scoreboard, this chapter focuses on the case of firms specializing in the "Made in Italy" industries (fashion, furniture, home products) to outline a framework explaining the new competitive opportunities for SMEs. Through a qualitative analysis the chapter presents four case studies of Italian firms that promote successful strategies based on a coherent mix of R&D-based innovation, experienced marketing, and design by leveraging on ICT.

INTRODUCTION

Global economy is transforming the sources of firms' competitive advantages and especially for firms embedded in local manufacturing systems. As in the case of Italy, during the '80s and '90s small and medium enterprises (SMEs) localized in industrial districts and specializing in low or medium-tech industries have built their success on productive flexibility, quality certification and incremental innovation. Literature on industrial districts has provided evidence of the sources of competitiveness of local systems (Pyke *et al.*, 1990). As opposed to the large multinational corporations, district SMEs emphasize an alternative model of economic organization (Piore & Sabel, 1984; Porter, 1998), in which external economies support distributed production

DOI: 10.4018/978-1-60566-348-7.ch014

processes within the local networks of firms. From this perspective, on the one hand, scholars focused on the advantages offered by proximity in terms of technology spillovers and economic externalities (i.e. Krugman, 1991) (collective goods). On the other hand, studies on the knowledge economy (i.e. Arora *et al.*, 1998; Becattini & Rullani, 1996) consider industrial districts as knowledge management systems, where the local context is able to sustain and facilitate creation, exploration and exploitation of (mainly tacit) knowledge, rooted into social practices.

SMEs are now facing competitive forces that impact on the sustainability of their strategies in the next years. First, manufacturing internationalization pushes firms operating in local supply chains to extend their networks beyond local boundaries to catch the opportunities of global value chains (Gereffi *et al.*, 2005). While, on the one hand, a growing part of local productive activities may be transferred internationally with cost advantages, on the other hand, those paths may reduce a small firm's control over economic processes with negative influence on learning-by-doing innovation.

A second major challenge refers to the development and management of sales networks on a global basis, in a framework of stronger connections with the market. As many scholars have outlined, the interaction between customers and the firm through sales networks, as well as the web, is crucial in order to understand the market and anticipate demand trends. More important, building relationships with active customers (lead users and communities of customers) is part of a firm's innovation strategy, to obtain profitable knowledge for product and brand management (i.e. Sawhney & Prandelli, 2000). From this perspective, SMEs have to improve their competencies in interaction with customers at the international level, overcoming local social and cultural boundaries as well as their traditional manufacturing approach. Such strategic options require more sophisticated marketing competencies, which are

not usually available within SMEs operating in local productive systems.

Thirdly, the evolution of information and communication technologies (ICT) contributes to the debate about the transformation of the district firm model and the advantages of local embeddedness (i.e. Chiarvesio *et al.*, 2004). Global supply chains and international commercial outlets ask the firm to increase control on processes at the organizational level and within the firm's extended value system. From this perspective, network technologies can strengthen information sharing, process transparency and interaction among players in the value system (final customers included). Large multinational companies were able to fill the gap with the flexible SME model in the 1990s, thanks to network technologies. These tools supported distance cooperative work, also increasing process monitoring, knowledge management and communication within a renovated firm model (Scott Morton, 1991). In the present scenario, SMEs are asked to update their strategies benefiting from network technologies. SMEs have to overcome the local environment as the prime source of innovation - local tacit knowledge, mainly manufacturing-oriented and informally managed - by developing new capabilities to manage extended networks including research centers, designers, and customers (Biggiero, 2006; Corò & Grandinetti, 1999).

Based on the theoretical contributions to knowledge management and industrial districts, this chapter describes alternative firm's strategies and upgrading options by exploring the relationships among innovation, marketing and networks technologies. The chapter focuses on the case of firms specializing in the "Made in Italy" industries (fashion, furniture, home products) to outline a framework explaining new competitive opportunities for SMEs. Our hypothesis is that the learning-by-doing innovation model that has characterized district firms in the past is no longer sufficient to sustain their competitive advantage. The R&D-based innovation, efficiently adopted in large corporations, can offer new strategic options to face international competition. However, it cannot be implemented easily in all district SMEs. Moreover, innovation cannot be limited to scientific knowledge management, but can benefit also from customer input and experience related to technical features as well as associations and symbols the product incorporates (i.e. Krippendorf & Butter, 1984). From this perspective, the capabilities of SMEs to manage networks of relationships and to translate customers' needs into products may open new competitive opportunities, under the condition of a well-defined ICT strategy.

In the first section this chapter analyzes the district SMEs' model and its impact on Italian competitiveness, based on the contributions and approaches to innovation of the Global Competitiveness Report and the European Innovation Scoreboard. The second section focuses on the drivers of competitive advantage and strategies of firms in terms of science-driven and market-driven innovation, also considering the role of ICT. Through a qualitative analysis, in the third section, this chapter discusses four case studies of Italian firms that promote successful strategies based on a coherent mix of R&D-based innovation, experienced marketing and design, by leveraging on ICT.

SMEs' COMPETITIVENESS IN THE EUROPEAN SCENARIO

Despite scholars' interests in the Italian economic model based on competitive local systems of SMEs (Piore & Sabel, 1984), international analysis stresses the marginal role of Italy in the global arena as regards SME's capabilities to manage codified innovation. The Global Competitiveness Report of the World Economic Forum put Italy 42nd in the international ranking. This study emphasizes the dynamics of growth and competitive factors of countries (with a focus on technology innovation, economic systems and institutional

framework) through a comparative approach and identifies then the competitive potentials of firms localized in each country. As opposed to its success during the '80s and '90s, the Italian economic system, and specifically SMEs specializing in the so-called "Made in Italy" industries (home products, fashion, mechanics, food), seems to lack competitiveness, due to low investments in R&D and patents. Even in the European Union framework, the tool used to evaluate competitiveness and performances of nations and regions – the European Innovation Scoreboard – describes a quite negative picture of Italian firms, based on a few indicators on firm's expenditure on R&D, the numbers of patents registered, investments in advanced services.

Italy (...) performs exceptionally badly in knowledge flow (...) Given the structural problems confronting innovation in Italy, as shown in EXIS, the Italian performance on innovation mode is above expectations (Arundel & Hollanders, 2005, p. 30).

As stressed by analysts, the prevalence of small and medium firms in the economic system is the principal reason for Italian weakness in managing innovation successfully. According to the data of European researchers, the Italian SMEs are characterized by learning-by-doing innovation. Thus, SMEs are not able to translate new knowledge into patents and codified outputs. Moreover, SMEs do not approach (formal) innovation with strategic intent and, hence, do not invest a relevant amount of resources in R&D, training and new technologies. Despite this negative picture, those studies mention a few Italian SMEs' strengths related to organizational innovation and strategic control on technical activities such as product design.

From our perspective, such contradictory results can be explained by considering a broader approach to innovation, which does not cover only R&D-based activities. Instead, innovation can also be linked with the development of intangible features of the product and customer experience as the main drivers of value creation. From this standpoint, there are many different ways through which innovation can be deployed: the value created through innovation and its impact on competitiveness is rooted in the variety of forms and processes of the innovation each firm is able to design in its own original way.

Following this approach, recently, the European Union has upgraded its framework of analysis by creating the Innovation Diversity Index, which is a measure oriented to capture the alternative forms of innovation characterizing countries and regions. Such an index is influenced not only by innovative firms that invest in R&D and patents, but also firms that have positive performances based on organizational innovation and innovation in marketing and design.

From this point of view, the competitive advantage of Italy becomes clearer. Despite their specialization in low or medium-tech industries, Italian SMEs rank at the top in Europe with regards to innovation management processes that develop and transform informal knowledge into value for the market. In this scenario, of near formalized procedures that lead to innovation – typically used in large corporations – one should also evaluate, on the one hand, the openness of the innovation cycle (innovation inputs beyond scientific knowledge and R&D) and, on the other hand, the results of innovation (outputs) and its use. Based on the Innovation Diversity Index of the EU, Italian SMEs show strong ability in the management of networks and collaboration. Traditional innovation drivers (R&D, skilled labor force and lifelong training) are weak in SMEs (ranked 21 out of 25). Instead, small firms are stronger in new knowledge generation and implementation.

According to the categories developed by the EU, Italian firms are classified as "modifier" in their innovation strategy because they capture and transform external knowledge into products through informal processes. Such approach is perceived either negatively, as it is not codified (and represents incremental innovation) or positively, as SMEs are flexible in knowledge management. Firms can reinvent products and processes in many original ways thanks to their reactivity to market inputs and demand and by developing differentiation strategies. This capability is supported by specific professional practices focused on product specialization available at the territorial level. We explain those results by referring to the economic district model, where small businesses belonging to local networks of production organize knowledge management through distributed innovation systems, instead of a large organization (Maskell, 2001).

During the fordism paradigm, the large firm model has been considered the best way and scientific knowledge (and R&D) was the main driver of innovation. In the open innovation paradigm, distributed networks sustain innovation (Chesbrough, 2003) and customers can contribute with their knowledge (von Hippel, 2005). Moreover, customers are available to pay for products that offer not only new features (technological innovation), but also which offer them an experience and the intangible value linked to associations with sensemaking supported by brand strategy, design and social participation (Prahalad & Ramaswamy, 2003). From this perspective, innovation cannot be limited to technological innovation, but should also include aesthetic and intangible elements created through marketing strategy (communication) (Bettiol & Micelli, 2005; Ravasi & Lojacono, 2005). According to this perspective, Italian firms may improve their position in the international competitive arena because of their specific capacity to face innovation.

STRATEGIES, KNOWLEDGE MANAGEMENT AND ICT

In low or medium-tech industries such as fashion or furniture, the competition is increasing and require firms to choose either cost leadership in the mass market or niche differentiation, while positioning in the middle-market is becoming more and more unsustainable (Silverstein & Fiske, 2003). As opposed to high-tech industries, in which the role of patents and collaboration with research institutions is crucial for product innovation, in the mentioned industries – as in the case of Italy – innovation cannot usually be perceived as patent-driven. Instead, innovation is linked to creativity, a firm's ability to manage variety (innovation as organizational capability), and mix inputs coming from the market, designers and marketing (Schmitt & Simonson, 1997). From this perspective, an evaluation of a firm's innovation performance and its strategy should not be limited only to R&D activities and its outputs. Rather, from our perspective, in the open-innovation paradigm (Chesborugh, 2003) it should also consider the extension and characteristics of the networks that sustain a firm's innovation (as inputs of knowledge) as well as innovation outcomes. Marketing scholars emphasize the role of the intangible as part of the innovation process and a result of the value offered to customers. Products are not sold only because of their new features and functionalities, but also, and often, due to the meaning they transmit through their shapes (design) and the experience they give to customers (Pine & Gilmore, 1999).

Studies on innovation process have stressed the role of codified knowledge in knowledge management cycles, while the analysis of social dynamics (Brown & Duguid, 2000) has outlined the situated learning system and the relevance of experience as a driver to develop and share complex knowledge. According to this point of view, SMEs operating in local manufacturing systems benefit from physical proximity to customers, suppliers and relevant communities of practices embedded into local contexts. However, the global competitive scenario forces SMEs to upgrade and develop new strategies where innovation processes are sustainable on a international level. In a complex and global market, where leading customers are far from the firm and there are numbers of potential knowledge sources for a firm's innovation (Tapscott & Williams, 2007), the local economic and social system is inadequate to offer SMEs all the relevant and useful knowledge to compete. On the one hand, modularity and codification can guarantee a more open and extended circulation and use of knowledge, across contexts. On the other hand, the more complex the knowledge to manage, the higher the difficulties in codification and the need for promoting more sophisticated sharing strategies based on "pragmatic collaboration" (Helper *et al.*, 2000) (people-to-people by face-to-face interaction or web-based).

Based on this distinction and the literature contributions on the topic, we can represent the sources of firms' competitive advantage (Grant, 1996; Kogut & Zander, 1996) by comparing the different role of knowledge developed by firms and the alternative strategies of knowledge management adopted. We identified alternative models (Figure 1). On the one side, we can identify firms that compete by leveraging on R&D and scientific knowledge. Codification allows firms to enter into global networks of innovation and exchange knowledge on a broad scale with universities and research centers (regional innovation systems, Asheim & Coenen, 2006). Local dynamics are supported by international connections, through which the firm is able to explore opportunities and exploit knowledge. On the other side, competitive advantage is based on customer relationship management built on experience. The firm is interested in selecting lead users and involving customer communities into the innovation processes, aiming at their sharing relevant knowledge (von Hippel, 2005). It is a form of entrepreneurial innovation, with a strong role of marketing, as the firm's organization and processes are oriented to the market and to interact with external players (customers and lead users) to co-develop the product and the meaning related to it (Muniz & O'Guinn, 2001). Our hypothesis is that in the complex competitive scenario, firms

Figure 1. Competitive advantage and firm strategy (Source: Authors)

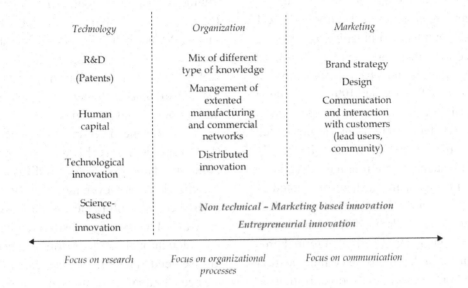

may develop sustainable competitive advantage by mixing the strengths of the opposite models, where patents and R&D-based innovation may be enhanced through marketing-based innovation and vice versa.

In such a competitive scenario, the analysis of a firms' strategy about innovation management cannot be developed without the study of their approach to information and communication technologies (ICT). On the one hand, these technologies support information management at a distance, by stressing the advantages of efficiency. On the other hand, thanks to multimedia tools, ICT allow the development of a virtual, interactive environment, where participants live the experience and are involved in social interaction on line. This environment offers opportunities related to knowledge creation and sharing, even in the case of complex knowledge (i.e. product innovation).

It is not our aim to describe the debate on the impacts of ICT on knowledge management in detail [1]. We would outline the SMEs' approach to ICT investment and its influence on innovation. The international reorganization of manufacturing activities, as well as sales networks, push firms to adopt technological solutions that sustain coordination of activities in extended networks and organizations (Scott Morton, 1991). Moreover, the transformation in the consumption models described above asks firms to interact with customers in order to exploit the linkages with lead users and communities for innovation purposes. In both the strategic options of a science-based, competitive advantage (i.e. patents) and value-driven by "customer intimacy" and sensemaking (Treacy & Wiersema, 1997), network technologies become key factors in supporting competitiveness. In the open-innovation paradigm, ICT is in fact the valuable infrastructure for knowledge management aims, where knowledge is spread across contexts, organizations, and people (employees, customers).

Computer-mediated communication offers tremendous advantages of tracking and tracing dialogues and interactive relationships, as well as content development and sharing (digitalization, multimedia solutions, social software) (Kuomi, 2002; von Hippel, 2005), even in complex situations. Hence, technologies can help firms overcome barriers and leverage the networks of connections characterizing the on-line environment (*in primis* among customers). Traditionally, ICT found primary application in large corporations, to solve coordination problems and support knowledge gathering and retrieval efficiently and effectively (Sproull & Kiesler, 1991). The role of technological infrastructure as a necessary condition for knowledge management did not match with the SME's competitive model. Especially within local systems, small firms have developed knowledge management mechanisms rooted in the social sphere of their contexts of embeddedness (Becattini & Rullani, 1996). Knowledge processes are usually not codified in formal procedures, but lie in the intensive communication and personal linkages within the organization, as well as outside the working domain, in the social fabric of places.

As shown in studies on ICT adoption in district firms (i.e. Chiarvesio *et al.*, 2004), as opposed to large corporations, small and medium firms localized in local manufacturing systems have focused their attention on commodity-based technologies, such as email and web sites. Those technologies can be considered ready-to-use tools, which can be implemented in the organizational structure with low financial investments, as well as limited organizational changes. In industrial districts, SMEs' strategies in ICT investments have been characterized by:

- selectivity in the technological solutions chosen;
- incremental innovation processes based on learning-by-doing paths;
- a bottom-up process (no "master mind" at the local level)

During the new economy many scholars and analysts stress the potentialities of e-commerce for SMEs in terms of market enlargement and efficiency. Instead, research on ICT adoption by Italian district SMEs show low rates of e-

commerce, while the web is exploited as an interactive marketing tool. Firms do not consider the e-commerce solutions available adequate to manage "Made in Italy" products for transactional purposes. Rather, firms stress the importance of web-based communication: the web becomes a medium to gather customers' feedback on products and support brand strategies.

More advanced technologies such as ERP (Enterprise Resource Planning) or groupware, tailored to large firms, are less diffused in small organizations. However, those solutions are considered crucial tools to increase process transparency and the control on distributed networks at the international level. In this perspective, the more extended the firm's value chain, the higher the need for upgrading the SMEs' strategy, where ICT sustains the firm's management beyond the local system. From our perspective, all the technological solutions available can be included in the framework of the knowledge management system, not limited to the organizational boundaries, but involving the players operating upstream (suppliers, designers, etc.) and downstream (sales agents, customers) in the product innovation as well as marketing activities.

COMPETITIVENESS IN "MADE IN ITALY" FIRMS

In this theoretical framework, we considered the strategies of firms specializing in low and medium-tech industries to explore the connection between R&D-based and marketing-driven innovation processes, and the role of ICT in supporting those activities at the local and global level (Di Maria & Micelli, 2007).

In order to explore the strategies of "Made in Italy" firms in the scenario described above, we carried out a qualitative study on district SMEs to analyze knowledge management processes and firms' innovation approach (Siggelkow, 2007; Yin, 1994). Based on a first selection of firms

Table 1. Case studies

Company		Innovation strategy	Main ICT investments
Alpinestars	100 Ml Euro turnover Car and motorbike apparel products (Montebelluna sport system district)	Focus on lead users, interaction in customer loci (Torrance, CA)	Web and multimedia, e-commerce
Lotto Sport Italia	120 Ml Euro - 230 employees Sport system: shoes and apparel (Montebelluna district)	Mix of R&D (patent, relations with universities) and design	ERP and explicit knowledge management processes
Horm	6 Ml Euro - 40 employees Furniture (Livenza furniture district)	Collaboration with external international designers Patents	Internet to support on-line distributed product design processes
Bisazza	100 Ml Euro - 350 (900) employees High-quality covering for private/public buildings (Vicenza, mosaic district of Spilimbergo, India, China)	Design and brand (luxury) R&D and craft competences	ERP and CRM, collaborative design, e-learning, e-commerce

specializing in "Made in Italy" sectors and located in North East Italy, we interviewed entrepreneurs and the managers of R&D, design and information system departments. Interviews focused on a firm's history and strategy, organizational structure and innovation management models and ICT adopted. The four cases discussed in the chapter are summarized in Table 1.

Alpinestars: Innovation Through Lead Users

Localized in the sport system district of Montebelluna, Alpinestars is a leading firm in sport apparel and accessories for motorcyclists and car drivers. Innovation in Alpinestars is perceived as a dynamic and interactive process, where the managers, the team of creative people and technicians work together to develop new innovative products for the markets. The source of innovation is not localized only in the province of Treviso (Alpinestars' headquarter), but also in California, where the lead users adopt a firm's products in their daily sport activities. According to long-term relationships Alpinestars was able to develop with customers, the firm can translate their needs and inputs into concepts and products, on an interactive basis.

The firm demonstrates having identified and implemented a successful strategy in recent years, where the positive economic performances stress its leadership in the district (characterized by negative trends). Alpinestars has obtained a leading international role through continuous product innovation and design. Based on a flexible and creative (not conventional) organization, the firm focuses on creating stable connections with the networks (the places and the players) of innovation in the market of sport apparel and accessories. In the framework of product innovation that couples technical performances and fashion components, Alpinestars relies on informal groups in charge of supporting the new product development. A fundamental component is played by California – Torrance, Agoura Hills – where the firm has located its own research center and interacts with most dynamic customers. In this scenario, innovation is not rooted in the management of suppliers or customers within the local system boundaries. On the contrary, the firm leverages on knowledge repositories available outside the district – in the customers' loci – to reinvent and originally transform those ergonomics and emotional inputs into products. Those relationships are also fundamental for the brand strategy of the firm.

In an international oriented organization as the one described, ICT is the key driver to support information sharing among the offices, as well as a tool (web) for communication. Multimedia allows rich and intense communication, where the discourse on the product and the brand meanings are nurtured also through videos and pictures shared on-line and created by the firm and lead users themselves. Alpinestars has also e-commerce solutions for customers.

Lotto Sport Italia: "Word Champions" in Mixing Design and Patents

One of the most famous companies of the Montebelluna sport system, Lotto started in 1973 producing tennis shoes, followed by shoes and other products for individual and team sports. During the '80s the company internationalized its business, thanks to soccer shoes and international partnerships with Italian and foreign athletes. Moreover, Lotto is among the first district firms that invested in internalization of productive activities beyond the local manufacturing system. As a leading firm in the Montebelluna district, Lotto invests in innovation to support its competitiveness by coupling R&D-based activities (scientific research on new materials, ergonomics, etc.) and the involvement of lead users. One of its latest products is, in fact, a pair of football shoes without laces (Zhero Gravity), designed in collaboration with athletes. Meanwhile, in a framework of global production and commercialization of products, network technologies have been considered key elements in the management of extended supply and sales networks with the district as the core.

In the new millennium the attention for the investment in product quality has been increased through an explicit strategy that emphasizes the role of design and innovation as drivers of competitiveness.

In the global competitive scenario, Lotto Sport Italia is oriented to reinforce its international presence. In this perspective, cost reduction as a key goal to face competition has to be coupled with continuous product innovation. The development of original ideas – where the "Zhero Gravity" comes from (launched for the German World Football championship in 2006) – is the starting point in Lotto's strategy. The management of internal knowledge is relevant both in terms of R&D and design – more than 20 patents have been registered or are in the process of registration. The development of research relationships with Italian and international universities stresses Lotto's interests in exploring knowledge paths beyond the local district networks to sustain the company internationally.

As an open network firm, Lotto Sport Italia has invested in network technologies systematically, by gathering different technology solutions – from their Web site, to e-commerce, ERP, groupware and supply-chain management applications. The technological infrastructure sustains information flows and communication between the company and its international networks of partners and markets, in a strategic and codified knowledge management approach. In fact, Lotto is interested in acquiring and sharing informal knowledge available within the organization through ICT (digital archives, database for intellectual property rights management).

Horm: From the District to International Design Networks

Horm is a small firm specialized in the production of high quality furniture and wooden complementary house products. It was founded in 1989 and is located in Azzano Decimo, in the furniture district of Livenza (North East Italy). Horm has developed its strategy by focusing on product differentiation through design. Since 1998, Horm has been obtaining economic success and growth thanks to the international recognition of a few of the firm's products – the Compasso d'Oro, a famous Italian Design Award promoted by the Italian Design Association - designed by one of Horm's founders (Lucian Marson) and the Grafite design studio. From these awards, this small firm started relevant collaborations with international designers. Due to Luciano Marson's and Paolo Chiarot's investments in developing personal relationships and connections with designers (Toyo Ito, Mario Botta and Steven Holl among others) all over the world (Japan, USA and Europe), the firm was able to increase the product range and international sales (60% of the turnover is export-based).

Horm's strategy is oriented to exploiting internal strong competencies in wood transformation and production of "natural wood" furniture. The manufacturing process is organized in small-scale stocks, with particular emphasis on product customization as regards to the material used and finishing activities. Specifically, a mix of hand-made and technological innovation processes characterizes Horm's made-to-order production.

As opposed to the typical district approach in which local suppliers are key players in the firm's innovation processes, Horm has developed innovation mainly internally, through R&D activities and patenting, and is able to increase the technological features of the products as well as their design characteristics (i.e. invisible hinges). In the global competitive scenario, Horm's approach to innovation is double: on the one hand, the focus is on design and aesthetical components of products as drivers of economic success; on the other hand, this small firm invests also in codified knowledge to protect their ideas against competitors (1 to 3 years is the average time of the product innovation cycle). Horm does not invest in market research. Instead, the firm exploits international designers and entrepreneur's knowledge about customers and future trends, as an emerging process.

The entrepreneur is confident about the strategic role of ICT to sustain the firm's competitive advantage. Network technologies are key tools to support creativity processes, while the Web infrastructure allows Horm to interact with its commercial networks. Specifically, the firm's exploitation of multimedia applications and broadband opens new opportunities in product design and development at the international scale. In fact, the product "Riddled" – obtained through a collaboration with the famous Steven Hollen's design studio based in New York and produced in 39 plus 39 items – has been made possible thanks to on line communication and document sharing at a distance between Italy and the USA. At the same time, Horm has also created an open and distributed digital archive concerning all the documents and digital contents about products and innovation processes to use them for marketing and knowledge management purposes.

Bisazza: Upgrading the Product Through Communication Strategy

Even if Bisazza cannot be considered a "strict" district firm, this family company acts as a local organization able to upgrade its strategy in the "Made in Italy" product towards international markets. More specifically, in the last few years, Bisazza has developed a new strategy based on a mix of local craft competencies, technological innovation and marketing (brand strategy and focus on distribution). Founded in 1956 in a small town in the Vicenza province (Alte, in the North East part of Italy), Bisazza is now a global leader in the production of glass mosaic and high-quality covering for private and public buildings. In the Italian context, Bisazza distinguishes itself because of its orientation to the culture of design-based products and its international vocation, by transforming its products into luxury ones.

The Bisazza group has now more than 1,000 employees, three factories, 11 branches and six shops, plus more than 6,000 points of sales worldwide. Since 2005, Bisazza has been a member of Altagamma, the Italian association of firms specializing in luxury products, and its turnover is about 100 million Euro. The firm is characterized for its focus on classic mosaic production (glass) and gold-leaf based mosaic. The upgrading transformation started in 2000, when Piero Bisazza (the founder's son) became CEO. Piero Bisazza outlined a twofold strategy. On the one hand, the focus is on product extension: the mosaic should overcome the covering use, to also become a fashionable product with furnishing applications. On the other hand, Bisazza's brand strategy is oriented to transform the meanings linked with the brand and upgrade product position to the luxury niche. To obtain such goals the firm invests in distribution and commercial sales networks (with brand stores, flagship stores and shop-in-shop), also participating in the most famous design fairs. Hence, the firm's strategy is difficult to imitate, while the market positioning is based on strong internal production competencies as well as an innovative communication approach: with a product application shift from bathroom and private house areas to living rooms and public spaces (i.e. museums).

Mosaic production is internally managed. Concerning the artistic and limited edition mosaic productions, Bisazza involves knowledge and competencies of the historical district of Spilimbergo (North East Italy). The manufacturing process includes local and international suppliers. All the processes are controlled through network technologies. Beyond ERP systems, Bisazza in fact supports information sharing about production steps and commercial details through digital connections (quality control, content management at a distance). It is important to stress the firm's investment in developing a customized software solution able to describe and manage mosaic production and its technical application. Through such a solution Bisazza can share key knowledge with its partners within the value chain. Moreover, the company also invests in customer relationship management (CRM) solutions to interact with its USA branch, in addition to e-commerce tools. Recently, the firm is oriented to create new technological collaborative tools to support interior designers and architects' activities, as well as an e-learning platform.

CONCLUSIONS

The four case studies are characterized by successful strategies based on a mix of R&D-driven innovation and marketing, where firms developed strong relationships with customers. Innovation processes blend codified knowledge and tacit knowledge based on specific practices related to consumption (i.e. sport) or professional profiles (exploitation as well as exploration in knowledge management, March, 1991). The firms interviewed coupled scientific innovation with product innovation based on design, the creation of experience and focus on communication. The local context in which these firms are embedded is important, but it is not the only source of knowledge in order to build their competitive advantage. On the one hand, these firms are interested in creating new connections with foreign research centers to promote projects for product, technology or material innovation. On the other hand, they develop relevant linkages with the loci of consumption and with key players for creativity, to nurture the innovation process interactively.

The local context offers competencies in the manufacturing domain and sustains the culture of the product. However, competitive SMEs are able to create and manage extended networks by operating in global value chains and approaching innovation through the entrepreneurial innovation model identified by the European Union. To be sustainable those strategies require information and communication technologies, where ERP systems support advanced process management and increase interoperability, while web-based solutions for communication and product (document) management are also implemented in supply chain and commercial sales networks.

Even if our study is still preliminary in its term, the case studies offer a few managerial implications in the way the innovation process is outlined as an open process. First, firms should understand the types of relationships characterizing the players involved in the innovation dynamics, in order to develop consistent mechanisms of management (codification vs. interaction). Second, there are interesting opportunities in combining different kinds and sources of knowledge, which have to be identified and coordinated. Today, firms are asked to develop capabilities in accessing external knowledge (exploration) through people-moving and electronic connections. In addition to this flexibility and openness they also have to pursue strategies and use tools (ICT) coherent with the relationships developed.

As described in the chapter, knowledge management emerges as a dynamic process where the selection of knowledge sources is crucial as well as the role of ICT.

Managers and practitioners should consider the advantages of connections with customers and lead users in general to improve the flow of valuable knowledge into the firm, for both product innovation and product improvement. More specifically, in low as well as in medium and even high-tech industries, focusing on the science-based inputs of product innovation can limit the firm's potentialities. The role of customers in the innovation framework refers also on the marketing domain, where they lead users and communities can support firm's brand strategy and sensemaking (non-technical innovation). Investing in identifying lead users becomes the starting point for the development of systematic relationships – on line and "off line" – between key customers and the firm. Those relationships allow managers to acquire insights about market perception of products and brands. Through lead users' (as well as designers) inputs (narratives about products, storytelling, etc.), firms can shape the offering towards new perspectives, where the value is linked to intangible elements instead of - or in addition to - technical features.

Information and communication technologies enable knowledge flows at distance, not only in terms of codified process, but also through more flexible solutions that sustain rich computer-mediated communication (i.e. multimedia). To enhance the knowledge management strategy,

managers should identify the right mix of technological tools that support the key relationships with knowledge owners – within and outside the firm (employees, suppliers, distributors, customers, researchers) – keeping in mind that codification and people-to-people connections are both important. On the one hand, technology solutions such as ERP can increase formalization of specific procedures and, hence, improving the firm's ability to extend their manufacturing and commercial processes at the international level. On the other hand, such solutions could co-exist with more open platforms where to manage interaction for knowledge exploration (on line communities).

REFERENCES

Antonelli, C. (2005). Models of knowledge and systems of governance. *Journal of Institutional Economics, 1*, 51–73. doi:10.1017/S1744137405000044

Arora, A., Gambardella, A., & Rullani, E. (1997). Division of labour and the locus of inventive activity. *The Journal of Management and Governance, 1*, 123–140. doi:10.1023/A:1009993430964

Arundel, A., & Hollanders, H. (2005). *EXIS: An exploratory approach to innovation scoreboard*. Retrieved on April 25, 2007, from http://www.trendchart.org

Asheim, B. T., & Coenen, L. (2006). Contextualizing regional innovation systems in a globalizing learning economy: On knowledge basis and institutional frameworks. *The Journal of Technology Transfer, 31*, 163–173. doi:10.1007/s10961-005-5028-0

Becattini, G., & Rullani, E. (1996). Local systems and global connections: The role of knowledge. In F. Cossentino, F. Pyke & W. Segenberger (Eds.), *Local and regional response to global pressure: The case of Italy and its industrial districts*. Geneva: International Institute for Labor Studies.

Bettiol, M., & Micelli, S. (2005). *Design e creatività nel made in Italy*. Milano: Bruno Mondandori.

Biggiero, L. (2006). Industrial and knowledge relocation strategies under the challenges of globalization and digitalization: The move of small and medium enterprises among territorial systems. *Entrepreneurship & Regional Development, 18*(November), 443–471. doi:10.1080/08985620600884701

Brown, J. S., & Duguid, P. (2000). *The social life of information*. Cambridge: Harvard Business School Press.

Chesbrough, H. W. (2003). *Open innovation*. Cambridge: Harvard Business School Press.

Chiarvesio, M., Di Maria, E., & Micelli, S. (2004). From local networks of SMEs to virtual clusters? Evidence from recent trends in Italy. *Research Policy, 33*(10), 1509–1528. doi:10.1016/j.respol.2004.08.009

Corò, G., & Grandinetti, R. (1999). Evolutionary patterns of Italian industrial districts. *Human Systems Management, 18*, 117–130.

D'Adderio, L. (2001). Crafting the virtual prototype: How firms integrate knowledge and capabilities across organizational boundaries. *Research Policy, 30*, 1409–1424. doi:10.1016/S0048-7333(01)00159-7

Davenport, T. H., & Prusak, L. (1998). *Working knowledge. How organizations manage what they know*. Boston: Harvard Business School Press.

De Sanctis, G., & Fulk, J. (Eds.). (1996). *Communication technology and organizational forms*. Thousand Oaks: Sage.

Di Maria, E., & Micelli, S. (2007). Imprese del *made in Italy*, competitività e innovazione. In G. Volpato (Ed.), *Il knowledge management come strumento competitivo. Un confronto intersettoriale*. Roma: Carocci.

Gereffi, G., Humphrey, J., & Sturgeon, T. (2005). The governance of global value chains. *Review of International Political Economy, 12*(1), 78–104. doi:10.1080/09692290500049805

Grant, R. M. (1996). Toward a knowledge-based theory of the firm. *Strategic Management Journal, 17*, 109–122. doi:10.1002/(SICI)1097-0266(199602)17:2<109::AID-SMJ796>3.0.CO;2-P

Helper, S., MacDuffie, J. P., & Sabel, C. M. (2000). Pragmatic collaboration: Advancing knowledge while controlling opportunism. *Industrial and Corporate Change, 9*(3), 443–488. doi:10.1093/icc/9.3.443

Kogut, B., & Zander, U. (1996). What firms do? Coordination, identity, and learning. *Organization Science, 7*(5), 502–518. doi:10.1287/orsc.7.5.502

Krippendorf, K., & Butter, R. (1984). Product semantics: Exploring the symbolic qualities of form in innovation. *The Journal of the Industrial Designers Society of America, 3*, 4–9.

Krugman, P. (1991). *Geography and trade*. Boston: MIT Press.

Kuomi, I. (2002). *Networks of innovation. Change and meaning in the age of the Internet*. Oxford: Oxford University Press.

March, J. G. (1991). Exploration and exploitation in organizational learning. *Organization Science, 2*(1), 71–86. doi:10.1287/orsc.2.1.71

Maskell, P. (2001). Towards a knowledge-based theory of the geographical cluster. *Industrial and Corporate Change, 10*, 919–941. doi:10.1093/icc/10.4.921

Muniz, A. M., & O'Guinn, T. (2001). Brand community. *The Journal of Consumer Research, 27*, 412–432. doi:10.1086/319618

Nonaka, I. (1994). A dynamic theory of organizational knowledge creation. *Organization Science*, *5*(1), 14–37. doi:10.1287/orsc.5.1.14

Pine, B. J., & Gilmore, J. (1999). *The experience economy*. Boston: Harvard Business School Press.

Piore, M. J., & Sabel, C. M. (1984). *The second industrial divide*. New York: Basic Books.

Porter, M. E. (1985). *Competitive advantage*. New York: The Free Press.

Prahalad, C. K., & Ramaswamy, V. (2003). The new frontier of experience innovation. *MIT Sloan Management Review*, *44*, 12–18.

Pyke, F., Becattini, G., & Sengenberger, W. (Eds.). (1990). *Industrial districts and Interfirm cooperation in Italy*. Geneva: International Institute for Labour Studies.

Ravasi, D., & Lojacono, G. (2005). Managing design and designers for strategic renewal. *Long Range Planning*, *38*, 51–77. doi:10.1016/j.lrp.2004.11.010

Sawhney, M., & Prandelli, E. (2000). Communities of creation: Managing distributed innovation in turbulent markets. *California Management Review*, *42*, 24–54.

Schmitt, B., & Simonson, A. (1997). *Marketing aesthetics. The strategic management of brands, identity, and management*. New York: The Free Press.

Scott Morton, M. S. (Ed.). (1991). *The corporation of the 1990s. Information technology and organizational transformation*. New York: Oxford University Press.

Siggelkow, N. (2007). Persuasion with case studies. *Academy of Management Journal*, *50*, 20–24.

Silverstein, J. M., & Fiske, N. (2003). *Trading up. The new American luxury*. New York: Portfolio.

Sproull, L., & Kiesler, S. (1991). *Connections. New ways of working in the networked organization*. Cambridge: MIT Press.

Tapscott, D., & Williams, A. D. (2007). *Wikinomics. How mass collaboration changes everything*. New York: Penguin Book.

Treacy, M., & Wiersema, F. (1997). *The discipline of market leaders: Choose your customers, narrow your focus, dominate your market*. New York: Perseus Books Group.

Von Hippel, E. (2005). *Democritizing innovation*. Boston: MIT Press.

Von Krogh, G., & Roos, J. (Eds.). (1996). *Managing knowledge. Perspectives on cooperation and competition*. London: Sage.

World Economic Forum. (2006). *The global competitiveness report*. Retrieved on April 20, 2007, from http://www.weforum.org

Yin, R. K. (1994). *Case study research: Design and methods*. Thousand Oaks: Sage.

ENDNOTE

[1]   Among the many contributions in this field consider: Nonaka (1994), von Kroogh and Roos (1996), Davenport and Prusak (1998), De Sanctis, Fulk (1996), D'Adderio (2001), Antonelli (2005).ff

Chapter 15

Knowledge Management for an Effective Sales and Marketing Function

Amit Karna
European Business School, Germany

Ramendra Singh
Indian Institute of Management, India

Sanjay Verma
Indian Institute of Management, India

ABSTRACT

In the last decade, knowledge management has been receiving managerial attention particularly in the post-Internet era. With advancements in information and communications technologies, the incentives to manage knowledge have far surpassed the costs associated with it. The sales and marketing (S&M) function is one of the important functions in an organization with a unique blend of internal and external stakeholders to cater to. Another unique feature of knowledge management in the S&M function is that it lies on the interface of the organization with its customers. Therefore, information that comes into the organization through sales and marketing employees is often collected, filtered, and assimilated in different forms and with time lags. This chapter is aimed at familiarizing the readers with the importance of managing a continuously churning ocean of knowledge in the S&M function. We address various knowledge management issues and opportunities in the context of S&M and recommend a set of guidelines to enable managers increase the effectiveness of the S&M function by using appropriate knowledge management tools and strategies.

INTRODUCTION

Knowledge is created and organized by the flow of information, anchored on the commitment and beliefs of its holder (Nonaka, 1994). In the context of Sales and Marketing (S&M), the holders are team members of S&M and their support functions. Compared to other functions, knowledge in the S&M context is more intricate yet unique because of the function's focus on building, maintaining,

DOI: 10.4018/978-1-60566-348-7.ch015

and enhancing relationships with customers, while keeping an orientation for activities of competitors. In the sales function, for instance, it has been shown that salespersons' declarative knowledge helps them in classifying selling situations as well as customers that ultimately leads them to adopt suitable strategies for successful selling (Sheth, 1975). Given that similar firms in the same space are targeting a similar set of consumers, knowledge creation and utilization becomes more dynamic in S&M functions than in any of the other functions inside the firm, mainly because of flow of information from markets to the firms and its employees.

The S&M function is overtly dependent on the skill set and information base of employees in the department. While the skills are developed over time, the information base can be managed with appropriate management of knowledge. The organization's market orientation, akin to an organization-wide culture, places emphasis on two primary activities: (1) profitable creation and maintenance of superior customer value, while considering the interest of other key stakeholders; and (2) providing norms for behavior regarding the organizational development and responsiveness to market information (Slater and Narver, 1995). While it is virtually impossible for any one employee to capture and utilize all knowledge at a given time, it becomes imperative for the organization to implement certain tools that can help it in capturing, sharing, and updating knowledge at various stages in the value chain. In order to help understand these tools, in this chapter, we cover different situations which will highlight the need for a KM system. More particularly, we will discuss how knowledge is created from information and leveraged in the various S&M functions such as new product development process, segmentation and targeting, and selling. We discuss knowledge creation and utilization at the employee and organization level. We also raise issues in KM applications in S&M function, and provide solutions to problems there. The chapter covers some key KM

tools in use such as customer relationship management (CRM), and business intelligence (BI). We conclude the chapter with a strategy for managerial action and implementation of KM, and directions for evolution of the field in future.

BACKGROUND

For long, organizations have been obtaining knowledge from the environment. Simon (1957) coined the term bounded rationality to explain the decision-making of business managers under the presumption that making perfectly rational decisions are often not feasible in practice, given the finite computational resources available at hand. However, over the years, with increased flow of information, decision-making within organizations has increasingly become more informed. In order to make better decisions, firms adopt various processes and practices – formally and informally – to ensure that knowledge within organizations is created, captured, shared, and utilized in an effective manner.

Knowledge in organizations can be broadly classified into two categories: tacit and explicit. Tacit knowledge is hard to articulate, and constitutes action-based skills which are difficult to document. Explicit knowledge, on the other hand, is codified using expressions and can therefore be easily communicated, transferred or diffused. Nonaka (1994) proposed different processes through which knowledge can be transferred from one person to another in the same form or another.

Tacit to Explicit: Articulation

Tacit knowledge is transformed into explicit knowledge using documentation of policies that define the philosophy of the firm. This is a gradual process, which Baumard (1999) termed as common knowledge that is articulated into explicit knowledge over the years.

Explicit to Explicit: Combination

Explicit knowledge can be converted into explicit knowledge by combining the knowledge through mechanisms such as conversations or exchange of documents. In this type of exchange, 'fitting together' dominates as an explicit combinative logic (Baumard, 1999).

Explicit to Tacit: Internalization

Visual or codified knowledge available within organizations can be internalized by employees by watching, reading, and observing the artifacts. At times, explicit manifestations of tacit knowledge can also be seen in body language or facial expressions.

Tacit to Tacit: Socialization

Tacit knowledge is difficult to transform and even more difficult to convert into tacit knowledge. This can happen only through one-to-one interaction and socialization of individuals. Since this type of knowledge is independent of symbols, this can also happen without use of any language.

While these processes inform us about transforming knowledge, knowledge within organizations exists at two levels – individual and collective. The transfer of knowledge from individual to collective level marks knowledge creation at organizational level. The spiral of organizational knowledge creation (Nonaka, 1994) describes the diffusion of knowledge that starts from socialization, followed by combination, externalization, and finally internalization. While embarking upon this spiral of knowledge creation, the firm faces challenges in sharing of tacit knowledge, as tacit knowledge is difficult to express and is very sticky. KM systems within organizations aim at capturing as much of this sticky knowledge as possible. In the next two sections, we look at KM issues in the context of S&M function and some solutions to overcome these challenges.

SALES AND MARKETING FUNCTIONS

Three most important S&M functions which create and deliver maximum value to customers are: new product development, segmentation and targeting, and selling process. We highlight their essential aspects as under:

New Product Development Process: Collective

The process of new product development includes generation of new ideas, concept development, test marketing, and product launch. This also involves knowledge about markets, consumers, and competitors to successfully target customers and make an offering to them. This knowledge is different from the technical knowledge of production possessed by the production department of the organization, with whom the S&M function needs to collaborate closely for developing new products. Generation of ideas for new products by customers, channel members, or employees of the firm, requires successfully capturing their ideas, sifting them through the feasibility funnel, and filtering the best ones into the next stage.

Since products and services are bundle of attributes that meet customer needs, new product development starts by collecting information on customer needs and transforming this information first into organizational knowledge about customer needs. This knowledge needs to be shared across departments to convert customer needs successfully into product design attributes. Most often this transformation takes place through a structured process. One of the most popular and structured processes is the quality function deployment – an application of the 'house of quality' concept. However it is extremely important that market knowledge in general is in explicit form, so that sharing across departments is easily facilitated to facilitate efficient and effective response to market needs in a timely manner. The concept of time-to-market of new product introduction also corroborates importance of knowledge about markets to move in explicit form within organizational sub-units. The desire to reduce the time-to-market of new products also underscores the dynamic nature of the external environment in which firms operate.

Segmentation and Targeting Process: Collective

Segmenting customers based on their common needs, wants or demands has been used by firms for several decades. A plethora of variables have been used for segmentation including demographic variables such as age, gender, education; psychographic variables such as consumer lifestyle patterns; or even geographic variables such as political boundaries within the market. Segmenting the market based on any combination of these variables increases the efficiency of targeting consumers with information on products, services or promotional programs. Needless to say, segmentation would require information from customers about these variables, and then choosing a reasonable basis for segmenting the market. The effectiveness of segmenting depends on the accuracy of information on each of the variables. Similarly, targeting customers with messages requires reaching them, getting their attention, and communicating the message. To enable effective targeting of messages it is essential to collect information from customers on their media consumption habits, attention spans, and other consumption habits. The most stringent test of segmentation and targeting customers takes place during test marketing of new products, when firms collect a lot of information on the marketing mix elements in each of the targeted segments so as to evaluate their success before the final roll-out. At each stage of segmentation, customer surveys are extensively used to collect relevant information, mostly with the help of market research agencies. This is later analyzed using sophisticated statisti-

cal techniques to derive meaningful trends and conclusions. Segmentation and targeting are not a one time activity for the firm. This is because of the constantly shifting nature of market segments. Customers keep changing their buying and consuming habits and therefore keep migrating to different segments. So it is imperative for firms to continuously keep a watch on their consumers and customers to discern any shifts in market segments. Firms also need to relentlessly look out for new demographic, psychographic and other relevant variables to better explain, new trends or shifts in consumer choices or demands, and predict them ahead of time. Segmentation of customers and targeting profitable ones has also been shown to be helpful in determining the market structure i.e. whether the market is monopolistic, duopolistic, oligopolistic, or near to perfect competition.

Selling Process: Individual to Collective

Sales people meet various types of customers in the course of their work. Through several interactions with customers, sales people build an accumulated stock of knowledge, which is also known as their experience. This experience helps them categorize customers, as well as selling situations. The classification helps sales people sell more effectively to new customers, using the a priori mental schema for classification. This knowledge is often called declarative knowledge. However, it has been shown that sales people use yet another type of knowledge called procedural knowledge when they exhibit an effective set of behaviors with their customers, as an outcome of their past learning. Simultaneous use of declarative and procedural knowledge by sales people is popularly called adaptive selling strategy.

Besides the functions mentioned above, knowledge about the firm's relationships with its customers is a highly valuable asset (also known as relational asset) which often resides with frontline employees.

ISSUES, CONTROVERSIES, AND PROBLEMS IN MANAGING S&M KNOWLEDGE

In this section, we discuss the key issues, controversies, and problems in knowledge management in S&M function of organizations.

To Create and Deliver Value to Customers

Creating and delivering value to customers requires the seller organization to continuously and successfully address the latent needs of the customer. Customer value is a function of customer benefits net of their costs, and a perceived measure of their utility. Besides the price paid, costs incurred by customers would include information search costs and transaction costs. Benefits may be either functional or experiential. While functional benefits can be explicated more clearly by providing information to customers, experience is something that a customer perceives as a gestalt. In delivering value, the organization faces a challenge in the form of reaching out to the customer at an appropriate location and time. The value that customers may perceive comes not only from possessing and consuming a product, but also from the service provided by the firm. This is especially true in the case of industrial and technology intensive products. On the other hand, the notion of value in services is highly contextual and more subjective. Value creation and delivery in the services context happens at the same time while the service is consumed. However, the holistic experience – perceived by customers as a gestalt - determines their perceived value. Moreover, customers evaluate services in the form of service quality which impacts their immediate and long term satisfaction with the service experience. Therefore, product selling is becoming more a game about management of customer expectations related to their service experience. There is also a buzz about co-creating value together with customers, where organizations prove an enabling environment to help customers create their own experiences with products and services that they buy.

The role of KM in creating customer value requires dual focus on time and delivery dimensions of information exchange with customers. The quality of information is as important as the magnitude of information collected. Information that is sub-par in either quality or quantity, or both, can lead to loss of credibility and trust, or to information overload for consumers, and can have detrimental consequences.

New Product Development (NPD)

The primary problem in NPD is that of generating and managing new ideas from customers, employees and channel partners. Most often the best ideas for developing new products come from customers and channel partners. The new idea generation process often becomes ritualistic or rhetorical, a baggage carried by the NPD department. It is difficult to find instances of organizations that have established a formal structured mechanism that really encourages, motivates and promotes their employees and other stakeholders to contribute 'really new' ideas. Within organizations practicing kaizen, new ideas that are contributed by their employees are either not really new, or not feasible to implement. At best they can be termed incremental in innovativeness. Very often, NPD is inspired by what the competition is doing in the market, which is another form of imitation. Such imitation has resulted more often in "me too" new products and services, contributing further to the increased clutter and reduced brand differentiation in the marketplace. Another source of irritation for the organizations is after the incubation of new ideas, in developing these products with customers and channel partners. However, since both these stakeholders are external to the firm, it often results in information asymmetry that reduces timely "buy in" by these stakeholders, thus creating an obstacle. This often adversely impacts the success of new products in the market. Some of the organizational concerns in sharing information with external stakeholders are genuine, since most new products fail anyway which adversely impacts the reputation of the firm. Even the remaining ones may get imitated by the competitors, thus reducing the relative competitive advantage for the innovator firm. Very often firms try to mitigate this problem by contractually binding their employees and business partners with non-competitive clauses, to restrict the outflow of proprietary information.

Targeting Customer Segments

Targeting customers poses several challenges for firms, affecting their marketing mix decisions. It is often said that half of advertising goes waste, as it is impossible to reach all the targeted customers. Therefore, knowledge management for targeting customers needs timely and customized information delivered to the right customer, using a right choice of media for delivery. Often the same information needs to be provided to customers using several media to reinforce their latent needs and to stimulate their purchase intention and reduce the purchase cycle. Most firms fail to provide timely and useful information to customers either because of poor choice of media or sub-optimal media planning. The constant dilemma for media planners and brand managers is optimal allocation of resources to distribute information to customers. Very often, product sales determine the advertising spent of the brand, which is treated as a function of the number of advertising exposures, with little attention paid to the quality of information in each ad exposure. Marketing and advertising scholars are yet to be fully convinced of the nature of the relationship between the number of ad exposures and product sales, purchase intentions, or brand attitudes. Therefore, the quality, quantity, and timeliness of information to customers need to

be more precisely understood before increasing marketing expenditures for any given media. Another source of irritation for firms is the mismatch between the product and the targeted customer, or market matching. At times, a wrong product may be targeted at customers because of lack of understanding of their latent needs (or improper segmentation), or an inability to transform their needs to desired product attributes.

Customers are often targeted by firms with promotions to increase short term sales, or to even engender and reward their loyalty. Problems similar to those related to targeting customers may occur here too, since the success of consumer promotions often depends on successful targeting. Therefore, firms need to collect information even at the micro-level, e.g. to look for price elasticity of demand for individual customer micro-segments. If this is known, the next objective can be to design a program to target the customers based on their specific price elasticities. Another parallel objective could be to target segments that want less price discounts, but more quantity discounts, and then the secondary objective is to design a consumer promotion program for this segment. Meeting such objectives requires collection and investigation of the micro-level data, which also needs to be studied at various levels of aggregation to decipher the meso and macro level trends. Merely collecting and analyzing this data is not often sufficient, but the data need to be continuously upgraded too.

Motivating and Sharing Knowledge with the Sales Force

The organization's sales force is often considered the "eyes and ears" in the market. This analogy arises because of collection of both verbal and non-verbal information by the sales force. This information includes data, cues, and tacit understanding of salespersons about customers, channel partners, and competitors. Once collected, this information is shared within and across the organization. In order to increase the efficacy of their "eyes and ears", organizations are increasingly resorting to sales contests to motivate their sales force to sell more to earn more, or even offering higher variable pay components, incentives, and trips abroad. However, the limitations of external motivators like monetary incentives to encourage sales force to sell more are rarely considered. Providing non-monetary incentives have much higher latitude, and probably more effective not only in driving results but also in effectuating long term organizational loyalty and commitment of the sales people. Very few organizations may have formal mechanisms for sharing information across the departments and sub-units other than emails, and some primitive forms of a web portal.

One common problem is with respect to managing tacit knowledge, specially that residing in knowledge workers. When knowledge workers leave the organization, they take away with them lot of tacit knowledge about the customers, markets, and the firms' environment itself. In the eventuality of their joining a competitor, such knowledge changes hands and could be easily replicated. The risk, however arises when customer relationship managers leave the organization, which may lead to customer migrating to other organizations. Very often firms do not calculate the cost of tacit knowledge. We call it as the *latent cost of owing the intellectual capital* of the firm.

RECOMMENDATIONS FOR MANAGING S&M KNOWLEDGE

We develop a list of corresponding solutions that we derive from instances of knowledge management in specific situations.

Managing Knowledge to Create and Deliver Value to Customers

Firms can increase customer value by providing relevant information to targeted customers using effective means. Correct, relevant, and timely information would not only reduce their search costs, but also expedite their decision making and perceived value from the exchange transaction. Firms are not always sure which information is most important for given customers. This mismatch in expectations often results in resource wastages and inefficiencies. Similarly, it is equally important for a reverse channel of information flow from customers to firms, which is often the source of complaints, or service guarantee failures. This can be a valuable feedback loop for firms to design their service recovery programs and redressal mechanisms to bring back the customers to their fold before it is too late. The most potent tool for companies is to increase the perceived customer value. Perceived customer value comes from building strong relationships with customers, which requires being close to them and meeting them quite often. Providing frequent information to customers is one way of doing it. However often direct mailers, e-mailers, and cold calls from call centers do more to irritate customers than build relationships with them. In such situations, the two-way flow of information between firms and customers gets stalled.

In Box 1, we present two examples. In the first example, the firm utilized its expert base to create a value proposition for its smaller customers. In the second example, the firm implemented a system to make use of the tacit knowledge of its employees to deliver value to the customers.

Managing Knowledge for New Product Development

In order to manage knowledge for new product development, firms have integrated themselves with their suppliers and customers. The sharing

Box 1. Managing knowledge to create and deliver customer value

X & Y – a consulting firm spread across several countries and domains – used an innovative service to deliver customer value. The product is in the form of online consulting service called 'Zee'. Through this service, the firm engaged with small customers that subscribe to 'Zee' for a period of one year, giving unlimited ability to post questions to the firm's experts. Within two days, the experts then responded to questions posed by the customers. Apart from this, the answers were also appended on a database of frequently asked questions which the customers could access. In addition, Zee started a custom-designed news clipping service, a business research service and proprietary content that added value to the customer as and when the customer required (adapted from a case by Chard and Sarvary, 1997).
Syscon Technologies – a software service provider from India – uses a practice to manage its knowledge that in turn is used to create value to its customers. Syscon introduced a system wherein the employees could log on to the system and provide their expertise in exchange for knowledge currency units. These currency units could be in the form of gift vouchers or coupons that they could use to buy music and books. By incentivizing the employees, Syscon was able to codify the tacit knowledge of its employees into expertise that managers of other similar projects could use it to deliver better services to their clients. The KM system was gradually institutionalized and imbibed into the company's culture, thus enabling it to not only deliver value to customers on an ongoing basis, but also reduce the lead time to deliver, thus increasing its productivity (adapted from a case by Verma, 2002).

of knowledge across the value chain is of key importance. Information about the application of products at the consumer end is a type of information that the new product development team expects to get from the sales and marketing team. The sales team however has the market information, but not in a form that is easy to share with others in an explicit manner. Secondly, since there is a time-lag between designing a new product and rolling it out in the market, it will help firms get a fast-mover advantage if the KM system acts as its eyes and ears, embodied within the sales and marketing team, to provide feedback in the form of relevant information to the new product development team. In order to do this, there needs to be a system that not only maintains a database of customer preferences and but also tracks the preferences over time. Automation of such an activity will help a lot in reducing the lead time, and reduce inefficiencies in the processes.

In Box 2, we present an example of a B2B food flavoring firm that was able to implement KM as a tool to bring its product development team closer to its customer's product development team in order to develop new flavors. This example gives insights into how organizational knowledge exists in a tacit form. The next example is of an online computer selling company that uses the direct selling approach to manage the customer knowledge and channelizes it in developing new products.

C. Managing Knowledge for Targeting Customer Segments

In order to target the right segment of customers, firms require knowledge about their preferences. Traditionally, companies produce different variants of products for different customer segments. However, customers are difficult to segment based on their service consumption. Some firms use BI to track the customer usage. Herschel and Jones (2005) point out that though KM and BI differ, they need to be considered together as necessarily integrated and mutually critical components in the management of intellectual capital. BI is increasingly being used to manage the overflow of information in the form of text and sound that is captured by various methods and stored within the organization. In order to scan through the data and provide information that can directly aid in decision-making, BI technologies help in identifying hidden patterns and unapparent trends within the data. With the help of BI programming, it is easier for firms to handle large amounts of data that otherwise would have been impossible to scan. It is not uncommon to find a separate department of BI in most banks and other organizations. BI has been often misconceived as a synonym of knowledge management. However, BI is more of a tool that helps in handling and making sense out of the knowledge existing in databases and data warehouses.

Box 2. Managing knowledge for new product development

Quality Foods – a firm that created food flavors and textures for food and beverages companies has implemented a novel way of developing new products. It relies on two methods of storing knowledge – in employees' minds, and through the process of codifying data. It sought feedback from the clients and employees on creative ideas about introducing new flavors for the market. The external arm of the KM system helped it to get sensitized to the local customers as well as country-specific tastes. The company implemented a system that was integrated with the customers' systems. It started with value-adding information to the clients and gradually planned to move towards an integrated supply chain management that will help it plan new flavors in accordance with the client requirements. This would not only enable it provide a cost-effective and efficient delivery to its clients, but also help it in responding fast to the market changes (adapted from a case by Everatt and Morrison, 2001).

Hitech Computers was founded with a simple philosophy of selling computer systems directly to customers, one who can understand their needs and efficiently providing them the most effective computing solutions. Innovation at Hitech is based on an unwavering commitment to delivering new and better solutions that directly address customer needs. In order to do this, it follows a three step "Listen, Solve, Impact" approach. It gathers requirements directly through tens of thousands of customer interactions daily, organized events, and customer panels. Partnerships with a wide variety of key industry software, hardware, and component suppliers give it a uniquely broad perspective on the computing landscape. Innovations begin in-house, led by a global team of top engineers, product designers, and technical experts. The mission is to deliver innovative and cost-effective solutions that meet today's real-life customer challenges and work seamlessly in existing environments and with other products. It partners, rather than compete, with top industry technology suppliers and original development manufacturers to develop new products (adapted from the company's website).

Another tool to manage this issue is CRM, which has been considered as the institutionalization of relationship marketing that adds to the existing knowledge store of the organization about its customers (Jayachandran, Kaufman, and Raman, 2005; Reinartz, Krafft, and Hoyer, 2004; Winer, 2001). It integrates an organization's marketing activities such as sales, service, and market research to increase customer acquisition, retention, and profitability. A CRM system captures information at various touch-points between the organization and its customers. It is stored in databases, and aggregated into data warehouses. This data is accessed using data mining techniques to fetch and transform it into information, which can be used. By making forecasts based on patterns and trends, knowledge is created by analytic tools in combination with data mining.

In Box 3, we present an example of a company that manages knowledge about customers using BI and CRM. The company was able to attract more profitable customers and was able to design the right kind of offers.

D. Managing Knowledge for Managing and Motivating Sales Force

Sales force constitutes the eyes and ears of the organization. However, merely collecting information from them is not sufficient. Salespersons want to leverage the information about external markets to suit their needs, and therefore unless suitable external and internal motivations are designed to capture and retain this information, it would remain largely untapped. Salespersons should be motivated to report relevant market information to all departments through an organization wide portal. It also gets motivated by rewards and recognitions such as publicly recognizing salespersons who share best quality information about customers and channel partners, or rewarding through cash incentives and 'salesperson of the month' awards. We recommend that salespersons' promotions and pay structure should also be linked to not only the quantity and quality of market information brought into the firm, but also the extent to which it is shared with other departments, and how it is successfully used for increasing value for the company, its customers and channel partners.

In order to address the employee turnover in the sales force, firms today practice relationship

Box 3. *Managing knowledge for targeting customer segments*

Gambler, Inc., a leading casino in Las Vegas, was able to implement Business Intelligence to track the customer purchasing patterns. Through a rewards program, customers earn credits each time they visit and play. Accumulated credits are traded for rewards, cash, coupons, or complimentary services, and tallied to determine customer loyalty levels of gold, platinum, or diamond. Associated services and privileges became increasingly valuable with each new level. Gambler's first established a segmented marketing approach in 1998. Using historical data which showed how often customers visited and how much they spent, these early modeling efforts provided basic segmentation based on various demographic trends. Historical data showed how often a customer visited Gambler's casinos but predictive models revealed which customer was likely visiting other casinos in the market as well. Once identified, Gambler targeted them for campaigns that will attempt to increase customer loyalty to their casinos (adapted from success stories available on http://www.sas.com).

Travelogue is an online travel portal that 'discovers' customer segment groups based entirely on the customers' purchasing behavior. Through this approach, it found a large number of travelers who turned out to be business travelers. This group's frequency of travel and the days and time they traveled better matched the established "business traveler group." Further analysis showed that this new customer segment was much more sensitive than leisure travelers in seeing a full range of options specific to their time needs, so Travelogue was able to create display by targeting specifically to appeal to its newly discovered customer profile (adapted from success stories available on http://www.sas.com).

marketing rather than transactional marketing. This creates life long relationships with customers, which helps firms to profitably monetize the relationship by fulfilling the customers' needs. Relationship marketing also increases the entry barriers for competitors, since building and sustaining long-term customer relationships can be costly in terms of executive man-hours spent by firm's employees with customers, and other forms of organizational resources. In addition to this, several CRM tools are also used that help them track the firm's relationship with clients on an ongoing basis, notwithstanding employee turnover. Although the basic idea of CRM is not new, it has evolved – with advancements in technology – to provide a highly personalized relationship with customers on a large scale. CRM automation system can be effectively used as a strategy to understand customers and to create and sustain long-term, profitable customer relationships.

In Box 4, we present an example of a company that successfully codified the knowledge embodied in its sales force, by offering adequate rewards and recognition.

KM STRATEGY FOR EFFECTIVE S&M

In order to tackle the issues and problems highlighted in the earlier section, we recommend a straightforward KM strategy that can help in increasing the effectiveness of the S&M function. Subsequently, we provide pointers towards the technology enablers that can act as effective KM tools.

The KM strategy for an effective S&M function should be clearly aligned with the vision and mission of the organization. For instance, the vision to become the most respected firm in the market would require the firm's KM strategy to be closely aligned with improvising its new product development competencies, honing its selling strategies, and increasing the service orientation among their salesforce. Depending on the product and market characteristics, the firm should place emphasis on one or more of these aspects of knowledge management:

1. Capturing Information: While the S&M team works relentlessly in the market with customers to sell the products by meeting the latter's needs successfully, information generated from the market must be captured and codified continuously. This information can include competitive intelligence, shifting

Box 4. Managing knowledge for managing and motivating the salesforce

ConsumerGood(CG), a direct selling company involved in selling consumer electronic equipment in India, manages the knowledge among its strong sales force using a very successful rewards and recognition scheme. CG has 5000 employees spread across 150 centers and building relationships with 90000 customers in 95 towns every day. In order to channelize the sales force knowledge, it has created a central and updated repository of best practices by codifying the tacit knowledge of sales force team. It encourages the sales force to share the best practices by offering them incentives and rewards to post their best practices. The incentives are provided in financial terms, whereas non-financial rewards come in form of a book compilation that contains the best practices from the sales champions of the organization. Apart from these, certificates and awards have also been introduced to recognize the initiatives of the knowledge sharing sales force (adapted from company material).

JobEx, an online career management portal, has categorized 1.4 million companies in a database and has ranked those not using the JobEx services. A group of sales representatives was hired and each of them was given the same mix of high, medium, and low probability clients to contact. After a fixed time, JobEx figured out which sales people were more successful and started to allocate important clients to these salespeople. This led to increase in sales productivity by 40 per cent (adapted from success stories available on http://www.sas.com).

Figure 1. KM Strategy for an Effective S&M Function

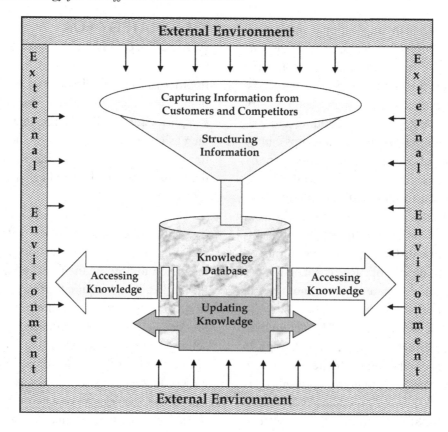

loyalties and trends in customers' buying behaviors, and customer satisfaction feedback on the firm's products and services that can accelerate managerial decision-making to get the much coveted market leadership.

2. Structuring Information: The captured information should then be converted into explicit knowledge such that it can discern various patterns in the movements of the firm's stakeholders, especially the customers and competitors. Observing timely and

relevant patterns such as future competitive moves or future consumer buying trends qualifies for good knowledge that can be utilized and developed by the firm to shape its subsequent strategies in the market.

3. Accessing knowledge: The knowledge created from arranging and logical structuring of the incoming information would then be made accessable to one and all on demand. Information asymmetry owing to any constraints in freely accessing relevant information in a timely fashion can not only mar the firm's performance in the market, but is also likely to fuel inter-departmental frictions. In particular, the sales team pitching to the prospects and customers needs real time information and knowledge on what is the best they can offer to the customer. This requires sophisticated sales force automation which is readily adopted and effectively leveraged by the salesforce, backed by managerial support, and their own autonomy and participation. The marketing team designing the communication programme for the target segment will also benefit from real-time access. It can keep itself updated with real-time salesforce and customer responses to the designed marketing mix elements, and use the knowledge available to customize these elements accordingly.

4. Updating knowledge database: Since the reach of the S&M team will be limited, the database of knowledge should have an inherent capability to continuously update itself through secondary sources within the environment, based on predefined internal actions. For instance, the customer purchase data and credit history can be directly fed into from the invoicing system, which gets updated on the next transaction of the customer with the firm. To facilitate such updation in an autonomous manner, firms must move beyond the mere implementation of ERP systems such as SAP, and make the

knowledge database sharing and updation a co-creating activity, to be performed with their supply chain partners.

FUTURE DIRECTIONS

Despite firms' continuous efforts in upgrading knowledge about their product markets, customers' changing preferences and demands have outpaced such efforts. With the changing profile of industrial and individual customers, firms are increasingly investing more on automation for KM. However, mere automation may not be enough as it creates entry and exit barriers that are not long lasting. In order to create a sustainable competitive advantage, firms need to make strategic investments in KM strategy implementation.

With the increasingly fragmented customer segments, there is a need for companies to move towards the paradigm N=1, R=G, i.e. one consumer experience at a time and resources from multiple vendors and often from around the globe (Prahalad and Krishnan, 2008). Under this paradigm, N=1 implies serving one customer at a time by segmenting the market to a level where it is possible to serve each and every individual as a separate segment. R=G implies resources to be global, and requires the seller organization to reach out globally to achieving very high scales. This makes it imperative for companies to move from customized CRM and KM solutions to specially designed ones. The financial meltdown of 2008 has compounded this problem by not only driving away customers, but also ensuring that customers are extremely choosy and highly experience-centric. This has brought capturing, measuring, and enhancing the customer experience to the center stage of S&M objectives. The solutions also need to be adapted to the needs of tracking customer experience. Managing this knowledge about experiences is currently being done through online product reviews on e-commerce sites and discussion forums. Going forward, this is expected to become more and more integrated with the selling process as well. Today if a customer logs on to the internet to book a hotel room or a car rental online, one of the major factors while deciding on the product is the reviews from the past customers; some budgets hotels like hihostels. com and hostelworld.com carry out this practice successfully. A way forward would be to capture the review about the product and normalize it on a scale and at the same time profile the prospective customer based on earlier purchases and experiences, similar to what www.amazon.com does. The e-commerce site would then be required to match the experiences that the product can provide with those desired by prospective customers. Experience-matching can be tough, given the subjectivity involved, but that can provide customers an edge over others, especially in the cut-throat race for attracting and retaining customers who are increasingly showing split loyalties. C2C sites are helping customers-both happy and irate- share their experiences with firms, their employees and product or service brands.

With the increasing usage of mobile and internet applications, a trend that has been seen unfolding in the last decade or so is the movement of the business model from B2B to B2C. Future business models are moving a step forward towards S2C (supplier to customer). This requires management of knowledge not only within the organization, but also at the supplier level. Innovations in this field have already begun in the form of efforts towards integrated supply chain management and ideas about having a Chief Supply Chain Officer (CSCO) in the organization. One of the main tasks of CSCO would be to make sure the knowledge chain is operating in sync with the supply chain so that firms can effectively implement an S2C model. This means that organizational boundaries would become more blurred than ever before and even meaningless, since the center of the business shifts towards customers like never before.

CONCLUSION

In this chapter, we have looked at some of the issues in KM practices in the sales and marketing function, and their plausible solutions. The KM strategy that we recommend may be used not only as a KM tool within the S&M function, but also as a generic tool for managing knowledge in other situations. The challenge for KM in the S&M context is more because of large number of external stakeholders. While on one hand the sales team and marketing teams within the organization work towards the objective of maximizing the value for the organization, the channel partners and customers aim at maximizing their own value from the exchange with their supplier organization. The challenge for the organization is in funneling the information received from innumerable transactions with its different stakeholders, and then converting it into knowledge so as to design and market better products for its customers, more effectively. In order to make the most out of KM investments, firms must realize that the S&M function thrives on the information present outside the organization's boundaries, and utilizing this information by converting it into knowledge in an efficient and effective manner. This requires an organization-wide approach that facilitates integrating KM strategies in S&M as an integral constituent of the organizational culture.

REFERENCES

Baumard, P. (1999). *Tacit knowledge in organizations*. Sage: London.

Chard, A. M., & Sarvary, M. (1997). *Knowledge management at Ernst & Young, case study*. Graduate School of Business, Stanford University.

Everatt, D., & Morrison, A. (2001). Quest foods. Asia Pacific and the CRM initiative. *Ivey Business Journal, 66*(1), 37–46.

Herschel, R. T., & Jones, N. E. (2005). Knowledge management and business intelligence: The importance of integration. *Journal of Knowledge Management, 9*(4), 45–55. doi:10.1108/13673270510610323

Jayachandran, S., Sharma, S., Kaufman, P., & Raman, P. (2005). The role of relational information processes and technology use in customer relationship management. *Journal of Marketing, 69*(4), 77–192. doi:10.1509/jmkg.2005.69.4.177

Nonaka, I. (1994). A dynamic theory of organizational knowledge creation. *Organization Studies, 24*(6), 831–857.

Prahalad, C. K., & Krishnan, M. S. (2008). *The new age of innovation: Driving cocreated value through global networks*. Columbus: McGraw Hill.

Reinartz, W., Krafft, M., & Hoyer, W. D. (2004). The customer relationship management process: Its measurement and impact on performance. *JMR, Journal of Marketing Research, 41*(3), 293–305. doi:10.1509/jmkr.41.3.293.35991

Sheth, J. N. (1975). Buyer-seller interaction: A conceptual framework. *Advances in Consumer Research. Association for Consumer Research (U. S.), 3*, 382–386.

Simon, H. A. (1957). *Models of man*. New York: Wiley.

Slater, S. F., & Narver, J. C. (1995). Market orientation and the learning organization. *Journal of Marketing, 59*(3), 63–74. doi:10.2307/1252120

Verma, S. (2002). Knowledge management at Infosys Technologies Ltd. In D. Remneyi (Ed.), *Third European Conference on Knowledge Management*. London: Academic Conferences Ltd.

Winer, R. S. (2001). A framework for customer relationship management. *California Management Review, 43*(4), 89–105.

Chapter 16
The Implications of the Development and Implementation of CRM for Knowledge Management

Diana Luck
London Metropolitan Business School, UK

ABSTRACT

Throughout the past decade, CRM has become such a buzzword that in contemporary terms the concept is used to reflect a number of differing perspectives. In brief, CRM has been defined as essentially relating to sales, marketing, and even services automation. CRM has also been increasingly associated with cost savings and streamline processes. Accordingly, the topic has been widely covered in terms of its alignment with business strategy. However, there appears to be a paucity of coverage with regards to the concept's alignment with knowledge management. This chapter demonstrates how CRM in fact pivots upon the dynamics of knowledge management. Furthermore, this chapter emphasises how by lieu of its conceptual underpinnings and operational dimensions, CRM is aligned with business development in the context of knowledge management. References have been made to specific strategies and tactics within the hotel industry in order to illustrate the relevance of this contended association.

INTRODUCTION

The general consensus is that Traditional Marketing tends to be essentially associated with the development, sale and delivery of products and services by means of short-term transactions (Ballantyne, 1996; Healy et al., 2001). However, since the 1980s, academic research has increasingly advocated for longer term exchanges. Relationship Marketing has emerged as an alternative to Traditional Marketing (Berry, 1983).

The reasons given for this shift of marketing thought and business development from an emphasis on single transactions and customer acquisition to relationships and customer retention have been varied. While such academics as Brodie et al. (1997) argue that Relationship Marketing has emerged from six distinct streams of research within the theoretical domain, others such as Zineldin (2000a) attribute this shift to the intensification of compe-

DOI: 10.4018/978-1-60566-348-7.ch016

tition and uncertainty in the marketplace. Still others regard the transition as the forthright effect of the attempt of companies to achieve optimum growth by means of knowledge management. In fact, academics such as Berry (1983), Grönroos (1994a,b) and Gummesson (1997a,b) go as far as to argue that organizations should restructure their efforts in line with the new paradigm that Relationship Marketing represents if they are to be able to survive and even develop their businesses within the increasingly competitive market environment.

CRM, a specialized component of Relationship Marketing, has been widely covered in terms of its alignment with business strategy. However, there appears to be a paucity of coverage with regards to its connection with knowledge management. This chapter demonstrates how CRM in fact pivots upon the dynamics of knowledge management. Furthermore, this chapter emphasises how through its conceptual underpinnings and operational dimensions, CRM is closely related to business development in the context of knowledge management. The examples included throughout this chapter are intended to clearly illustrate this link.

THE BACKGROUND TO THE CONCEPTUAL DEVELOPMENT OF CRM

In spite of much interest and effort, Relationship Marketing persistently remains ambiguous as a concept. In varied attempts to unravel its conceptual and fundamental underpinnings, several academics have defined Relationship Marketing (Harker, 1999). However, rather than clarify what the concept truly encompasses in reality, many of these definitions have instead arguably limited the scope of the concept. Consequently, depending on which position is being favoured, Relationship Marketing has been described as a specific type of marketing, such as database marketing or

services marketing, or even as a series of actions. At other times, the concept has been described as a single entity, which embraces almost every other marketing discipline (Berry, 1983; Gummesson, 1997a,b; Morgan and Hunt, 1994). As such, the precise meaning of Relationship Marketing is not always clear in literature.

Considering the conflict, which appears to prevail with regards to the actual dimensions of Relationship Marketing, it is not surprising that the concept of CRM has attracted just as many varied comparisons. Throughout the past decade, CRM has become such a buzzword that in contemporary terms, the concept has been used to reflect a number of differing perspectives. While it has at times been referred to as being synonymous to a form of marketing such as database marketing (Khalil and Harcar, 1999), services marketing (Grönroos, 1994a,b) and customer partnering (Kandampully and Duddy, 1999b), at other times CRM is specified in terms of more specialised marketing objectives such as customer retention (Walters and Lancaster, 1999a), customer share (Rich, 2000) and customer loyalty (Reichheld and Schefter, 2000).

In addition to being defined as essentially relating to sales, marketing and services automation, CRM is increasingly being aligned to processes such as "enterprise-resource planning applications", which are intended to "deliver cost savings and more streamlined services within organisations" (Keynote, 2002a:1). The tracking of the relationships, which organisations have with their customers and their suppliers, has also been considered integral to CRM (Gummesson, 1999; Keynote, 2002a). Indeed, as Lindgreen and Crawford (1999:231) succinctly summarise, this area of Relationship Marketing seems often to be "described with respect to its purposes as opposed to its instruments or defining characteristics".

Notwithstanding, the wide scope of objectives associated with CRM, the implication of knowledge management is becoming increasingly prominent in the concept's associations with customer retention and refined processes. Indeed, the significance of CRM with regards to business development is poignantly emphasised by Joplin (2001:81) when he contends that:

far from being a fad, it can be argued that CRM is the most important strategy that any organisation intending to stay in business must develop.

In contemporary terms, the term CRM is used to refer to both Customer Relationship Marketing and to Customer Relationship Management. Although Customer Relationship Marketing and Customer Relationship Management may be regarded as specialised fields of study, it is argued that they are in fact inter-related. Subsequently, within the premise of this chapter, the scope of CRM spans from the development and marketing of relationships between organisations and their customers to the day-to-day management of these relationships. As a matter of fact, as is demonstrated by the examples included from the hotel industry, both the marketing and management of customer relationships are considered integral to knowledge management in the context of business strategy.

DATABASE MARKETING: A REFINED KNOWLEDGE MANAGEMENT PROCESS

The Pareto Principle states that 80% of a company's income comes from 20% of its customers. According to Bentley (2005), the ongoing challenge for companies is to determine which specific customers represent that 20%. In an attempt to identify their profitable customers, companies are increasingly investing in database infrastructure. This important trend, in evidence centres itself on database marketing and on knowledge management.

As a concept, database marketing revolves around organizations acquiring and maintaining extensive files of information on past and current customers as well as on prospects. Although the objective of databases is to enable a better portrait of customers and their buying habits, ultimately they are intended to not only enable companies to market their products, services and even special offers more effectively, but to also provide an improved personalised service to customers (Bentley, 2005).

Although database marketing is traditionally associated with the specialised field of direct marketing, numerous authors including Moncrief and Cravens (1999) and Long et al. (1999) have acknowledged how its functions are being increasingly applied to enhance and refine relationships with customers within other areas of businesses too.

Databases can help companies manage their knowledge about their existing customers. However, the database has become a pivotal instrument within the CRM arena not only as far as interaction and the exchange of information between an organisation and its customers are concerned, but also in the facilitation of processes such as the segmentation and targeting of customers. Indeed, it seems that database marketing is closely aligned to knowledge management and business strategy.

THE DATABASE: THE PIVOTAL TOOL FOR KNOWLEDGE MANAGEMENT WITHIN CRM

According to Bradbury (2005), a database is a structured collection of information, which is not only set as indexes but also searchable. In general, databases are used for business applications such as the storing of customers' data. Thus, previous transactions and even communication exchanged may be held in a company's database. In layman's terms, databases may be compared to an electronic library, which receives fresh data, stores information and make the latter accessible to an organisation; thereby helping maintain a continuous learning loop (McDonald, 1998). In more implicit marketing terms, databases can be extended to form an extensive and multi-levelled process (Tapp, 2001).

Within the CRM arena, it could be argued that databases are used not only to promote and facilitate interaction between an organisation and its customers from the time of an initial response, but also to help with the measurement and analysis of such interactions. Simply put, the ongoing relationship between an organisation and a customer can be systematically recorded in databases. In fact, a sophisticated database can not only store data on active, dormant or lapsed customers but it may even have the potential to identify prospects (McDonald, 1998; Tapp, 2001). Subsequently, the increasingly integral role, which databases have come to play in CRM campaigns and in knowledge management appears well founded.

THE LINK BETWEEN CRM AND DATA MANAGEMENT

Developments in information technology have dramatically enhanced the scope for the collection, analysis and exploitation of information on customers (Long et al., 1999; Luck, 2008). Accordingly, data warehouses have been increasingly created by businesses. A data warehouse is essentially a giant database, which takes the raw information from the various systems within a hotel for instance, such as central reservations and room service, and converts the data collated from all the sources into one easily accessible and ideally user-friendly set of data (Davies, 2000).

When used effectively, data warehouses can not only gather data on a continuous basis but they can also allow the precise segmentation of information about customers. Subsequently, profitable interaction with customers can be increased and operations such as targeting and even personalised customer service improved. These

processes can not only be intricately linked with knowledge management but also with business development.

The ultimate aim of data warehouses can by all means to help create customer retention (Davies, 2000). Accordingly, large hotel chains have in evidence been acquiring and storing customer data in a combined attempt to achieve competitive edge and improve the experience of customers.

CRM is arguably a progression from data warehousing. At present, one of the principle functions of CRM systems is indeed to collect as much data about each customer as is possible. This information is then stored to be used at a later stage to give guests as much of a personalised service as possible when they return (Davies, 2001a). According to Cindy Green, the senior vice-president of Pegasus Business Intelligence, this will not only lead to a change in the sales and marketing arena but even more importantly this will imply that companies will need to become as advanced in the management of their customer relationships as technology will enable them to be (Davies, 2001a). This change of perspective is arguably expected to engender a transition from the management of data about the customers to the management of interactive relationships.

Accordingly, data that companies have compiled over the years about their customers, would need to be used intelligently in order to be enable predictions about consumer behaviour as well as the anticipation of needs or even problems. Such data can indeed be used to precisely target marketing campaigns. As succinctly summarised by Green, CRM is in actual fact simply about a company being willing and flexible enough to change its behaviour in line with what it is finding out from its knowledge management systems. Indeed, these systems and processes can not only consolidate what customers are saying but the data collated about the customers can reveal much about them; their attitudes and their intentions. Consequently, these processes can be crucial to business development.

THE PRINCIPAL STAGES OF ACHIEVING KNOWLEDGE MANAGEMENT FROM DATA

According to Cindy Estis Green, from Driving Revenue, a consultancy that aims to help hotel companies add value to the data they collect from and about the customer, the management of a database involves three crucial stages (Goymour, 2001).

Firstly, when all the data collected about a guest is consolidated into a usable set of information, the automated cleaning of data must be conducted. The general consensus is that an integrated and centralised database will enable a complete view of the customers. In the context of a hotel chain for instance, such a database is expected to collect ongoing information from all relevant sources and outlets, such as reservations and other point of sale systems located within the various hotels. Information from customer satisfaction questionnaires, surveys or even emails can also be fed into the database. The data would ideally be compiled so as to produce an integrated set of information in order to produce a unified profile about each customer (Bentley, 2005).

According to Jane Waterworth, the marketing director at Shire Hotels, the standardising of data is a process, which hotel companies should take seriously, as it is vital to ascertain that they in fact are inputting the right data in their CRM system. According to Steve Clarke, the account director at marketing database company CDMS, companies which are serious about CRM must consolidate their data. Otherwise not only may customers end up receiving the same information from various sources, thereby diluting marketing initiatives, but more specifically for the company, no full view of a customer's behaviour would be achievable. Indeed, as emphasised by Bentley (2005), without all the relevant information about a customer, any attempt to use data in a meaningful and precise way to enhance loyalty schemes or even marketing campaigns will be essentially flawed. Thus,

in order for a database to be a reliable component of knowledge management systems, it need to be consistently updated and meticulously integrated with other sources of knowledge.

Secondly, the analysis of the information about the guests must be undergone in order for the company to be able to precisely target the most attractive prospects and discard those suspects who do not meet the profiling criteria.

Although a central data warehouse can by all means combine information from many sources and help consolidate a comprehensive and reliable a picture of a company's clients, Velibor Korolija, the operations director with software specialist the Bromley Group, argues that for business and marketing analysts, data warehouses are by no means enough. In fact, it is data mining, a process which involves the analysis of the data in an attempt to seek meaningful relationships not previously known, which Korolija advocates to be of utmost importance with regards to knowledge management and business development (Davies, 2000).

In layman terms, data mining refers to the process of retrieving data from a data warehouse for analysis purposes. Data mining tools and technologies have been accredited by such academics as Nemati and Barko (2003:282) with having the potential

to enhance the decision-making process by transforming data into valuable and actionable knowledge to gain a competitive advantage.

Thirdly, the results of the targeting of specific guests must be tracked in order to determine which guests responded to the campaigns. This step will not only identify the profitable customers, but it will ultimately also indicate which promotions are successful. Subsequently, the adequacy of campaigns can be evaluated.

As identified by Bradbury (2005), CRM is meant to not only help companies collect information about guests, but even more importantly it is meant to help companies use the information collected about its customers more effectively. One of the ultimate steps within the data mining process is undeniably to cluster customers into segments, which are not only meaningful but also reachable by CRM campaigns.

According to Korolija, it is by all means possible to cluster a hotel's guests into very specific demographic groups (Davies, 2000). In serving a number of closely-related purposes, customer segmentation has been portrayed as a means of predicting behaviour (Clemons and Row, 2000), a method of detecting, evaluating and selecting homogeneous groups (Reichheld and Schefter, 2000) and a way of identifying a target market for which a competitive strategy can be formulated (Gulati and Garino, 2000).

In more general terms, customer segmentation is accredited with enabling the identification of key consumer groups so that CRM programmes can be targeted effectively. Some hotel chains in evidence acknowledge that the opportunities afforded by customer segmentation. For instance, in an attempt to precisely and cost effectively target its guests, De Vere Group Plc restructured its customer database in 2003 into a range of customer categories such as debutantes and devoted stayers. This strategy was also intended to enhance cross-selling across the various brands to existing customers. In the same year, Corus & Regal Hotels Plc divided its database, which consisted of 68,000 profiles, into categories. These spanned from cold prospects to loyal customers (Key Note, 2003c).

The varied outcomes of customer segmentation have been well documented. Benefits such as added protection against substitution, differentiation and pricing stability have been quoted by several authors including Walters and Lancaster (1999b) and Sinha (2000). Moreover, Ivor Tyndall, the head of customer intelligence at Le Meridien advocates that as the company segments their consumer base, they can precisely target different sectors or segments with different offers (Bentley, 2005). Although Botschen et al. (1999) support the importance of segmenting customers on the benefit-level, Long and Schiffman (2000) offer evidence to suggest that different segments of consumers may perceive benefits differently and consequently have differing degrees of affinity and commitment to CRM programmes. Consequently, the tracking of customers will uncover the relevance and degree of appropriateness of specific campaigns as well as general offerings and processes (Luck, 2008).

CONCERNS, CONTROVERSIES AND RECOMMENDATIONS WITH REGARDS TO DATABASE PROCESSES

The capability of databases to help track actual purchases of customers and enable inferences to predict future behaviour patterns may undoubtedly encourage the assumption that database marketing is routine within the embracing of CRM. Moncrief and Cravens' (1999: 330) contention that "customer service levels increase when customer information becomes so easy to obtain and disperse", could also by all means imply that databases are being efficiently and effectively used to acquire and maintain information on existing and prospective customers. Indeed, Abbott (2001:182) even advocates that refinements in technology has provided companies with increasing opportunities and well-structured channels to not only collect abundant amount of data but also to manipulate this data in various different ways so as to unravel otherwise unforeseen areas of knowledge and business development. However, several academics and practitioners have contended that databases are not being so optimally used.

Although many databases may by all means be deemed to be appropriate data warehouses, it has been argued that the data mining process associated with many of these has been consistently flawed. In actual fact, in spite of several academics acknowledging the technological trend to rely on database marketing to acquire and maintain extensive information on existing and potential customers (Krol, 1999; Long et al., 1999; Moncrief and Cravens, 1999), such academics as Dyer (1998), Rich (2000), Joplin (2001) and Overell (2004) provide evidence to confirm that companies are not adequately using the information at their disposal to build and strengthen relationships with customers.

According to Dyer (1998), many practitioners are failing to make optimum use of their client databases because not only is their information not being updated, but the available data is not even being analysed adequately so as to produce pertinent qualitative and quantitative information, from which future strategies and tactics could be based. Yet, Murphy (2001) advocates that not only does personalized data have to exist and be correct, but this data should also be correctly updated and be made available to the rest of the organisation. Indeed, the general consensus is that this process should be rigidly adhered to whichever channel of communication the customer uses to interact with an organization (Keynote, 2002).

Although this step may not yet be routinely be adhered to within the hotel industry, there is an indication that some hotel chains have integrated this process in their systems. For instance, from 2003 all bookings made for any of the hotels within the Corus & Regal hotel chain have been redirected via the central reservations office or to their new marketing database so that the information on the database can be continuously updated. Accordingly, the records about existing customers are consistently updated while the profiles of new customers are automatically created (Key Note, 2003c).

Highlighting a different shortcoming, Rich (2000) argues that companies are failing to use the information stored in their databases to build relationships with their customers even though the latter could prove vital for marketers in their attempts to outperform their competitors in terms of providing a better service to customers. Accord-

ing to Overell (2004), marketers and companies are not even attempting to adequately analyse the data to an accepted level of depth. In spite of such contentions, Michael Gadbury, the vice-president of Aremissoft, a CRM software company, advocates that while two years ago, arguably only ten percent of hotel companies showed interest in making use of the data, which they had collected about their customers, this percentage has risen to almost ninety percent in contemporary terms (Davies, 2001a). It is anticipated that in recent years, even more companies have shown interest in adequately mining their customer database.

Although the integrated process of capturing, sifting and interrogating data about customers is flawed, companies have been so eager to capturing data about their customers that according to Overell (2004:1), "many organisations are sitting on mushrooming stockpiles of data". This over zealous attitude towards the collection of data seems to have gripped the hotel companies too. Indeed, as is advocated by Geoffrey Breeze, the vice-president of marketing and alliance development at Hilton International, "hotels have far more information about their guests than they can actually use" (Caterer and Hotelkeeper, 2000:14). Yet, Overell (2004) advocates that the general consensus among database experts is that companies do not have much more understanding of customers than they did prior to their embracing of CRM.

Nemati and Barko (2003:282) offer a plausible explanation for the limited benefits reaped from data mining when they explain that although "management factors affecting the implementation of IT projects have been widely studied", "there is little empirical research investigating the implementation of organizational data-mining projects". Furthermore, in pointing to a plausible differential level of expertise between the collection of data and the actual mining and usage of this data, they also shed light on the inadequacy of training for the people at the various stages of the data mining process.

It is notable that within the hotel industry, technical systems tend not to be developed in-house (Luck and Lancaster, 2003) but commissioned through expert agencies. While CRM systems are developed by experts in line with specifications requested by a hotel company, once unfolded within an organization, such systems tend to be monitored in-house. Luck and Lancaster suggest that internal employees may not have the adequate level of expertise that some of the filtering processes may call for. Furthermore, they also suggest that the high financial, human and technological resources needed to keep a data mining system up to date may also place too high demands on some companies.

Arguably in attempts to curtail limitations and perhaps to also enhance their CRM opportunities, hotel companies have increasingly entered in partnerships with specialist agencies. While De Vere Group Plc enlisted the GB group to help create more targeted and cost effective database campaign, Thistle Hotels Ltd worked closely with Arnold Interactive to design, develop and handle its online strategy to increase its database from 50,000 to 500,000 profiles by the end of 2003 and its series of e-marketing campaigns (Key Note, 2003c).

Although academics and practitioners tend to agree that technical innovation is essential to ensure the future growth and success of businesses with regards to knowledge management and CRM, the embracing of technologies within operations appears to have been slower. In a survey of the use of information technology in the independent sector of the hotel industry in South Wales, Main (1995) found out that 65% of her sample felt that they did not maximise the potential of their existing system. Rather that deploy the lack of expertise of the hoteliers, Main (1995) argue that it is the suppliers of IT who seem to be unable to target their market. A study conducted in 1995 may seem very dated in terms of technological advancements. However their conclusion is considered still relevant in contemporary terms.

In recent times, this issue surrounding the expertise in data analysis appears to have been curtailed through partnerships between hotel chains and specialised IT agencies. For instance, in 2003 when De Vere Group Plc sought to restore its customer database to create more targeted and cost effective marketing campaigns, the GB group was enlisted. Later in the same year when Thistle Hotels Ltd engaged in a focused online strategy to increase its database, Arnold Interactive was appointed to handle that project (Key Note, 2003c).

The popularity of databases is increasing and as is highlighted by Abbott (2001:182), "vast databases holding terabytes of data are becoming commonplace". However, if companies do not follow the correct processes to tap into this valuable data they have in their databases, new knowledge about customers will be largely uncovered (Rich, 2000). Indeed, it is likely that the assiduous collection of information about customers will be largely wasted. Consequently, although in theory borrowing from the arena of direct marketing seems pertinent to CRM strategy, transferring the theoretical advantages into practice is an altogether different scenario.

Meanwhile, according to Felix Laboy, the chief executive officer of E-Site Marketing, when hotels are able to access more information about a guest and then be able to offer the latter the individual service he or she needs and indeed the benefits that is sought and valued, loyalty will be encouraged (Edlington, 2003; Goymour, 2001). Moreover such authors as Davies (2001a) and Bentley (2005) advocate that when the data is correctly structured and companies can target their marketing more effectively, it is expected that CRM and knowledge management schemes will become more effective.

In contemporary terms, the impetus surrounding CRM and knowledge management undoubtedly centres on technology and its respective tools. Technology has been hailed as having the potential not only to revive but also enhance more personalised service with customers (Gilbert et al., 1999) as well as optimise knowledge management. Companies are being faced with a multitude of complex choices in their structuring of relationships while the pace at which technology is being developed is arguably creating the significant problem of expensive investments potentially becoming rapidly obsolete shortly after being deployed (Davies, 2001a). Several authors including Davies (2001b) and Cushing (2004) thus recommend that instead of embracing technologies merely based on their infrastructural merit, companies should evaluate technologies in line with their own specific needs and CRM and knowledge management objectives and strategies. Only then, would they be able to remain focused on their business strategies as opposed to being led by technology.

CONCLUSION

CRM concept has grown out of companies' attempts to develop their business propositions. The various processes, which the concept is associated with, imply that CRM must be refined in line with companies' attempts to refine their knowledge management systems. Consequently, through its facilitation of knowledge management, CRM can only help companies offer better products and services to their customers than their competitors, but just as importantly CRM can help companies with their own business development. Indeed, as discussed throughout the above sections and illustrated by the examples taken from the hotel industry, CRM can help companies understand their customers by means of consistent knowledge management.

Technology has revolutionised operations within companies. In order to enhance their engagement in CRM, many hotel chains have invested in customised systems. Some applications have in evidence already managed to smoothly link front-office processes such as check-in, with back-office functionality such as reservation details. Notwithstanding, as is succinctly reminded by Chen and Popovich (2003:682), despite the crucial role that technology and people play within the CRM arena, "the philosophical bases of CRM: relationship marketing, customer profitability, lifetime value, retention and satisfaction" are in fact created through business process management. As such, practitioners must constantly remind themselves that technology is not equivalent to CRM.

The right combination of technological tools and strategies can arguably enable companies to develop and sustain their operations, but also to reap the opportunities, which CRM can provide in terms of knowledge management. Indeed, CRM can be a powerful tool in the quest for strengthening relationships with customers as well as the facilitation of knowledge management. However, the use of technology should be dichotomous. While on one hand, technology should help facilitate the enhancement of CRM initiatives and knowledge management opportunities, on the other hand technology should enable companies engaged in CRM to keep their finger on the customers' pulse and respond to not only the customers' changing needs but also to general market trends. Only then will the true interaction afforded by technological tools with regard to CRM and knowledge management arguably be genuinely achieved and exploited. This undoubtedly emphasises that practitioners must closely monitor their technological tools as well as their processes and knowledge.

Database marketing and database management have by all means driven CRM into a new era not only in terms of providing information and making sales, but also to access customers, gather data and even target campaigns. Indeed, the processes associated with the implementation, evaluation and monitoring of CRM and with knowledge management have been greatly enhanced by means of databases.

The importance of the database within CRM and knowledge management is unquestionable. Databases in fact represent the central tool of

CRM within many companies such as hotel chains. Indeed, hotel companies of all sizes appear to increasingly be developing and implementing database technologies. However many data mining processes have been somehow flawed. Yet, the popularity of databases is persisting. In attempts to maximise the effectiveness of their CRM systems and knowledge management strategies, companies are increasingly working in partnership with specialist external agencies. Such partnerships are bound to enhance the inherent strengths of CRM as well as increase the success of internal and external knowledge management. However, companies must first be clear about their objectives for engaging in CRM.

In spite of the great influence that technology, systems and processes can add upon the dynamics of CRM and knowledge management, it should however be reminded that customer retention and business development, the ultimate objectives of CRM and most knowledge management strategies are not achieved with just these dimensions. Instead, while customer loyalty is usually achieved with the delivery of a consistently superior customer experience, business development can only ever be afforded if the current needs and wants of the primary customers are being met profitably. Undoubtedly, such a balance would indeed be impossible to achieve without the right people within the organisation. Consequently, it is argued that more than any technological tool, listening and responding to one's customers still remains the pinnacle of knowledge management and of business development. For practitioners, this highlights how the customer is still very much at the centre of all business processes.

FUTURE DIRECTIONS

As companies look to possible customer needs for business development, it has been suggested that it is technology and its tools that will enable the greatest opportunities for creating long-term

and close relationships. However technology in itself cannot create knowledge management. It is in fact the examination of data and information that can create this. However, selecting the right technological resources and capabilities to consistently and continuously create a competitive advantage is undoubtedly one of the key challenges facing companies in contemporary terms. Responding to such an ongoing challenge requires continuous fresh thinking and expertise. Furthermore as Zahra et al. (1999:197) argued although it creates opportunities for technical innovation, market dynamism also challenges companies "to protect, upgrade or even revise its technological capabilities".

Although technology has been crucial in the facilitation of CRM and has as such attracted much investment, the optimisation of CRM also requires the organisation of business processes as well as a thorough understanding of customers; the internal and external ones. Genuine adoption of CRM thus requires that companies address their own cultures and subcultures. In fact, companies are expected to not only continuously view their organisations from the customers' perspective but just as importantly, gear operations to actively involve customer feedback and changes.

As a concept, CRM appears to call for the consistent application of best practices in the business processes too. When these processes are consistently and continuously integrated, applied and monitored, it is expected that companies would be able to use their resources in terms of people, technology and processes to optimally achieve their CRM objectives. However this chapter shed light upon how in order to be an effective tool in terms of knowledge management, CRM processes must be systematically and consistently monitored. Consequently, it is suggested that companies examine the short-term as well as the long-term validity of their systems.

As far as CRM is concerned, it is suggested that all bonds, whether internal or external, which may have an effect on the stability of relationships with customers and on knowledge management, should be actively cultivated. Indeed, the nurturing of employees, the listening to one's customers and the crucial commitment of senior management are arguably not only integral to CRM in contemporary terms, but for any strategy to stick in the long-term, it should be embedded in the organisation and be supported by adequate policies and processes. Indeed, successful CRM does not just emerge or simply exist. As a matter of fact, it is suggested that the creation and establishing of successful customer relationships confront companies with a complex range of relationship and network management tasks above the ones, which is inherent to their traditional operations and structures. These must be evaluated then implemented and evaluated.

Prior to even engaging in CRM and in knowledge management systems, it is proposed that companies ensure that they understand what their target customers are looking for as far as CRM is concerned. It is also important for the companies to assess what their objectives are in terms of CRM and in knowledge management systems. Thereafter, companies should ensure that the elements, which are genuinely deemed important by their core customers, remain the focus of their CRM endeavours. In fact, it is contended that the optimisation of CRM requires not only the understanding of customers and the prescribed organisation of business processes but also an understanding of the employees. Indeed, it is argued that employees, guests as well as the entire organisation are the building blocks of CRM. Technology and the database are simply but merely what bind all these entities, strategies and tactics.

REFERENCES

Abbott, J. (2001). Data data everywhere–and not a byte of use? *Qualitative Market Research: An International Journal, 4*(3), 182–192. doi:10.1108/13522750110393080

Ballantyne, D. (1996). Getting your way in business. *Asia-Australia Marketing Journal, 4*(1), 3–6.

Barnett, A. (2000, July 19). The customer wants to be anonymous. *Revolution (Staten Island, N.Y.)*, 25.

Bentley, R. (2005, August 25). Data with destiny. *Caterer & Hotelkeeper, 38.*

Berry, L. L. (1983). Relationship marketing. In L. L. Berry, G. L. Shostack, & G. D. Upah (Eds), *Emerging perspectives on services marketing* (pp. 25-28). Chicago, IL: American Marketing Association.

Birch, A., Gerbert, P., & Schneider, D. OC&C, & The McKenna Group. (2000). *The age of e-tail.* Capstone Publishing Limited.

Botschen, G., Thelen, E. M., & Pieters, R. (1999). Using means-end structures for benefit segmentation: An application to services. *European Journal of Marketing, 33*(1/2). doi:10.1108/EUM0000000004491

Bradbury, D. (2005, August 31). Technology jargon buster. *Caterer & Hotelkeeper*, Glossary.

Brodie, R. J., Corviello, N. E., Brookes, R. W., & Little, V. (1997). Towards a paradigm shift in marketing? An examination of current marketing practices. *Journal of Marketing Management, 13*, 383–406.

Buhalis, D., & Main, H. (1998). Information technology in peripheral small and medium hospitality enterprises: Strategic analysis and critical factors. *International Journal of Contemporary Hospitality Management, 10*(5), 198–202. doi:10.1108/09596119810227811

Buick, I. (2003). Information technology in small Scottish hotels: Is it working? *International Journal of Contemporary Hospitality Management, 15*(4), 243–247. doi:10.1108/09596110310475711

Cannon, J. (2000). *Make your Web site work for you.* McGraw-Hill.

Caterer & Hotelkeeper. (2000, September 7). *Hotel groups deny they're missing Web opportunities* (p. 14).

Caterer & Hotelkeeper. (2004, June 24). *Do the knowledge* (p. 34).

Chaffey, D., Mayer, R., Johnston, K., & Ellis-Chadwick, F. (2000). *Internet marketing.* Pearson Education Limited

Chen, I. J., & Popovich, K. (2003). Understanding customer relationship management (CRM), people, process, and technology. *Business Process Management Journal, 9*(5), 672–688. doi:10.1108/14637150310496758

Clemons, E., & Row, M. (2000, November 13). (in press). Behaviour is key to Web retailing strategy. *Financial Times (North American Edition).*

Collin, S. (2000). *E-marketing.* John Wiley & Sons Limited.

Curtis, J. (2000, July 12). Get some decent exposure. *Revolution (Staten Island, N.Y.),* 32–36.

Cushing, K. (2004, March 18). Time to get technical. *Caterer & Hotelkeeper,* 76.

Davies, A. (2000, June 29). Data's the way to do it. *Caterer & Hotelkeeper,* 31-32.

Davies, A. (2001a, July 26). Online, on course. *Caterer & Hotelkeeper,* 37–39.

Davies A. (2001b, July 26). Web's wonder. *Caterer & Hotelkeeper,* 37-39.

De Pelsmacker, P., Geuens, M., & Van den Bergh, J. (2007). *Marketing communications: A European perspective.* Harlow: FT Prentice Hall, 3rd ed.

Dyer, N. A. (1998). What's in a relationship (other than relations)? *Insurance Brokers Monthly & Insurance Adviser, 48*(7), 16–17.

Edlington, S. (2003, January 20). Future perfect? *Caterer & Hotelkeeper,* 26.

Fraser, J., Fraser, N., & McDonald, F. (2000). The strategic challenge of electronic commerce. *Supply Chain Management: An International Journal, 5*(1), 7–14. doi:10.1108/13598540010312936

Gabay, J. J. (2000). *Successful cybermarketing in a week.* Institute of Management, Hodder & Stoughton

Galbreath, J., & Rogers, T. (1999). Customer relationship leadership: A leadership and motivation model for the twenty-first century business. *The TQM Magazine, 11*(3), 161–171. doi:10.1108/09544789910262734

Gattiker, U. E., Perlusz, S., & Bohmann, K. (2000). Using the Internet for B2B activities: A review and future directions for research. *Internet Research: Electronic Networking Applications and Policy, 10*(2), 126–140. doi:10.1108/10662240010322911

Gilbert, D. C., Powell-Perry, J., & Widijoso, S. (1999). Approaches by hotel to the use of the Internet as a relationship marketing tool. *Journal of Marketing Practice: Applied Marketing Science, 5*(1), 21–38. doi:10.1108/EUM0000000004549

Gledhill, B. (2002, February 28). Learning from history. *Caterer & Hotelkeeper,* 33.

Goymour, A. (2001, July 26). Host in the machine. *Caterer & Hotelkeeper,* 43-45.

Grönroos, C. (1994a). From marketing mix to relationship marketing: Towards a paradigm shift in marketing. *Management Decision, 32*(2), 4–20. doi:10.1108/00251749410054774

Grönroos, C. (1994b). From scientific management to service management: A management perspective for the age of service competition. *International Journal of Service Management, 5*(1), 5–20. doi:10.1108/09564239410051885

Grönroos, C. (1994c). Quo vadis, marketing? Toward a relationship marketing paradigm. *Journal of Marketing Management, 10*, 347–360.

Gulati, R., & Garino, J. (2000, May-June). Get the right mix of bricks and mortar. *Harvard Business Review*, 107–114.

Gummesson, E. (1997a). Relationship marketing as a paradigm shift: Some conclusions from the 30R approach. *Management Decision, 35*(4), 267–272. doi:10.1108/00251749710169648

Gummesson, E. (1997b). In search of marketing equilibrium: Relationship marketing vs. hyper-competition. *Journal of Marketing Management, 13*(13), 421–430.

Gummesson, E. (1999). *Total relationship marketing–rethinking management: From 4Ps to 30Rs*. Oxford: Butterworth Heinemann.

Harker, M. J. (1999). Relationship marketing defined? An examination of current relationship marketing definitions. *Marketing Intelligence & Planning, 17*(1), 13–20. doi:10.1108/02634509910253768

Healy, M., Hastings, K., Brown, L., & Gardiner, M. (2001). The old, the new, and the complicated–a trilogy of marketing relationships. *European Journal of Marketing, 35*(1/ 2), 182–194. doi:10.1108/03090560110363418

Hoffman, D. L., & Novak, T. P. (2000, May-June). How to acquire customers on the Web. *Harvard Business Review*, 179–188.

Hunt, J. (2000, July 26). The lights are on but no one's home. *Revolution (Staten Island, N.Y.)*, 30–32.

Janal, D. S. (2000). *Guide to marketing on the Internet*. John Wiley & Sons, Inc.

Joplin B. (2001, March-April). Are we in danger of becoming CRM lemmings? *Customer Management*, 81-85.

Kandampully, J., & Duddy, R. (1999a). Competitive advantage through anticipation, innovation, and relationships. *Management Decision, 37*(1), 51–56. doi:10.1108/00251749910252021

Kandampully, J., & Duddy, R. (1999b). Relationship marketing: A concept beyond primary relationship. *Marketing Intelligence & Planning, 17*(7), 315–323. doi:10.1108/02634509910301124

Key Note. (2001a). *Internet usage in business*.

Key Note. (2001b). *Hotels*.

Key Note. (2002a). *Customer relationship management*.

Key Note. (2002b). *Hotels*.

Key Note. (2003a). *Customer relationship management*.

Key Note. (2003b). *Internet usage in business*.

Key Note. (2003c). *Hotels*.

Key Note. (2005a). *Hotels*.

Key Note. (2005b). *Internet usage in business*.

Key Note. (2006). *Hotels*.

Khalil, O. E. M., & Harcar, T. D. (1999). Relationship marketing and data quality management. *SAM Advanced Management Journal, 64*(2).

Krol, C. (1999, May). A new age: It's all about relationships. *Advertising Age, 70*(21), S1–S4.

Lee-Kelley, L., Gilbert, D., & Mannicom, R. (2003). How e-CRM can enhance customer loyalty. *Marketing Intelligence & Planning, 21*(4), 239–248. doi:10.1108/02634500310480121

Li, T., Nicholls, J. A. F., & Roslow, S. (1999). The relationship between market-driven learning and new product success in export markets. *International Marketing Review, 16*(6). doi:10.1108/02651339910300459

Lindgreen, A., & Crawford, I. (1999). Implementing, monitoring, and measuring a programme of relationship marketing. *Marketing Intelligence & Planning, 17*(5), 231–239. doi:10.1108/02634509910285646

Long, G., Hogg, M. K., Hartley, M., & Angold, S. J. (1999). Relationship marketing and privacy: Exploring the thresholds. *Journal of Marketing Practice: Applied Marketing Science, 5*(1), 4–20. doi:10.1108/EUM0000000004548

Long, M. M., & Schiffman, L. G. (2000). Consumption values and relationships: Segmenting the market for frequency programs. *Journal of Consumer Marketing, 17*(3). doi:10.1108/07363760010329201

Luck, D. (2008). The importance of data within contemporary CRM. In H. Rahman (Ed.), *Data mining applications for empowering knowledge societies* (pp. 96-109). Hershey, PA: Information Science Reference.

Luck, D., & Lancaster, G. (2003). E-CRM: Customer relationship marketing in the hotel industry. *Managerial Auditing Journal–Accountability and the Internet, 18*(3), 213–232.

Main, H. (1995). Information technology and the independent hotel–failing to make the connection. *International Journal of Contemporary Hospitality Management, 7*(6), 30–32. doi:10.1108/09596119510095370

McDonald, W. J. (1998). *Direct marketing: An integrated approach*. McGraw-Hill International Editions.

Moncrief, W. C., & Cravens, D. (1999). Technology and the changing marketing world. *Marketing Intelligence & Planning, 17*(7), 329–332. doi:10.1108/02634509910301142

Morgan, R. M., & Hunt, S. D. (1994, July). The commitment-trust theory of relationship marketing. *Journal of Marketing, 58*, 20–38. doi:10.2307/1252308

Murphy, J. M. (2001, March-April). Customer excellence: From the top down. *Customer Management*, 36-41.

Nemati, H. R., & Barko, C. D. (2003). Key factors for achieving organizational data-mining success. *Industrial Management & Data Systems, 103*(4), 282–292. doi:10.1108/02635570310470692

Overell, S. (2004, March 31). (in press). Customers are not there to be hunted. *FT Management*, 2.

Peppers, D., & Rogers, M. (1999, January-February). Is your company ready for one-to-one marketing? *Harvard Business Review, 77*(1), 151–160.

Reichheld, F., & Schefter, P. (2000, July-August). E-loyalty. *Harvard Business Review*, 105-113.

Reyes Pacios Lozano, A. (2000). A customer orientation checklist: A model. *Library Review, 49*(4).

Rich, M. K. (2000). The direction of marketing relationships. *Journal of Business and Industrial Marketing, 15*(2/3), 170–179. doi:10.1108/08858620010316877

Simeon, R. (1999). Evaluating domestic and international Web strategies. *Internet Research: Electronic Networking Applications and Policy, 9*(4), 297–308. doi:10.1108/10662249910286842

Sinha, I. (2000, March-April). Cost transparency: The Net's real threat to prices and brands. *Harvard Business Review*, 43–55.

Tapp, A. (2001). *Principles of direct marketing*. Prentice Hall, 2nd ed.

Van Niekerk, D. N. R., Berthon, J. P., & Davies, T. (1999). Going with the flow. *Internet Research: Electronic Networking Applications and Policy, 9*(2), 109–116. doi:10.1108/10662249910264873

Walters, D., & Lancaster, G. (1999a). Value and information–concepts and issues for management. *Management Decision, 37*(8), 643–656. doi:10.1108/00251749910291613

Walters, D., & Lancaster, G. (1999b). Using the Internet as a channel for commerce. *Management Decision, 37*(10), 800–816. doi:10.1108/00251749910302908

Walters, D., & Lancaster, G. (1999c). Value-based marketing and its usefulness to customers. *Management Decision, 37*(9). doi:10.1108/00251749910299066

Wang, F., Head, M., & Archer, N. (2000). A relationship-building model for the Web retail marketplace. *Internet Research: Electronic Networking Applications and Policy, 10*(5).

Werbach, K. (2000, May-June). Syndication: The emerging model for business in the Internet era. *Harvard Business Review*, 85–93.

Yelkur, R., & Da Costa, M. M. N. (2001). Differential pricing and segmentation on the Internet: The case of hotels. *Management Decision, 39*(4), 252–262. doi:10.1108/00251740110391411

Zahra, S., Sisodia, R., & Matherne, B. (1999, April). Exploiting the dynamic links between competitive and technology strategies. *European Management Journal, 17*(2), 188–201. doi:10.1016/S0263-2373(98)00078-4

Zineldin, M. (2000a). Beyond relationship marketing: Technologicalship marketing. *Marketing Intelligence & Planning, 18*(1), 9–23. doi:10.1108/02634500010308549

Zineldin, M. (2000b). Total relationship management (TRM) and total quality management (TQM). [f]. *Managerial Auditing Journal, 15*(1/2), 20–28. doi:10.1108/02686900010304399

Chapter 17
Quality and Continuous Improvement in Knowledge Management

Nicole M. Radziwill
Espresso Labs, USA

Ronald F. DuPlain
Espresso Labs, USA

ABSTRACT

Knowledge management requires people to synthesize and interpret information, and technologies to organize, make sense of, and draw conclusions from the collection of knowledge. Together, these people and technologies shape part of a sociotechnical system. The relationships between them make the sociotechnical system behave as a network, where communication and knowledge transfer can occur, and the network becomes a community once elements of the system interact in meaningful ways. The quality of a knowledge management system depends on how well these meaningful exchanges are promoted and cultivated. This chapter examines how to construct a high-quality knowledge management system, taking into consideration the challenging sociotechnical nature of such an effort. By relating the four stages of a continuous improvement process, the five measures of quality within a knowledge management system, and EASE (Expectations, Actionability, Sustainability, and Evaluation), we present an approach to examine the business processes associated with knowledge management. Managers can use this framework to assess the quality of knowledge management systems and formulate strategies for continually improving them.

DOI: 10.4018/978-1-60566-348-7.ch017

SOCIO-TECHNICAL SYSTEMS, NETWORKS AND COMMUNITIES

What is a Socio-Technical System?

A socio-technical system is a collection of people, projects, processes and products that engage in an *exchange* relationship with one another:

- **People** translate, transform and communicate within the system, and between the system and its environment
- **Projects and Processes** discover, interpret, constrain or transform aspects of the system (e.g. software, physical surroundings, laws, regulations, standards, and quality management systems)
- **Products** result from projects and processes, and provide a snapshot of the state of understanding at a particular time (e.g. documents, artifacts, software, hardware, and data)

People clearly provide the "social" part of the socio-technical system. Projects, processes and products are the mechanisms that people use to construct material objects and promote progress in general. As a result, they form the "technical" part of the socio-technical system.

Networks and Communities

Social systems and technical systems can be represented graphically as networks, which are collections of objects (called *nodes*) linked to each other via relationships (called *edges*). When represented as a network, *at least some* of the nodes of a socio-technical system are people. Thus socio-technical networks can be contrasted with social networks, where *all* of the nodes are people, and other types of networks (e.g. PERT/CPM) where *none* of the nodes are people. In a socio-technical network, people connect to one another, people connect to technologies, and technologies connect to other technologies.

A socio-technical network is the collection of the system's people, its technologies, and the relationships that connect them all. By definition, a relationship within the network represent an exchange between nodes, and nothing more – this relationship could be an information exchange, a relationship of accountability, an indication of trust. The relationship does not always have to be positive. When people have a choice, they will tend to seek information from the people who inspire them or make them comfortable (the "energizers"). But there are also "de-energizers" who may be pessimistic, combative, arrogant, or otherwise unpleasant to be around. The relationships between people and those who "de-energize" them can also be represented in a network. (Cross & Parker, 2004)

A community can be considered a special type of socio-technical network. In a community, members will cluster based on shared interests, where they will tend to cooperate and seek to add value within the context of their interests. A community is thus a collection of nodes related via *meaningful and mutually constructive exchanges*, where exchanges derive meaning from the collective purpose or interest of the community. An important difference between a network that is a community and a network that is not a community are the underlying motivations of the members. Participation in a network occurs when a member or node finds value in exchanging with others in the network. In this case, people want to find out "what's in it for *me*?" Participation in a community occurs when a member or node adds value to the common goals of the community. In contrast with a network that does not behave as a community, people in a community will tend to ask "what's in it for *us*?" This shift in perspective influences the group's ability to generate, codify and share knowledge.

Software Considerations in Socio-Technical Networks

Software for a knowledge management system should reflect the values and cultures of its stakeholders. Often, the stakeholders of a knowledge management system come from different departments, business units, or organizations. Rosen (2007) describes how cultural barriers impact the exchange of information in social networks as he reflects on an experience he had aboard a company cruise through San Francisco Bay. The purpose of the cruise was to bring the sales and marketing departments together to interact and share competitive intelligence. The group fell short of its goal:

"The marketing people, seeming uncomfortable amid unstructured interaction, retreated to the corners of the floating room. Half an hour into the cruise, the marketing people interrupted the party – and many good conversations – and announced that participants should take their seats. Then, one-by-one, marketing people took the floor and delivered presentations. The salespeople began drifting to the edges of the room, and disappeared..."

This is a social example that can be extended to understand cultural barriers in a socio-technical system. Although the marketing people valued stand-up presentations to deliver information, the salespeople preferred individual interactions. The difference in preferred styles blocked the groups from forming a true community based on mutual interests and trust. Similarly, knowledge management technologies that require wide participation should be implemented within socio-technical *communities* to deliver optimal value.

Consider a knowledge management system in place of the marketing group on Rosen's boat. Is the system aligned with the values of its stakeholders (the sales group on the boat), or does it subtly discourage participation? In other words,

building a community first may be an important (or perhaps even essential) aspect of deployment. Members of the community are more likely to connect with each other, and with the information resources they need, if they perceive that meaningful exchanges will be likely.

WHAT IS QUALITY?

To understand how to assess the quality of a socio-technical system for knowledge management, which may be a network or a community (or both), it is first important to define quality. The "quality gurus" of the 20th century described quality in these terms:

- Fitness for use (Joseph M. Juran)
- Zero defects (Philip B. Crosby)
- Conformance to requirements (Philip B. Crosby)
- Best for customer conditions (A. V. Feigenbaum)

In *Quality in America*, Hunt (1992) provided a categorization of these definitions of quality. This considers the definitions above a little more thematically:

- Transcendent (you know quality when you see it)
- Product-based (product is defect-free, or has required/positive attributes)
- User-based (the customer defines his or her needs)
- Manufacturing-based (the product conforms to its technical specifications)
- Value-based (the product provides the "best for customer conditions")

Despite the range of definitions, the goals underlying the pursuit of quality and continuous improvement are always the same: achieving conformity, reducing variation, eliminating waste and rework, eliminating activity which does not add value, preventing human error, preventing defects, improving productivity, and increasing efficiency and effectiveness (Okes & Westcott, 2000).

The most comprehensive definition comes from ISO 8402, which defines quality as **"the totality of characteristics of an entity that bear on its ability to satisfy stated and implied needs."** (ISO, 1991) An entity can be any technology - a product, a process, or a system. "Characteristics" covers both the attributes of that technology and the processes that produced it. "Stated and implied" acknowledges that customers will have needs, but other stakeholders can have needs too (e.g. you, your boss, your shareholders, or your company). If "you know quality when you see it," that means that something is meeting your stated and implied needs - your spoken and unspoken specifications.

Achieving quality means adding value. Because the essence of a high quality knowledge management system lies in is its ability to promote and support meaningful exchanges between people and knowledge resources, the outcomes that add value in these ways also contribute to improving quality. When quality is achieved, the implied needs of the system's users will be met in addition to their explicit specifications as they realize value from the system, even if they cannot define what is meant by quality.

QUALITY IN KNOWLEDGE MANAGEMENT

Because quality is fundamentally concerned with adding value, the *virtues* of knowledge management illuminate the nature of quality in the practice of managing knowledge.

Virtues and Value

Virtue can be defined as a "particularly efficacious, good, or beneficial quality or advantage." The virtues of knowledge management, according to this

definition, are aspects of (or practices relating to) knowledge management that deliver remarkable value. This value adds to the individual's personal advancement or professional development, to the team's completion of a project on time and on schedule, to the business unit's achievement of sales or production targets, or the organization's satisfaction of financial or growth objectives.

The Character of Knowledge Management

Before the virtues can be understood and enumerated, the character of knowledge management must first be identified. Ford (2001), through an extensive survey of the knowledge management literature, identified that all knowledge management practices can be considered *generation, codification, transfer* or *application.* De Long et al. (1996) extended this categorization when they surveyed hundreds of initiatives at clients of Ernst & Young LLP, and found that current or recent knowledge management initiatives fell into one of eight categories:

- capturing and reusing knowledge
- sharing lessons learned
- documenting expertise
- structuring and mapping knowledge
- measuring and managing the economic value of knowledge
- synthesizing and distributing external knowledge
- using technical infrastructure for knowledge exchange
- embedding knowledge in products and services

Using this categorization, Ruggles & Little (1997) surveyed the participants in these initiatives to identify the practices that drove the most value for the companies implementing knowledge management projects. The survey assessed that measuring the economic value of knowledge, although performed, had little or no value within 15 out of 18 organizations. Many of those surveyed attributed high value to documenting expertise and structuring and mapping knowledge, but few of the organizations actually acted on this impression.

The collaborations that derived the greatest value were those that introduced people to new people and new ideas over time, through synthesizing and distributing knowledge and using technical infrastructure for knowledge exchange.

The Virtues of Knowledge Management

Considering the results of these investigators, who aimed to understand the character and context of knowledge management, the following virtues of knowledge management (which suggest attributes that define high quality) emerge.

Knowledge management enables innovation, the force that establishes and sustains competitive advantage, by helping to create new value for organizations through accelerated exposure to new ideas. According to the surveys performed by Ruggles & Little (1997), this conclusion holds for both new growth and cost cutting circumstances. Oinas-Kukkonen (2004), by studying models for the knowledge-to-innovation transition, discovered that effective knowledge management practices "enable the sources of innovation quickly to multiply as organizations are able to *establish procedures to communicate experience in the organization and its business network.*"

Knowledge management helps to increase motivation, a factor necessary for innovation. Clark & Estes (2002) note that increased motivation is not sustainable without skills development and knowledge management. If the information is not available or accessible for an individual to satisfy his or her job objectives, motivation will be absent, resulting in blocked innovation. Longenecker et al. (1998) suggest that employee problem-solving circles can drive substantial

value, presumably through the two-stage process proposed by Clark & Estes (2002), where incentives drive the motivation to apply skills and knowledge, which results in increased performance. In this example, the natural incentive of an employee problem-solving circle is that employees support solutions to issues of key concern to the employees. With this promise, they are motivated to apply their skills and knowledge as a team and increased performance can result at the individual, team, and process levels.

Knowledge management provides an audit trail for emerging problems and solutions. Ruggles & Little (1997) noted synthesizing, distributing, and exchanging knowledge as highly value-adding results of knowledge management initiatives. Knowledge management solutions often make use of technology applied to these functional areas. This combination traces the genesis of ideas, the conversion of ideas into knowledge and actionable plans, and the process of eliminating or replacing old or outdated ideas. The process of tracing the information flow helps individuals and organizations to better identify the most value-adding aspects of knowledge management solutions.

Most significantly, **knowledge management increases trust.** Ford (2001) performed an extensive review of the knowledge management literature, both academic- and practitioner-oriented, to determine what relationships exist between knowledge management practices and trust. The findings report that interpersonal trust increases the success of groups and teams in knowledge generation. Further, the findings report that trust in the knowledge management system and trust of the organization itself, together, are associated with more knowledge codification.

Trust is required for the success of knowledge management implementations. However, there is a symbiotic relationship according to Ford, since knowledge management systems have been shown to *create* more trust. The accuracy and relevance of the codified knowledge will impart trust in the organizational system. Tangible evidence of codified knowledge, particularly if it is extensive and reliable, will suggest to an individual that organizational trust exists, and encourage him or her to in turn rely more on the organization, and on coworkers within the organization. The use of knowledge repositories by one's peers will also increase trust, since this demonstrates willingness between coworkers to believe the content produced by one another. Ford concludes that "as knowledge transfer becomes more prevalent [within an organization], interpersonal trust will naturally develop in the organization." Because this study also mentions that trust is associated with employee motivation and job satisfaction, it is clear that the strongest virtue of knowledge management is indeed its innate promotion of trust as a personal and organizational value.

In summary, four value-adding virtues of knowledge management are as follows. A virtuous knowledge management system will:

- Enable innovation (on an individual as well as an organizational level)
- Increase motivation
- Provide an audit trail for problem-solving
- Increase trust between the members of a network or community

These points establish *what a knowledge management system should do*, in the context of networks and communities, in order to achieve a high level of quality.

CONTINUOUS IMPROVEMENT OF A KNOWLEDGE MANAGEMENT SYSTEM

Three elements influence how effective the continuous improvement of a network-based knowledge management system will be. These are 1) the process of continuous improvement itself, 2) the measures, or quality attributes, that are used

to assess the quality of a knowledge base, and 3) the business practices associated with knowledge management within an organization.

The Continuous Improvement Process

Continuous improvement is the "planned, organized and systematic process of ongoing, incremental, and company-wide change of existing work practices aimed at improving customer performance." (Boer et al., 2000) This definition is very similar to another presented by Jha et al. (1996), which describes continuous improvement as the "collection of activities that constitute a process intended to achieve improvement," such as simplifying processes, reducing waste, enhancing individual and team empowerment, and improving customer service. Lillrank et al. (2001) provides a view that is more transcendent, and calls continuous improvement "a purposeful and explicit set of

Table 1. Stages and activities in continuous improvement (from Jha et al. 1996)

Stage	Activity
Understand and document the process	Identify value-added versus non value-added activities
	Analyze cost, quality and other relevant measures for
	equipment, material and labor inputs
Simplify and improve	Reduce, combine or eliminate activities
	Improve the performance of equipment, labor and material
	inputs with respect to cost, quality, or other criteria
	Increment "low-grade" or incremental automation
	Revise business rules as needed
Standardize and integrate	Reintegrate remaining activities
	Stabilize the process at its new level
Monitor performance	Measure and monitor
	Set new targets; identify new measures to track if necessary

principles, mechanisms and activities within an organization adopted to generate ongoing, systematic and cumulative improvement in deliverables, operating procedures, and systems."

According to these definitions, continuous improvement is both a philosophy and a process. The philosophy calls for a defined purpose, broad involvement, and collective pursuit of goals. The process unifies the participants behind the defined purpose, and provides a basis for action. To continually improve a body of knowledge, the typical stages of a continuous improvement effort should be addressed. These elements, which have been drawn from Jha et al. (1996), are in Table 1.

Quality Attributes in Knowledge Management

Studies such as Pfeffer (2007) and Hagan (2000) address five general attributes of a knowledge management system to determine its quality and to uncover ways to continually improve a body of knowledge. These are:

- **Utility**, where results are widely applicable to researchers and/or practitioners,
- **Novelty**, where new ideas are forming and spreading through the community,
- **Accessibility**, where the "barrier to entry" problem is addressed so that useful information is not blocked from being shared,
- **Permeability**, where there exists a resistance to biases that might prevent knowledge from being codified, and
- **Visibility**, where members of the community are able to view, browse, and explore the body of knowledge.

Using all of the information covered so far, continually improving a knowledge management system is *the planned, organized and systematic process of generating, codifying, transferring and applying knowledge, in an ongoing, incremental and cross-disciplinary manner.* This would

Figure 1. Quality attributes of information in a knowledge management system

include simplifying the processes required to make knowledge available, limiting the cost of production of useful information, promoting and catalyzing innovative ideas to expand the utility of the knowledge base, and enhancing accessibility to engender empowerment.

These actions realize the quality attributes of *utility, novelty, accessibility, permeability* and *visibility* listed in Figure 1.

Business Practices Common to Knowledge Management Systems

The business practices that are common to knowledge management systems also provide insights into how to promote continuous improvement. Recall that Ford (2001) identified four aspects of all knowledge management practices: generation, codification, transfer, and application. These correspond roughly to the business practices of information processing, business intelligence, organizational learning, and organizational development. Each of these areas in business engages in continuous improvement.

Continuous improvement in knowledge management focuses on the data warehouse, which may or may not include a knowledge base. Each of four areas relies on the data warehouse or knowledge base to store and index the information that represents the managed knowledge. In information processing, the quality of the data warehouse improves either by addressing data integrity issues or by improving the software or systems that access that data. (Loshin, 2005) With respect to business intelligence, quality enhances with more effective or more reliable reports, or with better ways to make decisions based on those reports. Quality improvement in organizational learning occurs when people can more readily internalize and act on new knowledge, gradually developing new capabilities that benefit themselves and their organizations. In organizational development, quality improvement refers to the collective development of new capabilities, enabled by organizational learning. (Christensen, 1997)

This information provides direction regarding what activities should occur to continually improve a collection of knowledge in an automated fashion. First, the **data integrity** within the knowledge base should be continually improved. **Search and reporting** functionality should also be continually improved. **Individual interactions** with the system, and feedback from the system, should also be continually improved so that people can more readily develop new capabilities within the system. Finally, a **monitoring** system should be in place to track growth and changes within the system, while detecting the emergence of new areas of interest.

EASE: A FOUR-POINT HEURISTIC

Quality and continuous improvement in knowledge management are complex subjects that are under active exploration by researchers. There are several facets to the problem, and many have been covered in previous sections. How can a manager address these problems? How can a manager make sense of this background information, and use it to continually improve a knowledge management system in his or her organization?

Our recommendation is to examine your specific situation in terms of EASE: Expectations, Actionability, Sustainability, and Evaluation. We developed the EASE heuristic to help us address each of the components of a socio-technical system - people, projects, processes, and products – in any problem-solving context. EASE also promotes a reflective cycle, prompting you to regularly reconsider the expectations and assumptions underlying your solution. This approach can assist in building a more complete view of a socio-technical system at any scale, and it can be used at any time in its life cycle. Similarly, EASE can be applied to a task as small as sending an email, as well as to evaluate more complex projects. Consider each of the four points of EASE:

- **Expectations:** What functions do you expect a complete system to have? What do other stakeholders expect from a complete system, and from the process of building or improving the system? What are your expectations for how the members of the network at large will interact with the system? How can you express these expectations in a simple and clear way?

- **Actionability:** Do you have tasks defined? Are those tasks well-defined and unambiguous? Are the roles associated with those tasks well-defined and unambiguous? Do you have enough information to actually complete those tasks? Do you have the expertise and the ability to follow through at the right time?

- **Sustainability:** Do you expect that you will have sufficient resources, expertise, and interest to prevent breakdown of all aspects of the system? In the future, will you be able to effectively support the processes and infrastructure? Will your stakeholders still be around, and will they still have similar needs and desires? Alternatively, do you need to plan for enhancing your system or phasing it out?

- **Evaluation:** How will you know you're making progress towards satisfying expectations? Have you selected appropriate metrics to gauge progress for each of the stakeholder groups that have expectations? How frequently must you observe your metrics, and what are your expectations for how they should evolve? How do you know that you've added value for each stakeholder group?

Table 2 integrates these four crucial points and relates them to the theoretical background provided throughout the chapter.

CONCLUSION

A socio-technical system is a collection of people, projects, processes and products that engage in an *exchange* relationship with one another. Socio-technical systems can be networks, communities, or both. A community is a special kind of network where members self-organize into smaller clusters based on shared interests, and engage in meaningful and mutually constructive exchanges. In this chapter we demonstrated that a community-driven knowledge management system will enable innovation, increase motivation, aid in problem solving, and increase trust (in both people and knowledge).

The four stages of continuous improvement are: 1) understanding and documenting the methods for generating, codifying, transferring and applying knowledge, 2) simplifying and improving this

Table 2. An integrated framework for applying EASE to assess quality and promote continuous improvement in the knowledge management domain

	Stage of Continuous Improvement	Measures	Business Practices
Expectations	Understand and document the process	What are my stakeholders' *expectations* for utility, novelty, accessibility, permeability, and visibility?	What are my stakeholders' *expectations* for continually improving the data integrity, search and reporting, individual interactions, and monitoring of the system?
Actionability	Simplify and improve the process	What specific actions can I take to move the system towards those expectations for utility, novelty, accessibility, permeability, and visibility?	Given those expectations, what specific actions can I *do* to continually improving the data integrity, search and reporting, individual interactions, and monitoring of the system?
Sustainability	Standardize the process and integrate it into regular operations	How can I ensure that the new standards for utility, novelty, accessibility, permeability, and visibility are supported? Will I have sufficient resources in the future to sustain these new needs?	How can I ensure that the continuous improvement aspects are adopted? Will I have sufficient resources to support the changes in the future, from the perspective of data integrity, search and reporting, individual interactions and monitoring of the system?
Evaluation	Monitor performance of the process	How can I measure utility, novelty, accessibility, permeability, and visibility? How are we enabling innovation, increasing motivation, aiding problem solving, and increasing trust?	What measures must be tracked to evaluate the accuracy of my expectations, the outcomes of my actions, and the success of my sustainability strategy?

process, 3) standardizing the process and integrating it into regular operations, and 4) evaluating progress and applying the feedback. Continuous improvement should address the key quality attributes for a knowledge management system: utility, novelty, accessibility, permeability, and visibility. Common business practices of improving data integrity, improving search capabilities and reporting, and improving individual interactions and monitoring practices provide direction for a continuous improvement process.

When these elements are combined with the EASE heuristic (Expectations, Actionability, Sustainability, and Evaluation), it provides a framework for putting the concepts in this chapter to practical use. The approach can help managers methodically start and sustain continuous improvement of a knowledge management system.

REFERENCES

Boer, H., Berger, A., Chapman, R., & Gertsen, F. (2000). *CI changes from suggestion box to organisational learning: Continuous improvement in Europe and Australia*. Ashgate, Aldershot.

Christensen, C. (1997). *The innovator's dilemma: When new technologies cause old firms to fail.* Cambridge, MA: Harvard Business School Press.

Clark, R. E., & Estes, F. (2002). *Turning research into results: A guide to selecting the right performance solutions.* Atlanta: CEP Press.

Cross, R., & Parker, A. (2004). *The hidden power of social networks.* Cambridge, MA: Harvard Business School Press.

Ford, D. (2001). *Trust and knowledge management: The seeds of success.* Working Paper WP 01-08. Kingston, Ontario, Canada: Queen's KBE Center for Knowledge-Based Enterprises, Queen's School of Business. Retrieved on October 25, 2006, from http://business.queensu.ca/knowledge/workingpapers/working/working_01-08.pdf

Hagan, L. (2000). *Improving journal quality with process improvement methods.* Whitepaper. The Sheridan Press.

Hunt, V. D. (1992). *Quality in America: How to implement a competitive quality program.* Chicago: Irwin Professional Publishing.

ISO 8402. (1991). *Quality management and quality assurance; vocabulary.* International Organization for Standardization.

Jha, S., Noori, H., & Michela, J. L. (1996). The dynamics of continuous improvement: Aligning organizational attributes and activities for quality and productivity. *International Journal of Quality Science, 1*(1), 19–47. doi:10.1108/13598539610117975

Lillrank, P., Shani, A. B., & Lindberg, P. (2001). Continuous improvement: Exploring alternative organizational designs. *Total Quality Management, 12*(1), 41–55. doi:10.1080/09544120020010084

Longenecker, C. O., Dwyer, D. J., & Stansfield, T. C. (1998, March-April). Barriers and gateways to workforce productivity. *Industrial Management (Des Plaines)*, 21–28.

Loshin, D. (2001). *Enterprise knowledge management: The data quality approach.* New York: Morgan Kauffman. virtue. (n.d.). *The American heritage® dictionary of the English language, fourth edition.* Retrieved on October 25, 2006, from Dictionary.com Web site http://dictionary.reference.com/browse/virtue

Oinas-Kukkonen, H. (2004). The 7C model for organizational knowledge creation and management. Retrieved on October 25, 2006, from http://www.oasis.oulu.fi/publications/OKLC-04-hok.pdf

Okes, D., & Westcott, R. (2000). *The certified quality manager handbook.* Milwaukee, WI: Quality Press.

Pfeffer, J. (2007). A modest proposal: How we might change the process and product of managerial research. *Academy of Management Journal, 50*(6), 1334–1345.

Rosen, E. (2007). The culture of collaboration: Maximizing time, talent, and tools to create value in the global economy. San Francisco: Red Ape Publishing.

Ruggles, R., & Little, R. (1997). *Knowledge management and innovation: An initial exploration.* Working Paper, Ernst & Young LLP Center for Business Innovations. Retrieved on October 24, 2006, from http://www.providersedge.com/docs/km_articles/KM_and_Innovation.pdf

Chapter 18
Translating Knowledge Management Practices into the Boundaries of Supply Chain

Ozlem Bak
University of Brighton, UK

ABSTRACT

This chapter aims to evaluate the application of knowledge management (KM) literature in supply chains. The underlying understanding derived from this evaluation can be used to devise a valid business strategy to encourage knowledge management practices in supply chains. The concept of a supply chain encompasses businesses organised around a common goal of delivering a product or service from the initial supplier to the end customers. In this respect, the importance of knowledge management within the boundaries of supply chain management has been iterated by many authors; some underline the strategic and tactical importance of knowledge management, whereas others focus on the advantages and tools used to create knowledge in supply chains. The difficulty of assessing knowledge management is twofold when considering supply chains–first, the underlying difficulty of locating the trail of knowledge creation in supply chains and secondly how this can be utilised to devise a business strategy. On close examination of the literature in this field, we can identify a salient need for the theoretical categorisation of existing theoretical frameworks of supply chain management (SCM) on KM-related practices. This chapter explicitly looks into three supply chains, namely learning chains, virtual chains and build-to-order supply chains, and the specific challenges that these create for knowledge management and devising a valid business strategy.

INTRODUCTION

In a supply chain, where the boundaries cannot be set easily, disseminating and sharing the knowledge between the members of the supply chain becomes of interest to academics and practitioners. Wang et al. (2008) acknowledge that research on knowledge management has been carried out on definition- and content-related aspects of SCM. However, in a rapidly changing environment it is also important

DOI: 10.4018/978-1-60566-348-7.ch018

to assess how these concepts and principles are translated into supply chains and their day-to-day operations. Several attempts in the literature have been made towards assessing the implications of knowledge management utilisation in the context of supply chains; however, an exhaustive literature review seems to be limited in its scope. This can be also evidenced by a study (Harry et al., 2007) which reflected on academic databases, such as the Elsevier online database, and noted that from a total 1500 supply chain-related articles only 149 referred to knowledge management and its practices within the supply chains. Given the limited range of the supply chain papers on knowledge management, it can be assumed that the nature of these papers and subject areas covered is dispersed in its scope. Therefore, some researchers when carrying out the literature review focus on specific areas of knowledge management in the supply chain management, rather than the application within the supply chains. Also found in the words of Harry et al. (2007:883) is the statement that "...there are only a few research papers that consider both knowledge management (KM) initiatives and the application of a knowledge management systems (KMS) written by academics and practitioners". Hence, the aim of the chapter is similar in as much that it does not intend to give an exhaustive review on knowledge management or knowledge management systems; rather it focuses on knowledge management and its implications within the boundaries of supply chains, and how these impact on the overall business strategy. In an effort to accomplish this task, this chapter will first explore knowledge management and how it is embedded within the supply chain literature. Secondly, this assessment will allow us to answer the question of how these concepts can be transferred into a successful business strategy. Before we examine the impact of knowledge management to supply chain management, let us examine how these two seemingly relevant themes merge.

THE USE OF KNOWLEDGE MANAGEMENT WITHIN SUPPLY CHAIN BOUNDARIES

Knowledge management has been referred to as the backbone – and in some cases the lifeblood – of the supply chain (Desouza et al., 2003). This notion stems from the boundaries of supply chain which encompass several (sometimes globally dispersed) organisations gathered around delivering a common goal, a product or service. It becomes difficult to assess at what stage, or by which supply chain member, knowledge is generated and how this knowledge can be shared throughout the boundaries of the supply chain because knowledge management caters not only for creating knowledge, but also preserving, using and sharing it (Warkentin et al., 2001). Desouza et al. (2003) argue that a disruption in knowledge in any areas, or in one or more entities of supply chain members, will lead to disruption within the supply chain as a whole. As a result, knowledge management at a tactical and strategic level will increase its importance for a supply chain's competitiveness.

In a supply chain, the dissemination of knowledge throughout requires knowledge flow from the initial supplier to the end customer. Hence, knowledge management resides within the boundaries of individuals, teams and sometimes in strategic business units of supply chains. The integration – or in other words, synchronisation – of knowledge becomes a difficult task to accomplish. In order to overcome the overstretching boundaries of supply chains (in some cases across different continents) to allow knowledge sharing, supply chains have invested in e-business applications such as customer relationship management (CRM) systems, enterprise resource planning (ERP), Intranet and Extranet tools and others. Although the use of such tools in the literature has been found to be beneficial for knowledge dissemination, there seem to be several underlying challenges despite the use of the aforementioned systems. The challenges associated with knowledge management in the literature can be summed briefly as:

- The difficulty locating where knowledge is generated within the boundaries of the supply chain;
- Even if knowledge is distributed freely, the dissemination of knowledge would take time to acquire throughout the supply chain;
- The level of willingness to share knowledge might differ throughout the supply chain (i.e. suppliers might be reluctant to share knowledge as they might be also part of other supply chains);
- The difficulty understanding what knowledge is worth acquiring and what is not for supply chain entities (knowledge acquired might be less important for some internal departments than for others);
- The initial learning/unlearning requires investments throughout the supply chain, and some supply chain members might be reluctant to make the necessary investments (i.e. one MNC automotive corporation needed to subsidise and encourage the adoption of B2B systems for its suppliers (Bak, 2007);
- Volatile market conditions dictate more flexibility, which thus requires the dissemination of knowledge in real time.

The aforementioned challenges might be influenced by the nature of the product, specific market conditions or the industrial arena. In order to understand to what extent and where knowledge is generated and disseminated within the supply chains, companies have created knowledge management departments. However, even with the appropriate knowledge management departments in place, if the individuals, members of the teams or strategic business units of the sup-

ply chain see themselves as a sole profit centre rather than a part of the supply chain, acquiring the knowledge will be difficult to accomplish and, hence, disseminate across the supply chain. In the supply chain literature, several researchers have looked into how knowledge management has been disseminated within the boundaries of supply chains and whether the collaboration tools that have been used increase the efficiency of the knowledge management integration. The next section will investigate the literature on knowledge management and its implications in regards to three specific types of supply chains: the learning chains, build-to-order chains and virtual supply chains.

CREATION OF LEARNING CHAINS

According to Cheng et al. (2007), knowledge management and learning have been two central notions that contribute to the competitiveness of supply chains. Maqsood and Walker (2007) go one step further and combine the so far distinctive concepts of knowledge management and the supply chain under the umbrella of 'learning chains'. They enforce the understanding that in order to be competitive, the integration of the supply chain and knowledge together is required, and are therefore rather complementary in nature. They refer to this notion as a learning chain in which knowledge management is an integral part that provides "... detailed guidelines as to what sort of knowledge is appropriate to share in a certain mode of interaction" within the boundaries of a supply chain (Maqsood and Walker, 2007:132).

One of the challenges facing learning chains is that learning requires the presence of trust between the supply chain members; without it this would be difficult, even impossible in some cases. Spekman et al. (2002) underline the importance of learning in supply chains and stipulate that a level of trust is required to openly share information and generate knowledge. However, the question on how and to what extent this level of trust can be created is a question which is not easy to answer. One of the attempts made to assess knowledge creation includes a case study involving a multinational automotive corporation's supply chain. In order to assess supply chain practices, the chain is divided into three distinctive and complementary levels (Bak, 2007). The first is the individual level in which the knowledge generated can be limited to an individual employee or group of employees. The second level contains a much wider context in which the knowledge is shared and distributed within individual supply chain members' strategic business unit departments. The last and final level is the supply chain level in which the knowledge that stems from the supply chain members is transmitted across the entire supply chain. To create the transmission of knowledge, ICT (Information Communication Technology) is necessary because without this infrastructure, knowledge dissemination will be localised and remain between the boundaries of the first (individual) and second levels (strategic business unit) rather than shared across the supply chain.

The distinction of the supply chain at three levels relies on ascertaining that knowledge dissemination is preserved through its translation to the next level. Similarly, Wang et al. (2008) define the first two levels in their Case Based Reasoning Model (CBR), in which they accommodate an individual organisation and the knowledge creation within, and thereafter translate the acquired knowledge to other supply chain members. Therefore, when trying to achieve a business strategy that encourages learning chains, the location of where knowledge is created, applied and augmented becomes important at each level (individual, business unit and supply chain level) of the supply chain. This again is an important strategic point where the supply chain design has an impact on the level at which knowledge sharing and dissemination can be structured.

A BUILD-TO-ORDER SUPPLY CHAIN'S IMPACT ON KNOWLEDGE MANAGEMENT

One supply chain structure that has an impact on the design of knowledge dissemination is the build-to-order supply chain (BOSC). According to Gunesekaran (2005), a BOSC can be defined as a supply chain that creates the flexibility required to respond to volatile market conditions (market/customer requirements). One of the best known examples of a BOSC is operated by Dell, with its pivotal operational approaches. Dell begins production on receipt of the customer's order, which enables them to hold low inventory and track the market data in real time. Here the knowledge of the customer in real time shapes Dell's operation and the customisation of the product. Therefore, knowledge management in this instance steps outside of the boundaries of the supply chain, where the supply chain is driven not only by customer demand but also by the market itself.

In a geographically dispersed BOSC, where the market, production and sourcing is placed separately, the more knowledge management becomes critical. If the geographically dispersed members cannot share knowledge in real time, they will not be able to react rapidly to changing market conditions. By sharing and disseminating knowledge across the supply chain, the BOSC can utilise this acquired knowledge in order to understand any rapid changes in the market and respond quickly to those changes. Adapting swiftly to market changes also requires flexibility within the supply chain; hence, knowledge management is also regarded in this context as the backbone of the BOSC, as it allows the creation of an environment that empowers supply chain members to be more agile when reacting to sudden market changes.

The use of e-business applications can also encourage timely access to relevant data, which can support collaboration and knowledge dissemination between the supply chain members. As stated by Chow et al. (2007), "...through the interaction and communication with each other, knowledge is created for enterprises to achieve their mutual goals". Here, again similar to learning chains, the central tenets of "mutual goals" and "trust" are seen as one of the key ingredients for knowledge dissemination in a BOSC. With these two key building blocks, knowledge can be exchanged with geographically dispersed multi-tier supply chain members. With this in mind, the development of knowledge management is considered to be a critical success factor for a build-to-order supply chain's business strategy.

VIRTUAL SUPPLY CHAINS AND THEIR IMPACT ON KNOWLEDGE MANAGEMENT

The final supply chain that we will look into is the virtual supply chain. A virtual supply chain is defined closely by its existence in the marketspace through electronic links with other supply chain members. In their initial work, Bal et al. (1999) identify the importance of e-business tools for knowledge management within the boundaries of virtual supply chains. In their (ibid) work, the loose decoupling of the supply chain structure in the marketspace has its challenges; however, the creation of a team in the virtual supply chain enables information flow and knowledge dissemination much more smoothly, and "...dampen[s] the turbulence through the ability of members to behave as a team sharing knowledge and expertise, regardless of location" (ibid:71).

The main difference between traditional supply chains and virtual supply chains lies in the nature of their designs. Virtual supply chains are designed around the notion of data and how this data is transferred as information leading to knowledge generation within the boundaries of the supply chain, hence creating a more agile structure

(Bal et al. 1999). This structure also encourages better knowledge dissemination, regardless of the location of the individual departments, strategic business units or independent entities that are part of the supply chains. Compared with earlier days in a turbulent environment, we can say that e-business tools were regarded initially as a coping mechanism or catalyst in response to the turbulence in the marketplace, whereas nowadays they are regarded as collaboration tools that encourage knowledge dissemination across the boundaries of virtual supply chains (Bak, 2007). Amazon, as an example, have created a virtual supply chain, in which the customer has a wider range of choices to select from (including third parties that are electronically linked through Amazon's platform), which allows the customers to opt specifically for a product based on terms of payment and delivery cost. Here also, although a part of Amazon's supply chain, other supply chain members' information provides Amazon with real time customer information relating to their buying behaviour, and also allows the other members to use the platform against a small fee.

To summarise, knowledge sharing at an individual level is successful; however, there is still the need to translate it to a rather broader level (strategic business unit). Although, when compared to physical supply chains, the virtual supply chains lack the proximity of location, this rather seems to have much less impact on knowledge dissemination because the supply chain can be designed to allow an existence in the marketspace that is created through a network of electronic connections – allowing the creation of individual, business unit and supply chain-level links. From the three distinctive, but rather complementary, types of supply chain we can see that e-business technologies have an impact on the generation, preservation and dissemination of knowledge across these three supply chains. Consequently, the next section will introduce a brief discussion on the supply chain literature and the impact of particular e-business technologies on knowledge management.

INFORMATION SHARING AND E-BUSINESS TECHNOLOGIES IN SCM, AND THEIR IMPACT ON KM

Through the use of information sharing, mediated with e-technologies, knowledge is generated with the aim of achieving a strategic goal (Harry et al. 2007). In order to utilise e-technologies effectively, the achievement of a common goal becomes important and hence diminishes the reluctance of sharing knowledge between supply chain members, despite the fact that they may have been designed or formed. The common goal does not need to be in conflict with any other supply chain members (Cheng et al. 2008), as this might lead to disruption of knowledge sharing across the supply chain. For this reason, the way in which knowledge sharing is designed through the application of e-technologies is in some cases limited to the knowledge that is disseminated. Grant (1996) argues that the most efficient knowledge dissemination will take place if the knowledge that has been transferred is explicit rather than tacit. Taking this point further, Hsieh et al. (2002) point out that having e-business technologies does not eliminate the actual decision making process; in some cases they lead to the creation of vast banks of information that the decision maker has to go through to eliminate any unnecessary knowledge. Therefore, having e-business technologies within supply chain management boundaries does not necessarily lead to efficiency in decision making. This is again related to knowledge management at an individual level (Bak, 2007). As at the first level of the supply chain (individual level), knowledge generation needs to be assessed in order to ascertain whether this is of strategic importance to the business unit (level 2) and the whole supply chain (level 3). One such example can be seen in Enterprise Resource Planning (ERP), that has been used to enhance data sharing and knowledge dissemination, but this system was set up solely for the purpose of internal information sharing and data dissemination – nowadays we can see that

ERP has extended its reach throughout the supply chain (Wang et al. 2008). This is an interesting picture that indicates that the use of knowledge management tools alone, if not shared at three levels (individual-business and supply chain), cannot be a source of competitive business strategy. Taking from a further step this standpoint, the next section will assess whether we can envisage a valid business strategy for encouraging the use of knowledge management in supply chains.

DEVISING A VALID BUSINESS STRATEGY THAT ENCOURAGES THE USE OF KM IN SUPPLY CHAINS

Having looked into the different structural settings of the supply chain, the challenges here can be seen as a) the dissemination of knowledge across the supply chain, b) the creation of a strategic business strategy beneficial for all supply chain members for knowledge management and c) the potential to encourage further knowledge generation by supply chain members. Thus, business strategy for the supply chain becomes an important issue when deciding whether the knowledge created can contribute to the competitive advantage of a supply chain. In some cases, knowledge generation takes place at one focal point (one supply chain member such as a supplier, distributor, etc.) within the supply chain, which allows the development of the idea/innovation as a product. The complex nature of supply chains also discourages the search for one best-fit strategy that is valid and generalisable to all supply chains. Although one business strategy can be devised for implementation purposes, how it will be translated to the supply chain members might vary depending on the way in which knowledge is generated and disseminated. For example, the implementation of B2B in an automotive supply chain case study had different levels of impact. The after-sales department found the system of limited use, whereas the marketing and planning department found it a valuable tool for knowledge generation and dissemination. Here, it is important not to assume that one business strategy can be of equal importance at three distinctive levels. Although the impact of knowledge generation can be of competitive importance, the knowledge itself may not be completely relevant to each of the three levels in the supply chains. By its very nature, a successful strategy might be right for another supply chain, and even to base the business strategy on such an assumption may create challenges as the associated learning in the supply chains (Cheng et al., 2007).

As it is difficult to devise one strategic fit (Fisher, 1987) for all supply chains, it is difficult to translate this to a framework for knowledge management and to establish how this disseminates within supply chains. However, if we base knowledge management and how it impacts on the supply chain, rather than by mapping the overall challenges, this might guide supply chain members to map out the associated risks and challenges that will allow them to set up a best-fit strategy for their own particular supply chain. The following table attempts to create an overview of the particular challenges that supply chains face, and tries to link this complexity to the associated knowledge management challenges. The final column discusses the challenges of translating KM into the business strategy. The following table therefore allows the identification of challenges and at which stage they occur, and associates the challenges ahead with setting up a business strategy agenda.

CONCLUSION AND IMPLICATIONS FOR PRACTITIONERS

This chapter creates a link between the walls of existing literature on knowledge management and three distinctive supply chains (learning chains, build-to-order chains and virtual supply chains), from the initial supplier through to the end cus-

tomer. In so doing, the aim is to assess knowledge management within the boundaries of a supply chain and how this can improve business strategy. When looking into knowledge management practices, different e-business technologies (B2B, ERP, Extranet, knowledge platform, etc.) are used in supply chains, each of which impacts at different degrees. The three distinctive levels of supply chain, from individual to strategic business unit to supply chain levels, enables the assessment of these technologies and determines in which way they contribute to the effectiveness of the overall business strategy. Hence, the implications for practitioners relate to a) the assessment of supply chain members' goals/business strategies, as without a common goal /business strategy knowledge dissemination is unlikely to take place across the boundaries of individual supply chain members, b) the supply chain design, which has an impact on how knowledge is generated and transmitted, and c) an understanding that in order to devise a valid business strategy for knowledge management, one has to identify the type of supply chains and the consequent impact of knowledge generation.

FURTHER RESEARCH

It is interesting to see that although a wide area is covered by the supply chain management literature, the way in which it shapes the business strategy of supply chains is underdeveloped. The literature review indicates that we can talk about and differentiate between supply chains at three distinctive levels in order to assess their knowledge management practices. However, a common framework on how they integrate and shape business strategy requires further research. As each supply chain will have its own peculiarities and structure, the commonalities/differences between these might contribute to a more detailed framework in assessing business strategy development and deployment across the supply chain. Having discussed the application of knowledge

Table 1. Summary of knowledge management applications in three distinctive supply chains

Use of knowledge management concepts within the existing supply chain (SCM) literature	Challenges related to supply chain management	Challenges related to knowledge management in the context of SCM	Challenges related to setting a supply chain business strategy
Learning Chains	• Allocation of learning circles • Understanding where learning is undertaken and, if so, to what extent. • Checking learning practices across the supply chains • Creating a coherent learning environment across the boundaries of the supply chain.	• Defining tacit/explicit knowledge. • Defining where knowledge has been generated. • Assessing to what extent this has been disseminated within the boundaries of the supply chain.	• The decision has to be taken at which supply chain level (Level 1-Level 3) the knowledge is created • Assessment of knowledge management practices and their performance at three distinctive levels to determine whether they improve the competitiveness of the whole chain.
Build-to-order Supply Chain (BOSC)	• Based on customer demand, usually at global scale	• Flexible and/or adaptable knowledge management structure that enables rapid knowledge sharing and dissemination when required.	• Recommendation and reasoning by market/customer analysis based on performance evaluation. • Use of knowledge platforms within the BOSC.
Virtual Supply Chains	• Multi-agent forecasting methods used, allocation of the best-fit for the requirements. • Overarching supply chain boundaries with less, sometimes non-physical, supply chain boundaries.	• Knowledge-specific allocation, strict guidelines and rules for knowledge dissemination. • Extensive use of knowledge management platforms and collaboration tools.	• Classification for storage and dissemination of knowledge and tools. • Creation of supply chain-wide knowledge management policies and procedures.

management in the context of a supply chain, this chapter has indicated the following potential research areas:

- Tools and techniques that can be implemented in a knowledge management framework/template for the supply chain'
- An assessment of performance to determine at which level the knowledge management is disseminated, and to what extent;
- An assessment to establish at which supply chain level knowledge dissemination/sharing has an impact on the overall business strategy;
- An assessment of the level of trust and the impact of knowledge dissemination between supply chain levels.

REFERENCES

Bak, O. (2007). The use of e-collaboration tools. In Z. Qingyu (Ed.), *E-Chain Technologies and Management* (pp. 162-178). Hershey, PA: Idea Group Inc.

Cheng, J. H., Yeh, C. H., & Tu, C. W. (2007). Trust and knowledge sharing in green supply chains. *Supply Chain Management: An International Journal, 13*(4), 283–295. doi:10.1108/13598540810882170

Desouza, K. C., Chattaraj, A., & Kraft, G. (2003). Supply chain perspectives to knowledge management: Research propositions. *Journal of Knowledge Management, 7*(3), 129–138. doi:10.1108/13673270310485695

Gunesekaran, A. (2005). Editorial, the build-to-order supply chain (BOSC): A competitive strategy for 21st century. *Journal of Operations Management, 23*(5), 419–422. doi:10.1016/j.jom.2004.10.004

Harry, K. H., Chow, K. L., & Lee, W. B. (2007). Knowledge management approach in build-to-order supply chains. *Industrial Management & Data Systems, 107*(6), 882–919. doi:10.1108/02635570710758770

Koh, S. C. L., & Tan, K. H. (2006). Translating knowledge of supply chain uncertainity into business strategy and actions. *Journal of Manufacturing Technology Management, 17*(4), 472–485. doi:10.1108/17410380610662898

Lee, H., & Choi, B. (2003). Knowledge management enablers, processes, and organisational performance: An integrative view and empirical examination. *Journal of Management Information Systems, 20*(1), 179–228.

McLaughlin, S., Paton, R. A., & Macbeth, D. K. (2008). Barrier impact on organisational learning within complex organisations. *Journal of Knowledge Management, 12*(2), 107–123. doi:10.1108/13673270810859550

Nissen, M. E. (2001). Beyond electronic disintermediation through multiagent systems. *Logistics Information Management, 14*(4), 256–275. doi:10.1108/EUM0000000005721

Sila, I., Ebrahimpour, M., & Birkholz, C. (2006). Quality in supply chains: An empirical analysis. *Supply Chain Management: An International Journal, 11*(6), 491–502. doi:10.1108/13598540610703882

Spekman, R. E., Spear, J., & Kamauff, J. (2002). Supply chain competency: Learning as a key component. *Supply Chain Management, 17*, 27–43.

Tayyab, M., Walker, D., & Finegan, A. (2007). Extending the "knowledge advantage": Creating learning chains. *The Learning Organization, 14*(2), 123–141. doi:10.1108/09696470710726998

Wang, C., Fergusson, C., Perry, D., & Antony, J. (2008). A conceptual case-based model for knowledge sharing among supply chain members. *Business Process Management Journal, 14*(2), 147–165. doi:10.1108/14637150810864907

Wu, C. (2008). Knowledge creation in supply chain. *Supply Chain Management: An International Journal, 13*(3), 241–250. doi:10.1108/13598540810871280

Compilation of References

Abbott, J. (2001). Data data everywhere–and not a byte of use? *Qualitative Market Research: An International Journal*, *4*(3), 182–192. doi:10.1108/13522750110393080

Abernathy, W. J. (1978). *The productivity dilemma*. Baltimore: John Hopkins University Press.

Adams, S. (1995). The corporate memory concept. *The Electronic Library*, *13*(4), 309–312. doi:10.1108/eb045380

Adamson, I. (2005). Knowledge management: The next generation of TQM? *Total Quality Management and Business Excellence*, *16*(8-9), 987–1000. doi:10.1080/14783360500163177

Adamson, I. (2005). Knowledge management–the next generation of TQM? *Total Quality Management & Business Excellence*, *16*(8/9), 987–1000. doi:10.1080/14783360500163177

Adler, P., & Kwon, S. (2002). Social capital: Prospects for a new concept. *Academy of Management Review*, *27*(1), 17–40. doi:10.2307/4134367

Ahn, J. H., & Chang, S. G. (2004). Assessing the contribution of knowledge business performance: The KP3 methodology. *Decision Support Systems*, *36*(4), 403–416. doi:10.1016/S0167-9236(03)00029-0

Ahokangas, P. (1998). *Internationalization and resources: An analysis of processes in Nordic SMSs*. Unpublished doctoral dissertation, Universitas Wasaensis, Vaasa.

Ajmal, M. M., & Koskinen, K. U. (2008). Knowledge transfer in project-based organizations: An organizational culture perspective. *Project Management Journal*, *39*(1), 7–15. doi:10.1002/pmj.20031

Alavi, M., & Leidner, D. (2001). Knowledge management and knowledge management systems: Conceptual foundations and research issues. *MIS Quarterly*, *25*(1), 107–136. doi:10.2307/3250961

Alavi, M., & Leidner, D. E. (2001). Review: Knowledge management and knowledge management systems: Conceptual foundations and research issues. *MIS Quarterly*, *25*(1), 107–136. doi:10.2307/3250961

Alavi, M., & Tiwana, A. (2003). Knowledge management: The information technology dimension. In M. Easterby-Smith & M. A. Lyles (Eds.), *Organizational learning and knowledge management* (pp. 104-121). London: Blackwell Publishing.

Alexander, R. (2004). Aspect-oriented technology and software. *Software Quality Journal*, *12*(2). doi:10.1023/B:SQJO.0000024109.11544.65

Almansa, A., Andreu, R., & Sieber, S. (2002). *La gestión del conocimiento en España-2001*. Cap Gemini, Ernst & Young.

Alvesson, M., & Kärreman, D. (2001). Odd couple: Making sense of the curious concept of knowledge management. *Journal of Management Studies*, *38*(7), 995–1018. doi:10.1111/1467-6486.00269

Ambrosini, V., & Bowman, C. (2001). Tacit knowledge: Some suggestions for operationalization. *Journal of Management Studies*, *36*(6), 811–829. doi:10.1111/1467-6486.00260

Amit, R., & Schoemaker, P. (1993). Strategic assets and organizational rent. *Strategic Management Journal*, *14*(1), 33–46. doi:10.1002/smj.4250140105

Anderson, J. R. (1983). *The architecture of cognition.* Cambridge, MA: Harvard University Press.

Antonelli, C. (2005). Models of knowledge and systems of governance. *Journal of Institutional Economics, 1,* 51–73. doi:10.1017/S1744137405000044

Appleyard, M. M. (1996). How does knowledge flow? Interfirm patterns in the semiconductor industry. *Strategic Management Journal, 17*(Special Issue-Winter), 137–154.

Appleyard, M. M. (1998). *Cooperative knowledge creation: The case of buyer-supplier codevelopment in the semiconductor industry.* Working Paper No. 98–06. Darden Graduate School of Business Administration. Retrieved on December 26, 2003, from http://papers.ssrn.com/abstract=287855

Argote, L. (1999). *Organizational learning: Creating, retaining, and transferring knowledge.* Berlin: Springer.

Argote, L., McEvily, B., & Reagans, R. (2003). Managing knowledge in organizations: An integrative framework and review of emerging themes. *Management Science, 49*(4), 571–582. doi:10.1287/mnsc.49.4.571.14424

Arora, A., Gambardella, A., & Rullani, E. (1997). Division of labour and the locus of inventive activity. *The Journal of Management and Governance, 1,* 123–140. doi:10.1023/A:1009993430964

Arundel, A., & Hollanders, H. (2005). *EXIS: An exploratory approach to innovation scoreboard.* Retrieved on April 25, 2007, from http://www.trendchart.org

Ashby, W. R. (1956). *An introduction to cybernetics.* London: Chapman and Hall.

Asheim, B. T., & Coenen, L. (2006). Contextualizing regional innovation systems in a globalizing learning economy: On knowledge basis and institutional frameworks. *The Journal of Technology Transfer, 31,* 163–173. doi:10.1007/s10961-005-5028-0

Atkinson, J. (1984). Manpower strategies for flexible organizations. *Personnel Management,* 28-30.

Auh, S., & Menguc, B. (2005). Balancig exploration and exploitation: The moderating role of competitive intensity. *Journal of Business Research, 58*(12), 1652–1661. doi:10.1016/j.jbusres.2004.11.007

Aurora Health Care (2009). *2007 Strategic Plan.* Retrieved from https://iconnect.aurora.org/ DotNetNuke/Default.aspx?tabid=2324

Aurora Health Care (2009). *2009-2011 Strategic Plan Chart.* Retrieved from http://heiwebaz031. aurora.org/DotNetNuke/portals/216/2009-2011_Strategic_Plan_Chart%20Final.pdf

Aurora Health Care (2009). *Aurora at a Glance.* Retrieved from http://iconnect.aurora.org/ portal/default.do?appId=EB416

Aurora Health Care (2009). *Aurora Pulse.* Retrieved from http://iconnect.aurora.org/ portal/default.do?appId=EB109

Aurora Health Care (2009). *Aurora Service – Aurora Star.* Retrieved from http://ahcweb03. aurora.org/aurora_service/aurora_star.htm

Aurora Health Care (2009). *Content Search "Aurora Quest."* Retrieved from http://iconnect. aurora.org/portal/default.do?appId=EBGOO&appParam=q%3Daurora%20quest

Aurora Health Care (2009). *Content Search "Aurora's Promise to Caregivers."* Retrieved from https://iconnect.aurora.org/portal/default.do?appId=EBGOO&appParam=q%3Dpromise

Aurora Health Care (2009). *Content Search "Innovative use of IT in the healthcare market."* Retrieved from https://iconnect.aurora.org/portal/default.do?appId=EBGOO&appParam =q%3Dthe%20innovative%20use%20of%20IT%20in%20the%20health%20care%20market

Aurora Health Care (2009). *Content Search "Learning Plans."* Retrieved from https://iconnect. aurora.org/portal/default.do?appId=EBGOO&appParam=q%3Dlearning%20lesson%20plan

Aurora Health Care (2009). *Content Search "loyalty index."* Retrieved from https://iconnect. aurora.org/portal/default.do?appId=EBGOO&appParam=q%3Dloyalty%20index

Aurora Health Care (2009). *Content Search "on boarding resources."* Retrieved from https://iconnect.aurora.org/portal/default.do?appId=EBGOO&appParam=q%3Don boarding%20process

Aurora Health Care (2009). *Content Search "Planetree Demystifying HealthCare."* Retrieved from http://iconnect.aurora.org/portal/default.do?appId=EBGOO&appParam=q%3D planetree%20demystifying%20healthcare

Aurora Health Care (2009). *Content Search, "Just Culture."* Retrieved from http://iconnect. aurora.org/portal/default.do?appId=EBGOO&appParam=q%3Djust%20culture

Aurora Health Care (2009). *Operating Principles.* Retrieved from http://iconnect.aurora.org/ DotNetNuke/LinkClick.aspx?link=Operating+Principles+(formerly+Leadership)+FINAL.doc&tabid=1630

Aurora Health Care (2009). *Patient Stories.* Retrieved from http://www.aurorahealthcare.org/ aboutus/stories/stories.asp

Aurora Health Care (2009). *Responsible Freedom.* Retrieved from http://www.aurora healthcare.org/jobs/why-aurora/respfreedom.asp

Aurora Health Care (2009). *Aurora Health Care – 2008 Report to the Community.* Retrieved from http://www.aurorahealthcare.org/aboutus/annualreports/2008/financial_ stewardship.html

Aurora Health Care (2009). *Aurora Health Care's Mission.* Retrieved from http://www.aurorahealthcare.org/aboutus/mission.asp

Aurora Health Care (2009a). *Number One Priority.* Retrieved from http://iconnect.aurora.org/portal/default.do?appId=EB416

Aurora Health Care (2009b). *Aurora Health Care fact sheet.* Retrieved from http://www.aurorahealthcare.org/aboutus/media/factsheet.asp

Aurora Health Care(2009). *Care Management/Quality.* Retrieved from http://iconnect. aurora.org/portal/default.do?appId=EB084

Australian Bureau of Statistics. (2006). *Labor force survey and labor mobility.* Retrieved on November 10, 2008, from http://www.abs.gov.au

Australian Bureau of Statistics. (2007). *Northern Territory at a glance.* Retrieved on November 10, 2008, from http://www.abs.gov.au

Bak, O. (2007). The use of e-collaboration tools. In Z. Qingyu (Ed.), *E-Chain Technologies and Management* (pp. 162-178). Hershey, PA: Idea Group Inc.

Ballantyne, D. (1996). Getting your way in business. *Asia-Australia Marketing Journal, 4*(1), 3–6.

Barley, S. R. (1986). Technology as an occasion for structuring: Evidence from observations of CT scanners and the social order of radiology departments. *Administrative Science Quarterly, 31,* 708–808. doi:10.2307/2392767

Barnett, A. (2000, July 19). The customer wants to be anonymous. *Revolution (Staten Island, N.Y.),* 25.

Barney, J. (1991). Firm resources and sustained competitive advantage. *Journal of Management, 17*(1), 99–120. doi:10.1177/014920639101700108

Baumard, P. (1999). *Tacit knowledge in organizations.* Sage: London.

Becattini, G., & Rullani, E. (1996). Local systems and global connections: The role of knowledge. In F. Cossentino, F. Pyke & W. Segenberger (Eds.), *Local and regional response to global pressure: The case of Italy and its industrial districts.* Geneva: International Institute for Labor Studies.

Becker, M. C. (2001). Managing dispersed knowledge: Organizational problems, managerial strategies, and their effectiveness. *Journal of Management Studies, 38*(7), 1037–1051. doi:10.1111/1467-6486.00271

Beltran-Martin, I., Roca-Puig, V., Escrig-Tena, A., & Bou-Llusar, J. C. (2008). Human resource flexibility as a mediating variable between high performance work systems and performance. *Journal of Management, 34*(5), 1009–1044. doi:10.1177/0149206308318616

Benner, M. J., & Tushman, M. (2002). Process management and technological innovation: A longitudinal study of the photography and paint industries. *Administrative Science Quarterly, 47*, 676. doi:10.2307/3094913

Benner, M. J., & Tushman, M. L. (2003). Exploitation, exploration, and process management: The productivity dilemma revisited. *Academy of Management Review, 28*(2), 238–256.

Bennet, A., & Bennet, D. (2003). The rise of the knowledge organization. In C. W. Holsapple (Ed.), *Handbook on knowledge management 1: Knowledge matters.* Berlin: Springer Verlag.

Bentley, R. (2005, August 25). Data with destiny. *Caterer & Hotelkeeper, 38.*

Berry, L. L. (1983). Relationship marketing. In L. L. Berry, G. L. Shostack, & G. D. Upah (Eds), *Emerging perspectives on services marketing* (pp. 25-28). Chicago, IL: American Marketing Association.

Bettiol, M., & Micelli, S. (2005). *Design e creatività nel made in Italy.* Milano: Bruno Mondandori.

Bierly, P., & Chakrabarti, A. (1996). Generic knowledge strategies in the U.S. pharmaceutical industry. *Strategic Management Journal, 17*(Special Issue-Winter), 123-135.

Bierly, P., & Daly, P. (2002). Aligning human resource management practices and knowledge strategies: A theoretical framework. In C. W. Choo & N. Bontis (Eds.), *The strategic management of intellectual capital and organizational knowledge.* Oxford University Press.

Biggiero, L. (2006). Industrial and knowledge relocation strategies under the challenges of globalization and digitalization: The move of small and medium enterprises among territorial systems. *Entrepreneurship & Regional Development, 18*(November), 443–471. doi:10.1080/08985620600884701

Biloslavo, R., & Trnavc̆evic, A. (2007). Knowledge management audit in a higher educational institution: A case study. *Knowledge and Process Management, 14*(4), 275–286. doi:10.1002/kpm.293

Birch, A., Gerbert, P., & Schneider, D. OC&C, & The McKenna Group. (2000). *The age of e-tail.* Capstone Publishing Limited.

Bishoff, L., & Allen, N. (2004). *Business planning for cultural heritage institutions.* Washington, D.C.: Council on Library and Information Resources.

Blackler, F. (1995). Knowledge, knowledge work, and organization: An overview and interpretation. *Organization Studies, 16*(6), 1021–1046. doi:10.1177/017084069501600605

Bloodgood, J. M., & Salisbury, W. D. (2001). Understanding the influence of organizational change strategies on information technology and knowledge management strategies. *Decision Support Systems, 31*, 55–69. doi:10.1016/S0167-9236(00)00119-6

Boer, H., Berger, A., Chapman, R., & Gertsen, F. (2000). *CI changes from suggestion box to organisational learning: Continuous improvement in Europe and Australia.* Ashgate, Aldershot.

Bogner, W. C., & Bansal, P. (2007). Knowledge management as the basis of sustained high performance. *Journal of Management Studies, 44*(1), 165–188. doi:10.1111/j.1467-6486.2007.00667.x

Bontis, N. (1996). *Intellectual capital: An exploratory study that develops measures and models.* WP 96-11. Canada: Richard Ivey School of Business.

Bontis, N. (1999). Managing organizational knowledge by diagnosing intellectual capital: Framing and advancing the state of the field. *International Journal of Technology Management, 18*(5-8), 433–462. doi:10.1504/IJTM.1999.002780

Bontis, N., & Fitz-enz, J. (2002). Intellectual capital ROI: A causal map of human capital antecedents and consequents. [from http://www.leighbureau.com/speakers/nbontis/essays/intel.pdf]. *Journal of Intellectual Capital, 3*(3), 223–247. Retrieved on June 25, 2009. doi:10.1108/14691930210435589

Bontis, N., Crossan, M. M., & Hulland, J. (2002). Managing an organizational learning system by aligning stocks and flows. *Journal of Management Studies, 39*(4), 437–469. doi:10.1111/1467-6486.t01-1-00299

Borgatti, S. P., & Cross, R. (2003). A relational view of information seeking and learning in social networks. *Management Science, 49*(4), 432–445. doi:10.1287/mnsc.49.4.432.14428

Botschen, G., Thelen, E. M., & Pieters, R. (1999). Using means-end structures for benefit segmentation: An application to services. *European Journal of Marketing, 33*(1/2). doi:10.1108/EUM0000000004491

Bower, J. L., & Christensen, C. M. (1995). Disruptive technologies: Catching the wave. *Harvard Business Review, 73*(1), 43–53.

Bowman, E. H. (1974). Epistemology, corporate strategy, and academe. *Sloan Management Review, 15*, 35–50.

Bradbury, D. (2005, August 31). Technology jargon buster. *Caterer & Hotelkeeper*, Glossary.

Braganza, A. (2004). Rethinking the data–information–knowledge hierarchy: Towards a case-based model. *International Journal of Information Management, 24*(4), 347–356. doi:10.1016/j.ijinfomgt.2004.04.007

Bresnahan, T., Greenstein, S., & Henderson, R. (2006, October). *Making waves: The interplay between market incentives and organizational capabilities in the evolution of industries.* Paper presented at Harvard Business School Strategy Conference, Retrieved on June 25, 2009, from http://mba.tuck.dartmouth.edu/digital/Programs/Seminars/HendersonPaper.pdf

Brickson, S. (2000). The impact of identity orientation on individual and organizational outcomes in demographically diverse settings. *Academy of Management Review, 25*(1), 82–101. doi:10.2307/259264

Brodie, R. J., Corviello, N. E., Brookes, R. W., & Little, V. (1997). Towards a paradigm shift in marketing? An examination of current marketing practices. *Journal of Marketing Management, 13*, 383–406.

Brooking, A. (1996). *Intellectual capital, core asset for the third millennium enterprise.* International Thomson Business Press/ London.

Brown, J. S., & Duguid, P. (1991). Organizational learning and communities-of-practice: Toward a unified view of working, learning, and innovation. *Organization Science, 2*(1), 40–57. doi:10.1287/orsc.2.1.40

Brown, J. S., & Duguid, P. (2000). *The social life of information.* Boston, MA: Harvard Business School Press.

Brown, J. S., & Duguid, P. (2001). Knowledge and organization: A social-practice perspective. *Organization Science, 12*(2), 198–213. doi:10.1287/orsc.12.2.198.10116

Brush, C. G., Greene, P. G., & Hart, M. M. (2001). From initial idea to unique advantage: The entrepreneurial challenge of constructing a resource base. *The Academy of Management Executive, 15*(1), 64–78.

Bryson, J. M. (2004). *Strategic planning for public and nonprofit organizations* (3rd ed.). San Francisco, CA: Jossey-Bass.

Buckman Laboratories. (2005). Retrieved from http://www.buckman.com/eng/AR/Buckman_AR_2005.pdf

Buhalis, D., & Main, H. (1998). Information technology in peripheral small and medium hospitality enterprises: Strategic analysis and critical factors. *International Journal of Contemporary Hospitality Management, 10*(5), 198–202. doi:10.1108/09596119810227811

Buick, I. (2003). Information technology in small Scottish hotels: Is it working? *International Journal of Contemporary Hospitality Management, 15*(4), 243–247. doi:10.1108/09596110310475711

Burgess, J. (1997). The flexible firm and the growth of non standard employment. *Labour & Industry, 7*(3), 85–102.

Burnet, S., Illingworth, L., & Webster, L. (2004). Knowledge auditing and mapping: A pragmatic approach. *Knowledge and Process Management, 11*(1), 25–37. doi:10.1002/kpm.194

Burstein, F., & Linger, H. (2003). Supporting post-Fordist work practices. A knowledge management framework for supporting knowledge work. *Information Technology & People, 16*(3), 289–305. doi:10.1108/09593840310489395

Burt, R. S. (2001). Structural holes vs. network closure as social capital. In N. Lin, K. Cook & R. S. Burt (Eds.), *Social capital: Theory and research* (pp. 31-56). Sociology and economics: Controversy and integration series. New York: Aldine de Gruyter.

Butler, R. (1998). Seasonality in tourism: Issues and implications. *Tourism Review, 53*(3), 18–24. doi:10.1108/eb058278

Callahan, S. D. (2002). Crafting a knowledge strategy. In *ACT Knowledge Management Forum (ActKM) Conference*, Canberra (ActKM). Retrieved on January 2, 2009, from http://www.anecdote.com.au/papers/CallahanCraftingKnowledgeStrategy.pdf

Camisón, C., Palacios, D., Garrigós, F., & Devece, C. (Eds.). (2009). *Connectivity and knowledge management in virtual organizations: Networking and developing interactive communications.* Hershey, PA: IGI Global.

Cannon, J. (2000). *Make your Web site work for you.* McGraw-Hill.

Carbery, R., & Garavan, T. N. (2003). Predicting hotel managers' turnover cognitions. *Journal of Managerial Psychology, 18*(7), 649–679. doi:10.1108/02683940310502377

Casillas, J., Crocker, P., Jr., Fehrenbach, F., Haug, K., & Straley, B. (2000). *Disruptive technologies: Strategic advantage and thriving in uncertainty.* Kellogg Tech-Venture 2000 Anthology (pp. 203–229).

Caterer & Hotelkeeper. (2000, September 7). *Hotel groups deny they're missing Web opportunities* (p. 14).

Caterer & Hotelkeeper. (2004, June 24). *Do the knowledge* (p. 34).

Chaffey, D., Mayer, R., Johnston, K., & Ellis-Chadwick, F. (2000). *Internet marketing.* Pearson Education Limited

Chalkiti, K., & Carson, D. (2009, in press). Knowledge cultures, competitive advantage, and staff turnover in hospitality in Australia's Northern Territory. In D. Harorimana (Ed.), *Cultural implications of knowledge sharing, management, and transfer: Identifying competitive advantage.* Hershey, PA: IGI Global.

Chan, K., & Liebowitz, J. (2006). The synergy of social network analysis and knowledge mapping: A case study. *Int. J. Management and Decision Making, 7*, 19–35. doi:10.1504/IJMDM.2006.008169

Chan, S. (2000). Information technology in business processes. *Business Process Management Journal, 6*(3), 224–237. doi:10.1108/14637150010325444

Chan, Y. (2002). Why haven't we mastered alignment? The importance of the informal organization structure. *MIS Quarterly Executive, 1*(21), 76–112.

Chan, Y. E., Huff, S. L., & Copeland, D. G. (1998). Assessing realized information systems strategy. *Strategic Information Systems, 6*(4), 273–298. doi:10.1016/S0963-8687(97)00005-X

Chandler, A. (1966). *Strategy and structure.* Garden City, NY: Doubleday & Company.

Chapman, C. B., & Ward, S. C. (2003). *Project risk management: Process, techniques, and insights* (2nd ed.). Chichester, UK: John Wiley and Sons.

Chapman, J. A., & Lovell, G. (2006). The competency model of hospitality service: Why it doesn't deliver. *International Journal of Contemporary Hospitality Management, 18*(1), 78–88. doi:10.1108/09596110610642000

Chard, A. M., & Sarvary, M. (1997). *Knowledge management at Ernst & Young, case study.* Graduate School of Business, Stanford University.

Chen, I. J., & Popovich, K. (2003). Understanding customer relationship management (CRM), people, process, and technology. *Business Process Management Journal, 9*(5), 672–688. doi:10.1108/14637150310496758

Chen, X. P., Hui, C., & Sego, D. J. (1998). The role of organizational citizenship behavior in turnover: Conceptualization and preliminary tests of key hypothesis. *The Journal of Applied Psychology, 83*, 922–931. doi:10.1037/0021-9010.83.6.922

Cheng, J. H., Yeh, C. H., & Tu, C. W. (2007). Trust and knowledge sharing in green supply chains. *Supply Chain Management: An International Journal, 13*(4), 283–295. doi:10.1108/13598540810882170

Chesbrough, H. W. (2003). *Open innovation.* Cambridge: Harvard Business School Press.

Chesbrough, H. W. (2007). Why companies should have open business models. *MIT Sloan Management Review, 48*(2), 22–28.

Cheuk, B. W. (2006). Using social networking analysis to facilitate knowledge sharing in the British Council. *International Journal of Knowledge Management, 2*(4), 67–76.

Cheung, C. F., Li, M. L., Shek, W. Y., Lee, W. B., & Tsang, T. S. (2007). A systematic approach for knowledge auditing: A case study in transportation sector. *Journal of Knowledge Management, 11*(4), 140–158. doi:10.1108/13673270710762774

Chiarvesio, M., Di Maria, E., & Micelli, S. (2004). From local networks of SMEs to virtual clusters? Evidence from recent trends in Italy. *Research Policy, 33*(10), 1509–1528. doi:10.1016/j.respol.2004.08.009

Cho, S., & Johanson, M. (2008). Organizational citizenship behavior and employee performance: A moderating effect on work status in restaurant employees. *Journal of Hospitality & Tourism Research (Washington, D.C. Print), 32*(3), 307–326. doi:10.1177/1096348008317390

Choi, B., & Lee, H. (2003). An empirical investigation of KM styles and their effect on corporate performance. *Information & Management, 40*, 403–417. doi:10.1016/S0378-7206(02)00060-5

Choi, B., Poon, S. K., & Davis, J. G. (2008). Effects of knowledge management strategy on organizational performance: A complementarity theory-based approach. *Omega, 36*(2), 235–251. doi:10.1016/j.omega.2006.06.007

Chourides, P., Longbottom, D., & Murphy, W. (2003). Excellence in knowledge management: An empirical study to identify critical factors and performance measures. *Measuring Business Excellence, 7*(2), 29–45. doi:10.1108/13683040310477977

Christensen, C. (1997). *The innovator's dilemma: When new technologies cause old firms to fail.* Cambridge, MA: Harvard Business School Press.

Chuang, S. (2004). A resource-based perspective on knowledge management capability and competitive advantage: An empirical investigation. *Expert Systems with Applications, 27*(3), 459–465. doi:10.1016/j.eswa.2004.05.008

Ciborra, C. U. (1997). De profundis? Deconstructing the concept of strategic alignment. *Scandinavian Journal of Information Systems, 9*(1), 67–82.

Clark, R. E., & Estes, F. (2002). *Turning research into results: A guide to selecting the right performance solutions.* Atlanta: CEP Press.

Clarke, J., & Turner, P. (2004). Global competition and the Australian biotechnology industry: Developing a model of SMEs knowledge management strategies. *Knowledge and Process Management, 11*(1), 38–46. doi:10.1002/kpm.190

Claycomb, C., Droge, C., & Germain, R. (2001). Applied process knowledge and market performance: The moderating effect of environmental uncertainty. *Journal of Knowledge Management, 5*(3), 264–277. doi:10.1108/13673270110401239

Clemons, E. K., & Row, M. C. (1992). Information technology and industrial cooperation: The changing economics of coordination and ownership. *Journal of Management Information Systems, 9*(2), 9–28.

Clemons, E., & Row, M. (2000, November 13). (in press). Behaviour is key to Web retailing strategy. *Financial Times (North American Edition)*.

Cohen, D., & Prusak, L. (2001). *In good company: How social capital makes organizations work.* Boston, MA: Harvard Business School Press.

Cohen, W. M., & Levinthal, D. A. (1990). Absorptive capacity: A new perspective on learning and innovation. *Administrative Science Quarterly, 35,* 128–152. doi:10.2307/2393553

Cohen, W. M., Nelson, R. R., & Walsh, J. P. (2000). *Protecting their intellectual assets: Appropriability conditions and why U.S. manufacturing firms patent (or not).* NBER Working Paper No. 7552.

Collin, S. (2000). *E-marketing.* John Wiley & Sons Limited.

Conner, K. R., & Prahalad, C. K. (1996). A resource-based theory of the firm: Knowledge vs. opportunism. *Organization Science, 7,* 477–501. doi:10.1287/orsc.7.5.477

Cooper, A. C., Woo, C. Y., & Dunkelberg, W. C. (1989). Entrepreneurship and the initial size of firms. *Journal of Business Venturing, 4*(5), 317–332. doi:10.1016/0883-9026(89)90004-9

Corò, G., & Grandinetti, R. (1999). Evolutionary patterns of Italian industrial districts. *Human Systems Management, 18,* 117–130.

Cotton, J. L., & Turtle, J. M. (1986). Employee turnover: A meta analysis and review of implications for research. *Academy of Management Review, 11,* 55–70. doi:10.2307/258331

Cross, R., & Parker, A. (2004). *The hidden power of social networks.* Cambridge, MA: Harvard Business School Press.

Cross, R., Parker, A., Prusak, L., & Borgatti, S. (2001). Knowing what we know: Supporting knowledge creation and sharing in social networks. *Organizational Dynamics, 30*(2), 100–120. doi:10.1016/S0090-2616(01)00046-8

Crossan, M. M., Lane, H. W., & White, R. E. (1999). An organizational learning framework: From intuition to institution. *Academy of Management Review, 24*(3), 522–537. doi:10.2307/259140

Curtis, J. (2000, July 12). Get some decent exposure. *Revolution (Staten Island, N.Y.),* 32–36.

Cushing, K. (2004, March 18). Time to get technical. *Caterer & Hotelkeeper,* 76.

D'Adderio, L. (2001). Crafting the virtual prototype: How firms integrate knowledge and capabilities across organizational boundaries. *Research Policy, 30,* 1409–1424. doi:10.1016/S0048-7333(01)00159-7

Dalton, D. R., & Krackhardt, D. M. (1983). The impact of teller turnover in banking: First appearances are deceiving. *Journal of Bank Research, 14*(3), 184–192.

Darroch, J. (2005). Knowledge management, innovation, and firm performance. *Journal of Knowledge Management, 9*(3), 101–115. doi:10.1108/13673270510602809

Davenport, T. H. (1993). *Process innovation: Reengineering work through information technology.* Boston, MA: Harvard Business School Press.

Davenport, T. H. (1995). The fad that forgot people. *Fast Company, 1*(1), 70–75.

Davenport, T. H., & Harris, J. G. (2007). *Competing on analytics: The new science of winning.* Boston, MA: Harvard Business School Press.

Davenport, T. H., & Prusak, L. (1998). *Working knowledge. How organizations manage what they know.* Boston: Harvard Business School Press.

Davenport, T. H., & Völpel, S. C. (2001). The rise of knowledge towards attention management. *Journal of Knowledge Management, 5*(3), 212–221. doi:10.1108/13673270110400816

Davenport, T., De Long, D., & Beers, M. (1998). Successful knowledge management projects. *Sloan Management Review, 39*(2), 43–57.

Davenport, T., DeLong, D., & Beers, M. (1998). Successful knowledge management projects. *Sloan Management Review, 39*(2), 43–57.

Davies A. (2001b, July 26). Web's wonder. *Caterer & Hotelkeeper,* 37-39.

Davies, A. (2000, June 29). Data's the way to do it. *Caterer & Hotelkeeper,* 31-32.

Davies, A. (2001a, July 26). Online, on course. *Caterer & Hotelkeeper,* 37-39.

Day, J. D., & Wendler, J. C. (1998). Best practices and beyond: Knowledge strategies. *The McKinsey Quarterly, 1*, 19–25.

De Boer, M., Van den Bosch, F. A. J., & Volberda, H. W. (1999). Managing organizational knowledge integration in the emerging multimedia complex. *Journal of Management Studies, 36*(3), 379–398. doi:10.1111/1467-6486.00141

de Gooijer, J. (2000). Designing a knowledge management performance framework. *Journal of Knowledge Management, 4*(4), 303–310. doi:10.1108/13673270010379858

De Long, D., & Seemann, P. (2000). Confronting conceptual confusion and conflict in knowledge management. *Organizational Dynamics, 29*(1), 33–44. doi:10.1016/S0090-2616(00)00011-5

De Pelsmacker, P., Geuens, M., & Van den Bergh, J. (2007). *Marketing communications: A European perspective*. Harlow: FT Prentice Hall, 3rd ed.

De Sanctis, G., & Fulk, J. (Eds.). (1996). *Communication technology and organizational forms*. Thousand Oaks: Sage.

Decarolis, D. M., & Deeds, D. L. (1999). The impact of stocks and flows of organizational knowledge on firm performance: An empirical investigation of the biotechnology industry. *Strategic Management Journal, 20*(10), 953–968. doi:10.1002/(SICI)1097-0266(199910)20:10<953::AID-SMJ59>3.0.CO;2-3

DeLong, D. W., & Fahey, L. (2000). Diagnosing culture barriers to knowledge management. *The Academy of Management Executive, 14*(4), 113–127.

Desouza, K. (2005). Vital dimensions of mission-critical organizations. *KM Review, 8*(3), 28–31.

Desouza, K. C., Chattaraj, A., & Kraft, G. (2003). Supply chain perspectives to knowledge management: Research propositions. *Journal of Knowledge Management, 7*(3), 129–138. doi:10.1108/13673270310485695

Dess, G. G., & Davis, P. S. (1984). Porter's (1980) generic strategies as determinants of strategic group membership and organizational performance. *Academy of Management Journal, 27*(3), 467–488. doi:10.2307/256040

DeTienne, D. R., & Koberg, C. S. (2002). The impact of environmental and organizational factors on discontinuous innovation within high-technology industries. *IEEE Transactions on Engineering Management, 49*, 352–364. doi:10.1109/TEM.2002.806719

DeTienne, K. B., Dyer, G., Hoopes, C., & Harris, S. (2004). Toward a model of effective knowledge management and directions for future research: Culture, leadership, and CKOs. *Journal of Leadership & Organizational Studies, 10*(4), 26–43. doi:10.1177/107179190401000403

Di Maria, E., & Micelli, S. (2007). Imprese del *made in Italy*, competitività e innovazione. In G. Volpato (Ed.), *Il knowledge management come strumento competitivo. Un confronto intersettoriale*. Roma: Carocci.

Dictionary.com. (n.d.). Pattern. In *Dictionary.com unabridged (v 1.1)*. Random House, Inc. Retrieved on June 11, 2007, from http://dictionary.reference.com/browse/pattern

Dijkstra, E. W. (1976). *A discipline of programming*. Prentice Hall. Henderson, J. C., & Venkatraman, N. (1992). Strategic alignment: A model for organizational transformation through information technology. In T.A. Kocham & M. Useem (Eds.), *Transforming organizations*. New York: Oxford University Press.

Dodgson, M. (1993). Organizational learning: A review of some literatures. *Organization Studies, 14*(3), 375–394. doi:10.1177/017084069301400303

Dodgson, M., Gann, D., & Salter, A. (2006). The role of technology in the shift towards open innovation: The case of Procter & Gamble. *R&D Management, 36*(3), 333–346. Retrieved on June 25, 2009, from http://espace.library.uq.edu.au/eserv/UQ:78772/RADM_03603002-2.pdf

Donate, M., & Guadamillas, F. (2007). The relationship between innovation and knowledge strategies: Its impacts on business performance. *International Journal of Knowledge Management Studies, 1*(3/4), 388–422. doi:10.1504/IJKMS.2007.012532

Dougherty, D. (1992). Interpretive barriers to successful product innovation in large firms. *Organization Science, 3*(2), 179–202. doi:10.1287/orsc.3.2.179

Dutton, J. E., Dukerich, J. M., & Harquail, C. V. (1994). Organizational images and member identification. *Administrative Science Quarterly, 39*(2), 239–263. doi:10.2307/2393235

Dyer, J. H. (1997). Effective interfirm collaboration: How transactors minimize transaction costs and maximize transaction value. *Strategic Management Journal, 18*(7), 535–556. doi:10.1002/(SICI)1097-0266(199708)18:7<535::AID-SMJ885>3.0.CO;2-Z

Dyer, J. H., & Singh, H. (1998). The relational view: Cooperative strategies and sources of interorganizational competitive advantage. *Academy of Management Review, 23*(4), 660–679. doi:10.2307/259056

Dyer, N. A. (1998). What's in a relationship (other than relations)? *Insurance Brokers Monthly & Insurance Adviser, 48*(7), 16–17.

Earl, M. (2001). Knowledge management strategies: Toward a taxonomy. *Journal of Management Information Systems, 18*(1), 215-233.

Earl, M. J. (1996). An organizational approach to IS strategy making. In M. J. Earl (Ed.), *Information management-the organizational dimension* (pp. 136–170). Oxford: Oxford University Press.

Ebert, C., & De Neve, P. (2001). Surviving global software development. *IEEE Software*, (March/April): 62–69. doi:10.1109/52.914748

Edlington, S. (2003, January 20). Future perfect? *Caterer & Hotelkeeper*, 26.

Edvinsson, L. (1996). Knowledge management at Skandia. *The Knowledge Challenge Conference*, MCE, Brussels, 30-31.

Edvinsson, L., & Malone, M. S. (1997). *Intellectual capital: Realizing your company's true value by finding its hidden brainpower.* New York: Harper Business.

Eisenhardt, K. M. (1989). Building theories from case study research. *Academy of Management Review, 14*(4), 532–550. doi:10.2307/258557

Eisenhardt, K. M., & Santos, F. M. (2002). Knowledge based view: A new theory of strategy? In A. M. Pettigrew, H. Thomas & R. Whittington (Eds.), *Handbook of strategy and management* (pp. 139-164). London: Sage Publications.

Elenurm, T. (2003). Knowledge management development challenges of transition economy organisations representing different value creation models. *Electronic Journal of Knowledge Management, 1*(2), 47-56. Retrieved on November 12, 2008, from http://www.ejkm.com/volume-1/volume1-issue-2/issue2-art5-elenurm.pdf

Emmanuelides, P. A. (1993). Towards an integrative framework of performance in product development projects. *Journal of Engineering and Technology Management, 10*(4), 363–392. doi:10.1016/0923-4748(93)90029-I

Ericsson.™ (2008). Retrieved on January 2, 2009, from http://www.ericsson.com/ericsson/press/releases/20050215-980794.shtml

Euroforum. (1998). *Medición del capital intelectual: Modelo intelect.* Madrid: Instituto Universitario Euroforum Escorial.

Everatt, D., & Morrison, A. (2001). Quest foods. Asia Pacific and the CRM initiative. *Ivey Business Journal, 66*(1), 37–46.

Fahey, L., & Narayanan, V. K. (1986). *Macroenvironmental analysis for strategic management.* St. Paul: West Publishing Company.

Farh, J. L., Christopher, E. P., & Lin, S. C. (1997). Impetus for action: A cultural analysis of justice and organizational citizenship behavior in Chinese society. *Administrative Science Quarterly, 42*(3), 421–444. doi:10.2307/2393733

Feldman, D. C., & Doerpinghaus, H. I. (1992). Patterns of part-time employment. *Journal of Vocational Behavior, 41*(3), 282–294. doi:10.1016/0001-8791(92)90030-4

Fiol, C. M., & Lyles, M. A. (1985). Organizational learning. *Academy of Management Review, 10*(4), 803–813. doi:10.2307/258048

Firestone, J. M., & McElroy, M. W. (2005). Doing knowledge management. *The Learning Organization, 12*(2), 189–212. doi:10.1108/09696470510583557

Fjeldstad, O. D., & Haanaes, K. (2001). Strategy tradeoff in the knowledge and network Economy. *Business Strategy Review, 12*(1), 1–10. doi:10.1111/1467-8616.00160

Fleming, L. (2001). Recombinant uncertainty in technological research. *Management Science, 47*, 117–132. doi:10.1287/mnsc.47.1.117.10671

Ford, D. (2001). *Trust and knowledge management: The seeds of success.* Working Paper WP 01-08. Kingston, Ontario, Canada: Queen's KBE Center for Knowledge-Based Enterprises, Queen's School of Business. Retrieved on October 25, 2006, from http://business.queensu.ca/knowledge/workingpapers/working/working_01-08.pdf

Fraser, J., Fraser, N., & McDonald, F. (2000). The strategic challenge of electronic commerce. *Supply Chain Management: An International Journal, 5*(1), 7–14. doi:10.1108/13598540010312936

Frery, F. (2006). The fundamental dimensions of strategy. *Sloan Management Review, 48*(1), 71–75.

Friedlander, F. (1983). Patterns of individual and organizational learning. In S. Srivastva & Associates (Eds.), *The executive mind: New insights on managerial thought and action.* San Francisco: Jossey-Bass.

Fry, L. W., & Slocum, J. W. (1984). Technology structure and workgroup effectiveness: A test of a contingency model. *Academy of Management Journal, 27*(2), 221–246. doi:10.2307/255923

Fuji Xerox. (2002). Retrieved from http://www.fujixerox.com/eng/company/ecology/report2002/2002e-01.pdf

Gabay, J. J. (2000). *Successful cybermarketing in a week.* Institute of Management, Hodder & Stoughton

Galbreath, J., & Rogers, T. (1999). Customer relationship leadership: A leadership and motivation model for the twenty-first century business. *The TQM Magazine, 11*(3), 161–171. doi:10.1108/09544789910262734

Garavelli, C., Gorgoglione, M., & Scozzi, B. (2004). Knowledge management strategy and organization: A perspective of analysis. *Knowledge and Process Management, 11*(4), 273-282.

Garcia, M. L., & Bray, O. H. (1997). *Fundamentals of technology roadmapping.* Strategic Business Development Department Sandia National Laboratories.

Gates, B. (1999). *Business @ the speed of thought: Using a digital nervous system.* New York: Warner Books, Inc.

Gattiker, U. E., Perlusz, S., & Bohmann, K. (2000). Using the Internet for B2B activities: A review and future directions for research. *Internet Research: Electronic Networking Applications and Policy, 10*(2), 126–140. doi:10.1108/10662240010322911

Geisler, E. (2001). Organizing for e-business: The implementation of management principles in electronic commerce. Retrieved from http://www.stuart.iit.edu/faculty/workingpapers/geisler/organizin g%20for%20 e-business.pdf

Gereffi, G., Humphrey, J., & Sturgeon, T. (2005). The governance of global value chains. *Review of International Political Economy, 12*(1), 78–104. doi:10.1080/09692290500049805

Ghosh, T. (2004). *Creating incentives for knowledge sharing.* Retrieved on June 25, 2009, from http://myoops.org/twocw/mit/NR/rdonlyres/Sloan-School-of-Management/15-575Spring-2004/72ACA0F6-3943-4C1F-AB7F-0013602D7A61/0/tanu_15575.pdf

Ghosh, T. (2004). Creating incentives for knowledge sharing. Retrieved from http://ocw.mit.edu/NR/ rdonlyres/Sloan-School-of-Management/15-575Spring-2004/72ACA0F6-3943-4C1F-AB7F0 013602D7A61/0/tanu_15575.pdf

Gilbert, D. C., Powell-Perry, J., & Widijoso, S. (1999). Approaches by hotel to the use of the Internet as a relationship marketing tool. *Journal of Marketing Practice: Applied Marketing Science, 5*(1), 21–38. doi:10.1108/EUM0000000004549

Gledhill, B. (2002, February 28). Learning from history. *Caterer & Hotelkeeper*, 33.

Gold, A. H., Malhotra, A., & Segars, A. H. (2001). Knowledge management: An organizational capabilities perspective. *Journal of Management Information Systems, 18*(1), 185–214.

Gottschalk, P. (2000). Knowledge management systems: A comparison of law firms and consulting firms. *Information Science, 3*(3), 117–124.

Gottschalk, P. (2002). Toward a model of growth stages for knowledge management technology in law firms. *Information Science, 5*(2), 79–123.

Goymour, A. (2001, July 26). Host in the machine. *Caterer & Hotelkeeper*, 43-45.

Granovetter, M. (1973). The strength of weak ties. *American Journal of Sociology, 78*, 1360–1380. doi:10.1086/225469

Granovetter, M. (1985). Economic action and social structure: The problem of embeddedness. *American Journal of Sociology, 91*, 481–510. doi:10.1086/228311

Grant, R. (1996). Toward a knowledge-based theory of the firm. *Strategic Management Journal, 17*(Winter Special Issue), 109-122.

Grant, R. M. (1991). The resource-based theory of competitive advantage: Implications for strategy formulation. *California Management Review, 33*(3), 114–135.

Grant, R. M. (1991). The resource-based theory of competitive advantage: Implications for strategy formulation. *California Management Review, 33*(3), 114–135.

Grant, R. M. (1992). *Contemporary strategy analysis: Concepts, techniques, application.* Basil Blackwell/Cambridge.

Grant, R. M. (1996). Toward a knowledge-based theory of the firm. *Strategic Management Journal, 17*, 109–122. doi:10.1002/(SICI)1097-0266(199602)17:2<109::AID-SMJ796>3.0.CO;2-P

Grant, R. M. (1996a). Prospering in dynamically-competitive environments: Organizational capability as knowledge integration. *Organization Science, 7*(4), 375–387. doi:10.1287/orsc.7.4.375

Grant, R. M. (1996b). Toward a knowledge-based theory of the firm. *Strategic Management Journal, 17*(Winter Special Issue), 109-122.

Grant, R. M. (2002). *Contemporary strategy analysis. Concepts, techniques, and applications* (4th ed.). Boston: Blackwell Publishers.

Grant, R. M., & Baden-Fuller, C. (2004). A knowledge accessing theory of strategic alliances. *Journal of Management Studies, 41*(1), 61-79.

Gray, P., & Chan, Y. (2000). *Integrating knowledge management practices through a problem-solving framework.* Queen's Centre for Knowledge-Based Enterprises, WP 00-03.

Gray, S. J. (1988). Toward a theory of cultural influence on the development of accounting systems internationally. *Abacus, 8*(1), 1–15. doi:10.1111/j.1467-6281.1988.tb00200.x

Grönroos, C. (1994a). From marketing mix to relationship marketing: Towards a paradigm shift in marketing. *Management Decision, 32*(2), 4–20. doi:10.1108/00251749410054774

Grönroos, C. (1994b). From scientific management to service management: A management perspective for the age of service competition. *International Journal of Service Management, 5*(1), 5–20. doi:10.1108/09564239410051885

Grönroos, C. (1994c). Quo vadis, marketing? Toward a relationship marketing paradigm. *Journal of Marketing Management, 10*, 347–360.

Guadamillas, F., Donate, M., & Sánchez de Pablo, J. D. (2006). Sharing knowledge in strategic alliances to build collaborative advantage. In S. Martínez-Fierro, J. A. Medina-Garrido & J. Ruiz-Navarro (Eds.), *Utilizing information technology in developing strategic alliances among organizations* (pp. 99-122). Hershey, PA: IGI Global.

Gulati, R., & Garino, J. (2000, May-June). Get the right mix of bricks and mortar. *Harvard Business Review*, 107–114.

Gulati, R., Nohria, N., & Zaheer, L. (2000). Strategic networks. *Strategic Management Journal, 21*, 203–215. doi:10.1002/(SICI)1097-0266(200003)21:3<203::AID-SMJ102>3.0.CO;2-K

Gummesson, E. (1997a). Relationship marketing as a paradigm shift: Some conclusions from the 30R approach. *Management Decision, 35*(4), 267–272. doi:10.1108/00251749710169648

Gummesson, E. (1997b). In search of marketing equilibrium: Relationship marketing vs. hypercompetition. *Journal of Marketing Management, 13*(13), 421–430.

Gummesson, E. (1999). *Total relationship marketing–rethinking management: From 4Ps to 30Rs*. Oxford: Butterworth Heinemann.

Gunesekaran, A. (2005). Editorial, the build-to-order supply chain (BOSC): A competitive strategy for 21st century. *Journal of Operations Management, 23*(5), 419–422. doi:10.1016/j.jom.2004.10.004

Gupta, A. K., Smith, K. G., & Shalley, C. E. (2006). The interplay between exploration and exploitation. *Academy of Management Journal, 49*(4), 693–706.

Gupta, A., & Govindarajan, V. (2000). Knowledge management's social dimensions: Lesson from Nucor steel. *Sloan Management Review*, Fall, *41*(1), 71–80.

Gustafson, J. P., & Cooper, L. (1985). Collaboration in small groups. Theory and technique for the study of small-group processes. In A. D. Golman & M. H. Geller (Eds.), *Group relations reader* (pp. 139-150). Washington, D.C: A. K. Rice Institute Series.

Hackney, R., Burn, J., Cowan, E., & Dhillon, G. (2000). Challenging assumptions for strategic information systems planning: Theoretical perspectives. [CAIS]. *Communications of the Association for Information Systems, 3*(9), 2–24.

Hafeez, K., Zhang, Y., & Malak, N. (2002). Core competence for sustainable competitive advantage: A structured methodology for identifying core competence. *IEEE Transactions on Engineering Management, 49*, 28–35. doi:10.1109/17.985745

Hagan, L. (2000). *Improving journal quality with process improvement methods*. Whitepaper. The Sheridan Press.

Hahn, J., & Subramani, M. (2000). A framework of knowledge management systems: Issues and challenges for theory and practice. *Proc. of the 21st International Conference on Information systems* (pp. 302-312).

Hai-yan, K., & Baum, T. (2006). Skills and work in the hospitality sector: The case of hotel front office employees in China. *International Journal of Contemporary Hospitality Management, 18*(6), 509–518. doi:10.1108/09596110610681548

Hall, R. H. (1977). *Organizations: Structure and process*. Englewood Cliffs, NJ: Prentice-Hall.

Hamel, G. (1991). Competition for competence and inter-partner learning within international strategic alliances. *Strategic Management Journal, 12*, 83–103. doi:10.1002/smj.4250120908

Handzic, M., Lagumdzija, A., & Celjo, A. (2008). Auditing KM practices: Model and application. *KM Research & Practice, 6*(1), 90–99. doi:10.1057/palgrave.kmrp.8500163

Hansen, M. T., Nohria, N., & Tierney, T. (1999). What's your strategy for managing knowledge? *Harvard Business Review, 77*(2), 106–116.

Hansen, M. T., Nohria, N., & Tierney, T. (1999). What's your strategy for managing knowledge? *Harvard Business Review, 77*(2), 106–116.

Harker, M. J. (1999). Relationship marketing defined? An examination of current relationship marketing definitions. *Marketing Intelligence & Planning, 17*(1), 13–20. doi:10.1108/02634509910253768

Harrison, A. W., & Rainer, R. K. (1992). The influence of individual differences on skill in end-user computing. *Journal of Management Information Systems, 9*(1), 93–111. doi:10.1080/10580539208906858

Harry, K. H., Chow, K. L., & Lee, W. B. (2007). Knowledge management approach in build-to-order supply chains. *Industrial Management & Data Systems, 107*(6), 882–919. doi:10.1108/02635570710758770

Healy, M., Hastings, K., Brown, L., & Gardiner, M. (2001). The old, the new, and the complicated–a trilogy of marketing relationships. *European Journal of Marketing, 35*(1/ 2), 182–194. doi:10.1108/03090560110363418

Helfat, C. E., & Raubitschek, R. S. (2000). Product sequencing: Coevolution of knowledge, capabilities, and products. *Strategic Management Journal, 21*(10-11), 961–979. doi:10.1002/1097-0266(200010/11)21:10/11<961::AID-SMJ132>3.0.CO;2-E

Helper, S., MacDuffie, J. P., & Sabel, C. M. (2000). Pragmatic collaboration: Advancing knowledge while controlling opportunism. *Industrial and Corporate Change, 9*(3), 443–488. doi:10.1093/icc/9.3.443

Henczel, S. (2000). The information audit as a first step towards effective KM: An opportunity for the special librarian. *Inspel, 34*(3/4), 210–226.

Henderson, R., & Clark, K. B. (1990). Architectural innovation: The reconfiguration of existing product technologies and the failure of established firms. *Administrative Science Quarterly, 35*, 9–30. doi:10.2307/2393549

Herschel, R. T., & Jones, N. E. (2005). Knowledge management and business intelligence: The importance of integration. *Journal of Knowledge Management, 9*(4), 45–55. doi:10.1108/13673270510610323

Hildreth, P. M., & Kimble, C. (2002). The duality of knowledge. *Information Research, 8*(1). Retrieved on May 2, 2006, from http://informationr.net/ir/8-1/paper142.html

Hill, C. W., & Rothaermel, F. T. (2003). The performance of incumbent firms in the face of radical technological innovation. *Academy of Management Review, 28*, 257–274.

Hinkin, T. R., & Tracey, J. B. (2000). The cost of turnover. *The Cornell Hotel and Restaurant Administration Quarterly, 41*(3), 14–21.

Hislop, D. (2003). Linking human resource management and knowledge management via commitment: A review and research agenda. *Employee Relations, 25*(2), 182–202. doi:10.1108/01425450310456479

Hjalager, A. M., & Andersen, S. (2001). Tourism employment: Contingent work or professional career? *Employee Relations, 23*(2), 115–129. doi:10.1108/01425450110384165

Hochschild, A. R. (2003). *The managed heart: Commercialization of human feeling.* CA: University of California Press.

Hoffman, D. L., & Novak, T. P. (2000, May-June). How to acquire customers on the Web. *Harvard Business Review*, 179–188.

Hofstede, G. (1991). *Cultures and organizations: Software of the mind.* New York: McGraw-Hill.

Hohl, A., & Tisdell, C. (1995). Peripheral tourism: Development and management. *Annals of Tourism Research, 22*(3), 517–534. doi:10.1016/0160-7383(95)00005-Q

Holden, N. (2001). Knowledge management: Raising the spectre of the cross-cultural dimension. *Knowledge and Process Management, 8*(3), 155–163. doi:10.1002/kpm.117

Holmes, J. S., & Glass, J. T. (2004). Internal R&D-vital but only one piece of the innovation puzzle. *Research Technology Management, 47*(5), 7–10.

Holsapple, C. W., & Joshi, K. D. (2003). A knowledge management ontology. In C. W. Holsapple (Ed.), *Handbook on knowledge management: Vol.1, knowledge matters* (pp. 89-124). Berlin/Heidelberg: Springer-Verlag.

Holsapple, C. W., & Wu, J. (2008a). Does knowledge management pay off? In *Proceedings of 41ˢᵗ Hawaii International Conference on System Sciences*, Hawaii.

Holsapple, C. W., & Wu, J. (2008b). In search of a missing link. *Knowledge Management Research & Practice, 6*(1), 31–40. doi:10.1057/palgrave.kmrp.8500170

Holsapple, C. W., & Wu, J. (2009). *An elusive antecedent of superior firm performance: The knowledge management factor.* Working paper.

Hooff, B., & Ridder, J. (2002). Knowing what to manage: The development and application of a knowledge management Scan. *European Conference Organisational Knowledge, Learning & Capabilities, Athens.*

Hospital Consumer Assessment of Healthcare Providers and Systems. (2009). *HCAHPS – Facts Page.* Retrieved from http://www.hcahpsonline.org/facts.aspx

Hsu, D. H., & Lim, K. (2005). Knowledge bridging by biotechnology startups. *The Wharton School Working Paper Series* (pp. 1-32). Retrieved on June 25, 2009, from http://knowledge.wharton.upenn.edu/papers/1320.pdf

Hsu, D. H., & Lim, K. (2007). *The antecedents and innovation consequences of organizational knowledge brokering capability.* Mimeo. Wharton School, University of Pennsylvania.

Huber, G. P. (1991). Organizational learning: The contributing processes and the literatures. *Organization Science, 2*(1), 88–115. doi:10.1287/orsc.2.1.88

Hughes. (2006, February). *Journal of Usability, 1*(2), 76-90.

Hult, G. T. M., Snow, C. C., & Kandemir, D. (2003). The role of entrepreneurship in building cultural competitiveness in different organizational types. *Journal of Management, 29*(3), 401–426.

Hunt, J. (2000, July 26). The lights are on but no one's home. *Revolution (Staten Island, N.Y.),* 30–32.

Hunt, V. D. (1992). *Quality in America: How to implement a competitive quality program.* Chicago: Irwin Professional Publishing.

Huplic, V., Pouloudi, A., & Rzevski, G. (2002). Towards an integrated approach to knowledge management: 'Hard,' 'soft,' and 'abstract' issues. *Knowledge and Process Management, 9*(2), 90–102. doi:10.1002/kpm.134

Hurley, R. F., & Hult, G. T. M. (1998). Innovation, market orientation, and organizational learning: An integration and empirical examination. *Journal of Marketing, 42*(July), 42–54. doi:10.2307/1251742

Huston, L., & Sakkab, N. (2006). Connect and develop: Inside Procter and Gamble's new model for innovation. *Harvard Business Review, 84*(3), 58–66. Retrieved on June 25, 2009 from http://randgaenge.net/wp-content/uploads/hbr-connect-and-develop.pdf

Hylton, A. (2002). A KM initiative is unlikely to succeed without a knowledge audit. Retrieved from Knowledge-Board.com

Iaquinto, A. L. (1999). Can winners be losers? The case of the Deming prize for quality and performance among large Japanese manufacturing firms. *Managerial Auditing Journal, 14*(1/2), 28–35. doi:10.1108/02686909910245531

Iazzolino, G., & Pietrantonio, R. (2005, November). Auditing the organizational knowledge through a balanced scorecard-based approach. *International Conference on Knowledge Management in Asia Pacific (KMAP 2005).*

Ichijo, K., & Kohlbacher, F. (2007). The Toyota way of global knowledge creation the 'learn local, act global' strategy. *International Journal of Automotive Technology and Management, 7*(2/3), 116–134. doi:10.1504/IJATM.2007.014970

Ichijo, K., & Kohlbacher, F. (2008). Tapping tacit local knowledge in emerging markets–the Toyota way. *Knowledge Management Research & Practice, 6,* 173–186. doi:10.1057/kmrp.2008.8

Ichijo, K., von Krogh, G., & Nonaka, I. (1998). Knowledge enablers. In G. Von Krogh, J. Roos & D. Kleine (Eds.). *Knowing in firms. Understanding, managing, and measuring knowledge* (pp. 173-203). London: Sage Publications.

Inkpen, A. (1998). Learning and knowledge acquisition through international strategic alliances. *The Academy of Management Executive, 12*(4), 69–80.

Inkpen, A. C. (2000). A note on the dynamics of learning alliances: Competition, cooperation, and relative scope. *Strategic Management Journal, 21,* 775–779. doi:10.1002/1097-0266(200007)21:7<775::AID-SMJ111>3.0.CO;2-F

Inkpen, A. C., & Beamish, P. W. (1997). Knowledge, bargaining power, and the instability of international. *Joint Ventures Academy of Management Review, 22*(1), 177–202. doi:10.2307/259228

Ireland, R. D., Hitt, M. A., & Vaidyanath, D. (2002). Alliance management as a source of competitive advantage. *Journal of Management, 28*, 413–446. doi:10.1177/014920630202800308

ISO 8402. (1991). *Quality management and quality assurance; vocabulary*. International Organization for Standardization.

Janal, D. S. (2000). *Guide to marketing on the Internet*. John Wiley & Sons, Inc.

Janis, I. (1972). *Victims of GroupThink*. Houghton Mifflin.

Jayachandran, S., Sharma, S., Kaufman, P., & Raman, P. (2005). The role of relational information processes and technology use in customer relationship management. *Journal of Marketing, 69*(4), 77–192. doi:10.1509/jmkg.2005.69.4.177

Jennex, M. E., & Olfman, L. (2004). Assessing knowledge management success/effectiveness models. *Proceedings of the 37ᵗʰ Annual Hawaii International Conference on System Science*. IEEE Computer Society Press.

Jensen, R., & Szulanski, G. (2004). Stickiness and the adaptation of organizational practices in cross-border knowledge transfers. *Journal of International Business Studies, 35*(6), 508–523. doi:10.1057/palgrave.jibs.8400107

Jha, S., Noori, H., & Michela, J. L. (1996). The dynamics of continuous improvement: Aligning organizational attributes and activities for quality and productivity. *International Journal of Quality Science, 1*(1), 19–47. doi:10.1108/13598539610117975

Johannessen, J., Olaisen, J., & Olsen, B. (2001). Mismanagement of tacit knowledge: The importance of tacit knowledge, the danger of information technology, and what to do about it. *International Journal of Information Management, 21*, 3–20. doi:10.1016/S0268-4012(00)00047-5

Johanson, J., & Mattsson, L.-G. (1993). Internationalization in industrial systems–a network approach, strategies in global competition. In P. J. Buckley & P. N. Ghauri (Eds.), *The internationalization of the firm: A reader* (pp.303-22). London: Academic Press.

Johanson, J., & Vahlne, J. E. (1990). The mechanism of internationalization. *International Marketing Review, 7*(4), 11–24. doi:10.1108/02651339010137414

Jolliffe, L., & Farnsworth, R. (2003). Seasonality in tourism employment: Human resource challenges. *International Journal of Contemporary Hospitality Management, 15*(6), 312–316. doi:10.1108/09596110310488140

Jones, O. (2000). Innovation management as a postmodern phenomenon: The outsourcing of pharmaceutical R&D. *British Journal of Management, 11*, 341–356. doi:10.1111/1467-8551.00177

Jones, P. (2002). When successful product prevent strategic innovation. *Design Management Journal, 13*(2), 30–37.

Joplin B. (2001, March-April). Are we in danger of becoming CRM lemmings? *Customer Management*, 81-85.

Kagono, T. (1988). *The cognitive theory of organization*. Tokyo: Chikura Shobou (in Japanese).

Kalleberg, A. L. (2001). Organizing flexibility: The flexible firm in a new century. *British Journal of Industrial Relations, 39*(4), 479–504. doi:10.1111/1467-8543.00211

Kandampully, J., & Duddy, R. (1999a). Competitive advantage through anticipation, innovation, and relationships. *Management Decision, 37*(1), 51–56. doi:10.1108/00251749910252021

Kandampully, J., & Duddy, R. (1999b). Relationship marketing: A concept beyond primary relationship. *Marketing Intelligence & Planning, 17*(7), 315–323. doi:10.1108/02634509910301124

Kaplan, R. S., & Norton, D. P. (1992). The balanced scorecard-measures that drive performance. *Harvard Business Review*, (January/February): 71–79.

Kaptelinin, V., & Nardi, B. (2006). Acting with technology-activity theory and interaction design. Cambridge, MA: The MIT Press.

Katila, R. (2002). New product search over time: Past ideas in their prime? *Academy of Management Journal, 45*, 995–1010. doi:10.2307/3069326

Kayworth, T., & Leidner, D. (2003). Organizational culture as a knowledge resource. In C. W. Holsapple (Ed.), *Handbook on knowledge management, volume 1: Knowledge matters* (pp. 235-252). Berlin/Heidelberg: Springer-Verlag.

Keenoy, T. (1999). Human resource management as a hologram: A polemic. *Journal of Management Studies, 36*(1), 1–23. doi:10.1111/1467-6486.00123

Khalid, S. (2006). Organizational citizenship behavior, turnover intention, and absteenteism among hotel employees. *Malaysian Management Review, 41*(1), 1–11.

Khalil, O. E. M., & Harcar, T. D. (1999). Relationship marketing and data quality management. *SAM Advanced Management Journal, 64*(2).

Khan, W. A. (1990). Psychological conditions of personal engagement and disengagement at work. *Academy of Management Journal, 33*(4), 692–724. doi:10.2307/256287

Khanna, T., Gulati, R., & Nohria, N. (1998). The dynamics of learning alliances: Competition, cooperation, and relative scope. *Strategic Management Journal, 19*, 193–210. doi:10.1002/(SICI)1097-0266(199803)19:3<193::AID-SMJ949>3.0.CO;2-C

Kiczales, G., Lamping, J., Mendhekar, A., Maeda, C., Lopes, C., Loingtier, J.-M., & Irwin, J. (1997). Aspect-oriented programming. *Proceedings of the European Conference on Object-Oriented Programming, 1241*, 220–242.

Kim, C. W., & Mauborgne, R. (2005). *Blue ocean strategy: How to create uncontested market space and make competition irrelevant*. Boston, MA: Harvard Business School Press.

King, W. R., Chung, R., & Haney, M. (2008). Knowledge management and organizational learning. *Omega, 36*(2), 167–172. doi:10.1016/j.omega.2006.07.004

Kirkpatrick, D. (1998). *Evaluating training programs*. San Francisco: Berrett-Koehler Publishers.

Kluge, J., Stein, W., & Licht, T. (2001). *Knowledge unplugged*. New York: Palgrave.

Knox, A. (2002). HRM in the Australian luxury hotel industry: Signs of innovation? *Employment Relations Record, 2*(2), 59–68.

Knox, A., & Walsh, J. (2005). Organizational flexibility and HRM in the hotel industry: evidence from Australia. *Human Resource Management Journal, 15*(1), 57–75. doi:10.1111/j.1748-8583.2005.tb00140.x

Koene, B., & Riemsdijk, M. (2005). Managing temporary workers: Work identity, diversity, and operational HR choices. *Human Resource Management Journal, 15*(1), 76–92. doi:10.1111/j.1748-8583.2005.tb00141.x

Kogut, B., & Zander, U. (1992). Knowledge of the firm, combinative capabilities, and the replication of technology. *Organization Science, 3*(3), 383–397. doi:10.1287/orsc.3.3.383

Kogut, B., & Zander, U. (1996). What firms do? Coordination, identity, and learning. *Organization Science, 7*(5), 502–518. doi:10.1287/orsc.7.5.502

Koh, S. C. L., & Tan, K. H. (2006). Translating knowledge of supply chain uncertainty into business strategy and actions. *Journal of Manufacturing Technology Management, 17*(4), 472–485. doi:10.1108/17410380610662898

Konovsky, M. A., Ellito, J., & Pugh, S. D. (1994). *The dispositional and contextual predictors of citizenship behavior in Mexico*. New Orleans, LA: Unpublished manuscript, Tulane University.

Kotha, S., & Vadlamani, L. (1995). Assessing generic strategies: An empirical investigation of two competing typologies in discrete manufacturing industries. *Strategic Management Journal, 16*(1), 75–83. doi:10.1002/smj.4250160108

KPMG. (2002). Retrieved from www.kpmg.com/aci/docs/aci_uk.doc

Krackhardt, D. M., & Porter, L. W. (1985). When friends leave: A structural analysis of the relationship between turnover and stayers attitudes. *Administrative Science Quarterly, 30,* 242–261. doi:10.2307/2393107

Krackhart, D., & Porter, W. E. (1986). The snowball effect: Turnover embedded in communication networks. *The Journal of Applied Psychology, 71*(1), 50–55. doi:10.1037/0021-9010.71.1.50

Kramar, R. (2002). Human resource management in Australia: Is it a hologram? *Employment Relations Record, 2*(2), 80–93.

Krippendorf, K., & Butter, R. (1984). Product semantics: Exploring the symbolic qualities of form in innovation. *The Journal of the Industrial Designers Society of America, 3,* 4–9.

Krogh, G., Nonaka, I., & Aben, M. (2001). Making the most of your company's knowledge: A strategic framework. *Long Range Planning, 34*(3), 421–439. doi:10.1016/S0024-6301(01)00059-0

Krol, C. (1999, May). A new age: It's all about relationships. *Advertising Age, 70*(21), S1–S4.

Krugman, P. (1991). *Geography and trade.* Boston: MIT Press.

Kuomi, I. (2002). *Networks of innovation. Change and meaning in the age of the Internet.* Oxford: Oxford University Press.

Kurzweil, R. (2005). *The singularity is near: When humans transcend biology.* New York: Viking Adult.

Kusunoki, K., Nonaka, I., & Nagata, A. (1998). Organizational capabilities in product development of Japanese firms: A conceptual framework and empirical findings. *Organization Science, 9*(6), 699–718. doi:10.1287/orsc.9.6.699

Kvist, A., & Klefsjo, B. (2006). Which service quality dimensions are important in inbound tourism?: A case study in a peripheral location. *Managing Service Quality, 16*(5), 520–537. doi:10.1108/09604520610686151

Lai, P. C., & Baum, T. (2005). Just-in-time labour supply in the hotel sector: The role of agencies. *Employee Relations, 27*(1), 86–102. doi:10.1108/01425450510569328

Lamming, R. C., Caldwell, N. G., Harrison, D. A., & Phillips, W. (2001). Transparency in supply relationships: Concepts and practice. *The Journal of Supply Chain Management, 37*(4), 4–10. doi:10.1111/j.1745-493X.2001.tb00107.x

Lane, P. J., & Lubatkin, M. (1998). Relative absorptive capacity and interorganizational learning. *Strategic Management Journal, 19*(5), 461–477. doi:10.1002/(SICI)1097-0266(199805)19:5<461::AID-SMJ953>3.0.CO;2-L

Lanjouw, J. O., & Schankerman, M. (2001). Characteristics of patent litigation: A window on competition. *The Rand Journal of Economics, 32*(1), 129–151. doi:10.2307/2696401

Lanzara, G. F., & Patriotta, G. (2001). Technology and the courtroom: An inquiry into knowledge making in organizations. *Journal of Management Studies, 38*(7), 943–971. doi:10.1111/1467-6486.00267

Lave, J., & Wenger, E. (1991). *Situated Learning: Legitimate peripheral participation.* Cambridge, MA: Harvard University Press.

Lee, C. C., & Yang, J. (2000). Knowledge value chain. *Journal of Management Development, 19*(9), 783–793. doi:10.1108/02621710010378228

Lee, C., & Moreo, P. J. (2007). What do seasonal lodging operators need to know about seasonal workers? *International Journal of Hospitality Management, 26*(1), 148–160. doi:10.1016/j.ijhm.2005.11.001

Lee, H., & Choi, B. (2003). Knowledge management enablers, processes, and organisational performance: An integrative view and empirical examination. *Journal of Management Information Systems, 20*(1), 179–228.

Lee, K. C., Lee, S., & Kang, I. W. (2005). KMPI: Measuring knowledge management performance. *Information & Management, 42*(3), 469–482. doi:10.1016/j.im.2001.09.001

Lee, S. M., Kim, Y. R., & Lee, J. (1995). An empirical study of the relationships among end user information system acceptance, training, and effectiveness. *Journal of Management Information Systems, 12*(2), 189–202.

Lee-Kelley, L., Gilbert, D., & Mannicom, R. (2003). How e-CRM can enhance customer loyalty. *Marketing Intelligence & Planning, 21*(4), 239–248. doi:10.1108/02634500310480121

Leonard-Barton, D. A. (1995). *Wellsprings of knowledge.* Boston, MA: Harvard Business School Press.

Lev, B. (nd). *Communication knowledge capabilities.* Retrieved on December 23, 2003, from http://pages. stern.nyu.edu/~blev/communicating.doc

Levinson, D. (1987). Making employee performance evaluations work for you. *Nonprofit World, 5*(5), 28–30.

Levinthal, D. A., & March, J. G. (1993). The myopia of learning. *Strategic Management Journal, 14*, 95–112. doi:10.1002/smj.4250141009

Lewin, K. (1997). *Resolving social conflicts: Field theory in social science.* Washington, D.C.: American Psychological Association. Original work published in 1943.

Li, A., Oppenheim, J., Chaplain, C., Dinkelacker, D., Elgas, J., Ramos, J., et al. (2002). *NASA, better mechanisms needed for sharing, lessons learned.* Washington, D.C.: GAO Report, GAO.

Li, T., Nicholls, J. A. F., & Roslow, S. (1999). The relationship between market-driven learning and new product success in export markets. *International Marketing Review, 16*(6). doi:10.1108/02651339910300459

Liebowitz, J. (2007). Developing knowledge and learning strategies in mobile organisations. *International Journal Mobile Learning and Organizations, 1*(1), 5–14. doi:10.1504/IJMLO.2007.011186

Liebowitz, J., Rubenstein-Montano, B., McCaw, D., Buchwalter, J., Browning, C., Newman, B., & Rebeck, K., & theThe Knowledge Management Methodology Team. (2000). The knowledge audit. *Knowledge and Process Management, 7*(1), 3–10. doi:10.1002/(SICI)1099-1441(200001/03)7:1<3::AID-KPM72>3.0.CO;2-0

Lillrank, P., Shani, A. B., & Lindberg, P. (2001). Continuous improvement: Exploring alternative organizational designs. *Total Quality Management, 12*(1), 41–55. doi:10.1080/09544120020010084

Lin, L.-H. (2009). Mergers and acquisitions, alliances and technology development: An empirical study of the global auto industry. *International Journal of Technology Management, 48*(3), 295–307. doi:10.1504/IJTM.2009.024950

Lin, N. (2001). *Social capital: A theory of social structure and action.* Cambridge, New York: Cambridge University Press.

Lindgreen, A., & Crawford, I. (1999). Implementing, monitoring, and measuring a programme of relationship marketing. *Marketing Intelligence & Planning, 17*(5), 231–239. doi:10.1108/02634509910285646

Long, G., Hogg, M. K., Hartley, M., & Angold, S. J. (1999). Relationship marketing and privacy: Exploring the thresholds. *Journal of Marketing Practice: Applied Marketing Science, 5*(1), 4–20. doi:10.1108/EUM0000000004548

Long, M. M., & Schiffman, L. G. (2000). Consumption values and relationships: Segmenting the market for frequency programs. *Journal of Consumer Marketing, 17*(3). doi:10.1108/07363760010329201

Longenecker, C. O., Dwyer, D. J., & Stansfield, T. C. (1998, March-April). Barriers and gateways to workforce productivity. *Industrial Management (Des Plaines)*, 21–28.

Lopez, K. (2001). How to measure the value of knowledge management. *Knowledge Management Review*, March/April.

Loshin, D. (2001). *Enterprise knowledge management: The data quality approach.* New York: Morgan Kauffman. virtue. (n.d.). *The American heritage® dictionary of the English language, fourth edition.* Retrieved on October 25, 2006, from Dictionary.com Web site http://dictionary.reference.com/browse/virtue

Lubatkin, M. H., Simsek, Z., Ling, Y., & Veiga, J. F. (2006). Ambidexterity and performance in small- to medium-sized firms: The pivotal role of top management team behavioral integration. *Journal of Management, 32*(5), 646–672. doi:10.1177/0149206306290712

Luca, L. M. D., & Atuahene-Gima, K. (2007). Market knowledge dimensions and cross-functional collaboration: Examining the different routes to product innovation performance. *Journal of Marketing, 71*(1), 95–112. doi:10.1509/jmkg.71.1.95

Lucas, R., & Deery, M. (2004). Significant developments and emerging issues in human resource management. *Hospital Management, 23*(5), 459–472. doi:10.1016/j.ijhm.2004.10.005

Luck, D. (2008). The importance of data within contemporary CRM. In H. Rahman (Ed.), *Data mining applications for empowering knowledge societies* (pp. 96-109). Hershey, PA: Information Science Reference.

Luck, D., & Lancaster, G. (2003). E-CRM: Customer relationship marketing in the hotel industry. *Managerial Auditing Journal–Accountability and the Internet, 18*(3), 213–232.

Luftman, J., & McLean, E. R. (2004). Key issues for IT executives. *MIS Quarterly Executive, 3*(2), 89–104.

Lun, J., & Huang, X. (2007). How to motivate your older employees to excel? The impact of commitment on older employees' performance in the hospitality industry. *International Journal of Hospitality Management, 26*(4), 793–806. doi:10.1016/j.ijhm.2006.08.002

Lundvall, B., & Nielsen, P. (2007). Knowledge management and innovation performance. *International Journal of Manpower, 28*(3/4), 207–223. doi:10.1108/01437720710755218

Luo, Y. (2008). Structuring interorganizational cooperation: The role of economic integration in strategic alliances. *Strategic Management Journal, 29*(6), 617–637. doi:10.1002/smj.677

Lyles, M. A., & Schwenk, C. R. (1992). Top management, strategy, and organizational knowledge structures. *Journal of Management Studies, 29*(2), 155–174. doi:10.1111/j.1467-6486.1992.tb00658.x

Maier, R., & Remus, U. (2002). Defining process-oriented knowledge management strategies. *Knowledge and Process Management, 9*(2), 103–118. doi:10.1002/kpm.136

Main, H. (1995). Information technology and the independent hotel–failing to make the connection. *International Journal of Contemporary Hospitality Management, 7*(6), 30–32. doi:10.1108/09596119510095370

Malone, T., & Crowston, K. (1994). The interdisciplinary study of coordination. *ACM Computing Surveys, 26*(1), 87–119. doi:10.1145/174666.174668

March, J. G. (1991). Exploration and exploitation in organizational learning. *Organization Science, 2*, 71–87. doi:10.1287/orsc.2.1.71

March, J. G., & Simon, H. A. (1958). *Organizations.* Cambridge, MA: Blackwell Publishers.

Marjanovic, O. (2005). Towards IS supported coordination in emergent business processes. *Business Process Management Journal, 11*(5), 476–487. doi:10.1108/14637150510619830

Marques, D. P., & Simon, F. J. G. (2006). The effect of knowledge management practices on firm performance. *Journal of Knowledge Management, 10*(3), 143–156. doi:10.1108/13673270610670911

Martin, J. (1995). *The great transition.* New York: AMACOM.

Martinsons, M. G., & Davidson, R. (2003). Cultural issues and IT management: Looking ahead. Guest editorial . *IEEE Transactions on Engineering Management, 50*(1), 3–7. doi:10.1109/TEM.2003.808299

Maskell, P. (2001). Towards a knowledge-based theory of the geographical cluster. *Industrial and Corporate Change, 10*, 919–941. doi:10.1093/icc/10.4.921

MatrixOne. (2008). Retrieved on February 2, 2005, from http://www.matrixone.com/index.html

McDavid, D. W.(n.d.). A standard for business architecture. *IBM Systems Journal, 38*(1).

McDonald, W. J. (1998). *Direct marketing: An integrated approach*. McGraw-Hill International Editions.

McGrath, R. G. (2001). Exploratory learning, innovative capacity, and managerial oversight. *Academy of Management Journal, 44,* 118–131. doi:10.2307/3069340

McKeen, J. D., & Staples, D. S. (2003). Knowledge managers: Who they are and what they do. In C. W. Holsapple (Ed.), *Handbook on knowledge management: Vol.1, knowledge matters* (pp. 21-41). Berlin/Heidelberg: Springer-Verlag.

McLaughlin, S., Paton, R. A., & Macbeth, D. K. (2008). Barrier impact on organisational learning within complex organisations. *Journal of Knowledge Management, 12*(2), 107–123. doi:10.1108/13673270810859550

Mesquita, L. F., Anand, J., & Brush, T. H. (2008). Comparing the resource-based and relational views: Knowledge transfer and spillover in vertical alliances. *Strategic Management Journal, 29,* 913–941. doi:10.1002/smj.699

Mikkola, J. H. (2001). Portfolio management of R&D projects: Implications for innovation management. *Technovation, 21,* 423–435. doi:10.1016/S0166-4972(00)00062-6

Miles, R., & Snow, C. H. (1978). *Organizational strategy, structure, and processes.* New York: McGraw-Hill.

Miller, B. K., Bierly, P. E., & Daly, P. S. (2007). The knowledge strategy orientation scale: Individual perceptions of firm-level phenomena. *Journal of Managerial Issues, 19*(3), 414–435.

Miltenburg, J. (2005). *Manufacturing strategy: How to formulate and implement a winning plan.* Portland, OR: Productivity Press.

Mintzberg, H., & Waters, J. A. (1985). Of strategies, deliberate and emergent. *Strategic Management Journal, 6,* 257–272. doi:10.1002/smj.4250060306

Moffett, S., McAdam, R., & Parkinson, S. (2002). Developing a model for technology and cultural factors in knowledge management: A factor analysis. *Knowledge and Process Management, 9*(4), 237–255. doi:10.1002/kpm.152

Moffett, S., McAdam, R., & Parkinson, S. (2003). An empirical analysis of knowledge management applications. *Journal of Knowledge Management, 7*(3), 6–26. doi:10.1108/13673270310485596

Mohsin, A. (2003). Backpackers in the Northern Territory of Australia-motives, behaviours, and satisfactions. *International Journal of Tourism Research, 5*(2), 113–131. doi:10.1002/jtr.421

Moncrief, W. C., & Cravens, D. (1999). Technology and the changing marketing world. *Marketing Intelligence & Planning, 17*(7), 329–332. doi:10.1108/02634509910301142

Mooney, L. (2007). BPM–a whole new world of opportunity. *KM World, January,* 54-55.

Moorman, R. H., & Harland, L. K. (2002). Temporary employees as good citizens: Factors influencing their OCB performance. *Journal of Business and Psychology, 17*(2), 171–187. doi:10.1023/A:1019629330766

Morgan, R. M., & Hunt, S. D. (1994, July). The commitment-trust theory of relationship marketing. *Journal of Marketing, 58,* 20–38. doi:10.2307/1252308

Mowery, D. C., & Rosenberg, N. (1979). The influence of market demand upon innovation: A critical review of some empirical studies. *Research Policy, 8,* 102–153. doi:10.1016/0048-7333(79)90019-2

Mowery, D. C., Oxley, J. E., & Silverman, B. S. (1998). Technological overlap and interfirm cooperation: Implications for the resource-based view of the firm. *Research Policy, 27,* 507–523. doi:10.1016/S0048-7333(98)00066-3

Mu, J., Peng, G., & Love, E. (2008). Interfirm networks, social capital, and knowledge flow. *Journal of Knowledge Management, 12*(4), 86–100. doi:10.1108/13673270810884273

Mukherji, A., Kedia, B. L., Parente, R., & Kock, N. (2004). Strategies, structures, and information architectures: Toward international gestalts. *Problems and Perspectives in Management, 3*(1), 181–195.

Muniz, A. M., & O'Guinn, T. (2001). Brand community. *The Journal of Consumer Research, 27,* 412–432. doi:10.1086/319618

Murphy, J. M. (2001, March-April). Customer excellence: From the top down. *Customer Management*, 36-41.

Mylonopoulos, N., & Tsoukas, H. (2003). Technological and organizational issues in knowledge management. *Knowledge and Process Management*, *10*(3), 139–143. doi:10.1002/kpm.174

Nahapiet, J., & Ghoshal, S. (1998). Social capital, intellectual capital, and the organizational advantage. *Academy of Management Review*, *23*(2), 242–266. doi:10.2307/259373

National Association of State PIRGs. (2004). *Mistakes do happen.*

National Electronic Library Health. (2001). *Conducting a knowledge audit.* Retrieved from http://www.nelh.nhs.uk/knowledge_management/km2/audit_toolkit.asp

Nelson, R. R., & Winter, S. G. (1982). *An evolutionary theory of economic change.* Boston, MA: The Belknap Press of Harvard University Press.

Nemati, H. R., & Barko, C. D. (2003). Key factors for achieving organizational data-mining success. *Industrial Management & Data Systems*, *103*(4), 282–292. doi:10.1108/02635570310470692

Nicolas, R. (2004). Knowledge management impacts on decision making process. *Journal of Knowledge Management*, *8*(1), 20–31. doi:10.1108/13673270410523880

Nissen, M. E. (2001). Beyond electronic disintermediation through multiagent systems. *Logistics Information Management*, *14*(4), 256–275. doi:10.1108/EUM0000000005721

Nissen, M., Kamel, M., & Sengupta, K. (2000). Integrated analysis and design of knowledge systems and processes. *Information Resources Management Journal*, *13*(1), 24–43.

Nonaka, I. (1994). A dynamic theory of organizational knowledge creation. *Organization Science*, *5*(1), 14–37. doi:10.1287/orsc.5.1.14

Nonaka, I. (1994). A dynamic theory of organizational knowledge creation. *Organization Science*, *5*(1), 14–37. doi:10.1287/orsc.5.1.14

Nonaka, I., & Peltokorpi, V. (2006). Objectivity and subjectivity in knowledge management: A review of 20 top articles. *Knowledge and Process Management*, *13*(2), 73–82. doi:10.1002/kpm.251

Nonaka, I., & Takeuchi, H. (1995). *The knowledge-creating company.* New York: Oxford University Press.

Nonaka, I., Toyama, R., & Konno, N. (2000). SECI, Ba, and leadership: A unified model of dynamic knowledge creation. *Long Range Planning*, *33*(1), 5–34. doi:10.1016/S0024-6301(99)00115-6

Nonaka, I., Toyama, R., & Nagata, A. (2000). A firm as a knowledge creating entity: A new perspective on the theory of the firm. *Industrial and Corporate Change*, *9*(1), 1–20. doi:10.1093/icc/9.1.1

Nousala, S., Miles, A., Kilpatrick, B., & Hall, W. P. (2005, November 28-29). Building knowledge sharing communities using team expertise access maps (TEAM). *Proceedings from KMAP05: Knowledge Management in Asia Pacific, Wellington, NZ.* Retrieved on June 25, 2009, from http://www.orgs-evolution-knowledge.net/Index/DocumentKMOrgTheoryPapers/NousalaEtAl-2005KnowledgeSharingCommunitesExpertiseMapping.pdf

Object Management Group. (2008). *Business motivation model.* OMG document number formal/2008-08-02. Standard document. Retrieved from http://www.omg.org/spec/BMM/1.0/PDF

Oinas-Kukkonen, H. (2004). The 7C model for organizational knowledge creation and management. Retrieved on October 25, 2006, from http://www.oasis.oulu.fi/publications/OKLC-04-hok.pdf

Okes, D., & Westcott, R. (2000). *The certified quality manager handbook.* Milwaukee, WI: Quality Press.

Oliveira, M. (1999). Core competencies and the knowledge of the firm. In M. A. Hitt, et al. (Eds.), *Dynamic strategic resources: Development, diffusion, and integration* (pp. 17-41). New York: John Wiley and Sons.

Olla, P., & Holm, J. (2006). The role of knowledge management in the space industry: Important or superfluous? *Journal of Knowledge Management, 10*(2), 3–7. doi:10.1108/13673270610656584

Opdahl, A. L. (1997, June). A model for comparing approaches to IS-architecture alignment. In B. Irgens, K. Ellingsen, E. Mathisen, N. M. Nielsen & Z. Uddin Quazi (Eds.), *Proceedings of "Norsk konferanse om organisasjoners bruk av IT"* (pp. 67-79). Bodö/Norway.

Organ, D. W., Podsakoff, P. M., & MacKenzie, S. B. (2006). *Organizational citizenship behavior: Its nature, antecedents, and consequences.* CA: Sage Publications Inc.

Orlikowski, W. (2002). Knowing in practice: Enacting a collective capability in distributed organizing. *Organization Science, 13*(3), 249–273. doi:10.1287/orsc.13.3.249.2776

Osono, E., Shimizu, N., Tackeuchi, H., & Dorton, J. K. (2008). *Extreme Toyota. Radical contradictions that drive success at the world's best manufacturer.* Hoboken, NJ: John Wiley and Sons Ltd.

Ossher, H., & Tarr, P. (n.d.). Multi-dimensional separation of concerns and the hyperspace approach. IBM, T.J. Watson Research Center.

Overell, S. (2004, March 31). (in press). Customers are not there to be hunted. *FT Management,* 2.

Oxley, J. E., & Sampson, R. C. (2004). The scope and gobernance of international R&D alliances. *Strategic Management Journal, 25*, 723–749. doi:10.1002/smj.391

Parikh, M. (2001). Knowledge management framework for high-tech research and development. *Engineering Management Journal, 13*(3), 27–33.

Paxton, L. J. (2006). Managing innovative space missions: Lessons from NASA. *Journal of Knowledge Management, 10*(2), 8–21. doi:10.1108/13673270610656593

Peppers, D., & Rogers, M. (1999, January-February). Is your company ready for one-to-one marketing? *Harvard Business Review, 77*(1), 151–160.

Perez-Soltero, A., Barcelo-Valenzuela, M., Sanchez-Schmitz, G., Martin-Rubio, F., & Palma-Mendez, J.

(2006). Knowledge audit methodology with emphasis on core processes. *European and Mediterranean Conference on Information Systems (EMCIS),* Alicante, Spain.

Peters, T. (1987). *Thriving on chaos.* New York: Harper and Row.

Pfeffer, J. (2001). Fighting the war for talent is hazardous to your organization's health. *Organizational Dynamics, 29*, 248–259. doi:10.1016/S0090-2616(01)00031-6

Pfeffer, J. (2002). To build a culture of innovation, avoid conventional management wisdom. In F. Hesselbein, M. Goldsmith & I. Somerville (Eds.), *Leading for innovation: And organizing for results* (pp. 95-104). San Francisco: Jossey-Bass.

Pfeffer, J. (2007). A modest proposal: How we might change the process and product of managerial research. *Academy of Management Journal, 50*(6), 1334–1345.

Phaal, R., Farrukh, C., & Probert, D. (2001). *Technology roadmapping: Linking technology resources to business objectives.* Centre for Technology Management, University of Cambridge.

Piccoli, G., Ahmad, R., & Ives, B. (2001). Web-based virtual learning environments: A research framework and a preliminary assessment of effectiveness in basic IT skills training. *MIS Quarterly, 25*(4), 401–426. doi:10.2307/3250989

Pine, B. J., & Gilmore, J. (1999). *The experience economy.* Boston: Harvard Business School Press.

Piore, M. J., & Sabel, C. M. (1984). *The second industrial divide.* New York: Basic Books.

Pitt, M., & Clarke, K. (1999). Competing on competence: A knowledge perspective on the management of strategic innovation. *Technology Analysis and Strategic Management, 11*, 301–316. doi:10.1080/095373299107375

Podsakoff, P. M., MacKenzie, S. B., Paine, J. B., & Bachrach, D. G. (2000). Organizational citizenship behaviors: A critical review of the theoretical and empirical literature and suggestions for future research. *Journal of Management, 26*(3), 513–563. doi:10.1177/014920630002600307

Polanyi, M. (1958). *Personnal knowledge: Towards a post-critical philosophy.* Chicago: University of Chicago Press.

Polanyi, M. (1966). *The tacit dimension.* London: Routledge & Kegan P.

Poon, A. (1993). *Tourism, technology and competitive strategies.* UK: C.A.B International.

Porter, M. (1996). What is strategy? *Harvard Business Review,* (November-December): 61–78.

Porter, M. E. (1980). *Competitive strategy.* New York: Free Press.

Portes, A. (1998). Social capital: Its origins and application in modern sociology. *Annual Review of Sociology, 24,* 1–24. doi:10.1146/annurev.soc.24.1.1

Powell, T. C. (1995). Total quality management as competitive advantage: A review and empirical study. *Strategic Management Journal, 16,* 15–37. doi:10.1002/smj.4250160105

Prahalad, C. K. (1993). The role of core competencies in the corporation. *Research in Technology Management, 36*(6), 40–47.

Prahalad, C. K., & Krishnan, M. S. (2008). *The new age of innovation: Driving cocreated value through global networks.* Columbus: McGraw Hill.

Prahalad, C. K., & Ramaswamy, V. (2003). The new frontier of experience innovation. *MIT Sloan Management Review, 44,* 12–18.

Press Ganey. (2009). *Home|Press Ganey.* Retrieved from http://www.pressganey.com

Pringle, C. D., & Kroll, M. J. (1997). Why Trafalgar was won before it was fought: Lessons from resource-based theory. *The Academy of Management Executive, 11*(4), 73–89.

Pyke, F., Becattini, G., & Sengenberger, W. (Eds.). (1990). *Industrial districts and Interfirm cooperation in Italy.* Geneva: International Institute for Labour Studies.

Quinn, J. B. (1992). *Intelligent enterprise: A knowledge and service based paradigm for industry.* New York: Free Press.

Quinn, J. B. (1999). Strategic outsourcing: Leveraging knowledge capabilities. *Sloan Management Review, 40*(4), 9–21.

Radebaugh, L. H., & Gray, S. J. (1997). *International accounting and multinational enterprises* (4th ed.). New York: John Wiley and Sons, Inc.

Raisch, S., & Birkenshaw, J. (2008). Organizational ambidexterity: Antecedents, outcomes, and moderators. *Journal of Management, 34*(3), 375–409. doi:10.1177/0149206308316058

Ravasi, D., & Lojacono, G. (2005). Managing design and designers for strategic renewal. *Long Range Planning, 38,* 51–77. doi:10.1016/j.lrp.2004.11.010

Raynor, M. E. (2007). What is corporate strategy, really? *Ivey Business Journal Online, 71*(8), 1-6. Retrieved on June 28, 2009, from ABI/INFORM Global (Document ID: 1451062821)

Regev, G., & Wegmann, A. (2003). Why do we need business process support? Balancing specialization and generalization with BPS systems. Introductory note to the *4th BPMDS Workshop on Requirements Engineering for Business Process Support.* Velden, Austria.

Reichheld, F., & Schefter, P. (2000, July-August). E-loyalty. *Harvard Business Review,* 105-113.

Reinartz, W., Krafft, M., & Hoyer, W. D. (2004). The customer relationship management process: Its measurement and impact on performance. *JMR, Journal of Marketing Research, 41*(3), 293–305. doi:10.1509/jmkr.41.3.293.35991

Reyes Pacios Lozano, A. (2000). A customer orientation checklist: A model. *Library Review, 49*(4).

Rich, M. K. (2000). The direction of marketing relationships. *Journal of Business and Industrial Marketing, 15*(2/3), 170–179. doi:10.1108/08858620010316877

Riley, M., & Lockwood, A. (1997). Strategies and measurement for workforce flexibility: An application of functional flexibility in a service setting. *International Journal of Operations & Production Management, 17*(4), 413–419. doi:10.1108/01443579710159996

Roberts, G., Seldon, G., & Roberts, C. (2005). *Human resources management.* Retrieved from http://www.sba.gov/library/pubs/eb-4.doc

Robertson, J. (2002). Benefits of a KM framework. Retrieved on January 12, 2002, from http://www.intranet-journal.com/articles/200207/se_07_31_02a.html

Robey, D., Boudrea, M.-C., & Rose, G. M. (2000). Information technology and organizational learning: A review and assessment of research. *Accounting . Management & Information Technology, 10,* 125–155. doi:10.1016/S0959-8022(99)00017-X

Robins, G., & Pattison, P. (n.d.). *Multiple networks in organizations.* Retrieved on December 10, 2008, from http://www.sna.unimelb.edu.au/publications/publications.html

Rodríguez, C. M., & Wilson, D. T. (2002). Relationship bonding and trust as a foundation for commitment in U.S.-Mexican strategic alliances: A structural equation modeling approach. *Journal of International Marketing, 10*(4), 53–76. doi:10.1509/jimk.10.4.53.19553

Rodwell, J., & Shadur, M. (2000). Management best practices in large firms of the Australian hospitality industry. *International Journal of Employment Studies, 8*(2), 121–138.

Roos, G., & Roos, J. (1997). Measuring your company's intellectual performance. *Long Range Planning, 30*(3), 413–426. doi:10.1016/S0024-6301(97)90260-0

Rosen, E. (2007). The culture of collaboration: Maximizing time, talent, and tools to create value in the global economy. San Francisco: Red Ape Publishing.

Rosenkopf, L., & Nerkar, A. (2001). Beyond local search: Boundary-spanning, exploration, and impact in the optical disc industry. *Strategic Management Journal, 22*(4), 287–306. doi:10.1002/smj.160

Rowley, G., & Purcell, K. (2001). "As cooks go, she went": Is labor churn inevitable? *International Journal*

of Hospitality Management, 20(2), 163–185. doi:10.1016/S0278-4319(00)00050-5

Royce, W. K. (1970, August). In *Proceedings of IEEE Wescon.*

Ruggles, R., & Little, R. (1997). *Knowledge management and innovation: An initial exploration.* Working Paper, Ernst & Young LLP Center for Business Innovations. Retrieved on October 24, 2006, from http://www.providersedge.com/docs/km_articles/KM_and_Innovation.pdf

Russ, M. (2008, January 28-30). *Do we need a new theory or a conceptual model to explain SME internationalization or do we need to apply existing theories and conceptual models by using a different epistemology?* Paper presented in the International Business Symposium at the International Academy of Management and Business Conference in San Diego, CA.

Russ, M. (2009, April 15-17). Knowledge management strategy in the age of paradox and transition. In *Proceedings of the Annual ISOneWorld Conference.* R. Hackney (Ed.), *Emergent challenges in IS/IT.* Washington, D.C.: Information Institute Publishing. ISBN: 978-1-935160-05-2.

Russ, M., & Jones, J. K. (2005). A typology of knowledge management strategies for hospital preparedness: What lessons can be learned? *International Journal of Emergency Management, 2*(4), 319–342. doi:10.1504/IJEM.2005.008743

Russ, M., & Jones, J. K. (2006). Knowledge-based strategies and information system technologies: Preliminary findings. *International Journal of Knowledge and Learning, 2*(1/2), 154–179. doi:10.1504/IJKL.2006.009685

Russ, M., & Jones, J. K. (2009, May 28-30). *International virtual industry clusters and SMEs: Early content and process policy recommendations.* Paper presented at the 40th MCRSA Annual Conference, Milwaukee, WI.

Russ, M., & Jones, J. K. (forthcoming). Knowledge management's strategic dilemmas typology. In D.G. Schwartz and D. Te'eni (Eds.), *Encyclopedia of knowledge management* (2nd ed.). Hershey, PA: IGI Reference.

Russ, M., & Jones, J. K. (forthcoming). Knowledge management's strategic dilemmas typology. In D.G. Schwartz & D. Te'eni (Eds.), *Encyclopedia of knowledge management* (2nd ed.). Hershey, PA: IGI Global.

Russ, M., Fineman, R., & Jones, J. K. (2010). How do we get there: Strategy action framework–"Action Engine."

Russ, M., Fineman, R., & Jones, J. K. (2010a). KARMA- Knowledge assessment review and management audit. In M. Russ (ed.) *Knowledge Management Strategies for Business Development.* Hershey PA: IGI Global.

Russ, M., Fineman, R., & Jones, J. K. (2010b). C³EEP taxonomy: Knowledge based strategies. In M. Russ (ed.) *Knowledge Management Strategies for Business Development.* Hershey PA: IGI Global.

Russ, M., Jones, J. G., & Jones, J. K. (2008). Knowledge-based strategies and systems: A systematic review. In M. Lytras, M. Russ, R. Maier & A. Naeve (Eds.), *Knowledge management strategies: A handbook of applied technologies* (pp. 1-62). Hershey, PA: IGI Global.

Russ, M., Jones, J. K., & Fineman, R. (2006). Toward a taxonomy of knowledge-based strategies: Early findings. *International Journal of Knowledge and Learning, 2*(1/2), 1–40. doi:10.1504/IJKL.2006.009677

Russ, M., Jones, J. K., & Jones, J. G. (2004). Knowledge-based strategies, culture, and information systems. *International Journal of Knowledge . Culture and Change Management, 4,* 427–452.

Ruzzier, M., Hisrich, R. D., & Antoncic, B. (2006). SME internationalization research: Past, present, and future. *Journal of Small Business and Enterprise Development, 13*(4), 476–497. doi:10.1108/14626000610705705

Sampson, R. C. (2005). Experience effects and collaborative returns in R&D alliances. *Strategic Management Journal, 26,* 1009–1031. doi:10.1002/smj.483

Sánchez de Pablo, J. D., Guadamillas, F., Dimovski, V., & Škerlavaj, M. (2008). Exploratory study of organizational learning network within a Spanish high-tech company. *Proceedings of Rijeka Faculty of Economics Journal of Economics and Business, 26*(2), 257–277.

Sanchez, R., & Mahoney, J. T. (1996). Modularity, flexibility, and knowledge management in product and organization design. *Strategic Management Journal, 17*(Special Issue-Winter), 63–76.

Sanchez, R., & Mahoney, J. T. (1996). Modularity, flexibility, and knowledge management in product and organization design. *Strategic Management Journal, 17,* 63–76.

Santa, R., Ferrer, M., & Pun, D. (2007). *Why do enterprise information systems fail to match the reality?* USA: ISRST.

Sarvary, M. (1999). Knowledge management and competition in the consulting industry. *California Management Review, 41*(2), 95–107.

Sathe, V., & Smart, G. H. (1997). Building a winning organization: The mind-body diagnostic framework. *Journal of Management Development, 16*(6), 418–427. doi:10.1108/02621719710174570

Sawhney, M., & Prandelli, E. (2000). Communities of creation: Managing distributed innovation in turbulent markets. *California Management Review, 42,* 24–54.

Saxena, S., & Shah, H. (2008). Effect of organizational culture on creating learned helplessness attributions in R&D professionals: A canonical correlation analysis. *Vikalpa, 33*(2), 25–45.

Saxton, T. (1997). The effects of partner and relationship characteristics on alliances outcomes. *Academy of Management Journal, 40*(2), 443–461. doi:10.2307/256890

Schein, E. H. (1985). *Organizational culture and leadership.* San Francisco, CA: Jossey-Bass Publishers.

Schilling, M. (2002). Technology success and failure in winner takes all markets: The impact of learning orientation, timing, and network externalities. *Academy of Management Journal, 45*(2), 387–398. doi:10.2307/3069353

Schmaltz, R., Hagenhoff, S., & Kaspar, C. (2004, April 2-3). *Information technology support for knowledge management in cooperation.* Paper presented at the Fifth European Conference on Organizational Knowledge, Learning, and Capabilities, Innsbruck, Austria.

Schmidt, K. (1990). *Analysis of cooperative work. A conceptual framework.* Risø National Laboratory, DK-4000 Roskilde, Denmark, [Risø-M-2890].

Schmidt, K., & Bannon, L. (1992). Taking CSCW seriously: Supporting articulation work. *Computer Supported Cooperative Work, 1*(1-2), 7-40. Retrieved on April 4, 2008, from http://citeseer.ist.psu.edu/schmidt92taking.html

Schmitt, B., & Simonson, A. (1997). *Marketing aesthetics. The strategic management of brands, identity, and management.* New York: The Free Press.

Scholl, W., König, C., Meyer, B., & Heisig, P. (2004). The future of knowledge management: An international delphi study. *Journal of Knowledge Management, 8*(2), 19–35. doi:10.1108/13673270410529082

Schultz, M., & Jobe, L. A. (2001). Codification and tacitness as knowledge management strategies: An empirical exploration. *The Journal of High Technology Management Research, 12,* 139–165. doi:10.1016/S1047-8310(00)00043-2

Schultze, U., & Boland, R. J. (2000). Knowledge management technology and the reproduction of work practices. *The Journal of Strategic Information Systems, 9*(2-3), 193–212. doi:10.1016/S0963-8687(00)00043-3

Schwartz, P. (1991). *The art of the long view.* New York: Doubleday.

Schwikkard, D. B., & Du Toit, A. S. A. (2004). Analyzing knowledge requirements: A case study. *Aslib Proceedings, 56*(2), 104–111. doi:10.1108/00012530410529477

Scott Morton, M. S. (Ed.). (1991). *The corporation of the 1990s. Information technology and organizational transformation.* New York: Oxford University Press.

Segev, E. (1989). A systematic comparative analysis and synthesis of two business level strategies typologies. *Strategic Management Journal, 10*(4), 487–505. doi:10.1002/smj.4250100507

Shahabuddin, S. (2008). Six sigma: Issues and problems. *International Journal of Productivity and Quality Management, 3*(2), 145–160. doi:10.1504/IJPQM.2008.016562

Shannon, C. E., & Weaver, W. (1949). *The mathematical theory of information.* Urbana, IL: University of Illinois Press.

Sharma, R., & Chowdhury, N. (2007). On the use of a diagnostic tool for knowledge audits. *Journal of KM Practice, 8*(4), 1–11.

Sheth, J. N. (1975). Buyer-seller interaction: A conceptual framework. *Advances in Consumer Research. Association for Consumer Research (U. S.), 3,* 382–386.

Siefe, C. (2006). *Decoding the universe: How the new science of information is explaining everything in the cosmos, from our brains to black holes.* New York: Viking.

Siggelkow, N. (2007). Persuasion with case studies. *Academy of Management Journal, 50,* 20–24.

Sila, I., Ebrahimpour, M., & Birkholz, C. (2006). Quality in supply chains: An empirical analysis. *Supply Chain Management: An International Journal, 11*(6), 491–502. doi:10.1108/13598540610703882

Silverstein, J. M., & Fiske, N. (2003). *Trading up. The new American luxury.* New York: Portfolio.

Simeon, R. (1999). Evaluating domestic and international Web strategies. *Internet Research: Electronic Networking Applications and Policy, 9*(4), 297–308. doi:10.1108/10662249910286842

Simon, H. A. (1957). *Models of man.* New York: Wiley.

Simonin, B. L. (1997). The importance of collaborative know-how: An empirical test of the learning organization. *Academy of Management Journal, 40,* 1150–1174. doi:10.2307/256930

Singh, N., Hu, C., & Roehl, W. S. (2007). Text mining a decade of progress in hospitality human resource management research: Identifying emerging thematic development. *Hospital Management, 26*(1), 131–147. doi:10.1016/j.ijhm.2005.10.002

Sinha, I. (2000, March-April). Cost transparency: The Net's real threat to prices and brands. *Harvard Business Review*, 43–55.

Skjølsvik, T., Løwendahl, B. R., Kvålshaugen, R., & Fosstenløkken, S. M. (2007). Choosing to learn and learning to choose: Strategies for client co-production and knowledge development. *California Management Review*, *49*(3), 110–128.

Skyrme, D. (2001). *Capitalizing on knowledge: From e-business to k-business*. Butterworth-Heinemann, Oxford.

Slater, S. F., & Narver, J. C. (1995). Market orientation and the learning organization. *Journal of Marketing*, *59*(3), 63–74. doi:10.2307/1252120

Smith, C. A., Organ, D. W., & Near, J. P. (1983). Organizational citizenship behavior: Its nature and antecedents. *The Journal of Applied Psychology*, *68*(4), 653–663. doi:10.1037/0021-9010.68.4.653

Smith, D. K., & Alexander, R. C. (1988). *Fumbling the future: How Xerox invented then ignored the first personal computer*. New York: William Morrow & Co.

Smith, P. G., & Reinertsen, D. G. (1998). *Developing products in half the time*. New York: Van Nostrand Reinhold.

Snow, C. C., & Hrebriniak, L. G. (1980). Strategy, distinctive competence, and organizational performance. *Administrative Science Quarterly*, *25*(2), 317–336. doi:10.2307/2392457

Snyman, R., & Kruger, C. J. (2004). The interdependency between strategic management and strategic knowledge management. *Journal of Knowledge Management*, *8*(1), 5–19. doi:10.1108/13673270410523871

Spekman, R. E., Spear, J., & Kamauff, J. (2002). Supply chain competency: Learning as a key component. *Supply Chain Management*, *17*, 27–43.

Spender, J. C. (1995). Organizations are activity systems, not merely systems of thought. In P. Shrivastava & C. Stubbart (Eds.), *Advances in Strategic Management* (Vol. 11, pp. 151-172). Greenwich, CT: JAI Press.

Spender, J. C. (1996). Making knowledge the basis of a dynamic theory of the firm. *Strategic Management Journal*, *17*(Special Issue-Winter), 45–62.

Spender, J. C. (1996a). Organizational knowledge, learning, and memory: Three concepts in search of a theory. *Journal of Organizational Change Management*, *9*(1), 63–78. doi:10.1108/09534819610156813

Spender, J. C. (2006). Getting value from knowledge management. *The TQM Magazine*, *18*(3), 238–254. doi:10.1108/09544780610659970

Sproull, L., & Kiesler, S. (1991). *Connections. New ways of working in the networked organization*. Cambridge: MIT Press.

Stacey, R. D. (1992). *Managing the unknowable: Strategic boundaries between order and chaos in organizations*. San Francisco, CA: Jossey-Bass.

Steensma, H. K. (1996). Acquiring technological competence through inter-organizational collaboration: An organizational perspective. *Journal of Engineering and Technology Management*, *12*(4), 267–286. doi:10.1016/0923-4748(95)00013-5

Stevens, L. (2000). Knowing what your company knows: A knowledge audit is a necessary precursor to a new KM initiative. Retrieved on January 12, 2006, from http://www.destinationcrm.com/km/dcrm_km_article.asp?id=475

Stock, G. N., & Tatikonda, M. V. (2004). External technology integration in product and process development. *International Journal of Operations & Production Management*, *24*(7), 642–665. doi:10.1108/01443570410541975

Storck, J., & Hill, P. (2000). Knowledge diffusion through 'strategic communities.'. *Sloan Management Review*, *41*(2), 2000.

Storey, J., & Barnett, E. (2000). Knowledge management initiatives: Learning from failure. *Journal of Knowledge Management*, *4*(2), 145–156. doi:10.1108/13673270010372279

Stringer, R. (2000). How to manage radical innovation. *California Management Review*, *42*(4), 70–88.

Stuart, T. E. (2000). Interorganizational alliances and the performance of firms: A study of growth and innovation rates in a high-technology industry. *Strategic Management Journal, 21,* 791–811. doi:10.1002/1097-0266(200008)21:8<791::AID-SMJ121>3.0.CO;2-K

Subramaniam, M., & Venkatraman, N. (2001). Determinants of transnational new product development capacity: Testing the influence of transferring and deploying tacit overseas knowledge. *Strategic Management Journal, 22,* 359–378. doi:10.1002/smj.163

Suchman, M. C. (1995). Managing legitimacy: Strategic and institutional approaches. *Academy of Management Journal, 20*(3), 571–610.

Sullivan, J. E. III. (2000). The often overlooked role of disclosure in asset protection planning: Part 1. *Asset Protection Journal, 2*(1), 1–14.

Sveiby, K. E. (2001). *Frequently asked questions.* Brisbane: Sveiby Knowledge Associates. Retrieved on July 16, 2001 from http://www.sveiby.com.au/faq

Szu, H., Jenkins, J., Hsu, C., Goehl, S., Miao, L., Cader, M., & Benachenhou, D. (2009). Digging for knowledge. In H. Szu, J. Jenkins, C. Hsu, S. Goehl, L. Miao, M. Cader & D. Benachenhou (Eds.), *Independent component analyses, wavelets, neural networks, biosystems, and nanoengineering VII.* Proceedings of the SPIE (Volume 7343, pp. 734304-734304-17). Retrieved on May 19, 2009, from http://adsabs.harvard.edu/abs/2009SPIE.7343E..26S

Szulanski, G., & Jensen, R. (2006). Presumptive adaptation and the effectiveness of knowledge transfer. *Strategic Management Journal, 27*(10), 937–957. doi:10.1002/smj.551

Takahashi, T., & Vandenbrink, D. (2004). Formative knowledge: From knowledge dichotomy to knowledge geography–knowledge management transformed by the ubiquitous information society. *Journal of Knowledge Management, 8*(1), 64–76. doi:10.1108/13673270410523916

Taleb, N. N. (2007). *The black swan: The impact of the highly improbable.* New York: Random House.

Tanriverdi, H. (2005). Information technology relatedness, knowledge management capability, and performance of multibusiness firms. *MIS Quarterly, 29*(2), 311–334.

Tapp, A. (2001). *Principles of direct marketing.* Prentice Hall, 2nd ed.

Tapscott, D., & Ticoll, D. (2003). *The naked corporation: How the age of transparency will revolutionize business.* New York: Free Press.

Tapscott, D., & Williams, A. D. (2007). *Wikinomics. How mass collaboration changes everything.* New York: Penguin Book.

Taxén, L. (2003). *A framework for the coordination of complex systems' development.* Dissertation No. 800. Linköping University, Dep. of Computer &Information Science. Retrieved on January 4, 2009, from http://www.ep.liu.se/smash/record.jsf?searchId=1&pid=diva2:20897

Taxén, L. (2006). Cognitive grounding of activity modalities. In *Proceedings of Action in Language, Organisations, and Information Systems (ALOIS 2006)* (pp. 75-93). Borås, Sweden: University College of Borås. Retrieved on January 8, 2009, from http://www.vits.org/?pageId=317

Taxén, L. (2007). Activity modalities–a multidimensional perspective on coordination, business processes, and communication. *Systems, Signs, & Actions, 3*(1), 93–133. Retrieved on January 4, 2009, from http://www.sysiac.org/?pageId=36

Taxén, L. (2007b). The activity domain theory–informing the alignment of business and knowledge strategies. In E. Abou-Zeid (Ed.), *Knowledge management and business strategies: Theoretical frameworks and empirical research* (pp. 253-280). Hershey, PA: Information Science Reference.

Taxén, L., & Svensson, D. (2005). Towards an alternative foundation for managing product life-cycles in turbulent environments. [IJPD]. *International Journal of Product Development, 2*(1-2), 24–46. doi:10.1504/IJPD.2005.006667

Taylor, D. W., Jones, O., & Boles, K. (2004). Building social capital through action learning: An insight into the entrepreneur. *Education & Training, 46*(5), 226–235. doi:10.1108/00400910410549805

Tayyab, M., Walker, D., & Finegan, A. (2007). Extending the "knowledge advantage": Creating learning chains. *The Learning Organization, 14*(2), 123–141. doi:10.1108/09696470710726998

Teece, D. J., Pisano, G., & Shuen, A. (1997). Dynamic capabilities and strategic management. *Strategic Management Journal, 18*(7), 509–533. doi:10.1002/(SICI)1097-0266(199708)18:7<509::AID-SMJ882>3.0.CO;2-Z

Tenkasi, R., & Boland, R. J. (1996). Exploring knowledge diversity in knowledge intensive firms: A new role for information systems. *Journal of Organizational Change Management, 9*(1), 79–91. doi:10.1108/09534819610107330

Tiemessen, I., Lane, H. W., Crossan, M., & Inkpen, A. C. (1997). Knowledge management in international joint ventures. In P. W. Beamish & J. P. Killing (Eds.), *Cooperative strategies: North American perspective* (pp. 370-399). San Francisco, CA: New Lexington Press.

Timo, N. (2001). Lean or just mean? The flexibilisation of labor in the Australian hotel industry. *Research in the Sociology of Work, 10*, 287–309. doi:10.1016/S0277-2833(01)80030-3

Treacy, M., & Wiersema, F. (1997). *The discipline of market leaders: Choose your customers, narrow your focus, dominate your market.* New York: Perseus Books Group.

Tsai, M. T., & Shih, C. M. (2004). The impact of marketing knowledge among managers on marketing capabilities and business performance. *International Journal of Management, 21*(4), 524–530.

Tsai, W., & Ghoshal, S. (1998). Social capital and value creation: The role of intrafirm networks. *Academy of Management Journal, 41*(4), 464–476. doi:10.2307/257085

Tsoukas, H., & Mylonopoulos, N. (2004). Introduction: Knowledge construction and creation in organizations. *British Journal of Management, 15*(Supplement 1), 1–8. doi:10.1111/j.1467-8551.2004.t01-2-00402.x

Tsui, E. (2005). The role of IT in KM: Where are we now and where are we heading? *Journal of Knowledge Management, 9*(1), 3–6. doi:10.1108/13673270510584198

Tuomi, I. (1999, January 5-8). Data is more than knowledge: Implications of the reversed knowledge hierarchy for knowledge management and organizational memory. In *Proceedings of the 32nd Hawaii International Conference on System Sciences* (pp. 1-12). Volume Track 1.

Tushman, M. L., Anderson, P. C., & O'Reilly, C. (1997). Technology cycles, innovation streams, and ambidextrous organizations: Organization renewal through innovation streams and strategic change. In M. L. Tushman & P. C. Anderson (Eds.), *Managing strategic innovation and change: A collection of readings* (pp. 3-23). New York: Oxford University Press.

Ulrich, D., & Smallwood, N. (2004). Capitalizing on capabilities. *Harvard Business Review, 82*(6), 119–127.

Un, C. A., & Cuervo-Cazurra, A. (2004). Strategies for knowledge creation in firms. *British Journal of Management, 15*(Supplement 1), 27–41. doi:10.1111/j.1467-8551.2004.00404.x

Uzzi, B. (1996). The sources and consequences of embeddedness for the economic performance of organizations: The network effect. *American Sociological Review, 61*(4), 674–698. doi:10.2307/2096399

Uzzi, B. (1997). Social structure and competition in interfirm networks: The paradox of embeddedness. *Administrative Science Quarterly, 41*, 35–67. doi:10.2307/2393808

Van den Bosch, F. A. J., Volberda, H. W., & de Boer, M. (1999). Coevolution of firm absorptive capacity and knowledge environment: Organizational forms and combinative capabilities. *Organization Science, 10*(5), 551–568. doi:10.1287/orsc.10.5.551

Van Niekerk, D. N. R., Berthon, J. P., & Davies, T. (1999). Going with the flow. *Internet Research: Electronic Networking Applications and Policy, 9*(2), 109–116. doi:10.1108/10662249910264873

Verilog. (2008). Retrieved on January 2, 2009, from http://www.verilog.com/

Verma, S. (2002). Knowledge management at Infosys Technologies Ltd. In D. Remneyi (Ed.), *Third European Conference on Knowledge Management*. London: Academic Conferences Ltd.

VHDL. (2008). Retrieved on January 2, 2009, from http://en.wikipedia.org/wiki/VHDL

Virkkunen, J., & Kuutti, K. (2000). Understanding organizational learning by focusing on "activity systems.". *Accounting, Management, and Information Technologies*, *10*, 291–319. doi:10.1016/S0959-8022(00)00005-9

von Baeyer, H. C. (2003). *Information: The new language of science*. London: Weidenfeld and Nicolson.

von Furstenberg, G. M. (2001). Hopes and delusions of transparency. *The North American Journal of Economics and Finance*, *12*, 105–120. doi:10.1016/S1062-9408(01)00040-7

Von Halle, B., et al. (2009). In Auerbach (Ed.), *The decision model*.

von Hippel, E. (1986). Lead users: A source of novel product concepts. *Management Science*, *32*(7), 791–805. doi:10.1287/mnsc.32.7.791

Von Hippel, E. (2005). *Democritizing innovation*. Boston: MIT Press.

von Krogh, G., & Roos, J. (1995). *Organizational epistemology*. London: MacMillan.

Von Krogh, G., & Roos, J. (Eds.). (1996). *Managing knowledge. Perspectives on cooperation and competition*. London: Sage.

Von Krogh, G., Nonaka, I., & Aben, M. (2001). Making the most of your company's knowledge: A strategic framework. *Long Range Planning*, *34*(4), 421–439. doi:10.1016/S0024-6301(01)00059-0

Walsh, J., & Deery, S. (1999). Understanding the peripheral workforce: Evidence from the service sector. *Human Resource Management Journal*, *9*(2), 50–63. doi:10.1111/j.1748-8583.1999.tb00196.x

Walters, D., & Lancaster, G. (1999a). Value and information–concepts and issues for management. *Management Decision*, *37*(8), 643–656. doi:10.1108/00251749910291613

Walters, D., & Lancaster, G. (1999b). Using the Internet as a channel for commerce. *Management Decision*, *37*(10), 800–816. doi:10.1108/00251749910302908

Walters, D., & Lancaster, G. (1999c). Value-based marketing and its usefulness to customers. *Management Decision*, *37*(9). doi:10.1108/00251749910299066

Wang, C., Fergusson, C., Perry, D., & Antony, J. (2008). A conceptual case-based model for knowledge sharing among supply chain members. *Business Process Management Journal*, *14*(2), 147–165. doi:10.1108/14637150810864907

Wang, F., Head, M., & Archer, N. (2000). A relationship-building model for the Web retail marketplace. *Internet Research: Electronic Networking Applications and Policy*, *10*(5).

Watt, P. (1997). Knowing it all. *Intranet*, 17-18.

Weaver, G. R., Trevino, L. K., & Cochran, P. L. (1999). Integrated and decoupled corporate social performance: Management commitments, external pressures, and corporate ethics practices. *Academy of Management Journal*, *42*(5), 539–552. doi:10.2307/256975

Welch, L., & Luostarinen, R. (1993). Internationalization: Evolution of a concept. In P. J. Buckley & P. N. Ghauri (Eds.), *The internationalization of the firm: A reader* (pp. 155-171). London: Academic Press.

Wenger, E. (1999). *Communities of practice: Learning, meaning, and identity*. New York: Cambridge University Press.

Werbach, K. (2000, May-June). Syndication: The emerging model for business in the Internet era. *Harvard Business Review*, 85–93.

Wernerfelt, B. (1984). A resource-based view of the firm. *Strategic Management Journal*, *5*(2), 171–180. doi:10.1002/smj.4250050207

Wertsch, J. V. (1991). *Voices of the mind: A sociocultural approach to mediated action.* Cambridge, MA: Harvard University Press.

Whitehouse, G., Lafferty, G., & Boreham, P. (1997). From casual to permanent part time: Non-standard employment in retail and hospitality. *Labour & Industry, 8*(2), 33–48.

Wiklund, J., & Shepherd, D. (2003). Knowledge-based resources, entrepreneurial orientation, and the performance of small and medium-sized businesses. *Strategic Management Journal, 24*(13), 1307–1314. doi:10.1002/smj.360

Wildes, V. J. (2007). Attracting and retaining food servers: How internal service quality moderates occupational stigma. *International Journal of Hospitality Management, 26*(1), 4–19. doi:10.1016/j.ijhm.2005.08.003

Willyard, C. H., & McClees, C. W. (1987). Motorola's technology roadmap process. *Research Management, Sept./Oct.,* 13-19.

Wilson, T. D. (2002). The nonsense of "knowledge management." *Information Research, 8*(1), paper no. 144. Retrieved on December 3, 2008, from http://InformationR.net/ir/8-1/paper144.html

Winer, R. S. (2001). A framework for customer relationship management. *California Management Review, 43*(4), 89–105.

Winter, S. G. (1987). Knowledge and competence as strategic assets. In D. J. Teece (Ed.), *The competitive challenge: Strategies for industrial innovation and renewal* (pp. 159-84). New York: Ballinger.

Winter, S. G., & Szulanski, G. (2001). Replication as strategy. *Organization Science, 12*(6), 730–743. doi:10.1287/orsc.12.6.730.10084

Wissensmanagement Forum. (2003). *An illustrated guide to knowledge management.* Graz Austria. Retrieved on February 14, 2008, from http://www.wm-forum.org/files/Handbuch/An_Illustrated_Guide_to_Knowledge_Management.pdf

Woods, R., Heck, W., & Sciarini, M. (1998). *Turnover and diversity in the lodging industry.* American Hotel Foundation.

Worden (2009). Making the case for the physical decision. In Auerbach (Ed.), *The decision model.* [1] OMG has been an international, open membership, not-for-profit computer industry consortium since 1989.f

World Economic Forum. (2006). *The global competitiveness report.* Retrieved on April 20, 2007, from http://www.weforum.org

Wu, C. (2008). Knowledge creation in supply chain. *Supply Chain Management: An International Journal, 13*(3), 241–250. doi:10.1108/13598540810871280

Wu, J. (2008). *Exploring the link between knowledge management performance and firm performance.* Unpublished doctoral dissertation, University of Kentucky.f

Yamada, J. (2004). A multidimensional view of entrepreneurship: Towards a research agenda on organisation emergence. *Journal of Management Development, 23*(4), 289–320. doi:10.1108/02621710410529776

Yelkur, R., & Da Costa, M. M. N. (2001). Differential pricing and segmentation on the Internet: The case of hotels. *Management Decision, 39*(4), 252–262. doi:10.1108/00251740110391411

Yin, R. K. (1994). *Case study research: Design and methods.* Thousand Oaks: Sage.

Zack, M. (1999). Developing a knowledge strategy. *California Management Review, 41,* 125–145.

Zack, M. H. (1999). Managing codified knowledge. *Sloan Management Review, 40*(4), 45–58.

Zahra, S. A., & George, G. (2002). Absorptive capacity: A review, reconceptualization, and extension. *Academy of Management Review, 27*(2), 185–203. doi:10.2307/4134351

Zahra, S., Sisodia, R., & Matherne, B. (1999, April). Exploiting the dynamic links between competitive and technology strategies. *European Management Journal, 17*(2), 188–201. doi:10.1016/S0263-2373(98)00078-4

Zajac, E. J., & Shortell, S. M. (1980). Changing generic strategies: Likelihood, direction, and performance implications. [f]. *Strategic Management Journal, 10*(3), 413–430.

Zander, U., & Kogut, B. (1995). Knowledge and the speed of transfer and imitation of organizational capabilities: An empirical test. *Organization Science, 6*, 76–92. doi:10.1287/orsc.6.1.76

Zaun, T. (2003, April 28). In Asia, Honda employs new tactic in building cars. *Wall Street Journal (Eastern Edition*), A11. Retrieved on June 28, 2009, from ABI/INFORM Global (Document ID: 329642741)

Zhang, H. Q., & Wu, E. (2004). Human resources issues facing the hotel and travel industry in China. *International Journal of Contemporary Hospitality Management, 16*(7), 424–428. doi:10.1108/09596110410559122

Zinchenko, V. (1996). Developing activity theory: The zone of proximal development and beyond. In B. Nardi (Ed.), *Context and Consciousness, Activity Theory, and Human-Computer Interaction* (pp. 283-324). Cambridge, MA: MIT Press.

Zineldin, M. (2000a). Beyond relationship marketing: Technologicalship marketing. *Marketing Intelligence & Planning, 18*(1), 9–23. doi:10.1108/02634500010308549

Zineldin, M. (2000b). Total relationship management (TRM) and total quality management (TQM). [f]. *Managerial Auditing Journal, 15*(1/2), 20–28. doi:10.1108/02686900010304399

Zollo, M., & Winter, S. G. (2002). Deliberate learning and the evolution of dynamic capabilities. *Organization Science, 13*(3), 339–351. doi:10.1287/orsc.13.3.339.2780

Zopiatis, A., & Constanti, P. (2007). Human resource challenges confronting the Cyprus hospitality industry. *EuroMed Journal of Business, 2*(2), 135–153. doi:10.1108/14502190710826022

About the Contributors

Meir Russ received his PhD in strategic management, entrepreneurship, and international business and his MA in Organizational Behavior/Theory from The Ohio State University. He also has an MBA and a BScEE from Tel Aviv University. He is currently an associate professor, the Frederick E. Baer Professor in Business, and the Chair of the Masters of Management program with the University of Wisconsin, Green Bay. Dr. Russ teaches undergraduate and graduate classes in management and marketing. He also teaches at BEM-Bordeaux School of Management and at the University of Pisa, GSA Master program. His research interests include knowledge-based strategies, the use of knowledge management for hospital preparedness, the new-knowledge based economic development, and human capital valuation methods among others. In addition to his academic focus, Dr. Russ serves in a consulting capacity with a number of multinational companies in the area of global strategic management and knowledge management and he chairs the incubator committee at the Green Bay Chamber Advance Board. Dr. Russ has provided reviews for numerous conferences and journals since 1992, and has presented and published numerous refereed presentations and papers. Dr. Russ joined the AIMB Advisory Board in April 2007 and is the founding editor of The International Journal of Management and Business (IJMB). Dr. Russ also serves on the Editorial Board for the Journal of Asia-Pacific Business.

***

Ozlem Bak is a senior lecturer at University of Brighton, United Kingdom, and currently teaches supply chain management, and operations related subjects. Her principal research interest is in the area of automotive manufacturing operations management and especially on e-business related value-shifts within the automotive supply chains. She has publications in the area of supply chain management, collaboration and knowledge management practices in e-supply chains. Before joining academia she worked in Multinational Automotive Corporations and on project management for companies in professional sectors in Germany, United Kingdom, and Turkey. Research interests: supply chain management, e-business applications, marketspace, transformation, automotive industry.

Montserrat Boronat-Navarro is a lecturer in Strategic Management and Operations Management at Jaume I University in Castellón (Spain). She received her PhD in November 2007 with Cum Laude qualification. She has been visiting researcher at London School of Economics and Political Science. Her research interests include knowledge development, dynamic capabilities, innovation, strategic alliances, and organizational structure. She has published chapters in international books and articles in *Organization Studies* and also in Spanish academic publications. She has presented her research in several international conferences organized by different associations such as European Academy of Management or European Group for Organization Studies.

César Camisón-Zornoza, Bachelor of Economic and Business Sciences (1980) with Extraordinary Prize, and PhD in Economics and Business Sciences on (1984) with Cum Laude and Extraordinary Prize, both by University of Valencia. Professor in Business Administration at University Jaume I of Castellón. He has an experience from 25 years in teaching, researching and university management, which he has developed in some Spanish Universities, and as Visiting Professor in different European and American Universities (Surrey, Universitá Commerciale Luigi Bocconi de Milán, Viena University, Université de Montpellier I, Texas A&M University). His fields of expertise are strategic management, intangible assets and dynamic / innovation capabilities, firm as a knowledge and learning organization, strategic alliances and competitive dynamic inside inter-organizational networks and industrial districts. He has published more of 60 books as author, co-author or coordinator by publishers as Prentice-Hall, Elsevier Science, John Wiley & Sons, Information Science Reference, Idea Group Publishing, Sage, Routledge, and Office for Oficial Publications of the European Communities. He has published articles in closely 100 journals as *Environment and Planning A, Organization Studies, International Marketing Review, and International Business Review.*

Kalotina Chalkiti (PhD Candidate) investigates staff turnover in the Australian accommodation sector. Her work looks at how hospitality businesses that operate in dynamic labour environments can remain both operational and competitive. She contributes to academic discourse by researching turnover from a qualitative perspective aiming to draw out the knowledge management and social networking effects staff turnover has on remaining employees. She is supervised by researchers from both Charles Darwin University (Australia) and the University of Melbourne (Australia); while sustains active co-authorship ties with researchers from the University of the Aegean (Greece). Kalotina has published her work in international peer reviewed scientific journals (e.g. Advances in Hospitality and Leisure, Current Issues in Tourism) co-authored with researchers from both Greece and Australia. Her research interests are social networks, knowledge sharing and staff turnover in hospitality businesses located in remote and peripheral tourism destinations.

Jesús D. Sánchez de Pablo is Assistant Professor at the University of Castilla-La Mancha. He teaches courses on Production Management and Business Administration at the Faculty of Chemical Sciences in Ciudad Real, Spain. His research mainly focuses on strategic alliances, knowledge management and organizational learning. He recently obtained his PhD from the University of Castilla-La Mancha.

Eleonora Di Maria is Assistant professor of business management at the University of Padua and Internationalization Head of Unit of the TeDIS Center. She has been involved in many national and international projects focused on innovation technology, industrial districts and local development. Her present research interests concern the internationalization process of SMEs and local economic systems and upgrading process of firms specializing in traditional industries.

Mario J. Donate is Assistant Professor at the University of Castilla-La Mancha in Ciudad Real, Spain. He teaches courses on Strategic Management, Ethics and Entrepreneurship at the Faculty of Law and Social Sciences. His research mainly focuses on knowledge management, strategic alliances, innovation and social responsibility issues. He obtained his PhD from the University of Castilla-La Mancha and his works have been published in specialised journals and books.

Hongwei Du is an associate professor of Information Technology Management in the College of Business and Economics at California State University, East Bay. He holds a PhD in Operations Research from Florida Institute of Technology and a MS in Computer Science from Bowling Green State University. Dr. Du possesses a broad knowledge in a wide range of areas. This has qualified him to teach and conduct research in multiple disciplines. His current research interests are artificial intelligence, database, electronic commerce, decision support systems, information technology management, computer networking and telecommunications. His works have been published in *International Journal of Innovation and Learning*, *International Journal of Electronic Healthcare*, *Journal of Economic Studies*, and *Journal of Communications of the IIMA*.

Ron DuPlain is a Co-Founder of Espresso Labs. He also currently serves as a software and Systems Engineer at the National Radio Astronomy Observatory. In this role, he applies agile development to web applications and telescope instrumentation. He also contributes to FPGA development at the Robert G. Byrd Green Bank Telescope (GBT) in Green Bank, WV, which is an initiative that he introduced to the Observatory. Ron has a B.S. in Computer Engineering from the University of Cincinnati, where he studied hardware systems, simulations, VLSI microchip design, and software engineering. He is completing an M.E. in Systems Engineering at the University of Virginia. His current research interest is exploring and developing novel content management systems that develop effective socio-technical communities.

Robert Fineman has over 25 years of experience working in both the private and public sectors in the areas of Project Management, Consulting, Business Analysis, Process Re-Engineering, and Quality Assurance. He has worked in a variety of industries including financial services, government, healthcare, and manufacturing. Much of his work has concentrated on the implementation of new IT systems and upgrading or re-engineering business processes to incorporate new systems and functionality into existing processes.

Thomas Ginter is currently the Director of Support Services for Aurora BayCare Medical Center in Green Bay, Wisconsin. He is responsible for all aspects of Building and Grounds, Food and Dietary Services, Housekeeping, and Telecommunications. He performs liaison duties with Aurora Health Care Corporate service departments of Distribution Management and Clinical Engineering. Other roles he serves for Aurora BayCare Medical Center include Emergency Management Coordinator, Life Safety Officer, Hazardous Waste Emergency Response Coordinator, along with Environment of Care Coordinator and Safety Officer. He began his medical career in the US Army as a medical equipment repair specialist. Mr. Ginter has been in leadership since 1992. He received his Bachelor of Science Degree in Business and Master of Science Degree in Management and Organizational Behavior from Silver Lake College in Manitowoc, Wisconsin. He is an Academy Fellow through the Health Care Advisory Board in Washington, D.C.

Fátima Guadamillas is Professor of Strategic Management at the Faculty of Law and Social Sciences in Toledo, Spain. She has a degree in Economics and obtained her PhD from the University of Castilla-La Mancha. She coordinates the MBA on Human Resources Management of this University. She teaches courses at the degree level on strategic and general management and on knowledge management, innovation and strategic management at the MBA and PhD levels. Her research focuses on innovation, knowledge management strategies and ethics and social responsibility in businesses. Her works have been published in specialised journals and books.

Jeannette K. Jones, RCC, is an associate professor and lead faculty member with American Intercontinental University (AIU) - Main Campus in the Master of Education program with concentration responsibilities in the Instructional Design and Instructional Technology content area. Prior to joining AIU, she was responsible for curriculum design of graduate and undergraduate programs and online faculty development instruction at the university level. Her research and publication interests include knowledge management strategies and technologies; online learning theory, practice, and design; coaching methodologies; and breast cancer survivor skills. In addition to her academic credentials, Dr. Jones is a Registered Corporate Coach certified through the World Association of Business Coaches. She serves on the Board of Directors for Star Charities, Inc., is a member of Association for Educational Communications & Technology (AECT), American Association of University Women (AAUW), Berea Women's Club, Berea Arts Council, Our Redeemer Lutheran Church, Community Chairperson- Cub Scout Pack 77, Chairperson, Madison Southern High School Tennis Boosters, and Women on Wheels. She volunteers as a guest lecturer for the American Cancer Society, Gear Up, and Women Supporting Women. Dr. Jones received her BS in Human Resource Management from George Mason University in Fairfax, Virginia, her MBA from Averett University in Danville, Virginia, and her Ed.D in Instructional Technology and Distance Education from Nova Southeastern University in Ft. Lauderdale, Florida.

Amit Karna is an Assistant Professor for Services Management with the Department of Strategy Organization and Leadership at the European Business School, Germany. Amit completed his PhD from Indian Institute of Management Ahmedabad's Business Policy area. He is involved in teaching courses like Management, Strategic Change, and International Strategy at European Business School. His research interests include development of organizational capabilities, knowledge management in service firms, and internationalization of firms from emerging economies. He has published in journals and conference proceedings, and presented his research at various conferences in the fields of management, strategy and knowledge management. Prior to his doctoral studies, he has an MBA and worked in the industry for five years.

Pengtao Li is an Assistant Professor of Computer Information Systems in the College of Business Administration at the California State University, Stanislaus. He earned his PhD degree in Decision Science and Information Systems from the Gatton College of Business and Economics at the University of Kentucky. His current research interests include human computer interaction, technology applications in learning and decision making, and e-commerce. He has published in various journals such as *Decision Sciences Journal of Innovative Education, International Journal of Information Management* and *Journal of Electronic Commerce Research*. His teaching activities include database management, system analysis and design, and system administration.

Xun Li is assistant professor of operations management at Nicholls State University. Her current research interests include work design in supply chains, supply chain agility, the effects of inter-organizational systems on supply chain performance, and privacy/security issues in information sharing. Her teaching activities include quantitative analysis in operation management, supply chain management, and IT applications in business. She can be contacted at xli@uky.edu.

Carolina López-Nicolás is an assistant professor in the Department of Management and Finance at the University of Murcia, Spain. She has been a visiting professor at Delft University of Technology in The Netherlands and Michigan State University in USA. Her current teaching and research relates to knowledge management, information systems, business strategy and mobile communications. She has published on these topics in such journals as the Information & Management, Journal of Knowledge Management, International Journal of Information Management, International Journal of Internet Marketing and Advertising, Journal of Enterprise Information Management, International Journal of e-Collaboration, among others.

Diana Luck is a Senior Lecturer in Marketing Communications within the London Metropolitan Business School at London Metropolitan University. She has been involved with the services industry since 1989. Her career started in the hotel and tourism industry. She then moved into Project Management and Marketing. She also worked in telecommunications and in consulting services. She left the industry for the academic arena at the beginning of 2002. Since 2001, her research interests and consultancy work have focused on Customer Relationship Marketing, Customer Relationship Management and Corporate Social Responsibility. Her current research is exploring the links between Customer Relationship Management and emerging key areas of business.

Philip Mattek is a Financial Advisor with Merrill Lynch in Green Bay, Wisconsin. He earned his Bachelors Degree in Accounting and his Masters Degree in Management from the University of Wisconsin-Green Bay. He is a member of Sigma Beta Delta – the International Honor Society for Business, Management, and Administration. He was honored by them as a Fellowship Award Recipient in 2008. He is also a member of St. Mary's Hospital Medical Center Community Advisory Council and Business Advisory Council.

Ángel L. Meroño-Cerdán is Associate Professor of Management at the University of Murcia in Spain. He holds a Master in Business and Foreign Trade including a three months training at USA-Spanish Chamber of Commerce in New York and a PhD in Business Administration (University of Murcia, Spain). He has published in International Journal of Information Management, European Journal of Information Systems, Journal of Computer Information Systems, Journal of Enterprise Information Management, Journal of Knowledge Management, International Journal of Electronic Business/, among others. His teaching and research are related to information systems, knowledge management and e-business.

Stefano Micelli is Associate professor of innovation technology at the Ca' Foscari University, Dean of Venice International University and Director of the TeDIS Center. He is also President of COSES (Consortium for Research and Training, Venice). He coordinated many national and international projects in the fields of ICT, local economic development and competitiveness of firms and regions. For many years his research has been focusing on the impacts of information technologies on business competitiveness, internationalization of industrial districts and design.

Riccardo Paterni is the Founder and President of Professione Lavoro ® by Knowledge for Action and Action for Knowledge; a network of professionals operating since 1999 in Europe and the US. He develops and coordinates innovative consulting and training projects focusing on Organizational and Human Capital development. He is the editor of two web-magazines: KnowledgeForAction.info (English language) and SaperePerFare.it (Italian language). He is the author of articles published on Italian management magazines and editor of the Italian edition of US management books. In 2009 he has co-authored the book published in Italy by the title "Rugby. From the Game Field to the Company Field. Going beyond simple team work dynamics"; the book focuses on the ethical, participative and shared leadership dimension of rugby relating it directly to organizational practices needed to compete within a complex changing global economy.

Nicole Radziwill is a Co-Founder of Espresso Labs. She is also a faculty member in the Integrated Science & Technology (ISAT) Department at James Madison University in Harrisonburg, Virginia. Nicole holds a Bachelor of Science degree in Meteorology from the Pennsylvania State University, an MBA from Regis University, Denver, CO, and a Ph.D. in Technology Management and Quality Systems from Indiana State University. Nicole has 15 years of industry experience at the senior and executive levels of start-ups, professional services organizations, and national laboratories. She is a 2009 National Examiner for the Malcolm Baldrige National Quality Award (MBNQA), a Certified Manager of Quality and Organizational Excellence (CMQ/OE), and is a Six Sigma Black Belt candidate. She is a Senior Member of the American Society for Quality (ASQ), where she is Chair-Elect of the Software Division, and a reviewer for *Software Quality Professional* and *Journal of Industrial Technology.*

Jane Root is currently Administrator of Clinic Operations for Aurora Health Care's medical group in their Green Bay, Wisconsin market. She is responsible for all aspects of the medical group practice for 20 clinic sites in 5 counties throughout Northeastern Wisconsin. Ms. Root has been in leadership roles with Aurora since July of 2001. She received her Bachelor of Science Degree in Nursing from Rush University in Chicago, Illinois, and her Master of Science in Management and Organizational Behavior from Silver Lake College in Manitowoc, Wisconsin. In 2006, she completed the 18-month Academy Fellowship Program through the Health Care Advisory Board in Washington, D.C.

Ramendra Singh is a PhD candidate in the Marketing, Indian Institute of Management Ahmedabad. His current research interests include salesperson's customer orientation, salesperson's performance, consumers' social well-being and marketing at the bottom of the pyramid. Ramendra has published in several international refereed journals including The Marketing Review, Journal of Medical Marketing, and Asia-Pacific Journal of Marketing and Logistics. Ramendra is a 2008 AMA-Sheth Doctoral Consortium fellow, and his research has been presented or accepted for several international conferences including 2009 Winter and Summer AMA Educators Conferences, 2008 EMAC Doctoral Colloquium, and the 2008 Academy of Marketing Conference.

Lars Taxén, (Associated Professor) received his M.Sc. from the Royal Institute of Technology in Stockholm in 1968. Between 1968 and 2003 he was employed at the Ericsson Telecommunication Company, where he held several positions related to processes and information systems for hardware and software design. From 1995 on he was engaged in the development and implementation of incremental development methods for large, globally distributed software development projects. The experiences from this work were reported in his PhD thesis "A Framework for the Coordination of Complex Systems' Development" (2003). In 2007 he became an associated professor at Linköping University in Sweden. He has published in various conference proceedings and journals and is now active as a researcher and consultant.

Sanjay Verma is a member of Computers and Information System group at Indian Institute of Management Ahmedabad. He is a Fellow of Management from Indian Institute of Management Calcutta with specialization in Management Information Systems (MIS) and Operations Research. Sanjay has an MBA in Marketing and Finance. His teaching interests are in Information System, Business Strategy, and Knowledge Management. Prior to his FPM, he has experience in the field of sales and marketing. He started his academic career with IMS Bikaner and later on taught at XIM Bhubaneswar. He is a regular faculty to various companies in India engaged in Insurance, Oil and Gas, Infrastructure etc. He has published papers and participated in conferences in India and abroad. Sanjay is also actively involved in consulting organizations engaged in the field of health, insurance, infrastructure and social sector. He has done significant work in understanding KM implementation process in organizations, and has written cases on KM implementation process in Infosys Technologies Ltd., Tata Steel and ONGC.

Daniel J. Worden is a principal with The RuleSmith Corporation. He has defined, designed, deployed and tuned communications based information systems since 1982. He has authored five books on a range of technologies including databases, storage networks, and Java. He has worked extensively with business requirements gathering and communication of strategies, priorities and constraints throughout organizations. His research for the past several years into new technologies, emerging techniques for business process management and agile alignment of IT with business strategy is also published in The Decision Model – A Framework for Business Logic and Business Driven SOA (Auerbach Press 2009, Von Halle et. al.) and Adaptive Cloud Computing (CRC Press 2010, Worden).

Jiming Wu is Assistant Professor in the Department of Management at California State University, East Bay. He received his Ph.D. from the University of Kentucky. His research interests include knowledge management, Internet-based business applications and IT acceptance, and computer and network security. He has published (or forthcoming) more than a dozen papers in *MIS Quarterly, The DATA BASE for Advances in Information Systems, Information Systems Frontiers, Knowledge Management Research & Practice, Journal of Electronic Commerce Research,* and elsewhere.

Index

V

W